COMMON SLAVIC
Progress and Problems
in its Reconstruction

by
Henrik Birnbaum

Slavica Publishers, Inc.
1975

189216

For a complete listing of our publications, please write to:
Slavica Publishers, Inc.
P.O. Box 312
Cambridge, Mass. 02139

Text set by Shirley H. Tabata. Editor of Slavica Publishers, Inc.: Charles
E. Gribble. Printed in the United States of America by LithoCrafters, Inc.,
Ann Arbor, Michigan 48106.

For Marianna

Table of Contents

Abbreviations

The following abbreviations are used throughout the text of this book (except in direct quotations and in headings and subheadings):

CS   = Common Slavic

OCS = Old Church Slavic

(P)IE = (Proto-)Indo-European

PS   = Proto-Slavic

In addition, the customary abbreviations for denoting languages are used to identify cited examples of relevant linguistic data or terminology; thus, e.g., Bg = Bulgarian, Cz = Czech, F = French, Gk = Greek, Goth = Gothic, Hitt = Hittite, Lat = Latin, Lith = Lithuanian, OHG = Old High German, OPr = Old Prussian, OR = Old Russian, P = Polish, etc.

Numerical and other symbols as well as abbreviations (for series titles and journals) used in the Selective Bibliography are explained on pp. 344-7.

Preface

The purpose for which this volume was designed is twofold: first, to serve as an introduction for the student in Comparative Slavic Linguistics to recent and current research in the particular field of CS, the term here used to designate the protolanguage underlying the present Slavic languages (as well as their now extinct sister idioms) as recoverable primarily by various methods of linguistic reconstruction; and, second, to provide a guide to the main issues of CS, i.e., to identify fundamental problems, resolved and unresolved, for specialists in other related areas of linguistic research. This book is *not* aimed, on the other hand, at furnishing a systematic outline, however succinct, of the changing structure of CS as such; to this end, the reader is referred to the several relevant titles listed in the appended Bibliography.

The limitations thus imposed reflect by necessity on the scope and selection of data and theory accounted for in this volume. Yet I have attempted to report on what appears to me the most essential achievements in the reconstruction of CS, particularly as accomplished over the last half century or so, and to outline at least briefly a number of crucial and challenging problems which to date resist satisfactory explanation.

While an effort was made to restrict to a minimum the discussion of such views as cannot be supported by incontestable evidence, it proved nonetheless unavoidable to present occasionally also certain conflicting opinions expressed, especially in recent years, on some basic issues in the reconstruction of CS (notably, its phonology). In doing so, I have not hesitated to indicate my own stand wherever I have seen reasons to favor one of the competing explanations. My contrary intention notwithstanding, some of my readers will therefore presumably find what they may construe as a certain measure of bias in the following presentation. However, not having been party to what I feel to be any major controversy of substance (though perhaps of terminology) in discussing the recovery of CS linguistic structure, I can only hope that such minor instances of possible subjectivism will serve as an incentive in the search for truth also in this field rather than jeopardize the striving for a maximum of achievable objectivity.

The manuscript of this report was completed by July 1, 1972. Any works that appeared or were brought to my attention after this date are therefore not included here except in a few instances in which I was aware of their imminent publication. Due to circumstances beyond the author's control, the appearance of this book was delayed by more than two years. A supplementary sequel, covering relevant literature of the period from 1972 through 1977, is planned for early 1978, in time for the Eighth International Congress of Slavists to be held in Ljubljana and Zagreb.

My sincere thanks go to Misses Marsha Gauntt and Shirley Tabata, my research assistants at UCLA, for their indefatigable technical assistance and advice in matters of style in the course of preparing the typescript of this book for publication. I am also indebted to Miss Irena Koschade, my assistant at the University of Munich, and to Miss Swantje Koch, of the University of Kiel, for their help and suggestions in editorial matters.

Los Angeles, January 1975

                                                    H. B.

1. INTRODUCTION

COMMON SLAVIC: Problems of Definition, Evidence,
and Approach

1.0. Terminology and Definition: Common Slavic and Pro-
toslavic.   CS and its equivalents in other languages (R
obščeslavjanskij [jazyk], F *slave commun*, G *Gemeinslavisch*,
etc.), used diachronically, i.e., with reference to a
stage in Slavic linguistic evolution, is one of the two
competing terms designating the generally posited protolanguage (parent language) underlying the entire course of
development of all individual Slavic languages, attested
as well as unattested, those currently in use and those
now extinct.   If used panchronically (or achronically),
i.e., with reference to all stages in Slavic linguistic
evolution (or without any reference to the time dimension
of this evolution), the term CS would obviously have different implications; it would then refer to some or all
features or characteristics common to — i.e., shared by —
all Slavic languages at one time or another.   Such connotations would therefore be primarily typological in nature
regardless of the fact that in most cases the historical
reasons for those structural agreements lie in the close
genetic relationship among the Slavic languages.   A similar meaning would also be implied in the term CS if used
synchronically, that is, with reference to one particular
time segment (moment, well-defined period) in Slavic linguistic evolution, for instance, to approximately the year
1000 A. D., to the early 13th century, or to the contemporary period.   However, when such connotations are intended,
to avoid possible misunderstanding it seems more appropriate to choose or coin some other term such as, e.g., Pan-
Slavic (in spite of the historical-ideological associa-

tions this term may evoke) or Generalized Slavic (preferable in a modeling-typological approach; cf. also, for example, the distinction between P *wspólnosłowiański* and *ogólnosłowiański* to render R *obščeslavjanskij*, the latter thus being more ambiguous).

Competing with CS as a diachronic term is PS (R *praslavjanskij* [*jazyk*], F *proto-slave*, G *Urslavisch*, etc.). To some extent, the preference for one term or the other is a matter of individual linguistic usage and scholarly tradition. Thus, e.g., F *slave commun* is more generally used than *proto-slave*, in part at least due to the impact of Meillet's classic text (1924, ²1934). G *Urslavisch*, on the other hand, continues to rank before *Gemeinslavisch*, notwithstanding some attempts to introduce the second term into scholarly literature (e.g., by Kiparsky 1934). R *praslavjanskij* still appears to have the upper hand over *obščeslavjanskij*, although the latter was preferred by Fortunatov, among others, and has gained ground, especially after the appearance of the translation of Meillet's text (1951). In English, CS and PS perhaps still keep the balance even though recent terminology, at least in American English, rather tends toward CS. (Notice incidentally that British usage prefers 'Slavonic' to American 'Slavic'.)

While, therefore, CS and PS may indeed be considered synonymous (at any rate, when used with reference to Slavic linguistic diachrony), the very availability of these two terms (and their equivalents in other languages) could suggest a slightly differentiated usage of them. Thus, in order to be able to distinguish between at least two major phases of the Slavic protolanguage — or, alternatively, two basic "synchronic slices," viz., its initial stage, just emerged from some larger language entity such as Balto-Slavic or a portion of Late IE, and its last more or less uniform stage, immediately preceding its subsequent disintegration into various Slavic linguistic subgroups — it was proposed some time ago to reserve the term PS for the earlier (or, if qualified by 'Early', first) phase of the common Slavic ancestral language and CS for its later (or, if qualified by 'Late', last) phase, roughly corresponding to the differentiation achieved by, e.g., G *Frühurslavisch* vs. *Späturslavisch* (cf. Bidwell 1963: 10-12; Birnbaum 1966a: 153-6; Hamm 1966: 45, 48). By recognizing the two terms PS and CS as partly overlapping in meaning (except when prefixed by 'Early' and 'Late', respectively), it would be possible to account for their near-synonymity while indicating at the same time the potential difference in reference. However, any absolutely clear-cut division into an earlier and a later period of the Slavic protolanguage remaining unattainable (in view of the relative and often controversial chronology of many of the sound changes on which such a tentative division must be based), it appears less advisable to utilize this possibility of a terminological distinction for the purpose of singling out two separate epochs in the history of the presumed protolanguage.

These terminological considerations, while not unchallenged (cf. Aitzetmüller 1967; Weiher 1967: 84-5), hinge on the further question of the relationship between the respective linguistic realities underlying the notions Early PS and (Common) Balto-Slavic, on the one hand, and, on the other, Late CS and differentiated Early Slavic, or more specifically the relationship between any particular Late CS dialect and a given preliterary individual Slavic language or language subgroup (such as Proto-Russian or rather Proto-East Slavic, Proto-Polish, Proto-Serbo-Croatian; Proto-Lekhitic, Proto-Czechoslovak, Proto-Slovene-Serbo-Croatian; see Birnbaum 1970c). In this context reference should be made to the view (first advanced by Ivanov and Toporov 1961: 303), according to which it may be methodologically difficult to draw a sharp line between what could be considered Late (Common) Balto-Slavic and what, Early PS, as the latter — to the extent that its basic phonological and morphological structure can be reconstructed on internal grounds — essentially is derivable from a hypothetical (and, to be sure, fragmentary) Proto-Baltic linguistic model (questionable as the establishment of the details of such a model might be), while, on the other hand, a reverse derivation tracing a Common (or rather Generalized) Baltic linguistic structure back to its Early PS counterpart appears to be virtually unfeasible (cf. also Birnbaum 1970b: 87, 117). It should further be noted, as pointed out, e.g., already by Trubeckoj (1922; 1924) and more recently by Toporov (1959: 19), that the upper time limit of Late CS is floating, that is, difficult to fix by means of incontestable inherent criteria, as many of the changes (primarily phonological, reflected in the earliest Slavic evidence, especially the OCS and Old Russian texts of the 10th and 11th centuries) are consistent with general tendencies already prevailing in the preceding centuries of preliterary Slavic linguistic evolution. Thus, while various developments of individual

Slavic languages and language subgroups were, no doubt,
largely anticipated in the divergent evolution of Late CS
of the preliterary period, justifying, consequently, at
least the theoretical positing of individual Slavic languages (prior to their being recorded in writing) or of
their immediate predecessors, a case could also be made
for setting the *terminus ad quem* of late CS only at the
approximate time — somewhat varying throughout the Slavic
language area — of the "fall of the weak jers" (i.e., the
disappearance of the so-called reduced vowels ь and ъ in
certain well-defined positions) and the concomitant or, at
any rate, immediately subsequent "vocalization of the
strong jers" (i.e., the developing of these reduced vowels
to regular full vowels in other positions). Therefore, at
least in certain parts of the overall Slavic language area,
notably in the East Slavic territory, the Late CS period
(in this broad sense) can be said to have lasted until
roughly the late 11th or even the early 12th century (for
details of the "fall" and "vocalization of the jers" in
East Slavic, see now also Isačenko 1970a). On the other
hand, for the recently challenged dating of some phonological processes long considered CS (viz., the Second and
Third Palatalizations of Velars), see below, pp. 50
and 265. Occasionally this time, spanning (preliterary
Late) CS as well as the first centuries of recorded Slavic,
is also subsumed under the rather vague term Early Slavic.
No intrinsic linguistic reasons can be adduced, of course,
to assume a coincidence in time of the end of the CS period and the purely accidental fact — determined entirely by
extra-linguistic factors — that Slavic writing happened to
take its beginning in the second half of the 9th century,
occasioned by Constantine's and Methodius' Moravian mis-
sion of 863. However, if we were to exclude from consideration all CS linguistic evolution characterized by some
degree of spatial variation, i.e., dialectal differentiation, the close of a more or less homogeneous development
of Slavic as a whole (viz., in the narrow sense of PS referred to above) might very well be dated somewhere around
500 A. D. as was also suggested by relevant research in
recent years (Shevelov 1964: 12-13, 307-9, 607-8; Stieber
1969/71, 1: 9-10, 68-73, 81-3).

Since, however, the following presentation is specifically designed to report on and evaluate recent and current findings and insights pertinent to the *reconstruction*
of the preliterary Slavic protolanguage as well as to
identify some as yet unresolved or only poorly understood

problems of that assumed language, the label CS stands here, in spite of the above terminological considerations, as a broad conventional cover term to designate the entire range of Slavic (but not pre-Slavic) linguistic evolution prior to its recorded history, i.e., its first attestation by written texts. Only where a distinction between (Early) PS and (Late) CS appears to be called for will these more specialized terms (used in their narrow sense) be used. In addition to basing theoretical inferences on attested Slavic language data strictly for the purpose of reconstruction, recorded evidence will be adduced also to elucidate such developments as can be assumed to have been at least incipient already in the preliterary period of Slavic even if their completion may fall only in the first centuries of recorded linguistic evolution.

*1.1. *Original Homeland and Early Expansion of the Slavs.* Any attempt to simply equate CS (or PS) with "the language spoken by the 'Proto-Slavs'" (as suggested some time ago by Aitzetmüller 1967: 89) cannot but be considered a futile shifting of the problem of defining CS from one level of argument to another, equally controversial one (cf. Birnbaum 1970c: 9-10). To be sure, the very delimitation in time and space of CS as a language is obviously closely linked with the problem of the original homeland (R *prarodina*, G *Urheimat*) of the primitive Slavs and its subsequent expansion in various directions up to the period of the disruption — caused by the advent of the Magyars in the late 9th and early 10th centuries — of the relative spatial unity of the Slavic community at large which had existed until then. A short account of our present knowledge in this respect, to the limited extent that it can be considered noncontroversial, may therefore seem in order.

Experts continue to disagree as to the exact location of the original territory settled by Slavs toward the end of the first millennium B. C. All that can be said with some degree of certainty is that this first homeland of the Slavs (or 'Proto-Slavs') must have been situated in Eastern Central Europe, somewhere north of the Carpathians and, though less likely, also their westward extension, the Sudetes. The Slavs had come to this earliest ascertainable region of settlement (as evidenced by archaeological finds and toponymic data) as one of the several ethno-linguistic groups emerging from the disintegrating Late Common IE community. Around the 4th century A. D.

the Slavs undoubtedly already occupied a wide area from
the basin of the Oder (Odra) in the west to that of the
central Dnieper (Dnepr) in the east and reaching in the
north up to the southern shores of the Baltic Sea, to the
Masurian Lakes, and to the Pripet (Pripyat', Prypeć)
Marshes. At some time in the 5th century a northeastward
expansion of the Slavs began, as a result of which the ancestors of today's Eastern Slavs settled the area around
the northern Dnieper and its tributaries and north of the
Pripet, formerly populated by Baltic tribes which were now
either assimilated by the Slavs or driven further toward
the northwest (for hydronymic evidence, cf. esp. Toporov &
Trubačev 1962; Sedov 1970). In the 6th century this
northeastward move continued into territories previously
occupied by Finnic peoples. About the same time the Slavs
expanded further toward the west, advancing from the Oder
basin to that of the central and lower Elbe. Also shortly
after ca. 500 A. D. a portion of the Slavs, pouring south,
seems to have crossed through the passes of the Carpathian
and Sudetic Mountains, while other Slavic tribes coming
from today's Ukraine reached the Balkan Peninsula by way
of the South Romanian Plain (Walachia). In the 6th century a part of the Slavs further settled the area of the
Eastern Alps (present-day Lower Austria, Styria, Carinthia,
and Slovenia). The Great Hungarian Plain (east and north
of the central Danube), previously settled by IE — Thracian, Illyrian, Germanic — as well as non-IE peoples
(Huns), was at that time probably only sparsely populated
by Slavs, soon to be subjugated by the non-IE Avars. In
the course of the 6th and 7th centuries Slavic population
waves inundated most of the Balkan Peninsula including
also Greece, where Slavs at that time made up a considerable, if not predominant, element, all the way to its
southernmost portion, the Peloponnesus. The gradual re-
Hellenization of Greece carried out by Byzantine imperial
administrators, feudal lords, powerful cities, and wealthy
monasteries was initiated in the 7th century and continued
for some six centuries.

Consequently, in the 7th through 9th centuries the
Slavs had come to occupy a vast territory in Eastern and
Central Europe, ranging from the Aegean and Adriatic Seas
in the south to the base of Jutland and the Baltic Sea in
the northwest, and the Gulf of Finland, Lake Ladoga, and
the upper Volga district in the northeast. In the west
the Slavs had reached the Eastern Alps, the Bohemian For-
est, the river Saale, and an area beyond the lower Elbe,

while in the east they soon came to cross the central
Dnieper. Only the Black Sea Steppe continued to be a land
of semi-nomadic Altaic and Ugric peoples, settling briefly
or passing through on their way from Asia and Southeastern
Europe toward the west.

However, at the beginning of the 9th century this
immense Slavic-populated area was by no means homogeneous
in its ethnic and linguistic composition. The Great Hungarian Plain (on both sides of the Tisza) and adjacent
lands (Pannonia, Transylvania) had until recently been
ruled by the Avars, an Altaic people, who, after having
subdued the sparse local Slavic population, had in turn
been conquered and virtually annihilated by the armies of
the Frankish Empire of Charlemagne. Romance peoples remained in parts of the Balkans, both in the interior of
the Peninsula (the ancestors of the present-day Romanians)
and along the shores of the Adriatic (the now extinct Dal-
matians). Other Balkan areas were occupied by Albanians
— at one time probably contiguous with the early Romanians — an IE people of Illyrian, Thracian, or Dacian de-
scent (or possibly descending from some combination of
these ancient IE ethno-linguistic groups and at any rate
subsequently heavily Romanized). In southern Bulgaria,
Macedonia, and in Greece proper, a large portion of the
Greek-speaking population withstood the onslaught of the
Slavs. Already toward the end of the 6th century the
Slavic population of what is now approximately Bulgaria
(and perhaps also Yugoslav Macedonia) had yielded to the
domination of the Bulgars, an Altaic people, a part of
which had entered the Balkan Peninsula, while another part
had first remained at the lower Volga and subsequently
moved upstream toward the mid-Volga area, founding there a
state of their own. Yet, while having militarily defeated
the Slavs, the outnumbered Bulgars were soon assimilated
by the earlier Slavic settlers, leaving behind only their
name and some loanwords. In the northeast of the vast
Slavic territory, Baltic and Finnic splinter groups undoubtedly survived for a long time, particularly in inaccessible tracts protected by impenetrable forests and
large bodies of water.

*1.2. Uniformity and Dialectal Differentiation; Internal
and Comparative Reconstruction of Common Slavic.* It is
not surprising that within such a large area as the one
occupied, with varying density, by the Slavs as early as
at the beginning of the 7th century a certain dialectal

7

differentiation must have prevailed. It seems, however,
that until ca. 500 A. D., i.e., prior to the southward
migrations of the Slavs, their common language, although
spread even then over a considerable geographic area, was
still largely homogeneous. This view is sustained by the
realization, reached only recently, that some of the phonological isoglosses on which a presumed early division
into two main dialect areas has usually been based can
actually, at least in their majority, be dated only from a
period after ca. 500 A. D. This traditional division posited a western group of CS dialects, supposedly yielding
the West Slavic languages, and an eastern dialect group,
claimed to underlie the East and South Slavic languages,
with the upper and central Bug as an approximate dividing
line (cf., e.g., Bernštejn 1961: 61-73). The relevant
isoglosses are: 1) the partly different results of the
so-called Second (regressive) and Third (progressive) Palatalizations of Velars in Slavic, specifically, the different reflexes of CS x and of CS kv, gv (xv); 2) the retention of the clusters tl, dl (West Slavic) as opposed to
their simplification ($> l$, East and South Slavic); 3) the
rise and retention of an epenthetic l (after palatalized
labials) in the east in contrast with the lack of such l
(at least in certain positions) in the west; and 4) the
different treatment of CS tj, dj, yielding by and large
hushing affricates (and secondarily in some cases fricatives) in the east (East and South Slavic), but corresponding hissing sounds in the west (West Slavic). However,
it can now be considered fairly certain that the Second
Palatalization of Velars did not begin to operate until
around 600 A. D. and that the Third Palatalization, while
probably partly overlapping in time with the Second Palatalization — some recent claims suggesting a radically
different relative chronology notwithstanding — did not
become effective prior to the 8th century (the outcome of
the two Palatalizations being identical, only differing in
their environmental conditions). There is further reason
to believe that the entire Slavic language area once had
developed an epenthetic l (in all positions after palatalized labials), and that its disappearance (in certain positions) in the west is secondary (as is, incidentally,
its disappearance in part of the South Slavic area, viz.,
in Macedo-Bulgarian where this process can be directly observed in the earliest Slavic evidence of OCS, whereas in
West Slavic it falls into a preliterary period). The various results of the assibilation of t', d' ($<$ CS tj, dj)

are also relatively late (after 500 A. D.). Only as regards the simplification of *tl*, *dl* in the eastern portion of CS is there some evidence suggesting that it took place prior to the 6th century; however, here also the situation is rather complex (*tl*, *dl* being retained in a northwestern part of South Slavic, while yielding *kl*, *gl* in a limited, northwestern region of East Slavic, not to mention other details obscuring the overall picture). Little, if any, significance can therefore be attributed to this one, possibly early, isogloss separating a western (subsequently West Slavic) from an eastern (subsequently East and South Slavic) portion of CS (cf. Birnbaum 1966a: 189-94; Shevelov 1964: 202, 370-5; Stieber 1969/71, 1: 10, 81-3).

Thus there are good reasons to assume that until ca. 500 A. D. or, in other words, prior to the southward migration of the Slavs and their moving into territories previously occupied by Finnic tribes, the common language of all Slavs was still to a high degree uniform.

No direct evidence is available on which to base any assumptions as to the phonological and grammatical (morphosyntactic) structure and the basic vocabulary of the fairly homogeneous development of CS prior to ca. 500 A. D. Virtually all attempts at recovering these earlier stages of the common Slavic protolanguage must therefore rely heavily on the methods of internal reconstruction, i.e., on techniques by which data of the last phase of an already disintegrating and dialectally differentiated CS of ca. 500-1000 A. D. can, as it were, be projected backward in time. This allows for some inferences from morphophonemic alternations, competing word forms, and coexistent syntactic structures of this late stage of CS as to primary (vs. secondary or partly even tertiary) sounds, forms, and, at least to some extent, also phrase, clause, and sentence patterns, suggesting the establishment of certain relative chronologies pertinent to CS linguistic change (cf. Birnbaum 1970b: 92-122). The validity of the results thus obtained can subsequently be verified in many instances by correlating the hypothetic primary data of earlier CS (= PS) with corresponding evidence from other IE languages, in particular those more or less closely related to Slavic, i.e., especially matching data of archaic Baltic, ancient Indo-Iranian (Aryan), and Early Germanic. Thus the methods of internal and comparative reconstruction can be used here to supplement each other and to corroborate each other's conclusions. The structure of disintegrating Late (post-5th century) CS can in turn be

9

reconstructed on the basis of comparative evidence drawn from the individual recorded Slavic languages, particularly in their earliest attestation. However, here the linguist is not entirely dependent on such circumstantial evidence alone but can, in addition, also resort to some data more immediately bearing on Late CS.

1.3. *The Earliest Slavic Texts.* What then is this direct evidence relevant to the period of emerging CS dialects (and subsequently individual Slavic languages) which at that time spread over a vast territory from the Peloponnesus in the south to the shores of the Baltic Sea and the Gulf of Finland in the north? It is in this period, or to be exact in the 9th century, that the "creation" of OCS, the first literary language of the Slavs, by Constantine-Cyril (d. 869) and Methodius (d. 885) falls. To be sure, no autographs of the two Thessalonian brothers or their immediate associates seem to have come down to us. The bulk of the extant OCS texts, copied from earlier originals, dates from the late 10th and the 11th centuries. Still, they reflect rather closely the Slavic vernacular spoken in the 9th and 10th centuries in Bulgaria (including its western portion, Macedonia). Of particular interest are, in addition, two short manuscripts, both possibly dating from the second half of the 10th century, whose highly archaic language, while generally OCS, exhibits traits of a more northwestern provenience (so that frequently these texts, despite their religious-ecclesiastic contents, are not included among the writings of "canonical" or "classical" OCS): the *Kiev Leaflets*, written in a particularly archaic form of Glagolitic script and containing a fragment or rather an abridged version (*libellus*) of a missal according to the Roman rite, adapted from a not fully identified Latin original; and the *Freising Fragments* (or *Freising Monuments*), rendered in awkward Latin spelling and consisting of a general confession, a short homily (penance sermon), and a baptismal vow, of which the first and last in part paraphrase Old High German (Old Bavarian) and possibly Latin sources, while the second, the homily, seems to go back to an original Slavic text. The preserved copy of the *Kiev Leaflets*, displaying a few phonological "Moravisms" (or Bohemisms) and one morphological feature characteristic of the northern Slavic languages rather than of South Slavic and, in addition, having its vocabulary interspersed with western elements (of Latin and/or Old High German origin; cf. Auty 1969),

10

is frequently believed either to have been written in Bohemia-Moravia or to be the work of a Moravian (or Czech) scribe who had come to the Balkans. More likely, though, the "Moravisms" of the *Kiev Leaflets* reflect certain characteristics of an earlier (or the original) Slavic version of this text, while the extant copy rather points to some northwestern region of the Balkan Peninsula. Less acceptable is the view that the language of the *Kiev Leaflets* is actually a specimen of the vernacular of a specific Slavic-speaking area, presumably Pannonia, and that the linguistic peculiarities of this text thus represent genuine traits of one particular Late CS dialect rather than merely being indications of some artificial admixture of West Slavic characteristics to a fundamentally Macedonian-Bulgarian OCS (cf. Stieber 1969/71, 1: 11-12; 1971). The basic character of the language encountered in the *Freising Fragments* is even more controversial: some linguists consider it essentially OCS (of the early, pre-Slovak or Pannonian-Moravian type) overlayered with secondary Slovenisms (cf. Isačenko 1943); others see in it a sample (or even the only recorded evidence, if one disregards the partly proto-Slovenian name forms inscribed in the Evangeliary of Cividale and some comparable onomastic data from legal and ecclesiastic documents, especially in the then German-Slavic borderlands of present-day Austria and Bavaria, dating from the late 8th-10th centuries) of Old Slovenian, superficially and incompletely adapted to the norms of OCS (cf. esp. *Freisinger Denkmäler*, 1968). ·

1.4. Ethnic Groupings and Linguistic Ties Within Disintegrating Late Common Slavic; the Testimony of Loanwords and Toponyms; Ultimate Division of the Slavic Language Area: Dialectal Tripartition and Core Region vs. Peripheral Zones. While not all details regarding the roads along which the Slavs moved southward from their "expanded homeland" have yet been established, it seems, as was already mentioned, that they followed two main tracks: one through present-day Romania into the heartlands of the Balkans, and the other one through the passes of the Carpathians and the Sudeten, first into what is now Czechoslovakia (Bohemia, Moravia, Slovakia), then further to Pannonia and the adjacent area of the Eastern Alps, and on to the western regions of the Balkan Peninsula. It was presumably here, in present-day Yugoslavia, that the Slavs coming from the north and northwest met and mingled with other, west-bound Slavic tribes moving from the shores of the

11

Black Sea. Two ethnic names, that of the Croats and that of the Serbs (or Sorbs), both probably of Iranian origin*, still testify to this early path-crossing of the Slavs in the Balkans. Until ca. 1000 A. D. the ethnonym *Croats* designated not only the predecessors of the contemporary South Slavic Croats but also some Slavic groups settling on the northern slopes of the Carpathian and Sudeten Mountains ("White Croats"); and *Serbs* is not only the name of one of the Balkan Slavic peoples but also — in an only slightly different form, *Sorbs* — that of the Western Slavs in Lusatia (between Silesia and Saxony in today's East Germany), the remnants of a once numerous Slavic population occupying in the Early and High Middle Ages an area between the central Oder and the Neisse (Nysa) in the east and the Saale in the west.

Close ties formerly existed between the language spoken in Slovenia (including a part of Carinthia) and the West Slavic linguistic area. In addition to a number of lexical and grammatical agreements, two phonological characteristics reflecting these ties deserve special mention: the partial retention of the clusters *tl*, *dl* in Slovene, shared with West Slavic; and contractions of the type *stati* (<*stojati*), *bati se* (<*bojati se*) which Slovene has in common with Czech, Slovak, and southern Polish (including contemporary standard Polish). A particularly close relationship between South Slavic and the southern (trans-Carpathian) portion of West Slavic is further suggested by the identical treatment of the CS sound sequences *tărt*, *tălt*, *tĕrt*, *tĕlt* (>*trāt*, *tlāt*, *trēt*, *tlēt*, where *t* stands for any consonant; notice also that, in accordance with present-day knowledge, we posit CS *ă* for traditional CS *o*). This sound change involved metathesis of the liquid with a concomitant lengthening of the vowel. These contacts were disrupted in the late 9th and early 10th centuries by the advent and eventual permanent settling of the Magyars in the Great Hungarian Plain and trans-Danubian Pannonia

---

*Iranian origin for the ethnonym of the Croats is generally assumed. The source of the name for Serbs is less certain; however, its early (mid-10th century) attestation in Constantinus Porphyrogenitus (Σέρβιοι, *De administrando imperio*, chap. 9) denoting an East Slavic tribe (hardly just a distortion of *sĕverjane*, as has also been suggested) seems to support the assumption of its Iranian origin as well.

(present-day Western Hungary). As was mentioned before,
the local population of Pannonia, subjugated by the Magyars, was predominantly Slavic, speaking some dialect or
dialects transitional between Proto-Slovak (or "Moravian")
and Proto-Slovene. (The occasionally expressed view that
the ancient Pannonian Slavs north of Lake Balaton spoke
Proto-Slovak, while those south and southwest of it spoke
an early form of Slovene, can hardly be substantiated; cf.
Sós 1969.) The so-called Yugoslavisms, i.e., South Slavic
features, of Slovak and, in particular, Central — historically South — Slovak dialects, are further remnants of
earlier linguistic connections between this area and the
Slavic South.

Loanwords that entered Early Slavic and Slavic borrowings in other languages are of great significance for
our knowledge of CS and its dialects. While this rich
source of information must be used with due circumspection,
it can supply important data concerning such controversial
chronologies as those of the CS and, as we now know, partly post-CS palatalizations of velars and their immediate
consequences; the rise of the so-called reduced vowels (or
jers: ь, ъ < PS $\breve{\imath}$, $\breve{u}$) and their subsequent disappearance
or modification ("fall" and "vocalization," respectively);
the denasalization (and, to a large extent, concomitant
change in timbre) of the — in CS, to be sure, only allophonic — nasal vowels (ρ, ϱ); etc. Particularly pertinent
are the Slavic loans from Finnic, Germanic, and the East
Romance languages and, on the other hand, Slavic borrowings found in Finnic, Baltic, Germanic, Balkan Romance,
Hungarian, Greek, and Albanian. Most revealing in this
respect are Slavic loanwords and toponyms in areas at one
time (namely, during the Late CS period) temporarily settled by Slavs. This applies, for example, to present-day
Hungary and a good portion of Greece whose lexical and
toponymic data of Slavic provenience therefore offer most
valuable insights into the phonology of the local CS vernacular of the 7th-9th centuries. Another area of Early
Slavic — non-Slavic symbiosis, reflected in a linguistically revealing Slavicization of mostly Late Latin/Early East
Romance place names, extends along the littoral from the
northern tip of the Adriatic Sea to Albania.

It is true that recent findings of CS dialectology
seem to confirm the statistical validity of the traditional tripartition of the Slavic languages (into West, East,
and South Slavic) while no longer supporting any rectilinear *Stammbaum*-like view of the complex processes of

divergence underlying the individual Slavic languages (cf. Furdal 1961; Birnbaum 1966a). At the same time it should be noted, however, that within each of these Slavic linguistic subgroups a peripheral portion has not undergone all the early modifications otherwise characteristic of that particular branch. Thus it can be shown that Polabian, the westernmost offshoot of the West Slavic group, developed in more than one respect differently from all the other West Slavic languages (cf., e.g., the treatment of the *jers* in Polabian). Similarly, Macedo-Bulgarian was affected at an early date by a far-reaching Balkanization which integrated this southeastern portion of South Slavic (including Bulgarian, Macedonian, and the Torlak dialects of Serbo-Croatian) into the Balkan linguistic convergence area and recast the phonological-prosodic and grammatical-phraseological structure of the languages involved in accordance with a linguistic model originally alien to the southern dialects of Late CS. The first indications of a typically Balkan linguistic evolution can, as a matter of fact, be ascertained already in OCS. Finally, Russian (or more precisely Great Russian), numerically the chief representative of East Slavic, developing largely on a territory of Baltic and Finnic linguistic substratum, does not — at least in most of its dialects and in its literary standard variety — share some old phonological and grammatical features found in Ukrainian (and/or Belorussian) and matched there by parallel phenomena in Slovak or Polish (partly also in Czech, Serbo-Croatian, etc.). As two cases in point, the special treatment of ь/ъ + j ($> i/y$ + j) and the reflexes of so-called compensatory vowel lengthening (largely yielding secondary high or diffuse vowels), not found in Russian, can be adduced. Alternatively, one could perhaps conceive of a development where the eastern dialectal segment of Late CS directly resulted in two separate individual Slavic languages — Proto-Ruthenian (or Proto-Ukrainian, if the emergence of Belorussian may be considered secondary) and Proto-Russian (Proto-Great Russian) — without first going through an intermediate shared stage of Common East Slavic (i.e., "Proto-" and "Old Russian" in the traditional sense). The heavy overlayer of Church Slavic elements (especially phonological features) may well have contributed to obliterating and making virtually indiscernible any possibly existing ancient distinction between Old Ruthenian and Old Russian proper (i.e., Old Great Russian) in the early, Kievan, period of East Slavic writing. Thus, while the

14

division of the Slavic languages into three branches remains generally valid also in the light of current CS dialectological research, another internal grouping of the Slavic linguistic area into a central region and a number of separate peripheral zones with a partly deviating (and often delayed) evolution can also be ascertained. This second internal grouping, too, was incipient already in the Late CS period.

1.5. Common Slavic (Proto-Slavic) as a Branch of Indo-European: Its Relationship to Cognate Language Groups, Especially Germanic, Indo-Iranian, and Baltic; the Assessment of Slavic—Non-Slavic Isoglosses. Thus, while fairly rich linguistic data from which to infer the structure and internal (dialectal) differentiation of Late CS is available, the same obviously cannot be said when it comes to the reconstruction of Early CS (PS). The methods of recovering the early stages of the Slavic protolanguage are by necessity less reliable, and the results must therefore be more tentative and remain only approximate. However, as was pointed out before, in addition to applying methods of internal reconstruction by taking as a point of departure the relatively well-established or at any rate easily reconstructable data of Late CS, the hypothetical model, if not the exact structure, of Early CS can to some extent also be established by resorting to the traditional, though constantly further improved, method of Comparative IE Linguistics; or rather, this model can be recreated with a greater degree of probability and in more detail by integrating the findings of the comparative approach with the general linguistic structure arrived at by internal reconstruction. In other words, if a comparison of the relevant evidence from other IE languages, particularly those closely related to Slavic, suggests the existence in PS of certain sounds or sound sequences and word forms (formation types, inflectional categories), as well as perhaps even a set of some basic syntactic patterns, such tentative data can be verified against internally reconstructed sounds and forms, possibly also sentence structures, and thus be either corroborated (and further elaborated) or refuted. Similar methodological considerations apply also to the stock of positable Early CS lexical items and their semantic structure (the latter to be understood both in terms of their semantic microstructure, i.e., their representing specific complexes of certain universal or near-universal semantic features, and in terms of their semantic macrostructure, i.e., their being constituents of some larger semantic domains or "fields").

Which, then, are the IE languages most closely related to Slavic, and what are the main points of their particular agreement with Slavic? As is well known, the traditional division of the IE languages into *centum* vs. *satǝm* languages according to their respective reflexes of original palatal velars (k', g', $g'h$), at one time considered to be of paramount significance, is now recognized to be only of secondary importance as a classificatory criterion, especially as it has been established that no other major isogloss line coincides with the *centum/satǝm* split. (As is well known, *centum*, the Latin word for '100', represents the group of languages in which these sounds, at least to begin with, remained velar stops, whereas *satǝm*, the equivalent numeral in Avestan, represents the group of languages in which they were shifted at an early date to hissing or hushing fricatives — s, z; $ś$, $ź$; $š$, $ž$.) Moreover, after the discovery of Hittite and the other cognate languages of Anatolia as well as the two dialects (A and B) of Tocharian, followed by the realization that these languages, despite their location in the south and east of the overall IE linguistic territory, belong to the *centum* group, it has become widely accepted that the "satemization" of a part of the IE language area must be conceived as an early innovation, characteristic of its central region. The *centum/satǝm* division can thus no longer be interpreted as due to some dialectal parallel development within Late PIE. The fact that the two IE language groups most closely related to Slavic — that is, Baltic and, although to a lesser degree, Indo-Iranian (Aryan) — share with Slavic the quality of being *satǝm* languages should not, therefore, be considered as significant a trait as a previous, *Stammbaum*-oriented, view of IE linguistic relationships may have been inclined to regard it.

When attempting to establish isoglosses shared by Slavic with some other IE language groups, it is often difficult to distinguish clearly between, on the one hand, instances of common inheritance, i.e., shared retentions ("archaisms") as well as jointly introduced innovations stemming from the period of disintegrating, dialectally differentiated Late PIE and, on the other hand, characteristics which Early Slavic may have in common with some related language or language group as a result of previous, though post-PIE, contacts — contiguity or, in some instances, even coterritorial symbiosis — and which there-

fore rather come under the heading of early borrowing,
lexical as well as phonological and grammatical, in addition to *substratum* and possibly also *Sprachbund* (convergence area) phenomena. It goes without saying that these
latter, secondary shared features or items have considerably less bearing on the reconstruction, by means of the
comparative method, of Early CS (PS) even though they, too,
occasionally may be revealing with regard to the CS sound
pattern at a given period, the same holding true, of course,
also for Early Slavic borrowings in unrelated languages,
notably Finno-Ugric; cf. also Polák 1969.

In particular, the difficulty of drawing a sharp
line between inherited shared characteristics and secondary, borrowed or otherwise passed-on linguistic phenomena
is felt with respect to the many and complex coincidences
occurring between Slavic and Baltic. Of these agreements
it is primarily in regard to some syntactic parallels (e.g.,
in the use of individual case forms — a predicative instrumental, an objective genitive in negative clauses, or
the dative absolute) that it is far from always clear whether they reflect influences exerted by one language group
on the other (in other words, by Slavic on Baltic or vice
versa) or whether they, along with some well-established
phonological and lexical correspondences, as well as a few,
generally less conspicuous morphological — mostly derivational — conformities, should be conceived as part of a
common Balto-Slavic heritage from PIE.

As regards the relationship of CS and Early Germanic
(especially Gothic) and that of preliterary Slavic and
Indo-Iranian (particularly Iranian), the instances controversial as to the nature of their origin, i.e., whether
commonly inherited or secondarily passed on, concern,
among other things, matching lexical items which, however,
often appear to have been borrowed by Slavic unless exceptionally they must rather be termed "migratory words" (G
Wanderwörter) of undetermined origin and untraceable
routes of travel. In other cases it seems still less
clear whether to count certain parallel phenomena among
jointly retained features (or perhaps rather their common
beginnings in Late Common IE), or whether to attribute
them to secondary influences — i.e., borrowing — or to independent, though coinciding or similar, developments.
This applies, for example, to the -*n* suffixation (and/or
infixation) in Germanic and Slavic (as well as Baltic) as
a means of deriving inchoative verbs and possibly also to
the first rise of the semantic-grammatical category of

17

perfective aspect (or its predecessor, a specific mode of
action with a comparable semantic function) and its formal
characterization by means of prefixation, rudimentarily
present in Germanic (with some parallels, to be sure, also
in Greek), further developed in Baltic, but fully systema-
tized only in Slavic.

In yet other instances a parallelism may only be
superficial, details being at variance and moving forces
operating universally or, at any rate, fairly generally.
Such appears to be the case with two seeming agreements or
parallels of sound change in Slavic, partly Baltic, and
Indo-Iranian:

1) IE $s > \check{s}$ in Indo-Iranian, x ($\sim \check{s}$ before front
vowel) in Slavic when preceded by $\check{\imath}$, $\check{u}$, r, k
(and their allophones); in Baltic, IE $s > \check{s}$ regularly only after r, k, sporadically also after
$\check{\imath}$, $\check{u}$ (moreover, this shift is clearly reflected
only in Lithuanian, but obscured in Latvian and
Old Prussian due to secondary developments —
$\check{s} > s$; sj, $tj > \check{s}$ — and, in the case of Old
Prussian, also by awkward orthography; cf. Birn-
baum 1971a);

2) IE k, g $(gh) > \check{c}$, $\check{z}$ ($= d\check{z}$) before primary front
vowels ($\check{\imath}$, $\check{e}$) in Indo-Iranian and in Slavic
(where $\check{z} > \check{z}$).

Chronological considerations (in addition to the potential generality of this sort of process; cf., e.g., Lat
centum [kentum] -> Ital *cento* [čento]) here virtually exclude the possibility of a genetically shared characteristic; while the CS First Palatalization seems to at least
have been efficacious still in the 5th century A. D. (cf.
Stieber 1969: 67), the equivalent Indo-Iranian consonant
shift must have been definitely concluded prior to the
Common Indo-Iranian vowel merger $\bar{e}/\bar{o}/\bar{a} > \bar{a}$ which falls
into the preliterary period, i.e., before ca. 1500 B. C.

Turning now to the particular agreements between
Slavic and its closest cognate, Baltic, various opinions
have been voiced both as to their presumed causes — ranging from the positing of a hypothetic Common Balto-Slavic
protolanguage to separate, though parallel, evolution from
a common dialectal base in Late PIE, possibly enhanced by
secondary convergence or even temporary coterritorial
symbiosis — and as to their exact number where assessments
have varied between as few as ten and as many as over

twenty; for a brief survey of various approaches to the problem see Birnbaum 1970a. The picture of the Slavic-Baltic linguistic relationships is further obscured by the fact that some of the features shared by the two language groups also have more or less direct counterparts in one or another additional branch of the IE language family (this applies, in particular, to Indo-Iranian and Germanic), while other conformities are characteristic for Slavic and Baltic only. Moreover, Slavic shares some features not with all of the recorded Baltic languages, but only with some portion of Baltic, usually either with West Baltic alone (represented by the scarce and often difficult-to-interpret Old Prussian evidence) or exclusively with East Baltic or even merely a part of it (i.e., Lithuanian and/or Latvian and/or some of their dialects). This situation, particularly, suggests an early disintegration of Common Baltic — if indeed the positing of a once spoken, fairly homogeneous Common Baltic protolanguage is at all realistic; a similar doubt, well-founded in the case of Baltic, would not be justified, incidentally, as regards the existence of a once uniform CS language.

Disregarding here, with a few exceptions, some particularly controversial, as well as some only partial, agreements between Slavic and Baltic (cf., e.g., the aforementioned shift IE s > CS x, Balt $\check{s}$ in certain phonetic environments), the following, without giving an exhaustive list, may be considered among the more important shared Balto-Slavic features:

1)   a great number of lexical items exclusively characteristic of Slavic and Baltic (for the best overall account see Trautmann 1923);

2)   the double reflex *ir/ur*, *il/ul*, *in/un*, *im/um* < IE $\underset{\circ}{r}$, $\underset{\circ}{l}$, $\underset{\circ}{n}$, $\underset{\circ}{m}$ (with or without a following laryngeal);[*]

3)   the parallel reflex Slavic *ju*, Baltic *jau* < IE $\bar{e}u$;[**]

---

[*]The *u*-series is, however, considered phonetically conditioned rather than regular ("spontaneous") by some linguists (e.g., Vaillant and, particularly, Kuryłowicz; cf. p. 61, below).

[**]The reflex *eu* (graphically *eu*, *ew*, and *eau* = $\bar{e}u$) in the Old Prussian *Enchiridion* seems to be secondary in relation to Common Baltic *jau*.

4) the reflex *r-*, *l-* < IE *ṳr-*, *ṳl-*;

5) some striking similarities in accentuation (intonation, place of stress) — vastly conflicting views as to their explanation notwithstanding;

6) the use of the original (IE) abaltive for the genitive singular in the *o*-stems: Slavic *-a*, Lith *-o*, Latv *-a* < East Baltic *-ā* (< *-ād̂) < IE *-oad;*

7) similar formation of long form ("definite") adjectives by means of a pronominal suffix (postposition of a form of the pronoun *îos* or *is* or a contamination of the two); cf., e.g., R *bosój*, P *bosy*, etc. < *bosъ-jь*, Lith *basàsis* (with some chronological and other details remaining controversial);

8) *-jo/-jā* stem declension of active (present and past) participles;**

9) coincidences in the formation of certain oblique case forms of the nongendered (personal) pronoun of the 1st person singular (*men-/*mon-/*mun-);

10) similar formation of collective numerals by means of the suffix *-er/-or*;

11) a great number of striking similarities in nominal derivation; cf., e.g., R *rátaj* < *ortajь* : Lith *artójis*; R *venéc* < *věnьcь* < *věnъkъ* / *venók* <*věnъkъ* : Lith *vainĩkas*, dial. Latv *vainuks* (stand. *vaiñuks*); OR *šьvьcь* : Lith *siuvĩkas*;

---

*In West Baltic (Old Prussian) the gen. sg. of the *-o* stems ends in *-as* < IE *-oso*. Since no formal distinction between gen. and abl. sg. can be ascertained for the other IE nominal stem classes, it has been suggested that Slavic and (East) Baltic have retained here an earlier general case identity of PIE rather than having introduced a common innovation; however, the West Baltic evidence does not seem to bear this out.

**The same declension type is attested for the present active participle also in Old Germanic. This type here being limited to West Germanic, it seems less likely that this feature represents an original common Balto-Slavic-Germanic isogloss.

R *pis'mó* < *pisьmo* : Lith *piešìmas*; OCS *krъvьnъ* :
Lith *krùvinas*;

12) some general as well as some specific parallels
in verbal derivation; cf. OCS *-ovati/-ujǫ* : Lith
-auti/-áuju, to be sure with a further, if less
close parallel in Greek; past tense stem formation in *-ē/ā-*; OR *damь*, *dastь* : OLith *duomi*,
duosti, etc.

For further details and discussion see especially Fraenkel
1950: 73-123; Arumaa 1964: 17-30, esp. 18-23; Stang 1966:
13-21; Senn 1966: 139-51. For a general survey of the
isogloss integration of Slavic and Baltic with other IE
language groups — notably, Indo-Iranian and Germanic;
further the ancient IE languages of the Balkans; Greek,
Armenian, and Hittite as well as Tocharian — see also, for
example, Porzig 1954: esp. 132-4, 135-7, 140-8, 164-77,
179, 180-1, 183, 184-7, 188-92, 204-9, 211-12.

Part One

PROGRESS IN THE RECONSTRUCTION

OF COMMON SLAVIC

(History of Research)

2. GENERAL TREATMENTS OF COMMON SLAVIC

2.0.   Preliminary Remarks.   It goes without saying that in
a survey of the accomplishments attained to date in the
reconstruction of CS the emphasis will have to be placed
on such works, mostly of a reference character, that summarize the state of accumulated knowledge in this field
at a given time, primarily during the last half century or
so. To be sure, this is not to say that new important
views and fresh data were not frequently first reported
elsewhere — in article form, in a monograph, or in some
other publication. However, as a rule, such findings and
theories were subsequently incorporated into textbooks and
reference works of a more general nature, designed for advanced classroom teaching and other academic pursuits. The
focus of attention in the following will therefore be on
comprehensive treatments of CS linguistic structure or, in
any event, of some of its major components (phonology,
morphology, syntax, lexicology). In addition, reference
will also selectively be made to some ground-breaking and
seminal specialized studies in the field of CS which have
made a lasting impact by virtue of either furnishing new,
heretofore unsifted linguistic data pertinent to the reconstruction of the preliterary protolanguage of the Slavs,
or opening up earlier unexplored approaches capable of
yielding such insights into the functioning and change of
this theoretically recovered common predecessor of the
historically attested Slavic languages as were previously
not conceivable or realized under the application of less
ingenious, if successfully tested, traditional methods.

   Of general reference works there are broadly four
categories that are devoted, entirely or in part, to CS.
Above all, preliterary Slavic linguistic structure is, of
course, the primary subject matter of those not too

numerous texts and handbooks that specifically deal with
CS, either with the full range of its presumed manifestations at all levels or with some particular component of
it. Usually the very terms CS or PS (and their respective
equivalents in other languages) appear on the title page
of these general reference books treating the ancestral
language underlying recorded Slavic. Of the particular
components of CS linguistic structure it is phonology that
has received the lion's share of attention, either because
of the individual scholar's preoccupation with phonology
rather than with some other portion of preliterary Slavic
(understandable in view of the greater degree of elaboration and sophistication in phonological reconstruction
and, generally, phonological diachrony as compared to other levels of linguistic change), or simply because phonology usually forms the first major part of any traditionally designed linguistic text- or handbook (preceded, at
most, by a general introduction), and the author concerned
has often left his work unfinished, completing only the
introduction and phonology sections of his book, originally conceived as a full-fledged reference grammar. After
phonology (including morphophonology), it is CS morphology,
inflectional as well as derivational, and lexicology (including etymology), in this order, that at least to some
extent have been treated comprehensively, while the reconstruction of CS syntax (or, to be exact, of some basic
models of CS phrase and sentence patterns) is still in its
beginnings and largely in the stage of discussing problems
of methodology, some first tentative attempts at revealing
fragments of CS syntactic and semantic deep structure only
recently having been undertaken.

Second in importance after the textbooks specifically designed for the study of CS rank the reference works
in Comparative Slavic Linguistics. Needless to say, texts
in this field are of vastly varying size, ranging from
concise introductory booklets of some thirty pages (such
as Jakobson 1955) to multi-volume sets of detailed research (such as Vaillant 1950-66). Moreover, among these
reference works, it is essentially only those which relate
to their common origin the pertinent data of the contemporary Slavic languages, as well as their earlier recorded
stages of development, in genetic rather than typological
terms — that is to say, project them, as it were, into
their CS prehistory — that may be considered germane to
the study of the theoretically reconstructed (or yet-to-
be-retrieved) Slavic protolanguage, and therefore fall

26

into the purview of this book. Depending on the significance of these reference works (in terms of their size,
general outlook, and original research reflected), they
will be briefly surveyed here, the selection being restricted, however, by considerations of space, in addition
to being inevitably influenced, at least to some degree,
by the present writer's awareness and assessment of the
relevant literature. It seems only natural that textbooks
of Comparative Slavic Linguistics, to the extent that they
are diachronically and genetically oriented, will tend to
emphasize the final stage of CS, i.e., Late CS and the
following period of disintegrating (and partly reintegrat-
ing) Early Slavic, immediately preceding and to some extent overlapping with the formation of linguistic subgroups and individual Slavic protolanguages (Proto-East
Slavic, Proto-Lekhitic; Proto-Polish, Proto-Serbo-Croatian,
etc.), rather than its initial stage, PS (having just
emerged from Common Balto-Slavic or from a particular
dialect group of Late PIE), or the details of its evolution from Early PS to Late CS. As suggested by the term
Comparative Slavic Linguistics, the procedure for reconstructing (Late) CS primarily utilized in these works is
the comparative method (in one or another of its formulations), not the set of techniques of internal reconstruction, the latter yielding, in particular, relative, but
not absolute, chronologies.

The comparative method (in some variety) will further find its application also in a third category of general reference works containing data from CS (and its
early and/or modern reflexes) and utilizing such data for
more far-reaching inferences and generalizations, namely,
in text- and handbooks of Comparative IE Linguistics.
Contingent upon the relative significance attributed to
the specifically Slavic data, as compared to evidence from
other branches of the IE language family, particularly for
the reconstruction of PIE (or rather its last stage), thus
identifying presumed retentions — partly in modified
form — and innovations as attested by Slavic — uniquely,
jointly with some other branch of IE, especially Baltic,
or frequently shared with several ancient dialect groups
of Late Common IE — the emphasis on various facets of CS
and Early Slavic linguistic structure (usually represented
by OCS) may be distributed accordingly, i.e., with corresponding unevenness, in these general treatments of Comparative IE Linguistics. Moreover, the particular emphasis will depend on the vast differences in detail and

thoroughness reflecting the specific purpose, ranging from first guideline to in-depth reference works, for which texts of this sort may be designed. Thus, the presentation of CS linguistic structure here will be both somewhat incoherent and disproportionate or, at any rate, less systematic than in any of the text- or handbooks purporting to give a full or balanced (if succinct) coverage of the makeup and functioning of the Slavic protolanguage (either as such or as a point of departure for the subsequent divergent evolution of the recorded Slavic languages). In addition to straight reference texts of Comparative IE Linguistics (or Grammar) — of which, however, only a few will be listed in the following as the data and theory contained in most of them are purely derivative — also some basic works accounting more particularly for the internal grouping of IE (or ancient IE dialects) will be considered in this general category. Naturally, the focus in the reference books of Comparative IE Linguistics is usually on the early phase of CS (i.e., PS) rather than on Late CS even though the illustrative data adduced is often taken from attested Slavic evidence (Early Slavic, especially OCS, archaic dialectal Slavic, or even contemporary standard as well as folkloric Slavic).

Finally, there is a fourth kind of general reference work that occasionally may, by way of introduction, give a short account also of CS linguistic structure. This category includes some diachronic (historical) treatments of individual Slavic languages, still in usage or extinct, especially those with a relatively early recorded history. Thus, in those textbooks of OCS representing or, in one way or another, continuing the neogrammarian vein, much attention is usually devoted to the sound and form systems of CS believed to be reflected, with only minor and easily accountable modifications, in the phonology and morphology of the earliest recorded Slavic literary language. Also in the few modern grammars of OCS designed primarily as introductions to the comparative and historical study of Slavic linguistics, the focus is on the close relationship, if not near-identity, between OCS — at least in its reconstructable, original Cyrillo-Methodian form — and Late CS linguistic structure. On the other hand, in some recent or fairly recent textbooks of OCS with a different, deliberately synchronic-descriptive (rather than diachronic-comparative) approach, their authors, while at least in one case even explicitly recognizing the preserved evidence of OCS as a specimen of a Late CS dialect (Lunt 1968: X),

28

have gone to great lengths to present the phonological and morphological data of the oldest literary language of the Slavs as an independent, self-contained structure, to be described in its own inherent terms rather than in those of Late CS, with the mere addition of a few minor modifications, or, as some linguists now would put it, low-level rules to account for the specifics of OCS. Also in some historical grammars of Russian, whose documented history, after all, reaches almost as far back in time as the period usually assumed for the OCS texts (i.e., the late 10th and 11th centuries; the oldest dated Russian Church Slavic manuscript, the so-called *Ostromir Gospel*, going back to 1056/57), a chapter or section is occasionally devoted to CS or at least its eastern (Proto-East Slavic or Proto-Russian) dialect. Similarly, in historical grammars of Polish, Czech, Serbo-Croatian, etc., the Late CS dialectal background of these individual Slavic languages has often been sketched. Again, only in the relatively few instances where these by and large peripheral treatments of CS within the context of the development of an individual Slavic language (including its prehistory) may be considered truly significant, will they be briefly referred to in the following.

2.1. *Common Slavic Structure.* The first grammar of CS that even today cannot be considered altogether obsolete and thus fully superseded by some more modern treatment of the same subject matter — as must be said to be the case, for example, with the two Russian textbooks by Porzeziński (Poržezinskij 1914; [2]1916) and Il'inskij (1916) — is J. J. Mikkola's *Urslavische Grammatik*, published in three installments over a period of nearly forty years (1. *Lautlehre: Vokalismus, Betonung* — 1913; 2. *Konsonantismus* — 1942; 3. *Formenlehre* — 1950); yet it was to remain a torso. Consistently neogrammarian in approach, this is the first promising attempt to clearly distinguish between CS as a preliterary, only theoretically reconstructable entity, on the one hand, and historically attested Slavic (including Early Slavic), on the other. Largely ignoring the diachronic dimension, the Finnish linguist (who has made a name for himself especially in the field of early Slavic-Finnic linguistic relations and contacts as evidenced by relevant loanword material) has endeavored to identify and in some detail describe, on the basis of comparative data drawn both from the recorded Slavic languages and from related IE language groups, a synchronic state in linguistic

29

evolution (to be sure, never existing, as such) rather than to account for the dynamics of this evolution itself. The numerous and intricate problems of changing and developing CS from its Early PS beginnings — whether or not these may be approximated to, or even equated with, Balto-Slavic — and down to the period of Late CS dismemberment (anticipating, and to some extent identical with, the first phases of a divergent development of Early Slavic) are not even tackled, much less seriously examined here. Thus, to take just a few examples, the modification of IE diphthongs (in tauto- and heterosyllabic positions, respectively) are presented by Mikkola in terms of a set of IE:CS correspondences (of the type: heterosyllabic IE ai, oi = CS oj, tautosyllabic IE ai, oi = CS word-medial $\check{e}$, word-final $\bar{\imath}$; word-final $\check{e}$ being held to be the reflex of IE $\bar{a}i$, $\bar{o}i$ only). Similarly, considerations of relative chronology are virtually excluded in the treatment of the various palatalizations of velars, the difference in phonetic conditioning (environment) rather than the difficult problems of periodization receiving primary attention. The author fairly consistently abstains from any — previously only all too frequent, if usually highly questionable — speculations regarding the physiological (articulatory) nature of any hypothetic intermediary stages in phonetic change and merely ascertains, in the best neogrammarian tradition, the positable point of departure and the unequivocal end result of a given sound shift. The concise outline of morphology, while arranged by inflectional rather than derivational categories, does take into account some basic aspects of word and stem formation as well. Spread in their publication over more than a generation, the three slim volumes of Mikkola's textbook display a slight change in emphasis also in terms of the method applied: although clearly neogrammarian in approach throughout phonology as well as morphology, a certain shift away from a largely atomistic toward a more holistic (though not yet structural) view of disparate linguistic phenomena can be perceived. For its time, the early years of this century, the treatment of Slavic accentology (in volume 1, chapter 4) must be considered a pioneering achievement.

Whereas Mikkola's grammar of CS was left unfinished or, to say the least, was not sufficiently elaborated and, despite its doubtless merits, must today be regarded as outdated in many respects, the same does not hold true for another reference work on the protolanguage underlying

attested Slavic, A. Meillet's *Le slave commun*, which first
appeared in 1924 and was subsequently revised and expanded
in a second edition in 1934, prepared in collaboration
with A. Vaillant. This text by the leading European comparatist of the first third of this century, as lucid and
precise in style as his famous, carefully structured oral
presentation in the classroom, has remained an unsurpassed
classic until this very day. It seems fair to say that,
given its particular concept, there is, in fact, not too
much in Meillet's book that would need fundamental rework-
ing even in the light of recent findings and newly gained
insights of modern scholarship. In large part this is due
to its author's definitive and, at the same time, cautiously phrased formulations and conclusions and to the
great acuity with which he has selected and interpreted
(but not overinterpreted) his data. Yet to some extent
this can also be attributed to the overall approach adopted in this broadly conceived and well-balanced, if synchronically compressed, treatment of the full range of CS
linguistic structure. While no longer strictly neogrammarian in method (as, e.g., Mikkola), Meillet, too, largely disregarded — or, perhaps, rather generalized away from
details of — spatial variation and temporal modification
as they can be ascertained within the limits of the Slavic
protolanguage in view of its ultimate territorial extension as well as the time span of its development. Meillet
reconstructed and interpreted CS not so much as a phenomenon of concrete, if hypothetic, reality, subject to constant change, but rather as an abstract sum total of a
number of specific (viz., Slavic) characteristics viewed
in their IE setting. In the words of G. Shevelov (1964:
16), Meillet's book "became a classic in the field not because it overcame the shortcomings and drawbacks of a non-
historical approach but because the author was aware of
its limitations and consciously did not extract from the
available data more than was possible when using that approach." And speaking of Meillet's treatment of CS phonology, Shevelov (*ibid.*) goes on to state that "he presented a projection of Sl(avic) phonetic developments onto
a surface of some abstract proto-language having no immediate connections in time and space (although, at the same
time, he made use of much historical data). The result
was a history compressed into one image, not an agglomera-
tion of facts, but a system which never existed in the
given form but which is still not antihistorical, an alge-
bra of CS." Some of the sections in Meillet's handbook

such as, for example, those on morphophonemic alternations, including ablaut, on the system of verbal stem classes and on aspect, or on nominal derivation — all problems he had previously treated in great detail in a number of specialized studies — will forever stand out as true masterpieces of concise formulation and profound insight, any minor revisions made necessary by subsequent research notwithstanding. It should further be noted that Meillet's text is rounded out by two brilliant sketches briefly outlining the basic features of CS sentence structure and the various strata of CS vocabulary, including lexical borrowing and early Christian terminology. In view of these truly exceptional qualities, it is quite understandable that a Russian translation of Meillet's reference work could appear as late as in 1951, especially as his text was here updated with the valuable comments by the outstanding Soviet specialist on Slavic diachronic linguistics, P. S. Kuznecov.

In 1964 a new grammar of CS began to appear, originally designed as a revised version of Mikkola's text. To date only the first volume of P. Arumaa's *Urslavische Grammatik: Einführung in das vergleichende Studium der slavischen Sprachen*, covering *Einleitung* and *Lautlehre* (1. *Vokalismus*, 2. *Betonung*), is available, but its immediate sequels treating the consonant system and derivational morphology (word formation) are expected shortly. I have given a detailed assessment of volume one of Arumaa's work elsewhere (cf. Birnbaum 1966b) and can therefore here limit myself to restating my main points. Both in concept and approach this is a traditional textbook regardless of the fact that the author acknowledges important achievements of structural methods as applied to Comparative IE and Balto-Slavic Linguistics. Still, the Estonian-Swedish linguist (whose own scholarly accomplishments lie primarily in the field of Balto-Slavic Linguistics and onomastics, especially hydronymics) has with much circumspection and keen understanding accounted in his work also for recent advances, particularly in the theory of ablaut and accentology, including some of the more generally accepted results of laryngeal theory, which in large measure were arrived at precisely by the application of a structural approach. The merits of using a strictly comparative method become particularly apparent in the section on accentology as the author here systematically proceeds from an analysis of the accentual (and other prosodic) patterns of the relevant individual Slavic languages to some insightful generalizations about accentuation and quantity, stress shifts and metatony in the preliterary period of Slavic. Cautious in matters of continued controversy while sober in its judgment of noncontroversial (or at any rate, less controversial) issues, Arumaa's book is of particular value by dint of its broad reference to, and utilization of, a wealth of Baltic (as well as other IE) data, convincingly demonstrating the relevance of such comparative material for the interpretation of some heretofore obscure sound changes in preliterary Slavic or their premises. While it is premature to assess the quality and significance of Arumaa's work as a whole, several volumes as yet outstanding, there is every indication that important new insights can be gained from this kind of research which takes into consideration relevant related linguistic data, in particular also in the to date insufficiently explored field of CS derivation in the broad sense (affixation and other processes of word formation). Though by and large an excellent guide to a multitude of bibliographical references, Arumaa's book shows in this respect also some striking gaps. The introduction, defining the scope and substance of CS and discussing the place of Slavic among the IE sister tongues as well as the earliest Slavic—non-Slavic linguistic relations, in addition to outlining the fundamental problems of the original (or, rather, earliest ascertainable) homeland of the Slavs, early Slavic tribal groupings, and the classification of the Slavic languages, is a fairly adequate account of our present knowledge in these areas. Fully aware and constantly taking into account the dynamics of linguistic change, Arumaa nonetheless, like Mikkola and Meillet, is primarily concerned with establishing what he considers the Early PS state in the evolution from PIE to Early Slavic. Thus, he specifically states his goal in the preface (p. 6) as follows:

> Der Verfasser hat . . . in erster Linie versucht, den frühesten uns erreichbaren Übergang vom Indogermanischen zum Urslavischen lautlich zu fixieren, d.h. die älteste und möglichst sichere Unterlage zur Rekonstruktion des Urslavischen aufzuzeigen. Darum ist hier auch von Versuchen, die urslavische Zeit in irgendwelche Perioden aufzugliedern, abgesehen.

Once completed, Arumaa's reference work will no doubt be one of the most useful tools for further explorations into the prehistoric past of the Slavic languages, more so, perhaps, by virtue of its riches of carefully selected and acutely observed linguistic data and the thoughtfully integrated conclusions of relevant modern scholarship, including some of Arumaa's own findings and interpretations, than thanks to any innovative, ground-breaking methodological approach of its author.

For a brief discussion of G. Y. Shevelov's textbook of CS phonology (1964), limited to this particular component of linguistic structure but commenting relevantly also on some general aspects of preliterary Slavic, see below, pp. 94-100.

An excellent, if quite succinct, account of our present knowledge of CS phonology and its development as well as of at least some major morphological modifications which occurred toward the end of the CS period can now be found under the appropriate heading "Prasłowiański język," in a brief sketch authored by the leading Polish Slavist, Z. Stieber (1970), in volume four, issue one, of the new monumental encyclopedia of Slavic antiquities, *Słownik starożytności słowiańskich*, published by the Polish Academy of Sciences. Another relevant entry in the same volume is that by K. Jażdżewski on the original area of settlement of the Slavs ("Praojczyzna Słowian"). Stieber's concise essay recapitulates briefly most of his partly original positions taken and more elaborately expounded in some of his recent writings (cf. Stieber 1964, 1965a, 1965b, 1967, 1968a, 1968b, 1968c, 1969/71). While the more significant ones among them will be merely enumerated here and discussed at some length only in subsequent paragraphs and sections, it should be noted already at this point that Stieber suggests a radical shortening of the assumed duration of the CS period, asserting that "CS emerged in all probability at the beginning of the first millennium of our era as one of the offshoots of the ancient PIE language." According to the Polish linguist, the majority of scholars are now of the opinion "that Proto-Balto-Slavic, which in all likelihood was spoken in the first millennium before our era, was an intermediary stage between PIE and PS." Among Stieber's original but generally very well-founded views on CS phonology are: late dating of the First Palatalization of Velars and of the monophthongization of diphthongs (end of 5th century and during 6th century, respectively); still later dating of the Second and Third Palatalizations of Velars (ca. 600 A. D. and thereafter), both incompletely — and not only

unsystematically, as long recognized for the Third Palatalization — implemented; specification of the phonetic
value of the intermediary stage between u_1 and y; short-
livedness (7/8th to 10/12th centuries) of CS ь, ъ (< PIE
i, u) before their "fall" and "vocalization," respectively.
In other cases, Stieber adheres, correctly in my opinion,
to one particular position in questions of continued controversy: allophonic (nonphonemic) status of CS ę, ǫ;
Late CS shift ă > ŏ (while denying any highly "archaic"
nature of Russian and Belorussian *akan'e*, allegedly, in
the view of some linguists, preserving the *a*-colored pronunciation of the CS short back vowel); late dating (8/9th
centuries, partly post-CS) of the so-called Metathesis of
Liquids, yielding divergent results in various Slavic linguistic groups.

2.2. Comparative Slavic Linguistics. Of older, now
largely obsolete comprehensive treatments of Comparative
Slavic Linguistics, the two volumes on derivation and syntax of F. Miklosich's monumental *Vergleichende Grammatik
der slavischen Sprachen*, conceived in the early, pre-neogrammarian vein of 19th century IE Linguistics, continue
to be of some value primarily as a reservoir of as yet
only partly tapped Slavic linguistic data. In view of
this continued usefulness, the respective volumes of the
first edition (2. *Stammbildungslehre*, originally published
in 1875; 4. *Syntax*, 1868-74) were photomechanically reprinted in 1926.

However, Miklosich's comparative grammar was essentially superseded by another comprehensive reference work,
designed along similar lines though in its approach following the neogrammarian method that meanwhile had become
virtually obligatory in comparative historical linguistics,
W. Vondrák's two-volume *Vergleichende Slavische Grammatik*.
Particularly in its second, revised and substantially augmented edition (1. *Lautlehre und Stammbildungslehre*, 1924;
2. *Formenlehre und Syntax*, neubearbeitet von O. Grünenthal,
1928), this well-informed text, rich in linguistic data
from all Slavic languages in their early attestation as
well as their early 20th century standard and, to some extent, even colloquial substandard form (to be sure, with a
marked preference for Czech, the author's mother tongue),
has served, along with Meillet's *Le slave commun*, as the
main reference work of Comparative Slavic Linguistics for
several generations of Slavists, particularly in the interwar period. Its systematic and detailed treatment of

Slavic phonology and morphology (at least as regards inflectional morphology), with frequent and more than merely
cursory retrospective glances at CS linguistic structure,
closely reflects the contemporaneous state of research in
matters such as accentology (accepting, for example,
Saussure-Fortunatov's stress shift law as applicable also
to Slavic), ablaut (positing, following H. Güntert, a PIE
reduced *schwa secundum* vowel, allegedly yielding CS ь and,
after labials and original labiovelars, ъ), or declensional endings, controversial as to their origin (making reference to the then novel findings and theories by O. Hujer,
J. Zubatý, and others). While many of Vondrák's own as
well as his secondhand explanations in these fields remain
valid or at any rate deserve continued consideration, some
of his relevant ideas and suggestions are now clearly outdated, proven inaccurate, and hence to be rejected. However, this applies only in a lesser degree to his (and
Grünenthal's) diachronic treatment of derivational morphology and syntax. The reason is primarily that in these
by and large less explored areas of inquiry no theoretical
framework and methodological approach were ever fully
elaborated and therefore the number of proposed explanations and hypotheses purporting to account for various
phenomena of word formation and sentence structure also is
generally much smaller. Yet the wealth of pertinent data
accumulated unquestionably continues to be of great importance as a mine of raw material, regardless of the fact
that much of it is still awaiting further and definitive
interpretation. After all, except for the fundamental
problem of defining the very scope of — traditional, surface — syntax (with at least some controversy as to whether to limit it only to the theory of sentence structure
or — as was done in Vondrák's reference work — to include
in it, in addition, the portion of grammar dealing with
the function of such grammatical categories as case, tense,
mood, etc., viewed in the narrower context of their syntagmatic utilization), the issues of word formation and
syntax were, for earlier generations of linguists, less a
matter calling for explanation and interpretation (in the
strict, scientific sense — requiring the application of a
particular set of sophisticated formalized techniques) but
rather a concern of mere data-gathering lending itself to
descriptive observations and taxonomic classification and
thus allowing, at best, for some vague theoretical generalizations. To meet these demands, modest by modern
standards, Vondrák's comparative treatment of the Slavic

36

derivational and syntactic surface structures provided
both the necessary factual material and an adequate system
of categorizing it.

Here another work should be mentioned which, although presumably of little international impact at the
time of its first publication, displays a new, relatively
modern concept of language and linguistic change approaching, though not yet fully adopting, the notions and overall framework of European structuralism, especially as
pertains to phonology (of the Prague School brand). N.
van Wijk's *Les langues slaves: de l'unité à la pluralité*
appeared in book form (in a second, improved edition) only
in 1956 but had previously been published in 1937 as five
separate essays in the semi-scholarly journal *Le Monde
slave*. The published version of these essays is based on
a series of lectures delivered by the Dutch Slavist at the
Sorbonne. Of the corresponding five sections of the posthumously assembled book it is particularly the first on
"Le slave commun dans l'ensemble indo-européen" and,
though to a lesser extent, the second on "Parallélisme et
divergence dans l'évolution des langues slaves" that need
to concern us here, while the three remaining sections on
East, West, and South Slavic, respectively, essentially
fall outside the purview of the present report. (For a
general assessment of the progress made through the early
sixties in the field discussed in van Wijk's second essay,
namely, the study of the parallel and divergent course of
Slavic linguistic evolution, see, among other things, R.
Auty's inaugural lecture of 1963; cf. Auty 1964). Couched
in a style which in lucidity and conciseness is in the
best Parisian tradition of Meillet and his school, van
Wijk's collection of essays naturally makes no claim to
being a systematic outline of the textbook kind but was
rather conceived as a number of synthesizing sketches focusing partly in a very personal tone — occasionally not
even free from some anecdotal ingredients no doubt intended to enliven the original oral presentation — on what in
the mid- and late thirties must have been considered the
most crucial and controversial issues of Slavic linguistic
diachrony. However, in doing so, van Wijk not only resorted to the obvious principles of genetic linguistics
but would also not hesitate to make occasional references
to some considerations of a typological nature (e.g., when
comparing certain predominant phonological tendencies
thought to be at work both in Early Romance and Early
Slavic). The sections concerned with the preliterary

evolution of Slavic discuss primarily general problems of
linguistic relationships, geographic distribution, and
chronology, but are largely limited to diachronic phonology when it comes to the substance of linguistic change.

In brief, van Wijk posits here a more than two-
thousand-year-long development of CS assumed to have been
preceded, despite Meillet's well-known objections, by a
period of Balto-Slavic linguistic unity of a clearly post-
PIE, i.e., not merely dialectal Late Common IE, character.
By and large, CS is said to have undergone only slow and
relatively few modifications during most of its long evolution, thus impressing on its earlier phases a stamp of
great homogeneity as well as considerable antiquity. It
is only during approximately the last five hundred years
of Late CS, beginning somewhere around the 4th century
A. D. and coinciding roughly with the expansion of the
Slavs from their original homeland (controversial as the
exact location of their primitive sites must remain), that,
according to van Wijk, their common protolanguage underwent a radical reshaping of its phonological and morphological structure. Ultimately this restructuring resulted
not only in a far more progressed state of development
away from the general IE linguistic type (which latter to
a large extent had been preserved during preceding periods
of Balto-Slavic and early PS linguistic evolution) but
also in a divergency within Late CS which already prefig-
ured the subsequent development of the individual Slavic
languages and language groupings. As for the specifics of
Late CS phonological modifications, the Dutch linguist was
to give a more detailed outline of his, by now largely
Prague-phonologist, view of it in a later paper (cf. van
Wijk 1950). However, at the time of his Sorbonne lectures
he was not yet entirely ready to accept the interpretation
of CS diachronic phonology in terms of the Prague School,
as sketched some years before by R. Jakobson (cf. Jakobson
1929; van Wijk 1956: 23); and one of the main principles
of CS phonology formulated by Jakobson, that of so-called
syllabic synharmonism, van Wijk still contested in an article published a few years later (cf. van Wijk 1941).
Instead he attempted not only to subsume but in fact to
explain a great number of the sound changes of Late CS by
suggesting that two other general tendencies were operating during the last centuries of CS: 1) a tendency toward
a syllable structure of rising (or increasing) sonority —
by which he sought to accomodate both the CS "law of open
syllables" and various instances of diphthong elimination,

including monophthongization proper as well as other modifications of original diphthongs in nasals and liquids, and the rise of prothetic consonants; and 2) a tendency toward palatalization — including several palatalization phenomena caused generally by post-consonantal *j* and, in the case of velars, also by front vowels; further vowel shifts of the *o*, *y*, ъ > *e*, *ĭ*, ь type caused by an original prevocalic *j* or by a preceding palatal affricate or fricative resulting from the progressive Third Palatalization of Velars. The same general phonological tendencies of Late CS and their assumed consequences van Wijk had, incidentally, sketched in some detail already in his earlier history of OCS (van Wijk 1931: 39-40, 46-80, cf. also below, pp. 70-1).

It is probably fair to say that neither the principle of syllabic synharmonism, originally formulated by Jakobson but contested by van Wijk and subsequently nonetheless providing the point of departure for yet another attempt at finding a general structural characteristic of CS phonology at least during some phase of its development, namely, that of the so-called group-phonemes, advocated by V. K. Žuravlev (for details see further pp. 142-4), nor the two overall tendencies just mentioned which van Wijk suggested as having determined most of the Late CS phonological restructuring can fully account for the actual causes underlying the various changes that these principles or tendencies were meant to explain. On the other hand, extracting, as it were, from a set of more or less disparate sound shifts a common, shared property, not necessarily reflecting causality (although perhaps hinting at some triggering factor) but expressible in terms of some general formula, has no doubt the purely pedagogical advantage of allowing for the structured presentation — and hence also the memorization — of the complexities of Late CS phonological modifications.

It is therefore not surprising that R. Nahtigal in his concise but at the same time fairly wide-ranging introduction to Slavic diachronic and comparative phonology and morphology, *Slovanski jeziki* (1938; [2]1952), adopted van Wijk's two general tendencies as handy headings under which to subsume a variety of CS sound changes. Although Nahtigal used the more traditional label "Law of open syllables," his introductory remarks to this section reveal unequivocally that what he had in mind here was van Wijk's more comprehensive principle of increasing syllabic sonority. In addition to this section and the one on "the palatal character of the CS sound system," the Slovenian Slavist treats in separate sections, inserted between the two just mentioned "Vowel quantity and the reduced vowels" as well as "Accentuation," the latter to a large extent reflecting Nahtigal's own original and important, if now partly obsolete, research in this area. A few short — in fact, overly short — appended notes on the CS reflexes of IE ablaut conclude the first major portion of his book, the one on the phonology of the prehistoric (preliterary) period. The second equally succinct and generally well-balanced portion contains a systematic presentation of CS nominal and pronominal declension followed by several sections on CS conjugation. The focus in these paragraphs is clearly on inflection, and derivational prerequisites are largely taken for granted or discussed only in brief outline. A number of surveys and summaries in tabular form further serve the purpose of facilitating memorization. The second part of the book, discussing the historical (literary) period of Slavic linguistic evolution, though occasionally making reference to underlying CS sounds and forms, is only of secondary import for this progress report. Designed originally as a textbook for students of Ljubljana University, the pedagogical merits of this text were rightly deemed so great that translations of it were made both into German (1961) and Russian (1963). While not structural in its basic approach, Nahtigal's book nonetheless incorporated also the most important and lasting insights gained by the application of structural, primarily Prague-phonologist, methods and can thus, in its second, 1952 edition (and the translations made from that version), be considered highly representative of a body of largely agreed upon general knowledge concerning CS phonology and (inflectional) morphology as still prevailing in many quarters at the beginning of the fifties.

At that time, however, another work had already begun to appear which, although retaining the format of an academic textbook, actually sums up a lifetime's intensive preoccupation with the history and prehistory of Slavic viewed on a comparative basis, A. Vaillant's *Grammaire comparée des langues slaves*. Of its three volumes (in five parts) which have appeared to date, the first (published in 1950) treats phonology (preceded only by a short general introduction), the second (in two parts, 1958) contains the morphology of the noun (substantive) and pronoun (pronouns proper, adjectives, numerals, and adverbs),

40

and the third (again in two parts, 1966) is devoted to the
verb (treating in three major sections verbal inflection
in general, the conjugations, and derivation and accentuation). Designed as a comparative grammar in the double
sense of placing the whole of the Slavic languages in its
broader IE context as well as tracing in considerable detail the divergent development of the Slavic linguistic
subgroups and individual languages throughout their recorded history, this is a most impressive attempt at presenting a thorough and well-rounded synthesis of Slavic
diachronic phonology and morphology; it is not known at
present whether further volumes of Vaillant's monumental
work, treating syntax and lexicology, may still be forthcoming. It goes without saying that a good portion of
Vaillant's *magnum opus* deals with the reconstruction of
preliterary Slavic and its pre-Slavic antecedents. In
this respect his work is in the best tradition of his
teacher Meillet's *Le slave commun*, in the preparation of
the second, revised and augmented edition of which
Vaillant took an important and active part and which his
new comparative grammar can in large measure be said to
replace (cf. above, p. 31).

Not genuinely innovative in method but rather continuing Meillet's precise, data-oriented approach and
lucid exposition, Vaillant's text incorporates a significant number of new facts and insights, including some
first brought to light or realized by the French Slavist
himself. Thus, for example, this is the first comprehensive presentation of Comparative Slavic Linguistics in
which the results of laryngeal theory — to be sure, in its
evolutionary phase of the late forties/early fifties —
have been fully utilized. (Vaillant denotes an unspecified laryngeal by h; cf. further below, pp. 61, 115-16).

However, among novel, if not entirely original,
assumptions made by Vaillant in his treatment of the CS
vowel system are also some that give rise to certain reservations. This is true, for example, of at least one aspect of his insistence on the a (rather than o) timbre of
the short back vowel not only for Balto-Slavic (for, contrary to Meillet, Vaillant accepts the hypothesis of a
period of Balto-Slavic linguistic unity of some duration
after the disintegration of Late Common IE; cf. 1: 14-15),
but also during most of CS times (cf. 1: 106-7). True,
this tentative reconstruction of the vocalic quality, justified, it seems, primarily by the evidence of Baltic
(having the general reflex a) and by the realization that

labialization — with concomitant raising of the tongue —
to the extent it may have occurred, was not phonemic in
CS, has gained wide acceptance. However, this should not
be confused with the claim, only cautiously hinted at by
Vaillant (and similarly, now more specifically, repeated
by Shevelov 1964: 151, 386-7) but subsequently pursued and
further developed with much vigor by Georgiev (cf. particularly Georgiev *et al*. 1968), that East Slavic — dialectal
and, secondarily, standard Russian as well as Belorussian —
akan'e and also some comparable (though genetically unrelated) phenomena elsewhere in Slavic (primarily the so-
called *akan'e* of some Bulgarian dialects of the Rhodope
district), conceived as archaisms, actually reflect or
even plainly preserve the CS state in this respect; for a
discussion of Georgiev's, in my view, erroneous theory,
see pp. 253-4. Also when it comes to the treatment of CS
e, for which Vaillant posits a pronunciation '*a* in Balto-
Slavic (again largely on the strength of the Baltic evidence), such a phonetic value is considered by him at
least as a variant also for CS with, once more, modern
dialectal evidence, said to preserve an earlier state, being invoked (cf. 1: 108-11). While it is possible, of
course, and perhaps even likely that the CS vowel traditionally denoted *e* (< PIE *e*) actually had an open articulation (and hence perhaps could be rendered more adequately *ä̧* rather than *e*; cf. also the occasional representation
ä̧ for traditional *e*, in Stieber 1969/71, 1: 25, or the denotation ₑ*ă* for *e*, along with ₒ*ă* for traditional *o*, in
Shevelov 1964: esp. 150-80), the positing of a CS '*a* (i.e.,
supposedly of a vowel which was not only quite open but
which also was preceded by, or had some sort of on-glide
of, presumably, phonemic softness or iotation, affecting —
it must be assumed — a preceding consonant) for traditional CS *e* seems less felicitous since it can be considered a
firmly established fact that front vowels did not as such
phonemically (but only perhaps to some degree phonetically) palatalize preceding consonants in CS. On some further, in my opinion devious, elaboration of Vaillant's interpretation of CS *e* as '*a* (or '*ä* by Weiher and some other
Slavists), see below, pp. 251 and 330. Generally it may be
said that Vaillant, while to be commended for having widely
adduced comparative Baltic linguistic data, handles the
evaluation of the evidence from this closely related language group in its bearing on CS with somewhat less circumspection and insight than, for example, experienced
Baltologists like Arumaa or Stang.

The above slightly critical remarks regarding some
points in Vaillant's treatment of CS phonology were not
intended, however, to detract from the overall unquestionably great merits of his reference work. Thus, to take
another instance from the first volume on phonology, the
two concluding chapters on accentuation and morphophonemic
alternations (1: 221-308) can be regarded as truly master-
ful sketches not only ably summarizing and interpreting
the relevant facts — partly still highly controversial —
but also presenting a balanced, well-rounded account of
the problems at hand.

Vaillant's treatment of Slavic morphology, viewed
diachronically, is extremely thorough and offers occasionally new, ingenious explanations, usually based on the
keen observation of a rich body of Slavic as well as cognate non-Slavic linguistic data. On the other hand, not
even his broad reference to comparative IE, especially
Baltic, parallels always permits the French Slavist to
come up with new convincing solutions to old resistant
problems so that he frequently is forced to seek at least
tentative answers in line with those earlier offered by
his teacher Meillet. One such problem, still not quite
satisfactorily resolved, is, for instance, the origin of
the dative singular ending in *-u* of the *-o* stems, said to
go back to PIE *$*-\bar{o}i$ < $*-o-ei$, with circumflex intonation,
for which Vaillant posits a hypothetic intermediate triphthongal stage *$*-uoi$ in Balto-Slavic, yielding various reflexes in Baltic: Lith *-ui*, dial. *-ou*, OPr *-u* (cf. 2, 1:
31). Similarly, the instrumental plural ending in *-y* of
the same stem class is traced back by Vaillant to PIE
*$*-\bar{o}is$ < $*-o-\bar{\imath}s$ or $*-\bar{o}-\breve{\imath}s$, the latter in the lengthened
vowel grade of its first component ($<-o$ + laryngeal),
possibly representing the original instrumental singular
ending of the *-o* stems; cf. Lat adv. *$u\bar{e}r\bar{o}$*. Again Balto-
Slavic triphthongal *$*-uois$ is assumed to underlie the
Slavic reflex while East Baltic *-ais* here shows a deviating, analogical development (cf. 2, 1: 31-2, 37-8; on
the alleged different treatment of PIE *$*-uoi$ > $*-uo$ > PS
*$*-\bar{u}$ > $-u$ vs. PIE $*-uois$ > $*-uoi$ > $*-ui$ > -y$, see also 1:
118-22, 213). The genitive singular in *-y* of the *-ā* stems
does not conform, as noted by Vaillant, to the Baltic,
Greek, and Germanic evidence, all pointing to PIE *$*-\bar{a}s$ (<
*$*-\bar{a}-es$, with circumflex intonation). He therefore has to
resort to a rather far-fetched, "analogical" explanation,
suggesting that here *-y* is patterned after the soft counterpart of *-y* (in this declensional class) represented by

OCS $-(j)ę$, with $-y$ (regularly developed from $*-\bar{a}ns$ in the accusative plural) extended to the nominative plural (for expected $*-a$ from $*-\bar{a}s$) by analogy with the generalization of $-i$ in the genitive singular and nominative-accusative plural of the feminine $-i$ stems (cf. 2, 1: 80-1). These and similar cautious explanations of irregular and unexpected — in terms of the known phonetic development — declensional endings do not essentially go beyond earlier speculation, practiced with great ingenuity by Vaillant's teacher as well as, for example, by Hujer. Yet they can no longer fully satisfy the requirements of a more modern concept of linguistic change, skeptical, to say the least, of all unqualified recourse to the magic agency of analogy, particularly where the prerequisites for its conceivable operation are not readily discernible. More bold and imaginative solutions to the problems of reconstructing the pre-Slavic and Early PS declensional system, exploring new avenues of approach, if occasionally running into some unavoidable blind alleys, have in recent years been proposed by F. V. Mareš in a series of relevant studies (cf. below, pp. 155-6 and 276-7).

By and large more convincing or at any rate less controversial than his discussion of moot points in the prehistory of Slavic declensional desinences, both nominal and pronominal, is Vaillant's excellent exposé, scattered over several sections and paragraphs, of the principles and details of CS nominal derivation — a field, of course, in which his great predecessor had already laid a solid foundation (cf. pp. 166-7).

Considerations of space preclude a further discussion and exemplification of the merits and shortcomings of Vaillant's impressive reference work. It should only be added that his relatively recent (1966) treatment of the diachronic morphology of the Slavic verb (3, 1-2), while based to a large extent on Stang's relevant findings and conclusions of 1942 (see pp. 159-61 and 170), but treating the attested evolution of the verb system in greater detail and, in general, giving a more systematic and complete presentation, is rich in subtle observations and acute insights, utilizing, among other things, the newest achievements of Comparative IE Linguistics, especially in the field of laryngeal theory and Slavic-Hittite (or, more generally, Balto-Slavic-Anatolian) comparative studies; notice, for example, the comparison of the Slavic thematic verb inflection with the denominative $-\hbar i$ conjugation attested in Hittite (3, 1: 20-1 and *passim*); on the significance of the Hittite evidence for Slavic, see especially also Ivanov 1957 and 1965 (discussed below, pp. 67-8, 224).

On the whole, then, there can be little doubt that Vaillant's *Grammaire comparée* is to date the most important comprehensive reference work of its kind, covering the full range of diachronic Slavic phonology and morphology. Fairly traditional in approach, it is extremely rich in factual data, generally up-to-date with the accomplishments of recent (if, for obvious reasons, not always with current) relevant scholarship, but it usually shuns new, boldly exploratory explanations of heretofore insufficiently understood developments and does not offer any radical reinterpretations resulting from the application of any fundamentally novel methods or techniques in linguistic research.

Also conventional, though continuing a different tradition of Slavic linguistic studies, and equally solid is another, more succinct textbook of Comparative Slavic Linguistics which began to appear in the early sixties, H. Bräuer's *Slavische Sprachwissenschaft*, published in the well-known *Göschen* series of condensed outlines. Trained in the late neogrammarian vein of his teacher, the leading German Slavist M. Vasmer, and consonant with the general makeup of the *Göschen* précis, Bräuer has managed to cram a surprisingly large amount of thoughtfully commentated linguistic data into the three slim volumes that have so far appeared (1. *Einleitung, Lautlehre*, 1961; 2. *Formenlehre*, part 1; 3. *Formenlehre*, part 2, both treating the substantive and published in 1969). A general characteristic of his presentation, again in keeping with the overall goal of the particular series in which it appears, is that Bräuer has reduced to an absolute minimum the discussion of such issues of Comparative Slavic Linguistics as must still be considered to some extent controversial so that whatever has been included in his text bears the stamp of solid and unquestionable fact. As for forms and especially endings, difficult to explain in terms of the assumed regular sound changes, the reader is left with the impression that all available alternative solutions, briefly discussed, have been exhausted. To be sure, this makes his work reliable and instructive reading for the newcomer to the field (and also the more advanced Slavist will profit from finding a multitude of interesting, carefully selected data in Bräuer's introduction), but, by the same token, it lacks to a large extent the challenge and

interest that only a confrontation of previously unexplained or disputed, though well-documented phenomena with
more or less ingenious new theories or hypotheses to account for them can arouse. When studying Bräuer, the engaged reader is therefore hardly given a real opportunity
to evaluate the explanatory power of the suggested interpretation.

Contrary to Vaillant's text, which (following Meillet's and other French linguists' example) contained only
an extremely limited selection of bibliographical references, Bräuer, continuing an established German tradition
(adhered to, for example, also by Arumaa), offers a broad
and varied range of titles, noticeably deficient only in
his coverage of early structural (Prague-phonologist) work
on CS. Also, while Vaillant presented his readers merely
with the bare minimum of general background information
regarding the place of Slavic among the IE languages, the
relationships between Slavic and contiguous language
groups (including unrelated ones like Finno-Ugric and
Altaic), the temporal and spatial bounds of CS, and the
divergent development and grouping of the various Slavic
languages, Bräuer — like Arumaa (both linguists in this
respect further pursuing the scholarly concerns of their
teacher Vasmer) — opens his survey with a fairly detailed
discussion of these issues. As for the controversial
problem of the original homeland of the Slavs, the German
scholar adopts Vasmer's pertinent view in slightly modified form, allowing for some flexibility as to the western
(and northwestern) boundaries of the primitive Slavs by
taking into account, in particular, recent findings of
Polish linguists and prehistorians (Lehr-Spławiński,
Ułaszyn, Kostrzewski, Czekanowski, Moszyński; cf. 1: 29-
32).

While Bräuer's textbook is designed both as an introduction to the prehistory of Slavic and to the historical development of the various Slavic languages, the emphasis in his treatment of phonology is particularly on
CS; pre-Slavic reconstructions, corroborated by comparative IE evidence, play rather a subsidiary role, providing
merely a point of departure, and the divergent development
of attested Slavic is sketched in rough outline only. In
the parts on morphology, available to date, the focus is
less predominantly on CS (any morphological reshaping in
the course of CS being less evident and conclusions in
this respect therefore largely conjectural), and a proper
balance between the discussion of the preliterary phases

46

of Slavic and that of the recorded periods in the evolution of the separate Slavic tongues is maintained. Yet
also the historically attested phenomena and developments
are frequently viewed in relation to the assumed (Late) CS
stage — that is, as either retentions, perhaps with some
minor modifications, or innovations. Among the former,
the Slavic vestiges of archaic IE declensional types (remnants of original consonantal stems, including heteroclites), in particular, have received succinct but apt
treatment (cf. 3: 99-112). In his discussion of the controversial origin of certain declensional endings (such as
those of the previously mentioned genitive singular of the
-$\bar{a}$ stems or dative singular and instrumental plural of the
-o stems) Bräuer's judgment is usually more guarded and
noncommittal than that of, say, Vaillant (cf. 2: 22, 27,
103-4). The German Slavist's traditional, if not to say
somewhat old-fashioned, approach becomes apparent by the
fact that he has not found it necessary to posit, in his
presentation of the underlying PIE vowel system, including
its modifications by qualitative and quantitative ablaut,
any laryngeals (or even one general unspecified laryngeal),
but continues to operate with the conventional *schwa indogermanicum* (*ə*; cf. 1: 66-9, 160-2). It will be interesting to see whether Bräuer will see fit to avoid introducing the laryngeal(s) also in his forthcoming discussion of
CS accentuation.

CS (as well as pre-Slavic) linguistic — including
lexical — structure is also taken into account to a considerable degree in the 1966 introduction to Comparative
Slavic Linguistics coauthored by a team of Ukrainian linguists headed by O. S. Mel'nyčuk, *Vstup do porivnjal'no-
istoryčnoho vyvčennja slov'jans'kyx mov*; cf. especially
the following sections on: the place of Slavic in the IE
language family and the PS homeland (16-21), CS phonology
(26-79), substantival word formation in CS (113-25), adjectival word formation in CS (175-9), formation of numerals in CS (196-9), adverbs in CS (205-6), verbal word
formation in CS (214-27), substantival declension in PIE
and CS (256-71), pronominal declension in PIE and CS (279-
85), adjectival declension in PIE and CS (288-92), gradation in PIE and CS (299-300), declension of numerals in CS
(302-3), conjugation in CS (310-23), CS vocabulary (500-
35); many interspersed comments on CS sentence structure
are also found in the section on syntax (335-499). While
generally reliable and well-documented, this is, however,
on the whole, a fairly traditional treatment of CS (and

pre-Slavic) data.

A fortunate combination of Vasmer's basic methodological principle of letting the facts speak for themselves (largely adhered to, e.g., by Bräuer) and the Prague-phonologist approach (in the definitive formulation given it by Trubeckoj) can be found in the first part of a new outline of Slavic Comparative Grammar, Z. Stieber's *Zarys gramatyki porównawczej języków słowiańskich. Fonologia*, published in 1969 and appropriately dedicated to the memory of Vasmer. As I have in some detail reviewed the great merits and few shortcomings of Stieber's comparative Slavic phonology elsewhere (cf. Birnbaum 1971b), I can confine myself here to merely giving a brief characterization of his text, which follows the methodological approach adopted with much success by the same linguist in his outline of Polish diachronic phonology, already a classic. Crammed into only eighty-two pages, this is a highly condensed but nonetheless exceptionally lucid treatment of primarily CS and Early Slavic phonology (i.e., roughly up to the 13th century), providing merely a few sketchy comments on the subsequent developments of Slavic vocalism (post-13th century) and consonantism (after ca. 1000 A. D.). The hypothetical state of Early CS (PS) serves as the point of departure for Stieber's succinct discussion. Thus, sound shifts believed to have occurred in a period preceding the Slavic linguistic evolution proper (i.e., in a conceivable period of Common Balto-Slavic or in dialectally marked Late PIE) are here only summarily mentioned or even omitted altogether, despite the fact that some of these changes provide the very criteria on the basis of which the emergence of a uniquely Slavic language can be posited. As in Bräuer's outline, the amount of data and theory susceptible to varying interpretation is kept to an absolute minimum. In some instances, notably as regards the treatment of prosodic phenomena (62-5), this self-imposed reticence has forced Stieber to limit his observations to an extent hardly allowing him to discuss even the most basic, if disputed, issues of CS accentology. Unlike Bräuer, Stieber does not avoid offering new, often original explanations of well-known (but, actually, so far poorly understood) CS phenomena and data, deliberately limiting himself, however, to propounding only such theories as can be proven by facts and refraining from other hypotheses that as yet cannot be substantiated by incontestable evidence. In theorizing — but not speculating! — about CS phonology Stieber has acknowledgedly been influenced particularly by Shevelov's monumental text of 1964 (cf. pp. 94-100, below); yet his own treatment, rich in original ideas and conclusions, can by no means merely be considered an abridged or in some points modified version of Shevelov's thought-provoking and detailed reference work. In an article published a few years earlier and preliminary to his own textbook, the Polish Slavist has indicated his assessment of some of the most important recent accomplishments in Comparative Slavic Linguistics, singling out, in particular, a number of newly suggested interpretations and solutions by Shevelov (cf. Stieber 1967).

Like Bräuer's text (and Arumaa's grammar) Stieber's treatment of phonology is preceded by an introduction in which he briefly discusses the presumed location of the original homeland of the Slavs, cautiously adhering to the western theory of the Polish school, placing the earliest ascertainable habitat of the Slavs somewhere north of the Carpathians and Sudetes between the Oder basin in the west and the central and upper Dnieper in the east. He then proceeds to outline the first expansionary moves of the Slavs, critically reassessing earlier theories about the primary dialectal split into a western and eastern (subsequently eastern and southern) dialect group of CS, to trace the further migrations of the Slavs and their linguistic, including ethno- and toponymic, vestiges, and to describe briefly the three traditional subgroups of Slavic. Included in the introduction is further a survey of the first recorded evidence of Slavic, mentioning, in addition to the linguistically controversial *Freising Fragments* and the still earlier entries of Slavic pilgrims' and visitors' names in the ancient Evangeliary of Cividale, particularly also the *Kiev Leaflets* concerning which he reiterates his previously stated (and since contested) view that this text constitutes a specimen closely reflecting the 9th/10th century Slavic vernacular of Pannonia rather than, as is traditionally assumed, representing Macedo-Bulgarian OCS with an admixture of Early Czech-Moravian elements (see also Stieber 1971).

In the strictly phonological sections of his book Stieber suggests, for good reasons it seems, a number of new, generally fairly late chronologies for several CS sound shifts hitherto usually held to have occurred rather early in the CS period. This applies, for example, to the rise of the so-called reduced vowels (ь, ъ < i, u), assigned by Stieber to the 8th century A. D. (28-30), the various monophthongizations, dated by him to the 5th/6th centuries (23-5), and in particular to the Palatalizations of Velars. The First Palatalization is said to have still been fully in effect in the 3rd/4th centuries during the Gothic-Slavic symbiosis and to have ceased to operate only by the following two centuries (66-8). The (regressive) Second Palatalization is said not to have been carried out completely in CS since, as indicated by dialectal evidence gathered particularly from the northwest and the east of the Russian linguistic territory, forms with unshifted as well as only partly shifted consonant (k', etc. and t', etc., respectively) are known to have persisted; the Second Palatalization is therefore dated by him to approximately the 6th/7th centuries (73). On other points, especially as pertains to the CS vowel system, Stieber adopts a sound original or generally modern view. Thus, based on his own previous research, he posits an intermediary stage (denoted ω) for the vowel shift $\bar{u}_1 > y$ (23; cf. also Stieber 1963); he now accepts the notion, most recently advocated by me (cf. Birnbaum 1963), that the CS nasal vowels cannot be assigned phonemic status but must be considered allophones of sound combinations of the type AN (eN, oN); and he shares the now rather commonly embraced view that the timbre of the CS short back vowel presumably was a. (However, this CS a is said to have generally shifted to o in Early Slavic of the 9th/10th centuries. Thus, Stieber rightly, in my opinion, rejects the theory that Russian and Belorussian *akan'e* be interpreted as an archaism, allegedly preserving the CS pronunciation; cf. 18-20, 30.)

Among other keen observations and cogent arguments found in Stieber's text may be mentioned his insistence on the significance of the minimal acoustic-perceptual difference between k', g' and t', d' (in his discussion of the reflexes of CS $t' < tj$, kt', $d' < dj$; 77) and his comment that, while voiced and voiceless consonants are phonemically distinguished in Slavic only by the feature voiced/unvoiced, they are phonetically (subphonemically) differentiated also by the *tenuis/lenis* (tense/lax) opposition. It is this second difference that is said to have triggered the further partial development of voiced affricates to fricatives ($\tilde{\ʒ} > \tilde{z}$, $\acute{ʒ} > \acute{z}$, $ʒ > z$) as well as the spatially restricted shift $g > (\gamma >) h$ (80-1, 89). Stieber's acute revealing of common factors underlying seemingly disparate sound changes in CS and Early Slavic runs largely parallel with the reasoning independently proposed by Andersen (1969).

Part two, issue one, of Stieber's *Zarys* published in
1971, treating nominal inflection, is as condensed and
terse a presentation as the secions of part one on phonology. Yet the basic approach here is essentially a different one due, above all, to the very difference in the
interpretability of the data itself. While the phonological evidence would allow making valid inferences also regarding relatively remote stages in the development of the
CS protolanguage by applying the techniques of the comparative method as well as those of internal reconstruction (resorting, in addition, to early Slavic linguistic
evidence and to the data of closely related language
groups, also to direct — extraneous, as it were — clues
provided by loan word material and toponymic data for the
establishment of chronologies, both absolute and relative,
of various sound shifts), such or similar procedures can
hardly be followed when it comes to reconstructing morphological changes. Here, only the last preliterary stage of
the already disintegrating CS form system can be restored
on the basis of the pertinent evidence found in the earliest Slavic texts, especially OCS and Old Russian. At
best, this reconstructed morphological structure can then
be related, wherever possible, to the hypothetical protoforms of Late PIE as suggested by a comparison with matching data of a number of ancient and/or archaic IE languages. Thus, generally speaking, in CS morphology only
two distinctly separate stages can be reconstructed with
some degree of certainty: the fairly complete system of
Late CS forms, directly traceable from Early Slavic recorded data, and, on the other hand, the only partially
recoverable point of departure for many of these Late CS
forms in a remote Early PS or even pre-Slavic (Balto-
Slavic, Late PIE) past. Stieber, in his comparative
treatment of the Slavic declension, has chosen to focus
almost exclusively on the Late CS situation and to follow
in some detail the development of nominal (and pronominal)
inflection in the various Slavic language groups and individual languages almost up to the present. As an introduction to a major segment of the morphology of CS proper
this part of his textbook is therefore but of limited value, especially as his few, unsystematic references to the
ascertainable Late PIE protoforms underlying the Late CS
data hardly ever deviate from, or go substantially beyond,
standard knowledge of Late PIE or its pre-Slavic (Balto-
Slavic) dialect group. This is not to be construed as a
criticism against Stieber's discussion of the Slavic

declensional system but merely by way of comment, pointing out that, due to its particular emphasis, this portion of his text has much less to offer for the study of CS than his comparative treatment of Slavic phonology including its preliterary phase.

Among the controversial issues of CS, and partly also PIE, morphology where Stieber's position deserves attention (whether one agrees with him or not) at least a few may be mentioned here for exemplification purposes. Thus, for instance, in discussing the origin and early development of the differentiation of gender, the Polish linguist tentatively advances the hypothesis (10) that the primitive speaker of PIE in a distant past may have conceived of all objects in his environment as animate, assigning to them (largely arbitrarily, it seems) masculine, feminine, and neuter gender. While such a hypothesis appears indeed plausible (though hardly provable), it could, on the other hand, also be argued that only the masculine and feminine genders of PIE actually reflect an earlier category of animation, whereas it is precisely the neuter gender that continues, although probably not exclusively, an original category of inanimate objects (in addition to including various living creatures not specified for gender or rather originally not identified with natural sex). It therefore seems at least possible that the gender subdichotomy of animate vs. inanimate, found in Slavic from the very beginning of its attestation, is not in fact merely a general Early Slavic (i.e., post-CS) innovation, as suggested by Stieber (15), but may in some way also be related to a PIE initial bipartition of a similar kind.

The ending -ъ in the nominative singular of the old -ŏ stems is explained by Stieber as rather due to analogy with that of the old -ŭ stems (< *-ŭs) even though he at least considers the possibility of a phonetic development *-ŏs > -ъ (along with *-ŏm > *-ŏn > -ъ in the accusative singular; cf. 12, 22). As keenly noted by the Polish Slavist in this context, the hypothesis of a morphological-analogical rather than phonetic development seems to be corroborated here by, among other things, the introduction into the -jŏ stem declension of the ending -ju (or its earlier form) in the vocative singular, an ending originally belonging to the -jŭ stems, extinct, it seems, already in the CS period. Interesting is, moreover, Stieber's observation (81) that the West Slavic inflectional type represented by P *dobrego, dobremu,* Cz-Slk *dobrého, dobrému,* etc., is a further development of the CS long

adjectival forms *dobrajego, *dobrujemu (found and partly
modified in OCS and Bulgarian), as indicated by the long
-ě- of Czecho-Slovak (cf. also dial. P dobrěgo) pointing
to contraction (< -aje-, -uje-, following the elimination
of intervocalic -j-) rather than to pronominal origin as
in East Slavic (-ogo, -omu; cf. togo, tomu), with the interpretation of the adjectival inflection in NW South
Slavic (Serbo-Croatian, Slovene) being more complex. Except for the CS forms *tysǫtja, *tysętja for the numeral
'thousand', assumed by Stieber (100), parallel, if not
original, forms in -i must be posited, as indicated by
both Slavic and comparative IE evidence (cf. OCS tysǫšti/
tysęšti, Lith tūkstantis, dial. tukstuntis, Goth þusundi
< Gmc *þūs-hundī < PIE *tūs-k'm̥tī). Unjustified seems
Stieber's skepticism as to the CS character of present active participles of the type OCS idy, vědy (104-5), particularly since his own explanation of some of the participial forms in -a (OCz nesa, bera, OR moga, živa) as
solely due to analogy with the soft type (in -ę and its
reflexes), with only five isolated instances of rzeka
(graphically reca) in the earliest Old Polish text allegedly unexplained, is not necessarily quite convincing; cf.
also below, pp. 145 and 157-8.

    Characterized by the same unprejudiced, sober reex-
amination of the available linguistic data as his earlier
writings (notably his textbooks), Stieber in part two of
his outline of Slavic comparative grammar primarily discusses, as was already mentioned, problems of the development of the Slavic declensional patterns from Late CS
through the historical period. He therefore has been able
to avoid taking a stand on such major, as yet unresolved
or only tentatively settled, questions as the origin of
the ending -u of the dative singular of the original -ŏ
stems, of the ending -y of the instrumental plural of the
same stem class, or of the ending -y of the genitive singular of the former -ā stems (given the firmly reconstructed PIE case endings of these forms) or as that of
the precise relationship of CS (j)azъ 'I' to PIE *eg'hō(m),
possibly with a variant *ēg'hom, underlying the Slavic
form, to mention just a few examples. That his interpretation of the Late CS and Early Slavic developments and
his occasional comments on the prehistory of the Late CS
declension, although mostly suggestive and well argued,
can also give rise to some doubts was shown by the sampling of a few controversial instances briefly discussed
here.

Contrary to the German tradition (of Arumaa and Bräuer) and also, for example, to the rich documentation found in Shevelov, Stieber does not offer even a selected bibliography. While this procedure may be understandable in view of the purpose for which his textbook was designed (and also, perhaps, can be explained in terms of his professed preference for extreme succinctness), it nonetheless somewhat reduces the usefulness of his book as a tool for research and independent study. The disadvantage for the initiated reader will not be overly great, however; he will be able to sort out the broad hints and vague references to previous and contemporary scholarship and to translate them into concrete titles and bibliographical data. The less advanced student of Comparative Slavic Linguistics, on the other hand, will have to rely on the word of the author. This he can do, in most cases, without too much hesitation for this is an excellent introduction to the field, some very minor deficiencies notwithstanding. There is every reason to assume that its sequel will be of the same overall high quality in substance as well as in approach and style of exposition. (Part two, issue three, treating verbal inflection has since appeared — in 1973 — and will be discussed in the companion volume to this one, scheduled to appear in 1978 and providing an updating of the present research report through 1977.) For a brief statement of the Polish Slavist's view of the earliest Slavic dialectal differences, see further Stieber 1968b (in Polish and French variants).

In addition to the various treatments of Comparative Slavic Linguistics reviewed here, there are of course others, some of considerable merit, which would deserve mention. This applies, in particular, to the following texts: R. Trautmann 1947, M. Braun 1947, W. J. Entwistle and W. A. Morison 1949, T. Lehr-Spławiński, W. Kuraszkiewicz, and F. Sławski 1954, R. Jakobson [2]1955, K. Horálek 1955, [2]1962, N. A. Kondrašov [2]1962, and S. Ivšić 1970. However, these as well as some further texts designed for a similar purpose do not, by and large, substantially add to our knowledge of CS beyond that conveyed in the above discussed works.

Trautmann's introduction focuses on the various subgroups (South, West, East Slavic) and the languages constituting them and touches only very briefly on the problems of CS, adopting van Wijk's view of a few major tendencies dominating the restructuring of its phonological system (15-17). Braun's text treats CS in somewhat

54

greater detail (14-22) without, however, imparting any particularly important new insights. Interesting, if not fully convincing, is his grouping of the Late CS dialects (and their successor languages) into two initial units, one cis-Carpathian and one trans-Carpathian. The comparative treatment of *Russian and the Slavonic Languages* by Entwistle and Morison discusses the general aspects of "Balto-Slavonic and Proto-Slavonic" in a separate chapter (II: 50-9), establishing a firm but questionable periodization on the basis of rather definite (though, in fact, highly disputable) chronologies ("Primitive Slavonic," "Early Proto-Slavonic," "Middle Proto-Slavonic," "Late Proto-Slavonic"). The adduced illustrative data, both Slavic and comparative IE, is generally accurate and instructive. Lumped together with OCS ("Old Bulgarian," in the British scholars' terminology) is a long chapter on CS "Sounds," "Forms and Their Uses," and "Words" (IV: 71-170), providing a fairly comprehensive and reliable account of the respective data covered. However, not all of the generously offered explanations of underlying causes will withstand critical evaluation, and the occasional failure to clearly distinguish between reconstructed CS and attested Early Slavic (primarily, though not exclusively, OCS) adds to blurring the emerging overall picture. Particularly useful is the section on lexicology ("Words"), focusing on early borrowings and word formation.

Jakobson's *Slavic Languages* is, as suggested by the subtitle of his booklet, an extremely condensed survey, tersely restating his fundamental views on Slavic linguistic diachrony. A short section on "Protoslavic; Expansions" (4-5) identifies the earliest specifics of Slavic (in contrast to other IE languages) and provides basic background information. The sections on "Comparative Phonology" (13-17, also reprinted together with the first section on "Protoslavic" in Jakobson 1962: 413-17) and "Comparative Grammar" (17-21, now reprinted in Jakobson 1971: 115-18) sketch in brief outline the evolution of Slavic diachronic phonology, morphology, and syntax as conceived (and partly in much greater detail treated elsewhere) by the leading American Slavist (cf. pp. 85-8, below). The introductory text by the Polish team of linguists mentioned above (with the section on CS authored by Lehr-Spławiński), the one by Horálek, and the one by Kondrašov, all provide valuable, partly detailed, information also on CS without, however, essentially going beyond a traditional treatment of the subject.

In the classical neogrammarian tradition, and today therefore primarily of historical interest, is finally also the posthumous textbook *Slavenska poredbena gramatika* by S. Ivšić (edited and in terms of references slightly updated by J. Vrana and R. Katičić) giving a fairly detailed account of CS phonology, morphology, and — though less completely — syntax as well as the further modifications of these subsystems in the various Slavic languages, especially Serbo-Croatian. While amply testifying to the Croatian linguist's vast erudition, lucid style, and profound insight (given the state of methodological progress and factual knowledge attained roughly during the first third of our century) this, consequently, must be considered a book largely obsolete already at the time of its first appearance. Only some particular sections, notably those on Slavic accentuation, one of the chief research interests of the author and even today a matter of much controversy, retain a good deal of their original topicality (cf. 150-78, chapters XI-XIII, on accentuation in general, CS accentuation, and the accent system of Serbo-Croatian — the latter being the text of a much noted Ivšić lecture of 1953, integrated by the editors with the rest of the author's lecture scripts of essentially a considerably earlier date).

2.3. *Indo-European Grammar and Dialectology; Prehistory of Common Slavic*. Turning now to some major comprehensive treatments of Comparative IE Linguistics, it should be noted that neither the detailed, authoritative codification of the IE linguistic material according to the neogrammarian doctrine undertaken jointly by K. Brugmann and B. Delbrück in their monumental *Grundriss der vergleichenden Grammatik der indogermanischen Sprachen* (2nd edition of the first two volumes: volume I — introduction and phonology, volume II — morphology, by Brugmann, 1897-1916; volumes III-V — syntax, by Delbrück, 1893-1900, with volumes III and IV partly superseded, however, by Brugmann's 2nd edition of volume II), nor the 1904 abridged one-volume version, based on the five-volume set, by K. Brugmann alone, *Kurze vergleichende Grammatik der indogermanischen Sprachen*, while rich in data also from Slavic (notably OCS) and Baltic (notably Lithuanian), contain any crucial information or discussion essentially going beyond data and theory found, to some extent, already in Miklosich's broadly designed reference work of Comparative Slavic Linguistics. The latter, it is true, was still

56

conceived in the pre-neogrammarian vein. Nor does Brugmann's work contain any information not also found, though
in greater detail of course, in Vondrák's comparative
grammar of Slavic which, on the other hand, fully adhered
to the methodological principles proclaimed by the neo-
grammarians (cf. above). More immediately, the treatment
and assessment of Slavic (and Baltic) material, viewed in
its overall IE context, as presented in Brugmann's (and
Delbrück's) reference works, reflect the intimate knowledge and keen evaluation of such data by a close fellow-
neogrammarian of the Leipzig School and a then leading
Slavist, A. Leskien, laid down in his historically tinged
textbooks of Lituanian (1919b), OCS (cf. Leskien, 1919a;
[8]1962), and Serbo-Croatian (1914), and in a number of specialized monographs and articles concerned with Balto-
Slavic Linguistics.

   The large-scale reference work designed to replace
the neogrammarian edifice of Comparative IE Linguistics at
least in the German-speaking world, H. Hirt's strongly
opinionated *Indogermanische Grammatik* (in seven volumes,
1927-37), while no doubt challenging and intriguing in
areas of its author's special scholarly concerns, primarily ablaut and accentuation (in which field Hirt's theories
were fully superseded only by Kuryłowicz 1952, [2]1958a,
1956, 1968a), does not, generally speaking, represent any
real advancement over Brugmann's or, when it comes to
Slavic, Leskien's findings and utilization of the relevant
linguistic evidence. In any case, for the progress of reconstructing CS, Hirt's work is, for all intents and purposes, negligible.

   The same is definitely not the case, on the other
hand, with A. Meillet's magistral outline of Comparative
IE Linguistics, *Introduction a l'étude comparative des
langues indoeuropéennes* (1903, 8th, posthumous edition,
1937), a brilliant condensation of this great and many-
sided Indo-Europeanist's compounded research in which, incidentally, the Slavic component provided one of the cor-
nerstones. Still, having summed up his findings and
thinking on CS linguistic structure in greater detail in a
work specifically devoted to that subject (Meillet 1924;
cf. above), Meillet's *Introduction* does not, in terms both
of factual data and its interpretation, add substantially
to his own more complete treatment of the reconstructed
Slavic evidence, but merely provides a wider framework into which hypothetic CS can be integrated. Moreover, for
the student of IE linguistics not primarily concerned with

Slavic, the more broadly comparative approach of the *Introduction*, adducing a limited amount of carefully selected relevant and reliable Slavic data along with evidence from a number of other IE language groups, may present a certain (at least practical) advantage.

V. Pisani's *Glottologia indeuropea* ([3]1961), placing particular emphasis on Greek and Latin and arranging its subject matter predominantly in tripartite sections treating, in this order, IE, Greek, and Latin, naturally does not focus on Slavic but does, as shown also by the numerous OCS ("Old Bulgarian") items listed in the appended word index, take into account Slavic data as reflected in its earliest literary attestation.

Also the best among recent outlines of Comparative IE Linguistics, O Szemerényi's *Einführung in die vergleichende Sprachwissenschaft* (1970), treating primarily phonology (including morphophonemics) and morphology and applying largely contemporary methods of diachronic linguistics, adduces a considerable amount of Slavic (mostly OCS) and Baltic (mostly Lituanian) evidence and is impressively up-to-date in its broadly selected bibliographical references. Critical about Kuryłowicz's interpretation of some phenomena of Balto-Slavic accentuation as to a large extent being due to secondary developments, i.e., as supposedly not immediately traceable to any PIE origins (71-4, cf. also below), Szemerényi's own treatment of ablaut (76-87) is perhaps partly overly traditional and therefore does not take into account certain recently gained insights into some of the submechanisms of IE vowel alternation (cf., e.g., so-called *Schwebeablaut*, explored by Anttila 1969). A revised English edition of Szemerényi's generally excellent and most useful introduction is presently in preparation.

Both volumes, published to date, of the new *Indogermanische Grammatik* (under the general editorship of J. Kuryłowicz) designed to replace the controversial and, in fact, inadequate IE grammar by Hirt are of immediate bearing also on some crucial aspects of CS. The second volume (*Akzent, Ablaut* 1968), which appeared first and is authored by Kuryłowicz, summarizes the leading Polish Indo-Europeanist's relevant research, previously set forth in two bulky monographs (cf. Kuryłowicz 1952, [2]1958; 1956), adding only a few minor modifications and tightening the exposition for the purpose of textbook presentation. While Kuryłowicz's treatment of IE accentuation and specifically his interpretations of Balto-Slavic accentology (regarded

by him as not directly relatable to the prosodic patterns
of PIE) have not gained complete or even particularly wide
acceptance, there can be little doubt that his new, structural approach to the many intricate problems involved —
definitely breaking with the neogrammarian as well as some
other, post-neogrammarian yet traditionalist attempts to
handle them — represents a tremendous advance over previous directions of relevant research and has already yielded highly significant, novel insights into the moving
forces which underlie the overt patterns of IE, including
Balto-Slavic, accentuation. It is a different question,
of course, whether all solutions proposed by Kuryłowicz to
account for the whole of IE accentology will ultimately
stand up to critical scrutiny.

After discussing in the first sections of the introduction to the accentological portion of his book the conceptual and definitional prerequisites adopted, viewing
accentuation as a phonological means utilized in morphology, i.e., as a phenomenon of morphophonemics in the broad
sense, and briefly characterizing the nature of intonation
(pitch) as divisibility (analyzability) of the long core
of a syllable (i.e., a long vowel or a diphthong) into two
morae of which one is stressed ($\acute{o}\smile$ = falling pitch, $\smile\acute{o}$ =
rising pitch), Kuryłowicz in the following devotes a long
chapter (IV) to "The special development of Balto-Slavic."
Strictly speaking, the term *Balto-Slavic* is here slightly
inappropriate and ought to be qualified as including, in
addition, Baltic *and* Slavic as separate units, since the
Polish linguist assumes two distinct prehistoric developments of stress and pitch of considerable duration and
complexity in each of the two language groups subsequent
to an initial phase of shared Balto-Slavic accentual evolution. Here is not the place, of course, to even attempt
to summarize the Polish comparatist's theory of Balto-
Slavic prosody. Suffice it to say that it comprises one
of two, partly conflicting, conceptions of CS accentology
deserving serious consideration today, the other one belonging to Chr. Stang (cf. Stang 1957b; see also below pp.
117-19). Whereas Greek prosody can be interpreted as a
further development of the accentual system prevailing in
PIE, more closely reflected in Vedic, the patterns of
stress and pitch found in Baltic and Slavic cannot, according to Kuryłowicz, be directly related to the IE system. The Polish comparatist considers the rise of phonemic pitch in Balto-Slavic a result of the shifting back of
the stress from word-medial to word-initial syllables

59

(while in Greek it is said to be conditioned by prehistoric vowel contractions). Vowel quantity is believed to have played a crucial role here as the stress was retracted only from word-medial short vowels (and diphthongs) and phonemic pitch (acute intonation) appears in first syllables with long vocalism. Thus, in word-initial position a phonemic opposition is said to have obtained by which new and old stress are contrasted as acute vs. circumflex intonation, respectively. Word-medial syllables with long vocalism carry merely phonetic (subphonemic) acute intonation, not contrasting with circumflex which is inadmissible in this position. The incompatability of the Greek and Balto-Slavic intonation systems is said to be borne out by the fact that phonemic pitch oppositions are limited in Greek to the word-final syllable where, on the other hand, intonational distinctions are neutralized in Balto-Slavic, and that in Greek falling pitch is the marked member of the correlation while in Balto-Slavic it is rising pitch that is marked. The shortening of long diphthongs ($\bar{e}i > ei$, $\bar{e}r > er$, etc.) led to (phonemic) intonability of all (short) diphthongs ($\acute{e}i : e\tilde{i}$, $\acute{e}r : e\tilde{r}$, etc., diphthongs with falling pitch representing original short diphthongs). Subsequently Kuryłowicz goes on to discuss the function of intonation and stress in various morphological categories (of nominal inflection, composition, and derivation, verbal inflection and derivation). In describing and analyzing this function he heavily relies on phonological and morphological (as well as, to some extent, semantic) types and patterns, in part conceived and coined by himself, such as oxytone (marginal) : barytone (columnal) fixed stress as opposed to mobile stress, non-motivated (primary) : motivated (secondary, derived) formations, strong : weak cases, etc. As for the controversial stress shift rule known as "Saussure's law" (though more appropriately to be labeled "Leskien-Saussure's law"), Kuryłowicz, like Saussure (but contrary to Fortunatov who misread parallel surface realizations as implementations of identical underlying factors), restricts the applicability of this low-level rule to Lithuanian while giving it a new and quite different interpretation; according to Kuryłowicz, primary here is the shortening of certain word-final long vowels, and the shifting of the stress to the last syllable is merely a corollary of the vowel shortening. As a result, acute (being the marked member of the intonation correlation) is in Lithuanian — at least phonemically — reversed to equal the mora sequence ‿ (as

opposed to Balto-Slavic ⌣̑) with an automatic reversion
of circumflex intonation from Balto-Slavic ⌣̑ to ⌣̑ .
This reinterpretation of "Saussure's law," here briefly
summarized, has become the subject of much controversy and
misunderstanding. Other, perhaps equally significant re-
evaluations of known Balto-Slavic or Baltic and Slavic
prosodic phenomena, proposed by Kuryłowicz, cannot be surveyed here for lack of space.

As is well known, the morphophonemic mechanism subsumed under the term ablaut, qualitative as well as quantitative, is closely connected with prosodic phenomena,
particularly in Balto-Slavic. Thus, acute intonation is
here frequently an indirect reflex of a lost laryngeal
(*erH* or *erₐ >ḗr > ér*, etc.). Apophonic alternations play
an important role also in Balto-Slavic, and Kuryłowicz,
the originator of the "laryngeal theory" (based on Hittite
evidence first properly interpreted by him following
purely theoretical assumptions made previously by Saussure), has contributed many new insightful comments also
on the Balto-Slavic data. By and large it is less the
qualitative ablaut (*e/o*, etc.) that presents a problem in
Slavic even if this alternation, too, is well represented
here. More difficult to interpret and hence controversial
are Balto-Slavic phenomena of quantitative ablaut, especially zero-grade and its secondary lengthening. Thus,
Kuryłowicz regards the well-known double reflexes *ir/ur*,
il/ul, *in/un*, *im/um* of Balto-Slavic not as directly reflecting a qualitative distinction of the PIE reduced
grade (*ₑr/ₒr*, etc.) but is rather inclined to interpret
ir, *il*, etc., as the regular reflex of PIE zero-grade *r̥*,
l̥, etc., attributing the reflexes (considerably less frequent and partly etymologically obscure) of the *u*-series,
ur, *ul*, etc., to phonetic conditioning in the position
after velar (*kr̥ > kur*, etc.). Therefore, the double reflexes of Balto-Slavic, as such, cannot be said to be due
to any special phonological development particular only to
Balto-Slavic but must, according to the Polish comparatist,
rather be seen in connection with the rise of the correlation palatal vs. nonpalatal in the consonant system of
these languages (cf. 240-3). Ingenious as this theory is
(and it should be pointed out that Vaillant has previously
pursued a similar line of reasoning), it nonetheless
raises some serious chronological doubts since it is perhaps not easy to subscribe to Kuryłowicz's view that it
does not really matter in this connection whether the opposition of palatalized vs. nonpalatalized consonants

represents a Balto-Slavic isogloss or developed independently in both language branches (241); cf. also Stieber's
late dating of the First Palatalization of Velars, discussed above. As for the PIE reduced grade proper, the
Polish linguist does posit, as shown in greater detail in
his larger work on ablaut, such an earlier stage (with reduced e, o or perhaps rather only o resulting from the
shift $e > o$, merging the two sounds into one) but suggests
that this was an unstable phase which was either further
reduced to zero ($or > r̥$) or was subsequently restored to
full vocalism ($ot > et/ot$). For the further reduction of
prehistoric IE (i.e., reduced > zero grade), Slavic, according to Kuryłowicz, provides a telling parallel, not to
be taken, however, for a direct reflex of the pre-Slavic
development (cf. PS *vĭlkŭ* or *vьlkъ* > CS *vl̥'kъ/vl̥kъ*; CS
bьrati > R *brat'*, P *brać*, etc.). Also the utilization of
qualitative ablaut and, in particular, of secondary quantitative ablaut (including lengthening of zero grade) in
the morphology of the Baltic and Slavic verb (and in deverbative derivation) is treated at some length by Kuryłowicz (cf. 293-7, 318-26). For some reservations concerning certain points in Kuryłowicz's ablaut theory, see T.
Mathiassen 1970a, 1970b, briefly discussed below (p. 250).

In part one of the third volume of the new IE grammar, written by C. Watkins and treating conjugation (3:
Formenlehre, 1: *Geschichte der Indogermanischen Verbalflexion,* 1969), a chapter is also devoted to Balto-Slavic
(XV: 210-25). Viewed in its IE setting which the author
has discussed in previous chapters, the Slavic (and Baltic) verb is treated here strictly as a further development
and modification of a set of morphological categories of
IE. Thus, a new, post-PIE category such as the imperfect,
being a CS innovation (of controversial origin), is not
even mentioned, while other specifically or primarily
Slavic categories, such as full-fledged aspect (perfective : imperfective) and its formal characteristics, will
possibly be dealt with only in a subsequent volume treating verbal derivation.

As far as I have been able to determine, Watkins'
discussion of Slavic data does not suggest any altogether
novel, original explanations of phenomena previously unaccounted for or controversial. Rather, he summarizes, with
good judgment and circumspection, relevant (and mostly recent) research in the field, weighing the merits and
shortcomings of work by Fortunatov, van Wijk, Kuryłowicz,
Stang, Vaillant, Kuznecov, Ivanov, Toporov, and others.

Modifying Kuznecov's explanation and adhering to Toporov's
pertinent view, the American Indo-Europeanist considers
bare stem forms of the type OCS *veze* (ending in the thematic vowel -*e* with zero desinence, to be sure, rare in OCS)
primary as compared to the more regular endings of the 3rd
person singular (in -*tъ*, -*tь*); this enables him to link
the Slavic evidence with parallels in Greek and Celtic.
This hypothesis Watkins sees corroborated by the imperative (earlier "injunctive") form OCS *bǫdǫ* < *-*ont* (not <
*-*oint* as Vaillant claims) which he interprets as reflecting the original ending of the 3rd person plural of the
present indicative. The -*tъ* of OCS *veze-tъ*, *vezǫ-tъ* Watkins — not too convincingly, it would seem to me — explains, following Fortunatov and Kuznecov, as a generalization of a first optionally added subject pronoun (*tos =
OCS *tъ*, Lith *tàs*, OPr suffixal -*ts*). For -*ǫ* of the 1st
person singular Watkins (in accordance with Stang and
others) assumes underlying PIE *-*ō* + secondary ending
*-(*o*)*m* while rejecting Vaillant's derivation *-*ōm* < *-*ōmi*.
Following Kuryłowicz, Watkins traces the Slavic verb type
represented by OCS *mьněti*, *mьnitъ* (class IV b) to old perfect forms and considers the inflection of the type *xvali-
ti* or *saditi* (class IV a) due to analogy with that of
mьněti (thus eliminating the alleged "semi-thematic" inflectional type, still posited by Stang). OCS *mьni*(*tъ*)
(= Lith *mìni*, with shortened -*i*), providing the basis for
the whole paradigm, he reconstructs as PIE *m₀n-ei.

Already these brief remarks, mentioning only a few
points discussed in the *Indogermanische Grammatik*, will
indicate the great importance of this new reference work
also for the reconstruction of CS. It goes without saying
that the volumes yet to appear (phonology to be treated by
W. Cowgill, the rest of morphology by C. Watkins, and syntax by V. V. Ivanov) can be expected to further add substantially to our understanding also of CS linguistic
structure and its prehistory.

In addition to comprehensive text- and handbooks of
IE grammar, general studies surveying the dialects of IE —
whether these are conceived as actual regional varieties
of the Late Common IE protolanguage or as primitive,
largely preliterary (and hence only reconstructed) forms
of individual IE language groups, early attested (like
Hittite, Greek, or Old Indic) or archaic in character
(like Baltic or, at least to some extent, Slavic) — are of
some significance also for the reconstruction of CS and
its immediate predecessors. Foremost among the earlier

outlines of IE dialectology in terms of lucidity of style
and exposition ranks A. Meillet's *Les dialectes indo-
européens*, first published in 1908 and thereafter in a
second, slightly revised edition in 1922. While largely
superseded today by more recent scholarship allowing for a
deeper understanding of the structure and mechanisms of
the IE protolanguage and its ultimate disintegration,
Meillet's brief outline, based on a course given at the
Collège de France in 1906/7, was still considered insightful and precise enough to warrant an English translation
as late as in 1967. Moreover, for the history of the
problem of Balto-Slavic linguistic relationships, his work
marks a milestone, as it was in this book that Meillet for
the first time at some length propounded his view that
"Baltic and Slavic had identical points of departure and
that they developed under the same conditions and influences." According to Meillet, "there may even have been
some period of common development, but, if so, neither
Baltic nor Slavic, the most conservative of the Indo-
European languages, produced any notable innovations in
the course of it." Therefore, as he saw it, "Baltic and
Slavic provide a fine example of two parallel, but long
autonomous, developments" (cf. 67 in the English translation). Previously also Meillet had expressed similar
opinions more succinctly; cf. Meillet 1902/5, 2 (^{2}1961):
201-2. This view, while accepted in slightly modified
form by some Baltologists (for example, J. Endzelīns and
more recently A. Senn), was challenged by others who have
suggested different approaches to account for the no doubt
striking agreements of the two language groups concerned
(cf. Birnbaum 1970a; see also pp. 317-22, below).

Already Meillet (in chapter V of his IE dialectology,
on "The gutturals") had attached only secondary importance
to the *centum/satəm* division, once considered the chief
watershed separating all IE dialects into two major groups.
The deemphasizing of this particular feature has subsequently continued (cf. above, p. 16) and it plays merely
a subordinate role in the so far best overall study
on the language groupings of the IE area, *Die Gliederung
des indogermanischen Sprachgebiets* by W. Porzig (1954).
Here the relevant Slavic data is firmly integrated with
comparable features and phenomena of other IE languages,
both those considered more or less closely related (i.e.,
above all, Baltic, Indo-Iranian, and, on the other hand,
Germanic) and others to which Slavic is only more remotely
related (e.g., Armenian, Thracian, Illyrian, Hittite,

Tocharian, Celtic). The extremely complex picture, emerging from Porzig's presentation, of the connections holding Slavic firmly embedded, as it were, among the various IE sister idioms is therefore apt to supplement and partly supersede earlier surveys of the specific relationships obtaining between Slavic and some cognate language groups (cf. for example, E. Fraenkel 1950: 73-123 — as related to Baltic; H. Arntz 1933 — as related to Indo-Iranian). For relevant page references to Porzig's book, see above, p. 21.

A somewhat different approach was taken in the volume *Ancient Indo-European Dialects*, edited by H. Birnbaum and J. Puhvel (1966), in which are recorded a number of papers read at a conference on IE Linguistics, held at the University of California, Los Angeles, in 1963. Of the two contributions concerned with Slavic material, A. Senn's "The relationships of Baltic and Slavic" (139-51) and "The dialects of Common Slavic" (153-97) by the present writer, only the former addressed itself to one aspect of the broader issue of the place of Slavic among the IE languages. Polemicizing with a then recent article by O. Szemerényi (1957) surveying the Balto-Slavic problem, Senn discusses points of agreement and, mainly, disagreement between himself and Szemerényi, restating his previously known position, admitting "the term 'Balto-Slavic' in the sense of 'Baltic and Slavic' and in the meaning of the 'Proto-Indo-European of Northeastern Europe in its last phase.'" It is, according to Senn, "the residue of Proto-Indo-European, the remainder left after all adjacent parts had entered into history and developed into independently regulated languages" (143). Among the fourteen allegedly common Balto-Slavic innovations enumerated by Szemerényi and discussed by Senn, it is notably the to some extent justified criticism of the first two, namely, 1) Balto-Slavic palatalizations, and 2) the development of i and, after velars, u before r, l, n, m (< PIE $\underset{.}{r}$, $\underset{.}{l}$, $\underset{.}{n}$, $\underset{.}{m}$), adopted from Kuryłowicz, that deserves mention (cf. also above on Kuryłowicz's treatment of ablaut). Cf. now also Senn 1970, once more restating his earlier position but also making some quite untenable, even unscholarly, it would seem, assumptions and claims; cf. below, pp. 318-20. In my discussion of CS dialects, taking as a point of departure A. Furdal's monograph of the disintegration of CS (cf. Furdal 1961; for a brief discussion, see below, pp. 106 -9, 234). I attempted to reassess, after having examined admissible criteria and available data, both the ultimate division of CS dialects (subsequently developing into the separate Slavic languages) and their underlying, earlier grouping, commenting in passing on some problems of relative chronology. In summing up, I concluded (197) "that the traditional tripartition into East, West, and South Slavic languages respectively remains valid in the light of CS dialectology. However, such a classification should be considered primarily as based on statistically derived synchronic data, since the underlying, many-layered diachronic phenomena do not represent any consistent, rectilinear evolution, as the adherents of the *Stammbaum* theory would have been inclined to believe."

A brief sketch of Late CS dialectology was recently propounded by Z. Stieber (1968b). However, this short outline does not add substantially to suggestions made by the same linguist elsewhere (cf. Stieber 1967, 1969/71).

CS linguistic structure as a whole or some major component of it, viewed against the background of its IE origin, has also been the subject of monographic treatment. Among earlier attempts in this direction, retaining some significance though now partly obsolete, the book by J. M. Kořínek, *Od indoeuropského prajazyka k praslovančine*, published posthumously in 1948, ought to be mentioned for its wealth of pertinent data and keen observations. Prepared for publication from an unfinished manuscript, written largely before World War II, this broad sketch was originally designed as section one of a comprehensive history (and prehistory) of Slovak which, however, was never completed. Strictly neogrammarian in approach, Kořínek's text, after an introductory discussion of the methods used in linguistic reconstruction (with special regard to the prehistory of Slavic), sketches the vowel and consonant systems of PIE, as conceived by late neogrammarian theory of the interwar period (positing, for example, in addition to the traditional *schwa indogermanicum* also a second *schwa*, allegedly representing the reduced grade of full-grade short vowels, a theory elaborated in Güntert 1916) and traces the development of these systems down to Early CS (PS) or rather to those sound changes which usually have been considered to mark the emergence of Slavic as an independent branch of the IE language family. In the discussion of the vowel system and its modifications a few comments on accentuation are inserted as well. Of the morphological outline only the portion treating nominal inflection (including some remarks on derivation) was completed, while the section on the pronoun has remained a fragment and only a few scattered notes on the verb were found in the author's bequest, not warranting their inclusion in the published version of his work.

Whereas Kořínek's outline, while unfinished, was originally designed as a systematic treatment of the major facets of phonology and morphology in their evolution from Late Common IE to Early CS (PS), this is not the case with another work on a similar theme which, rather than attempting to provide any complete coverage, on the contrary dwells on particularly controversial problems and previously insufficiently explored areas of IE Linguistics, with a special emphasis on Slavic (as well as Anatolian) data, V. V. Ivanov's monograph *Obščeindoevropejskaja, praslavjanskaja i anatolijskaja jazykovye sistemy (sravnitel'no-tipologičeskie očerki)*, published in 1965. Fully up-to-date with recent and then current research in the field and applying the most modern linguistic methods (including those of typological linguistics), this monograph, as pointed out by its author in the preface, is "the result of an endeavor to reconsider the new possibilities opening up before the comparative-historical study of the IE languages (including Slavic) thanks to the new, significant discoveries connected with the decipherment of previously unknown IE languages."

The slight disproportion of its four loosely connected sections is due, as further explained by Ivanov, to the fact that part of his relevant research had been previously published so that, in order not to make his book bulky, the first sections on "Some questions of phonology and morphophonology" and "Some questions of the morphology of the noun" are relatively short and largely supplementary to findings reported elsewhere, while the two subsequent sections on "The morphology of the verb" and "The reconstruction of syntactic structures" are not only considerably more extensive but also contain substantial, original contributions to our knowledge in this area; in addition, these are the sections focusing particularly on Slavic evidence. Thus, in the chapter on the "Two Indo-European sets of verbal forms" Ivanov, partly following and partly arguing against Stang (as well as others), discusses, among other things, some Slavic items attested already in OCS as thematic formations while originally belonging to the athematic root verb type (*ženǫ/gъnati, žьnǫ/žęti; strěgǫ/strěšti*; with some qualifications, further, R *torotorit'* and OCS *glagoljǫ*, both with reduplication, possibly also *borjǫ, koljǫ, sopǫ, pojǫ, godǫ*, OR

stonju, Cz *stůňu*; cf. also Ivanov 1970: 207). Discussing
verbs of the Hittite -*ḫi* conjugation (relatable to perfect
and mediopassive formations), Ivanov points out their connection with such partly reduplicating verbs as OCS *deždǫ/*
děti (with the derivative *dějǫ/dějati*) and *dadętъ* (ptc.
dady) /*dati* (with the derivative *dajǫ/dajati*). Other
Slavic verb forms discussed in this context include:
stǫpiti/stǫpati, *stanǫ*, *vedǫ*, -*spějǫ*, *sějǫ*, *vějǫ*, *sędǫ/*
sěsti (: *sěděti*), *moliti* (Cz *modliti*), OR *měniti*, OCS
mъnitъ/mъněti. OCS *vědě* (Lat *uīdī*), an original perfect
(though, according to Ivanov, hardly mediopassive) is said
to testify, along with Hitt -*ḫi* (archaic Hitt -*ḫe*) to the
confusion of the two sets of verbal forms in IE, OPr -*mai*
(cf. *asmai*, along with *asmu*, *asmau*) providing further
proof. Treating "Verbal forms in *-*s*- and *-*sḱ*-*," Ivanov
finds Slavic parallels to Anatolian -*s* and -*sk'* formations; cf., e.g., OCS *pas-ti* (Lat *pās-tum*, *pās-tor*), Hitt
paḫš-; OCS aor. *ěsъ* (*jasъ*), SCr *ješa*, Anat **ad-s*- (Luw
azzaš), further OCS *jasli*, Latv *ēsli*(*s*) (< **ēd-s-li*); OCS
aor. *věsъ*, Hitt *ḫuez-ta* (< **Huedh-s-tHo*); OCS *slušati* (:
sluti), Lith *klaŭso*, *kláusia*, Toch B *klyaus*-, Toch A
klyos-, cf. OHG *lüschen*. Discussing "Some other types of
verbal stems," the Soviet linguist adduces Hittite and IE
counterparts to the Slavic formations with nasal affix;
cf. OCS (*vъz*)*niknǫti*, Lith (*ap*)*nikti*, -*ninka*, Hitt *ninink*-;
OCS *lęgǫ*, Hitt *lak-nu*. Similarly, equivalents are further
quoted for verbs with the suffix *-*i̯o*-; cf. OCS (*u*)*tajǫ*,
Hitt **tai̯*(*a*)*zi*- (reconstructable from the attested Early
Hittite deverbative noun *tai̯azil*-; note also OCS *tatъ*, Ir
táith, *taid*).

While the just cited, largely new collocations of
Slavic and other IE (particularly Hittite) linguistic
items are most revealing, affording new insights into the
underlying morphological structure primarily of the Slavic
verb, Ivanov's utilization of Slavic (Early Slavic as well
as archaic, folkloric Slavic), Hittite, and other IE material for the purpose of tentatively reconstructing some
syntactic patterns and models of the common protolanguage
must be considered truly pioneering, especially from a
methodological point of view. By examining in three chapters the "Reconstruction of the schema for the basic type
of projecting the tree of the Indo-European verbal sentence," the "Reconstruction of the schema for projecting
the tree of the sentence with the verb in initial position," and the "Reflection of traces of the ancient type
of the nominal sentence," Ivanov has been able to retrieve

with appreciable accuracy a substantial body of primitive IE sentence structure. The Soviet comparatist's achievements in the field of syntactic reconstruction (shortly to be summed up in the portion on syntax of the new collective *Indogermanische Grammatik* referred to above, but, as applied to CS, already to a considerable extent reported and demonstrated in a number of specialized studies, partly in collaboration with V. N. Toporov) will be discussed in some detail in following sections of the present account and need therefore only brief mention here.

Other recent studies treating the development from (Late Common) IE to CS (PS) focus mostly on some specific problem, usually one of phonology (cf., e.g., Martynov 1968; Mathiassen 1970a, 1970b) but occasionally also on a problem of morphology (as well as functional syntax; cf. Kølln 1969).

2.4. Diachrony of Individual Slavic Languages. Finally, as was mentioned before, there is still another kind of general reference work which occasionally, usually by way of introduction, though sometimes also integrated into the various sections on phonology and morphology, may include at least a brief outline of CS linguistic structure and the major changes it underwent — the text- and handbooks covering the history of individual Slavic languages.

It is only natural, of course, that information on the underlying development of CS will be found in textbooks and reference grammars of OCS, the earliest attested written language of the Slavs and, in fact, scarcely more than the first literary recording of a Late CS dialect, namely, primarily that of the Macedo-Bulgarian region. Yet, not all texts of OCS will necessarily provide a brief introduction to CS as well. Thus, the best descriptive (synchronic) handbooks on the oldest Slavic literary language, whether predominantly philological in their orientation (such as the excellent detailed textbooks of Diels and Vaillant) or rather adopting a structuralist approach (as found, for example, in the OCS grammars of Trubeckoj and Lunt) will contain little, if any, or usually at most oblique, reference to CS linguistic data and its interpretation. On the other hand, textbooks of OCS conceived diachronically, i.e., designed primarily as introductions to the early history (and prehistory) of Slavic, obviously use the data of OCS to illustrate the first attested phase in the evolution of the Slavic languages and therefore frequently dwell at some length also on the stages

preceding the one recorded by the oldest texts preserved.
Such was the attitude, for example, of the neogrammarian
school and it is therefore not surprising that in the two
textbooks of OCS written by one of its foremost proponents,
A. Leskien, *Grammatik der altbulgarischen (altkirchenslavischen) Sprache* (2nd & 3rd editions, 1919) and *Handbuch der altbulgarischen (altkirchenslavischen) Sprache*
([5]1910; posthumous 6th, 7th, and 8th editions, 1922, 1955,
1962), much space is devoted to preliterary changes and
their respective points of departure in PIE. Particularly
Leskien's *Handbuch* was long considered a model tool for
classroom teaching as, incidentally, suggested by the
relatively recent date of its last, updated and augmented
edition. Yet, the language, especially as presented in
the many complete paradigms of Leskien's reference works,
is more a normalized (or standardized) ideal OCS, closely
reflecting the norm of "Proto-Church Slavic" (to use
Trubeckoj's term) of the Cyrillo-Methodian period, than
the already slightly distorted and modified Early Slavic
actually attested in the extant manuscripts. Whereas the
Handbuch at least indicates some of the differences in
spelling and forms encountered in the various OCS texts,
samples of which are appended together with a glossary,
the *Grammatik*, being more theoretically oriented, focuses
primarily on the comparison of the OCS sounds and forms
with their presumed reconstructed CS and PIE antecedents.
Further, the *Grammatik* includes a sketch of nominal word
formation (missing in the *Handbuch*) while containing only
a few scattered remarks on the syntax of the verb (viz.,
on aspect in the broad sense). Although in terms of factual information Leskien's textbook treatment of the OCS
data and its underlying CS sound and form system has long
been superseded, it nonetheless deserves mention here as
the firmly established framework of CS linguistic structure to which many generations of beginning Slavists — in
some instances until quite recently — were first exposed
in the course of their academic pursuits.

Although van Wijk in the preface to his *Geschichte
der altkirchenslavischen Sprache*, published in 1931 (of
which, unfortunately, only the first volume on phonology
and inflectional morphology appeared while the manuscript
of the second volume, analyzing word formation, the use of
word forms, and syntax, perished in the turmoils of World
War II), announced his intention to exclude, wherever possible, any reference to CS — in view of an envisaged special treatment of CS to appear in the same series — the

closeness of the OCS phonological and inflectional systems
to the linguistic structure of CS nonetheless occasionally
led him to discuss also the immediately underlying last
phase of the Slavic protolanguage. Thus, it was in this
textbook that the Dutch Slavist for the first time developed in detail his concept of the two dominant tendencies
of Late CS phonology — the tendency for increasing (rising) sonority of the syllable and the tendency for palatalization (§ 7), subsuming under them a great many sound
shifts preceding the attested OCS evidence (§§ 9-19). But
also in his analysis of other data of the earliest Slavic
literary language van Wijk sometimes had to resort to commenting, if only briefly, on phenomena of CS and even PIE
(cf., e.g., § 36 on ablaut, or § 47 on heteroclites).
Still it should be stated that, by and large, van Wijk's
excellent handbook, reliable and accurate in its presentation of data while partly already foreshadowing a post-
neogrammarian approach, is primarily a history, not a prehistory, of OCS phonology and (inflectional) morphology,
as indicated in its title.

The same is hardly true of another unusually original and important textbook of OCS which, like van Wijk's,
remained a torso due to the personal hardships and untime-
ly death of its author, A. M. Seliščev. His *Staroslavjanskij jazyk* (1: *Vvedenie, Fonetika,* 1951; 2: *Teksty.
Slovar'. Očerki morfologii,* 1952) is more than a mere
handbook for university use; it is, in addition, a synthetic account of the great Soviet Slavist's own penetrat-
ing research in the field of Comparative IE and Slavic
Linguistics, supplemented by the testimony of his thorough
knowledge of Balkan Linguistics and great erudition in
Early Slavic philology. While designed as a tool for the
study of recorded OCS, his reference work is, at the same
time, a general introduction to Comparative Slavic Linguistics in its diachronic aspect. Of the two parts
available, the first one, worked out in full detail, surveys in an introductory section the external history of
the language examined, the body of relevant texts, and the
sound system of OCS (including some remarks on the effi-
cacy of certain phonological tendencies as reflected in
the rendering of loanwords as well as on the relationships
of OCS to other Slavic languages) and treats, in a subsequent section, phonology. The second part (originally
conceived as part 3), containing a selection of texts, a
glossary, and a brief outline of OCS morphology, was primarily designed as a practical tool, a classroom workbook;

71

its theoretical portion, the morphological sketch, is
therefore quite succinct. The manuscript of a more elaborate treatment of morphology, syntax, and lexicology,
planned for the (original) second part, was unfortunately
never completed by Seliščev. Even so, his concise treatment of the morphological categories of OCS, discussed on
a broad comparative basis, serves the double purpose of
both acquainting the student with the basic paradigms derivable from the recorded evidence of OCS and elucidating
the underlying, preliterary processes reflected in the
actually attested form system of the oldest literary language of the Slavs. In particular, systematic treatments
of Early Slavic derivation (and other word formation processes, viz., reduplication and composition) being scarce,
Seliščev's outline of nominal stem formation 2: 53-87),
including also some preliminary notes on Slavic remnants
of original root nouns, and his remarks on the derivational morphology of the pronouns, adjectives, and numerals,
as well as the verb, interspersed in the sections discussing these word classes (2: 111-204) is one of the few existing synopses, still in most respects meeting modern
standards for a diachronic analysis and a synchronic description of the pertinent surface data.

The bulk of the detailed treatment of phonology in
part one of Seliščev's work (1: 107-259) is for all intents and purposes a full-fledged discussion of the CS (as
well as pre-Slavic) sound system and its development, as
indicated, incidentally, also by the subheadings of this
section: "The social and linguistic situation of the
Slavs in the prehistoric epoch" (1: 107-75), analyzing,
after a few preliminary remarks on the external prehistory
of the Slavs, the CS vowel system, its origin and further
modification, including some incidental comments on quantity and intonation, and treating also the combinations of
reduced or full vowel plus liquid; and "The place of the
Slavic language group among other IE languages with regard
to consonants" (1: 176-219). Shorter subsequent chapters
examine further the particularities of word-initial and
word-final position (1: 219-33), the quantity of the syllable (1: 233-4), pitch and stress (1: 235-42), and apophonic vowel alternation (1: 242-59). Only thereafter
follows a relatively brief subsection on "The phonological
features of the language of the OCS texts" (1: 259-330).
It goes almost without saying that Seliščev's treatment of
CS and pre-Slavic phonology, while extremely thorough and
full of fresh and subtle observations, by and large

reflects the general late neogrammarian view on sound systems and their changes as still prevailing in the mid- and late thirties. Yet, quite a few of the Soviet Slavist's own interpretations and explanations display a degree of independent, original thinking only rarely encountered in traditionalist linguistic quarters.

By comparison to Seliščev's superior treatment of the historically underlying sounds and forms of the first Slavic literary language, the two more recent diachronic treatments of OCS phonology and morphology, that by B. Rosenkranz (*Historische Laut- und Formenlehre des Altbulgarischen*, 1955, stronger in its comparative IE portions than in its comments on the attested Slavic data) and that by G. Nandriş (*Old Church Slavonic Grammar*, 1959, generally reliable and rich in factual material but fairly traditional in approach), do not substantially add to our knowledge or understanding of CS.

As was mentioned above, reference to CS linguistic structure is made, in more or less general terms, also in a number of diachronic treatments of other Slavic languages, even though such reference is usually less detailed and specific than in historically oriented grammars of OCS. While the entire course of development of OCS — from its no longer textually attested Cyrillo-Methodian beginnings in the 860s until ca. 1100 — spans only slightly more than two centuries, this language most closely reflects Late CS (or rather, perhaps, represents a particular Late CS dialect for the first time recorded in writing). The following brief remarks do not claim, of course, to give a complete account — or even provide a full listing — of all those not yet quite outdated text- and handbooks of the history of individual Slavic languages in which more than only cursory mention is made of CS. Rather, what follows is a hopefully representative sampling of such titles (including also some monographic treatments).

As is well-known, OCS is not only accounted for in greater or lesser detail in a number of reference works specifically designed for that purpose, but a brief outline of its structure (particularly in its phonological and morphological aspects) is frequently also included in historical grammars or outlines of the history of Bulgarian and more recently of Macedonian. This is the case, for example, with the noted history of the Bulgarian language (published in German in 1929) by S. Mladenov. Yet this thorough, if now slightly obsolete, reference work does not contain any systematic or near-systematic survey

of the CS (or Late CS) background of Early Bulgarian, including its first, OCS, phase. Still, reference is made
in various sections of the book to hypothetic CS sounds
and forms underlying the Bulgarian data. The same applies
also to a more recent treatment of Bulgarian diachrony, K.
Mirčev's *Istoričeska gramatika na bălgarski ezik* (²1963)
which, in addition, devotes short sections to the periodization of the history of Bulgarian, beginning with the
preliterary period (§4.1), Bulgarian and the other Slavic
languages (§7), and a subsequent more detailed discussion
of the preliterary period (§9). Similarly, the short
history of Macedonian by B. Koneski (*Istorija na makedonskiot jazik*, 1965; Serbo-Croatian translation, 1966) does
not provide even a basic characterization of the Late CS
point of departure of the Macedonian linguistic evolution
(as the first phase of which OCS, here referred to as Old
Macedonian, can be rightly considered), but merely quotes,
sporadically, underlying sounds and forms identifiable as
CS in addition to briefly discussing, in an introductory
paragraph, the place of Macedonian in its Balkan linguistic setting and in its relationship to continguous Slavic
languages.

Largely the same approach is further taken in the
published version of the lecture scripts on the history of
Serbo-Croatian by A. Belić (*Osnovi istorije srpskohrvatskog jezika,* 1: *Fonetika,* 1960; *Istorija srpskohrvatskog
jezika,* 2:1: *Reči sa deklinacijom*; 2: *Reči sa konjugacijom,*
⁴1969) in which, after two quite brief sections on "Our
language and the other Slavic languages; the Slavic protolanguage" and "The South Slavic protolanguage" (1: 5-7),
CS sounds and reconstructed word forms are only occasionally adduced. Incomparably more space is devoted to various aspects of the prehistory of Serbo-Croatian and thus
also to the gradual breaking up of the CS linguistic unity
in I. Popović's generally very well-documented, though
partly controversial book *Geschichte der serbokroatischen
Sprache* (1960) where, in the first chapters, linguistic
data is combined and integrated with other, historic and
prehistoric evidence to give a rounded picture of the
southward migrations of the Slavs from their original (or
rather, earliest ascertainable) homeland and the ultimate
occupation by a portion of them of what is now the Serbo-
Croatian linguistic territory. Thus, the first chapter
(1-47) of Popović's history of Serbo-Croatian treats at
considerable length, quoting many bibliographical references, "Das Ursüdslavische in der alten Heimat," i.e., the

Late CS dialectal basis for the subsequent development of
the South Slavic languages. Another chapter (III: 104-77)
titled "Die Slaven in Mitteleuropa und auf dem Balkan"
discusses the Southern Slavs in their new environment,
both their transitory sites (in present-day Austria,
Northern Italy, Hungary, Romania, Albania, Greece) and
their permanent settlement (predominantly within the fron-
tiers of present-day Yugoslavia and Bulgaria). And only
in the following chapter (IV: 178-95), after first in some
detail having analyzed early superstrata in the previously
Slavicized areas of Central and Southeastern Europe as
well as the consolidation of the Southern Slavs in their
new homeland, does the Serbian linguist turn to commenting
on their definite breaking away from the bulk of the Slavic community — the speakers of the North Slavic languages
— i.e., on the final disintegration of CS (192-5). Also
the best presentation to date of the history of Slovenian,
F. Ramovš's *Kratka zgodovina slovenskega jezika*, 1 (1936,
containing four introductory chapters and a section on vocalism — to be supplemented by his previous *Historična
gramatika slovenskega jezika*, 2: *Konsonantizem*, 1924, 7:
Dialekti, 1935, and the published version of his lecture
scripts, *Morfologia slovenskega jezika*, 1952), briefly
discusses in its preliminary section (in the chapters on
"Primitive Slovenian" and "The place of Slovenian among
the Slavic languages") such problems as "The PS language"
(16-19), "The PS period and homeland" (19-20), "The development of PS" (21-2), "PS dialectal innovations" (69-70),
and "On the South PS dialect" (70-2). In addition, reconstructed, prehistoric Slavic sounds and forms are frequently posited throughout the Slovenian linguist's diachronic treatment of his native tongue.
　　Turning to the historical treatments of the West
Slavic languages, it may be noted that the most extensive
(and generally best) history of Slovak — the West Slavic
language having the closest ties with South Slavic — J.
Stanislav's *Dejiny slovenského jazyka* (2 volumes, 1st volume in 2nd augmented edition, 1958; a 3rd volume, 1957,
contains texts) not only throughout its presentation refers to reconstructed (CS or otherwise pre-Slovak as well
as comparative IE) data but also, in its "Introduction to
the history of the Slovak language," surveys "The first
references to the Slavs" (1: 85-91), "The earliest sites
and the origin of the Slavs" (1: 91-106), "The Balto-
Slavic group" (1: 113), "The PS language" (1: 114-16), and
"The place of Slovak among the Slavic languages" (general

75

remarks and development up to the 10th century; 1: 116-28). (Two further volumes, 4 and 5, treating syntax, have since appeared, in 1973, and will, as they pertain to CS syntax, be briefly mentioned in the sequel volume to this state-of-the-art report scheduled for publication in early 1978.) Ample references to CS linguistic material are also contained in F. Trávníček's *Historická mluvnice československá* (1935), treating the development of both Czech and Slovak. In particular, the CS basis of Czech and Slovak is briefly sketched in the section discussing the place of Czecho-Slovak in the Slavic language family (10-21, esp. §6). Slightly fewer reconstructed sounds and forms (substituting for them, wherever possible, attested OCS evidence) are found in the more recent *Historická mluvnice česká* written by a team of Czech linguists (1: *Hláskosloví* by M. Komárek, with an introduction by K. Horálek, 1958; 2: *Tvarosloví*, 1: *Skloňovaní* by V. Vážný, 1964; 2: *Časování* by A. Dostál, 1967; 3: *Skladba* by F. Trávníček, 2nd revised edition by A. Vašek, 1963). The CS and Common West Slavic basis of Czech is briefly outlined in K. Horálek's introduction. In this connection also S. E. Mann's *Czech Historical Grammar* (1957) deserves mention. While rather weak and deficient in its treatment of the Czech linguistic evolution proper, this textbook emphasizing a comparative approach is particularly (indeed, even disproportionately) rich in references to the CS as well as the more remote general IE background of Czech.

It will come as no surprise that two fairly long initial chapters of the external history of Polish by T. Lehr-Spławiński (*Język polski. Pochodzenie, powstanie, rozwój*, [2]1951; Russian translation, 1954) are devoted to "The PS community" (17-45) and to "The Western Slavs" (46-60), considering the fact that the late Polish linguist was one of the leading experts on CS, having authored numerous monographs and specialized studies on this and related subjects (cf. Bibliography). Similarly, the authoritative *Gramatyka historyczna języka polskiego*, coauthored by Z. Klemensiewicz, T. Lehr-Spławiński, and S. Urbańczyk ([2]1964) discusses in the first section treating phonology "The Slavic languages and the place of Polish among them," singling out, among other things, especially "The Balto-Slavic linguistic community," "The PS linguistic community," "The dialectal differences in PS," and "The West Slavic linguistic community" (22-34). Moreover, while frequently referring to underlying sounds and forms posited for CS throughout the entire book, special paragraphs

are devoted to "The PS evolutionary basis of the Polish
vowel system," "Quantity and accentuation: General characterization," "The development of accentuation and quantity in the early phase of PS," "The further development
of the PS prosodic system," and "The development of the PS
intonation system on the Polish-Pomeranian territory" (41-
52). A short survey of the CS consonant system opens the
discussion on the development of the Polish consonants
(129). Further paragraphs briefly state the CS basis for
the development of inflectional paradigms in Polish (265),
especially the twofold adjectival inflection in CS (323),
and the CS (or general Slavic) prerequisites of syntactic
change in Polish (393-4). Also in volume one of Z. Klemensiewicz's *Historia języka polskiego* (1: *Doba staropol-
ska*, 1961), a text somewhere between an external history
of Polish and a Polish historical grammar, special paragraphs (of section I, treating the preliterary period) are
devoted to "The Balto-Slavic linguistic community and the
PS language" and "The disintegration of the PS linguistic
community into a Western, an Eastern, and a Southern linguistic group" (12-14) while making little reference, in
the remainder of the book, to reconstructed (CS) sounds
and forms. Considerable information on CS (as well as
PIE) is further provided in some other outlines of Polish
historical grammar such as, for example, the text by B.
Wieczorkiewicz and R. Sinielnikoff, *Elementy gramatyki
historycznej języka polskiego z ćwiczeniami* (1959); cf.
especially 4-6, 20-32, 45-6, 49-56, 59-60, 69-70, 128-9.

Except for OCS (in the broad sense, i.e., including
also such non-Macedo-Bulgarian or, at any rate, not
strictly Macedo-Bulgarian archaic Slavic texts as the
Freising Fragments and the *Kiev Leaflets*), it is of course
Russian, or rather East Slavic, among all the Slavic languages, that can claim the earliest records and, in view
of the short time span of OCS (9th-11th centuries), East
Slavic has the longest documented history and, therefore,
in its earliest attestation is closest to Late CS of all
the extant Slavic languages. Thus, it is only natural
that brief sketches of its CS basis will be included in
many diachronic treatments of the East Slavic linguistic
evolution, notably that of Russian. To be sure, the Early
Old Russian (Kievan) period, i.e., 11th-13th centuries,
can with at least equal right be considered the first literary phase also of the history (or prehistory) of Ukrainian. Nonetheless it is not often that specific reference
to (Late) CS linguistic structure will be found in

Ukrainian historical grammars or outlines of Ukrainian
linguistic history since the beginnings of Ukrainian (or
more generally Ruthenian) as an independent language, i.e.,
clearly separate from Great Russian or Russian proper, is
usually dated only to the 13th-14th centuries. Still, to
take just one example, a sketch of the early phase of
Ukrainian like the one by T. Lehr-Spławiński ("Początki
języka ukraińskiego," forming part one of the outline
Dzieje języka ukraińskiego w zarysie, coauthored by T.
Lehr-Spławiński, P. Zwoliński, and S. Hrabec 1956) contains, along with other data, basic information on Late
CS and Common East Slavic linguistic structure.

Textbooks or monographs dealing specifically with
the early period of East Slavic naturally have to take into consideration also its Late CS prehistory. This is
true, for example, both of the methodologically now obsolete but as yet unmatched (in terms of the wealth of its
factual linguistic material) *Očerk drevnějšago perioda
istorii russkago jazyka* by A. A. Šaxmatov (1915) and of
L. P. Jakubinskij's original (if not to say strongly opinionated, though thought-provoking) *Istorija drevnerusskogo
jazyka* (1953), in many respects continuing Šaxmatov's tradition. In Jakubinskij's text frequent reference is made
to PS and CS sounds, forms, and grammatical categories
(primarily in the sections on "Phonology" and "Grammar,"
121-269). In the first section of his book on "The Russian language as one of the Slavic languages" (43-70), the
Soviet linguist discussed such overall issues as "The
Slavic languages" (47-52), "The relationship of the Slavic
languages" (52-63, to be sure, with some references to not
overly relevant dicta from the classics of Marxism), "On
the problem of the origin of the PS tribal dialect" (using
a coinage of F. Engels, 63-7), and "The East Slavic
tribes" (67-70). In the section on phonology the first
two chapters are devoted specifically to "Some phonological phenomena of CS" (121-5) and "Common East Slavic phonological phenomena" (125-39).

In the first Russian historical grammar meeting modern (if by now not the most recent) standards of diachronic linguistics, N. Durnovo's *Očerk istorii russkogo jazyka*
(1924, reprinted 1959), much emphasis is placed on viewing
the Old Russian, or rather the preliterary Proto-Russian,
phonological and morphological systems as, to a large extent, directly inherited from CS. Thus, in the section
treating the "History of the sounds of Russian," the first
chapter is devoted to "Sounds which have come down to

78

Russian from CS" (109-38). Similarly, in the section on
historical morphology, both the portions treating the
"History of declensional forms" and the "History of conjugational forms" open with a chapter on "Forms which have
come down to Russian from CS" (243-64 and 309-26, respectively). Each of these chapters on CS phonology, declension, and conjugation is in turn followed by chapters discussing the respective modifications in "Common Russian"
(i.e., Common East Slavic): "Common Russian sound
changes" (143-72, with a subdivision into "Prehistoric
changes" and "Changes of the historical epoch," and preceded by a brief inserted chapter on "The relationship of
Russian to other Slavic languages," 138-42), "Common Russian changes in declensional forms" (264-79), and "Common
Russian changes in conjugational forms" (326-9). Somewhat
different is the share of space devoted to linguistic prehistory in two other historical grammars of Russian which,
although not entirely up to an expectable level, nonetheless are widely used at various universities: P. Ja.
Černyx's *Istoričeskaja grammatika russkogo jazyka* (^{3}1962;
German translation, based on the 2nd edition, 1957) and
W. K. Matthews' *Russian Historical Grammar* (1960). Whereas in Černyx's controversial textbook Common East Slavic
(Proto-Russian), but not CS, provides, generally speaking,
merely a point of departure sketched in brief outline (cf.
73-6, "The phonological system of the language of the
Eastern Slavs"; 338-44, "The basic word stock"), Matthews'
presentation, by and large more carefully thought through,
includes also a section on "Linguistic prehistory," discussing in some detail both (1) "Indo-European" (13-34)
and (2) "Common Slavonic" (34-52), where a general characterization as well as at least a cursory survey of all
major segments of linguistic structure during these two
preliterary epochs can be found. Presumably because CS is
the subject of another course in the curriculum of Soviet
students of Russian and Slavic, virtually no systematic
reference to CS linguistic structure is made in the relatively most adequate of the historical grammars of Russian
currently in use in the Soviet Union, *Istoričeskaja grammatika russkogo jazyka* (2nd, augmented edition, 1965),
jointly authored by V. I. Borkovskij and P. S. Kuznecov.
Only indirectly can the user of this textbook derive some
information on Late CS phonology from reading the chapter
on "The sound system of Old Russian," particularly its
preliminary remarks (45-65, where, incidentally, the "law
of open syllables" and syllabic synharmonism are mentioned

as the two predominant tendencies of Early Slavic phonological development) as well as the two first subsections
on "Differences between Old Russian and the other Slavic
languages" (65-79) and on "The reflexion of the characteristics of CS accentuation in Russian" (79-85). In addition, for some of the quoted Old Russian sounds (or sound
sequences) and forms, underlying (i.e., reconstructed)
equivalents are occasionally cited. CS proper is generally only mentioned in passing also in the undoubtedly best
historical grammar of Russian available to date, V. Kiparsky's *Russische historische Grammatik* (1: *Die Entwicklung
des Lautsystems*, 1963; 2: *Die Entwicklung des Formensys-
tems*, 1967; further volumes on lexicology and on syntax,
the latter to be authored by H. Bräuer, are forthcoming;
for some reservations concerning volume 1, see Birnbaum
1965c). Still, the Finnish Slavist's reliable textbook
contains an instructive general characterization of East
Slavic (1: 13-18) as well as a section on preliterary
Proto-Russian (1: 75-84), including some highly relevant
remarks also on the sound system of Late CS, primarily as
it can be reconstructed on the basis of early loanword
material (especially Old Scandinavian loanwords and name
adaptations in Old Russian as well as borrowings from East
Slavic in Baltic and Finnic). Again, for certain Old Russian (and other Slavic) items, asterisked protoforms are
sometimes cited.

    Parenthetically and more as a matter of curiosity,
it may be noted that fairly extensive information on the
dynamics of CS phonology (as well as some pre-Slavic processes), once more conceived as being largely determined by
the two general tendencies of rising sonority of the syllable and palatalization (as formulated by van Wijk), has
been included as a major portion of the preliminary, theoretical notes of a Russian language text, devised osten-
sibly for the mere practical purpose of serving as a tool
for improving the mastering of a basic vocabulary of Russian, *Russische Wortkunde* (1966, [2]1969), compiled by a
team of East German linguists (R. Eckert, G. Kirchner, R.
Růžička, W. Sperber). By revealing primarily phonological
processes (underlying the synchronic lexical data of Contemporary Standard Russian and their paradigmatic interrelations) the authors have with great pedagogical perspi-
cacity provided a shortcut to an early ability of manipu-
lating an essential core of the Russian word stock (for CS
and a few pre-Slavic rules, see 9-42).

For a discussion of R. Jakobson's pioneering reinterpretation of CS phonology, viewed in the framework of Russian (and Comparative Slavic) sound change, see below, pp. 84-8.

Finally, in surveying briefly the treatments of, or in some cases merely the cursory references to, CS linguistic structure as found in various textbooks of Russian (and East Slavic) historical grammar as well as some comparable handbooks, mention should here also be made of a monograph which, while not specifically designed as a reference work, nonetheless is of a somewhat similar nature as it summarizes its author's relevant research within a well-defined area, F. P. Filin's *Obrazovanie jazyka vostočnyx slavjan* (1962). Here two major portions (together making up 140 of the book's total of 294 pages) are devoted to problems of CS and its speakers: the section "On the origin and development of the CS (PS) language and the original homeland of the Slavs" (83-151) and the section discussing "The beginning of the disintegration of the CS language" (152-223). In the first section the Soviet linguist discusses, after some preliminary remarks, such issues as the IE problem, the periodization of CS (PS), the vocabulary of CS (PS) and the significance of lexical data for determining the original habitat of the Slavs, the Balto-Slavic (linguistic) community as related to the problem of the Slavic homeland, Balto-Finno-Ugric and Slavo-Finno-Ugric relations, the ancient Slavs as the southern neighbors of the Balts, the problem of Slavo-Germanic and Slavo-Iranian linguistic relations, some aspects of tree nomenclature, and — summing up his relevant observations and considerations — once more the question of the location of the original homeland of the Slavs. In the second section Filin then addresses himself to such problems as the geographical distribution of the ancient Slavic tribes, the Early Slavic tribal designations as related to this distribution, the period of the disintegration of CS, the dismemberment of CS in the light of lexical borrowings, the rise of phonological differentiation (sound changes with twofold results), and Early Slavic dialect zones in the light of lexical data — all of the aforementioned leading up to some general conclusions concerning the process of disintegration of CS. While this is not the place to enter into a discussion of the many interesting points raised in Filin's thoughtful, well-documented, partly imaginative reasoning, suffice it to say that it is notably in his superior control and

utilization of lexical data that his own strength as a
scholar is revealed and that it is therefore in this field
that he is able to arrive at his most significant and convincing conclusions. At the same time it should be pointed out, however, that his investigation does not, in fact,
substantially change the hitherto existing overall picture
of CS and its speakers, or, to be more precise, some of
the earlier relevant views, but that it is rather bound to
only more exactly define a detail or two in the previously
held opinions relating to this field of research. (Another book by Filin, *Proisxoždenie russkogo, ukrainskogo i
belorusskogo jazykov*, appeared in 1972; to the extent it
pertains to CS and its dialectal disintegration it will be
discussed in the sequel to this volume due to appear in
1978.)

In addition, CS or mostly the dialectal basis of a
part of Late CS is briefly referred to in some outlines of
South, East, and West Slavic dialectology (cf. Sławski
1962; Kuraszkiewicz 1954; Stieber 1956) as well as also
being touched upon in various introductions to South, West,
and East Slavic linguistics (cf., e.g., Sławski 1955;
Seliščev 1941; Stieber 1955; Kuraszkiewicz 1955).

Concluding this survey of general treatments of CS
in various reference works (and a few related monographs),
it should further be mentioned that CS linguistic structure (or some part thereof) is discussed also in a number
of scholarly works focusing on the prehistory and early
history of the Slavs. Although partly written by professional linguists (cf., for example, Vasmer 1926, now also
reprinted in Vasmer 1971: 31-56; Lehr-Spławiński 1946a,
1946b, 1953, 1958a, 1960a; Rudnicki 1959/61; Ułaszyn 1959;
Rospond 1968a), these studies are not primarily in the
field of linguistic research proper but rather attempt, in
some instances, to integrate linguistic findings with other evidence, anthropological, ethnographic, archeological.
Other relevant introductions and monographs have been authored by anthropologists (cf. Czekanowski 1957), ethnog-
raphers (cf. Moszyński 1957), historians (cf. Dvornik
1956; Nalepa 1967 — for some criticism of Nalepa's linguistic positions, see Popowska-Taborska 1970), and, above
all, archeologists (cf. Kostrzewski 1946; Tret'jakov 1948,
1966; Jażdżewski 1948/49, 1968, 1970; Ljapuškin 1968;
Sedov 1970; Gimbutas 1971). Particularly those published
in Poland endeavor to corroborate the "western" (or autochthonic) hypothesis of the origins of the Slavs in the
Vistula-Oder area (for an assessment of the linguistic

aspects of this hypothesis, see, not too convincingly, it must be said, Martynov 1963a). The evaluation (or even systematic enumeration) of these and similar works falls beyond the scope of the present state-of-the-art report.

3. PHONOLOGY

3.0. Preliminary Note. As was pointed out above (p. 26),
phonology — including morphophonology — is that component
of CS linguistic structure which has been relatively the
most thoroughly investigated and discussed. In this chapter some monographic treatments of CS phonology (to the
extent they do not form part of some broader presentation
of CS, Comparative Slavic or IE Linguistics, or the history and prehistory of some individual Slavic language,
and therefore have not been previously mentioned) will
first be surveyed; thereafter, a selection of important
specialized studies on specific issues of CS phonology
(and of its utilization in morphology) will be briefly
commented upon.

3.1. Monographic Treatments of Common Slavic Phonology.
The first significant non-traditionalist — i.e., post-
neogrammarian — sketch of CS phonology, while not claiming
complete coverage of all major phonological phenomena of
CS diachrony, yet boldly reinterpreting a substantial body
of relevant data, was contained in some of the earlier
sections (notably III and IV) of R. Jakobson's terse outline of the prehistory and subsequent evolution of the
Russian sound system, viewed against a comparative Slavic
background, *Remarques sur l'évolution phonologique du
russe comparée à celle des autres langues slaves*, published in 1929 (reprinted in Jakobson 1962/71, 1: 7-116).
While displaying generally a negative attitude toward the
neogrammarian doctrine of the Leipzig School (though
equally committed to demonstrating the systematic character of linguistic change), Jakobson's study — the longest
one ever written by him on phonology — "was the greatest
event in the development of diachronic methods since the

neogrammarian breakthrough in the 1870s," to quote Ivić's well-balanced, enthusiastic, and at the same time critical assessment of Jakobson's *Remarques* (cf. Ivić 1965: 42). In particular, Jakobson's conception of CS phonology marked a turning point in the history of relevant research, notwithstanding N. van Wijk's (to be sure, then still pre-phonologist) judgment about this "monographie très sugges-tive" stating that "sa reconstruction de l'histoire du système phonologique préhistorique me paraît moins heu-reuse que les considérations renfermées dans d'autres chapitres du même ouvrage" (cf. van Wijk 1956: 23). In-deed, Jakobson, too, was at that time not without certain predecessors who had profoundly influenced his own fresh approach to the prehistory of Russian (and Czech) dia-chronic phonology. Foremost among them were his Moscow teacher N. N. Durnovo (who had further developed the lin-guistic tenets of the Moscow School, headed by Fortunatov, a particularly sophisticated variety of the neogrammarian vein of linguistics, and who for some time himself was as-sociated also with the Prague Circle; cf. especially Dur-novo 1924; 1924-5; 1927-8; 1932a) and his friend N. S. Trubeckoj, together with Jakobson, the leading theoreti-cian of the Prague phonologist group. In the 1920s, Trubeckoj had published a series of important studies on various problems of the prehistory of Slavic, all prelim-inary to a broadly conceived, never-to-be-completed larger work (cf. Trubeckoj 1921, 1922, 1922-3, 1923, 1924, 1925a, 1925b, 1925c, 1927, 1928-9, 1930; see also Jakobson 1966: 535-9), but at that time he was still wrestling with fun-damental questions of theory and method and, as Ivić puts it, "did not yet possess mastery of the phonological meth-od, and especially of its application to diachronic prob-lems. Thus it happened that the work ripened in Jakob-son's mind earlier than in Trubeckoj's" (cf. Ivić 1965: 45). It should also be noted that an extensive corre-spondence between Jakobson and Trubeckoj (of which a major part is finally to be published in the near future) served as a vehicle of their interchange of ideas (cf., e.g., footnote 20 in the *Remarques*, Jakobson 1962/71, 1: 30-1, quoting at length from a private letter of Trubeckoj out-lining his view on the development of the diphthongs *o/e* + *r/l*, *i* in CS).

Applying his theoretical notions to a vast body of factual material, Jakobson in his *Remarques* improved his phonological theory (in comparison with his own earlier formulations) by redefining the phoneme, by reaching a more insightful understanding of positional variants, and, most important, by introducing the new powerful concept of the archiphoneme. Though subsequently — and it seems prematurely — abandoned by Jakobson himself (definitely by 1937, i.e., around the time his universalized distinctive feature theory began to take shape), this concept, as well as the related notion of (phonological) neutralization, has a firm place, albeit partly under the disguise of a new terminology, in the morphologically oriented "item-and-process" approach to linguistic structure and its consistent further development in generative grammar (at least at first primarily syntactically oriented, but recently increasingly semantically anchored). Also in the system of concepts on which recent developments of distinctive feature theory is based the archiphoneme seems to be able to assert itself as "that bundle of features which appears in positions where not all features of the given (morpho)phoneme are distinctive" (cf. Ivić 1965: 43-4).

Underlying Jakobson's *Remarques* is the overall view that sound evolution is explicable in terms of the (sound) pattern. According to Jakobson, various forces govern sound evolution, thus causing the pattern to undergo ever new chain reactions of change in order to maintain threatened distinctions (carrying semantic implications) and to restore lost equilibrium. The sound system itself is conceived as the passive object of change confined, as it were, to a defensive role against the — mostly implicit — change-triggering factor of shifting the boundaries between stylistic variants, a view inspired by Jakobson's strong literary leanings. "The causes giving the first impulses to change remain unnamed: inner factors such as the principle of economy and the tendency to simplify overloaded patterns, and external influences emerging from contacts between languages," to cite Ivić (1965: 44). Yet, in at least one case, Jakobson did undoubtedly pinpoint precisely such a striving for economy and simplification of overcharged sound patterns, namely, the claimed and subsequently much debated trend toward syllabic synharmonism in Late CS (cf. above, pp. 38-9; and below, pp. 141-4). By formulating this tendency toward "uniformization of the syllable," Jakobson not only established a second major principle of Late CS sound change geared to the structure of the syllable (the other one being the "law of open syllables," to be reformulated by van Wijk as a tendency for rising syllabic sonority and extending over a period of scholarly debate from Leskien to Martinet and

Shevelov, cf. below, pp. 142, 145-6, 268-9), but was also
able to accommodate under one common denominator a great
number of seemingly disparate processes, substantially ex-
ceeding those covered by various phenomena of palatalization in the broad sense (*ke > če, ik > ic, jo > je*, etc.);
cf. Jakobson 1962/71, 1: 25-8. In particular, the Russian-
American linguist managed to account for certain difficult instances of presumed progressive as well as regressive assimilation (e.g., *tert > ter't > ter^e t > ESl teret*,
but *telt > tel't/tolt > ESl tolot*). In other cases, a reinterpretation of the phonetic value of a given CS phoneme
(in part following Durnovo but also Šaxmatov) would allow
for an integration of a seemingly contradictory process
with the overall principle of syllabic synharmonism (e.g.,
the change *jě, kě > ja, ča* reinterpreted as *> jä, čä*, i.e.,
palatal consonant + front vowel); cf. further also the
phonetic reinterpretation of traditional *'u/ju* as *ü**, *'o/
jǫ* and *'o/jo* as *ǫ̈* and *ö*; on the other hand, *ē* (= *ě₂ < oľ*)
> ie, suggesting a questionable difference in the pronunciation of CS *ě₁* and *ě₂*, etc. While the interpretation
(or rather reinterpretation) of these as well as a number
of other developments subsumed under the posited consequences of the Late CS principle of syllabic synharmonism
may indeed be considered ingenious, it is of course far
from certain that Jakobson's explanations always stand up
to contemporary criticism. To be sure, he himself was
fully aware of the provisional nature of some of his findings and hypotheses when referring to M. Grammont's well-
known dictum, "Une théorie inexacte amène une rectifica-
tion, tandis que l'absence de théorie n'amène rien" (Jakobson 1962/71, 1: 109). Thus, many of his ideas and observations embodied in this work, while no doubt striking and
keen for their time, must today be recognized as outdated
or in need of substantial revision. The very concept of
syllabic synharmonism has in recent years served as a
point of departure for yet another, kindred phonological
doctrine, V. K. Žuravlev's theory of group-phonemes (see
further below, pp. 142-4). As was also noted by Ivić
(1965: 46), some weak or at any rate debatable points in
Jakobson's outline of CS phonology concern the positing of
a split of velar phonemes in connection with the First and
Second Palatalization or the assertion that prothetic

---

*However, also *žiltu > žültu* for traditional *žьltъ >
žьltь*; cf. Jakobson 1962/71, 1: 26).

consonants (j-, v-) had to first be eliminated in order to obliterate the contrast of front and back vowels. Other shortcomings, including an occasional confusion of phonetic and phonemic facts, not to speak of his long since abandoned insistence on a (as it now seems, purely accidental) parallelism of certain isotherms and isoglosses in ancient Russia (first observed by Savickij but still seriously referred to, e.g., by Kiparsky 1963: 19) need not be dealt with here.

Jakobson's *Remarques* make no easy reading; on the contrary, they put extremely high demands on the reader's intellectual capacity, ability for concentration, and expected familiarity with then current technical terminology and relevant literature. As a tool for classroom teaching (if ever used as such) this sketch could hardly have been successful. Yet it ushered in modern diachronic phonology, demonstrated on concrete linguistic data. A good portion of this data was CS.

The notion of a few underlying general tendencies (if not outright moving forces) determining CS sound evolution as well as its direct continuation in Early East Slavic is also the leitmotiv of another study viewing the chief phenomena and processes of Old Russian diachronic phonology and its CS prehistory from a holistic angle, B. Calleman's 1950 Uppsala dissertation *Zu den Haupttendenzen der urslavischen und altrussischen Lautentwicklung*. Conceived, like Jakobson's earlier sketch, as a reinterpretation of previously known data rather than as a formulation of new insights on the basis of fresh linguistic material, Calleman's synthesis explicitly rejects Jakobson's (and argues, despite some points of agreement, against van Wijk's) attempt at defining the basic factors, if not the causes, responsible for the regular modification of the CS and Early Slavic sound pattern. Utilizing the findings of Slavic (especially Polish) dialectology — among them, data gathered in the field by the Swedish linguist himself — Calleman's fundamental thesis is that CS sound evolution was characterized by the interplay of two major alternating and contrasting types of articulation, produced by two pragmatically defined "articulatory bases," one ("palato-labio-nasal") centered in the front part of the oral cavity, the other ("velar") in the back part of the mouth. Adducing relevant dialectal data, Calleman endeavors to characterize each of these two types of articulation and to determine the purely physiological (articulatory, i.e., speech-producing, not acoustic-auditive, i.e., speech-

perceiving) parameters of the two "articulatory bases."
In large part Calleman here relies on the then available
measurements and data — now vastly improved and hence substantially modified — of instrumental phonetics. The concept of labiovelarization (typified by k^u and applied to
Slavic phonetic data, e.g., by O. Broch) is rejected by
Calleman; cf. also the distinctive feature oppositions
compact/diffuse and grave/acute, more recently, in generative phonology, redefined in slightly different terms and
by other parameters. Velarization, one of the two predominant tendencies of CS sound development — manifested in
open syllables and increased sonority (not increasing or
rising sonority of the syllable, as van Wijk would have
it) — is, according to Calleman, continued in East Slavic.
The opposite trend, also found in CS, toward palatalization and/or labialization, on the other hand, resulting,
among other things, in palatalized consonants (p, t, k >
p', t', k'), prothetic consonants (or on-glides, j-, v-)
and "nasalization" products (or, more precisely, the outcome of *Nasalierung*, i.e., the quality of turning nasal or
evolving nasals, as opposed to *Nasalisation*, the quality
of being nasal or having nasality, exemplified by the distinction tot > $toNt$ vs. $toNt$ > tot, the latter said to result primarily from velarization) is typically found in
Polish — cf., in particular, the "decomposed" pronunciation of the graphemes "ę", "ą" before stops and affricates — and, especially, in some West Polish dialects
(of *Wielkopolska*). A set of analogous distinctions (in addition to *Nasalierung* vs. *Nasalisation*, also *Palatalisierung* vs. *Palatalisation*, *Labialisierung* vs. *Labialisation*,
Velarisierung vs. *Velarisation*, terminologically difficult
to render in English or French; cf. 115-16, with exemplification) has provided the Swedish Slavist and phonetician
with a refined tool for tracing the effects of these po-
larized comprehensive processes posited by him. In particular, when it comes to his analysis of the Slavic (CS,
Polish) nasal vowels, studied by Calleman also in an earlier work, his observations are keen and his conclusions
insightful. A fair overall assessment of Calleman's relevant research is nonetheless not easy. Clearly his conception presents an alternative to that previously outlined by Jakobson. A serious drawback of Calleman's study
is the almost complete lack of any chronological considerations (except for the broad distinction of CS versus

post-CS), thus shunning any discussion of the essential
issue of the time sequence obtaining between any alternation (or possibly several alternations) of the assumed two
types of articulation during the CS period, granted the
well-known difficulties of establishing any firm chronologies, absolute or even relative, for CS (cf. below, pp.
228-33). Also in some other respects, especially as concerns Calleman's disregard for the acoustic-auditive side
of phonological phenomena as well as his antimentalistic
attitude toward linguistic processes in general, his monograph seems almost like a step backward. After all, it
was conceived, if not written, subsequent to the formulation of the Prague School phonological doctrine and even
after at least the first stages of distinctive feature
theory and kindred conceptions of the sound pattern had
been set forth. Yet, in other respects his work points
toward further deeper insights into the underlying mechanisms (and perhaps causes) determining the sound changes
of CS and subsequent periods of Slavic diachrony.

The monograph *Nasoki i razvoja na fonologičnite sis-
temi na slavjanskite ezici* by I. Lekov (1960), surveying
the phonological development of Slavic from a diachronic-
typological viewpoint and resorting to the conceptual
framework of modern linguistic and information theory, also applies the notion of "tendency" (here following the
corresponding usage by some Soviet linguists) to some of
the patterned regularities of sound change. In his book,
the Bulgarian linguist discusses a number of CS phenomena
in addition to those of the Slavic languages of the historically attested period. However, except for a few details, his treatment does not substantially add to our
deeper understanding of CS diachronic phonology.

In 1954 the Soviet Slavist S. B. Bernštejn, a former
student of Seliščev whose broad approach to Comparative
Slavic as well as Balkan Linguistics he adopted, published
an article outlining his view of "the basic tasks, methods,
and principles of the comparative grammar of the Slavic
languages" (cf. Bernštejn 1954). This programmatic statement was followed, in 1961, by the same scholar's text
Očerk sravnitel'noj grammatiki slavjanskix jazykov in
which he endeavored to realize a major portion of the task
as outlined by him. Yet, despite its title, Bernštejn's
Očerk, based on two lecture courses given at Moscow University in 1952/3 and 1953/4 but slightly updated before
publication, is limited to providing a general Introduction (7-120) and treating Phonology (121-306) only. A

fairly comprehensive (though still highly selective) bibliography and various useful indexes round out the presentation. Word formation and — inflectional — morphology
are said in the preface to have been reserved for a separate volume which, however, has not appeared to date. (It
was recently learned, though, that Bernštejn is now close
to completing work on this sequel volume.) As the general
purpose of his undertaking, the Soviet linguist proposes,
"to give the students a textbook which in systematic form
would contain the history of PS and of the major CS processes" (p. 3). Particular attention is further said to
have been paid to problems of methodology and to presenting the current state of research, to be sure in traditional terms.

Among the merits of Bernštejn's book should be mentioned the lucidity of his style and the structuredness
of his exposition, notwithstanding the fact that his
treatment of phonology is not subdivided into any larger
chapters but is merely organized into sixty-two more or
less equally important sections (§§ 19-80). In the Introduction the Moscow Slavist discusses, in addition to a
brief statement about the scientific significance of Comparative Slavic Linguistics (§1), a number of largely
methodological questions: "Comparative grammar and language relationship" (§2), "Comparative grammar and substratum theory" (§3), "The object of comparative grammar"
(§4) , "The method of comparative grammar" (§5), and
"Identity in substance, structure, and function" (§6).
Following these general considerations, detailed factual
background information is provided on the IE languages and
PIE (§7), Balto-Slavic linguistic relationships (§8),
the Slavic languages and their classification (§9), PS,
the methods of studying it, and the periodization of its
history (§10), the earliest PS language area (§11), the
earliest PS dialects (§12), the extension of the PS language area in the 2nd-3rd centuries A. D. and the PS isogloss regions of that period (§13), the Slavic landtaking in the Balkan Peninsula (§14), Slavic ethnonyms
(§15), lexical borrowings in PS (§16), and accounts of
the Slavic languages in non-Slavic sources, the earliest
Slavic texts, and the dialects of Slavic (§17). Concluding his Introduction, Bernštejn gives a brief sketch of
the history of Comparative Slavic Linguistics adducing
some basic bibliography (§18). Also his treatment of
Phonology — couched essentially in phonemic terms and thus
freely operating with the "functional" concept of the

phoneme — opens with a lengthy section on "General Principles" (§ 19).

While much valuable standard information as well as
some original observations and thoughts are contained in
Bernštejn's book, it goes almost without saying that much
controversial material, too, is included here. Thus, for
example, his conception of the dialects of CS, their initial grouping and subsequent regrouping (assuming a first
West/East split along a line following the upper and central Bug and a short northward extension, that is, partly
continuing views earlier expressed by Šaxmatov and others;
cf. 66-82), although not lacking certain merits and even
intriguing ideas, seems by and large not very realistic as
was, incidentally, pointed out by me already on some previous occasions (cf. Birnbaum 1965b: 12-14 and 1966a:
191-3). Likewise, Bernštejn's view of the nature of the
linguistic ties existing between Baltic and Slavic, interpreting them as characteristic of an early Balto-Slavic
convergence area (G *Sprachbund*, R *jazykovoj sojuz*; cf. 27-
37 and 154-7, similarly also Bernštejn 1958a), does not
coincide with any of the more common notions regarding the
underlying causes for this particular linguistic relationship — though, for example, Stang at one time entertained
analogous ideas (cf. Stang 1942: 278) — but may provide a
useful point of departure supplementary to other approaches to the Balto-Slavic language problem (cf. Birnbaum 1970a: 74). However, positing a period of Balto-
Slavic convergence (viz., of two previously already established, separate branches of the IE language family),
causes Bernštejn to assume a period of Early PS with a
well-defined sound system preceding the time of closer
Balto-Slavic contacts (or rather even of a Balto-Slavic
linguistic symbiosis or "community," R *soobščnost'*, G
Verkehrsgemeinschaft; 133-54). In the discussion of the
sound pattern of this hypothetic Early PS period Bernštejn
devotes a special section (§ 22) to "the earliest structure of the syllable, pitch, and stress" (the latter two
phenomena, in his view, being largely conditioned by the
syllable structure) in connection with which the effect of
the loss of laryngeals also is mentioned. Cf. further
182-200 and 257-9 on the CS and second, Late CS, restructuring of the syllable and its consequences; on laryngeals
(in word-medial position), see also 147-8. Subsequently,
Bernštejn returned to the problem of the syllable in CS
(PS) in a separate study (Bernštejn 1963). Fully up to
date with current research in some respects, the Soviet

linguist in other instances lags behind the modern development of CS phonological studies. This applies, for example, to his interpretation of the reduced vowels (ь, ъ)
as being allegedly "extra-short" (R *sverxkratkie*), i.e.,
in effect introducing a phonemically highly improbable
third degree of quantity (in addition to the opposition
short : long or non-long : long) — again, a relic of a now
obsolete Russian linguistic tradition; cf. 177-80 and
passim.

   Whereas Bernštejn's keen observation of his data in
many cases has allowed him to reach correct or at least
potentially or partly correct conclusions (cf., e.g., his
assessment of various secondary phenomena of vowel reduction subsumable under the term *akan'e*, 291-2), in other
cases his interpretations and deductions seem less felicitous or, in some instances, even patently incorrect. Not
too-well-founded is, for example, his interpretation of
the timbre of the CS (PS) short back vowel where Bernštejn, on insufficient grounds, it seems, posits labialized o or possibly weakly labialized o^a rather than delabialized or unrounded a (143-7). An instance of a clearly
incorrect conclusion is, in my opinion, Bernštejn's claim
that P *rzɑd* (< CS *rędъ*) would indicate that any depalatalization (or "umlaut") $e > ǫ$ (alternatively, $\ddot{a} > \mathring{a}$ or the
like), usually believed to have taken place in Lekhitic
and paralleling the sound shift $e > o$ and $\breve{e} > a$ (to use
traditional notation) in the same phonetic environment,
did not actually occur since in that case the Polish end
result presumably would have been **rɑd* (and not *rzɑd*). I
have tried to show the fallacy of Bernštejn's reasoning
elsewhere (Birnbaum 1965a) and can therefore here limit
myself to the statement that Bernštejn's incorrect conclusion ultimately seems attributable to his failure to
clearly realize the fact that sound change proper takes
place not so much at the phonemic level (if indeed autonomous phonemes are to be recognized as legitimate linguistic units also in the light of recent generative claims
concerning the nature of phonological structure) but rather at the subphonemic (or feature) and allophonic levels.
Cf. also below, pp. 113-14.

   Despite these and a number of comparable shortcomings, primarily of a theoretical nature, it should be
pointed out, however, that Bernštejn's introduction to
Comparative Slavic Linguistics and, in particular, to many
of the specific problems of reconstructing CS as well as
his outline of CS and Early Slavic phonology on the whole

constitute a successful endeavor to adduce and interpret a
substantial body of relevant data and to summarize the
major achievements of recent research in the field, contributing in many cases valuable, often original, observations and suggestions. Of the relatively few comprehensive treatments of CS phonology that have appeared in the
Soviet Union, Bernštejn's *Očerk* is no doubt the best.

However, only a few years after the publication of
Bernštejn's *Očerk* another reference work on CS phonology
appeared which, in thoroughness of treatment, originality
of thought, and methodological grasp, by far overshadows
the Soviet Slavist's description and interpretation of the
sound system of prehistoric and early attested Slavic, G.
Y. Shevelov's *A Prehistory of Slavic: The Historical Phonology of Common Slavic*, published in identical editions,
1964 and 1965, for the European and American market, respectively. Before going into a brief discussion of this
monumental work, it should be unequivocally stated that in
the considered estimation of the present writer Shevelov's
combined textbook and research synthesis is clearly the
best overall treatment of CS phonology available to date.
While fully aware of certain drawbacks and controversial
aspects unavoidable in an undertaking of this size (xx +
662 pp.) and complexity, attempting both to critically
evaluate past achievements and to suggest, in many instances, new solutions, I thus find unjustified and,
indeed, unfair the harsh rejection with which Shevelov's
magnum opus has met in some quarters. Cf. Lunt 1966a; Van
Campen 1966; note, on the other hand, e.g., the overall
very positive assessment by Stieber 1967 and the balanced
and reasonable review by Kiparsky 1969b, recognizing the
book's great merits while at the same time indicating some
objectionable points. The purely negative attitude of
some American Slavists toward Shevelov's work largely be-
trays their own narrowly dogmatic approach to linguistic
(and specifically phonological) theory which is incapable
of accepting the sort of sound and open-minded eclecticism
adopted by the Ukrainian-American Slavist. Shevelov's
flexibility in approach, his preparedness to apply an integrated methodology resorting to any specific technique
considered best fit to describe or explain a given phenomenon rather than strictly adopting one particular coherent
doctrine of (diachronic) phonology regardless of its inability, in some instances, to account for sound change
and related matters, in short, Shevelov's unwillingness to
break with all past achievements of earlier, more

traditionalist historical linguistics (though certainly also not shunning criticism of some of its tenets) for the sake of new insights gained on the basis of more recent theoretical considerations — this compromising or, better, integrating attitude may well be explicable in terms of Shevelov's own scholarly career. Having received a thorough training with the leading, essentially traditionalist Ukrainian Slavist L. A. Bulaxovs'kyj (Bulaxovskij), whose most outstanding student he became, Shevelov was subsequently exposed to West European and American structuralist linguistic thought, holding teaching positions first in Sweden and thereafter in the United States. Shevelov's failure to systematically and consistently analyze the many CS (and pre-CS) sound shifts in terms of feature substitution or switching — not even necessarily using Jakobsonian or post-Jakobsonian distinctive feature specifications — has imposed a limitation on his approach and interpretation that occasionally may seem hampering and thus not warranted. To be sure, this drawback can be explained at least partly, by the fact that in the late fifties when the general ideas of Shevelov's book took shape, linguists were still largely unaware of the fact that sound change does not primarily take place at the phonemic level (while its repercussions and implications in various ways affect and modify the sound system as a whole, i.e., in particular also at higher, viz., the phonemic and morphophonemic or "systematic phonemic," levels where also some of the triggering forces must be sought).

Writing "a prehistory of Slavic" (if only in its phonological aspect) implies by definition doing linguistic reconstruction. Shevelov handles its two fundamental sets of techniques, the comparative method or, rather, its improved version, the "integrated comparative method" (ICM; for discussion, see 6-7), and the method of internal reconstruction, with great circumspection and skill, applying them to a multitude of linguistic data and combining them thoughtfully to achieve maximum results.

Shevelov's book, which is designed for both the newcomer to the field and the experienced specialist, does not make easy reading, but it should be acknowledged that the author has at least tried to cope with this inherent incompatibility of the two vastly differing points of view (and purposes of his handbook) by subdividing, wherever feasible, the material covered in most of his chapters into three portions. The first one contains a general statement and presents the basic facts, adducing by and large

generally accepted views only. The final section in each
chapter (usually labeled "Conditions and effects") summarizes the author's own interpretation of the phenomenon
under scrutiny and therefore, by its very nature, is often
speculative and hypothetic; it is primarily intended to
stimulate further discussion. The intervening sections of
each chapter focus on details of chronology and spatial
limitations. However, even with this internal organization of the individual chapters, Shevelov's book must be
said to be more rewarding and indeed more epoch-making
reading for the specialist rather than a particularly
helpful tool for classroom teaching (except perhaps in advanced seminars and special courses). Yet ample bibliographical references following each chapter, handy indexes
of authors, words, and subjects, as well as two appendices
providing a synopsis of the principal sound changes in CS
and Early Slavic and summarizing the systems of consonantal phonemes in the modern Slavic languages and Polabian
(for the purpose of comparison with their CS point of departure), in addition to a map showing dialectal divisions
in disintegrating CS and some diagrams, add to the practical usefulness of the book. The notation used is largely
traditional with a few notable exceptions, however, of
which some, but not all, carry substantive implications.
Thus, $_o a$ ($_o \breve{a}$ = traditional o or, more recently, $\breve{a}$; $_o \bar{a}$ =
traditional a or, for an earlier period, $\bar{a}$) and $_e a$ ($_e \breve{a}$ =
traditionally e; $_e \bar{a}$ = traditionally $\breve{e}$ or rather $\breve{e}_1$) is not
merely a new way of attempting to graphically represent a
slightly changed pronunciation of the monophthong (cf.
previous notations such as $\mathring{a}$ for traditional o, $\overset{\circ}{\ddot{a}}$ for traditional a, $\ddot{a}$ or $\mathring{a}$ for $\breve{e}$, etc.) but is meant to denote an
a-sound with an actual o- or e-colored on-glide. On the
other hand, the symbols b^ς, d^ς, g^ς, $\hat{g}^\varsigma$, $g^{w\varsigma}$ simply stand
for aspirate sounds otherwise usually denoted bh, dh, gh,
$\hat{g}h$ (or $\hat{g}h$), $g^w h$ (or $g^{u}h$), by Shevelov still considered
voiced stops, a view that today is no longer shared by all
Indo-Europeanists.

Shevelov's treatment spans the entire sound development from Late PIE to disintegrating dialectal CS (or
actually post-CS Early Slavic), altogether, in his view,
roughly three millennia. Compared to the chronologically
monolithic concept of CS of a Mikkola or Meillet (but to a
large extent also found, for example, in Arumaa's text)
and, as it may seem at first, even when set against the
notion of CS as largely falling into two major periods,
Early CS (or PS) and Late CS, Shevelov's differentiation

of forty major sound changes ranging from somewhere around 2000-1500 B. C. (i.e., sound shifts 1 through 6 in his synopsis on p. 633) to the 10th, 11th, and mid-12th centuries A. D. (shifts 39 and 40) reflects the dynamics of diachrony of preliterary and early literary Slavic as well as some pre-Slavic, Balto-Slavic, and/or dialectal Late Common IE developments. However, on closer inspection this difference in chronological conception does not in actual fact differ so widely from the view distinguishing only two major periods of CS proper just referred to. For while Shevelov groups his forty principal sound changes into five periods, it should be noted that his last period (corresponding to sound shifts 34 through 40, ca. mid-9th to mid-12th centuries) largely fall outside the upper limit of CS, granted the fact that some scholars, among them Trubeckoj, Toporov, and the present writer, have argued that only the last general Slavic change, namely, the loss of the *jers*, marks the definite close of the Late CS period. Moreover, at least Shevelov's two first periods (covering processes 1 through 9 and lasting, supposedly, until sometime before the 6th-5th centuries B. C.) and even the relatively short third period (characterized primarily by the coalescence of o and a into $_oa$ and the development $e > {}_ea$ in the 6th-5th centuries B. C.) are still pre-Slavic, partly perhaps Balto-Slavic. This would therefore narrow down the time range of a strictly CS phonological evolution to a period from approximately the first pre-Christian centuries through the early 9th century A. D., a total of not much more than one millennium only. This concept thus comes quite close to the one proposed more recently by Stieber (cf. pp. 34-5 and 48-50, above). Within this relatively short time span one could then, again, distinguish between an earlier, relatively stable PS (or Early CS) period (processes 11-15, last pre-Christian centuries to ca. 500 A. D.) and a later, CS (or Late CS) period of radical changes (sound shifts 16-33, ca. 5th through early 9th centuries).

Shevelov's masterly utilization of comparative IE data to elucidate pre-Slavic as well as CS phonological processes is most impressive. This applies, for example, to his skillful and knowledgeable manner of integrating the findings of laryngeal theory into CS phonological structure and, especially, accentology (28-31, 46-7, 91-2, 96, 113, 116, 126, 246). Extremely useful is further his broad recourse to loanword and toponymic (as well as other onomastic) material enabling him, among other things, to

posit new absolute chronologies or to corroborate and more
firmly fix previously established ones. The ease with
which Shevelov handles the techniques of internal reconstruction permits him to determine convincingly a number
of relative chronologies (on such chronologies as establishable for CS phonology cf. especially also Ebeling
1963). A firm grasp of the principles of linguistic geography (areal linguistics) afford the Ukrainian-American
Slavist the opportunity to locate focal points of certain
CS, especially Late CS, phenomena unevenly spread over the
Slavic linguistic territory. Thus, for instance, Shevelov
conceives of the chronologies of the Second (regressive)
and the Third (progressive) Palatalizations of Velars as
partly overlapping (chapters 21 and 23, esp. 351-4; for a
generative approach to this problem and a demonstration of
its limitations, see Birnbaum 1970c: 103-13) and places
the center of the Third Palatalization in the southwestern
part of the Slavic language area (345-6). Contrary to
some other contemporary researchers (including Stieber
1967: 19-20; 1969/71,1: 10, 81-3; cf. also above, *passim*),
Shevelov finds sufficient evidence to establish an approximate time range 600-850 A. D. (i.e., at any rate later
than ca. 500 A. D.) for the partial simplification tl, dl
> l in Late — dialectally differentiated — CS (373-4).
The *jers* are by Shevelov considered to have evolved only
relatively late (early 9th century), to have been short-
lived, and, articulatorily, not to have been generally
"reduced" but only "reducible" (viz., in weak position)
but pronounced with a more "neutral" (central) articulation (i.e., with less tense lips and flattened tongue)
than i and u (chapter 29). As in many other instances,
Shevelov's view here coincides rather closely with that
expounded more recently by Stieber (cf. p. 49, above).

     While Shevelov's reference to loanwords and onomas-
tic data hardly ever evokes any doubts as to its justification and accuracy, the same is not necessarily always
true when it comes to his resorting to etymologies. Etymological collocations provide, of course, a further important and, on the whole, legitimate source from which to
draw information also relevant to certain sound changes.
Without going into any detail here, it may be stated that
not all of the etymologies adduced by Shevelov are generally recognized as correct so that some of the reconstructions built on them are at least open to debate. Yet it
should also be mentioned that the number of controversial
etymologies found in Shevelov's book is relatively small

and that, as a rule, he indicates their tentative nature
(cf., e.g., 191-3 where such lexical items as OR *stryi* =
stryjь and RChS *nestera*, OP *nieściora*, SCr *nèstera* are
discussed to illustrate, in cautious terms to be sure, a
possible shift $pt > st$ in Early CS, first suggested, it
seems, by Vey 1931; cf. also Birnbaum 1972a: 155-6). Thus
it is less any uncritical acceptance of uncertain etymologies on Shevelov's part than it is his willingness to
even consider such controversial items in a standard reference work that may perhaps give rise to some methodological (as well as pedagogical) objections.

Upon closer scrutiny the attentive reader will find
a number of subtle observations and original ideas in
Shevelov's text which at first glance may have escaped
him. Some of these thoughts and suggestions provide interesting clues for the interpretation of heretofore unexplained irregularities (or rather seeming deviations) in
the phonological development of CS and/or its closest cognates. Thus, for example, Shevelov attributes considerable importance to affective factors in sound change which
are claimed to account not only for one of the sources of
PS (Early CS) x (132-5) but also for some instances of
palatalization in Indo-Iranian and Baltic (lacking an
equivalent in Slavic), depalatalization, and affricatiza-
tion (evidenced in Slavic, 141-5, 275), nasalization (321-
2), alveolarization ($s > \check{s}$, especially before k and p,
592), and voicing (366, 368).

Naturally, a book so rich in data and interpretations will by necessity also always contain some claims
with which not everyone will find it easy to agree. One
such instance, already mentioned above (p. 42), is Shevelov's explicit assertion that the *akan'e* pronunciation
of the reflex of the CS (originally short) back vowel
found in Russian (southern dialects and standard variety
which is based on the Moscow pronunciation) and Belorussian, directly continues the *a*-coloring of that vowel in
the Slavic protolanguage (151, 386-7). As we have seen,
this idea was at least hinted at already by Vaillant (cf.
p. 42, above) and subsequently carried *ad absurdum* by
Georgiev (cf. especially Georgiev 1963; Georgiev *et al.*
1968; for a critical evaluation of Georgiev's theory, see,
in particular, Birnbaum 1970c: 47-61; 1971b: 350). For my
part, while not denying the *a* timbre of the (short) back
vowel for most of the CS period, I cannot accept this view
of the allegedly archaic nature of Russian and Belorussian
akan'e (and some comparable phenomena elsewhere in Slavic,

especially in Bulgarian); for further discussion, cf. below, pp. 253-4.

Many other, indeed most, details deserving mention
in Shevelov's CS phonology must be omitted here for lack
of space. It should be stated, however, that while in
some instances his conclusions may seem objectionable
(though even then they are always well considered and
forcefully argued), in the vast majority, his observations
and inferences are not only keen and cogent but frequently
have a flavor of novelty and freshness allowing for new
and deeper insights into the structure and dynamics of CS
phonology. Relying on a supreme command of relevant data
and adopting a flexible, eclectic, undogmatic, but never
inconsistent approach, Shevelov has laid a new foundation
for the study and reconstruction of prehistoric Slavic in
its phonological aspect. Its impact can hardly be overestimated. The fact that some — though on the whole few —
of the many views advanced in his book are merely tentative and may, in some instances, eventually not stand up
to critical scrutiny is only natural and can in no way detract from the overwhelming general significance of his
achievement.

If Bernštejn's *Očerk*, despite frequent recourse to
phonological (phonemic) terminology, retained a largely
traditionalist basic conception of sound change, and even
Shevelov's *Prehistory*, while displaying some awareness of
modern (though to be sure pre-generative) phonological
theory and adopting holistic (i.e., non-atomistic) approaches to complex and interrelated phenomena and processes of CS, still managed to remain on the firm ground of
traditional linguistics, this can hardly be said to apply
to yet another outline of CS and Early Slavic phonology
which attained its — at least so far — definitive formulation only by 1969, having previously gone through several
stages of published preliminary versions, F. V. Mareš's
Diachronische Phonologie des Ur- und Frühslavischen (earlier variants: Mareš 1956, 1965a, 1965b; integrated into
the final version were further findings and theories reported in Mareš 1958a, 1958b, 1959, 1962b, 1963b, 1963c).
In the new version a notational system has been adopted
which does not differ substantially from the traditional
one as was the case, on the other hand, with the somewhat
peculiar phonemic notation used in much of Mareš's earlier
work. Fostered in the tradition of the Prague School, the
Czech-Austrian Slavist in his book (as well as in the preceding studies) has striven to give a synthetic interpre-

tation of the CS and Early Slavic sound changes which in
more than one way could be considered a direct continuation of similar, innovative attempts undertaken in the
twenties and thirties by some of the theoreticians of the
Prague brand of phonology, notably Jakobson (1929). The
reception of Mareš's endeavors in this field has consequently varied considerably, ranging from his being re-
proached for pursuing mere "paper phonology" (*bumažnaja
fonologija*; cf. Bernštejn 1961: 147, rejecting his hypothesis of an Early CS delabialization of vowels, see also
176) to being commended for providing a truly structuralist view of CS diachronic phonology, by a usually overly
critical colleague to boot (Lunt 1966a: 92). There can
indeed be little doubt that Mareš's treatment of CS and
Early Slavic diachronic phonology has great merit as it
offers a number of new, intriguing insights and suggests
some original, subtle explanations along with resorting to
previously recognized factors and elaborated concepts such
as syllable harmony (= syllabic synharmonism) or the law
of open syllables. Of course, this does not mean, however,
that all of his assertions and suggestions are necessarily
convincing or acceptable. It should further be noted that
Mareš's outline focuses on Late CS and early attested
Slavic rather than on Early CS (PS) or even Balto-Slavic
phases of the prehistoric evolution (notwithstanding his
occasional, hardly always justified claim as to the high
antiquity of certain sound shifts, e.g., the progressive
Third Palatalization of Velars; cf. 59-63).

The overall arrangement of Mareš's presentation is
as follows: Introduction (discussing principles of synchronic and diachronic phonology, the time limits of CS,
the sound system of pre-Slavic dialectal Late PIE, and a
suggested tripartition of sound classes into vowels, consonants, and sonants, §§ 1-3), delabialization (§§ 4-14 a),
syllable harmony (§§ 15-16), the law of open syllables
(§§ 17-39), the so-called Third Palatalization of Velars
(according to Mareš, more appropriately numbered Second,
§§ 40-48), palatalization of alveolars (§§ 49-55), modification (rather than metathesis which would literally
translate his G *Umstellung*) of the timbre-quantitative
vowel system (§§ 56-66), the nasal vowels (§§ 67-73),
notes on the evolution of word-final position (§§ 74-76),
and — summarizing — the period of Slavic linguistic unity
in the light of the phonological system (§§ 77-78). In
this connection, it ought to be pointed out that under
some of the just listed subheadings certain phenomena and

developments are subsumed which, while generally related, do not strictly fall under a given rubric (cf., e.g., the positionally conditioned shifts $kt > t'$ and $gn/kn > gň/kň$ or the development of epenthetic l', all dealt with in the chapter on the palatalization of alveolars, 76-9).

Paraphrasing Mareš's statement of his overall conception of the CS phonological evolution (117-19), the following general picture emerges. The consistent delabialization of vowels is allegedly the first decisive factor identifying the Slavic sound system as such (i.e., as an autonomous entity). A symmetric and self-contained vowel system developed which was based on vocalic quality, graded according to the place of the vowels on the vertical (high-to-low or closed-to-open) axis of articulation (degree of aperture), and on the consistent maintenance of the phonemic timbre and quantity correlation. This constituted a fundamental distinctive characteristic singling out the Slavic system of phonemes from that of other IE languages. This vowel system was the primary and specific system of CS. It gave immediate rise to syllable harmony, markedly affecting consonantism as well (1st and 2nd, partly also 3rd Palatalizations). The two principles of syllable harmony and open syllables underlie, directly or indirectly, all major sound changes of CS. As regards word-final syllables, the law of retaining the mora value of the syllable must be added. However, the development subject to the law of open syllables resulted in new labialized vowels, thus affecting the main phonological substance of CS, i.e., the vowel system. The disintegration of this vowel system and its restructuring on the basis of quality differences of labiovelarity mark, from a phonological point of view, the end of the Slavic linguistic unity and simultaneously signal the emergence of clearly differentiated, autonomous entities ultimately yielding independent Slavic languages. Put differently, the gradual elimination of the earlier system foreshadows the approaching end of CS (in phonological terms), and the gradual emergence of the labiovelar system has as its corollary the rise of the basic units underlying the individual Slavic languages. The earlier and subsequent dialectal differentiations are contingent on two basic factors: (1) the existence of, generally speaking, two focal points with different locations in the Slavic language area; and (2) various phenomena involving the overlapping of a number of developments in accordance with their shifting relative chronology. Toward the end of the period of Slavic (relative) linguistic unity, a number of modifications take place triggered by general, common tendencies; however, owing to the two focal points and differences in relative chronology, their results are so manifold that they clearly go beyond the limits of a single coherent system. New light is also shed on the historical classification of the Slavic languages according to phonological criteria; two entities clearly emerge, a northern (yielding the West and East Slavic languages) and a southern. The agreements between the southern and the eastern group, supposedly much overestimated since Dobrovský's days, are rather said to be accidental in kind (e.g., *cw*, *zw*; epenthetic *l'*; *tl/dl* > *l*). Also here, for a general assessment of the genetic relationships, the principle "non numerantur, sed ponderantur" is claimed to be applicable to the various phenomena. In the dissolution of the Slavic linguistic unity these two groups are most patently characterized in their respective systems by the rise vs. lack of a correlation of softness (palatality) in the consonants.

It is readily clear, of course, that even in this brief account of Mareš's overall view of CS and Early Slavic phonological development several points are debatable. Thus, as was already mentioned, his notion of a general vowel delabialization as the first major event setting apart a specifically Slavic sound evolution from that of other IE languages and language groups (including apparently Baltic) is questionable. To be sure, the early developments $\bar{o} > \bar{a}$, $\bar{u} > y$ (or rather first to some other intermediary stage in the sound shift, however already delabialized; cf. Stieber 1969/71, 1: 23), and probably also $\breve{o}$ (partly < ∂) > $\breve{a}$ (with a general shift > o only in Late CS), all imply a process of delabialization. But it now appears unlikely that (delabialized) ь < (rounded) $\breve{u}$ represents an early development of CS (cf. Stieber 1969/71, 1: 21-2, and above, p. 98). Also Mareš's belief in the primacy of the vowel system (in contrast to the consonant system) as the cornerstone on which everything hinges in CS phonology is at least arguable. And his assertion that all major sound changes of CS were somehow triggered by a few general tendencies, or even laws, obviously echoes earlier attempts at holistic explanations (van Wijk, Jakobson, etc.) but is hardly in keeping with more recent systematic treatments of CS phonology (Shevelov, Stieber). The assumption of a labiovelar system and of labiovelarity as a unified characteristic feature of Late CS and Early Slavic,

while having had its advocates, has more recently been
questioned if not plainly rejected (Calleman). The emphasis on spatial differentiation (singling out different
focal points) in Late CS and the insistence on a first
dialectal division north : south (i.e., ultimately West-
East vs. South Slavic) rather than west : east (i.e., West
vs. East-South Slavic, an initial split advocated by Šaxmatov, but still maintained, e.g., by Lehr-Spławiński and
especially Bernštejn) seems indeed well-founded. However,
the notion of relative chronology appears in Mareš's conception to assume added — unfamiliar — spatial-temporal
connotations, relating time differences of identical or
collocatable phenomena as ascertainable in various parts
of the Slavic language area, rather than carrying merely
temporal (diachronic) implications, relating the time (or
time range) of a particular process or phenomenon to the
time (range) of a different (though usually causally connected) preceding or following linguistic event (i.e., establishing precisely relative, but not absolute, chronologies).

In addition, several other points in Mareš's account,
not included in the above given summary statement, deserve
closer scrutiny. It was already mentioned that Mareš belongs to the decreasing number of Slavic linguists who
argue for a reversal of the chronological order of the
Second and Third Palatalizations of Velars (another well-
known advocate of such a reversed chronology before Mareš
was Ekblom 1951; further earlier adherents of this order
include, among others, Il'inskij, Ščepkin, Hujer, Vondrák,
Trubeckoj, Lehr-Spławiński, and Kořínek). It seems, at
least to the present writer, that the arguments for an
early date of the progressive palatalization of k, g, x
set forth by Mareš (as well as by previous advocates of
such a chronology) cannot be considered cogent (cf. also
Stieber 1968b: 93-5, 104-5; for a refutation of a chronological reversal recently proposed by Chomsky & Halle, see
below, p. 264). Another point on which I find myself unable to subscribe fully to Mareš's treatment concerns the
so-called nasal vowels. Thus, while discussing phonetic
(articulatory-acoustic) problems of the nasal vowels in CS
and Early Slavic, Mareš suggests (p. 104) a development
$\breve{a}\eta > \breve{a}N > \tilde{a} > \varrho(N)$ as underlying those Slavic languages
where nasal vowels were preserved (i.e. primarily Lekhit-
ic). However, such an evolutionary series strikes one as
inherently unlikely. And from a phonological point of
view, it is of course much more important to pose the

question as to just what was the phonemic status of the CS
and Early Slavic nasal vowels (whatever their realization,
namely, as nasal "diphthongs" of the Polish type or pure
nasal vowels of the French type). Some years ago I tried
to show, modifying a suggestion along similar lines by
Trubeckoj, that the nasal vowels cannot have functioned as
autonomous phonemes prior to the loss of the "weak" *jers*
but must at that time merely have been allophones of sound
sequences of the type *EN/ON* (i.e., front/back vowel + nasal consonant) even if perhaps pronounced (realized, implemented) as nasal vowels proper (ϱ, ϱ; in this latter
assumption I maintained a view different from Trubeckoj's);
cf. Birnbaum 1963: esp. 29-34. Also the fact that in some
parts of the Slavic language area (notably on East Slavic
territory) nasal vowels were replaced by oral vowels even
earlier than the elimination of the *jers* in "weak" position, in no way invalidates the given assertion since it
seems that it is not primarily phonemes as such that undergo sound change (which, as we now know, largely takes
place at the subphonemic level); cf. Birnbaum 1965a: esp.
285-9. For further discussion see p. 114, below. A par-
ticularity encountered in Mareš's discussion of the nasal
vowels (107-8, 111-13) and elsewhere in his book is his
effort, at least partly successful, to derive relevant
phonological information directly from the Old Slavic
(Glagolitic and Cyrillic) writing systems (cf. also, e.g.,
102-3).

Much more could of course be adduced by way of com-
mentary, both favorable and critical, to Mareš's concept
of CS and Early Slavic diachronic phonology. However, to
keep within reasonable space limitations we may conclude
this brief evaluation of his original contribution to the
field by stating that, while not everything in his approach to, and analysis of, the CS sound system and its
development through time as well as its specific modification according to spatial diversity may coincide with our
own (or some other linguists') view of these matters, the
Czech-Austrian scholar certainly has succeeded in sketching a fairly coherent and internally consistent outline of
CS and Early Slavic sound change viewed in an overall
structuralist framework.

Much more traditional in approach is another fairly
recent systematic treatment of Late CS phonology where the
focus, however, is exclusively on the period of the final
disintegration of the Slavic protolanguage. Indeed, the
decomposition of CS as such is the primary concern of the

author, while the Late CS and Early Slavic phonological evolution merely provides the parameters for measuring and describing the rate and directions of this divergent development. The monograph referred to, A. Furdal's *Rozpad języka prastowiańskiego w świetle rozwoju głosowego* (1961), is a product of the Polish tradition of research in the field of CS represented in particular by the late T. Lehr-Spławiński (for relevant titles, see Bibliography). Since the data adduced in this study as well as some of its conclusions have previously been utilized and discussed by me (Birnbaum 1965b and 1966a), I can here summarize the upshot of the Polish Slavist's findings adding only a few general remarks by way of comment.

Following Lehr-Spławiński, Furdal posits a first period of CS dialectal differentiation (concurrent with generally shared CS innovations and lasting until approximately the 5th century A. D.) which was marked by an East: West split and manifested itself in the isoglosses related to the Second Palatalization of Velars ($\check{s}$ vs. s', $\check{s}\check{c}$ vs. $s'c'$, kv' vs. cv') and the simplification of the clusters tl, dl. The second — more important — period of dialectal developments within Late CS is far more complex. Based on relative chronologies of various sound shifts and of certain partly related morphological changes, the author attempts to demonstrate that no clear-cut time sequence of internal regroupings can be established for that period as regional modifications intermingle with dialectal phenomena of a different spatial range. The only chronological distinction applicable to the second period of CS dialectal differentiation is that of an earlier phase of preserved areal unity of all Slavs as opposed to a subsequent phase of territorial disruption into a northern and a southern portion of the Slavic language area caused by the settling of the Magyars in Pannonia and the adjacent area east of the Danube (present-day Hungary) shortly before 900 A. D. During the second period, Late CS is still said to have been characterized by some overall innovations such as, for example, the delabialization $\check{u} > $ ь, the emergence of syllabic $\underset{\circ}{r}$, $\underset{\circ}{l}$, $\underset{\circ}{r}'$, $\underset{\circ}{l}'$ ($< \check{u}r$, $\check{u}l$, $\check{i}r$, $\check{i}l$ < PIE $\underset{\circ}{r}$, $\underset{\circ}{l}$), or the establishment of the phonemic front : back vowel correlation. Some of the general Slavic developments, among them the "weakening" of the *jers* (in certain positions) and of the nasal resonance in nasal vowels, subsequently provided the basis for regionally limited or chronologically uneven phenomena such as the denasalization of ρ and ϱ and concomitant sound changes and —

transcending the CS period proper — the loss of the weak
jers. Regional innovations of varying extent are introduced in the second period, e.g., $eT > 'aT$ in Lekhitic (T
here marking a hard dental) or the merger of the reflexes
of *tj* and *stj*, *skj* in pre-Macedo-Bulgarian. More decisive, however, for defining the second period of CS dialectal differentiation are the innovations which contrast
all the North Slavic area with the Slavic South. These
more wide-ranging developments are either independent or
related to other modifications of a more limited extent.
Among the former are, for example, the change $\delta rt- > rot-$
(in the north) vs. *rat-* (in the south) or the substitution
of the ending $-\text{ь}mъ$ for $-omъ$ (in the instrumental singular
of the $-o$ stems) in North Slavic; among the latter are the
rise of phonemic palatalization of all consonants before
front vowels in the Slavic North (interpreted by Furdal as
a shifting of the correlation of palatality from the vowel
to the consonant system) and the emergence of the so-
called $-\bar{e}_3$ ($< -jenъ$) in North Slavic, both phenomena connected with, among other things, the denasalization $\rho > a$.
Yet, while the most important modifications of this period
are those separating North and South Slavic, the gap between West and East Slavic continues to widen and new sub-
groupings take shape in South and West Slavic.

The Polish Slavist has attempted to reveal some of
the underlying factors in the development of CS dialectal
features and to relate these factors to the overall evolution of CS phonology. In particular this applies to the
second period of (Late) CS dialectal differentiation.
Thus the emergence of a front : back vowel correlation is
explained as the combined result of the delabialization
$\bar{u}, \breve{u} > y$, ь, the coalescence of $\bar{a}$ and $\bar{o}$, and the shift $\bar{e} >$
$\breve{e}$ (implying a more open articulation, i.e., a lowering of
the tongue). The Lekhitic depalatalizations of front vowels before hard dentals ($eT > 'aT$, etc.) and the denasalization $\rho > a$ in the rest of North Slavic are said together
to have caused the shifting of the correlation of palatality from the vowel to the consonant system. In South
Slavic the vocalic front : back correlation soon broke down
in the Serbo-Croatian-Slovene area, while in Bulgaria it
persisted for some time due, in particular, to the delabialization of ρ ($> \breve{a}$). The shift $\rho > a$ in turn is explained in terms of the particular position of nasal vow-
els in the overall vowel system, favoring a more open
articulation, as well as the tendency for denasalization,
that is to say, the fading of the nasal resonance char-

acteristic for most of the Slavic language area. According to Furdal, the change $e > a$ was probably not only one of the factors triggering the shifting to the consonant system of the phonemic correlation of palatality (replacing the previous front : back distinction in the vowels) but may also be responsible for the emergence of $-\check{e}_3$ and — unrelated to the latter — the closed articulation of $\check{e}$ (or rather its reflexes) in part of North Slavic. A tendency toward labialization is claimed to account both for the sound shifts $telt > tolt$, $t\check{\imath}lt > t\check{u}lt$ (subsequently $t\underset{\sim}{l}t$) in East Slavic as well as West Lekhitic (Polabian-Pomoranian) and for such developments as $je- > o-$, (strong) $ь > o$, $e > o$, etc., in East Slavic.

Advancing a new theory of the relationships between the Slavic languages, based on a partly redefined distinction of innovations vs. archaisms (retentions) peculiar for each Slavic language, the Polish linguist arrives at the conclusion that, while the traditional synchronic tripartition into West, East, and South Slavic remains valid, the fundamental division of the Slavic languages is that between North and South Slavic, firmly anchored in the underlying grouping of Late CS dialects, and not any east : west bipartition. Furdal sees the chief criterion for the north : south division in the modification of the phonological system as it relates to the phonemic correlation of palatality. The North Slavic languages, for some time actively continuing to introduce innovations which were CS in kind, must, according to Furdal, be considered more closely related internally than the South Slavic languages for which the existence of a preceding period of relatively homogeneous unity (Common South Slavic) cannot, in fact, be posited as many of the South Slavic characteristics either extend beyond the South Slavic territory or are clearly of an archaic nature.

Attempting to assess the significance of Furdal's work, it must be stated that in the light of recent research (especially by Shevelov and Stieber, to be sure, after the appearance of his work) his positing of the two clear-cut periods of CS dialectal differentiation seems at least questionable. For of the phenomena linked by Furdal (following in this respect Lehr-Spławiński) with an earlier (pre-5th century) phase of CS, only the different treatment of tl, dl can possibly be assigned to such an early period. On the other hand, the coalescence of PIE $\bar{o}$ and $\bar{a}$ into one sound (presumably $\bar{a}$, with or without some degree of nonphonemic labialization) seems to belong to a

very remote period in the prehistoric development of Slavic (if not perhaps even pre-Slavic). In view of the Late
CS shift $\bar{a} > \breve{o}$, dialectal developments such as *telt >
tolt, je- > o-*, strong ь *> o* qualify as instances of labialization only if they are assumed to have occurred quite
late, i.e., very much toward the end of the Late CS period
(perhaps 9th-10th centuries), since otherwise the resulting vowel was not yet *o* but (nonlabialized or merely in-
significantly labialized) $\breve{a}$. While it may indeed seem ap-
pealing to lump together the developments $\bar{u} > y$ and $\breve{u} > $ ь
as instances of — the same — delabialization, it is nonetheless doubtful whether these two sound shifts were causally and temporally connected, the change $\breve{u} > $ ь seeming to
have occurred only late (cf. also Stieber's and Mareš's
conflicting relevant views, referred to above, pp. 49
and 103). Some further reservations as well as the ones
just mentioned notwithstanding, one of the major conclusions arrived at by the Polish Slavist is no doubt convincing. This refers to the fact that the division into
North vs. South Slavic, based on CS dialectal differences
(of which phonemic palatalization of all consonants before
front vowels in the north may indeed have been the most
important), is more fundamental than that between West
Slavic and the rest of the Slavic languages. And also
Furdal's corollary that the internal differentiation of
South Slavic must have begun prior to the arrival of a
portion of the Slavs in the Balkan Peninsula (and the
Eastern Alps) appears plausible.

   Finally, concluding this section on monographic
treatments of CS phonology, it can be noted that the brief
outline by C. E. Bidwell, *Slavic Historical Phonology in
Tabular Form* (1963), opens with a chapter titled "From
Indo-European to Common Slavic" (9-15). However, except
for the terminological distinction of an earlier, PS, and
a subsequent, CS, period, Bidwell's treatment has little
new to offer and does not afford any particularly important insights into the structure and development of CS
phonology but contains, on the other hand, some inaccuracies and inadequacies; for a critical evaluation, see
Stankiewicz 1963: esp. 420-1.

3.2. Specialized Studies in Common Slavic Phonology.
Turning now to some studies on specific subfields and topics of CS phonology, we shall limit ourselves in this section to briefly discussing or at least listing a few important relevant contributions published up to a recent

period (using 1965 as an approximate, though by no means firmly fixed, cut-off point). Assessment or, in some instances, merely cursory mention of most recent and current work in these areas of research (roughly since 1965) is reserved for a subsequent section of Part Two of this book dealing with as yet unresolved, insufficiently explored, or only tentatively or partly elucidated problems in the reconstruction of CS phonology (see pp. 242-71). A similar division between previous (including fairly recent) and current (as well as most recent) research will further be adopted in the following when discussing progress made and problems identified and now being explored in CS morphology (cf. pp. 272-91), in CS syntax (cf. pp. 292-8), and in CS lexicology (cf. pp. 299-311). The same bipartition will also be applied when dealing with some overall aspects of CS structure as they relate to the general IE setting of CS, its particular relationship to certain language groups (primarily IE, but occasionally also to some unrelated language family), its immediate emergence from the more narrow framework of Balto-Slavic (whatever the latter's linguistic status and reality), its outer time limits, internal periodization, and specific chronologies (absolute as well as relative), and, finally, its ultimate disintegration and dialectal differentiation (cf. pp. 220-35, 312-38).

3.2.1. General Problems. Among more important contributions to general problems of CS phonology, first two articles by N. S. Trubeckoj from the early twenties, already referred to in the preceding, deserve mention. In his "Essai sur la chronologie de certains faits phonétiques du slave commun" (1922), the Russian linguist sketched a broad outline, based on phonological data, of the chronology of CS linguistic evolution which he conceived as divided into three distinct phases: (1) The PS period during which CS was merely a Late PIE dialect sharing common changes (notably sound shifts) with other IE dialects. It is only the nonrecurring totality of these changes that allows us to refer to this CS of the early period as a separate dialect of Late PIE. Considering that most (though not all) of the changes falling into this period can also be posited for the common predecessor of the Baltic languages, the thus qualified term Balto-Slavic may be applied to this period. (2) The phase of unitary independence during which CS was a language fully apart from all other IE idioms but did not yet exhibit any dialectal

features. (3) The period of dialectal differentiation.
It is within this tripartite chronological framework that
Trubeckoj proposes to view the well-known major phonetic
changes of CS (monophthongizations and other modifications
of diphthongs in the broad sense, palatalizations, etc.),
however excluding from this particular examination the developments of the first ("Balto-Slavic" or narrowly defined PS) period in view of the fact that virtually all of
them are shared with one branch or another of IE and thus
do not, considered individually, qualify as strictly Slavic innovations but rather fall within the purview of Comparative IE Linguistics. The relative chronologies established by Trubeckoj and discussed in this article largely
belong to the second period of independent Slavic homogeneity. In a subsequent study, "Einiges über die russische
Lautentwicklung und die Auflösung der gemeinrussischen
Spracheinheit" (1925b), Trubeckoj treated in some detail
diachronic phonological phenomena which, in most instances,
do not even fall within the Late CS period; only a few of
the preliterary East Slavic sound shifts discussed qualify
at best as Late CS dialectal features (e.g., $g > \gamma$; $\check{c} \times$
c; tl, $dl > l$ / kl, gl; partial modification of $\check{z}\check{c}$, $\check{z}\check{z}$).
Important from a methodological point of view is Trubec-
koj's rejection of any mechanistic *Stammbaum*-type interpretation of the process of dialectal differentiation of
Common East Slavic as well as his claim that no Proto-
Great-Russian linguistic unity can be ascertained at the
dialectological level, suggesting instead an early breakup
into North (Great) Russian, South (Great) Russian, and
Ukrainian (or Ruthenian, underlying both Ukrainian proper
and essentially also Belorussian) rather than the traditional tripartition into (Great) Russian, Ukrainian, and
Belorussian, frequently believed to reflect a corresponding incipient preliterary division. Moreover, Trubeckoj
in his article, as elsewhere, points out that the treatment of the *jers* (i.e., their "fall" and vocalization)
represents the last generally shared characteristic of all
Slavic languages, granted differences in implementation,
and that it thus marked the final event in the development
of Late CS. For a general and more complete assessment of
Trubeckoj's contribution to CS phonology, including some
of his writings which will be mentioned only in subsequent
sections of this state-of-the-art report, as well as of
its impact on the relevant thinking of some other members
of the Prague School, see in particular Horálek 1959.
      Following earlier critical remarks, N. van Wijk in

an article published in 1941, "Zum urslavischen sogenannten Synharmonismus der Silben," subjected to substantial
criticism the concept of syllabic synharmonism, formulated
more than a decade earlier (1929) by R. Jakobson in an attempt to find a common, fairly generalized motivating
force to account for a number of partly disparate phonetic
changes of CS (including dialectal Late CS) for which van
Wijk had introduced the more vague and general notion of
"tendency for palatalization," contrary to Jakobson's more
strictly defined concept not specifically connected with
the structure of the syllable. For some particular points
of van Wijk's critical argumentation, see below (pp. 141-
2).   A new, holistic view of the phonological system of
Late CS and its gradual transformation, clearly influenced by the structual approach of the Prague School, can
be found in the great Dutch Slavist's posthumous sketch
"K istorii fonologičeskoj sistemy v obščeslavjanskom jazyke pozdnego perioda," published in the 1949/50 volume of
Slavia but originally submitted for publication in a
planned volume to honor M. Murko. Except for problems of
intonation (and syllable quantity) not treated in this article (for which time was not yet ripe, as was stated by
the author in the closing paragraph), a fairly coherent
picture of the relative chronologies of all major sound
changes of the Late CS period, as conceived by van Wijk
toward the end of his life, emerges from this lucid presentation. Not all of it of course remains acceptable to
contemporary scholarship and van Wijk himself hastened to
point out some of the aspects not covered by his brief
discussion; in particular, the rules of phoneme concatenation within larger linguistic units had not been formulated as this article merely endeavored to provide a paradigmatic description of a set of successive phonological
systems but did not pursue the aim of exploring the diachronic dynamics of syntagmatic Late CS phonology.
     Of more recent contributions to the problems of
chronology, relative as well as absolute, in CS phonology,
C. E. Bidwell's solid and insightful study on "The chronology of certain sound changes in Common Slavic as evidenced by loans from Vulgar Latin," for obvious reasons
focusing on Late CS and dialectal Early Slavic (notably
pre-South Slavic), once again demonstrated the immeasur-
able value of extraneous linguistic evidence for the establishment of firm chronologies for some controversial sound
shifts previously resisting incontestable dating. Some of
the lexical and, particularly, onomastic data involved,

allowing in some instances for a fairly narrow chronology, will be cited below (pp. 231-2).

Only peripherally concerned with CS phonology or rather with the Late CS phonological system as a theoretical point of departure is the joint 1963 paper by M. Čejka and A. Lamprecht titled "K otázce vzniku a differenciace slovanských jazyků" in which an attempt was made to establish definite chronologies for many of the divergent phonetic developments characterizing the period of CS disintegration by resorting to the — to be sure, highly controversial — methods of lexicostatistics (or glottochronology). Still, the general conclusion that the period of the breaking-up of Late CS can be dated to approximately the 10th century and that OCS (at least in its original, Cyrillo-Methodian form) therefore must be considered only one of the dialects of spatially already differentiated (Late) CS is of course quite plausible while by no means new.

Considerations of chronology, as applied to two dialectal phenomena of Late CS and with further theoretical implications regarding sound change at the allophonic level (in addition to such change at the phonemic and/or, in particular, subphonemic, i.e., feature, levels), were also discussed in my article "Lautwandel und Phonologisierung: Ein chronologisches Problem, erläutert an zwei dialektischen Erscheinungen des Spätgemeinslavischen" (1965a). As was already mentioned above (p. 93), I here tried to show the fallacy of S. B. Bernštejn's argument against the, in his view, unjustified positing of a Lekhitic vowel shift $ę > ǫ$, generally believed to parallel the changes $ě > a$ and $e > o$ under identical phonetic conditions and in the same or a similar geographic area, while obscured by the subsequent Old Polish merging of $ę$ and $ǫ$ (or $ą̈$ and $ą̊$) in one nasal vowel ($ą$), merely on the basis of such forms as P $rząd$ (rather than *$rąd$) < CS $rędъ$ (cf. R $rjad$, SCr $rêd$, etc.). In my reasoning, it was the shift $r'ęd(ъ)$ (with only allophonic $r'-$) > $r'ǫd(ъ)$ that, by introducing palatalized r' also in the position before a back vowel, rendered the at first merely phonetically palatalized liquid an independent phoneme (thus creating the phonemic contrast /r'/ : /r/; whereas, according to Bernštejn, an early, Lekhitic change *$ę > $*$ǫ$ (contested by him) would necessarily have led to the loss of phonetic palatalization in the position before a back vowel: *$r'ęd(ъ)$ (= /ręd[ъ]/) > *$rǫd(ъ)$, a development unequivocally contradicted by the Polish evidence ($rząd$). More-

113

over, and arguing the same basic point of autonomous phonetic change (of allophones), I further contended in the
same article that the preliterary East Slavic ("Proto-
Russian") reflexes a ($'a$, ja) and u < CS $ę$ and $ǫ$ (allophonic, in my view, i.e., representing one of the possible
realizations of /EN/, /ON/) could not be cited as proof
against the assumption of the allophonic (rather than phonemic) status of the CS and pre-jer-fall OCS nasal vowels
argued by me elsewhere (cf. Birnbaum 1963, and below,
p. 128), a consideration that may well suggest itself in
view of the relatively late date (late 11th – early 13th
centuries) of the elimination and vocalization of the reduced vowels on East Slavic soil.

Problems embracing the entire range of CS (and, for
that matter, pre-CS) phonology, but in particular pertinent to the field of accentuation and vocalism (including
apophonic vowel gradation), and carrying some far-reaching
implications, were discussed in several papers published
in the late fifties and early sixties, elaborating on and
summing up the insights of laryngeal (and ablaut) theory
as applied to Slavic (and Baltic) material and projectable
to Early PS (and, presumably, Proto-Baltic). Thus, the
1959 article "O nekotoryx refleksax indoevropejskix
'laringal'nyx' v praslavjanskom" by V. M. Illič-Svityč,
whose promising career was prematurely cut short by his
tragic death, examines the presumed intonational reflexes
of PIE laryngeals in certain verbal categories, notably
the present and infinitive of $-o/e-$ and $-ī-$ verbs. Proceeding from the basic, partly contradicting assumptions
of C. S. Stang (esp. 1942), J. Kuryłowicz (esp. 1952), A.
Vaillant (1950/66, 1), A. Martinet, V. V. Ivanov, and
others, and striving to corroborate by additional evidence
the rather commonly made connection between the posited
former presence of laryngeals and acute syllable intonation (or, at any rate, primary long vocalism) in Slavic
(and Baltic), the brilliant young Soviet linguist was able
to define more exactly an important body of relevant data;
this applies, among other things, to verbs of the type
*$bьrati$, $berǫ$, $berèši$, etc. (cf. esp. 9-12). While Illič-
Svityč's examination of traces of former (PIE) laryngeals
and their reflexes in CS pitch patterns remained merely a
fascinating fragment, his corresponding studies of Baltic
and Slavic nominal accentuation and its PIE background
were rounded out in a book-length monograph in which, however, any reference to underlying laryngeals is conspicu-
ously absent (Illič-Svityč 1963; see below, p. 120).

114

Quite skeptical about the possibility of establishing an incontestable and clear-cut connection between
Balto-Slavic intonations and lost PIE laryngeals (as
claimed, e.g., by W. P. Lehmann and A. Martinet) is C.
Watkins in his terse report "Evidence in Balto-Slavic" appearing in the volume *Evidence of Laryngeals* (1965; first
read in 1959, preliminary version of conference proceedings published in 1960). According to Watkins' cautious
formulation (116):

> From the intonations attested in certain Baltic and
> Slavic languages we may determine the original
> existence in certain positions of long vowels in
> Balto-Slavic, whether or not the vocalic length has
> been preserved in the historical languages. But
> there is no direct and unmediated connexion between
> the laryngeals of IE and the intonations of Balto-
> Slavic.

Yet, the American Indo-Europeanist soon goes on to qualify
his statement by asserting (117):

> The unique and characteristic feature of Balto-
> Slavic, however, is that an IE or perhaps early
> Proto-Balto-Slavic sequence $ER\partial$ (including $iR\partial\ uR\partial<$
> IE [RH]) before stop or resonant yielded tautosyl-
> labic diphthongal sequences $\bar{E}R$. The long vowel of
> these sequences was subsequently shortened, but the
> original length is reflected by an acute accent as
> opposed to the circumflex on original short diph-
> thongs. It is the former presence of these long
> vocalic nuclei, $\bar{E}R$ from IE ERH plus C, which is at-
> tested by acute accent. But the intonability of
> these long nuclei is on exactly the same footing as
> that of other simple long vowels of the system, $\bar{\imath}\ \bar{e}$
> $\bar{a}\ \bar{o}\ \bar{u}$. Thus, the result of an IE sequence EHR will
> be likewise $\bar{E}R$, though such cases are rather rare in
> Balto-Slavic. The original position of the laryn-
> geal is irrelevant; only the original (i.e., Balto-
> Slavic) quantity is significant in the appearance of
> the intonation.

But Watkins then, once more, cautions against any too far-
reaching conclusions (117-18):

> In the absence of corroborative data from other lan-
> guages, Balto-Slavic quantity alone cannot be taken
> as indicating a laryngeal unless it can be shown

conclusively that no other origin for that quantity
is possible. This view of the absence of direct
connection between the laryngeal as such and the intonations of Balto-Slavic, maintained by Kuryłowicz,
has been recently upheld by V. V. Ivanov, and seems
the most likely yet offered. We may conclude that
Balto-Slavic, in parallel fashion to the great majority of other Indo-European languages, furnishes
by its intonations and quantities evidence for a
laryngeal only there where the loss of that laryngeal resulted in a long vowel by compensatory
lengthening . . . One must, however, insist on the
fact that the intonations are by no means unambigu-
ous in a great number of cases; they can be used
effectively only as supporting evidence, never as
conclusive evidence. On the one hand there are
cases, due to accent shift or otherwise, which result in so-called 'unhistorical' acute or circumflex accent; on the other hand the laryngeals are by
no means the only source for long vowels with acute
even in Proto-Balto-Slavic, which is one of those
languages which has most widely innovated in the development of the intra-dialectal lengthened grade
(Dehnstufe) formations.

3.2.2. Accentology. As the only potential and, to be
sure, indirect reflex of a lost PIE laryngeal in CS can be
found in original (nonmetatonic) acute intonation, inquiries into laryngeal theory based on Slavic data fall
primarily within the field of accentology. The assumption
of underlying laryngeals (or a single unspecified laryngeal) thus plays a major role in a great many of the more
recent contributions to the study of CS accentuation — one
of the continuously most intriguing and at the same time
most controversial areas of Comparative Slavic Linguistics
projected into the preliterary, CS (PS, and Balto-Slavic)
period. The number of contributions, both synthesizing
and exploring one detail or another, is accordingly also
particularly great and only a few selected relevant titles
can therefore be discussed or even mentioned in the following.

Among modern, synthesizing treatments of CS accentuation (including its Balto-Slavic antecedents and, partly,
its historically attested reflexes) there are two in particular that deserve more than merely cursory mention:
the long third chapter (pp. 162-356) on Balto-Slavic and

116

the pertinent conclusions (pp. 362-8) in J. Kuryłowicz's monumental study *L'accentuation des langues indo-europé-ennes* (1952, [2]1958), reassessing and integrating previous relevant research, including the author's own (cf. especially Kuryłowicz 1931 and 1938), and, on the other hand, C. S. Stang's summing up of his accentological investigations in the book *Slavonic Accentuation* (1957b). These two syntheses thus superseded the now largely obsolete, if for its time impressive, monograph of 1923 by N. van Wijk, *Die baltischen und slavischen Akzent- und Intonationssysteme: Ein Beitrag zur Erforschung der baltisch-slavischen Verwandtschaftsverhältnisse*, based, to some extent, on the Dutch linguist's own inquiry (cf., e.g., van Wijk 1916b) and yet to be followed over a decade later by some further contributions on Slavic prosody — the breakdown and restoration of vocalic quantity, North Kashubian polytony, and metatony — now largely viewed from the Prague-phonologist standpoint (cf. van Wijk 1937b, 1941b, and 1941/42). Compared to Kuryłowicz's and Stang's fundamental and thorough reinterpretations of the entire range of problems connected with CS (and Balto-Slavic) accentology, even an important, and for classroom use exemplary, monographic treatment like L. Sadnik's *Slavische Akzentuation*, 1: *Vorhistorische Zeit* (1959) can be considered largely derivative. Yet it is not without considerable scholarly merit and partly even utilizes findings derived from the author's own, independent research (cf. especially Sadnik 1957). It also provides one of the points of departure for further inquiries into the historically attested reflexes of Balto-Slavic prosody (for Slovak, e.g., see Nonnenmacher-Pribić 1961). Since Kuryłowicz himself has subsequently summarized, with only very minor modifications (cf. his relevant theoretical considerations in Kuryłowicz 1962a), his conception of IE accentology and the particular place of Balto-Slavic prosodic phenomena within that larger framework in volume two (1968a), authored by him, of the new comparative IE grammar now appearing under his general editorship (briefly accounted for above, cf. pp. 58-61), there is no need to repeat here the basic tenets of his overall view. Suffice it to reiterate that, while interpreting with great ingenuity and acuity the many intricate mechanisms of prehistoric Slavic accentuation, the Polish comparatist does not see fit to directly relate the prosodic phenomena of preliterary Balto-Slavic to the hypothetic accentological system of PIE as inferable from the evidence of Old Indic (i.e., primarily Vedic) and

Greek, though in the latter instance to a considerably lesser extent and essentially only secondarily. Considering Kuryłowicz's dismissal of any direct link or close connection between the prosodic patterns of PIE and Balto-Slavic accentuation, it will come as no surprise that, when discussing in three appendices stress and/or pitch of Iranian, Latin and Romance, and Scandinavian (the latter exhibiting distinctive intonation contrasts), his conclusions are primarily of a typological nature but do not imply any genetic relationship whatsoever with earlier prosodic phenomena, ultimately traceable to PIE. In this, then, Kuryłowicz differs from the attitude taken, for example, by Ekblom (1930) who, when comparing and contrasting the rise and evolution of Balto-Slavic and Nordic accentuation, in addition to purely typological and descriptive considerations, made at least some broad hints as to a potential genetic relationship pointing to a common origin.

Contrary to Kuryłowicz, Stang views the specifics and characteristics of reconstructed Slavic (and Baltic) accentuation as an immediate continuation of PIE prosody and thus as interpretable only in this context and against the setting of the prosodic evidence of other IE languages testifying to stress and pitch inherited from prehistoric times, notably the ancient varieties of Indic (Vedic) and classical (and preclassical) Greek. In this, therefore, he may be considered a traditionalist — following a well-established trend in Slavic (and Balto-Slavic) accentology (cf., e.g., Meyer 1920). Yet nothing would be more inaccurate than labeling Stang's own relevant results traditional. While in essential points irreconcilable with Kuryłowicz's position, Stang's own findings, too, are in many ways highly novel. It should be noted, however, that in some respects, for example, in the assessment of de Saussure's law and its previously usually alleged applicability also to Slavic, the Norwegian Slavist is quite close to Kuryłowicz's notions. Wherever there is disagreement in their points of view, Stang's solidly founded interpretations are usually — at least in the opinion of the present writer — more convincing than some of the Polish linguist's far-reaching and bold assumptions. Stang's conclusions were summarized as follows (p. 179; here in slightly rephrased wording):

(1) De Saussure's law did not operate in Slavic.

(2) Neoacute intonation is not due to metatony but

to a retraction of the stress from a reduced vowel (*jer*) or from a non-initial vowel with falling intonation.

(3) Neocircumflex intonation is not a CS phenomenon.

(4) CS had three (distinctive) intonations: a) acute, which can occur on any syllable and does not shift its stress throughout the paradigm; b) neoacute, which can occur on any syllable, provided other forms of the paradigm or the etymological group concerned have the stress on the following syllable and provided, further, no skipping of syllables ever takes place in the process concerned; c) circumflex, which occurs on the first syllable when other forms of the paradigm have the stress on the last syllable.

(5) All paradigms, nominal and verbal, could be: a) immobile, with either the stress on the first syllable or the stress on a medial syllable (the stress was retracted from a circumflex vowel in a medial syllable and, in verbs, analogically from -*e*-/-*o*-; the newly stressed syllable would have neoacute intonation); b) mobile, with stress in some forms on the first syllable, in others on the last, skipping the medial syllables (in the verb few traces of mobility are preserved; in most forms stress has analogically been transferred to the last syllable).

(6) The mobile nominal paradigms of Slavic are closely related to those of Baltic. The immobile type with the stress on the last stem syllable, which in some cases coalesced with the ending, has disappeared in Lithuanian.

(7) In Slavic, acute intonation was characteristic of the paradigms with constant root stress, neoacute of those with recessive stress in certain forms, and circumflex of those with mobile stress.

Research in comparative Slavic accentology aiming, in particular, at reconstructing the prosodic system of CS, its modifications and dynamics, has, as was already mentioned, a long and impressive history in Slavic

Linguistics. Many of the numerous contributions in this field, starting at the very beginning of the century, have either retained some of their intrinsic value or, where they have been entirely superseded by more recent research, at least permit us, in a most instructive way, to retrace the course of progress, hampered by more than one pitfall, made over the last seventy years or so. For an assessment of the state-of-the-art by the end of the fifties and the early sixties, see Horálek 1960/61 (unfairly underrating, in particular, the truly innovative achievements of C. S. Stang) and Lunt 1963 (rather unsystematic while including some extraneous comparative material); for a critical appraisal of Stang's monograph by Kuryłowicz, identifying differences of methodological approach, see Kuryłowicz 1958. Thus, for example, A. Meillet in his brief remarks on some irregularities of Slavic nominal stress patterns (1902) had already tackled some of the problems eventually and systematically (though perhaps still not definitively) dealt with only by V. M. Illič-Svityč in his 1963 monograph on nominal accentuation in Baltic and Slavic where the findings and conclusions of modern relevant research (including that of Kuryłowicz and Stang) have been fully utilized. It should be noted, incidentally, that among Illič-Svityč's tentative conclusions (pp. 162-4) is the assertion that the mobility of stress, as attested in Balto-Slavic, may represent not an early innovation of dialectal Late PIE (as occasionally claimed) but rather an archaic feature obliterated in Old Indic and Greek (with their pronounced tendency for columnar paradigmatic stress). On the other hand, the manifestation of a barytone (non-final) stress pattern in nouns with nonapophonic vocalic length in the root, implying stress retraction, according to the Soviet linguist, seems to be due to an early IE dialectal innovation, however not limited to Balto-Slavic alone but embracing also Italo-Celtic (as shown by Dybo 1961) while at the same time constituting the oldest ascertainable shared Balto-Slavic prosodic process.

Largely obsolete today, though representing significant advances at the time of their first publication, are the extensive accentological writings of A. Belić (1913, 1914, 1920, 1925) and T. Lehr-Spławiński (1917, 1918a, 1918c, 1921/22, 1928b, 1935, and, slightly revising the last title, 1957a); in particular, Belić's *Akcenatske studije* (1914) and Lehr-Spławiński's *O prasłowiańskiej metatonji* (1918a) were at their appearance rightly saluted

as major contributions to the field of Slavic accentology.
Also essentially superseded now is the relevant work by
D. V. Bubrix (1922, 1926), important as his assessment
especially of A. A. Šaxmatov's accentological studies must
have been for its time. Similarly, M. Dolobko's once
acute observations (1926/27) on certain stress shifts (of
the type R *noč'* : *nočés'*, *ósen'* : *osenés'* as compared to
zimá : *zimús'*, *léto* : *létos'*) and their diachronic interpretation have long since been incorporated in the standard
body of data and theory of Slavic accentuation. Even
N. S. Trubeckoj's studies on CS intonations (1921; cf.
also 1922/23, on the type *mogǫ́*, *móžešь*), antedating his
own structural-phonologist orientation, no longer fully
stand up to critical evaluation, and his later thinking in
these matters (as taught in his classes at Vienna University in the thirties) are perhaps best echoed in a contribution by his most prominent student, A. V. Isačenko
(1939), discussing Slavic stress shift phenomena in
Prague-phonologist terms primarily from a synchronic point
of view but adding some insightful remarks also regarding
their underlying prehistoric motivation. A. Vaillant's
brief discussion of the problem of Balto-Slavic intonations (1936), while stirring up some controversy when discussed by subsequent specialists in the field, is now
largely rejected and at any rate superseded by more recent
work including that of the French Slavist himself (Vaillant
1950/66, 1). By contrast, much of the accentological writings of L. A. Bulaxov'skyj, elaborating, in particular, on
the reflexes of the CS prosodic system in East Slavic
(1946, 1958b — the latter on the East Slavic manifestations of former neoacute intonation), West Slavic (1950,
1953/56, cf. also Romportl 1953), and Bulgarian (1955,
1958a), but also — to refer to just a few of his many accentological studies — discussing the controversial accent
law attributed to Šaxmatov (1947) and tackling the problem
of the Balto-Slavic linguistic unity in the light of prosodic data (1959), has retained most of its validity and
significance. Among more recent contributions to particular problems of CS accentology can further be noted the
articles by F. Ramovš (1950, on chronology of Slavic prosodic phenomena; 1951, on metatony), E. Koschmieder (1956,
likewise on metatony, or rather attempting to refute van
Wijk's objection to the interpretation of its "second
phase," originally proposed by Lehr-Spławiński), and L.
Ossowski (1965, rejecting Šaxmatov's law on phonemic
grounds). Another relevant contribution worth mentioning

is H. Lüdtke's attempt (1959) to sketch the further development of the CS prosodic system in Serbo-Croatian. While
not free from some oversights, untenable generalizations,
and outright mistakes, understandable in view of the fact
that the author is not a specialist in Slavic accentology
or Serbo-Croatian diachrony but trained as a Romanist and
phonetician, this is on the whole an interesting and important reinterpretation of the Serbo-Croatian prosodic
data and its underlying CS antecedents, particularly in
its typological aspect. For a critical review of Lüdtke's
work (listing some of its more grave deficiencies), see
Illič-Svityč 1964.

Whereas Trubeckoj never published a strictly phonologist overview of the CS prosodic phenomena and Kuryłowicz's structuralist accentological investigations,
crowned by his wide-ranging synthesis, conceived prosodic
patterns primarily as a morphological means (or morphophonemic, paradigm-shaping device), a purely phonemic approach to the complex problems of (Late) CS prosody was
sketched by R. Jakobson in the first half of the sixties.
In his contribution to the Fifth International Congress of
Slavists (Sofia, 1963), "Opyt fonologičeskogo podxoda k
istoričeskim voprosam slavjanskoj akcentologii: Pozdnij
period slavjanskoj jazykovoj praistorii," Jakobson discusses in strictly binary terms the prosodic features
(long [marked] : short; high-pitched [marked] : low-pitched)
as they combine with two sets of inherent features (diffuse : compact, acute : grave) of the phonemic vowel system
and are integrated into the syllabic structure of Late CS,
describing and analyzing the various functions (culmina-
tive vs. demarcative, distinctive vs. redundant) of the
features of the prosodic pattern in its diachronic modifications. On the basis of chronological and areal considerations, in addition to taking into account the inherent
dynamics of the Late CS accentual system, Jakobson singles
out four dialectal types, each characterized by its peculiar prosodic pattern and its respective reflexes: Czech-
Lusatian, Slovak-Lekhitic, Serbo-Slovenian, and Bulgarian-
Russian (or simply Eastern). The full implications of
this radical reductionist reinterpretation of the complexities of the Late CS prosodic pattern, based on the constant dichotomies (marked : unmarked, distinctive : redundant) of Jakobsonian linguistic theory and further elaborated, now in the broader conceptual framework of information theory, in a subsequent paper, "Information and
redundancy in the Common Slavic prosodic pattern" (1965a,

appropriately contributed to a volume honoring J. Kuryłowicz), are yet to be fully explored. It seems safe to
assume, however, that their potential impact on current
and further research in the field can hardly be overrated
(the first testimonies of which have already begun to appear; cf., e.g., Ossowski 1965; Stankiewicz 1966a).

The important accentological work resumed in the
Soviet Union by V. M. Illič-Svityč is fortunately being
continued, after his tragic death, by his close collaborator and colleague V. A. Dybo. Having first focused his
attention on the prosodic phenomena of the CS verbal paradigms (Dybo 1958 and 1962) and on relevant problems of
Comparative IE Linguistics (cf. especially Dybo 1961), the
two scholars, in a joint paper presented at the Fifth International Congress of Slavists, Sofia (Dybo & Illič-
Svityč 1963), could submit some first generalizations
bearing "on the history of the Slavic system of accentual
paradigms" ("K istorii slavjanskoj sistemy akcentuacionnyx
paradigm"). It should be noted that, while the approach
to the problem here is similar to that of Kuryłowicz (focusing on accentual types as determined by morphological
paradigms), the solutions suggested rather lie in line
with those of Stang (and previously Meillet) and, among
Soviet comparatists, Ivanov.

The two Soviet scholars assume for Slavic a secondary trifurcation into a triple system of accentual paradigms, reducible to an earlier bipartite opposition of
mobile vs. barytone-oxytone (nonfinal-final-stressed),
with the latter representing an original barytone type (as
evidenced by Baltic). While identifying and defining certain redistributions of accentual-paradigmatic types in
various branches of IE (Balto-Slavic as well as, separately, Baltic and Slavic, among others), they conclude that
with the exception of one major deviation (explicable,
however, in terms of a Late Common IE tendency) the Balto-
Slavic system (barytone vs. mobile paradigm), and hence
also the Slavic system derived from it, reflects directly
(i.e., is structurally identical with) the posited prosod-
ic-morphological system of PIE (barytone vs. oxytone-
mobile paradigm). In more recent years Dybo has turned in
his investigations to the evidence of individual Slavic
languages, partly in their earlier attestation, for the
purpose of extrapolating additional data relevant to the
reconstruction of the CS prosodic pattern and its morphological utilization. The first of these contributions
(Dybo 1963) discusses the reflexes in Upper Sorbian of

former quantity and intonation differences. Some additional more recent relevant studies will be briefly discussed in Part Two of this report (cf. pp. 247-8).

3.2.3. Vocalism. The term *vocalism* when applied in the following to CS, pre-CS, and Early Slavic data will be used broadly to include not only the vowel system proper and its various modifications but also the treatment of original diphthongal (tautosyllabic) sound sequences combining a vocalic element with a nonsyllabic high (diffuse) vowel (or, rather, semi-vowel, $i̯$, $u̯$), a liquid (r, l), or a nasal (n, m). Reference will also be made here to some significant discussions of the prehistoric Slavic reflexes of IE ablaut phenomena (as they can be reconstructed on the basis of historically attested data) as well as the particular Slavic variety of morphophonemic vowel gradation, productively utilized in verbal derivation (especially in the formation of imperfective, formerly iterative, verb stems). On the other hand, some work on peculiar developments of CS (and pre-CS) vocalism as conditioned by a specific position within the word (or syllable), notably in auslaut, will be surveyed only in a subsequent section (cf. 3.2.5.).

On the borderline between the fields of prosody and vocalism falls N. van Wijk's succinct contribution to the 1937 *festschrift* for H. Pedersen, discussing the decline (or rather virtual breakdown) and subsequent restoration of the Slavic system of distinctive vowel quantities where the point of departure and a substantial portion of the gradual obliteration of quantity contrasting lie within the CS period. A useful outline of the CS vowel system as a whole had earlier been provided by M. Weingart (1919, [2]1923), devised primarily as an aid for classroom teaching, while the vocalism of a particular morphological category, the comparative, had been the subject of a brief study by A. Vaillant (1929). More recently, K. Žuravlev (1963a) has discussed some problems in the evolution of Late CS vocalism in the light of his theory of group-phonemes (see below, pp. 142-4).

As was already mentioned, H. Güntert's original theory of a presumed reduced vowel in PIE, by him labeled *schwa secundum* (1916), seemed for some time to have important implications also for the study and proper interpretation of CS vocalism as some of his most striking evidence appeared to be corroborated by Slavic data (cf., e.g., Gk τέσσαρες/τέτταρες, R *četýre*, SCr *četiri*, etc. vs.

124

Gk dial. [Aeol.] πίσυρες, Lat *quattuor*, P *cztery*, Cz
čtyři, etc.). The positing of a PIE *schwa secundum* therefore also found its way into some reference works of Comparative Slavic Linguistics and CS of the neogrammarian
vein (Vondrák 1924; Kořínek 1948; cf. above, pp. 36 and
66), and it was only J. Kuryłowicz's new overall theory
of IE ablaut that put an end to all further speculation
about a possible second reduced vowel of undetermined (or
"neutral") coloring in PIE. Still, Kuryłowicz continues
to operate with two at first qualitatively distinct reduced vowels (denoted $_e$, $_o$, perhaps, after a shift $_e > _o$,
merging in $_o$) which, however, already in the protolanguage
tended to either drop out or develop into a full, short
vowel (*e*, *o*; cf. esp. Kuryłowicz 1956: 169, 179-80; see
also above, p. 62). Apophony, its manifestations and morphological utilization in various branches of the IE language family, had of course long been one of the main concerns of Kuryłowicz's discerning inquiry into the structure of reconstructed and recorded IE. In this context,
some aspects of the relevant evidence of Balto-Slavic had
attracted his particular interest. Among the published
evidence of this interest, still preliminary to the Polish
comparatist's grand synthesis of his life-long researches
in the field, is Kuryłowicz's intriguing, though controversial, article "Le degré long en balto-slave" (1950)
outlining his view of the particular nature of the long
ablaut grade in Balto-Slavic and its utilization primarily
in verbal derivation and inflection; for some criticism,
see Mathiassen 1969, 1970a, 1970b. The findings and hypotheses of the 1950 article were subsequently integrated,
along with much other material and theory, in Kuryłowicz's
fundamental *L'apophonie en indo-européen* (1956). This is
not the place to discuss Kuryłowicz's monumental monograph,
particularly as we have already briefly commented on his
more recent discussion of IE ablaut, summing up and tightening the Polish comparatist's earlier monographic presentation, in the framework of the new IE grammar edited and
partly authored by him (cf. above, pp. 61-2). Kuryłowicz's monograph on ablaut, contrary to his book of comparable significance on accentuation, is not arranged entirely by language groups but falls, above all, into three
major parts treating (1) the "ancient processes" (qualitative ablaut *e:o*, quantitative ablaut *e/o* : zero, and the
long grade), (2) the "ultimate transformations of the zero
grade" (in the languages of the South, those of the North,
and in Indo-Iranian), (3) the "secondary long grades" (in

Greek, in the languages of the North, and in Indo-Iranian).
Appended is a chapter on consonantal alternations in IE
(the labio-velar stops, the palatal stops and their assibilation, and the voiceless aspirants). Suffice it to
merely note here that Kuryłowicz's approach to ablaut, as
could be expected, is strictly functional-structuralist,
viewing phonological phenomena and processes (alternations) as expressions of the morpho-semantic dynamics inherent in any language, thus also in PIE and its descend-
ents. Particular attention is paid to relative chronology
and to the intricate synchronic coexistence of sounds and
forms representing different evolutionary phases within a
single functioning linguistic system. Balto-Slavic, including CS, manifestations of primary and secondary ablaut
are discussed in particular in the chapters analyzing the
relevant phenomena in the languages of the IE North. On
the treatment of CS reflexes of IE ablaut in the broader
framework of morphophonemic alternations, both vocalic and
consonantal, sketched by P. S. Kuznecov (1954), see below
(p. 149). A purely synchronic description of the vowel
alternations of the OCS verb in terms of R. Jakobson's
analysis of the Slavic conjugation (originally applied by
him to Russian and subsequently adapted to the corresponding data of OCS by M. Halle) was offered some time ago by
J. A. Van Campen (1963). To be sure, while presented in
rigorous synchronic terms, much, if not most, of Van Camp-
en's material can be interpreted as representing reflexes
of IE and secondary CS ablaut operating in the Slavic verb
system.

The scanty Slavic evidence of the submechanism of
"double ablaut" (or, to use Anttila's recent apt term,
schwebeablaut) occurring in diphthongal roots, nominal as
well as verbal, was examined by J. Schütz (1963). He
dates the relevant phenomena as ultimately going back to
the Balto-Slavic period which in this context is tantamount to saying that we have to do here with the morphological utilization of a phonological means resorted to
already in PIE. Schütz's account has now been superseded
by the more thorough discussion also of the Slavic (and
Baltic) data, viewed in its broader IE setting, found in
Anttila (1969).

As for the CS monophthongization of diphthongs prop-
er (*ĕi*, *ŏi* or rather *ăi*; *ĕu*, *ŏu* or rather *ău*) it is, understandably, in particular those tautosyllabic sequences
combining heterogeneous elements, i.e., *ŏi* (*ăi*) and *ĕu*,
that have been repeatedly scrutinized. In the case of the

change $\breve{o}i$ ($\breve{a}i$) $> \breve{e}_2$, at least the outcome is indisputable
and the attention of linguists, especially in earlier
years, therefore had focused primarily on speculations as
to the presumed intermediary stages in this process of monophthongization (considering such possibilities as $oe >$
$\bar{o}$, $ae > \bar{a}$ or, on the other hand, perhaps rather first
metathesis $> i̯o$, $i̯a > i̯e$, $i̯\bar{a}$, the double reflex in auslaut
position, $-\breve{e}_2$, $-i_2$, to be sure presenting special problems). As for the monophthongization of original $\bar{e}u$, even
the "regular" end result ($> u$ or, as now more generally
held, $> ju$, $'u$) has long been a matter of considerable
controversy. Thus, the regular CS reflex of PIE $\bar{e}u$ was
much discussed already around the turn of the century (cf.,
e.g., Berneker 1899; Mikkola 1904; Il'inskij 1907). In
recent years, a phonologist reinterpretation of the CS monophthongization of $i̯$- and $u̯$-diphthongs was suggested by
F. V. Mareš (1959, subsequently incorporated in Mareš
1965a, 1965b, 1969). As regards the CS monophthongization
processes much attention has been devoted to the problem
of chronology, relative (i.e., vis-à-vis other sound
shifts of CS) as well as absolute, the latter ascertainable in particular on the basis of topo- and hydronymic
material (cf. of recent work especially that by Z. Stieber). The somewhat inconsistent and complex treatment of
original diphthongs (in the broad sense) in the position
before $-j-$ ($< -i̯-$) as found at the morpheme boundary of
verbs of the third and fourth classes (in Leskien's classification), exemplified by OCS $kujǫ$ (: $kovati$) vs. $lovljǫ$
(: $loviti$) $<$ *$kou̯i̯ōm$, *$lou̯i̯ōm$ (in traditional phonetic reconstruction), was discussed with great insight by P. S.
Kuznecov (1958).

The origin (from diphthongs ending in a nasal) and
development of nasal vowels in CS and their retention,
while undergoing certain modifications, in a part of disintegrating, dialectally differentiated Late CS and Early
Slavic have been dealt with in several special publications. Thus, already in the twenties N. S. Trubeckoj
argued that the nasal vowels of CS (and Early Slavic as
represented by OCS) were in fact not monophthongs but had
a diphthongal pronunciation (oral vowel + nasal consonant)
comparable to that found in contemporary standard Polish
in certain positions (cf. Trubeckoj 1925b, 1927/28: 673-
84). This view (reiterated also in Trubeckoj 1954: 68-9,
78-9) was criticized, in particular, by T. Lehr-Spławiński
(1926, 1929a) and, more recently, again by E. Koschmieder
(1958a), the latter arguing against the presentation in

Trubeckoj 1954 and the claimed parallelism with the situation in modern Polish. At the beginning of the thirties the then prevailing views on the rise of nasal vowels in CS were summed up by T. Milewski (1931b). Proceeding from Trubeckoj's conception of the phonemic status of the nasal vowels in CS and Early Slavic, I ventured (Birnbaum 1963) to demonstrate the biphonemic nature of pre-*jer*-fall nasal vowels in Slavic on the basis of distributional-syntagmatic considerations, differing from Trubeckoj's analysis, however, in that I assumed not only a consonantal archiphoneme (/N/) but also one of two vocalic archiphonemes (/E/ and /O/), and hence interpreted CS ę and ǫ phonemically as /EN/ and /ON/ rather than accepting Trubeckoj's /eN/, /oN/, /öN/, and /aN/. Moreover, and contrary to Trubeckoj, I proposed that while the structure of the nasal vowels in this early period of Slavic was biphonemic, their phonetic (allophonic) realization might very well have been that of monophthongal nasal vowels proper. Subsequently I had occasion to elaborate my relevant view on some points (cf. Birnbaum 1965a; 1967b: 333-4). As was mentioned before (see p. 50), this view has now been accepted by Z. Stieber, among others. In the same 1963 Sofia Congress paper I further suggested a tentative reinterpretation of Late CS *jǫ/'ǫ* (graphically rendered by a special ligature in OCS) as indeed consisting of /j/ plus /ON/ or /ǫ/ (in the pre- or post-*jer*-fall period, respectively). Thus I preferred not to adhere to an interpretation of this nasal vowel as — isolated — /ǫ̈/ (lacking an oral counterpart */ö/ in the phonemic inventory of CS and OCS), as originally advanced by F. Fortunatov and subsequently further underpinned by N. Durnovo and R. Jakobson (the latter bringing such an interpretation in line with his concept of syllabic synharmonism). Yet my own seemingly more traditional interpretation of CS and OCS *jǫ* differed from the earlier one insofar as I proposed, with some qualifications, to consider /j/ not an independent consonantal phoneme but merely a suprasegmental feature (prosodeme) of palatality, materializing phonetically as *j* in the position of consonantal zero segments of the sound chain but manifesting itself otherwise (i.e., in the position of segments occupied by single consonants or consonantal clusters) as the concomitant feature of softness. When discussing, at approximately the same time, the origin of this particular nasal vowel, F. V. Mareš interpreted it in the orthodox phonologist tradition as /ǫ̈/ (1963b). Among other special problems pertaining to the

CS (as well as OCS) nasal vowels and their origin, the
treatment of diphthongs ending in a nasal in the position
before another nasal, yielding divergent results in different dialectal zones of CS ($eN + N > \rho N$ or $\check{e}N$) was discussed, for example, by N. Durnovo (1927/28), while the
problem of the puzzling coexistence (or alternation?) of ρ
and u in Slavic lexical doublets has been tackled repeatedly (cf., e.g., Brückner 1931; Lehr-Spławiński 1937c;
Sławski 1947; Machek 1964).

If some aspects of the development of original nasal
diphthongs in CS and Early Slavic have been controversial,
the same is true of several facets of the various modifications of original diphthongs in a liquid in Late CS and
its dialects. In addition to occasionally lengthy discussions of relevant problems in all textbooks, reference
works, and monographic treatments of CS and Comparative
Slavic Linguistics as well as in overall discussions of CS
dialectology, there already exists a sizable body of specialized literature on the subject of the development of
tautosyllabic sequences containing a liquid in prehistoric
Slavic. What follows is therefore merely a highly selective sampling of references to some of the more significant relevant titles.

Thus, already in 1903 V. Vondrák published an article addressing itself to some of the main issues of this
complex problem, and even shortly before that the Swedish
Slavist T. Torbiörnsson had made the CS "liquid metathesis" the topic of an extensive dissertation (in two parts,
1901/03). Criticized for some of his assertions, Torbiörnsson later returned briefly to the treatment of liquid diphthongs in CS (1922), now viewed more broadly together with the parallel phenomenon of the rise of nasal
vowels. A new approach to the development of the liquid
groups in Slavic was soon thereafter explored by another
Swedish Slavist, R. Ekblom, in a longer monograph (again
in two parts, 1927/28), while at about the same time the
Polish linguist T. Milewski (1927) focused his attention
on a specific instance of the overall phenomenon, namely,
the Lekhitic reflex $tart$ for CS $tort$ (in conventional sym-
bolization), mistakenly seeing in it the result of an
actual development (sound change); and, simultaneously,
also F. Ramovš briefly discussed the treatment of CS $tort$
and $tert$ (1927). Ekblom's and Milewski's views were subsequently critically scrutinized by T. Lehr-Spławiński
(1931b). This same Polish Slavist shortly thereafter
(1932b) attempted an original contribution to a particular

aspect of the problem, the fusion of the reflexes of original *telt* and *tolt* (as well as *tьlt* and *tъlt*, in conventional notation) in North, notably East, Slavic while relying on a traditionalist (neogrammarian) approach. And
Milewski, in the following year (1933), offered an overall,
modified and improved interpretation of the liquid groups
in Lekhitic. In 1939 Š. Peciar discussed the "liquid metathesis" as a criterion for classifying the Slavic languages, and in 1952 the same linguist made a general survey of the research in the field. Also in 1952, the
Danish Slavist H. C. Sørensen published a partly old-
fashioned, partly exceedingly bold — indeed fantastic —
article on the treatment of the liquid groups in Slavic,
suggesting, in fact, that the pleophonic forms of East
Slavic (or, at any rate, the general, vowel + liquid +
vowel formula they represented) might be more or less directly equated with some highly hypothetic reconstructed
specimens of alleged pre-IE "Nostratic" (as gropingly en-
visioned by H. Møller). Sørensen's to be sure quite bi-
zarre surmises were sharply and immediately criticized by
R. Jakobson (1952). In this article his polemic remarks
were preceded by a set of succinct statements with regard
to the Slavic evolution of liquid diphthongs, distinguishing clearly between (a) "processes common to the whole
Slavic domain," and (b) "rules of implication for dialectal mutations." In 1957 W. K. Matthews discussed "the
phonetic basis of pleophony in East Slavonic," without,
however, essentially advancing our understanding of the
processes involved. Particularly intricate has been the
question of absolute chronology when it comes to the sound
changes subsumed under the term "liquid metathesis." Needless to say, evidence from adjacent language groups which
borrowed from and in turn loaned to Slavic, and which exhibit Slavic topo- and hydronyms on their own territories,
can be most helpful here. Earlier and recent researches
in this field by E. Schwartz (1927a, concerning Slavic-
German language contacts), V. Kiparsky (1954, regarding
relevant evidence in Baltic Finnic), and Z. Stieber (1965b,
discussing language contacts between Slavs and various
Balkan peoples, largely based on previous findings by M.
Vasmer, especially 1941b, C. E. Bidwell 1961, and others),
to mention just a few, have shed much-needed light on some
of these difficult chronological issues.

    Closely connected with the problem of liquid diph-
thongs and their modification in CS and its dialects is
the question of the Slavic reflexes of the PIE syllabic

liquids in CS (and, more generally, in Balto-Slavic) as
well as the further development of these reflexes (ir/ur
and il/ul, Late CS ьr/ъr and ьl/ъl) back into — new — syllabic liquids at least in part of the Slavic language
area. The latter problem was tackled in a special study
by Š. Peciar (1941), whereas the more conservative evolution of CS *jer* plus liquid in East Slavic was discussed in
a posthumously published article by N. van Wijk (1949/50b).
Naturally, the relevant data and theories have, in addition, received due attention in all textbook and many
monographic treatments of CS and Comparative Slavic Linguistics. The same is true, of course, also of a number
of other special problems regarding the reduced vowels of
CS, including their "tense" varieties (before *j*), already
discussed in 1910 by A. A. Šaxmatov. While the relational
place and the function of the *jers* in the CS sound system
seem to be at least fairly well understood (some details,
to be sure, calling for further clarification), little is
known even today about their approximate pronunciation.
To tentatively ascertain it, the testimony of the reflexes
(correspondences) of the CS *jer*-vowels in other, adjacent
languages is of particular value. Here, therefore, a contribution specially devoted to this particular problem
such as that by G. Décsy (1958), discussing the Finnish
and Hungarian equivalents of the CS *jers*, is of considerable importance. Another kindred problem that in recent
years has again attracted much attention concerns the details (chronology, conditions, spatial discrepancies,
etc.) of the so-called *jer* shift, by which term we designate (following Isačenko 1970a) the interrelated processes
of the "fall" (dropping) and the — full — vocalization of
the Late CS *jers*, marking, in the opinion of a sizable
number of Slavists concerned, the very end of the (Late)
CS period (cf. below, pp. 223, 234). For an insightful
discussion of the somewhat blurred relevant developments
on East Slavic territory, see Koschmieder 1958c (now, however, partly superseded by Isačenko 1970a; see below, pp.
255-6). For an overall coherent interpretation of the fall
of the *jers*, methods employing techniques of information
theory and mathematics (especially statistics) were tested
by R. Abernathy (1963) and V. V. Kolesov (1964).

    Of individual vowels, it is particularly two, *ě*
(*jat'*) and *y*, that have been much discussed in terms of
their presumed actual pronunciation (phonetic value) in
(Late) CS and Early Slavic. For both, a diphthongal articulation has been at least considered. As for *ě*, the

reason for the interest in its actual pronunciation can be explained in view both of the heterogeneous origin of this sound in Slavic, its ambiguous denotation in the oldest Slavic writing system (Glagolitic having only one symbol for etymological $\check{e}$ and $ja/'a$), and, in particular, its divergent development in various historically attested Slavic languages and dialects, ranging from i to a and, in its less extreme reflexes $\hat{e}$ - e - $\ddot{a}$, competing and partly merging with (originally short) e. As for y, on the other hand, it is presumably its particular graphic rendition in the Slavic alphabets (by means of a ligature or digraph combining an — originally always "back" — jer with i) that has frequently, though, it seems, without sufficient justification, been taken as an indication (if not as proof) of its presumed earlier diphthongal pronunciation. The origin of CS y (< PIE $\bar{u}$, controversial only in its chronology), its relation to related sounds in the CS vowel system (ь, i, u), and its partial merger with i (phonemically and largely also phonetically) would hardly, by themselves, have warranted a particular interest in its phonetic value.

The assumed actual pronunciation of CS jat' was discussed, for example, by N. van Wijk (1923/24), two decades later by F. Ramovš (1944; cf. also Hamm 1957), and, again two decades later, by Z. Stieber (1964) who suggested that the term jat' in fact is a misnomer for the qualitatively "indifferent" (or "neutral") long counterpart of short e. It should be added, perhaps, that Stieber's conclusion about the pronunciation of CS $\check{e}$ generally (though not in all details) coincides with that arrived at, on the basis of different reasoning, by van Wijk forty years earlier. Less convincing, in my view, though more cautious and therefore also rather noncommittal, are the "tentative conclusions" summing up the pertinent discussion of the phonetic value of Late CS jat' in M. Samilov's book on *The Phoneme Jat'* in Slavic (1964; cf. 80-129, especially 128-9). According to Samilov, "the reconstructions of the late Common Slavic jat' as a broad monophthong or diphthong seem better founded than other reconstructions. The scholars favoring the latter have not devoted much effort to the elaboration of their respective assumptions. As the problem stands now, the $*\ddot{a}$ and the $*ea$ theories have a relatively more substantial foundation." While considering it "less easy to choose between $*\ddot{a}$ and $*ea$," Samilov mentions one circumstance allegedly speaking "in favor of $*ea$: the distribution of the 3rd Palatalization of Velars

132

which has occurred after *i, *$ь$, *$ę$, but not after *$ě$, *e." This argument turns out to be hollow, however, if we consider that the Third Palatalization only occurred after (originally) i-colored vowels; also $ę$ causing progressive palatalization reflects an earlier *$į$ (especially in the suffix -$ęz$- < Gmc -ing-). The fact that the Third Palatalization therefore did not operate in the position after (originally) e-colored vowels (e, $ě$, $ę$ < eN) does not yet speak in favor of any diphthongal interpretation of Late CS $ě$ as $eä$. Rather, the assumption that Late CS (but perhaps not Early Macedo-Bulgarian) $ě$ was in fact a monophthong ($ē$ or, possibly, $\ddot{a}$) therefore seems more acceptable at least to the present writer. Much of Samilov's relevant reasoning echoes the views of his teacher, G. Y. Shevelov, who, as we have seen (p. 96), posited $_e\bar{a}$ (or $\widehat{_e a}$, with an on-glide $_e$) for CS $ě$. Shevelov has further elaborated this opinion in an article (1965a) treating two particular instances, however, without adducing any incontestable evidence.

As was mentioned above, the chronology of the sound shift $\bar{u} > y$ is still disputed in some respects. Among earlier contributions toward the solution of this particular problem, an article by E. Schwartz (1929), the outstanding expert on German-Slavic language contacts as evidenced in onomastic data and loanword material, deserves to be singled out. At about the same time, T. Milewski (1929) opened a discussion concerning the pronunciation of CS y which more recently has been continued, in particular, by his fellow countryman Z. Stieber (1963; cf. further Stieber 1966; 1969/71, 1:23). As was noted before (p. 50), Stieber posits an intermediary stage, symbolized by ω, in the development from original (PIE) $\bar{u}$ ($\bar{u}_1$) to Early Slavic y.

Finally, among the monophthongs of the CS vowel system, the short back vowel, traditionally denoted o but for most of the PS and CS period probably more correctly to be rendered $\ddot{a}$, has attracted the renewed interest of many Slavists. The problem of the chronology of CS $\ddot{a} > o$, now generally considered a vowel shift efficacious only toward the end of the Late CS period, had previously been studied, for example, by E. Schwartz (1927b), while N. van Wijk some years later discussed the parallelism (and divergence) between Germanic, Slavic, and Baltic with regard to the overall treatment of short and long back vowels (1934). However, it was the unsettled issue of the potential antiquity or relatively recent date of so-called

133

akan'e in part of Russian (as well as in Belorussian) that
again brought the question of the original timbre of the
CS short back vowel to the fore. A gradually increasing
labialization $\breve{a} > \breve{o}$ seems to have been phonemically redundant, at least initially. Thus, while R. I. Avanesov
(1947) had advanced some powerful arguments for the relatively recent date of *akan'e*, V. I. Georgiev (especially
1963; Georgiev *et al.* 1968), taking as his point of departure some, in my view, exceedingly far-reaching statements regarding the pronunciation of the CS short back
vowel in Vaillant 1950/66, 1, soon being further backed up by
G. Y. Shevelov (1964; cf. above, pp. 42, 99), launched a
theory about East Slavic *akan'e* as being a retention (i.e.,
a surviving "archaism") from CS times, supposedly further
corroborated by some *akan'e*-like phenomena in Bulgarian
dialectal vocalism (of the Rhodope region). Although
Avanesov's reasoning for a relatively recent date of Russian and Belorussian *akan'e* was subsequently further supported by additional arguments advanced by, among others,
P. S. Kuznecov (1964) and J. Rigler (1964), following
somewhat different lines of argumentation (cf. further
also V. I. Lytkin 1965), Georgiev has until quite recently
continued to insist on his interpretation of *akan'e* as
reflecting a CS state of affairs; for a more detailed discussion of the various arguments and counterarguments, see
below, pp. 253-4. Proceeding, like Georgiev, from some
unfortunate formulations in Vaillant and quoting also
some pertinent statements by G. Y. Shevelov, R. Aitzetmüller (1965) not only identifies traditional CS *o* with *a*
(= $\breve{a}$) but also, without sufficient justification in my
opinion, reinterpreted CS *e* with (what seems to be not
only phonemic but apparently also phonetic) *'a*. This line
of reasoning, fairly close also to Shevelov's relevant
views (cf. his *e* = $_\bullet\breve{a}$), was subsequently continued by
Aitzetmüller (1967) and E. Weiher (1967); its validity
will be briefly discussed below (p. 330).

Of only limited relevance for a purview of research
on CS vocalism are some studies on vowel contraction —
largely a post-CS or, rather perhaps, dialectally focused
Late CS or Early Slavic phenomenon. Of earlier work in
this field, notably N. S. Trubeckoj's discussion of the
chronology of vowel contraction in West Slavic (1928/29)
deserves mention, while, more recently, R. Krajčovič
(1962) has attempted to reveal the underlying causes for
the various West Slavic modifications falling under this
label. On the most recent and current work pertaining to

Early Slavic vowel contraction, especially by J. Marvan, see below, pp. 256-8 and 334.

3.2.4. Consonantism. As regards the consonant system (in the narrow sense) and its modification in the CS period, it is particularly various palatalization phenomena that have received the lion's share of attention. Above all, this applies to the three Palatalizations of Velars and the controversial relative chronology of the Second and Third Palatalizations. Thus, the number of specialized studies treating the much-debated Third (i.e., progressive, also so-called Baudouin's) Palatalization alone by now approaches two hundred. But the two other — regressive — Palatalizations of Velars, triggered by a following front vowel (or j) as well as instances of palatalization of whole consonantal clusters containing a velar have also been scrutinized in a great number of articles and monographs devoted exclusively to these and related processes. It goes without saying that only a few selected titles from this highly specialized literature, echoed in the textbooks and reference works listed or briefly discussed in previous sections of this report, can even be mentioned here.

A contribution from the (Prague) phonologist point of view to the general problem of palatal consonants in Slavic, reflecting a CS or, rather, dialectal Late CS state of affairs and resulting from the palatalizations affecting velar plus front vowel and consonant plus j, was made by B. Havránek (1939b) who critically evaluated some assumptions propounded some years earlier by N. S. Trubeckoj (1930). In his article Trubeckoj had given an original and rather complex chronological explanation of the particular West Slavic outcome of the Second and Third Palatalizations (especially $\check{s}$ vs. $\acute{s}/s'$ in East and South Slavic; further West Slavic retention of kv-, gv- in the position before front vowel as opposed to substitutive softening of the velar of these clusters in the Slavic East and South).

Also in the thirties, R. Ekblom offered a new overall interpretation of the three Palatalizations of Velars, *Die Palatalisierung von* k, g, ch *im Slavischen* (1935), where the emphasis, as in most of the Swedish Slavist's work, was on articulatory (rather than on functional or acoustic) factors involved in the sound shifts discussed. Another aspect to which Ekblom paid much attention was that of relative chronology (see also below). This problem had previously been examined by K. Nitsch (1926), among others, who based his analysis in part on the methodological experience gained in the field of Polish dialectology — the chief object of his scholarly concern. From the unusually rich specialized literature dealing specifically with the progressive Third Palatalization, at least the following references (prior to 1965) ought to be listed: Lehr-Spławiński 1911 (discussing work by A. A. Šaxmatov and J. Zubatý) and 1954 (attempting to establish an absolute chronology); A. Belić 1921 and 1928; V. Vondrák 1923/24 (discussing the later Palatalizations of Velars in their chronological relationship); K. Knutsson 1925; J. Otrębski 1948 (suggesting a morphological interpretation of the inconsistent occurrences of progressive palatalization); R. Ekblom 1951 (elaborating and slightly modifying some of his earlier ideas); I. Grickat-Virk 1951/52; V. Machek 1958b (discussing the pertinent Slavic data along with comparable Baltic evidence). However, of the scholars just listed, Vondrák, Lehr-Spławiński, Knutsson, Ekblom, Machek (in addition to Il'inskij, Trubeckoj, Kořínek, Mareš, and some others) placed the progressive palatalization temporally somewhere between the two regressive Palatalizations of Velars or, in any case, before the regressive Second Palatalization. The special phonetic conditions under which the Third Palatalization occurred or failed to take place have been much discussed both in the studies just referred to and in other contexts, but no consensus about the additional environmental factors affecting its operation has to date been reached. Among the factors considered are: stress on the following vowel or, more generally, lack of stress on the preceding i-colored vowel; following, faded (or, rather perhaps, absorbed) j; the origin of a preceding $\bar{\imath}$ from PIE $\bar{\imath}$ or $\breve{e}i$, the latter presumed not to have caused palatalization; strong original labialization of following vowel ($\bar{\bar{u}} > $ CS $y/\text{ь}$), believed to have prevented palatalization. For the most recent dating of the two later palatalizations only toward the very end of the CS period or, partly, even in the time of Early Slavic dialectal differentiation, see below (p. 265).

The dialectally divergent development of the clusters kv, gv, xv, the former two in word-initial, the latter in word-initial as well as word-medial position, and some related phenomena have been reanalyzed fairly recently in articles by myself (Birnbaum 1956), F. V. Mareš (1958a, discussing also the treatment of tvj or $tu\underset{\sim}{i} > tjv$

136

or $t\underset{\frown}{i}u > \check{s}tv$, etc.), and M. Jurkowski (1963). The development of CS (and pre-CS) sk, zg has been discussed in
different contexts by N. Durnovo (1926), N. S. Trubeckoj
(1927), T. Lehr-Spławiński (1931a), and É. Décaux (1957),
while J. Endzelīns in a separate article (1939) commented
on the Balto-Slavic reflex of PIE sk'. The OCS replace-
ments for CS tj, dj and their phonetic characteristics and
phonemic status have been studied by N. S. Trubeckoj
(1936) and, more recently, by W. Diver (1955), whereas V.
Kiparsky (1954) contributed to elucidating chronological
problems of the development of CS tj, dj on the basis of
extraneous evidence from Baltic Finnic.

For some time the question of whether Polish dialectal *mazurzenie* and some comparable phenomena in other
Slavic languages (notably Russian *cokan'e* and Serbo-
Croatian *cakavism*), i.e., the fusion of the hushing ($\check{c}$,
$\check{\check{z}}/\check{z}$, $\check{s}$) and hissing (c, χ/z, s, partly with a further palatal, $\acute{c}$, $\acute{\check{z}}/\acute{z}$, $\acute{s}$, or palatalized, c', χ'/z', s', variety)
sound series into one — usually hissing — sound series
represents a retention ("archaism") from the period of
Late CS dialectal differentiation has been raised and
usually judiciously discarded. Work by A. M. Seliščev
(1931), W. Węglarz (1937/38b), S. Rospond (1954), and L.
Moszyński (1960) helped to further clarify the issues at
hand.

The CS dialectal beginnings of, and/or prerequisites
for, phonemic palatalization as an overall correlation
splitting up the whole Slavic consonant system have been
studied extensively. In particular, the implications of
phonemic palatalization also for a proper interpretation
of the phonemic vowel system, given concomitant instances
of "dephonologization," and its subsequent role as a criterion for the classification of the historically recorded
Slavic languages have been analyzed. Largely from a phonologist point of view, though with shifting emphasis,
these problems have been dealt with in separate contributions by N. van Wijk (1937/38), H. G. Lunt (1956), E.
Koschmieder (1958b, 1966), and L. É. Kalnyn' (1961), among
others. Lunt, concerned particularly with the repercussions on the system of vocalic phonemes, and Koschmieder
(1958b), arguing especially with some contentions made by
F. V. Mareš (1956), maintained that phonemic palatalization as a general correlation can be considered essentially only a post-CS development, hinging on the fall of the
jers. The discussion in the more recent contributions by
Kalnyn', assuming syllabic synharmonism as a chief deter-

mining factor of Late CS phonology, and Koschmieder (1966),
taking issue primarily with some of the points made by
the Soviet Slavist while acknowledging the merits of her
well-systematized linguistic material, centers on the
question of the palatalized (or "semisoft") consonants occurring before front vowels and their potential allophonic
status already in CS. In his earlier work, Koschmieder
had simply denied the existence of any palatalized (as opposed to palatal) consonant in CS by summarily referring
to the situation prevailing in South Slavic. However,
subsequently he modified his position somewhat on the
basis of evidence from certain South Slavic languages and
dialects adduced by Kalnyn'. Yet he continued — with good
reason, it seems — to maintain a skeptical attitude as to
the claimed proof value of the relevant South Slavic data
concerning the allophonic status of the palatalized
("semisoft") consonants already for the CS rather than
only for a post-CS, namely, Common South Slavic or perhaps
merely Proto-Macedo-Bulgarian period. He also questioned
the presumed equal relevance of this data for the entire
sound system, that is, as applicable to all consonants and
valid for the position before all front vowels.

Of the somewhat controversial developments of consonantal clusters in the Late CS period, partly reflecting
a spatial differentiation, the discussion of the treatment
of CS *tl*, *dl* in several studies devoted especially to the
subject and approaching it from different methodological
positions (Trubeckoj 1925a; R. Ekblom 1928; L. Tesnière
1933; H. Schuster-Šewc 1964a) ought to be referred to at
least briefly. The major points made by F. V. Mareš
(1958b) regarding the development of the cluster *gn* (*kn*) in
CS have since been integrated into his systematic treatment of CS and Early Slavic phonology (1965a, 1965b, 1969).

Instances of possible Slavic reflexes of PIE k^s (>
Gk *kt*, Skt *kš*, CS *s*, by contrast to PIE *ks* > *kš/*kx* > CS
x) were discussed by V. Machek (1965a), adding to the already known, fairly certain Slavic example (*tesati*, cf. Gk
τέκτων, Skt *tákšan-*) three more cases with presumed word-
initial k^s- attested in Slavic (*sědlo*, *sěnъ*, *sesti/sedati
sę*).

As for the development PIE *s* > CS *x* in certain phonetic environments, most of the special studies on this
subject published prior to 1965 limit themselves to discussing this sound shift when occurring in word-initial
(anlaut) position (cf., e.g., V. Machek 1939; T. Lehr-
Spławiński 1952a; S. E. Mann 1958/59; V. M. Illič-Svityč

1961) and will therefore be briefly mentioned along with
some other work examining CS sound changes conditioned by
such positioning (see below, pp. 147-8). Only the earlier short article by G. Laziczius (1933) discusses this
sound shift regardless of position and retains some interest (cf., however, also H. Andersen 1968 and H. Birnbaum 1971a, briefly accounted for below, pp. 261-2).
Also, the conceivable, while by no means certain, sound
shift PIE *pt* > CS *st* seems to have been considered first
by M. Vey (1931); however he posited this change for anlaut position only although it possibly operated also in
word-medial (inlaut) position; cf. OR (RChS) *nestera*, P
nieściora, SCr *nèstera* < **neptera*, OLith *neptě*, Skt *naptī*
(see further, e.g., G. Y. Shevelov 1964: 191-2). On the
appearance of secondary, prothetic consonants, analyzed
by, among others, G. Y. Shevelov (1963), see below, pp.
145-7.

3.2.5. *Special Factors Conditioning CS Sound Change: Syllable Structure, Word-Final and Word-Initial Position.*
In addition to being subject to the — assimilatory, dis-
similatory, etc. — effect of phonetic environment, sound
change is usually determined by the next larger (or "higher") unit of the same "linguistic articulation" (in the
sense of A. Martinet's felicitous coinage) of which the
individual segment (phone) also forms a part, namely, the
syllable. To be more specific, phonetic change is governed by the particular requirements and constraints imposed on the syllable structure of a given language at a
given time. These include some related factors such as
word-final (auslaut) and word-initial (anlaut) position
whose rules in CS are binding for syllable-final and syl-
lable-initial position as well. In fact, in Slavic Linguistics there is a long tradition of recognizing that
sound change, where it does not occur spontaneously, is
due not only to the immediate or, in some rare instances,
also noncontiguous environment of a particular segment
(sound, phoneme) but, in addition, may be explicable in
terms of some special overall factors at work. To be
sure, referring to sound change as "spontaneous" is essentially only tantamount to saying that it occurs for reasons, as yet not well understood, inherent in the always
prevailing imbalance and dialectic dynamics of a given
sound pattern. One such overall factor, the "law of open
syllables," operative in Late CS and clearly reflected in
OCS, was first identified and formulated by members of the

neogrammarian Leipzig School, especially A. Leskien, subsequently discussed by J. J. Mikkola (cf. esp. Mikkola
1921), and only more recently reexamined in modern linguistic terms by A. Martinet (1952 and 1955) and G. Y.
Shevelov (especially 1969), cf. below, pp. 142, 268-9.
Its slightly modified successor at least for some time, N.
van Wijk's "tendency for rising (increasing) sonority (of
the syllable)," accomodating a greater number of disparate
processes falling into the (Late) CS period, while not
necessarily providing a uniform explanation for them, was,
above all, geared to the structure of the syllable as it
was conceived for that period. Palatalization, the other
chief tendency operating in Late CS according to van Wijk
and his followers, was not as unequivocally conditioned by
the structure of the syllable, but was primarily due to
contiguous sounds affecting each other, regressively (*ke*
> *če*, *sj* > *š*, etc.) as well as progressively (*ik* > *ič*,
ćo > *će*, *jo* > *je*, etc.). The more comprehensive "law" or
rule, formulated by R. Jakobson (1929) to replace the
notion of palatalization as a general underlying factor
determining the course of sound change, namely, that of
syllabic synharmonism, understood as a trend toward "uniformization of the syllable" (cf. above, pp. 86-7) on the
other hand, very much hinges on a specific interpretation
of the presumed syllable structure in CS. The same also
applies, of course, to the direct outgrowth of the notion
of syllabic synharmonism, V. K. Žuravlev's theory of
group-phonemes or "syllabemes" (cf. below, pp. 142-4).

Given this situation, it is a bit surprising that a
general treatment of the role and development of the syllable in CS should appear only in 1963: S. B. Bernštejn's
"K istorii sloga v praslavjanskom jazyke," discussing many
(but not all) of the specific theories briefly referred to
above as well as some aspects of general linguistic theory
concerning the syllable, and adducing selected illustrative Slavic data (cf., however, also Hjelmslev 1937).
Bernštejn's own conclusions could be summarized as follows: The "law of open syllables" determined many instances of shifting the syllable boundary which in turn
led to some significant phonetic modifications. Prior to
the operation of this "law," the syllable structure of CS
was characterized by great stability as regards the syllable boundary, giving the syllable considerable autonomy
(within the word) and thus shielding it from the effect of
contiguous sounds of other syllables. However, the shifting of the syllable boundary did not imply any breakdown

of the earlier autonomy of the syllable. Rather, toward the end of the CS period, this autonomy of the syllable was even reinforced by the rise of "syllabemes," i.e., by the assimilation in quality (timbre) of neighboring sounds within one syllable. This has left a profound imprint on the CS syllable structure as a whole. The period of "syllabemes" lasted until the "fall" of the *jers*. The latter obliterated the previously clear-cut opposition of hard and soft consonants, brought about a sharp reduction in the number of syllables within the word, and introduced a mobile syllable boundary. Instances of hiatus (vowel contact), sandhi phenomena, etc., became possible only in a subsequent period in the history of Slavic syllable structure, following the "fall" of the *jers*.

The most significant criticism leveled against R. Jakobson's theory of syllabic synharmonism (incidentally, strangely enough not mentioned in Bernštejn's account) came from N. van Wijk in his posthumously published article "Zum urslavischen sogenannten Synharmonismus der Silben." Concluding his article with a few fitting words by A. Sommerfelt cautioning against too much optimism and confidence when it comes to revealing the causal factors of linguistic change, van Wijk sums up his considerations in the following statement (van Wijk 1941a: 48):

> Zusammenfassend können wir sagen, dass von einem späturslavischen Silbensynharmonismus nur in sehr beschränktem Umfange die Rede sein kann, und dass die phonologischen und nichtphonologischen Lautprozesse, welche man als die Symptome einer Tendenz zum Silbensynharmonismus betrachtet hat, von Haus aus extraphonologische Palatalisierungserscheinungen gewesen sind, welche sowohl innerhalb der Silben wie auch über die Silbengrenze hinaus (*otьk- > otьc-) gewirkt haben und im letzten Grunde auf einer intensivierten gegenseitigen Beeinflussung der aufeinanderfolgenden Laute beruhen. Weshalb im Späturslavischen die Laute angefangen haben, einander stärker als früher zu beeinflussen, das wissen wir nicht.

Granted that van Wijk's critique contains an element of truth, a similar general point (implied, by the way, also in Sommerfelt's statement quoted by van Wijk) could be made against his own attempt to "explain" vastly different phonological developments of (Late) CS by viewing them as manifestations of one single "tendency" for rising

141

sonority within the syllable.

As was mentioned before, the thesis of CS as having been a language favoring — and ultimately tolerating only — open syllables, i.e., syllables ending in a vowel, first clearly stated by A. Leskien, was again taken up in the fifties by A. Martinet and put in a contemporary terminological and methodological framework. The French linguist's article "Langues à syllabes ouvertes: le cas du slave commun" (1952) was subsequently slightly revised for incorporation under the heading "Les syllabes ouvertes du slave commun" in his magistral introduction to diachronic phonology, *Économie des changements phonétiques* (1955: 349-69, with some further relevant remarks in the introductory section of this chapter, 326-32). Martinet quotes numerous examples illustrating the relevant evidence in addition to adducing many partly controversial instances not having immediate bearing on the problem at hand (cf., e.g., his discussion of various phenomena of palatalization or of issues concerning vowel quality), and makes ample reference to the secondary literature. Above all, he offers an insightful general linguistic interpretation of the phenomenon of "open-syllabicity" (G *Offensilbigkeit*) by drawing typologically revealing parallels, especially with Romance, and by viewing this phenomenon against a background of linguistic universals or near-universals. Also Martinet's cautious concluding remark as to the implications of the theory of open syllables in CS, a characteristic not matched by Baltic, for the controversial problem of Balto-Slavic (quoting and arguing with A. Senn) can hardly give cause for any objections. As was already indicated, Martinet's typological line of reasoning concerning this topic has more recently been taken up by G. Y. Shevelov in a paper (written jointly with J. J. Chew, Jr., 1969) juxtaposing the CS evidence with comparable data of Japanese and appropriately published in a volume of studies honoring Martinet.

In a series of specialized studies, the Soviet Slavist V. K. Žuravlev has elaborated a theory, essentially taking as its point of departure R. Jakobson's concept of syllabic synharmonism, according to which, at a certain evolutionary stage of CS, the basic unit at the phonemic level was not so much the individual phoneme but rather a larger (though not "higher," in terms of linguistic level) unit, labeled by him group-phoneme, R *gruppofonema* (cf. also "group synharmonism," R *gruppovoj singarmonizm*). Cf. in particular Žuravlev 1961, 1963b, 1965a, 1965c; for

142

some more recent, post-1965 relevant work, see below, pp. 267-8. Žuravlev's theory operates with a slightly modified system of distinctive features (essentially of the Jakobsonian kind) and claims that, while group synharmonism exhibited a marked tendency for developing into full-fledged syllabic synharmonism, the group-phoneme and the syllable never entirely, i.e., in all instances, coincided. Besides, the main tenets of the theory as applied to the evolution of the CS phonological system can be briefly stated as follows:

Phase 1: Formation of group-phonemes. The process of delabialization in vowels can be interpreted as a shifting of the feature flat (^{O}) from the vowel to the preceding consonant: $C + {}^OV \longrightarrow C^OV$, e.g., $t\bar{u} \longrightarrow t^O\bar{y}$. Connected with this is the fusion of $\tilde{o}$ and $\tilde{a}$. Following the same pattern, the feature sharp of a front vowel is shifted to the preceding consonant ($C + {}'V \longrightarrow C'V$). The analysis of the combinations symbolized C^OV and $C'V$ shows that here the feature sharp is distinctive not for the phonemes entering these combinations (front/nonfront and palatalized/nonpalatalized merely being positional variants) but for the whole group-phonemes ($C'V \longrightarrow {}'\widehat{CV}$) as indivisible units at the phonemic level with the feature flat turning redundant (integral). It is here that the tendency for palatalization develops and becomes operative.

Phase 2: Generalization of the group-phoneme system. After the processes of Phase 1, group-phonemes and individual phonemes, mostly consonants, coexisted at the phonemic level of CS. The processes of Phase 2 can best be subsumed under the notion of generalization of the group-phoneme system and the elimination of the residues of the system of phonemes by either their integration into the group-phonemes or their elimination, i.e., dropping of word-final consonants and rise of word-initial prothetic consonants (dealt with separately by Žuravlev 1965b), simplification of consonantal clusters and iotation, monophthongization of diphthongs. In this context it is easy to demonstrate, provided the correctness of the theory, that, in the process of integrating the sonorants into the group-phonemes, a transphonologization of the feature distinction long/short into an intonational feature distinction (acute/circumflex) has to take place. Consequently, the so-called law of open syllables develops and becomes efficacious.

Phase 3: Decline of the group-phoneme system. In the process of monophthongization of heterogeneous diphthongs (*ai̯*, *eu̯*) a situation obtains where the features sharp and flat again assume distinctive status separately for vowel and consonant phonemes. This marks the beginning of the decline of the group-phonemes and of the formation, or rather re-emergence, of a system of vowel and consonant phonemes. The logical conclusion of this process was the "fall" of the reduced vowels concomitant with the shifting of distinctive (inherent) and prosodic features from the fading weak *jers* to the preceding segments. Connected with this are the phenomena of metatony and stress retraction. At this point the "laws" of palatalization and open syllables cease to operate.

Even this highly condensed account of the basic points of Žuravlev's notion of group-phonemes as applied to the main phases of CS linguistic evolution, displaying some fundamental affinity with the holistic conception of F. V. Mareš, notwithstanding some important differences of detail, will reveal some of the great merits inherent in this consistently conceived theory. Yet it suffers from some general shortcomings, for example, regarding the theoretical status of linguistic units in relation to the presumed levels at which they operate, and specific inadequacies, for instance, regarding some chronological details, which, however, would lead us too far afield to even sketch in broad outline. Moreover, the obsessive, not to say monomaniac, propounding of the theory almost exclusively by its originator has rather been harmful to its general acceptability.

As is well known, sounds occurring in word-final and word-initial position are frequently subject to particular modifications explicable both in terms of their exposed place at the word boundary, some special peculiarities of syllable structure in these positions, and, especially as regards word-final position, morphological (inflectional) factors of frequency, economy, and grammatical-semantic explicitness. It is therefore only natural that most of the discussion of auslaut development in CS and, for that matter, also in historically recorded Slavic would have as

144

much of a morphological emphasis, taking into account
factors of inflection such as the effect of analogy and
paradigmatic leveling, as it would focus on purely phonetic aspects. This is characteristic of earlier work, for
example, by J. Zubatý (1893), suggesting an explanation
for the CS dialectal discrepancy $-y : -a$ in the nominative
singular of the active present participles by assuming underlying PIE or, rather, dialectal IE forms in $-\bar{o}n : -\bar{o}$,
respectively. P. Diels (1914), like Zubatý, discussed the
problem of $-ę : -\breve{e}_3$ with the same geographic distribution
as $-y : -a$, reflecting CS dialectal differences; cf. also
Otrębski 1921. A. Meillet (1914/15 and 1916) and J. Rozwadowski (1914/15) both dealt with the treatment of $-o-$ in
CS word-final syllable, while N. van Wijk (1924) argued
against Zubatý's explanation of the $-onts > -y : -a$ differentiation just referred to, but is unable to offer a more
convincing interpretation, operating with allegedly shifting timbre shades of $-o-$, namely, $-\mathring{a}-$ in the North as opposed to $-\hat{o}-$ in the South, and, parenthetically, adhering
to the views held by Meillet as regards the controversial
endings $-u$ and $-y$ of the dative singular and instrumental
plural, respectively, of the $-o$ stems. T. Milewski also
discussed some minor details of CS nominal and verbal inflection in terms of a combined morphological and phonological approach (1931a) before giving, in 1932, a thorough survey of all the problems and evaluating the by then
proposed solutions relevant to the development of the
word-final position in CS in his article "Rozwój fonetyczny wygłosu prasłowiańskiego." More recently, V. Mažiulis
(1965) has, in a rather speculative manner, discussed some
aspects of Balto-Slavic inflection, taking into account
also phonological considerations. And, G. Y. Shevelov has
ventured an "inquiry into the allophonic structure of CS"
in a discussion "On endings with nasal consonants after
palatal and palatalized consonants" (1965b), offering a
few new, tentative explanations for some much-debated
controversial phenomena. For additional references to
work on CS auslaut, see below, pp. 152-64, in the discussion
of CS declension and conjugation; for some more recent,
post-1965 relevant discussion (esp. Lüdtke 1966), cf. pp.
269-70 in Part Two of this report.

    G. Y. Shevelov is also the author of an important
contribution on "Prothetic consonants in Common Slavic"
(1963), adopting "an historical approach" and discussing
controversial issues regarding the rise of consonantal
prothesis. He rejects the traditional notion that

secondary word-initial *j-* and *v-* developed mainly or even exclusively to avoid hiatus across the word boundary, as would have been the case with words originally beginning in a vowel at a time when all preceding words had come to end in a vowel in CS. Rather, Shevelov is inclined to subscribe to a view combining the hiatus argument with a theory only slightly modifying van Wijk's principle of a rising wave of sonority, applicable, according to the Ukrainian-American Slavist, not only to the entire sylla- ble — as van Wijk would have it — but also to the indi- vidual vowel whose sonority peak is said to have been cen- tered in its last part, a view fully in agreement with his own interpretation of CS $e/\check{e}$ as $_{e}\tilde{a}$, and CS $\check{a}$ (traditional o)/$\bar{a}$ as $_{o}\tilde{a}$. Pointing out that Slavic, contrary to some other eastern IE languages (e.g., Iranian, Armenian, Greek) did not develop prothetic vowels (the only poten- tial exception *istьba*, R *izbá*, etc., being a loan from Rom **estufa* rather than from Gmc *stuba*), Shevelov sketches a tentative chronology for the various stages in the de- velopment of CS prothetic consonants: (1) *v-* before $\check{u}$ and *j-* before $\check{i}$ prior to loss of final consonants, ca. 1st-5th centuries A. D.: (2) *v-* before $_{o}\tilde{a}$ and *j-* before $_{e}\tilde{a}$ after loss of final consonants, ca. 6th century; (3) *v-* eliminated before $_{o}\tilde{a}$ or its reflexes at a time when the $_{o}$ on-glide was disappearing, ca. 8th century; (4) *j-* de- veloped dialectally before $\bar{a}-$ < $_{o}\tilde{a}-$ at the time of the ultimate disintegration of CS. This chronology he matches with causal conditions: prothesis conditioned (1) by vowel structure alone: *v-* before $\check{u}$ and *j-* before $\check{i}$; (2) by vowel structure and hiatus: *j-* before $_{e}\tilde{a}$ and presum- ably *v-* before $_{o}\tilde{a}$; (3) by hiatus only: *j-* before $\bar{a}$. Re- gardless of whether this theory can be accepted without further qualifications — Shevelov's positing of $_{e}$ and $_{o}$ on-glides causing the greatest difficulties for this writer — its ingenuity and explanatory power are beyond doubt. As was mentioned above, V. K. Žuravlev in a spe- cial article has elaborated his view of the rise of CS prothetic consonants in the light of his theory of group- phonemes and group synharmonism (1965b), largely following a different line of reasoning than Shevelov.

Problems of word-initial position where a prothetic *j-* alternates with vocalic anlaut, reflecting, in part at least, a CS alternation, have been treated in a number of specialized publications. Thus, for example, T. Lehr- Spławiński discussed the diverse reflexes of CS *jь-* in the dialects underlying West Slavic (1918b), while A. Meillet added a note on the treatment of word-initial *ju-* in Slavic (1922d). A particular instance of CS *ju-* was the subject of an article by E. Nieminen (1956) discussing Slavic *(j)utro/(j)ustro* and its IE cognates. Particularly lively, during the twenties, was the discussion of the alternation *(j)e-* : *o-*, the latter being the normal reflex in East Slavic (cf. Lang 1922; Il'inskij 1923, 1925; Durnovo 1924/25; Ekblom 1925). It was only R. Jakobson who, once and for all rejecting the interpretation of the alternation *je-* : *o-* as reflecting an instance of PIE qualitative ablaut (still seriously considered by Il'inskij), posed the question of whether the loss of word-initial *j-* (before *e*) was indeed an indispensable precondition for the shift **e-* > *o-* in East Slavic or the CS dialect underlying East Slavic, and arrived at a less than clearly affirmative answer (cf. Jakobson 1929 = 1962/71, 1: 44-52).

Another problem of CS anlaut treatment that has attracted Jakobson's attention is that of word-initial **ūr-*, **ūl-*, yielding, in his view, various reflexes (cf. *ryba* : R *výrej*, OR *izyrьja*) depending on their position before consonant or vowel, tauto- or heterosyllabic position, respectively (cf. Jakobson 1962b). For some sharp criticism of the derivation *ryba < *ūr-b-*, considered also by O. Szemerényi, see Shevelov 1971: 308.

Of other than prothetic consonants in word-initial position, it is particular *x-* that needs explanation since CS *x*, as is well known, is the regular reflex of PIE *s* only in the position after *ĭ*, *ŭ*, *r*, *k*, and their allophones, and, in addition, can in some instances have developed by analogy with forms where this position obtained (e.g., after *a* in the locative plural of the *-ā* stems patterned after *-xъ < *-su* in the same case form of the *-ŏ*, *-ĭ*, and *-ŭ* stems: *-ěxъ < *-oisu*, *-ьxъ < *-isu*, *-ъxъ < *-usu*, or in the 1st person aorist *pisaxъ* or *znaxъ*, by analogy with *xvalixъ* or *prosixъ < *-ī-s-on*). Therefore, word-initial CS *x-* poses a particular problem. In addition to occurring in CS loanwords from Germanic where *h-* (*hv-*, Goth ƕ) was fairly common in anlaut, PIE *ks-*, reflexes of which are rather numerous in Indo-Iranian, is a possible source of CS *x-*, assuming a development with an intermediary state **kx-* or, possibly, *kš-*. These as well as other potential origins of CS *x-* are considered and discussed in a number of studies specially devoted to this subject (cf. especially Brückner 1923; Machek 1939; Lehr-Spławiński 1952a; S. E. Mann 1958/59; V. M. Illič-Svityč 1961). Thus, for example, Lehr-Spławiński considers the

147

possibility of CS x- resulting under sandhi conditions
from s- in the position after $-i$, $-u$, $-r$, and, in particular, $-s$ > $-x$ of a preceding word, while Illič-Svityč suggests PIE sg-, sgh-, with s- here being of the "s mobile"
kind, as an additional possible source of CS x-. On the
other hand, PIE sk-, once considered by Brückner a potential origin of CS x-, but dismissed by Machek, seems to
have yielded CS sk- only, while sk- appears to have been
the regular reflex of PIE sk-, sg-, and sgh- in Baltic and
Germanic.

Of the other specialized discussions concerning the
treatment of word-initial consonantism in CS, the important article by M. Vey (1931) suggesting that CS st- in
some instances may reflect PIE pt-, an assumption possibly
applicable also to word-medial position, has already been
referred to as have also some more recent treatments of
the divergent reflexes of CS kv-, gv-, and (-)xv- (Birnbaum 1956; Jurkowski 1963). It may be added that in a recent note A. Vaillant (1963) rejected Slavic $rota$ as an
instance of "Lidén's law" which states that word-initial
PIE ur-, ul- are simplified in Balto-Slavic > r-, l-.

3.2.6. Morphophonemics. In addition to the more or less
thorough treatments of the morphophonemic alternations
operating in CS which can be found in various text- and
handbooks of CS, Comparative Slavic Linguistics, and outlines of CS phonology, many of the numerous discussions
of ablaut as reflected in CS, of systematic consonantal
alternations, and of modifications due to the particular
position of a given sound sequence (notably vowel plus
semi-vowel or glide, liquid, or nasal; in relation to the
syllabic structure; in tauto- vs. heterosyllabic position)
analyze, in effect, some portion of the mechanism of morphophonemics during the CS period. Moreover, aspects of
morphophonemics are implicitly or explicitly treated also
in the context of morphology, in particular, for example,
in the discussion of the contrast between "hard" and
"soft" stem classes in the declensional paradigms or in
the diachronic analysis of ab- and umlaut phenomena in
Slavic conjugation. This applies, among other things, to
the present stem classes in $-e$-/$-o$-, $-ne$-/$-no$- vs. $-je$-/
$-jo$- > $-je$- or to the problem of the o-coloring of the
thematic vowel in the 1st person singular and 3rd person
plural as opposed to the e-coloring of the 2nd and 3rd
person singular and the 1st and 2nd person plural. Thus
it is not particularly surprising that for a long time

there seems to have been no need for a systematic a thorough treatment of all aspects and manifestations ⊾ morphophonemics, i.e., of the morphological utilization both vowel and consonant alternations as reconstructable for the prehistoric period of Slavic. To be sure, attempts to sketch at least the morphophonemic vowel alternations of Early Slavic (OCS), viewed in their IE setting, had been previously undertaken by A. Meillet (1906/08 and, though not specifically focusing on Slavic, 1927). But it was only in 1954 that P. S. Kuznecov in a study titled "Čeredovanija v obščeslavjanskom 'jazyke-osnove'" gave a truly well-argued analysis of all major aspects of CS morphophonemics, covering vocalism as well as — although perhaps somewhat more sketchily — consonantism and relating, wherever appropriate, the reconstructed Slavic system to its IE origins while adducing standard Old Slavic, mostly OCS and OR, material along with previously unsifted Slavic linguistic data, freshly gathered by the Soviet linguist himself. In the future, no researcher setting out to tackle either the overall problem or some particular facet of the mechanism of morphologically motivated vowel and/or consonant alternation in preliterary Slavic can afford to ignore Kuznecov's excellent study of the subject.

4. MORPHOLOGY

4.0.   General Remarks.   Unlike phonology, the CS morphological system can be reconstructed with some prospect of
success essentially only in the very earliest and the
latest phases of its development, in other words, in the
states of its emergence and ultimate disintegration, while
details of the intervening evolution must largely remain
conjectural at best.   For it is only a relatively insig-
nificant portion of the reshaping of the morphological
structure as still discernible in the early recorded evidence, especially of OCS, that can be assumed to reflect
major modifications of the form system in earlier prehistoric, i.e., pre-Late CS, times.   Thus, for example, the
transition from a complex nominal stem class system (as
reconstructed for PIE) to a primarily gender-determined
system (as largely characteristic for historically attested Slavic) may have been incipient in a remote period
of CS (PS), if not earlier.   Largely prehistoric is further the regrouping in terms of a general hard versus soft
stem class opposition in Slavic declension, as both these
uniformization processes can be noted to be still operative in OCS.   Generally, in morphology the Late CS state
is adequately represented by the evidence of OCS, supplemented, in the fairly few instances of deviation reflecting dialectal differentiation, by corresponding Old Rus-
sian data (cf. $-\ę : -\tilde{e}_3$, $-y : -a$, $-om\hdsymbol : -\hdsymbol m\hdsymbol$, $-t\hdsymbol : -t\hdsymbol$).   By
and large, however, the diversity in early Slavic attesta-
tion as regards morphology is minimal.   Early PS morphological structure, on the other hand, can be recovered —
to be sure, only fragmentarily — by combining techniques
of the comparative method applied to IE linguistic data
and of internal reconstruction.   The latter implies that
the Late CS data is being projected backward in time, thus

filling in the blanks, as it were, in the overall picture
established on the basis of comparative evidence from
other IE languages. In brief it can be stated that in any
attempt at reconstructing the morphology of Slavic linguistic prehistory a polarization, focusing primarily on
the initial and final phases only, is inevitable. For
some methodological considerations along similar lines,
see now also Andersen 1971: 950-1, and Birnbaum 1973.

Slavic morphology can be broadly divided twofold:
(1) into inflection versus derivation, and (2) into
nominal versus verbal categories. Derivation is here understood in the comprehensive sense of including not only
word formation by means of affixation (suffixation, prefixation, infixation), partly combined with ablaut modification of the root, but also by way of composition and reduplication, the former fairly rare, the latter barely
vestigial in CS. Nominal (or, put differently, declinable) categories — here also referred to under the cover
term *noun* — include not only the substantive (subsuming
the cardinal numeral) and the adjective (subsuming the
ordinal numeral as well as the participle, the latter,
however, in regard to inflection only) but also the pronoun, serving as the replacement of the substantive or the
adjective. Verbal categories include foremost the finite
forms of the verb but also the nominal verb forms, participles, infinitive, and supine, as regards their respective derivation. As can be seen from the categorization
suggested, there is a certain overlap when it comes to the
participle, this subclass being considered a nominal category in its inflectional, but a verbal category in its
derivational aspect. Infinitive and supine, being indeclinable, do not pose this problem and can, in morphology,
be dealt with entirely as verbal categories. The two
principles of overall division just indicated combine,
therefore, as follows: (1a) nominal inflection = declension; (1b) verbal inflection = conjugation; (2a) nominal
derivation (noun formation); (2b) verbal derivation (verb
formation). The discussion in this chapter will reflect
this categorization. It should be noted, however, that
some studies and monographs mentioned in the following
will transcend the narrow scope of one of these four subfields and deal most often with the broader aspects of
either all of inflection or derivation, treating the noun
as well as the verb, or the overall problems of the noun
or the verb, i.e., not limiting themselves to either inflection or derivation. Occasionally, some of the work

reported will even cover, or at least touch upon, the entire range of CS morphology. In such instances, the work
will be treated in the section under the heading of which
most of its discussion falls. Where a decision to this
effect is impossible or inappropriate, inflection will
take precedence over derivation and nominal over verbal,
following the order of presentation just suggested. Only
items covered by the categories of inflective word classes
and the research concerning them will be accounted for under Morphology, while noninflective word classes such as
adverbs, prepositions, and conjunctions will be considered, where appropriate, under Syntax (in the case of
prepositions and conjunctions, as regards their syntactic
function and, along with other word classes, with respect
to word order) and/or under Lexicology (as concerns their
etymology and derivation — partly identifiable as petrified morphological forms, e.g., case forms yielding adverbs, or fixed underlying phrases).

Here, as in Phonology, the approximate cut-off date
for relevant research discussed in Part One will be 1965,
while more recent and current work (up to mid-1972) pertaining to CS morphology will be briefly discussed in a
separate chapter on Morphology in Part Two (cf. pp. 272-
91).

4.1. Research on Common Slavic Inflection. The most
broadly conceived work dealing specifically with CS morphology is, not surprisingly, P. S. Kuznecov's 1961 monograph *Očerki po morfologii praslavjanskogo jazyka.* While
not aimed at providing a systematic coverage of all aspects of the CS form system, as indicated by its title,
the range of problems dealt with in this book is quite
wide indeed, the emphasis clearly being on inflection.
Fully up-to-date with recent achievements in Comparative
IE Linguistics, for example, as regards laryngeal theory,
Kuznecov, after a short introductory chapter, discusses at
some length problems of declension as well as of the verb
in CS. Specifically, in the part treating nominal inflection, the Soviet Slavist focuses on such problems as "the
structural means for differentiating case forms in PIE and
CS," "the cases and their forms in CS," "the basic types
of changes leading up to the formation of the CS declensional system," "the distribution of nouns according to
declensional types and the relationship of these types to
grammatical gender," "the correspondences between the
forms of one case and the total range of syntactic

meanings expressed by them as applied to grammatical num-
bers," "phonetic changes resulting in changes in the declensional system," and "the forms of the plural in CS."
In the second part, Kuznecov discusses controversial
issues concerning the personal endings, the aorist and imperfect, the problem of the — residual — form of a simple
future tense (type *byšęšt-*), and aspect, examining as regards the latter not only matters of terminology, conceptual framework, and meaning but also problems of verbal
derivation.

As with most of Kuznecov's work, this book, too, is
full of original observations and well-taken points, particularly when it comes to analyzing the relationship between grammatical form and meaning, sometimes reasoning
along lines similar to those followed by R. Jakobson. It
thus testifies to its author's vast erudition and keen
perception. Though modern and unprejudiced, Kuznecov does
not attempt to break with all established tradition or to
test an altogether novel method. Thus, while this book
may not entirely revolutionize our previous notion of CS
morphological structure and its prerequisites, it certainly contributes, in a number of instances, important eluci-
dations and new insights.

The treatment of *The Inflectional Categories of
Indo-European* (1964) by J. Kuryłowicz, more bold and novel
than Kuznecov's book, at times borders on the speculative
but also displays flashes of genius in approach and interpretation. Here, along with ample instances of adducing
comparative data from other IE language groups, frequent
reference is also made to Slavic linguistic material. For
example, when discussing "Perfect and voice" in chapter
two, Kuryłowicz first analyzes "the functional successors
of the IE passive" in Balto-Slavic and other language
groups, and then devotes several paragraphs (§§ 24-9) to
"the Balto-Slavic type *miněti/mьněti*." He offers some new
suggestions for rejecting the explanation of this type as
'semi-thematic' and submits instead "that the paradigm of
Slav. *mьn-i-tь*, Lith *mìn-i* is nothing else than a continuation of the IE 'mediopassive' perfect . . . Slav.
mьni(tь) < IE $*m_o nei$" (p. 81; cf. Watkins' echoing of this
explanation, referred to above, p. 63). In chapter three
on "Aspect and tense" much of the illustrative material is
of course Slavic; cf. further in particular the exemplification of "the renewal of the present system" by Slavic
(and Gothic) data (98-105). In chapter five, discussing
"Person and number," the Polish linguist comments briefly

on the controversial origin of the ending -тъ in the 2nd
and 3rd person singular of some Slavic aorists (type
u-mrě-tъ; among previous explanations, cf. especially van
Wijk 1926 and 1937a). And, again, when discussing "Gender" in chapter nine, Kuryłowicz naturally devotes a few
paragraphs (§§ 13-14) to the problem of "The animate and
the personal gender in Slavic." Finally, Slavic, along
with Germanic and Greek, provide the evidence in chapter
ten on "Comparison" to substantiate the presumed adverbial
origin of the vowels in the comparative suffix (§6). As
was indicated, the preceding is merely a sampling of the
many instances where the Polish Indo-Europeanist, as in
much of his writing, is ready to back up his claims and
theories with Slavic data. Whether one agrees with his
reasoning or occasionally remains unconvinced, Kuryłowicz's
book no doubt has much to offer the interested student of
IE and Slavic Linguistics.

     Whereas in Kuryłowicz's penetrating study of IE in-
flection the Slavic material is only embedded among
comparative evidence from many other IE languages, Slavic
provides one of the two terms of comparison in V. V.
Ivanov's pioneering article "O značenii xettskogo jazyka
dlja sravnitel'no-istoričeskogo issledovanija slavjanskix
jazykov" (1957), abundantly demonstrating the fruitfulness
of a comparison between Slavic and Hittite data, in particular also as regards inflectional and derivational
morphology. Ivanov's findings and surmises have since
been incorporated to a large extent in the latest standard
works on Comparative IE and Slavic Linguistics.

4.1.1. Declension. F. Specht's *Der Ursprung der Indogermanischen Deklination* (1944), discussing, particularly in
its second part, the presumed early development of the IE
declensional system, is largely obsolete today and proven
erroneous in its overall concept. The author suggests,
among other things, an origin of the major nominal stem
suffixes from demonstrative pronouns, a view that has
since been refuted. This book, written by an Indo-Europeanist with a particular interest in Balto-Slavic, on the
other hand contains a wealth of valuable factual material
and many keen observations of detail, based on a great
number of generally still valid etymologies and some revealing collocations of individual lexical items. P. S.
Kuznecov's sketchy essay "Razvitie indoevropejskogo
sklonenija v obščeslavjanskom jazyke" (1961), originally
presented at the Fourth International Congress of Slavists

(Moscow, 1958), is superior to Specht's presentation in overall approach as well as in the control of the secondary literature and interpretation of his selected data, and focuses on the further development of the IE declension specifically in CS. Discussing many of the controversial issues raised in connection with case endings of Slavic and their prehistory, Kuznecov frequently takes a stand for one of the proposed solutions, occasionally adding a powerful argument of his own in favor of a particular explanation or pointing to earlier, now often half-forgotten interpretations deserving continued consideration. Also, Kuznecov's reasoning concerning the theoretical foundations of the case system in CS, acutely analyzing the intricate interplay of semantic and formal factors in a way similar to, if not always coinciding with, the views of R. Jakobson, is most impressive.

Of earlier work treating the prehistoric evolution of Slavic declension, O. Hujer's relevant writings, the monograph *Slovanská deklinace jmenná* (1910), the essay "K slovanské deklinaci zájmenné" (1911), and the textbook *Praslovanské tvarosloví* 1: *Praslovanské skloňování* (1920/21), deserve mention. In particular the first one, though today obviously outdated in many respects, retains a good deal of its significance both by virtue of some of its original explanations and interpretations and as an accurate state-of-the-art report representative of its time. Being one of the best documented and most detailed accounts, Hujer's monograph long served as one of the basic reference works in the field.

Several studies by F. V. Mareš, echoing some of the views of O. Hujer (and of J. Zubatý) but also affording important new insights into the functioning of the mechanisms underlying the development of Slavic declension in the prehistoric period, theorize, in particular, about the moving forces and determining factors of the various modifications and overall restructuring of the nominal and pronominal inflection in CS and Early Slavic (cf. Mareš 1962a, 1963a, 1963d, 1964; more recently continued in Mareš 1967b and 1968 where the emphasis is primarily on the historically attested languages, however). Applying his structuralist approach to both the phonological and morphological aspects of Slavic inflection (including an original analysis of the categories involved), Mareš is able to shed considerable new light on the data at hand and to suggest some explanations partly unexplored heretofore, especially as regards changes affecting the whole

system or at least a well-defined major subsystem of prehistoric Slavic declension. Thus, in one of his studies
(1964: 163) the Czech-Austrian linguist states the basic
assumptions from which he proceeds as follows:

> The morphological development can be derived from
> phenomena traced throughout the whole declension.
> Even so there remain a certain number of examples
> where the declension form cannot be explained either
> by the ascertained laws of phonology or of morphol-
> ogy. In all these cases it is possible to explain
> the origin of the forms on a phonological basis, but
> it is necessary to start with another Indo-European
> form and not with that formerly used; in some cases
> we presuppose for the IE origin forms which were
> taken into consideration by scholars years ago, but
> the meaning of which was not commonly accepted.

It is on the basis of such considerations that he does not
hesitate, by the same token, to resort to earlier explanations where considered appropriate (cf., e.g., his derivation CS *igǎ* < PIE *i̯ugo*, i.e., from a bare-stem form, without *-m*, proposed in Agrell 1925/26, or his acceptance of
Zubatý's and Hujer's derivation North Slavic *bera* < PIE
bherō, i.e., without *-n*, and not < *-ons* < *-onts*).

Of other fairly recent work analyzing more than
merely one or two controversial case forms in prehistoric
or Early Slavic, one may single out H. Schelesniker's
relevant essays, loosely gathered together in the slim
volume *Beiträge zur historischen Kasusentwicklung des
Slavischen* (1964), discussing, after some theoretical pre-
liminaries, the genitive singular of the *-ā* and *-i̯ā* stems;
the genitive plural; the accusative plural in *-y*, *-'ę*,
-'ě; functional remodeling of the Slavic case system;
word-final *-o*; the *-g-* of the pronominal declension; and
the so-called genitive-accusative. Based on a thorough
knowledge of the IE foundations of the development of the
case system in Slavic, Schelesniker in his study, following in some major points A. Vaillant's position, has contributed a number of keen observations and intriguing suggestions, challenging, in particular, the outmoded method
of arriving at purely hypothetic case form reconstructions
by means of mechanistic equations (such as, e.g., OCS *ženy*
= Goth *qinōns* for the genitive singular) or empty assumptions of a "regular" (G *lautgesetzlich*) phonetic change
(e.g., of the type OCS *rǫky* < *-āns* for the accusative
plural). Although the share of his own independent and

new interpretations is not overly impressive and constructive criticism therefore was not altogether out of place,
Schelesniker's findings and conclusions certainly did not
deserve the kind of harsh, purely negativistic reception
given them by E. Dickenmann (cf. Schelesniker 1967 for a
rebuttal).

The role of analogy (conceived broadly and labeled
induction), a few years ago much decried in some quarters
of linguistic theory but (as shown more recently by R.
Anttila, among others) undoubtedly one of the determining
factors in the shaping of morphological paradigmatics, was
reexamined with much insight by L. A. Bulaxovs'kyj (1956,
1957) in regard to the diachrony, including prehistory, of
the Slavic case system, with special attention being paid
to the accusative. The effect of analogy was considered
also in some studies dealing with the phonetic shape and
the underlying, notably CS, developments of individual
Slavic case forms. Among such studies, the following may
be noted: Meillet 1922c (on the nominative-accusative
masculine in CS); Stang 1964 (on the instrumental singular
of the $-o$ stems in CS); Ferrell 1965 (on the nominative
and vocative singular of the $-o$ and $-\dot{\iota}o$ stems in CS); Lohmann 1930 (on the genitive singular of the $-\bar{a}$ stems in
Slavic); Vaillant 1935 (on the genitive plural in $-\breve{o}n$);
Milewski 1931a (on the genitive plural in $-\text{ъ}/-'\text{ъ}$ and on
the modifications, including gender shift, of the nominative-accusative singular of original neuters in $-om$, exemplified by such items as Slavic *darъ*, *dvorъ*, *jezerъ*, along
with *jezero*, cf. Gk δῶρον, Lat *forum*, OPr *assaran*); Mareš
1963c (on the dative singular in Slavic); Karstien 1936
(on some petrified Slavic instrumental forms in $-a$);
Schmalstieg 1965 (on Slavic $-o$ and $-\bar{a}$ stem accusative
forms). For some more recent, post-1965 work in this
field, see below (pp. 276-81).

As was already indicated, the problem of the $-\varrho/-\breve{e}_3$
and $-y/-a$ doublets have been treated in a number of special studies. Among the older ones, see especially Zubatý
1893; Diels 1914; van Wijk 1916a; Otrębski 1921; Noha 1924.
For studies dealing only with the form of the active present participle in dialectal CS and Early Slavic (OCS, Old
Russian, etc.), see further Ekblom 1915/16, Torbiörnsson
1922/23 (attempting to identify the secondary OCS type *nesę*,
encountered in *Codex Zographensis* and *Codex Marianus* and
replacing *nesy*, with OR, etc., *nesa*), van Wijk 1925 (arguing against Zubatý, but unable to come up with a more
convincing explanation; cf. above, p. 145) and, marginally,

Jacobsson 1963 (his attention being focused primarily on derivation and function).

The nominative-accusative of -*s* stem neuters (type *nebo*, *nebese*) was discussed in Szober 1927, while problems of inflection, derivation, and semantics concerning the Slavic neuters in -*nt* (type *telę*, *dětę*) were tackled in Aitzetmüller 1954, covering the full time range from their PIE origins to the modern Slavic reflexes and modifications. The relevant considerations on inflection and derivation (including instances of switch of stem class) by Karaś (1965) are more specifically limited to CS, though utilizing data from recorded and even contemporary Slavic, and taking into account all consonantal stem classes. The impressive monograph by Toporov (1961b) on the locative in Slavic, devoting a whole section (268-347) and part of the conclusion (352-3) also to CS, addresses itself primarily to the syntactic functions of the various forms subsumed under this label rather than discussing its formal aspects (cf. below, pp. 187-8).

As for the long-form (compound) adjectives, the origins of which date back to PS and possibly even Balto-Slavic times, the relatively short contribution on this topic by Kurz (1958) focuses chiefly on the problem of the original meaning (function) of these formations and on the time of their first appearance and only in passing touches upon some aspects of their inflection. By contrast, the paper by Tolkačev (1959) discusses primarily the earliest, preliterary changes in the declension of the long-form adjectives.

The inflection of Slavic pronouns, including the prehistoric period, has repeatedly been the subject of scholarly attention. Among more important contributions on this subject, at least the following may be quoted: Meillet 1913 (on the declension of Slavic demonstrative pronouns in the plural and dual feminine); Dolobko 1925 (on the enclitic forms of the pronoun for the 1st and 2nd person in the dative dual in CS); Szober 1930 (on the CS forms of the genitive and accusative singular of personal pronouns, suggesting the existence of inherited forms **me*, **te* along with the accentuated *mene*, *mę* and *tebe*, *tę*); Schelesniker 1963 (on the -*g*- and -*s*- in *kogo*, *togo*, *jego*, *česo*, identical with chapter seven in Schelesniker 1964); and — last but not least — Ferrell 1963. The latter, a lengthy, thoughtful essay titled "Some notes on Slavic gendered pronominal inflection," comments at some length, critically but often also appreciatively, on much of the previous work in the field while analyzing and elucidating many aspects of the relationship, agreements as well as differences, between nominal and pronominal inflection in the course of Slavic linguistic evolution, mainly prehistoric and early historic (represented by OCS). Admittedly slightly "melodramatic" in his presentation, Ferrell, in addition to discussing pronominal inflection proper, also offers several suggestions relevant to the derivation (word formation) of gendered pronouns in CS and Early Slavic, all set against a broad IE background.

4.1.2. Conjugation. Compared to the CS declensional system which can be considered fairly conservative, at least if measured by the rate of change of some other branches of IE, in spite of its overall development from a system of essentially PIE stem classes to one largely determined by gender, conjugation (and, generally, the verb system of the Slavic protolanguage), as it can be reconstructed, points to a far more progressed evolution away from its PIE origins and can thus be characterized as rather innovative at both the formal and functional (syntactic) levels. This marked difference in the pace of development between the noun and the verb systems of prehistoric Slavic has long been recognized and commented upon on several occasions by A. Meillet, in particular. Yet the great French comparatist acknowledged, in concluding his survey "Des innovations du verbe slave" (1922b), that "révolutionnaire à beaucoup d'égards dans la forme, le verbe slave est, sur un point au moins, très conservateur dans le fond." However, this one point referred to is the aspect *function* (compared by Meillet to that of Homeric Greek), not the aspect *form*, of the Slavic verb. As to its form system, therefore, that is in its morphology, derivational as well as, especially, inflectional, the Slavic verb already in its reconstructable prehistoric and early attested stages exhibits a far advanced degree of independent development. In this respect, it should be noted, Slavic differs from its closest cognate among the IE languages, Baltic, which by and large is fairly conservative not only in the morphology of its nominal categories, like Slavic, but also in that of its verbal system.

This difference between Slavic and Baltic had been observed and discussed by several linguists, particularly, of course, by those interested in the controversial problem of the Balto-Slavic linguistic relationship. Thus, in 1931, J. Endzlīns devoted a special article to some aspects of Slavic and Baltic as regards their conjugation. But it was only in 1942 that C. S. Stang in a broadly conceived monograph, *Das slavische und baltische Verbum*, strove to provide a systematic confrontation of the relevant data of the two closely related language branches. At the outset (7-14) he discusses the IE point of departure for the development of the verb system in Slavic and Baltic and sums up, in conclusion (268-78), his findings in general outline, contrasting, where especially revealing, the Slavic and Baltic material with that of other IE language groups. He suggests, among other things, that some of the common features of the Slavic and Baltic verb, having some parallels also in Germanic, may go back to a period of a secondary Germanic-Baltic-Slavic linguistic convergence, in essence tantamount to some form of an early *Sprachbund* linking together these three language groups. The bulk of Stang's book contains a detailed account of the Slavic and Baltic verb systems (14-97, 98-212), focusing on derivation (specifically, in the Slavic portion, on: aspects, 14-21; the present stems, 21-63; the aorist stems, 63-81; the imperfect, 81-5; the infinitive stems, 85-8; the constitution of the verb paradigms, 89-95; and the nonfinite verb forms, 95-7). Subsequent sections treat conjugation proper, i.e., the endings of the finite verb forms (the Slavic data, 213-24), and the — marked, i.e., non-indicative — mood forms (for Slavic, conditional and imperative, 238-42). As is the case with everything published by the Norwegian linguist, in this study, too, the reader comes away with the impression that virtually each line and most certainly every moot point (and there are many of them when it comes to this in part highly controversial subject matter) has been weighed carefully and from all possible angles by the author before a solution or explanation is suggested, to be sure often in qualified terms, indicating its tentative nature. While not all of Stang's contentions may eventually stand up to critical scrutiny (so, e.g., his interpretation of the Slavic $-\bar{\iota}$ verbs as 'semi-thematic'), there can be no doubt that every argument set forth in his monograph is well thought through and merits meticulous consideration even in the few instances where it ultimately may have to be rejected. Among the novel points in Stang's book should be mentioned his appreciative taking into account the then recent findings of laryngeal theory (in its early stage of development around 1940, linked, above all, to the name of J. Kuryłowicz) and the parallels drawn with Hittite evidence (with its significant distinction of *-mi* vs. *-ḥi* conjugations; cf. Ivanov

1957). As regards some of the controversial points of the
Slavic verb inflection, Stang considers the 1st person
singular of the thematic verbs in -ǫ as unequivocally derivable from the old IE ending -ō (> CS -ā) expanded by
means of a final -n patterned on the secondary ending (cf.
aor. *mogъ* < **mogŭn* < **mogon*). Stang is less sure of the
origin of the endings -si and -ši in the 2nd person singular (type OCS *jesi*, *bereši*), and also of OCS -tъ (OR -tь)
in the 3rd person singular and plural of the present and —
secondarily — in the 2nd and 3rd person singular of some
aorists. While he weighs the merits and shortcomings of
several possible explanations, he does not take a definite
stand in favor of any particular one. This is not the
place, of course, to attempt anything near a complete account of the many, partly new and usually cogent explanations suggested by Stang or to seek to identify in detail
the considerable body of lasting, generally accepted insights provided by his book. Suffice it to say here that
Stang's fundamental treatment of the prehistory of the
Slavic (and Baltic) verb, summing up with great erudition
and keenly evaluating previous work in the field while, at
the same time, opening up new avenues of research, will
continue to remain the very basis for all future relevant
studies for many years to come.

Among work that has appeared since Stang's monumental monograph and that addresses itself to the same overall issue of comparing the development of the verb system
in Slavic and Baltic, the relevant articles by E. Fraenkel
(1950b) and by V. N. Toporov (1961a), the latter, in particular, once more tackling many of the controversial
problems earlier discussed by Stang, deserve mention.

Of a fundamentally different orientation are some
other studies examining Early Slavic conjugation and the
Slavic verb system as a whole. Thus, to quote just two
instances, I. Lekov's *Praslavjanskite glagolni formi i
otraženjata im v dnešnite slavjanskite ezici* (1934) simply
uses, as suggested by the title, the reconstructed CS verb
forms as a convenient common point of departure, taken for
granted without any further discussion of its prehistory,
to explain and comment on the divergent development of the
conjugational paradigms as reflected in the present-day
Slavic languages. M. Halle's article "The Old Church
Slavic conjugation" (1951), on the other hand, applies the
descriptive technique of the so-called one-stem system,
devised for contemporary standard Russian by R. Jakobson
(1948), to the data of OCS, that is to say, in this

particular context for all intents and purposes, to the
data of Late CS. Economic, elegant, and powerful as a
descriptive device, operating with a clearly counter-
historical stem-truncation rule, this analysis is explicitly not aimed at a diachronic interpretation of the actual, partly reconstructable evolution of the Slavic verb
system and its paradigmatic functioning up to Late CS and
OCS, but is merely intended as an adequate synchronic account of the data at hand. As such it has, no doubt, considerable merit.

When it comes to the individual tense and other categories of the Slavic verb in the prehistoric period, the
discussion of the present tense forms has focused in particular on the athematic inflection and its gradual restriction in CS (or pre-CS, the secondary spread of -*m* at
the expense of -*ǫ* and its reflexes in the 1st person singular, being a phenomenon largely of the historical period
only); cf., e.g., Vaillant 1934; Szemerényi 1948 (on the
inflection of *damь*, etc., 7-12; on the same subject see
now also Kuryłowicz 1967); Aitzetmüller 1962c (on *imamь*,
etc.; see also Aitzetmüller 1962a).

In addition, such controversial endings as the 1st
person singular in -*ǫ* (where, besides the explanation adhered to by Stang, i.e., $< -\bar{a}n < -\bar{o}$ + secondary -*n*, an
original injunctive desinence in -*ām* has been considered
by A. Meillet, among others) or the 3rd person singular
and plural in -*tъ* (as found in OCS, in contradistinction
to OR -*tь*, the latter obviously more in agreement with the
comparative IE, especially Greek and Sanskrit, evidence;
cf., e.g., Milewski 1931a) have received continued attention. Yet other studies only peripherally treat problems
of the present tense inflection, and focus primarily on
the derivational aspect of present tense stem formation;
cf. esp. Vaillant 1937; Machek 1937, 1938, 1942, 1951/52,
1957c, and 1965b (the latter also on syntactic function
and lexical semantics); Sadnik 1962. Some of these will
be briefly discussed below in the appropriate context.

However, among the Slavic simple tenses it is particularly one, the imperfect, generally held to be a Slavic innovation but controversial as to its precise origin,
that has attracted the interest of diachronically oriented
linguists. The existing theories about the origin of the
Slavic imperfect can be roughly divided into two kinds:
one that assumes that underlying the Slavic forms concerned (OCS *nesěaxъ*, *žьdaaxъ*, etc.) are original compound
tense forms, subsequently synthesized, consisting of a

verbal stem in $-\check{e}$ and/or $-a$ (cf. the Baltic preterits in
$-\bar{e}-$, $-a-$) plus some form of the copula verb (PIE $es-$, either in an old imperfect form, marked by augment, or in an
ancient perfect form); the other one, positing original
simple (i.e., noncompound) forms, namely, preterit (ao-
rist) stems of the type $*nes\check{e}ja-$, $*vid\check{e}ja-$, $*d\check{e}laja-$ as
supposedly underlying the Slavic imperfect; cf. Stang
1942: 81. In fact, there already exists a fairly extensive body of specialized literature on the subject of the
Slavic imperfect and its origin. Of more important, still
to a varying degree significant contributions, at least
the following should be listed: Kuryłowicz 1937 and 1959
(the latter, p. 1, boldly suggesting that "l'imparfait
slave en $-\check{e}a\check{s}e$ est le successeur direct de l'imparfait de
l'itératif en $-\bar{a}i\underset{\cdot}{e}/o-$, et continue par conséquent un $-\bar{a}i\underset{\cdot}{e}t$
primitif"); Otrębski 1938; Vaillant 1939b; Karstien 1956a,
1956b; Sadnik 1960 (arguing against Kuryłowicz and, in
part at least, also against Karstien and attributing special significance to the type $ved\check{e}a\check{s}e$).

While the IE origins of both the root and the sigmatic aorist forms of Slavic are generally recognized, it
is primarily the obscure and, it seems, secondary ending
$-t\mathsf{b}$, occurring in the 2nd and 3rd person singular of some
aorist types (OCS $byst\mathsf{b}$, $dast\mathsf{b}$; $pit\mathsf{b}$, $p\check{e}t\mathsf{b}$, $j\underset{\cdot}{e}t\mathsf{b}$, $umr\check{e}t\mathsf{b}$,
etc.) and its possible connection with the formation of
past passive participles in $-to-$, pointing, perhaps, to a
parallelism with Germanic, that has been the object of
some brilliant though not entirely conclusive theorizing.
Among the most intriguing attempts in this direction,
taking into account also accentual factors and considering
a likely origin in the 2nd person singular desinence of
the old IE perfect and/or the middle voice form of the IE
paradigm represented by the Hittite $-\hbar i$ conjugation, see
especially van Wijk 1926 and 1937a (discussing further the
enigmatic, possibly nonpresent form OCS $s\underset{\cdot}{e}t\mathsf{b}$) and, more
recently, Vaillant 1953/54 (making reference also to Meil-
let's and Stang's well-argued earlier hypotheses); for a
still more recent discussion, see Kuryłowicz 1968b (cf.
also below, pp. 281-2).

Related problems, namely, the residues of a medial
(middle voice) conjugation in CS and the reflexes of the
IE perfect tense in Slavic, were dealt with by Lehr-
Spławiński (1965) who also discussed the origin of the OCS
form $v\check{e}d\check{e}$ (in Slavic reinterpreted as a present tense
form), and Kuryłowicz (1965) who suggested that the type

represented by OCS *mьn-i-tъ* is nothing but a semantic reinterpretation and formal transformation of the IE mediopassive perfect; cf. Lat *(me-)min-i(t)* < PIE **-mₒnei*, a
view repeated subsequently by the Polish comparatist and
also adopted by C. Watkins (1969; cf. above, pp. 63 and
153).

The irregular present tense inflection represented
by R *xóčeš'*, *xotíte* (< **xotješъ*, **xotīte*) was tentatively
traced back to an old IE optative by N. Trubeckoj (1922/
23: 17-21). The roots of the Slavic imperative in the IE
optative were discussed at some length in an article by A.
Vaillant (1930/31b); and more recently F. V. Mareš (1962b),
proceeding from and modifying Vaillant's view in this
respect, has sought to reconstruct the underlying IE protoforms of the 3rd person plural *bǫdǫ* (optative-impera-
tive) and *bǫ* (conditional) as **bhundoi̯n̥t* and **bhu̯oi̯n̥t* (>
PS **bundont, **bont*).

Resuming his 1951-52 discussion of Slavic *bǫdǫ* (1st
person singular) and its reflexes, V. Machek (1965b) examined phonetic, derivational, and semantic problems as
they pertain to this verb's functioning as an auxiliary
verb in periphrastic (analytic) future tense forms in combination with present participles and the infinitive.
Machek's reasoning concerning the factors predisposing
this verb (in contradistinction to some other, largely de-
lexicalized verbs governing the infinitive) to eventually
becoming fully grammaticalized, i.e., turning into a formal means of expressing the future, seems fairly cogent.
On the other hand, his implication that the type *bǫdǫ* +
infinitive, although not recorded in OCS and only relatively late in East Slavic, but found in West Slavic from
the beginning of its literary attestation, may very well
be of CS origin does not seem convincing to this writer,
notwithstanding the fact that Machek makes reference precisely to my relevant findings in order to corroborate his
assertion. However, in my study of the OCS periphrases
denoting the future (Birnbaum 1958a: 276-8) I merely
stated that the not yet fully grammaticalized analytic
future expressions with the infinitive (fairly frequently
imamь or *xoštǫ* + infinitive of either aspect, rarely *-čьnǫ*
+ infinitive of the imperfective aspect only), if at all
inherently Slavic, in view of other ancient IE parallels,
may, at least in part, have further developed under the
influence of foreign, primarily Greek, models. This applies, at any rate, to the *imamь* and *xoštǫ* constructions
whose indigenous Slavic origin is not quite certain,

however; the -čьnǫ + infinitive phrase, on the other hand, well represented also in Old Russian, seems indeed to have been a genuinely Slavic (though not necessarily truly CS) means of expressing the future. Clearly, there is no evidence whatsoever suggesting a grammaticalized use of the phrase bǫdǫ + infinitive in prehistoric times, but also the phrases containing one of the three other auxiliary verbs (retaining some of their modal or other semantic coloring) appear to have been functioning as syntagmatic phrases and not yet as full-fledged analytic verb forms. Their discussion would therefore fall under syntax rather than under inflectional morphology.

4.2. *Research on Common Slavic Derivation.* It is quite clear that any definition of the exact range of derivational morphology will always remain arbitrary to some extent. For it is virtually impossible to draw a sharp line between derivational morphology, on the one hand, and lexicology, including in the latter etymology and lexical semantics, on the other, as both these subfields of linguistic research are eminently concerned with the various processes of word formation. Much work pertaining to CS derivation will therefore be surveyed or briefly referred to only in a subsequent section of this report discussing lexicology, especially the CS vocabulary inherited from PIE (pp. 204-13). Applied to Slavic linguistic prehistory and early attested history, the overlap (necessitating, for purely practical reasons, an arbitrary division in any attempt at subcategorization) becomes patently apparent already in the ground-laying work by A. Meillet, *Études sur l'étymologie et le vocabulaire du vieux slave* in two volumes (1902/05), still unsurpassed despite its by now respectable age. This work was originally conceived as a series of preliminary studies meant to lead up to a full-fledged etymological dictionary of OCS, an ambitious project envisaged but, it seems, never really embarked upon by the French comparatist. Thus, volume one of Meillet's *Études* contains two model essays, one derivational-morphological, the other functional-syntactic, on the verbal category of aspect, examining the relevant evidence of the OCS gospel translation (section 1: 1-104). Also included in this volume are five studies on grammatical subjects (section 2: 105-49) of which two deal with problems of phonology, two with inflectional morphology (one treating the controversial -tъ of the aorist), and one specifically with verbal derivation, namely with the Slavic verb stems

165

in -ujǫ, -ovati (147-9). While quite succinct in its
three-page presentation, this short essay nonetheless soon
set the pattern for all subsequent research on this puzzling verbal stem class by pointing to the resemblance of
this type (as well as its Baltic counterpart in -auju,
-auti) with the Greek verbs in -ευω (type βασιλεύω, νομεύω)
and the possible connection with -ēu/-ōu stems underlying
forms such as Gk πάτρως, πάτρωος (cf. also Gk πατρυιός,
Skt pítr̥vyaḥ, Early Latin patruos, etc.). On the Slavic
verb stems in -ujǫ, -ovati, see further also below, pp.
172-3. However, it was primarily Meillet's research on
Slavic nominal derivation, contained in volume two of his
Études, that proved to be of lasting significance, occa-
sioning the republication of this volume in 1961.

4.2.1. *Nominal Derivation.* Though never intended to give
a systematic coverage, volume two of Meillet's *Études*
ranges in fact over a wide scope of problems in OCS and,
by the same token, Late CS nominal derivation, thus serving as a manual-like introduction to the field. As such
it came to replace the by then largely outdated, though
still useful second volume of Miklosich's comparative
Slavic grammar (1875, ^{2}1926 = 1852-1926, 2) without subsequently itself being fully superseded even by the portion
treating derivation in volume one of Vondrák's corresponding reference work (^{2}1924 = 1924/28, 1); cf. above, pp.
35-7. After a brief introduction, reflecting the contemporary state of IE derivational theory, Meillet's work in
twenty-five chapters treats the following topics: (1) the
nouns with a zero suffix, (2) the suffix -arjь, (3) nouns
characterized by the element -e/o-, (4) -ь (-ŭ) stems,
(5) *-ā stems, (6) -ь (-ĭ) stems, (7) Slavic -y stems,
(8) suffixes with -b-, (9) the suffix -tь (-tĭ), (10)
(substantival and adjectival) stems in -to and -ta, (11)
*-teu formations, (12) the suffix -tel-, (13) nomina in-
strumenti in *-dlo, (14) formations characterized by -d-,
(15) the suffix -ko (and feminine equivalents), (16) suffixes containing -g-, (17) -s stems, (18) the suffix
-vo, (19) suffixes with -j-, (20) suffixes showing -r-,
(21) suffixes characterized by -l-, (22) residues of the
IE suffix *-men-, (23) suffixes characterized by -m-,
(24) the suffix -ǫt-, and (25) various (substantival and
adjectival) suffixes characterized by -n-. This brief
summary of contents alone may suffice to indicate the degree of variety and complexity of the problems dealt with
in Meillet's monograph. The French Indo-Europeanist's

proven method of presentation, limiting himself to drawing, in a most succinct and lucid style, only such unequivocal conclusions as are borne out by the adduced data
itself while clearly indicating in the few instances, where
a theoretical consideration may have to leave the firm
ground of the attested evidence, its tentative, merely suggestive nature, has salvaged much of the scholarly significance of this most valuable selection of reliable relevant data in spite of the fact that Comparative IE Linguistics has made some of its most important advances precisely in the field of derivational theory since the first
appearance of Meillet's work.

In his article "Les formes nominales en slaves"
(Meillet 1923) he later returned to some of the many problems presented by the noun in CS and Early Slavic, not
limiting himself, however, to the derivational aspect only
but discussing also questions of inflection (case forms),
syntactic function (use of case and number), and grammatical category and semantic meaning (gender, substantive vs.
adjective, etc.).

The appearance in 1935 of *Origines de la formation
des noms en indo-européen* by É. Benveniste, one of Meillet's most brilliant students and his subsequent successor
in the academic profession, marks a major step forward in
the theory of IE nominal derivation. While the amount of
data quoted from Slavic is relatively modest (totaling
twenty-nine items), this book, by discussing and shedding
new light on such important, if partly controversial problems as ancient IE heteroclites (particularly of the *-r/-n*
type, residues of which can be found also in Slavic),
formations of *-l*, *-i* and *-u* stems as well as archaic nominal derivations, and sketching a new theory of the root in
IE and, at least by way of exemplification, adducing some
relevant Slavic evidence, is of paramount significance
also for the prehistory of Slavic (and Baltic) nominal derivation, especially as regards "IE nominal formations
submerged in Slavic" (cf. Birnbaum 1972a, and below, pp.
283-5).

Among the few ancient compounds in Slavic, *nevěsta*
'bride' has long presented a particular challenge as its
etymology and original meaning are not readily transparent.
Among the explanations suggested, a rather ingenious (but
not universally accepted) one, advanced by N. Trubeckoj
(1922/23: 12-14), shall be briefly stated here. In his
view, *nevěsta* is not originally the reflex of an old compound consisting of the negation *ne* plus a form of the

167

verbal root *věd-* 'know' or *ved-* 'lead', but goes back to an ancient IE superlative **neu̯isthā* (from **neu̯os* 'new, young') yielding Slavic **nevьsta*. It was supposedly at this stage that the word was reinterpreted and subsequently reshaped to *nevěsta* under the influence of, and in connection with, the semantic breakup of the ablaut variants of the root * *u̯ei̯d*(> CS *vid-* 'see') / **u̯oi̯d* (> CS *věd-* 'know') / **u̯id* (> CS **vьd-*, at first found in the past passive participle, but soon going out of use in Slavic and being replaced by the ablaut grade *věd-*: **věd-t-věst-*). According to Trubeckoj, as a result of this transformation where an original adjectival superlative was reinterpreted as a negated past passive participle form, Slavic *nevěsta* emerged.

The Slavic masculine nouns in **-ēn* (type *korenь*, *jesenь*, *grebenь*; cf. also *kamy*, *kamene*) were examined by A. Vaillant (1930/31a), and E. Hermann (1935) briefly discussed the origin of the Slavic feminines in *-yńi* (/-*yni* <**-ūnī*, type *bogyńi/bogyni*). The Slavic suffix *-dlo* (type **or-dlo* or *ăr-dlo* > *radlo/ralo*) was treated by J. J. Mikkola (1937), and V. Machek (1949) contributed some thoughts on the origin of the Slavic neuter nouns in *-ęt* (type *telę*, *dětę*). R. Eckert (1959) turned his attention to the old *-u* stems (type *medъ*, *vьrxъ*) in CS and subsequently (Eckert 1963) made an important contribution to the study of the largely covert remnants of archaic IE heteroclitic nominal stems in Slavic and Baltic, ascertainable, at least in Slavic, only in petrified form, as it were, in nominal derivation but not in inflection (the latter being the case, e.g., in Latin, Greek, or Hittite; cf. *voda/vědro*, *vydra/*-vodn-*; **sьl-n-ь*, R *sólnce*, R dial. *pósolonь*, etc., and, from the Germanic domain alone, E *water*, G *Wasser* vs. Sw *vatten*, ONorse *vatn*; E *sun*, G *Sonne* vs. Sw *sol*, etc.). In the same year, F. Liewehr (1963) contributed to the discussion concerning the Slavic stems in *-en* (and *-men*, masculines and neuters; cf. *kamy*, *kamene*; *imę*, *imene*) and *-ū* (feminines of the type *ljuby*, *svekry*), and about that time S. M. Šur (1963) provided a fairly detailed formal and semantic analysis of the various Slavic nouns in **-ti* (> *-tь*, types *datь*, *čьstь*, *sьmьrtь*, *milostь*, *pamętь*, *nitь*, etc.).

Turning to the adjectival stems (originally not distinguishable formally from the substantival nominal stems), it may be noted that N. S. Trubeckoj (1923) briefly discussed the Slavic adjectives in *-ъkъ*, i.e., old *-u* stems expanded by a *-k* suffix (type *sladъ-kъ*, cf. Lith *saldùs*).

168

A more detailed treatment was given the adjectival -*u*
stems in Balto-Slavic by P. Arumaa (1948/49). The remnants, even more difficult to detect, of old adjectival -*i*
stems in Slavic (type *svobodъ*, *različь*, indeclinable and
therefore partly reinterpreted as adverbs) were surveyed
by C. S. Stang (1939b). A particular variety of adjectival doublets in *-ont*, often carrying emotional connotations (cf. Cz *běloučký* 'nicely white', P *malutki* 'small
and cute'), was discussed by V. Machek (1961). Problems
regarding the formation of the Slavic comparative were
analyzed by A. Vaillant (1931) and, more recently, J. Hamm
(1963), among others, the latter also taking into account
considerations of phonology, especially accentuation. A
short article on the origin of the compound (or long-form,
"definite") adjective in Baltic and Slavic from the Indo-
Europeanist's point of view is Rosenkranz 1958, while F.
Kopečný in the same year published an interesting contribution (in the *festschrift* for E. Petrovici) discussing
the adjectival deverbative formation in -*l* (type Cz *dbalý*,
vzteklý, P *dbały*, *wściekły*, etc.), pointing to interesting
parallels not only in Tocharian and Armenian (where -*l*
formations were "paradigmatized," i.e., integrated into
the inflectional pattern) but also from other IE language
groups (Latin, Greek, Hittite, Germanic, Baltic, where
remnants of the IE verbal adjectives can be found; Kopečný
1958). From a methodological point of view Kopečný's attempt to distinguish between deverbative -*l* adjectives,
genuine -*l* participles, and the fully "paradigmatized" -*l*
component of the old perfect (and subsequent generalized
past tense form) is of particular importance; cf. now also
Damborský 1967, discussed below, pp. 287-8. Strictly
synchronic in its orientation but nonetheless most valuable also for any further diachronic study is M. Brodowska-
Honowska's monograph *Słowotwórstwo przymiotnika w języku
staro-cerkiewno-słowiańskim* (1960), providing a complete
listing — grouped by (1) productive simple suffixes, (2)
complex suffixes, (3) nonproductive suffixes — classification, by formal as well as semantic criteria, and general characterization, including statistical data, of the
short-form adjectives as found in the eight chief OCS
texts. Demonstrating the great variety and wealth of productive adjectival suffixes in OCS, this monograph can
serve not only as the point of departure for any study of
adjectival derivation in subsequent periods and particular
areas of Slavic linguistic evolution, but also as the concrete basis for any attempt at reconstructing earlier,

prehistoric phases of the formation of the Slavic adjective. For additional research on long-form adjectives, see also above, p. 158.

4.2.2. Verbal Derivation. The single most important and, for its time, novel comprehensive study on the prehistory of Slavic (and Baltic) verbal inflection as well as verbal derivation is, in the opinion of the present writer, the now classic 1942 monograph on the Slavic and Baltic verb by Stang, briefly surveyed above (*sub* 4.1.2. *Conjugation*, pp. 159-61). As was already mentioned there, some of Stang's partly hypothetic assertions — couched, to be sure, in appropriately cautious, circumspect terms and presented, for the sake of achieving a fairly complete and systematic picture, merely as tentative suggestions for the consideration of the more qualified reader along with other, generally recognized and well-understood processes and phenomena — may today seem no longer fully acceptable (cf., for example, Stang's considering the -$\bar{\imath}$ stem conjugation 'semi-thematic', in addition to a few other controversial points). Yet this work is by and large a most well-founded and thorough overall interpretation of the CS verb system in its derivational as well as inflectional aspects, set against its IE background with keen insight and full command of the comparative evidence. At the same time, Stang utilizes to the maximal extent possible data of the historically recorded development of the Slavic verb in all its variety and complexity down to uncovering suggestive clues and potential indications provided even by dialectal detail. This book will thus long remain the basis for all further inquiry also into Slavic verbal derivation of the prehistoric period. The only more complete and systematic treatment of all facets of the morphology of the verb in CS published since, namely, the relevant portion of A. Vaillant's *Grammaire comparée* (1950/66), relies heavily on the Norwegian linguist's findings and conclusions, occasionally carrying them even a bit farther due to the availability of new data and insights (cf. pp. 44-5). For some additional observations by Stang on verbal derivation in Slavic (and Baltic), see also Stang 1961 (on *čekati/čakati* and various verbal suffixes).

Most of the specialized literature dealing with problems of verbal derivation in CS (and/or pre-Slavic linguistic evolution) can be grouped into two main kinds of studies — those discussing verbal stem formation (and notably present stem formation) per se, with or without

taking into account functional (syntactic) and semantic
factors, and, on the other hand, those treating the origin
and first crystallization in Slavic of the dichotomy of
aspect (perfective : imperfective) and related phenomena,
including a discussion of the morphological, i.e., derivational, means by which the formal characterization of this
typically Slavic grammatical category (in its marked vs.
unmarked members) was achieved. Only relatively few of
the studies to be briefly discussed or at least referred
to in the following do not belong to one of these two
groups but either fall somewhere in between them or, in
two instances, lie altogether outside the indicated range
of problems. The subsequent survey will follow this general order of topics.

Quoting the abstract of A. Vaillant's article on
"L'origine des présents thématiques en -*e/o*-," published
in 1937,

> Les présents thématiques, dont l'importance en indo-
> européen était au moins égale à celle des présents
> athématiques, ont une double origine: ils sont
> issus, soit de présents thématiques de la flexion en
> -*mi* (type skr. *tudáti*), soit de dénominatifs en
> *-oh*- de la flexion en -*hi* du hittite (type gr.
> φέρει). Le prétérit des dénominatifs en *-oh*- se
> continue dans le prétérit en -*ē*- du balto-slave,
> dans le suffixe verbal -*ē*- et dans le subjonctif en
> -*ē/ō*-.

While, to be sure, not particularly drawing on Slavic material, Vaillant's article obviously also contains a great
deal of Slavic data, explaining, among other things, the
Slavic imperfect (type *nesě-aše*, *živě-aše*) as a vestige of
the ancient preterites of the *-oh*- (i.e., -*o* + laryngeal)
type conjugation. H. Kølln, in his 1961 study "Die *e/o*-
Verba im Slavischen," penetrated deeper into the specifically Slavic problems of the -*e/o*- verbs. Kølln, who has
published several studies on the verbal categories of CS
and Early Slavic and their IE background, also acknowledges that the -*e/o*- verbs in Slavic (as well as in other
IE languages) have absorbed many originally athematic
verbs. He then goes on to investigate the aorist, distinguishing for this verb class between -*s* and -*e/o*- formations (type *věsь*, *něsь*, *rěxь* and *idь*, *mogь*, *vrьgь*) as opposed to expanded aorist formations in -*a* and -*ě*. Moreover, Kølln comments on various problems of the present
stem formations, especially accentuation (studied also by

V. A. Dybo).

The origin of the Slavic -*ne*/-*no* verbs (inf. -*nǫ-ti*, Leskien's class II) was discussed by V. Machek (1938), while ten years later P. Tedesco (1948: 346) was able to show, in a thorough and well-documented study, that "a large part of the Slavic *ne*-presents, probably all imperfectives," and, in particular, the principal subtype of this class, namely, the intransitives from consonant roots, "have replaced older *je*-presents, a number of which are still preserved in Old Church Slavic and Later Church Slavic, especially Old Russian," to quote the abstract of his article. Subsequently, the place of the nasal presents, both those with nasal suffix and with nasal infix (type *lęžetъ*, *sędetъ*), within the Early CS (PS) verb system was once more examined by L. Sadnik (1962). A certain subtype of Slavic -*ne*/-*no* verbs, to wit, the transitive -*n* verbs (type OCS *dvignǫti*, *stignǫti*), and their origin were discussed in a paper by I. Němec (1964). OCS *bǫdǫ*, *bǫdetъ* and its Slavic cognates (< *bhū-n-d-*), studied from several points of view by V. Machek (1951/52 and 1965b; cf. above, p. 164), is also a formation with a nasal infix (and -*d* suffix).

The -*je*/-*jo* verbs (Leskien's class III) present at least some problems that have occasioned discussion. Thus, for example, N. van Wijk (1929b) suggested that the puzzling coexistence in Slavic of a relatively small group of primary (nonderived) verbs in -*ajǫ*, -*ati* and -*ějǫ*, -*ěti* (type OCS *želajǫ*, *želati* / *želějǫ*, *želěti*, *pitajǫ*, *pitati* / *pitějǫ*, *pitěti*) finds its parallel in the CS alternation of -*a* : -*ě* stem of the athematic verb *ima-mь*, *imě-ti*. While retained in the paradigm of this highly frequent and generally "irregular" verb, the same — or similar — verb stem alternation was, according to van Wijk, eliminated within one and the same paradigm of the just mentioned, less frequent verb group, with generalization of either the -*a* or the -*ě* stem throughout the entire paradigm (present and infinitive stem), thus -*ajǫ*, -*ati* or -*ějǫ*, -*ěti*. On Slavic *iměti* and its formal origin in an old perfect (< *im-ē-*), see also Aitzetmüller 1962a. The Slavic verbs in -*ujǫ*, -*ovati*, previously briefly discussed by A. Meillet (1902/05, 1: 147-9; cf. above, pp. 165-6), were reexamined by V. Machek (1937). Contrary to Meillet's opinion that these verbs are based on diphthongal long -*ōu* stems (a view, incidentally, independently arrived at also by some other scholars), Machek suggested the explanation that the -*ujǫ*, -*ovati* verbs, as well as their Baltic counterparts, could be derived from regular nominal -*u* stems, modeled after the type *cělovanъ* (: *cělъ* as Ved. *tákav-āna-* : *táku-*), providing the basis for the infinitive *cělovati* and further the present *cělujǫ* (< **cěl-oу̯-jǫ* or, rather, **kai̯l-oу̯-i̯-ō-*). He notes such correspondences as *cělъ*, *sladъ-kъ* (adjectival -*u* stems) and *cělovati*, *sladovati* (the latter, however, not attested in canonical OCS, as also noted, e.g., in Vondrák 1924/28, 1: 718 before him) and proceeds from the realization reached by J. Zubatý (on the basis of Indic parallels) that Slavic infinitive formations of the type *sъpati*, *lъzati*, *čekati*, *zъvati* were patterned on the participles (going back to original adjectives) **sъpanъ*, *lъzanъ*, *čekanъ*, *zъvanъ*, leading to such new — analogical — formations as *dělanъ*, *dělati*, etc. On the type *zějǫ*, *zъjati*, cf. esp. Schmalstieg 1960a.

Machek (1942) explained the difference in the infinitive stem (-*ě-ti* vs. -*i-ti*) of the Slavic -*i* verbs (Leskien's class IV) by resorting to underlying adjectival forms (subsequently largely transformed into and reinterpreted as participles) as well as genuine, primary participial formations (cf., on the one hand, the type OCS *trъpělъ*, triggering the rise of the secondary forms *trъpěnъ* and *trъpěti*, with, on the other hand, *pilъ*, paralleling — not forming the basis of — the primary formations *pitъ*, participle and supine, and *piti*, infinitive). As for the origin of the Slavic -*i*- in the present stems of this class, Machek assumed, in most cases, an underlying -*ei*- (partly shortened from older -*ēi*-, cf. OCS *sědimъ*, Lat *sedēmus*), considering the Old Indic and Greek counterparts reflecting **-ei̯o/e*- (Skt -*aya*-, Gk -ει̯ο-) instances of secondary thematization (an expansion, comparable to Skt *bhárti* = Lat *fert* vs. later *bhárati* < **bhérti* vs. **bhéreti*). According to Machek, an original suffixal -*ī*- (and not -*ei*-) may, however, underlie formations represented by OCS *gostitъ* (OR *gostitь* < **gostī-ti*). The particular form of the 1st person singular of this class, reflecting CS suffixal -*i̯*- (as opposed to -*ī*- in the rest of the paradigm; cf. OCS *nošǫ*, *kloñǫ*, *trъpljǫ*, etc. vs. *nositъ*, *klonitъ*, *trъpitъ*, etc.), Machek explained as due to quantitative ablaut (full grade before consonantal endings vs. zero grade before vocalic endings, i.e. *ei/i* or, in the latter position, rather, allophonic *i̯*) of this "strange" (*merkwürdig*, as he put it) verbal derivational suffix. A somewhat different opinion both as regards the claimed secondary character of the Indic and Greek thematized formations and the 1st person singular (as well as the apparently irregular forms of the 2nd and 3rd person singular of the verb *xotěti*) was expressed by W. R. Schmalstieg (1959b) who, in this respect perhaps closer to Stang's views, suggested (183) that

> the forms of the Slavic statives and the Sanskrit passives can be related easily if one presupposes an early morphemic alternation of */ey/ - /ye-ō/, the generalized */ey/ explaining the Slavic /ī/ (e.g., O.C.S. *smr̥d-ī-ši̇*, *smr̥d-ī-tŭ*, etc.) and the *ye-o [= */ye-o/, H.B.] explaining the remaining Slavic forms (e.g., *smr̥ždǫ* < *smr̥d-yǫ*, *xoštǫ* < *xot-yǫ*, *xošteši* < *xot-ye-ši̇*, *xoštetŭ* < *xot-ye-tŭ*, etc.). The short /i/ of Lithuanian statives is a later formation based on analogy with the 3rd plural.

Schmalstieg's interpretation, relevant, to be sure, only to a particular portion of the Slavic -*i* verbs, while less convincing to my mind, deserves further consideration. Cf. also Schmalstieg 1960b (referred to below), and for a different explanation of the irregular present tense paradigm of *xotěti* (best reflected in Russian, not in OCS, however), Trubeckoj 1922/23, briefly mentioned above, p. 164.

Questions of semantic and syntactic function were further discussed in connection with verbal derivation (stem formation) also in papers by O. Szemerényi (1948: 13-14, on -*d* verbs), V. Machek (1957c, on -*sk* verbs, more recently touched upon in passing also by Ivanov 1970), Schmalstieg (1960b, on "-*ǐ*- as marker of the determinative aspect").

Research on Slavic aspectology, notably on the origin and early development of the aspect dichotomy (perfective vs. imperfective), can be roughly divided into two schools of thought. One of them holds that the aspect category of Slavic represents merely a further development and full systematization of categories inherent, latently and/or overtly, in the IE (PIE or perhaps post-PIE, dialectal IE) verb system. According to this view, aspect can thus be studied, in the formal (morphological) manifestation and semantic (and partly syntactic) functions of its subcategories, also in certain other ancient or archaic IE languages, especially Greek (where in particular the Greek originals of the OCS translations lent themselves to fruitful comparison; cf. esp. Meillet 1902/05,

1: 1-104, as regards the OCS gospel translation,cf. above, p. 165), Gothic, and Lithuanian. The other school of thought concerning the origin of aspect in Slavic is inclined to see in this category essentially a Slavic innovation with some kind of continuity from pre-Slavic IE times only in the sense that certain inherited morphological categories, of the semantic-lexical rather than grammatical type of *modes of action* (G *Aktionsarten*, R *sposoby dejstvija*), may have provided some formal basis or a part thereof, and to some extent perhaps also the semantic impetus, for the rise and development of the category of aspect in the narrow sense of perfective vs. imperfective. As a corollary of these two general trends in Slavic aspectology, one group of scholars will tend to view Slavic aspect in close connection with comparable, though by no means identical, phenomena in Early Germanic (esp. Gothic) and Baltic (Lithuanian) and consider the perfective : imperfective dichotomy as almost wholly developed already in prehistoric Slavic and hence fully functioning in early attested Slavic (OCS and Old Russian), some, by and large minor differences in aspect usage in Early and Modern Slavic notwithstanding. The other group of aspectologists will rather tend to see aspect as a category in the making during the first centuries of recorded Slavic linguistic evolution, only in the process of gradually taking over some of the functions of and replacing the formerly highly complex tense system, already in a state of beginning decay in the early medieval period.

As aspectology is one of the most thoroughly researched fields of Slavic Linguistics and the body of relevant literature therefore is quite extensive, even if one is to limit oneself to diachronic studies and synchronic work on early stages of Slavic linguistic development, a discussion, no matter how succinct, of more than just a few of the many important monographs and articles on the formal and/or functional facets of Slavic aspect would exceed the scope of this state-of-the-art report. In most cases we will thus have to limit ourselves to a mere listing of references and abstain from any evaluative comments. It should only be indicated at the outset of this survey that this writer generally adheres to the views of those experts in the field who consider full-fledged aspect a relatively recent phenomenon in Slavic (and hence also no more than an emerging category in CS and Early Slavic) rather than sharing the view of those who see in it a completely developed category of CS and Early Slavic directly inherited from pre-Slavic IE (or PIE). Further, within each school of thought concerning the origin and early development of Slavic aspect there exists a wide range of views on a variety of questions of detail. Moreover, as both morphological (derivational) and purely syntactic (functional) considerations are involved in the formation and development of the double category of perfective vs. imperfective aspect, and as most relevant studies deal with both form and function, this body of research should be accounted for or at least referred to under Morphology (more specifically, *Verbal Derivation*) as well as under Syntax (more specifically, *Grammatical Categories and Functions*). However, for purely practical reasons and considerations of space, the pertinent literature will be briefly discussed or listed only in this section of Morphology, whereas, in the appropriate section of Syntax only a cross-reference to this section will be given (cf. below, p. 192). However, where, in a few instances, relevant studies are concerned exclusively with the syntactic (functional) side of the aspect category, they will be mentioned under Syntax only.

While Meillet still saw a fairly close correlation between the aspectual dichotomy of OCS and certain tense oppositions in ancient Greek (which, according to him, did not necessarily continue a corresponding tense contrast from PIE, however), his two former students J. Kuryłowicz and C. S. Stang took a somewhat different view of the development of the aspect category in Slavic. According to Kuryłowicz (1929 & 1932), the Slavic aspect system has its origin in the opposition obtaining between presents in -*ajǫ* and -*nǫ*. A similar view was, incidentally, also held by Kuryłowicz's fellow countryman, T. Milewski (1937a and 1938, the latter with a polemical note by J. Safarewicz). Later, Kuryłowicz's concept of the origin of the Slavic aspect dichotomy was criticized, for example, by R. Růžička (1962: especially 19). Meanwhile, returning to the problem of aspect in Early Slavic, Kuryłowicz had already somewhat modified his own relevant views when analyzing the particular formal and functional relationship between the OCS imperfect and the aspect correlation, in particular the imperfective formations in -*ajǫ*, -*ajetъ* (see Kuryłowicz 1959). Stang (1942: 14-21, especially 18-19), while generally sympathetic toward Kuryłwicz's original explanation of the development of aspect in Slavic, cautions nonetheless against seeking the beginnings of the aspect correlation exclusively in the formal present opposition invoked by Kuryłowicz, especially since, as he puts it,

> Es herrscht aber immer wieder Zweifel, inwiefern Verba auf -$(a)j\varrho$ und -$n\varrho$ von Alters her nebeneinander standen, ob nicht das eine oder das andere eben auf Grund des schon vorhandenen Aspektsystems gebildet worden ist.

While partly disagreeing as regards the point of departure for the formation of the Slavic aspect category, the above mentioned scholars (possibly with the exception of Meillet) all belong to that school of thought which conceives of aspect (in the narrow sense of perfective vs. imperfective) as a purely or, at any rate, predominantly Slavic phenomenon, at most developed from certain formal prerequisites inherited from pre-Slavic IE. Among the same group of scholars one may also count N. van Wijk (1929a) who seems to have been the first to consider the possibility of an ancient opposition of determinate versus indeterminate verbs (i.e., a lexical-semantic rather than grammatical dichotomy, falling under the label *mode of action* rather than under *aspect*) serving as the original formal basis for the subsequent development of the aspect contrast in Slavic. His ideas were later further developed and partly modified, especially by C. G. Regnéll (1944), V. V. Borodič (1953), I. Němec (1956 and 1958), and H. Kølln (1957 and 1958; cf. further also Kølln 1966). Among proponents of the other camp, viewing Slavic aspect as a direct continuation and systematization of a categorial opposition inherent already in PIE, A. Belić (in several studies) can be mentioned. A somewhat different stand was taken by A. Senn (1949). Pointing out that, with some qualifications, "Gothic and Old High German represent very much the same picture, especially in the use of perfective present to express future action," Senn concludes that, while Baltic, notably Lithuanian, must have borrowed its aspect system from Slavic and more specifically Russian, "it remains only to establish the relationship between Slavic and Germanic. If both groups inherited this system from Proto-Indo-European, we are forced to assume that Pre-Germanic and Pre-Slavic lived more closely together than has been believed . . ." Alternatively (*ibid.*, 408-9), in

> answering the question whether this aspect system originated in the Slavic or in the Germanic group,

it must be kept in mind that our Gothic documents
were written 500 years earlier than the Old Church
Slavic gospel translation. Furthermore, it should
be remembered that the entire Slavic area was for
some time under Gothic domination. A strong linguistic influence exerted by the Goths is evident
from the numerous loan words in the Slavic languages. Therefore, it is not improbable that the
Slavs received the aspect system from the Goths and
passed it on to the Baltic people.

While not uninteresting, Senn's view of the Germanic origin of the Slavic aspect system has had few adherents. A.
Dostál, somewhat more cautious when it comes to explicit
statements as to the origin and development of aspect in
Slavic, seems to consider the contrast perfective vs. imperfective a fully developed opposition already in canonical OCS. Invaluable as an exhaustive reference work on
aspect in OCS, Dostál's monumental monograph *Studie o
vidovém systému v staroslověnštině* (1954) cannot, however,
in the view of the present writer, be accepted as regards
its theoretical premises and conclusions. The underlying
theory finds its expression in Dostál's functional analysis of certain OCS verbs (which, it would seem, have not
yet been embraced by the aspect category or have remained
for some time indifferent toward it) as in fact susceptible to both aspects, perfective and imperfective, taking
the preexistence of the aspect opposition as such for
granted. Of other important research on Slavic aspect
and, in particular, its prehistoric (CS or pre-CS) origins,
see further, for example, Vaillant (1939a), Machek (1958a),
Schelesniker (1959), Maslov (1959 and 1961), Dombrovszky
(1962 and 1967). In concluding this survey of past and
recent research on aspect in CS and Early Slavic times,
its formal prerequisites, first emergence, and subsequent
morphologization, it should be pointed out, once more,
that the above references represent merely a very incomplete sampling of some of the more significant relevant
titles. Ample additional references will be found in many,
if not most, of the selected works listed here.
    Of studies dealing with derivational aspects of non-
finite verbal categories in CS, at least two ought to be
mentioned here: G. A. Il'inskij's brief discussion of the
infinitive in CS (1930) and G. Jacobsson's 1963 article on
"the Slavic active participles: original structure and
interference" where, arriving at a preliminary conclusion

(125), the Swedish Slavist summarizes his view of the CS and OCS participles analyzed as follows:

> To sum up, it can be said that *-nt-* and *-us-* forms so frequent in O. C. S. are adjectives with pronounced verbality inherited from Indo-European, and it is just this verbality which makes participles of them.

In the tradition of Zubatý and Machek, Jacobsson then proceeds to corroborate his notion of the Slavic participles as original adjectives by examining some comparative evidence of other IE languages before turning to the data of Slavic languages other than OCS; cf. also Večerka 1959.

This, then, concludes our brief account of research up to 1965 on CS derivation and, at the same time, on CS morphology as a whole.

5. SYNTAX

5.0. Some General Problems of Defining Syntax and of Reconstructing Common Slavic Syntactic Patterns. The term *syntax* will be used here in the traditional double sense. On the one hand, it refers to the theory of grammatical functions of various rank and kind (such as *predication*, *possessiveness*, *indicativeness*, or *past time*, the latter two as opposed to *indicative* and *past tense* or *preterit*, denoting morphological categories) and to the theory of the broader and more abstract notion of grammatical categories (such as *gender*, *case*, *mood*, or *tense* or, rather, the respective underlying generalized grammatical meanings, as opposed to their morphological expression in terms of a particular form designating, say, masculine, a specific case form, e.g., the genitive, indicative, or past = preterit). On the other hand, *syntax* refers to the study of sentence structure, including its components (i.e., clauses and syntactic phrases, the latter roughly equivalent to *syntagms* or word-groups, R *slovosočetanija*). Strictly speaking, it would suffice, of course, to define syntax simply as the study (or theory) of sentence structure, subsuming under this term also the theory of grammatical functions (and their generalized abstractions, i.e., grammatical categories) since grammatical function in turn can be defined as the particular — grammatical — meaning a given word form (R *slovoforma*) assumes within the framework of a syntactic phrase (syntagm, word-group). To be sure, word-group in this conception would presumably include also the narrow verbal expression of the subject — predicate relationship (i.e., of *predication*) regardless of whether the subject is explicit — expressed by a separate word, a noun or pronoun — or implicit — implied in a word carrying other functions as well, usually in the

finite verb form. Generally, only the grammatical functions expressed formally by the vocative case and the imperative mood would, at least in Slavic, fall outside the
scope of such a definition of syntactic function or grammatical meaning; cf. the various attempts at integrating
these functions in overall semiotic models of language
communication, sketched or elaborated in some detail by
C. S. Peirce, C. Morris, K. Bühler, R. Jakobson, and
others. These exceptional instances may be ignored for
practical purposes, however, by treating — as is usually
done — the vocative along with other case forms, and the
imperative together with other moods (in the case of
Slavic, the indicative and the conditional or new subjunc-
tive).

Obviously, certain theoretical objections could be
raised even regarding the fairly broad definition of the
field of syntax just given. Yet, this is not the place to
enter into a detailed argumentation for the purpose of
theoretically further underpinning the suggested definition. Rather, this definition was briefly expounded here
merely in order to indicate the exact scope and kind of
research qualifying, in principle, for consideration in
this section. Therefore, following a discussion of some
fairly recent general studies pertinent to CS syntax, relevant work will be dealt with under the two headings of
Studies on the Grammatical Categories and Functions of CS
and *Studies on the Sentence Structure of CS*, the latter —
rather meager for the pre-1965 period — consequently excluding research on specific functions obtaining within
the syntactic phrase.

It should be readily clear that research on CS syntax, i.e., the syntactic patterns of a reconstructed protolanguage, encounters particular difficulties of a methodological nature. This applies, above all, to the grop-
ing attempts at recreating CS sentence structure or, more
specifically, syntactic models underlying real sentences,
not to speak of the even more ambitious endeavors, undertaken in recent years, to restore, if only in a rather
general and fragmentary manner, whole CS texts. Also, in
view of the basic fact that no samples of CS discourse
from which one might abstract the syntactic patterns and
their workings have been preserved, the overall reconstruction of a certain portion of the syntactic component
of CS linguistic structure, if not all of it, is still
struggling with considerable problems of method and approach. Only when it comes to the particular grammatical

functions of individual word forms and morphological categories do we stand on somewhat firmer ground as one here, to some extent at least, can project functions ascertainable in the early recorded evidence back into a prehistoric, Late CS period.

Two approaches one may explore in an attempt to gain some insight into CS syntax as a whole are either to try to establish CS syntactic patterns inherited from a previous, presumably Balto-Slavic, period by comparing relevant Slavic and Baltic features in an effort to ascertain shared syntactic archaisms; or, one may try to sort out from the complex system of syntactic patterns encountered in the earliest attested Slavic evidence all those features that can be identified, with a fair degree of probability, as originally foreign to Slavic, thus arriving at a "purified" system of archaic Slavic syntax (or some portion thereof), equaling, in principle, Late CS syntactic structure. Both approaches have been tested, but neither one, so far, with particular success. Thus, for example, P. Trost (1958b) studied some aspects of the Balto-Slavic syntactic relations without, however, arriving at any definitive conclusions. The main difficulty here, of course, is the fact that Baltic is recorded only from a relatively very late period (Old Prussian beginning around 1400, Old Lithuanian only from the first half of the 16th century on) so that in many instances — e.g., the use of a predicative instrumental or the genitive to denote the direct object governed by a negated verb — it is virtually impossible to decide whether certain Slavic-Baltic syntactic parallelisms are due to secondary influences (usually from Slavic on Baltic) dating presumably from sometime between ca. 1000 and 1500 A. D., or whether they point to a common origin and hence could be considered truly Balto-Slavic also in a genetic sense (and therefore also PS and CS). As for syntactic "foreignisms" found in the oldest recorded Slavic language, in 1958 I undertook an effort to outline at least some of the methodological problems and to suggest some techniques for the purpose of identifying the syntactic Grecisms of OCS (Birnbaum 1958b), setting out to separate "echt Slavisches, Altererbtes von Nachgeahmtem und Entlehntem . . . und dadurch in manchen Punkten ein deutlicheres Bild der ältesten genuin slavischen Syntax, ihrem Bau und den ihr zu Gebote stehenden Ausdrucksmitteln, [zu] gewinnen" (241). Notwithstanding the considerable progress made since 1958 in improving the methods and techniques for identifying and assessing the impact of

Greek (and, to a lesser degree, Latin) models on OCS syntax (cf., especially, the relevant studies by J. Bauer, R. Večerka, and R. Růžička, in addition to my own subsequent research in this area), it must be conceded, frankly, that we are still far from gaining that "clearer picture of the oldest genuinely Slavic syntax." I, for one, realizing the full extent of the complexity of the Greek-OCS syntactic patterns prevailing, both at the surface and at deeper levels, in the oldest literary language of the Slavs, have lately pinned greater hopes on the syntactic yield of the relatively unaffected segments of Early Old Russian evidence (mostly from the northern area), ascribing to the relevant data of OCS only secondary importance as a useful control instrument (cf. Birnbaum 1968a: 62-3).

A more balanced and well-rounded discussion of the goals, problems, and methods of reconstructing CS syntactic structure was presented by J. Bauer (1963b) in his programmatic contribution to the 5th International Congress of Slavists, Sofia, entitled "Úkoly a metody rekonstrukce praslovanské syntaxe." While not entering into a detailed discussion of all the difficulties encountered in this kind of linguistic reconstruction, this is a well thought through essay identifying major problems and commenting on and tentatively exploring some promising avenues of research in this difficult area. Together with another, similarly conceived programmatic article on the "basic problems of the comparative-historical study of Slavic syntax," published almost simultaneously (Bauer 1963a), this paper stands out as a kind of spiritual legacy of the prematurely deceased Czech syntactician.

An ambitious though highly abstract attempt at reconstructing a CS text was made by the two Soviet linguists V. V. Ivanov and V. N. Toporov in their joint report presented at the 5th International Congress of Slavists, Sofia (Ivanov & Toporov 1963). As stated in the English summary of their paper,

> It is suggested that the reconstruction of a Proto-Slavic text should be made possible by the recent development in the field of the basis of linguistic theory. . . It is possible to describe the process of generation of a Proto-Slavic text in two ways: by constructing a synthetic model where a text is generated from the upper levels (starting with the content) to the lower levels (such as morphological and phonological) or by building an analytic model

starting from the lower levels . . . For practical reasons the second way was chosen in the present report. For each level . . . special systems of notation are introduced. Thus, for the phonological level the symbols for distinctive features, phonemes and their relations are introduced; by means of this notation several rules of distribution . . . are expressed. In connection with the phonological description the main characteristics of Proto-Slavic verse are discussed. For the morphological level the symbols for different positional classes of morphemes, grammemes (elementary members of grammatical oppositions) and word-forms are introduced and the rules describing the restrictions laid on the combinations of grammemes in a given word-form are expressed. The syntactical level is described by means of a set of rewriting rules (several restrictions laid on the possibility of the cyclic application of the rules are discussed). The transformational level is described by means of a set of equivalence relations between different syntactical constructions that express the same syntactical meaning (that is, the meaning-preserving mapping of syntactical constructions is made the basis for the transformational level).

In what follows, the techniques resorted to for defining stylistic aims and restrictions are briefly described. The English resumé continues:

The last part of the report is dedicated to the analysis of several examples of reconstructed texts beginning with the shortest and simplest forms. As a first example several simple (noncompound) Proto-Slavic names of gods are discussed . . . The Proto-Slavic compound personal names are described on the basis of the material collected in separate Slavic languages . . . Proto-Slavic compounds discussed in the report are taken as the basis for the reconstruction of the corresponding Proto-Slavic phraseological combinations . . . The report ends with a discussion of larger texts such as charms . . ., lamentations . . ., fragments of Proto-Slavic epics and fairy-tales (based on the comparison with Lithuanian material) . . .

As can be seen even from the authors' own summary, this is

indeed a holistic approach toward reconstructing CS texts
(or, for the most part, text fragments), utilizing modern
tools of linguistic research and extending, in addition to
analyzing the linguistic structure at all levels, into the
realms of anthropology, sociology, folklore, and mythology, formal-structural as well as comparative-historical.
This line of semantically based research was subsequently
continued in part three of the monograph on *Slavjanskie
jazykovye modelirujuščie semiotičeskie sistemy* (1965), coauthored by the same scholars, where they first discuss
the notational system (including logic symbolism) on
various levels (218-21) and then provide "examples of formalized notation of reconstructed texts and their elements" (222-39). Regarding the possibility of interpreting certain compound personal names as petrified rudimentary sentences, see also T. Milewski 1962/63.

*5.1. Studies on the Grammatical Categories and Functions
of Common Slavic.* Among earlier studies in Slavic comparative and historical case syntax touching upon the problem
of the grammatical function of individual cases in CS, the
essay by E. Fraenkel "Der prädicative Instrumental im
Slavischen und Baltischen und seine syntaktischen Grundlagen" (1926) may be quoted as an example. While containing some keen observations and subtle interpretations, it
also demonstrates the methodological difficulty, referred
to above, of establishing unequivocal criteria for distinguishing between common heritage and secondary borrowing
as regards parallel syntactic features found in two closely related language groups known to have been subject to
mutual influences (in this particular instance, to be
sure, much more from Slavic on Baltic than vice versa)
long after their original divergence. Many of Fraenkel's
conclusions as to the prehistoric period must therefore
remain tentative at best.

An attempt at sketching the various functions (or
meanings) of the dative in CS was made by A. B. Pravdin
(1957) who previously had investigated in some detail certain functions of the dative in OCS and Old Russian.
Taking as his point of departure the evidence of early
attested Slavic and, in those instances where there is no
reason to assume any secondary developments of a particular function found in all or most Slavic languages, the
testimony of modern Slavic as well, Pravdin first discusses the primary function of the dative as expressing
the indirect object, i.e., the addressee of a delivery or

communication. Semantically close to that meaning is the use of the dative with the preposition *kъ*, carrying primarily spatial connotations, however. Other functions of the dative in CS include its use as *dativus commodi* and *incommodi*, partly retained in contemporary Slavic, and, close to this meaning, the subjective-possessive use of the dative in connection with the verb *byti* or some of its substitutes or near-synonyms (cf. also the use of the dative in such phrases as R *mne žal'*, where *žal'* is assigned by some linguists the status of a separate — relatively newly emerged — word class labeled *category of state* or *predicative*; cf. below). Whereas, according to Pravdin, the combinations of the prepositions *kъ* or *po* with a dative in the CS period still expressed primarily concrete, spatial meanings (while the more abstract connotations of these prepositional phrases, expressing the goal with *kъ*, the cause or basis with *po*, etc., largely belong to the history of the individual Slavic languages), CS seems to have known a much wider use of an adverbial dative without a preposition than recorded Slavic; yet, as Pravdin points out, the adverbial function (with its various semantic shades of goal and location) was not the primary function of the dative even in CS since these connotations were also expressed at that time mainly by means of prepositional phrases. The basic function of the dative, preserved in modern Slavic but inherited from PIE and paralleled in the other IE languages, was that of the indirect object.

On the Slavic construction *sъ* + accusative in expressions of measure and on the origin of this phrase, see Stang 1956.

While the predicative function of the Slavic instrumental, also in its diachronic aspect, has been discussed on several occasions and in various contexts, the further functions of the Slavic instrumental have been less investigated, especially from a comparative-historical point of view. This deficiency was largely remedied by the publication in 1958 of the monograph *Tvoritel'nyj padež v slavjanskix jazykax*, coauthored by a team of young researchers at the Institute of Slavic Studies of the Soviet Academy of Sciences under the editorship of the well-known Slavist S. B. Bernštejn. Here all ascertainable functions of the Slavic instrumental (except its predicative use) were discussed in separate chapters, preceded by an introduction on the methods and tasks of the historical study of the meanings and functions of the cases in Slavic and summed up in a concluding chapter presenting the overall results of the book. Since, as pointed out in the beginning of the final chapter, "all above indicated basic meanings of the instrumental were already represented in CS" and "many of them go back to an even earlier period" (351), these meanings and functions, discussed in the monograph on the basis of an impressive sampling from ancient, folkloric, dialectal, and modern literary text material of various Slavic languages, shall be briefly listed here: the associative instrumental proper (i.e., *casus instrumenti*), discussed in chapters two and three by D. S. Staniševa; the instrumental in passive constructions and in impersonal sentences (i.e., denoting the logical subject), the instrumental of cause, and the instrumental of transformation and comparison (the latter two uses believed by some scholars to underlie the secondary, subsequently widespread predicative use of the instrumental), treated in chapters four, five, and six by K. I. Xodova, well-known also for her research on the case syntax of OCS; the instrumental of totality (expressing the whole or its divisibility), dealt with in chapter seven by D. S. Staniševa; the instrumental of delimitation, analyzed in chapter eight by M. A. Gadolina; the instrumental of time, discussed in chapter nine by L. S. Malaxovskaja; the instrumental of location with and without a preposition, examined in chapters ten and eleven by A. M. Bulygina; the adnominal instrumental, studied in chapter twelve by M. A. Gadolina; and the process of adverbializing the instrumental, discussed in chapter thirteen by T. S. Tixomirova.

If the just mentioned monograph on the Slavic instrumental suffers from some minor flaws of coherence and consistency caused by its being the result of team work, the same cannot be said about another monograph which grew out of the same broad research project conducted at the Institute of Slavic Studies, V. N. Toporov's *Lokativ v slavjanskix jazykax* (1961b). Part one of this monograph (9–267) is devoted to an analysis of the locative in all the attested individual Slavic languages, part two (268–347) discusses the prehistoric period, notably the bare locative (285–309) and the locative with a preposition (*vъ* and *na*, *o*, *po*, and *pri*, 309–47) in CS, and the concluding section (348–53) deals largely with prehistoric and comparative aspects of the Slavic locative. This study relies heavily on the method of internal reconstruction in the rather general sense of taking into consideration other IE, non-Slavic data only where corroborated or at least not contradicted by the — to be sure, comparative — evidence of Slavic, a method providing for superior linguistic as well as philological control of the pertinent Slavic material. The author also displays a great deal of ingenuity of interpretation and inference both internally, in terms of drawing the line between productive uses of the Slavic (including CS) locative and instances of its ceasing to be a paradigmatic means of nominal inflection by turning into petrified, adverbialized forms and phrases; and externally, in terms of integrating the Slavic phenomena into their broader IE context. This truly model study proves, once again, the fruitfulness of combining a sound and solid philological method with insightful, imaginative linguistic theory. As for the purely syntactic aspect of the Slavic locative, the upshot of Toporov's investigation is that while the meanings and functions of the prepositional locative are largely determined by the semantics of the prepositions governing it, the fairly limited use of the bare (i.e., non-prepositional) locative, ascertainable beyond doubt only in OCS (and Middle Bulgarian), Early Old Russian, and Old Czech, can be roughly divided into three areas, namely, expressions indicating: (1) location (usually place-names) or (2) time (mostly of words with an implicit time connotation), and (3) in verb phrases (as a rule with verbs exhibiting "strong" government) indicating a spatial, directional, or object meaning (285-6).

While Toporov's ability to draw the line between a productive use of the locative as an inflectional means and its unproductive use in adverbial phrases hardly calls for any critical comment (notwithstanding some possibly controversial details), the same cannot be said about a highly intriguing though questionable theory advanced by the Polish-Swedish Slavist J. Trypućko, regarding the origin of certain adverbial expressions formally identical with plural case forms with or without a preposition. Thus, in his study *Le pluriel dans les locutions adverbiales de temps et de lieu en slave* (1952), Trypućko tried to prove, not too successfully, I would suggest, that the plural endings of the oblique cases can be traced back to adverbial suffixes and that the frequent use of plural case forms in adverbial function in ancient and modern IE languages (in the latter usually an archaism) is a manifestation of a tendency, still in effect, to utilize these desinences for derivational rather than inflectional purposes; cf. also Trypućko 1949 and 1957. In its somewhat unfortunate combination of profound erudition and vivid imagination, Trypučko's bold theory in more than one respect brings to mind Specht's abstruse theorizing about the origin of IE declension, now generally rejected (cf. p. 154, above).

The controversial origin of the OCS dative absolute construction was reexamined by R. Růžička (1961) who stated (592) that

> der dativus absolutus ist ein fester, echter und nicht unproduktiver Bestandteil des syntaktischen Systems der altslavischen Sprache. Unter Echtheit verstehe ich, dass die Konstruktion nicht als gezwungen und unorganisch gelten kann und dass sie sich nicht als fremd zu erkennen gibt. Diese Echtheit ist vereinbar mit der Behauptung, dass der absolute Dativ eine komplizierte syntaktische Entlehnung darstellt.

And he goes on to say (*ibid.*)

> Die Schlüsselfrage ist in jedem Falle, ob die Existenz des dativus absolutus für das Urslavische angenommen werden muss oder nicht.

Subsequently, Růžička arrives at the conclusion (593)

> dass der dativus absolutus in den altslavischen Übersetzungen zum ersten Male auf slavischem Boden erscheint und eine syntaktische Entlehnung aus der griechischen Vorlage ist, freilich keine platte Entlehnung, kein 'calque', sondern eine komplizierte, deren Gestalt und Modifizierung von der Struktur des Altslavischen selbst bestimmt worden ist.

While Růžička thus in the final analysis only considers the choice of the dative (over some other potential case form) as dictated by the semantic-structural factors inherent in the Slavic case system itself, others have subsequently gone one step further considering the Slavic dative absolute either a 'covert category' of CS (as well as several other ancient IE languages) only activated and "raised" under the influence exerted by the Greek model (of the genitive absolute) or even integrating it as an entirely genuine Slavic construction (cf. Birnbaum 1968a: 57-60; 1970b: 43-5; Andersen 1970b). For some additional considerations concerning the origin of Slavic active participial constructions, see also Večerka 1959. It should be noted, incidentally, that both Růžička and

Večerka have worked extensively on the syntax of participles in OCS, each publishing a monograph on the subject
in which the complex and controversial problem of the origin of participial constructions in OCS is discussed at
length. The category of gender in the broad sense (i.e., including the dichotomy animate : inanimate) has not yet been
made the topic of monographic treatment as regards Slavic
diachrony. Nonetheless, many of its peculiarities and
problems have received ample attention not only in systematic textbook coverage but also, for example, in the
discussion of the so-called genitive-accusative in Slavic
beginning with Meillet's early monograph of 1897 treating
the relevant OCS data. Subsequently Meillet returned to
the question of gender in Slavic in a short article (1920a),
viewing this category in its comparative IE context and
using the history of gender in Slavic as an example to
illustrate the conservative and at the same time innovative character of Slavic linguistic evolution. The replacement of the accusative by the corresponding genitive
in the singular of masculine animate nouns, "a well-known
fact attested in all Slavic languages and going back to a
prehistoric period," more recently served J. Kuryłowicz
(1962b) as a point of departure for some considerations on
"personal and animate genders in Slavic" of a primarily
typological nature; cf. on gender in prehistoric Slavic
also Milewski 1950.

While B. Rosenkranz (1958) in his discussion of the
origin of the definite adjectives in Baltic and Slavic was
primarily concerned with formal (and phonological) aspects
of derivation (cf. above, p. 168), J. Kurz's contribution
to the volume in honor of F. Trávníček, published in the
same year (1958), deals largely with syntactic and semantic problems. Suggesting that the close syntactic combination of the (simple) adjective with the anaphoric pronoun (CS *jь*) dates back to the Balto-Slavic period (or its
chronological equivalent), Kurz is inclined to attribute
the morphological synthesization of these two elements
into new, compound lexical units (i.e., long-form, 'definite' adjectives whose crystallization, to some extent at
least, was affected by the gradual syntactic polarization
of an attributive : predicative function) only to a subsequent period of separate CS and Common Baltic.

The emergence of a new word class, assumed by some
linguists and termed by them *category of state* (R *kate-
gorija sostojanija*) or *predicatives*, particularly well-

developed in modern Russian but ascertainable at least in rudimentary form also in other Slavic languages, was studied by A. V. Isačenko (1955). Regardless of whether one accepts this category of words used predicatively as forming a new, separate and clear-cut word class (as claimed, in any event for contemporary standard Russian, by V. V. Vinogradov, Isačenko, and others) or prefers to consider it merely a somewhat loosely clustered group of words, syntactically and semantically interrelated (cf. the generally explicit or implicit presence of the copula verb for these words to express predication and the some-what fuzzy range of this category even in modern Russian, where it is not quite clear, for example, whether short-form adjectives are to be counted among the *category of state* words or not), there can be no doubt that some of the semantic-syntactic characteristics of these *predica-tives* date back to Early Slavic or even CS times as was shown by Isačenko. Yet this eminent Slavist, too, clearly qualifies his position by stating (Isačenko 1955: 58) that

> in CS the normal sentence types were the verb and the copula sentences while sentences without the copula were extremely rare and limited to particular instances. Therefore, the occurrence of a great number of sentences of various types in Russian without the copula is not a direct continuation of the IE or CS state of affairs but an innovation peculiar only to the eastern group of the Slavic languages and manifesting itself in the loss of the copula in the present tense. This innovation be-longs, to judge by the data available, to the pre-historic period.

As was indicated above (p. 165), the verb peri-phrases expressing the future (OCS *imamь*, *xoštǫ*, *-čьnǫ* + infinitive) were not yet fully morphologized in Early Slavic. A study of them undertaken by me some time ago (Birnbaum 1958a) falls therefore largely under the heading of syntax. My relevant monograph, *Untersuchungen zu den Zukunftsumschreibungen mit dem Infinitiv im Altkirchen-slavischen* with the specific subtitle *Ein Beitrag zur his-torischen Verbalsyntax des Slavischen*, focuses on the OCS evidence and attempts to relate this data to its Slavic (as well as other, Balkan and IE) parallels. The Greek models for these expressions are discussed, and a cautious and qualified conclusion is arrived at regarding the pos-sible CS roots of some of these periphrases, particularly the $-\check{c}$ьnǫ + infinitive phrase (see above, pp. 164-5).

Research on Slavic aspectology and especially its prehistoric phase was reported in the section on *Verbal Derivation* (pp. 174-8), as most of the pertinent studies deal both with the formal expression (derivation) and the syntactic (and semantic) function of the category of aspect. Only work addressing itself primarily, if not exclusively, to the question of the functional relationship of aspect and tense, particularly with regard to the prehistoric period of Slavic, was not referred to above and therefore needs brief mention here.

The incompatibility of aspect and tense — and between aorist as a simple past tense form in Slavic (as such opposed to the imperfect) and the aspectual "aorist" meaning inherent in the Greek aorist stem (as opposed to the present stem from which also the Greek imperfect is formed) — within one overall combined aspectual-temporal category, envisaged by some linguists, was demonstrated with extreme clarity using Early Slavic (mostly OCS) data by B. Havránek in his seminal paper "Aspect et temps du verbe en vieux slave" (1939a), contributed to the *Mélanges* for C. Bally. There the Czech Slavist states specifically (229):

> De ce que nous avons exposé ici, il ressort que l'indépendance des systèmes du temps et de l'aspect est dans les langues slaves un fait primaire et que dans les cas où l'on rencontre une confusion de ces deux systèmes, il s'agit d'un fait secondaire . . . Quant au sens futur que le présent des verbes perfectifs exprime en vieux slave, il ne faut pas y voir le résultat d'une confusion des deux systèmes . . .

A fundamentally different (and, in my view, much less convincing) stand concerning the relationships between aspect and tense was taken by A. Belić (1955/56), one of the advocates of an allegedly fully developed aspect system already in CS (cf., e.g., his remark to this effect on p. 9). In the group of verbs with both aspects, known from earlier as well as modern Slavic, Belić saw a residue of the claimed original contrast between an imperfective present and a perfective preterit, i.e., generally speaking, the contrast as found also between the present and the aorist of ancient Greek although, to be sure, expressed by different formal means (cf. especially 9-10). A compromise view, suggesting that the Slavic aorist,

while originally "neutral" vis-à-vis aspect, subsequently
developed into a carrier of the double tense (preterit)
and aspect (perfective) function, was sketched in the concluding chapter on "Der Übergang vom Indogermanischen zum
Slavischen" (128–33) of H. Galton's controversial monograph *Aorist und Aspekt im Slavischen. Eine Studie zur
funktionellen und historischen Syntax* (1962), primarily
discussing the historically attested Slavic evidence on a
comparative basis though occasionally deviating also into
an "Exkurs zum Futurum in den slavischen Sprachen" (88–93)
and engaging in some sharp polemics particularly against
the view of I. Němec who had derived the perfectivity of
certain present stems from their presumed future meaning.
The rise of the future function in the Slavic perfective
present was reexamined with great competence by F. Kopečný
(1962b) who, while in more than one respect in agreement
with Němec's relevant views (rather than with Dostál's),
concludes on a cautious note (180):

> Wenn wir auch die wesenhafte Bedingtheit der Zu-
> kunftsbedeutung beim slavischen perfektiven Präsens
> bestritten und zeigen wollten, dass die Zukunfts-
> bedeutung schon voraspektale Wurzeln hat — so ist
> damit noch nicht gesagt, dass etwa das pf. Präsens
> doch nicht eine bessere Veranlagung zur Futurbe-
> deutung hätte als das imperfektive . . . Der Ver-
> balaspekt entstand . . . mit dem Auftauchen von
> Formen der aktuellen Präsentia vom Typus *sъbirajetь,
> prilětajetь* und *padajetь*. Nach ihrer Entstehung
> wurde das pf. Präsens (*sъberetь, priletitь* usw.)
> immer mehr nur auf die Sphäre der nicht aktuellen,
> eigentlich atemporalen Präsensbedeutung beschränkt —
> während die imperfektiven Neubildungen daneben noch
> die Aufgabe hatten, das echte, aktuelle Präsens zu
> bezeichnen, also funktionell mehr belastet waren.
> Auch deswegen — hauptsächlich aber wegen der Per-
> fektivierung der ingressiven Präsentia bei Beibe-
> haltung ihrer Zukunftsbedeutung — wurde das perfek-
> tive Präsens allmählich auch bei den übrigen Perfek-
> tiva für den Futurgebrauch spezialisiert.

Further, the absence of a separate future tense form in
Slavic — after the prehistoric loss of the IE -*s* future —
is attributed some, though only secondary, importance by
Kopečný. Baltic, where the old -*s* future had been preserved, never developed a full-fledged aspect category,
although the beginnings of a development similar to that

which actually occurred in Slavic (especially in North
Slavic) are evident. The Lithuanian present forms with a
pa- prefix have a similar, basically atemporal function as
that of the perfective presents of South Slavic which in
this respect represents an earlier evolutionary stage.
The situation in CS was, according to Kopečný, strikingly
similar to that of Germanic. And, returning to Havránek's
(and the Prague School's) position, the Czech Slavist
states at the end of his article (181) that, as regards
aspect, the two aspectually marked forms — the present and
the preterit — are unmarked for temporal meaning.

On the borderline between functional syntax proper
and the theory of sentence structure (if this distinction
serves anything more than purely practical purposes), one
may place research pertaining to the use of conjunctions,
this word class linking together both individual words,
phrases, clauses, and occasionally even sentences, or contrasting them. In addition, the study of CS conjunctions
also falls under the heading of Lexicology. Of recent
work in this field, the studies by L. Bednarczuk (1962/63
and especially 1963, lately also 1967) deserve mention.
Thus, of particular interest for our present purpose is
his discussion (1963) of three chronological layers of
paratactic (coordinate) conjunctions in CS, the oldest,
consisting of PS items partly inherited from PIE, being
generally Slavic, the second, resulting from a CS trend
which, however, did not prevail throughout the entire
Slavic linguistic territory, and the third, limited to CS
dialectal innovations. As for the conjunctions of the
earliest layer, it is particularly Bednarczuk's remarks on
a and *i*, their semantic-functional competition and final
distribution (with *i* never finding its way to the westernmost zone of Slavic, including the Resian dialect of Slovenian, Sorbian, Polabian, Slovincian, and part of Kashubian, and *a* retaining and secondarily enhancing its purely
copulative function in Czech and probably also Slovak)
that clarify previously moot points (cf. 1963: 61-2). The
alternative conjunctions *ljubo* and *libo*, though belonging
to different chronological layers, the second and third
(dialectal), respectively, do not merely represent various
evolutionary stages of the same lexical item as the phonetic development known from Czech might seem to suggest
(cf. 1962/63: 15-16; 1963: 63). And *da* as a paratactic
(copulative-adversative) conjunction — in addition to
functioning as a subordinate conjunction, in South Slavic
predominantly so — turns out to be of relatively recent,

dialectal Late CS dating (see 1963: 63-4). For some comments on the IE background of the pleonastic use of paratactic conjunctions in Slavic (discussed in Bednarczuk 1967), see below, p. 294.

5.2. *Studies on the Sentence Structure of Common Slavic.*
More directly concerned with sentence structure is the study of word order within the boundaries of the individual sentence. Insofar as certain conclusions regarding word order in CS can be drawn on the basis of a systematic (or representative) comparison of the relevant evidence of attested Slavic, especially in its earliest historical phase, to be further corroborated by comparative data from other ancient or archaic IE languages, such research is indeed germane to the reconstruction of the basic sentence models of the Slavic protolanguage. An endeavor in precisely this direction was made as early as the turn of the century by E. Berneker with his thesis, published in a somewhat abridged form under the title *Die Wortfolge in den slavischen Sprachen* (1900), a dissertation straight out of the neogrammarian school of his teacher A. Leskien and greatly influenced also by the research of one of the other chief representatives of the same group of linguists, the syntactician B. Delbrück. Analyzing in five chapters the position of the verb in the sentence, of the enclitics, of the case forms (especially the dative and the genitive), of the attribute, and of the infinitive in the chief Slavic languages in their early and modern periods, and distinguishing frequently between the vernacular (substandard) and standard varieties and quoting fairly consistently also parallel Lithuanian evidence, Berneker, in the final, sixth chapter on "word order in Slavic compared to that of the other IE languages," arrives at the conclusion (155) that word order "in sämtlichen slav. Sprachen ist so einheitlich, dass man mit vollem Recht eine urslavische feste Wortstellung annehmen darf, welche die einzelnen Sprachen in ihr Sonderleben mitgenommen und nur wenig umgebildet haben." He then goes on to formulate six general rules governing word order in Slavic:

(1) The (finite) verb originally occupied the first or last place in the sentence. Sentences with the verb in the middle (formula: SVO) were at first rare but gradually achieved equivalent status with the two other typical positions (VSO and SOV).

195

(2)   The enclitics gravitate toward the beginning of
      the sentence and "lean on" the first word of
      the sentence with the strongest stress (Wacker-
      nagel's rule). Where several enclitics come
      together their internal distribution follows
      definite rules.

(3)   The dative normally precedes the accusative of
      the (direct) object in Slavic (as well as in
      Lithuanian). The attributive genitive occupies
      a different place in the two language branches:
      Baltic (Lithuanian) uses it prepositively,
      Slavic postpositively.

(4)   In CS the attributive adjective could precede
      or follow the substantive; the same applies to
      the demonstrative pronoun. Possessive pronouns
      and adjectives would always follow the noun.
      Numerals, at any rate the cardinals, would be
      placed before the substantive. The situation
      in modern Slavic can be derived from this state
      of affairs.

(5)   The infinitive followed the finite verb; the
      object is usually placed in between. Also the
      supine followed the finite verb; however, an
      object, originally always in the genitive,
      would not be inserted but would follow the
      supine. Once the infinitive replaced the su-
      pine, the position of the object could vary,
      either it would retain its final position or it
      would shift into the middle position.

(6)   Words receiving emphatic stress could be sin-
      gled out also positionally in violation of the
      above general rules.

No overall revision of the word order rules as
stated by Berneker has been suggested to date. The closest to such a thorough reformulation of the laws governing
word order in CS and preceding phases of linguistic evolution can be found in the work of V. V. Ivanov, especially
in the syntactic portion of his 1965 monograph on PIE, PS,
and Anatolian, briefly referred to above (pp. 68-9). Particular aspects of Early Slavic word order have, on the
other hand, been studied on the basis of data from one individual language. Thus, for example, M. Widnäs (1953)
has analyzed the position of the adjective in Old Russian,

arriving at the conclusion, contradicting Berneker's view, that the postposition of the attributive adjective is largely of foreign (Byzantine Greek) origin (194). The few corrections of Berneker's findings regarding the position of enclitics and the more precise definitions given by R. Jakobson (1935, reprinted in Jakobson 1962/71, 2: 16-22) affect, at most, certain segments of the Slavic linguistic territory or, rather, some of its underlying Late CS dialects and/or typological groupings; cf., e.g., his assertion, based on a combination of phonological, morphological, and syntactic considerations, that in the Slavic languages with free stress Wackernagel's rule does not apply to inflected enclitics since this rule does not operate in Bulgarian (as shown by Havránek, Seliščev, and Beaulieu) in addition to not being applicable to East Slavic (as Berneker had already realized).

If comparative research on word order in Slavic and attempts to formulate appropriate rules also for the prehistoric period thus address themselves to one facet of the reconstruction of CS sentence structure, serious efforts to retrieve the basic models determining the makeup of the simple and the compound and complex sentence in the Slavic protolanguage have until fairly recently been lacking. To a large extent this is due to the methodological dilemma in which diachronic research on syntax has found itself. In particular, when it comes to reconstructing prehistoric syntactic patterns and models, the methodological difficulties have long seemed almost insurmountable. Thus, for example, the proper assessment of syntactic agreements and conformities, observable among closely related languages (such as Slavic) has often been the subject of heated theoretical debates hinging on the question of whether such coincidences testify to secondary (and perhaps irretrievable) influences occurring between these (or some of these) languages, or whether they instead, or perhaps in addition, point to a common — prehistoric — origin of some of these patterns and models. There is some indication that the emergence, in the framework of generative grammar, of the notion of an underlying, abstract *deep structure*, more generalized than the particular *surface structure* of a given sentence in a specific language (and partly perhaps even maximally generalized, i.e., universal), by grouping and relating some of the fundamental functions expressed in the overt sentence manifestation, may ultimately prove to be a powerful tool in the reconstruction of prehistoric sentence structure;

for further details, cf. Birnbaum 1970b: 9-70, especially
42-7, and below, pp. 292 and 296-7.

The inherent problems of reconstructing the models
of the compound and complex sentence in CS were ably discussed by J. Bauer in his programmatic article "Problema
rekonstrukcii praslavjanskogo složnogo predloženija"
(1958). Pointing to some of the particular difficulties
mentioned above and suggesting ways of overcoming them,
Bauer's summary of his relevant views can be rendered as
follows (54-5): The only way to gain knowledge of the CS
state of affairs is through a thorough study of the development of the compound and complex sentence in the individual Slavic languages and an extension (projection) of
these lines of development into the past. The CS state of
affairs lies at the intersection of the lines of development thus ascertained. In doing so we must pay due attention to the transitional phase — the borderline between
the stage of the compound and complex sentence in the preliterary and in the literary language. At the same time
a comparative semantic analysis has to be carried out of
all the connective (conjunctive) elements whose CS origin
can be considered probable. Here it can be stated that
the grammatical function is usually derived from the lexical meaning (conjunctions frequently developing from
particles, especially deictic ones, and from adverbs).
Also an etymological analysis, applied with discretion,
can be useful by revealing related means in other IE languages. The attempt to sketch an overall picture of the
compound and complex sentence in CS leads to the surprising realization of how few conjunctions can be directly
projected into CS. Not even such commonly used conjunctions as i and a had a distinct and stabilized conjunctive
function. Even less can the means expressing hypotactic
(subordinate) function be posited for CS. This also applies to the conjunctions derived from the old relative
stem *jo-; only the relative pronoun itself was in the
process of emerging during the CS period. The objection
that there may have existed syntactic means that subsequently have disappeared or were replaced by various conjunctions in the individual languages does not withstand
close scrutiny. Each change in the sphere of conjunctions
or relative pronouns represents the result of a restructuring of the compound and complex sentence type as a
whole. Further, it cannot be assumed that the subordination of ideas was expressed asyndetically (Brugmann's
"Hypotaxis ohne grammatische Kennzeichnung"). Not only

grammatical hypotaxis but also the subordination of one idea to another idea developed from original juxtaposition, i.e., from a "free stringing" of clauses. The beginnings of these processes are old, but this development could attain full completion only in the literary language. Additional research will show how far this development had already progressed in CS.

The realization of a research program along the lines sketched by Bauer has just begun, partly with the help of new, powerful techniques. Some of the preliminary results will be briefly reported in a subsequent section on current research in the field of CS syntax (cf. below, pp. 296-8).

6. LEXICOLOGY

6.0. Preliminary Note on the Method and Scope of Lexicology, Especially in Relation to Derivation, as Applied to Common Slavic; General and Theoretical Works. As was indicated before, the precise division between derivational morphology (or, in somewhat broader terms, the theory of word formation) and lexicology is largely a matter of approach and arbitrary categorization. As a general rule one may say, of course, that when the principles of word formation applicable to an individual lexical item are viewed in their paradigmatic context of morpheme concatenation (in particular, affixation, i.e., derivation proper) and in addition, perhaps, are being related to or contrasted with some general principles underlying paradigmatic word form variation by means of inflection, such analysis falls within the realm of derivational morphology (in the broad sense) rather than within that of lexicology. By contrast, where a specific lexical item or a set of such items is juxtaposed with other lexical items of the same or a related meaning, in other words, when it is viewed as a constituent part of a larger "building block" of a language's vocabulary or, at any rate, of some sphere of its word stock, and, especially, where the focus is on lexical meaning as opposed to grammatical function, such research may appropriately be reviewed under the heading of lexicology. Put somewhat differently, derivational morphology deals primarily with the constituent morphemes and the processes operating on them for the purpose of forming words, while lexicology focuses more on the ready lexical items as such and their clustering and grouping into larger semantically defined subdomains of the vocabulary of a language. It goes without saying, that the considerations just suggested in no way draw a clear-cut line between the two fields of linguistic structure; nor can they claim to eliminate all instances of ambiguity as to under which heading a particular phenomenon or process may be treated. Rather, they were suggested here merely to indicate, in a general and informal fashion, the reasons followed in this report for treating research of one kind under one heading, while research with a somewhat different orientation is dealt with under another rubric.

Included in lexicology, as conceived under the broad definition just outlined, are semantics and etymology. Semantics is understood in this context as limited to the study and theory of lexical meaning, i.e., the meaning of individual words, where this meaning may be viewed in terms of its microstructure, that is to say, the hierarchically structured conglomeration of various primary semantic units (semantic features or *primes*) into a complex semantic whole expressed by the linguistic unit *word* (whatever its theoretical definition); or lexical meaning may be conceived in its opposite, macrostructural aspect, that is to say, the meaning of an individual word or one of its constituents (morphemes) is integrated with the appropriate overall semantic categories and their formal expression, together making up all or part of the general structural network of meanings of a given language at a certain stage of its development. To be sure, such a view of lexical semantics may be more theoretical than consistently applied in actual practice, at least as regards the analysis of the pertinent data of CS. Excluded from this largely traditional domain of semantics is, on the other hand, the semantic (or generally semiotic) interpretation of grammatical form at the morphological, syntactic (surface-syntactic), or transformational (deep-syntactic) level, in recent years — and particularly in generative semantic theory — utilized as a powerful tool for linguistic description and explanation. Also etymology, definable as the theory of the original meaning and initial form of attested and/or reconstructed lexical items and their morphemic constituents — resorting for purposes of reconstruction to comparison with cognate data of related languages — is best treated under the cover term of lexicology.

In this context, the largest body of analyzed and explicated lexical data will no doubt be found in the many existing etymological dictionaries, uneven as their quality may be. As regards the CS material, the comparative etymological dictionaries of IE, Balto-Slavic, and, above

all, Slavic in general are of particular importance. Under
the first category, the dictionary by A. Walde (1927/30,
edited by J. Pokorny) used to be the standard reference
work but has now largely been superseded by that of J.
Pokorny (1959/69). For Balto-Slavic as a whole, R. Trautmann (1923) is still the main reference work; its data can
now be supplemented with the material contained in the
Lithuanian etymological dictionary by E. Fraenkel (1962/
65). For the general Slavic data, E. Berneker (1913/14)
served many generations as a useful source of information,
remaining only a torso, however; see now also the recently
launched endeavor of the same kind, still in progress, by
L. Sadnik and R. Aitzetmüller (1963-). Where applicable,
the data, particularly of the general Slavic lexicological
reference works, may be collated with relevant information
contained in etymological dictionaries of ancient languages that may be assumed to have served as sources of
large-scale lexical borrowings by CS; cf., e.g., S. Feist
1939, for Gothic. Also the selected comparative and partly processed vocabulary data listed in The Basic All-
Slavic Word Stock (*Základní všeslovanská slovní zásoba*
1964), provisionally published (as working materials) by
a team of researchers of the Brno Etymological Section of
the Institute of Languages and Literatures of the Czecho-
slovak Academy of Sciences under the editorship of F.
Kopečný, is overwhelmingly CS: cf. the statement by the
editor (p. 4) that only about half a percent of the nearly
two thousand items listed are of post-CS origin (dating,
to be sure, the end of the CS period to the 10th century).

    Of almost equal significance for reconstructing the
vocabulary of CS are further the various etymological dictionaries of individual Slavic languages, beginning with
OCS (cf. L. Sadnik & R. Aitzetmüller 1955, with a special
etymological section, 211-341) and going on to the other
Slavic languages: Bulgarian (cf. S. Mladenov 1941, and
more recently the collective Bulgarian etymological dictionary now in progress, edited by V. Georgiev *et al.*
1962-; see also V. Georgiev 1960); Serbo-Croatian (cf. the
posthumously, belatedly published work by P. Skok 1971/73);
Russian (cf. of older publications A. Preobraženskij 1910/
14 & 1949, now largely replaced by M. Vasmer 1953/58, annotated Russian version, 1964/73; see further also the
generally much less successful attempt in this area by N.
M. Šanskij 1963-); Ukrainian (cf. J. B. Rudnyc'kyj 1962-);
Polish (cf. the semi-scholarly etymological dictionary by
A. Brückner 1927, [2]1957, now quite obsolete and superseded

by the much more reliable work of F. Sławski 1952-);
Polabian (see T. Lehr-Spławiński & K. Polański 1962-);
and Czech (cf. J. Holub & F. Kopečný [3]1952) as well as
Czech and Slovak combined (cf. the generally very well-
researched dictionary by V. Machek 1957b).

Research in the field of Slavic comparative etymology, including CS etymology, in the fifties and partly
also in the early sixties was centered primarily in Brno
and Cracow, but activity in this field has somewhat slowed
down there in recent years, particularly after the death
of the leading scholars engaged in the reconstruction of
the vocabulary of CS, V. Machek and T. Lehr-Spławiński.
Yet efforts are being continued locally by equally competent specialists, F. Kopečný and E. Havlová in Brno, F.
Sławski and K. Polański in Cracow (and Poznań/Katowice) to
mention only the most prominent experts in the field (cf.
also *Słownik prasłowiański* 1961, and *Etymologický slovník
slovanských jazyků* 1966). More recently, a new center for
Slavic comparative and CS etymological research has become
increasingly active in Moscow where O. N. Trubačev is
heading a group of promising scholars working under the
auspices of the Soviet Academy of Sciences. A foretaste
of the major work to come from this group can be found in
the series of "Slavic etymologies" — now totaling 47
items — by Trubačev, appearing in various publications
during the late fifties and early sixties (cf. Trubačev
1957c, 1957d, 1958, 1959b, 1960b, 1960c, 1962, 1964a,
1964b). Another testimony of the major project now in
preparation is the same scholar's sample prepublication of
his and his associates' forthcoming Slavic etymological
dictionary (cf. Trubačev 1963a; see more recently also
Trubačev 1967b). To be sure, a certain division of labor
between the Moscow and Cracow groups (one working on an
etymological dictionary of the Slavic languages, the other
one on a dictionary of CS) now seems to have been tentatively envisaged. Cf. further also the irregular publication of annual volumes titled *Ètimologija* under the chief
editorship of Trubačev, containing contributions by members of the Moscow group as well as by other Soviet and
foreign scholars (1963, 1965, 1967, 1968, 1969, and 1971).
See now also Kopečný 1972.

Problems of theory and method in the field of Slavic
etymology and lexical reconstruction, based on the experience of published as well as heretofore unpublished research, were tackled in a number of special articles and
state-of-the-art reports authored by F. Sławski (1957),

T. Lehr-Spławiński jointly with F. Sławski (1958), and Z. Gołąb and K. Polański (1960), all largely drawing on the Cracow project initiated by Lehr-Spławiński, and, on the other hand, by O. N. Trubačev (1957b, 1963d), giving an account of his and his group's current work and defining future research tasks.

6.1. Studies on the Common Slavic Vocabulary Inherited from Indo-European. The brief references and comments given in the following two sections of this chapter on lexicology cannot, of course, claim to provide even a fairly representative selection of studies of the CS word stock inherited from pre-Slavic IE (viz., from PIE or post-PIE dialectal IE). For a highly selective listing of works on the inherited vocabulary (G *Erbwortschatz*) of CS, the reader is referred to the titles marked for Lexicology (i.e., V, especially V:2 and V:3) in the appended Bibliography. Also, works previously mentioned in this report in a different context will, as a rule, be omitted in the following discussion. The titles cited or briefly referred to will merely serve the purpose of exemplification, not of representative or systematic coverage. At any rate, the sheer volume of specialized studies in this field precludes a more ambitious attempt as that would far exceed the stringent limits of a state-of-the-art report such as this.

Among writings by A. Meillet not referred to before, his two studies of 1925, subsumed under the common title "Les origines du vocabulaire slave," discussing two different sets of problems (1. "Le problème de l'unité balto-slave" in the light of lexicological evidence, and 2. "De quelques noms de nombre") deserve mention. Of considerable and lasting scholarly weight are also several of the scattered relevant studies by J. Zubatý, usually viewing the Slavic evidence in its IE context, which were assembled posthumously in a volume of *Studie a články* (1: *Výklady etymologické a lexikální*, č. 1-2, 1945/54). Other minor contributions to Slavic comparative, mostly Balto-Slavic, lexicology and etymology, published prior to 1965, include studies by F. P. Preveden (1932, on "Some Balto-Slavic Terms of Acoustic Perception"), M. Vasmer (1957, on two Balto-Slavic word equations), C. S. Stang (1957a, on a Prussian-Slavic or possibly general Baltic-Slavic special agreement in word formation, represented by the Slavic prepositions in -*dъ*: *nadъ*, *podъ*, **perdъ*, and some related items), V. V. Ivanov (1958, on the Balto-Slavic name of the god of thunder, Lith *Perkúnas*, Slavic *Perunъ*), and V. Machek (1957a), dealing with common Italic(Latin)-Slavic etyma, collocating such items as *caperrāre* : **korpati, dubāre* : *dъbati, dūrāre* : *trъvati, fovēre* : *xovati, lacere* : *lakati*, G *locken*. On Italic-Slavic lexical correspondences, see also Safarewicz 1963 and 1964.

    While the studies just quoted all viewed Slavic lexicology and etymology from a comparative IE angle, another approach was taken in a number of different investigations proceeding from the lexical data of one particular Slavic language and tracing it back to its CS past. The first and best known of these studies is T. Lehr-Spławiński's 1938 contribution to the *festschrift* for S. Kutrzeba, "Element prasłowiański w dzisiejszym słownictwie polskim," listing and classifying a substantial body of relevant modern Polish lexical items and allowing for some important statistical and other inferences; cf. more recently also Orłoś 1958 (for Czech), and Radewa 1963 (for Bulgarian). By contrast, the singling out as such of the CS lexical heritage was not the main purpose of L. Wanstrat's characterization of a segment of the contemporary Russian vocabulary (1933); rather, the author had set out to define various, essentially chronological, layers of the exclusively Russian word stock. In doing so and by further restricting the scope of her dissertation to those inherited lexical items (*Erbwörter*) which have undergone some semantic or formal modification on Russian (or generally East Slavic) soil, Wanstrat excludes, for example, such words of CS origin as *v'juga* 'blizzard' or *ljaguša* 'frog' (cf. 2-4), and discusses only a highly selective list of modified lexical items inherited from prehistoric times (6-29). She makes an exception to her own criteria for inclusion only in the case of *devjanosto* '90' where she posits CS and, tentatively, even PIE protoforms and assumes no basic change of meaning or, at most, only a slight one from 'small hundred' to 'ninety' (29-30; cf. now, however, also the slightly different treatment by Stang 1965). Moreover, she lists a number of etymologically obscure words, some of them possibly of CS origin (98-107). While today largely superseded by more recent research, especially that of her own teacher, M. Vasmer, Wanstrat's study nonetheless deserves mention as a relatively early and methodologically interesting attempt at projecting lexical data of one Slavic language back into the CS period. O. N. Trubačev set a similar task for himself when discussing the CS lexical dialectisms preserved in Sorbian (1963c) even though this was not intended as a systematic endeavor and the Soviet linguist had recourse to a much more advanced methodology.

Telling examples of the inextricable intermeshing of derivational morphology and lexicology (especially in its etymological aspect) are provided by the studies by A. V. Isačenko (1954, on the neuters in *-men, representing one of the oldest layers of the "basic word stock of Slavic") and the predominantly theoretical considerations of Ž. Ž. Varbot (1963a), illustrated with Slavic data, largely ancient and reconstructed. Among the lexical items covered by Varbot in this article is the adjective *naglъ* 'sudden', previously treated in its comparative (Slavic as well as IE) context by P. Tedesco 1951 (also discussing, with a semantic emphasis, another Slavic adjective, *pilьnъ* 'diligent', boldly considered by the American Indo-Europeanist a formational variant of OCS, etc., *priležьnъ* with the same meaning). Subsequently, Varbot returned to the etymology of *naglъ(jь)*, proposing a different explanation and discussing, along with it, also some other etymologically controversial items (1965). Of somewhat earlier etymological studies of individual CS adjectives, we may quote C. S. Stang's brief article (1949) on *istъ*, its IE parallels and a possible Slavic cognate (*prisnъ*). Examples of recent contributions attempting to further elucidate etymologies of CS nouns (and partly verbs) are the articles by W. Krogmann (1956, on *gospodъ*, cf. more recently also Machek 1968), V. I. Abaev (1957, on *mědъ*), E. Nieminen (1957, on *gatję/ě*), V. N. Toporov (1963, on *myslъ*), A. Vaillant (1963, on *rota*, rejecting, as was already mentioned, the applicability of "Lidén's law" to this item), and Ž. Ž. Varbot (1963b, on *vad-*, encountered as root morpheme in both verbal and nominal formations).

Semantic considerations, of course, play a prominent role in many of the above listed etymological studies. However, in none of them (possibly with the exception of Tedesco 1951) are the semantic factors the clearly decisive ones. In the following, a few additional studies on CS lexicology, including etymology, shall be quoted in which various lexical items are grouped together primarily on the grounds of their semantic affinity and close coherence. Most of these studies can therefore be said to investigate an entire, more or less well-defined "semantic field," without, however, excluding other, phonological and morphological, considerations altogether from examina-

tion. In some instances, as will be noted, an individual
study may analyze, to be sure, only one particular lexical
(or morphemic) item, but the overall scope of the relevant
research of the investigator concerned (in the case used
here as an example, G. Jacobsson) ranges over a whole,
generally clearly defined area of related concepts. A
sampling of additional studies with a still more one-sided
semantic focus will be discussed in the following section
of this presentation. Here, as on other, previous occasions, the line separating the two categories of studies
is somewhat artificial and had to be drawn rather arbitrarily.

   Because of its usually archaic shape and inherent
archaic structure, kinship terminology has often been
chosen as a word group particularly lending itself to in-
depth semantic examination. As far as the Slavic material
is concerned, an important attempt at sketching a synthesis of the CS nomenclature of terms designating family relations, viewed in their IE setting, was undertaken some
time ago by A. V. Isačenko (1953); in this study the
emerging hierarchic-sociological kinship structure is, in
general, solidly backed up by linguistic data, some of it
newly interpreted. Isačenko's linguistically well-argued,
often quite imaginative reasoning — operating on the assumption that the IE kinship terminology reflected in
Slavic came into being during an epoch of matriarchal
social order — would probably have made an even greater
impact on future research in this subfield of Slavic semantics (some controversial etymologies and a thin coat of
ideological, Marxist, phraseology notwithstanding), had it
not soon been superseded by an even more thoroughly researched study on more or less the same subject by the
leading Soviet etymologist, O. N. Trubačev. After some
preliminary work in a related area (Trubačev 1957a), he
published his monograph *Istorija slavjanskix terminov
rodstva i nekotoryx drevnejšix terminov obščestvennogo
stroja* (1959a). Conceived on a broad comparative basis,
both within Slavic and against its IE background, this
study covers in three extensive chapters (1) the terms of
blood relationships, (2) relationships by marriage, and
(3) designations closely connected with kinship terminology as well as some ancient terms denoting social institutions. In chapter two Trubačev also discusses Slavic
nevěsta, rejecting both Trubeckoj's earlier explanation
(cf. pp. 167-8) and Isačenko's more recent attempt to
again link this term with *vedǫ*, *vesti* (cf. Lat *uxorem*

207

ducere). Instead, he subscribes to the more traditional etymology of this word, adhered to also by M. Vasmer, as **ne-věsta* 'the unknown one' (90-5). Opening with a general introduction which discusses theoretical problems and surveys previous relevant research, and rounded out by some concluding remarks on some derivational aspects germane to kinship terminology, Trubačev's excellent monograph will long remain the most important piece of relevant research, serving at the same time as a useful reference tool in this particular segment of Slavic lexicology and semantics, which to a large extent was inherited from (P)IE. Of minor contributions in this field that have appeared since, E. Stankiewicz's article (1962) on "The Etymology of Common Slavic **vъnǫkъ/*vъnukъ*" may be noted.

Among other etymological-semantic studies examining a particular segment of the CS (and Balto-Slavic) vocabulary, the research pertaining to various time notions and their linguistic expression (as well as some semantically now seemingly removed but formally cognate, and, to be sure, originally also semantically related items), conducted over a number of years by G. Jacobsson, deserve mention; cf. Jacobsson 1947 and 1960 (on Slavic *lěto*), 1958b (on *časъ*), 1958a and 1961 (on Balto-Slavic **temp-* 'to cut', claimed to be related to Lat *tempus*). See now further Jacobsson 1969. In this connection E. Nieminen's earlier mentioned essay of 1956 on Slavic (*j*)*ustro*, (*j*)*utro* and cognates (cf. Lith *aušrà*, Latv *àustra*, Lat *aurōra*, etc.) comes to mind as an example of a similar kind of investigation. Yet another lexical domain particularly suited for a systematic and comparative semantic analysis, because of its indistinct objective transitions for one thing, is that of the color spectrum, studied for Slavic by G. Herne (1954), among others.

Botanical terminology is another semantic area whose core lexical items, whether inherited in CS from pre-Slavic times or definable as ultimately borrowed from another adjacent language group (cf., e.g., the Germanic origin of the name of the beech in Slavic), may provide significant data for a better understanding of certain aspects of the prehistory of the Slavs, their everyday life and their earliest settlement. Their proper etymological analysis is therefore not without consequences. Of recent work in this field, the contributions by V. A. Merkulova on some principles of etymologizing botanical terms (1965a) and on relative chronology with regard to Slavic mushroom designations (1965b) can be quoted as examples. Among older studies, those on the Slavic name of the oak (with derivations, CS *dǫbъ*, *dǫbrava*, etc.) are typical (cf., e.g., Lehr-Spławiński 1937b, also discussing the etymology of Slavic *ognь*; Falk 1958; more recently also Otrębski 1966/67, viewing *dǫbъ*, etc., as an instance of nasal infixation).

Semantic considerations play an important role but are not the only aspect under which the CS root morpheme *kot-* is treated by V. N. Toporov (1962) who, despite the formal resemblance and semantic closeness, assumes no direct connection between *kotъ*/*kotę* 'cat, kitten' and the root in *kotiti* (*sę*) 'to litter', etc. (cf. also Trubačev 1960a: 97-8). More than merely considerations of meaning also enter, for example, into V. A. Merkulova's discussion (1963) of the Slavic (and ultimately CS) word family exhibiting the root morpheme *-žab-* (cf. *žaba* 'frog', etc.); cf. also Plevačevá 1968.

6.2. Research Specifically Focusing on Common Slavic Semantics (Lexical Meaning).

The studies quoted or referred to in the preceding section, and particularly in its latter part, all have a heavy semantic emphasis while, in most instances, taking into consideration other — phonological, morphological, etc. — factors as well. Nonetheless, many of them could equally well have been listed in this section of the present report discussing work with a primary focus on CS semantics. In the following, a few additional titles whose orientation is predominantly toward — lexical — meaning shall be briefly surveyed.

From a theoretical point of view the most interesting single contribution in this field, in the opinion of this writer, is the book *Slavjanskie jazykovye modelirujuščie semiotičeskie sistemy: Drevnij period* (1965) by V. V. Ivanov and V. N. Toporov. Following the line of research begun with the same two linguists' joint 1963 congress paper on the reconstruction of a CS text and continuing their discussion in the volume mentioned with a section on "some fragments of reconstructed Slavic texts" (218-39), briefly mentioned above (p. 185), the bulk of this monograph deals, in two major sections, with "some fragments of the Slavic model of the world" (analyzing the primary religious system, i.e., the Slavic pantheon proper, 11-62) and with some aspects of "the question of reconstructing the content plane of the ancient Slavic religious system" (63-217). Drawing heavily on contemporary

structural approaches to comparative IE mythology and
anthropology (especially as expounded in the writings of
C. Lévi-Strauss) and utilizing the method of "semiotic
modeling," elaborated among Soviet linguists and logicians
(among them, I. I. Revzin, the official reviewer-editor of
this book, and A. A. Zaliznjak), the Soviet scholars also
incorporate in their theoretical framework some of the semantic and typological insights of the glossematic (Copenhagen) school of linguistics and at the same time acknow-
ledge the advice of R. Jakobson in matters of Slavic
mythology, philology, and etymology. They provide a systematic analysis and interpretation of the functional
characteristics and relationships of the attested Slavic
pagan deities (*Velesъ/Volosъ, Dažьbogъ, Mokošь, Perunъ,
Svarogъ, Stribogъ, Svętovitъ, Triglavъ, Jarovitъ*, etc.)
and suggest a few general conclusions bearing on the reconstructed language as well as on the world view of the
prehistoric Slavs. In the second section the emphasis is
primarily on a semantic analysis of some fundamental
antinomies: fortune/misfortune, life/death, right/left,
top/bottom, sky/earth, south/north, sea/dry land, day/
night, spring/winter, sun/moon, light/dark, own/alien,
male/female, old(er)/young(er), sacred/wordly (with many
variants and subtypes), etc. — all of which are conceived
as serving as a kind of set of semantic distinctive features for the definition of the earliest Slavic religious
system. Two shorter chapters on the possibility of describing this system at various semantic-mythological
levels and on some pertinent typological aspects conclude
this section. While it may be said, perhaps, that the
very general title of Ivanov's and Toporov's book promises
in scope even more than it actually offers, their accom-
plishment in capturing an important portion of Slavic
mythology and reality as linguistically conceptualized in
a remote, preliterary period has brought about not only a
deeper understanding of some concrete Slavic data known
earlier, but also marks a major advance in developing a
new methodology for covering and semantically interpreting
large segments of the vocabulary of a lost, reconstructed
language.

As for contributions to the problem of reconstruct-
ing the original, prehistoric meaning of an individual
Slavic lexical item, reference was already made to G.
Jacobsson's 1960 article "Polysemie und semantische Struk-
tur," subtitled "Betrachtungen anlässlich des slavischen
Wortes *lěto*" and constituting a theoretical sequel, as it

were, to his earlier in-depth study of this word in Slavic (1947).

The orientation is also primarily semantic in the 1954 study "Abstraktní význam u nejstarších vrstev slovanských substantiv (kmenů souhláskových)" by A. Mátl, a member of the Brno etymological group, even though he deliberately limits his material on morphological grounds to the original consonantal stems, these archaic formations, including their secondary modifications, exhibiting a tendency for abstract meaning of various degrees (cf. also Birnbaum 1972a). The opening remarks, paying lip service to the "wisdom" of Stalin also in linguistic matters, should not detract from the otherwise considerable merits of Mátl's contribution.

Preliminary to his more comprehensive monograph on the Slavic terminology of craftsmanship (1966) to be discussed below (pp. 307-8), O. N. Trubačev's study "Formirovanie drevnejšej remeslennoj terminologii v slavjanskom i nekotoryx drugix indoevropejskix dialektax" (1963b) focuses especially on the CS data while drawing on a broad spectrum of comparative Slavic material. Among the results arrived at by examination of the relevant evidence and particularly the Early Slavic textile designations are some revealing statistical conclusions: compared to six reliable Slavic-Baltic lexical-derivational agreements, there are sixteen, i.e., almost three times as many, Slavic-Germanic correspondences in this semantic subfield (33). And in summing up his analysis, Trubačev singles out two basic observations: on the lexical level — a marked quantitative predominance of Slavic-Germanic and Slavic-Latin correspondences over incontestable Slavic-Baltic ones; on the derivational level (cf. the influential model in *-dhlo/*-tlo) — a clear predominance of Slavic-Latin formational agreements over other correspondences, including some indisputable Slavic-Baltic ones.

Another area of semantics that Trubačev explored was the origin of the Slavic designations for domestic animals; cf. his study *Proisxoždenie nazvanij domašnix životnyx v slavjanskix jazykax* (1960). Here, too, he was able to come up with some interesting and important results, pointing to cognates in other IE languages and evaluating competing etymologies, and to rather firmly establish the CS and partly pre-CS origin of a number of names for domestic animals attested, in part, only by some but not all Slavic languages. In this context it seems surprising that in her thorough investigation of the

Slavic nomenclature pertaining to live nature (*Słowiańskie słownictwo dotyczące przyrody żywej*, 1965), containing also a special chapter on "names of domestic animals" (55-78), W. Budziszewska fails to make any reference to Trubačev's relevant study, published several years earlier. Budziszewska's otherwise impressive monograph covers, in addition, designations for the body, its parts, organs, etc. (11-54) as well as names of wild animals (79-164). Part two (165-290) investigates Slavic plant and tree names, another layer of the vocabulary comprising many archaic or at any rate early items. Designed at first as a study of the relevant West Slavic data (with the focus on Polish, but examining also the cognate evidence of Polabian, Sorbian, Czech and Slovak), the Polish linguist's original scope was soon broadened to include also Ukrainian, South Slavic, and ultimately the rest of the Slavic languages. The primary goal of her investigation was to identify lexical items of considerable range (i.e., occurring in more than one Slavic language) and antiquity, including also early loans into CS; on the other hand, the specialized, professional terminology of zoology and botany, not belonging to the everyday vocabulary, was excluded from her consideration. In a fairly lengthy final chapter, summing up the conclusions of her study (291-327), Budziszewska arrives at a somewhat different picture of the earliest grouping of the Slavic languages — or, rather, their prehistoric predecessors, the Late CS dialects — using the occurrence and frequency of certain terms pertaining to living beings (and their parts) as a yardstick, as compared to the traditional classifications based on phonological and grammatical criteria. Quite revealing are also her findings as to the degree of stability in the core vocabulary of this particular semantic subfield and its determining factors. A detailed word index and two appended diagrams showing the distribution of selected, diagnostic items further enhance the value of this generally useful reference work.

As examples of some other recent studies relevant to CS lexicology and having a semantic emphasis, the two articles on Slavic terms for peasant and serf written by H. Schuster-Šewc (1964b) and V. Machek (1965c), deserve mention (on one of the items discussed, *smrъdъ*, see now also Aitzetmüller 1971). Also Z. Stieber's brief contribution (1965a) on CS *věža* (*veža*), again connecting it with *voziti*, and suggesting two different original meanings, 'entrance hall, gate' in the dialects underlying South and

West Slavic, 'caravan, tent-covered vehicle' in East Slavic (attested in this meaning in Old Russian), both apt to
yield the secondary meaning 'tower', found in a large portion of North Slavic, could be cited in this context.   On
some further specialized studies, published even more recently (after 1965), see below, pp. 305-8.

6.3. *Studies on Lexical Borrowing in Common Slavic.*
Lexical borrowing in CS turns out to be a two-way street.
In other words, we know of a sizable number of lexical
items borrowed by CS from another, usually adjacent language or language group; on the other hand, instances are
also known where Slavic lexical material was borrowed into
another language during the period of relative CS unity
or, in particular, toward the end of this period, i.e., in
the time of increasing Late CS dialectal disintegration.
The study of both kinds of phenomena contributes substantially to our overall conception of CS.

When it comes to the study of individual CS loanwords from other languages and, to a lesser extent, lexical borrowings from prehistoric Slavic in other languages,
the results of the accumulated research in this field are,
again, most readily available in the various etymological
dictionaries, Slavic as well as non-Slavic. The student
interested in a particular lexical item or group of items
should therefore first consult these standard reference
works. However, in what follows we will briefly survey
some of the more important areas of research on which the
relevant data of these dictionaries is based or — where we
deal with relatively recent publications — from which the
results will be culled and digested in future etymological
dictionaries (or as yet outstanding sequels of such work)
and in new, improved editions of already existing ones.

In this context we must disregard, at least for the
time being, the language group most closely related to
Slavic, i.e., Baltic, since it is virtually impossible to
distinguish between, on the one hand, commonly inherited
lexical items (in a number of instances retained exclusively in Baltic and Slavic; cf. Trautmann 1923) and, on
the other hand, potential prehistoric loanwords which have
penetrated from Baltic into CS or vice versa, from CS into
Baltic (or into one of the preliterary Baltic languages or
dialects). Later, post-CS loanwords in Baltic (say,
Lekhitic or even more specifically Polish in Old Prussian,
Polish or Belorussian in Lithuanian, etc.) can, as a rule,
be reasonably well ascertained and identified as to their

immediate source language on the basis of phonological and other linguistic criteria.

The linguistic contacts between CS and other language groups that have found their expression in a considerable number of borrowed lexical items pertain particularly to Germanic and Iranian. Of non-related languages, it is primarily Finno-Ugric that has long been considered as potentially entering into such contacts, to be sure mostly on the receiving end, already in CS or, at any rate, Late CS times. Other linguistic contacts involving prehistoric lexical loans from or to Slavic (e.g., with Latin, including Late Latin or Early Balkan Romance, Greek, Celtic) are of more subordinate importance while in some instances not without significance for considerations of chronology (cf. below, pp. 231-2, and esp. Bidwell 1961).

As regards the field of prehistoric Germanic-Slavic loan relations, the unsurpassed standard work is still V. Kiparsky's 1934 dissertation *Die gemeinslavischen Lehnwörter aus dem Germanischen*, essentially superseding also the monograph on a closely related subject by A. Stender-Petersen, *Slavisch-Germanische Lehnwortkunde*, published a few years earlier (1927). Previous research in the field has been thoroughly and critically scrutinized by Kiparsky, and the results, where generally tenable (as, e.g., in the case of K. Knutsson's solid study on *Die germanischen Lehnwörter im Slavischen vom Typus* buky, 1929), have been utilized and incorporated. After having reviewed, in the introduction to his book, the methods and results of the preceding relevant research, Kiparsky subsequently arranges his material in three major groups: (1) words that cannot be considered CS loanwords from Germanic — assertions to the contrary notwithstanding; (2) genuine CS loanwords from Germanic; and (3) controversial instances. Kiparsky concludes with a section, drawing phonological inferences about sound correspondences in nonfinal syllables, about the treatment of auslaut as well as stress and intonation. Of particular interest is, naturally, the section discussing the genuine CS loans from Germanic (165-270). Here, after having set the *terminus a quo* for Germanic-Slavic linguistic contacts to the third century B. C., i.e., after the first (Germanic) consonant shift, Kiparsky then proceeds to analyze the Slavic loans from Proto-Germanic, Gothic, Balkan Germanic, and West Germanic dialects. In the first section, reviewing the lexical material that cannot be considered CS borrow-

214

ing from Germanic, the chapter on those words which themselves are the source of their alleged Germanic models
(96-101) is of particular interest. Kiparsky's and
Stender-Petersen's findings as well as some additional
minor contributions to the field (by R. Ekblom, K. Knutsson, T. Lehr-Spławiński , and others) were subsequently
critically reviewed by J. Kuryłowicz in an article
"Związki językowe słowiańsko-germańskie" (1951). While
agreeing with many of Kiparsky's (and partly also Stender-
Petersen's) conclusions, Kuryłowicz criticized both scholars for not having sufficiently taken into consideration
the overall structure of the languages involved (having
important repercussions, for example, as regards the adaptation of gender) and added some keen observations relevant to prosody (quantity and accentuation) in connection
with lexical borrowing from Germanic to Slavic. Of more
recent studies in the field of Slavic-Germanic lexical
relations it is in particular the pertinent writings of
V. V. Martynov that deserve to be mentioned here. Having
outlined his basic theoretical position in a previous
paper (Martynov 1961; cf. also Martynov 1963a), the Soviet
linguist in his monograph *Slavjano-germanskoe leksičeskoe
vzaimodejstvie drevnejšej pory. K probleme prarodiny
slavjan* (1963b) attempted to substantiate his adherence to
the "western" (or "autochthonic," i.e., Vistula-Oder)
hypothesis of the original homeland of the Slavs by reexamining the entire body of potentially eligible lexical
data. Breaking up his material into two main sections,
one discussing the "lexical penetrations and borrowings
from Proto-Germanic into CS" (43-107), the other reviewing, analogically, the "lexical penetrations and borrowings from CS into Proto-Germanic" (108-234) and subgroup-
ing his data in each section into three chapters of decreasing relative reliability, Martynov uses this data
primarily as an important — in his view, the single most
important — argument in favor of the "western" hypothesis
of the CS homeland. The published portion of his relevant
research only covers the period 5th century B. C. through
1st century A. D. and excludes the period not relevant to
the corroboration of this hypothesis, the 2nd to 5th centuries A. D. (yielding Gothic - CS and West Germanic - CS
evidence). While no doubt contributing some new, interesting etymological interpretations and modifying, in some
respects, previously held views, Martynov's monograph cannot, in my opinion, be considered an unqualified success
in what it sets out to prove: generally speaking, his

reasoning seems not to have added substantially to the likelihood of the western, Vistula-Oder hypothesis of the original sites of the Slavs.

Turning now to the early Slavic-Iranian relations as reflected in the Slavic vocabulary (whereas any potential Slavic impact on the word stock of one of the Old Iranian languages or dialects is mostly irretrievable or, at any rate, minor to negligible), it should first be pointed out that the more or less agreed upon Iranian component in the oldest lexical strata of Slavic appears surprisingly small in view of the well-established fact of a century-long symbiosis of Slavs and Iranians (Scythians, Sarmatians, etc.) in the "Pontic" area north of the Black Sea (cf. the onomastic and other evidence examined especially by M. Vasmer 1923 and 1924). Possibly this alone, it has been argued, would speak against any even tentative placing of the original homeland of the ancient Slavs very far to the southeast. A skeptical attitude toward Slavic lexical borrowing from Iranian was taken by A. Meillet who, in addition to treating this problem in some of his various manuals, devoted a special article to the common aspects of the ancient Slavic and Indo-Iranian vocabulary (1926). According to the French comparatist, the only incontestable ancient Slavic item borrowed from Iranian is *toporъ* 'axe, hatchet'. Subsequently, the pertinent data was reviewed in the lexical portion of H. Arntz's 1933 study *Sprachliche Beziehungen zwischen Arisch und Balto-Slawisch* (35-57; cf. also 58-63: "Kultur- und Lehnwortbeziehungen") and again, now taking into consideration all relevant previous research and applying an advanced, modern method, by A. A. Zaliznjak in his article "Problemy slavjano-iranskix jazykovyx otnošenij drevnejšego perioda" (1962, especially 30-41: "Predpolagaemye zaimstvovanija iz iranskogo v praslavjanskij ili v vostočnoslavjanskij"; of more recent contributions to this problem, see also Benveniste 1967, Trubačev 1967a, and Toporov 1971).

Latin occupies a prominent place among other possible IE source languages for CS loanwords. The relevant lexical material was screened by T. Lehr-Spławiński in his article "Les emprunts latins en slave commun" (1929; Polish version, "Zapożyczenia łacińskie w języku prasłowiańskim," 1957), listing a considerable number of items presumably borrowed from Latin into CS. Comparing the accentual treatment of loanwords from Latin with those from Germanic, Lehr-Spławiński arrives at the conclusion that only long stressed syllables in words of Latin

provenance were perceived by the Slavic hearer as corresponding to acute intonation, thus retaining the original
place of stress, while the stress on short Latin syllables was identified by the Slavic hearer as circumflex
(or neoacute) intonation of the pretonic syllable and
therefore caused a stress shift to the following — usually
final — syllable. According to the Polish Slavist, the
reason for the different perception of Latin and Germanic
stressed syllables can be found either in chronological
differences or in the qualitative difference of stressed
syllables in Germanic as compared to Latin. Lehr-Spławiński's concluding appeal for a thorough examination to define the exact period and area, i.e., precisely when and
where Latin lexical items penetrated into Slavic has, in
part at least, found its response in C. E. Bidwell's revealing study of 1961, to be briefly discussed below (pp.
231-2).   While Bidwell focused primarily on the Western
Balkans and adjoining areas, less is known about Vulgar
Latin words that may have penetrated into Late CS from the
Eastern Balkans (i.e., in particular, present-day Romania).
Certainly one can only agree with those scholars who reject G. Gunnarsson's attempt (1937) to derive the Slavic
word for 'church' (OCS *crъky*) from Rom *beserecă, biserică*
< Lat *basilica*, assuming truncation of the first syllable,
rather than from Germanic **kirikō* (cf. OBav *kirkō*) or Gk
κυρι(α)κόν (cf. more recently also Menges 1966). As for
Greek loanwords in Slavic, they seem to stem largely from
the earliest literary (OCS, Old Russian) period of Slavic
linguistic evolution, while previous linguistic contacts
between Greeks and Slavs, beginning in the 6th-7th centuries (cf. above, p. 13), are evidenced by onomastic
(mostly toponymic and hydronymic) material; cf. further in
particular Vasmer 1941b.
    Among neighboring non-IE languages, some exhibit
borrowings that possibly, in part at least, may go back to
a prehistoric (CS, Early Slavic) period. Thus, as shown
particularly in I. Kniezsa's unfinished major monograph on
the Slavic loanwords of Hungarian, *A magyar nyelv szláv
jövevénszavai* (1: 1-2, 1955), a certain portion of the
borrowings from Slavic found in Hungarian cannot be easily
identified in terms of one particular Slavic source language or even language group. Many of these items may
therefore have entered Hungarian already during its speakers' first settlement in Pannonia, previously inhabited by
Slavs, and in the course of the frequent incursions by the
militant Magyar nomads or semi-nomads into Slavic-held

territory. The assumption that a number of Hungarian loanwords originated from Late CS or one of its dialects thus appears fully conceivable.

On the other hand, the genuinely CS (= PS) origin of Slavic loanwords in Finnic, especially Baltic Finnic, seems less likely. Thus, while J. Kalima (1929, 1955, and elsewhere) still assumed at least the possibility of a certain, to be sure, relatively small portion of the Baltic Finnic lexical borrowings as dating back to a period of undifferentiated CS (PS), E. Nieminen (1957b) took a much more cautious position, ascertaining that "by a closer analysis of the phonetic form of words of Slavic origin existing in the Baltic Finnic languages it is easy to convince oneself that the majority of words assumed to be loans from CS do not permit one to narrowly define the period of their borrowing. These words can be derived equally well also from the language of the Eastern Slavs, viz., from Old Russian of the prehistoric period" (497). And returning to his basic assumption, Nieminen further states (501) that "I do not consider conclusive those words which are cited by scholars in support of their thesis that the oldest stratum of Baltic Finnic borrowings from Slavic dates back to as early a period as that of CS". While differing with Nieminen in some details of assessment concerning the Finnic loanwords from Slavic, V. Kiparsky, the foremost living specialist in the field, shares the view, embraced also by his teacher, J. J. Mikkola, that no definite loanwords from CS can be ascertained in Finnic. This is the gist of Kiparsky's discussion in his article "O xronologii slavjano-finskix leksičeskix otnošenij" (1958) in which the Finnish Slavist not only argues against the by now obsolete views of scholars such as Setälä, Vilkuna, Ariste, Šaxmatov, Sobolevskij, Rozwadowski, and Lehr-Spławiński, but also refers the reader to his own earlier publications concerning these matters. Cf. subsequently also Kiparsky 1962, where (223-4) he professes to see "die Quelle der ins Ostseefinnische eingedrungenen ältesten slavischen Lehnwörter im 'Urrussischen', d. h. dem vorliterarischen Russisch des 7. bis 9. Jhs. n. Chr." and where, toward the end of his article (230), he speaks of the "Annahme der ältesten finnisch-slavischen Beziehungen erst für das 6.-8. Jh. n. Chr."; see also Polák 1969.

Generally speaking, then, and as further substantiated by research on lexical borrowing in CS, it may be stated that the impact of other languages, notably

Germanic, on the vocabulary of CS was by and large stronger and more significant than the, to be sure, also ascertainable influence exerted by CS on the lexical component of any of its neighboring languages.

7. SOME SPECIAL PROBLEMS OF COMMON SLAVIC RELATED TO TIME AND/OR SPACE

7.0. Preliminary Remarks. Various aspects of CS have already been touched upon in earlier sections of this research report, including those pertaining to the temporal and spatial limits and divisions of the protolanguage of the Slavs to the extent it can be reconstructed internally and by applying the comparative method. Therefore some repetition will prove to be unavoidable in the following three sections discussing studies, published up to 1965 and addressing themselves specifically to some special problems of CS related to time and/or space; however, work already dealt with at some length previously will not, at this point, again be surveyed in any detail but at most will be summarily referred to here. The three sections devoted to these special problems of CS will discuss, in this order: (1) studies on CS in its IE and non-IE settings and the problem of Balto-Slavic, (2) research on the time limits, periodization, and chronology of CS, and (3) treatments of the disintegration and dialectal differentiation of CS. While the first section thus focuses on the initial period of CS (PS) and the emergence of the Slavic protolanguage from among its sister idioms, notably within the more narrow framework of Balto-Slavic, and the last section ·deals primarily with work concerning the end phase and disintegration of CS and the immediately following period of Early Slavic, the intervening second section surveys some attempts at establishing the outer temporal boundaries, periodization, and chronologization of CS or some major component of its structure (e.g., phonology) and only makes brief reference to some other work involving chronology mentioned elsewhere in this volume.

However, before going into a discussion of these problems, mention should be made here of two summarizing

studies which appeared almost simultaneously but which reflect two significantly different approaches to the overall problems of reconstructing CS — one largely traditional, the other more modern. The first of them, T.
Lehr-Spławiński's essay "Szic dziejów języka prasłowiańskiego" (1958c), is a highly condensed restatement of the
Polish Slavist's relevant opinions expressed on previous
occasions and now partly revised in the light of more recent findings and newly gained insights. Truly representing the summing up of a life-long preoccupation with the
multifaceted problem of CS, this essay does not, therefore, easily lend itself to a brief review, attempting to
convey even the mere essence of Lehr-Spławiński's position
on this subject. Probably his overall concept of CS could
be characterized as continuing in the vein of and slightly
modifying N. van Wijk's notion of the Slavic protolanguage
and its development through time, referred to above
(cf. pp. 37-9; see also below, pp. 229-30). Contrary to
van Wijk, however, Lehr-Spławiński attached great importance also to extra-linguistic considerations, mainly to
the findings of archeology. Thus, while explicitly stating that the unsettled but much debated question of the
nature of the prehistoric Balto-Slavic relationship —
i.e., essentially whether Baltic and Slavic go back to a
common, distinctly post-PIE protolanguage or simply represent two closely related but separate branches of IE exhibiting an early parallel development (cf. below, pp.
225 - 8) — is not really crucial (248), Lehr-Spławiński
subsequently nonetheless seems to take for granted the
existence of an original Balto-Slavic linguistic community
(or unity). He suggests that the independent development
of Baltic and Slavic began sometime around 1300 B. C.
(253) after a part of the earliest Balto-Slavic homeland,
stretching allegedly from the Oder and Vistula basins to
the upper Dnieper and Volga (249; cf. especially also
Lehr-Spławiński 1946 and 1964a), had been conquered by
some other IE tribes, identifiable merely as the bearers
of the so-called Lusatian culture of the Bronze Age (251-
2). While Baltic, which had not been exposed to these incursions, subsequently evolved at a slow pace, accounting
for the generally highly archaic and conservative character of this language group, prehistoric Slavic, according
to Lehr-Spławiński (in this respect closely following van
Wijk, granted some minor differences of opinion), developed in two chronological phases, one earlier and longer,
marked — like Baltic — by a relatively slow pace (though

yielding different results), and a second shorter one, characterized, on the other hand, by radical changes and a thorough reshaping of the entire linguistic structure of CS. It should be noted that Lehr-Spławiński, in addition to carefully assessing various linguistic, notably phonological, criteria for the purpose of establishing, tentatively in some instances, relative as well as absolute chronologies, also emphasizes the significance of the substantial modifications and additions (by means of loanwords) ascertainable in the vocabulary of CS. Though these few remarks can in no way do full justice to the wide range of Lehr-Spławiński's many keen observations and acute assertions — whose lasting value, incidentally, is not even diminished by his generally traditional, now no longer entirely acceptable outlook — they will have to suffice to convey at least a general impression of the importance of this synthesis of the Polish Slavist's thinking on CS.

Whereas Lehr-Spławiński in his essay had primarily been concerned with the relevant data itself and methodological considerations played only a subordinate role in his discussion except for the insistence on a multidisciplinary approach, the situation is almost reversed in V. N. Toporov's thought-provoking article "Nekotorye soobraženija otnositel'no izučenija istorii praslavjanskogo jazyka" (1959a). Here, problems of method and approach are clearly in the foreground, while the data as such is assumed to be known and therefore adduced only for purposes of illustration; thus, for example, some controversial interpretations of factual material serve to demonstrate the greater or lesser adequacy of different techniques. And, if for Lehr-Spławiński the point of reference and argument was provided particularly by van Wijk, Toporov primarily proceeds from certain assumptions first advanced by N. S. Trubeckoj (and in part by his follower in the Prague School tradition as regards Slavic prehistoric phonology, F. V. Mareš), while more traditional approaches to the specific problems of CS, such as those advocated by van Wijk and Lehr-Spławiński, are not ignored either. The Polish specialist on CS had already argued in favor of viewing Slavic prehistory not merely in static terms as the end phase of the Slavic protolanguage, i.e., as nothing more than the point of departure for the historically attested development of the individual Slavic languages, but also as a dynamic entity subject to constant change. The appropriateness of such an approach was even

more strongly stressed by Toporov (for a still more extreme emphasis on this aspect both of Balto-Slavic and CS,
see Žuravlev 1970 and, for an assessment, Birnbaum 1973;
cf. further below, pp. 312-15). Among the many points
discussed in Toporov's article is also the question of the
applicability of and relationship between the comparative
method and internal reconstruction, the latter yielding,
in particular, relative chronologies. Believing in certain general factors (if not outright causes) underlying
interrelated developments in the reconstructable prehistory of Slavic, and discussing, with some reservations,
previous attempts in this direction (e.g., by van Wijk,
Nahtigal, Martinet, Galton, Calleman), Toporov's approach
is a truly structuralist one. Following Trubeckoj and
others, the Soviet linguist accepts the view that CS in
the broad sense can be said to have lasted until the 10th-
12th centuries, i.e., up to the time of the *jer* shift
(fall and vocalization in weak and strong position, respectively), this being the last genuinely CS phonological
process. In setting such a late *terminus ad quem* for CS,
he sees no fundamental contradiction as regards the indisputable fact that OCS and Old Russian already existed
in the given period, since the proper chronological division ultimately is a matter of approach on the side of the
particular linguist (viz., as determined by his specific
topic); cf. 19-20. For reasoning along similar lines, see
Birnbaum 1970c: 20-35, recently criticized by Weiher 1971;
cf. also below, pp. 327 and 330-1.

*7.1. Studies on Common Slavic in Its Indo-European Set-
ting; Possible Common Slavic — Non-Indo-European Linguistic Contacts; the Problem of Balto-Slavic.* Among the many
specialized studies dealing with the setting of CS among
its IE sister idioms or the relationship of prehistoric
Slavic to several of the other IE language groups, only a
few can be listed here. For the treatment of this problem
or some of its aspects the reader is referred to the works
already discussed in a previous section (2.3.; pp. 56-69,
above). Reference should also be made here to N. van
Wijk's published lecture "Le slave commun dans l'ensemble
indo-européen" (1937c), subsequently included as part one
in his book *Les langues slaves. De l'unité à la pluralité*
(1956), briefly reviewed in the preceding (pp. 37-9).
Among general discussions of some basic aspects of the
prehistory of CS, the contribution by B. V. Gornung, *Iz
predystorii obrazovanija obščeslavjanskogo jazykovogo*

edinstva, presented at the Fifth International Congress
of Slavists, Sofia (1963), deserves mention for its many
interesting observations and suggestions, some of which
may be somewhat too speculative, however. Slavic-Hittite
parallels were discussed, for example, by T. Milewski
(1950) and, especially, V. V. Ivanov (1957 and 1965), already referred to. Similarly, the particular relationship
of Slavic and Tocharian within the broader framework of IE
was the topic of considerations set forth by T. Lehr-
Spławiński (1957/58) and V. Georgiev (1958b), the latter
including also Baltic in his discussion. The closer ties
ascertainable between Slavic (or Balto-Slavic) and Germanic, and partly also between Balto-Slavic, Germanic, and
Indo-Iranian, were scrutinized, with different emphasis,
in papers by J. Kuryłowicz (1951), A. Senn (1954), and V.
Georgiev (1958a and 1959). Of these contributions, the
one by Senn somewhat exaggerates, it seems, the active
part allegedly played by Germanic in what by some scholars
(C. S. Stang, for example) has been referred to as an
early Balto-Slavic-Germanic *Sprachbund*.

If the relationship between Slavic (or even Balto-
Slavic) and Indo-Iranian as a whole does not appear to
have been a uniquely close one, the contacts — original
(i.e., dialectal Late PIE) or secondary — between Slavic
(and especially the eastern branch of dialectal Late CS)
and Iranian (or, rather, a part of the Iranian language
group, namely, that which can be located in the area north
of the Black Sea) appear to have been fairly intimate at
times, as testified also by the, to be sure, limited,
lexical borrowings that penetrated from Iranian to Slavic
(cf. above, p. 216). In addition to the studies by
Arntz (1933) and, above all, Zaliznjak (1962), already
referred to, two additional contributions, one by K.
Treimer (1957/58), discussing "Skythisch, Iranisch, Urslavisch" in the somewhat dubious context of his peculiar
hypothesis regarding the ethnogenesis of the Slavs, the
other one by É. Benveniste (1956), examining the Slavic
preposition *kъ* and its Iranian parallel, may be quoted
here; cf. now also Toporov 1971. Further, as regards
studies of the prehistoric relationships between Slavic
and other — European — members of the IE language family,
the articles by J. Safarewicz (1963 and 1964) on Italo-
Slavic ties were already mentioned (see above, p. 205), so
that here only T. Lehr-Spławiński's reexamination of the
once fashionable hypothesis, which was later rejected and
only recently reconsidered, concerning possible direct

224

contacts between CS and Celtic, "Kilka uwag o stosunkach językowych celtycko-prasłowiańskich" (1956b), ought to be mentioned; cf. further also Machek 1963.

The highly questionable CS – Finnic linguistic contacts, assumed by some scholars (cf. Polák 1969) but rightly, it would seem to me, rejected by others (Nieminen 1957b; Kiparsky 1962 and elsewhere) need not concern us here (cf. above, pp. 217-18). The same also applies to any possible direct contact and linguistic interchange between Slavs and Turkic (Altaic) peoples occasionally considered already for the prehistoric (CS) period. If indeed any such contacts between one of the Altaic peoples (one may think of the Huns, the Proto-Bulgars, or the Avars) and the CS linguistic community as a whole (and not only one of its subbranches or dialects) could have existed, their linguistic yield at least for Slavic seems to have been nil (or virtually so, in view of the very few isolated lexical items in need of closer scrutiny).

When it comes to the genetic relationships obtaining between Slavic and any other single linguistic branch of IE, by far the most extensive body of specialized literature concerns, of course, the still largely controversial problem of Balto-Slavic. Here, the opinions continue to range from the assumption of a complete linguistic unity (i.e., the existence of a Balto-Slavic protolanguage), preceding the emergence of Baltic and Slavic (PS) as independent branches of IE, to the positing of a merely parallel development of two clearly separate, though closely related language groups stemming from a common dialectal base in Late PIE, with a variety of compromise views — including suggestions as to a secondary yet prehistoric convergence between Baltic and Slavic (as well as possibly additional branches of IE, notably Germanic) — formulated in an effort to overcome the apparent difficulties in substance and terminology; cf. also above, pp. 18-21, generally on the problem of Balto-Slavic linguistic relationships and pp. 64 - 5, on the theory of a parallel, separate evolution of Baltic and Slavic, inaugurated by Meillet. The following listing of, and occasional brief commenting on, some relevant references is therefore highly selective but includes several contributions which in themselves summarize and evaluate previous research on the Balto-Slavic problem; for titles appearing after 1965; see below, pp. 317-22.

Of earlier, now largely superseded work in this field, one may still mention two lengthy articles by W.

Porzeziński (1911) and J. Rozwadowski (1912), and, in
particular, the important monographic treatment by J.
Endzelīns, *Slavjano-baltijskie ètjudy* (1911), representing, on the whole, a detailed elaboration and, at the same
time, slight modification of Meillet's then fresh views on
the subject; cf. further the Latvian Baltologist's more
recent contribution to this problem, "Drevnejšie slavjansko-baltijskie jazykovye svjazi" (1952), in which he maintained at least some of his original basic positions while
analyzing additional data and taking issue with some of
the contemporary work in the field. Meillet's extreme
separatist position found a follower in A. Senn (1941) who
has taken the general view (more recently elaborated in
Senn 1966 and 1970) that Baltic and Slavic can be regarded
as some sort of entity only in the sense of representing
the residual portion of Late PIE after all other branches
of the common protolanguage had already embarked on their
respective independent development. A view fairly close
to that of Endzelīns was expressed by E. Fraenkel (1950a:
73-123); C. S. Stang, too, does not belong to the adherents of the hypothesis of a uniform, homogeneous Balto-
Slavic protolanguage (1939a, 1963, and, more recently,
1966: 1-21). On the other hand, among the cautious proponents of a common epoch of shared Balto-Slavic linguistic
prehistory we find, for example, J. Otrębski (1954, 1957,
1958), P. Arumaa (1955, 1963) and even A. Vaillant (1957),
who on this point abandoned his teacher Meillet's more
extreme view. Close to the concept of an actual Balto-
Slavic protolanguage prior to the emergence of Baltic and
Slavic as separate branches of the IE family are, in somewhat varying formulations and with a slightly different
emphasis, also the comparatists J. Safarewicz (1945), M.
Leumann (1955), O. Szemerényi (1957) and, in particular,
J. Kuryłowicz (1957). Among Slavists adhering essentially
to the same view, T. Lehr-Spławiński (1953, 1958a, 1958b)
deserves to be singled out. Somewhat more qualified positions in this respect were taken, for example, by A. Erhart (1958), W. K. Matthews (1958), V. Mažiulis (1958),
and P. Trost (1958a, 1958b, the second contribution, however, concerned almost exclusively with Balto-Slavic syntactic parallels which are much harder to assess in terms
of their potential proof value).

As can be gathered even from the brief survey just
given, the interest in the Balto-Slavic problem reached a
peak around 1958 when it was one of the main topics discussed at the Fourth International Congress of Slavists in

226

Moscow. About that time, therefore, several critical
state-of-the-art reports appeared, especially in the
Soviet Union. Of those, at least a few, in part contributing constructive criticism and fresh ideas, deserve
mention: V. N. Toporov 1958 and 1959b; Bogoljubova and
Jakubajtis 1959; B. V. Gornung 1958 and 1959.

Also presented at the Moscow congress were two
papers of particular significance, opening up new avenues
to the interpretation of the striking features shared by
Baltic and Slavic. These two contributions are S. B.
Bernštejn's "Baltoslavjanskaja jazykovaja soobščnost'"
(1958) and the joint paper by V. V. Ivanov and V. N.
Toporov, "K postanovke voprosa o drevnejšix otnošenijax
baltijskix i slavjanskix jazykov" (1961). The first one
is an attempt to explain the many Balto-Slavic agreements
less as a result of a genetically exclusive origin (i.e.,
a common Balto-Slavic protolanguage) and more in terms of
an early secondary convergence between prehistoric Baltic
and Slavic due to conditions of symbiosis and coterritorial existence. While the convergence approach to the
Balto-Slavic problem is not without predecessors (cf.,
e.g., Stang 1942: 278), Bernštejn is the most explicit
advocate of this theory. Subsequently, he adopted the
same approach also in his textbook of Comparative Slavic
Linguistics (1961: 27-37; for a partly similar explanation, see more recently also S. Karaliūnas 1968a). The
paper by Ivanov and Toporov attacks the Balto-Slavic problem from a different angle; theirs may be termed a modeling approach. Resorting, primarily, to the method of internal reconstruction, the two Soviet linguists have here
sketched a theory according to which, by abstracting from
the ascertainable data of Baltic and Slavic, it is possible to construct two linguistic models (at least on the
phonological and morphological levels) that can serve as
the respective points of departure for the retrievable
Baltic and Slavic developments. By superimposing, as it
were, these two abstract models, the authors arrive at the
conclusion that the Slavic model is derivable, in principle, from the Baltic, but not vice versa. Translated into
prehistoric linguistic reality, this would suggest that,
granted some difficulties of method and terminology, it
still remains meaningful to posit an intermediate Balto-
Slavic stage — perhaps too abstract and dynamic, to be
sure, to qualify for being considered an actual, homogeneous protolanguage — in the evolution from Late PIE to PS
(and CS), while such an intervening phase need not be

postulated for the prehistory of Baltic, derivable directly from Late PIE; for a reasoning along somewhat similar
lines, see now also Ossowski 1971, assuming an unaccept-
ably narrow area, roughly Western Polesia, as the original
homeland of the Slavs, however. For a brief assessment of
these two, relatively new approaches and the more traditional ones, conceiving of Balto-Slavic either as originally one single branch (subsequently to split up into two
subbranches) or as two distinct, parallel offshoots of the
IE *Stammbaum*, see Birnbaum 1970a.

*7.2. Research on the Time Limits, Periodization, and
Chronology of Common Slavic.* A good deal of research
falling under this rubric has, obviously, already been
discussed or at least touched upon in previous sections
of this report, particularly those on General Treatments
of CS and on Phonology; it is therefore not necessary to
survey it here. For an attempted systematic indication of
selected works concerned in one way or another with the
outer time limits, internal periodization, and problems of
absolute as well as relative chronology of CS, the reader
is referred to the relevant titles listed in the appended
Bibliography and marked with the appropriate numerical
symbol (namely, VI:2). In the following we shall thus
focus primarily on some of the more important contributions elucidating some facet of the time dimension of CS
not dealt with before or at most only mentioned in passing, and limit ourselves in Part One of this report, as
usual, to publications that have appeared no later than
1965.
     Of earlier work in this field, a short article by
A. Belić, "O praslovenskom jeziku" (1922), dealing largely
with questions of time limits and periodization, retains
some interest. As is well known, Belić, in this and other
writings, was inclined to set the upper limit of CS relatively early (somewhere around 500 A. D.), considering
the first ascertainable dialectal features and spatially
limited innovations to signal the end phase of CS rather
than, with Durnovo, Trubeckoj, and their modern followers
(H. G. Lunt, R. Auty, V. N. Toporov, and the present
writer, among them), placing the *terminus ad quem* considerably later, namely, at approximately the time of the
last generally shared sound shift of Slavic as a whole,
i.e., the fall of weak, and vocalization of strong *jers* in
in the 10th-12th centuries (with some locally conditioned
time discrepancy); for a different opinion, recently

expressed by E. Weiher (1967 and 1971, in a polemic with me), see below, pp. 330-1. In this particular article, Belić, arguing against Meillet's view that the CS period lasted until at least the 9th century, rejects the suggestion that the various Slavic reflexes of the word for 'king', *korl' < Gmc Karl (i.e., Charlemagne) support the theory that at the time when this word was borrowed from Germanic, viz., in the 9th century, Slavic as a whole must still have been rather homogeneous. As for the stem vowel of this word, we know today, of course, that at the time of its borrowing it was probably ă not only in Germanic, but also in Slavic, hence Late CS kărl'ь; cf. also Lunt 1966b. Likewise, Belić argues that the distinct local reflexes of CS clusters and other sound sequences in various parts of the Slavic territory, attested by OCS (e.g., št, žd < t', d'), speak against any positing of Late CS in the second half of the 9th century, i.e., the time of the first — no longer extant — OCS texts.

Of greater significance for the problem of dividing CS into distinct periods was N. van Wijk's article "O dwóch okresach w rozwoju języka prasłowiańskiego i o ich znaczeniu dla językoznawstwa ogólnego" (1927), conceived, in a sense, as a response not only to Belić's position but also to Trubeckoj's earlier attempt (1922) to divide, on the basis of phonological criteria, the CS time span into three separate epochs, the first of which would, for all intents and purposes, coincide with the period of Balto-Slavic (cf. above, pp. 110-11, and for some thoughts along similar lines now also Žuravlev 1970 and Birnbaum 1973, discussed below, pp. 312-15). In his article, van Wijk for the first time clearly outlined his concept (subsequently elaborated on various occasions, especially in the first two of his 1937 Sorbonne lectures, but also, e.g., in van Wijk 1949/50a) of CS linguistic evolution as falling into two distinct periods, the first one considerably longer, lasting for roughly two thousand years, and exhibiting only relatively few changes (notably, sound shifts) taking place at a slow pace, the second, much shorter one, characterized by many radical changes, all of which supposedly developed within only a few centuries. A fundamentally similar view about the periodization of CS as that professed by van Wijk had also been held, for quite some time, by T. Lehr-Spławiński. However, in an article, published in 1956 and occasioned by the republication, now in book form, of van Wijk's Sorbonne lectures on the Slavic languages (cf. above, pp. 37-9, and passim),

"Bemerkungen zu N. van Wijks Periodisierung des Urslavischen," the Polish Slavist suggested some fundamental
modifications in van Wijk's tentative periodization. According to Lehr-Spławiński, who in his later years — and
definitely ever since the publication of his book on the
origin and first homeland of the Slavs in 1946 — strove to
combine his linguistic findings and views with the results
of contemporary archeological research, the second period
of CS must have lasted longer than van Wijk had assumed
and was now dated by him to approximately the last three
pre-Christian and first three Christian centuries, thus
allegedly coinciding in time with the "post-Lusatian"
phase of the CS ethnic and linguistic community. Lehr-
Spławiński dates the first signals of a beginning dissolution of the CS linguistic unity to the 2nd-3rd centuries
A. D. (i.e., shortly after the Gothic migrations through
Slavic territory), in this respect coming fairly close to
Belić's concept briefly related above (but definitely at
variance, for example, with the more recent relevant
chronological views of Z. Stieber, mentioned above, pp.
49-50, and further discussed below, pp. 331 - 3), Lehr-
Spławiński's contribution to the volume in honor of S.
Mladenov (1957c), "Z dziejów języka prasłowiańskiego
(Urywek z większej całości)," is essentially only a
slightly more elaborate variant of his 1956 "Bermerkungen."

A very interesting attempt to define the outer time
limits of CS, which, however, went almost unnoticed, was
made by A. Mayer in his contribution to the Third International Congress of Slavists, scheduled to be held in
Belgrade in 1939, but canceled because of the outbreak of
World War II. Mayer's paper, "Die zeitliche Bestimmung
der urslawischen Periode," utilizes not only phonological
criteria but resorts also, to a large extent, to morphological (inflectional as well as derivational) phenomena.
In doing so, the Slavic evidence is viewed against its IE
background with great expertise, in terms of the state of
knowledge at that time. Positing the beginnings of a
separate, post-PIE Balto-Slavic linguistic evolution somewhere at the turn of the 3rd to the 2nd millennium B. C.
and not specifying any even approximate date for the initial phase of a specifically Slavic development (while
assuming the continued existence of Balto-Slavic in the
12th century B. C.), Mayer associates the emergence of
Slavic as an independent linguistic branch with the pre-
sumed shift (PIE $s >$) $*\check{s} > x$ in the position after $\check{\imath}$, $\check{u}$,
r, k (cf. also Andersen 1968 and Birnbaum 1971a). The

upper (or in his usage: lower) limit of CS, Mayer sets at approximately the end of the 9th century, i.e., the time of the Magyar landtaking. For a more recent detailed discussion of these problems, see also Birnbaum 1970c, with some additional comments below, pp. 325-8.

Important and generally cogent, as usual, are the chronological considerations suggested by V. Kiparsky (1948) on the basis of data testifying to Slavic-Baltic and Slavic-Finnic linguistic ties; cf. also Kiparsky 1958 and 1962. While dating the beginning of the Slavic-Finnic and Slavic-Baltic relations, as evidenced by loanwords, to a period prior to the fall of the weak *jers* and probably prior also to the development of pleophony, and, at least as concerns the contact with Finnic tribes, before the denasalization of nasal vowels, Kiparsky nonetheless considers these contacts as falling into the Old Russian and partly Proto-Russian period rather than into an epoch of as yet undifferentiated CS (cf. especially p. 46).

C. E. Bidwell's excellent and thorough study "The Chronology of Certain Sound Changes in Common Slavic as Evidenced by Loans from Vulgar Latin" (1961) is a fine example of successful utilization of the evidence provided by loans (in the broad sense, i.e., loanwords proper as well as, in particular, Slavic adaptations of foreign names, mostly place names) for establishing absolute chronologies of certain sound shifts of Late CS and, by the same token, setting a more precise upper time limit for dialectally differentiated CS, at least in one specific geographic area. As pointed out in the opening section, Bidwell's paper attempts

> an evaluation of loanwords (especially place-names) from Vulgar Latin of the Balkan peninsula and adjoining areas with a view to dating certain sound changes of the late Common Slavic period. While the evidence adduced here and the conclusions based upon it relate, strictly speaking, only to the speech of those Slavs who moved southward into the Balkans (the linguistic forerunners of the present-day South Slavs), it may be assumed that the same developments were proceeding with a roughly parallel chronology in the other Slavic dialects.

Sifting a great number of Late CS loans from Late Latin (and commenting briefly also on some foreign words or names that entered Slavic from other languages, namely, Greek and Germanic), Bidwell arrives at the following

conclusions regarding some absolute chronologies of Late
CS phonetic change (126):

(a) The first palatalization ceased operation before
circa 600 A. D. (*terminus ad quem*: Slavic settlement in the Balkans). (b) Restructuring of the
Slavic vowel system, involving monophthongization
and replacement of phonemic length by other distinctions, was operative during the earliest period of
Slavic settlement in the Balkans (circa 600 A. D.),
but was completed by the time such Christian names
as *Laurentius* > *Lovreč* began to be borrowed (sometime after 750 A. D.). (c) The second palatalization was operative around 600 A. D., was still
operative at the time Slavic colonization reached
the Adriatic coast, probably ceased by 750 A. D.,
and certainly ceased before the appearance of the
first documents late in the ninth century. (d)
Metathesis of liquids began after c. 750 A. D. and
was complete before c. 900 A. D. (e) The third
palatalization likewise was operative about A. D.
600 and continued to be operative in South Slavic
until sometime prior to c. 900. (f) In the western
varieties of South Slavic *y* and *i* early merged into
one phoneme *i*; there was probably an accompanying
merger of *ŭ* and *ĭ* and a loss of allophonic palatalization before front vowels. This merger took place
after monophthongization and after the borrowing of
crucem > *kryžĭ* and *Rōmam* > **rymŭ* (say sometime after
650-750 A. D.) and before transmittal of these words
to the western Slavs (sometime after 850), most
probably before the eleventh century.

Bidwell's keen observations and cogent reasoning have influenced the thinking in these matters of such scholars as
G. Y. Shevelov and, in particular, Z. Stieber, the latter
shifting forward in time a number of traditional chronologies for CS sound change; cf. above, pp. 49-50 and 230;
and below, 331-3. For some specific items discussed by
Bidwell, see also Stieber 1966.

Finally, some interesting remarks on the problem of
the outer time limits of CS and its internal periodization
can also be found in A. Dostál's short but thoughtful article "Několik úvah o praslovanštině" (1963), containing,
in addition, some acute comments on the problem of one
linguistic system (with its specific set of grammatical
categories) replacing another one in the course of the

prehistoric evolution of protolanguages. However, although stressing the significance of relative chronology also, Dostál perhaps sketches a somewhat too rigid and abstract scheme of periodization for the Slavic and pre-Slavic linguistic development (73-4).

7.3. Treatments of the Disintegration and Dialectal Differentiation of Common Slavic. Problems pertaining to the time, causes, and details of the disintegration and beginning dialectal differentiation of the CS protolanguage, preceding or, rather, gradually changing into the emerging individual Slavic languages, has of course long attracted the attention of Slavists. The more important research in this field through the early sixties was briefly accounted for in my stock-taking survey on "The Dialects of Common Slavic" (1966a), mentioned above (pp. 65 - 6); for a slightly abridged variant of this paper, see Birnbaum 1965b. Among earlier contributions to this particular set of problems, three studies appearing in the proceedings of the First International Congress of Slavists, held in Prague, 1929 (published in 1932), deserve to be singled out. One is J. Czekanowski's "Różnicowanie się dialektów prasłowiańskich w świetle kryterium ilościowego" where, on the basis of a detailed quantitative-statistic analysis mostly of phonological criteria, an attempt is made to compute, as precisely as possible, the exact degree of relationship between the individual Slavic languages and to arrive, by this method, at a partly new view of the pace and direction of CS dialectal differentiation. Among the more interesting results of this study, undertaken by a professional anthropologist, though with deep insights also into Slavic and Comparative IE Linguistics (cf. also Czekanowski 1957), are the particular linguistic ties (suggesting, presumably, earlier ethnic connections) between the forerunners of a northern portion of the Eastern Slavs and the predecessors of the speakers of the Lekhitic branch of West Slavic, previously assumed also by N. S. Trubeckoj and later, e.g., by B. V. Gornung (1963). Concerning an isogloss ("isophone") of West Slavic extending also into North East Slavic, see further Lehr-Spławiński 1931a. Reading Czekanowski's application of quantitative linguistics to a problem of linguistic relationship with a view to measuring it in exact terms, it is hard not to see in it an early anticipation of some crucial aspects of the particular method later known as glottochronology or lexicostatistics, doubtful, to be sure, in some of its results; for an application of this method to Slavic linguistic differentiation, see, e.g., Lotko 1965. The second of the relevant studies occasioned by the Prague congress is the contribution by N. Durnovo, titled "K voprosu o vremeni raspadenija obščeslavjanskogo jazyka" and culminating in the statement (524, rendered here in English translation):

> Thus, there are no difficulties in assuming that the Slavic language up to the so-called fall of the *jers*, i.e., up to the loss of ь and ъ in weak position and their shifting into full vowels in strong position, was homogeneous and that the differences between the Slavic languages whose rise must be dated to an earlier period were merely dialectal differences for that language.

This view was shared, as we have seen, also by Trubeckoj and has been adhered to, more recently, by V. N. Toporov and, with some qualifications, myself. The third contribution in this volume is T. Lehr-Spławiński's brief essay, stating his basic position on this subject, elaborated, before and after, elsewhere. In this connection, N. van Wijk's second Sorbonne lecture, "Parallélisme et divergence dans l'évolution des langues slaves," first published in 1937 and reissued as part of the publication of these lectures in book form in 1956 and referred to above (pp. 37 - 9), should further be noted.

Taking Lehr-Spławiński's periodization of CS and his overall concept of its disintegration and dialectal regrouping as his own point of departure, the complex problem of the dissolution of CS was reexamined, primarily in the light of the phonological development, by A. Furdal in his 1961 monograph *Rozpad języka prastowiańskiego w świetle rozwoju głosowego*. Furdal's detailed and keen analysis of the pertinent linguistic data led him to revise, in some important respects, the general concept elaborated by Lehr-Spławiński. As I have discussed Furdal's findings and conclusions in some detail in my own work on CS dialects (especially Birnbaum 1966a), I can here limit myself to the general remark that Furdal's work, while by and large conceived in traditional terms and not revolutionizing our previous assessment, is a piece of thorough research, some minor disagreements on my part notwithstanding.

The monograph by F. P. Filin, *Obrazovanie jazyka vostočnyx slavjan* (1962), based primarily on lexical data and in part relevant to the problem of Late CS dialectal differentiation, was briefly reviewed above (pp. 81-2) and therefore need not be discussed again here.

The article by L. Moszyński, "Przyczyny rozkładu prasłowiańskiego systemu językowego" (1965b, appropriately contributed to a volume in honor of Z. Stieber), is, as suggested by the title, an attempt to reveal the underlying causes for the ultimate breakup of CS. Moszyński assumes that phonological evolution in the CS period was subjected to three major tendencies, to wit, (1) the substitution of old (inherited) quantity distinctions by new quality contrasts in the vowel system; (2) the so-called rule of open syllables, prompting, among other things, monophthongizations of former diphthongs, including supposedly (PIE $\bar{u} > u\underset{\frown}{u} >) u\underset{\frown}{i} = ьi > y$; and (3) assimilation in terms of palatalization, tending toward, though not fully accomplishing vowel harmony. Proceeding from these tendencies and their specific effects, in part leading to a mutual cancellation of conflicting developments and to an overall reshaping of the sound system of CS, Moszyński arrives at a set of basic isoglosses characterized by the following linguistic phenomena: (1) the combination of quantity and various types of intonation (pitch); (2) a strengthening of the trend toward assimilation by way of palatalization extending beyond the syllable boundary; (3) different treatment of CS y or, rather, its assumed earlier stage ьi, yielding (a) i in the South, (b) front y, as an allophone of /i/, in the West, and (c) back y, resulting from monophthongization of $*u\underset{\frown}{u}$ (rather than $*u\underset{\frown}{i}$) in the East; (4) different treatment of new (secondary) clusters with j; and (5) a renewed tendency to differentiate between long and short vowels by means of qualitative distinctions. While, to be sure, the approach as such chosen by Moszyński is not new, his observations and interpretations capture phenomena in groupings and classifications to some extent not previously considered.

With this, we conclude Part One of our report, accounting for the progress achieved through the mid-sixties in the reconstruction of CS.

Part Two

PROBLEMS IN THE RECONSTRUCTION

OF COMMON SLAVIC

(Current Research)

8. SOME GENERAL PROBLEMS OF CURRENT RESEARCH ON COMMON SLAVIC

Turning now to the current research situation as regards the reconstruction of CS, a few introductory remarks
on the problems at hand and the methods resorted to for
the purpose of attacking and, whenever possible, resolving
them, as well as some comments on the manner of presentation adopted in the following, seem in order. As was indicated before, when subsuming relevant work published by
and large after 1965 under what here is labeled *current
research*, this approximate date was chosen at random for
practical rather than for any inherent reasons. It should
also be noted that in Part Two of this book only specialized studies that have appeared in the recent past will
actually be taken into consideration, while textbooks and
reference works of a broader scope as well as general
treatments, for example, of phonology have already been
accounted for in previous sections of this report regardless of their date of publication. Such works will therefore not be dealt with again in the following but at most,
in a few instances, be cited for cross-reference.

In very general terms, current research on CS (and
earlier phases in the prehistory of Slavic) can be divided
into two kinds of relevant work: that which can be viewed
primarily as a direct continuation of previous attempts —
varying in nature, to be sure — at reconstructing the
Slavic protolanguage roughly along *traditional* methodological lines and, on the other hand, linguistic research
that introduces an innovative element, exploring new approaches and techniques to gain heretofore inaccessible
insights into the structure and functioning of prehistoric
Slavic. It goes without saying, however, that *innovative*
in this context is used as a very relative term: much of
the previous relevant research was certainly also innova-

tive, indeed at times even revolutionary if measured by
the standards of the accepted methods of its own period.
The Prague School's approach, and in particular the then
new concepts launched and applied to the reconstructed
linguistic data of prehistoric Slavic in the writings of
such eminent scholars as Durnovo, Trubeckoj, and Jakobson,
provide only one set of outstanding examples of a kind of
methodological innovation that has paid off richly. The
reference above to recent innovative research as opposed
to a more traditional approach is therefore used here with
this time-relative qualification. And even what is innovative by contemporary standards is often by no means
without its immediate antecedents in previous periods of
relevant research. For, again, some of the most important
work on CS now in progress was begun prior to and sometimes far in advance of 1965/66 so that in this sense also
the cut-off point adopted here is largely artificial,
though no more arbitrary than any other year would be.
Thus, to take a few examples, much of the relevant work
achieved by Kuryłowicz, first conceived and in part already elaborated in the twenties and thirties, but vigor-
ously pursued into the sixties and seventies, or, more recently, by Ivanov and Toporov, in large measure initiated
in the fifties, can rightly be considered modern and truly
innovative today as much as when it was first embarked
upon. Moreover, while the novel character of some of the
writings to be reported will be pointed out where appropriate, current research on CS as an integrated whole will
be reviewed in Part Two of this volume in separate sections closely paralleling those of Part One, slightly differently phrased section headings notwithstanding; in
other words, no attempt will be made here to treat separately exploratory and more traditional writings, particularly where they pertain to the same or related issues.

Yet it seems appropriate, in this context, to point
to some major advances in general linguistic theory and
method of the recent past that have begun to yield some
first important results also in their application to CS
and promise to continue to do so. This is said here in
reference, especially, to distinctive feature theory as it
was originally devised by R. Jakobson (in collaboration
with some other scholars, M. Halle foremost among them)
and, in more recent years, has been modified and integrated into the overall framework of generative grammar in
the form of generative phonology, elaborated by M. Halle,
N. Chomsky, P. Postal, and others, and, on the other hand,

as it has been developed in a somewhat different direction, stressing the semiotic concept of markedness, by H. Andersen in particular who has tested his new models and theoretical apparatus on Slavic diachronic data. While the early assertion of some generative phonologists about an alleged full parallelism, indeed coincidence, of the order of synchronic phonological rules and the relative chronology of diachronic sound shifts have been proven erroneous or, at any rate, grossly exaggerated, distinctive feature theory and its various recent refinements have no doubt furthered the realization that phonetic change takes place, to a large extent at least, at the subphonemic feature level rather than at any higher and more abstract — phonemic, morphophonemic, etc. — level of representation; for some further details, with CS examples, see Žuravlev 1967b. Even those who reject some of the more far-reaching assumptions and claims of generative phonology have been provided by this theory with, or — to say the least — have been stimulated to intensify the search for, a more accurate understanding of the intricate relationship and interaction obtaining between the rule component of a language and its feature hierarchies peculiar to a set of segments (roughly corresponding to the traditional phonemes) on which the rules operate, as they pertain to sound change. In other spheres of linguistic structure, namely, at the syntactic and semantic levels, generative theory, as applied to diachrony, in some instances has been able to reveal and identify underlying more or less covert categories and patterns of sentence structure as well as whole sets of invariant elements of meaning (universal semantic features) combining into complex lexical units. This, therefore, suggests, on the one hand, a higher degree of stability at an often typologically definable deep structure level than what the surface data of a given syntactic structure might otherwise have led linguists to assume, and, on the other hand, allows for a more adequate interpretation of semantic micro- and macrostructure pertaining to the lexical makeup also of protolanguages recoverable only by means of linguistic reconstruction such as CS. As was indicated, some of these newly gained theoretical insights have already in various ways made an impact on the quest for solutions to heretofore resistant problems in the reconstruction of CS to be briefly accounted for in the subsequent sections of this state-of-the-art report.

9. SOME CURRENT VIEWS ON THE SOUND PATTERN OF COMMON SLAVIC

9.0. General Problems. An important paper, touching on
several problems of CS phonology (e.g., the coexistence
and succession of different phonological systems in CS,
the CS reflexes of PIE syllabic liquids and nasals and
their further development, to mention just a few), is K.
Dejna's "Prasłowiańskie systemy fonologiczne" (1968). The
last synthesis to date of F. V. Mareš's overall view of CS
and Early Slavic phonology (Mareš 1969) was discussed
above (pp. 100 - 5) and therefore need not concern us here.
For some comments on recent contributions to the theory of
so-called group-phonemes in CS by V. K. Žuravlev (1966 and
1967a), see below (pp. 267 - 8). In a paper titled "O
stepeni dokazatel'nosti dialektizmov-'arxaizmov'," appearing in the *festschrift* for R. I. Avanesov (Birnbaum 1972b),
I discuss the hazards of attributing CS status to some
dialectal features, rightly or wrongly considered to represent an archaic sound system. As this contribution is
basically a variant of a major section of another, larger
essay of mine, concerned with the problems arising in connection with defining the outer time limits of CS (Birnbaum 1970c), commented upon elsewhere (see below, pp. 325-
8), the reader is referred to the discussion of my more
comprehensive paper.

One of the new features of generative phonology is
its insistence on relating phonological data directly to
the linguistic units and processes obtaining at the semantically interpreted morphological and syntactic levels.
As is well known, in standard generative theory, the 'systematic phonemic' level corresponds to some extent, though
not entirely, to the traditional morphophonemic level
whereas the approximate equivalents of the traditional

morphemes serve as the basic units of the syntactic component. To be sure, modified semantically-based generative
theory, also referred to as *generative semantics*, recognizes the fact that the borderline between syntax and
semantics is anything but well-defined, if not artificial
or, in fact, fictitious. It is only natural, therefore,
that some of the first attempts at systematically describing and analyzing, in generative terms, the inventory and
workings of the phonological system of a given language
would view this system as operating within a particular
major segment of morphology. For Early Slavic such an attempt was undertaken by T. M. Lightner in his article "On
the Phonology of the Old Church Slavonic Conjugation"
(1966; cf. also Van Campen 1963, briefly referred to
above, p. 126). As stated at the outset of his article,
Lightner claims to "show how application of the theory of
generative phonology can help us to gain insight into the
nature of OCS phonological processes." And although "the
analysis given here is strictly synchronic," much if not
most of the data analyzed can be readily equated with that
of Late CS. In concluding his paper, Lightner points out
(20-1) that

> We have been concerned with finding a descriptively
> adequate analysis of OCS phonology. In order to
> account for underlying regularities we have regarded
> phonological description from an abstract point of
> view. The abstractness of our description is evi-
> dent not only in its partial dependence on syntactic
> structure but also in the nature of the underlying
> forms and ordered rules which derive phonetic repre-
> sentation. To explain the different phonetic shapes
> in which morphemes may appear, we were obliged to
> posit underlying representations which often bore no
> obvious relation to actual phonetic representations.
> Thus, for example, to explain the stem alternation
> in l sg. *kazujǫ* ~ inf. *kazovati*, we had to posit an
> underlying diphthong *ău*, although no diphthong oc-
> curs in phonetic representation. To explain the re-
> lation between the l sg. endings -*mь* for athematic
> verbs and -*ǫ* for thematic verbs . . . we had to
> posit that the underlying form of some words ends in
> a consonant, although no words may end in a conso-
> nant in phonetic representation.

And commenting on the earlier suggested parallelism between synchronic description (in terms of generative

rules) and diachronic processes, alluded to above (p. 241), the American Slavist takes this stand (24-6):

> Although the difference between synchronic and diachronic description is very clear-cut, synchronic description may *reflect* diachronic processes and still retain its synchronic nature. Whether a particular synchronic description does or does not mirror diachronic description is not relevant to an evaluation of that synchronic description . . . In evaluating the fragment of grammar proposed here, then, the issue is not whether it reflects diachronic development or not, but whether to accept the notion of abstract underlying forms and fairly long derivations mediated by a series of ordered phonological rules. Failure to use such abstract phonological description as we have proposed here, however, may lead to a grammar which lists many related forms as exceptional or suppletive. Such a grammar would fail to explain the synchronic relationship between clearly related forms . . . Such a grammar could not reach beyond the level of observational adequacy.

While this sort of abstract phonology, largely operating with underlying units subject to processes not readily ascertainable (and certainly not paralleling any reconstructable diachronic phonetic change), may seem too far removed from the tangible linguistic reality to some, its potentially added synchronic descriptive adequacy (in terms of economy, precision, and comprehensiveness), rather than any particular implicit explanatory power, as regards diachrony or otherwise — which to my mind it cannot in fact claim — will be apparent to many.

Based on the well known "law," first formulated by the American linguist G. K. Zipf, to the effect that frequently used linguistic units tend to be smaller (shorter) than less often used ones, the Polish Romanist and theoretical linguist W. Mańczak, in an article, "Nieregularny rozwój fonetyczny spowodowany częstością użycia w prasłowiańskim" (1969; cf. also Mańczak 1970a, in part based on this article), critically annotated by B. Havránek, the editor of the journal in which it appears, has attempted to come up with some new explanations — all reducible to the one principle of frequency — for irregularities in the phonological development of CS and preceding evolutionary phases, notably as regards inflectional endings (auslaut position; cf. further Mańczak 1970b; Lüdtke 1966). Although occasionally offering an interesting, even convincing point of view and generally arguing his theoretical position fairly well, Mańczak's paper on the whole fails to provide a consistent and cogent explanation for the manifold instances of irregular sound change adduced by him. Some factual oversights and inaccuracies do not contribute to strengthening the case of this self-avowed anti-structuralist.

A variety of controversial or, at any rate, topical issues of CS phonology, ranging from general linguistic theory, terminology, and chronology to details of vocalism (phonetic value of individual vowels, vowel shifts, monophthongization, etc.) and consonantism (e.g., Second and Third Palatalization), were touched upon in the somewhat casually phrased article (or, rather perhaps, selective state-of-the-art report) "Phonologische Erwägungen: Das Urslavische" by J. Hamm (1970). Full of interesting observations and ideas worthy of further consideration, this paper does not give the impression of pursuing one particular point or attempting to corroborate any one single thesis but is rather to be understood as a set of informal marginal notes commenting on various points in a multitude of loosely connected problems and phenomena, lately again much debated. Hamm's phonological interpretation of graphic (Glagolitic as well as Cyrillic) evidence (70-2) deserves, as usual, special attention.

Illustrative material partly from CS and Early Slavic was adduced by P. Ivić in two closely related articles discussing, from a theoretical point of view, the increase of the phoneme inventory as related to the number of distinctive possibilities in a language (Ivić 1967 and 1970). Thus Ivić quotes here examples of the type (PIE $k\bar{e}iatei >$) CS *čäjati > čajati* (where *č* must be considered phonemic only when followed by a back vowel, /ča/, whereas *č* in *čäjati* was merely an allophone of /k/ before a front vowel, [čäjati] = /käjati/) or CS and Early OR *danь* > OR and CSR *dan'* (where *n* before ь in Early Old Russian and possibly also in Late CS was at most phonetically soft, [n'], while *n'* after the fall of the final weak *jer* became phonemically palatalized as well, i.e., /n'/, contrasting with /n/).

9.1. The Common Slavic Prosodic System. An excellent, detailed survey of Slavic (and pre-Slavic) accentuation, grouped in sixteen chronological stages numbered A1 through A15, plus an additional stage labeled "Stage Štok.

245

16" (Štok. = Štokavian), can be found in the paper "Historical Laws of Slavic Accentuation," C. S. Ebeling's contribution to the 1967 *festschrift* for Roman Jakobson. Reminiscent in its pedagogical striving for lucidity and systematicness of the Dutch linguist's earlier endeavor to supply relative chronologies for some major developments in CS and Russian phonology (Ebeling 1963; cf. above, p. 98), Ebeling's paper for methodological considerations avoids the term CS, not held by him to be "a chronological term" (578). While one may argue about the merits of this terminological preference, it is clear that most of his chronological stages fall precisely into what has been traditionally referred to as the CS (or PS) period. As, incidentally, noted by Ebeling himself (*ibid*.), "in the history of Slavic accentuation, the oldest change differentiating dialects is to be found in stage A6, but a much later development such as Stang's law (A15) is still Common Slavic in the literal sense." It is hard to conceive of a more clear, succinct, yet fairly detailed and, on the whole, reliable overview of the highly complex prehistoric — and to a lesser degree also historic — evolution of Balto-Slavic and Slavic accentuation than this exposition by Ebeling. It should further be noted that the fairly recent findings contained in the standard monographs of leading accentologists, such as J. Kuryłowicz (1952, ²1958) and C. S. Stang (1957b), reviewed above (pp. 117-19), not to mention many earlier experts active in the field are included in his summary of significant accentological research. In addition, many of the relevant insights (partly modifying our previous views) gained by the chief representatives of the Moscow group working on problems of Slavic accentuation, the late V. M. Illič-Svityč and V. A. Dybo (cf. pp. 123-4), have been digested in this remarkable presentation.

The major contribution made to Balto-Slavic accentology by Illič-Svityč, his book on nominal accentuation in Baltic and Slavic paradigms (1963, see pp. 114 and 120, above), was scrutinized in a lengthy review article by M. Pešikan (1966/67, with a Russian resumé), who suggests, in sections V-VII of his discussion, a number of improvements on the Soviet accentologist's argumentation, in general acknowledged to be sound and objective, however. In concluding his analysis and criticism of Illič-Svityč's relevant views (sections VIII-IX), the Yugoslav linguist sketches a slightly modified overall pattern of the development of the prosodic means inherited from PIE in the CS

and/or pre-Slavic period, making — in Pešikan's opinion at
least — the basic concept elaborated by the Soviet scholar
more readily acceptable.

As was mentioned before, Illič-Svityč's accentological research has been continued after his death by his
close collaborator V. A. Dybo. In 1968 Dybo published a
major contribution, presented at the Sixth International
Congress of Slavists, Prague, which in a way may be considered a counterpart to Illič-Svityč's book on Balto-
Slavic declensional accentuation while, at the same time,
supplementing Dybo's own accentological work (cf. esp.
Dybo 1958 and 1962; Dybo & Illič-Svityč 1963, briefly discussed above, pp. 123 - 4). In his Prague congress contribution, Dybo examines in great detail the interdependence
of "accentology and word formation in Slavic," limiting
himself to nominal (substantival, adjectival) derivation
proper, i.e., to derivation by means of suffixation, and
focusing primarily on CS, while, to be sure, liberally
adducing comparative data from attested Slavic. Among the
particularly important general conclusions reached by the
Soviet Slavist is the confirmation of the view (first tentatively advanced by Ivanov & Toporov 1958, but firmly
corroborated with accentological data only by Illič-
Svityč) that the relevant CS forms and patterns can be
derived from — or, rather perhaps, reduced to — corresponding accentual types of Baltic (theoretically Balto-
Slavic) whereas a reversed process of derivation (generation) is inconceivable. More specifically, this suggests
(220) that

> the Slavic rules for generating accentual types of
> derivations [i.e., derived nouns, H. B.] can be
> formed from the Baltic ones by means of superim-
> posing the rule of V. M. Illič-Svityč, which is to
> say that the law of V. M. Illič-Svityč operated not
> only in the sphere of simple [i.e., nonderived,
> H. B.] nouns but also in the sphere of nominal deri-
> vation which, in turn, proves its universal and con-
> sequently phonetic character. The same is borne out
> also by the possibility of rigorously identifying
> the accentual curves, resulting from the application
> of the generative rules for the accentual types of
> derived nouns ("chains of accentual types"), with
> the accentual paradigms (or, more precisely, "chains
> of accentual paradigms") of the CS verb.

Other, even more recent work by Dybo has focused — contin-

uing earlier explorations in similar directions by L. A.
Bulaxovs'kyj (see p. 121) — on Old Russian and Middle
Bulgarian textual evidence as a source for reconstructing
CS accentuation (as regards the present tense, Vasil'ev-
Dolobko's law; cf. Dybo 1969a, 1969b, 1971). For a diachronic interpretation of the South Slavic evidence,
especially East and Central South Slavic, relevant to the
present tense accentuation (including underlying CS protoforms), see also S. Gustavsson 1969: esp. 5 and 14; cf.
further the general inferences as to the Late CS prosodic
pattern arrived at on the basis of Slovenian linguistic
material by E. Stankiewicz 1966a.

   Based on recent relevant research by Kuryłowicz,
Stang, Jakobson, and, in particular, Illič-Svityč, B. J.
Darden has lately (1972) reexamined the problem of Baltic
and Slavic nominal accentuation, suggesting, in the vein
of standard generative theory and quoting P. Kiparsky's
attempt to define constraints on possible changes in rule
ordering, that this much-invoked mechanism (i.e., rule
ordering) is a decisive factor accounting for the specific
differences and simultaneous, discernible interrelations
between the pertinent Baltic and Slavic accentual types.
In this respect, Slavic is more complex (exhibiting a
secondary development involving two innovations in rule
reordering) than Baltic which displays the original, common Balto-Slavic state of affairs. According to Darden
(79-80),

> the two innovations [of Slavic] may justifiably be
> considered part of a single process, a process which
> might logically have been triggered by the neutrali-
> zation of length in diphthongs. Once the neutral-
> ization of length in diphthongs had undermined the
> dependence of intonation on quantity, Slavic moved
> in the direction of making intonation predictable
> from the type of accentual paradigm.

Clearly, the explanation offered by the American linguist
not only contends to be more explicit and hence more adequate than previous descriptions of the underlying mechanisms (in synchronic terms), but also implies a claim to
greater explanatory power of the diachronic processes involved. Whether the latter is indeed the case would merit
closer examination.

   The problem of stressed vs. unstressed *jers* in Late
CS (and Proto-Russian) was tackled by V. Kiparsky (1969d)
in a discussion of the factors causing, and irregularities

observable in, the so-called fall and vocalization of the
"weak" and "strong" reduced vowels in Early East Slavic.
Some of the points raised by Kiparsky will be further
touched upon at the proper place in the section on vocalism where recent work relevant to the *jer* shift in East
Slavic (or dialectal Late CS) will be discussed (p. 255).
A few recent remarks by J. Kuryłowicz (1968b) on some intonational peculiarities of a particular category of the
Slavic verb (2nd and 3rd person singular aorist in *-tъ/
-tь*) will be cited below (pp. 281-2).

9.2. The Common Slavic Vowel System. Among general, synthetic treatments of the CS vowel system and its modifications, one may note the essay by T. Milewski, "Ewolucja
prasłowiańskiego systemu wokalicznego" (1965, [2]1969;
slightly abridged English version, 1967, showing some instances of careless, unfortunate wording). However, while
making the important distinction between phonetic and
phonemic change (and phonetic vs. phonemic level), this is
a rather traditional presentation — some, keen, original
observations notwithstanding — intent on incorporating and
accomodating a number of recently advanced, controversial
or even wholly untenable hypotheses. To be sure, Milewski's account pursues a relatively modest goal: to replace the neogrammarian concept of CS vocalism with a more
modern one, based on the achievements of structural linguistics (represented, in Milewski's opinion, by such linguists as Vaillant, Žuravlev, and Georgiev as regards research relevant to CS phonology).

The reflexes of IE ablaut in Slavic and CS secondary
apophony continue to attract the interest of researchers.
The important monograph *Proto-Indo-European Schwebeablaut*
(1969) by R. Anttila, adducing ample Baltic and Slavic
evidence (cf. the long listing of items belonging to these
language groups in the Index, 224-30, with further page
references), was already referred to above (p. 126).
Undoubtedly Anttila's dissertation provides us with a better understanding of this particular and somewhat puzzling
submechanism of IE ablaut as reflected also in the relevant Slavic (and Baltic) data. A special case of ablaut,
found in OCS but representative, of course, of the CS
state of affairs, was reexamined by L. Sadnik (1966) who,
following Vaillant, sees an instance of secondary zero
grade in the root vocalism of imperatives of the type OCS
rьci (: present *rekǫ*). Sadnik posits an earlier present
form **rьkǫ*, along with attested *rekǫ* (cf. also the derived

imperfectives *-ricati* : *-rěkati*), the zero grade present
form presumably having had nondurative, hence future function. Contrary to seemingly analogical formations such as
-mьrǫ or *-dьrǫ*, for which IE parallels outside of Slavic can be adduced, **rьkǫ* seems to have been a secondary Slavic derivational type. Also *rek-* (both in the present:
rekǫ, and in the infinitive: **rek-ti* > OCS *rešti*) was,
according to Sadnik, nondurative in a previous, pre-aspec-
tual stage of development; the durative and, subsequently,
imperfective function of **rek-* is said to be secondary.
For the parallel imperative forms *tьci*, *pьci* (*sę*) no zero
grade present forms can be assumed, which suggests that
here **rьkǫ*, *rьci* served as the model. Based on the
ground-breaking work on IE ablaut by J. Kuryłowicz, who
had ascertained a few instances of the particular variety
of IE ablaut usually referred to as *vṛddhi* also for Slavic
(*ljubъ*, *vórna*, *zimà*), Z. Gołąb, in an article published in
the Jakobson *festschrift* (1967, "The Traces of *Vṛddhi* in
Slavic"), was able to enlarge this list by another twelve
(or thirteen) items of Slavic reflexes of *vṛddhi*, suggesting that these traces provide additional evidence of ancient linguistic ties between Slavic and Indo-Iranian.
Taking issue with some of the major tenets of Kuryłowicz's
ablaut theory (as well as C. Watkins' more derivative
thinking in these matters) and discussing, among other
things, also some instances of putative *vṛddhi* in Baltic
and Slavic, T. Mathiassen has recently reexamined certain
facets of IE ablaut as they pertain to Baltic and Slavic
data, including repercussions on Balto-Slavic prosody
(metatony, etc.). In particular, Mathiassen's relevant
research has to date focused primarily on the lengthened
grade and the Slavic sigmatic aorist (1969) and on the
chronology and significance of the shortening of long
diphthongs in Baltic and Slavic (1970a). A large-scale
study by the Norwegian linguist on problems of long vocalism in Slavic and IE (Mathiassen 1970b), announced as
having been published some time ago (cf. the brief summary
given by the author in *Scando-Slavica* 16, 268-9) is not
yet available to the present writer, if indeed it has appeared at all. Testifying, in part, to the same kind of
ingenuity, indispensable for any fruitful discussion of
these difficult problems, as has been so frequently exhibited by some of the scholars with whom he takes issue
(Kuryłowicz foremost among them), Mathiassen's fresh look
at some manifestations of IE and secondary ablaut in Baltic and Slavic certainly merits serious attention.

Also the recent discussion of the development of the
IE sonorants ($\underset{\circ}{r}$, $\underset{\circ}{l}$, $\underset{\circ}{n}$, $\underset{\circ}{m}$) in CS by L. Moszyński (1969) is
related peripherally to the problem of Slavic reflexes of
IE ablaut. Arguing against the standard view (formulated,
e.g., by Shevelov) that the syllabic sonorants of PIE were
reflected in Balto-Slavic by biphonemic sequences of the
type *ur/ir* (ъr/ьr), etc., before further developing in CS,
Moszyński suggests (following, in part, ideas previously
expressed by T. Milewski) that PIE $\underset{\circ}{r}$, $\underset{\circ}{l}$ yielded directly
CS $\underset{\circ}{r}/\underset{\circ}{r}'$, $\underset{\circ}{l}/\underset{\circ}{l}'$ while PIE $\underset{\circ}{n}$, $\underset{\circ}{m}$ resulted in CS ę/ǫ without
any intermediate evolutionary stage, once the nasal vowels
had been established as reflexes of PIE *en*, *em*, *on*, *om* (in
tautosyllabic position). As for the realization (phonetic
implementation) of CS syllabic liquids, Moszyński believes
that it was of the type [r°], as attested in OCS (cf. the
graphic renditions *r*ъ, *r*ь, *l*ъ, *l*ь), rather than of the
type [°r], the latter type considered secondary and dialectal, originating in connection with rendering weak *jers*
optional (facultative) phonemes. This secondary type
(*t°rt*) is said to then have further developed in part of
North Slavic (cf. OR *p*ъ*rv*ъ, P *kark*, *wilk*). While not
without interest, this interpretation of the treatment of
original syllabic liquids and nasals in CS does not, at
least in my view, appear fully convincing. Even less cogent is, to my mind, the attempt recently undertaken by L.
Sadnik (1969) to account for the shift IE *ei* (*ei̯*) > CS *ii̯*
(ьj) in heterosyllabic position by assuming substitution
(G *Lautsubstitution*) of *i* (> ь) for allophonic '*e* (allegedly a positional variant — in tautosyllabic position before *i* — of phonemic '*ä*, the latter supposed to be the
regular CS reflex of PIE *e*). It is hard to imagine, I
would think, a more far-fetched and inherently less likely
explanation for PIE *ei* > CS *ī* (in tautosyllabic position)
and PIE *ei̯* > CS *ii̯* (> ьj, in heterosyllabic position)
than the one suggested by Sadnik, namely, on the one hand,
ei > '*äi* > '*ei* > *ī* (where the posited second stage seems
entirely superfluous) and, on the other hand, *ei* > '*äi* >
'*ei* > *ii̯* (ьj), the last change supposedly by substitution
in connection with the shifting of the syllable boundary
(where assimilation of *e* > *i* before *j* or, rather perhaps,
analogy with other instances of *ī* vs. *ii̯* > *i* vs. ьj, like
ū vs. *uu̯* > *y* vs. ьv, in tauto-ˑ vs. heterosyllabic position, respectively, would have provided a more natural explanation). For a somewhat different but rather attrac-
tive interpretation of the Slavic monophthongization *ei*,
ou > *i*, *u* in terms of distinctive feature theory and

resorting to the concept of markedness, see Andersen 1972: 25.

Expanding on some ideas set forth in work especially by Jakobson, one of his former students, E. Scatton, has given a highly interesting analysis (1968) in terms of distinctive feature theory (and rule ordering) of the CS elimination of PS liquid diphthongs (of the TORT type), claiming that the Late CS dialectal differences can be explained as due to "(1) the slightly different ordering of three changes in two of the areas under consideration, and (2) the absence of one of these changes in the third area" (286). Somewhat more complex conditions obtain in the elimination of diphthongs symbolized by the ORT formula where retention of quantity oppositions in most of the areas defined complicate the overall picture (287). On the treatment of word-initial *ort-* (or *art-*), see also Schelesniker 1969, discussing the doublets *rabъ* and *robъ* from a phonological and semantic point of view and polemicizing, in part, with the relevant views set forth by V. Georgiev. Prosodic quality (intonation) rather than quantity (length) as a decisive factor was assumed by Schelesniker 1967/68 not only for the treatment of CS *tart*, *talt* (= traditional *tort*, *tolt*) but also for *art*, *alt* (= traditional *ort-*, *olt-*), thus rejecting the notion of vowel lengthening in connection with metathesis in South Slavic (and South West Slavic). R. Abernathy's Prague congress paper, "The Slavic Liquid-Metathesis" (1968) discusses with great insight and sagacity factors, other than accentual, at work in the processes subsumed under this label and in terms of motivation goes beyond the "open syllable law" (or any of its variants).

My reinterpretation of the phonemic status of the CS modifications of PIE nasal diphthongs (Birnbaum 1963, further developing some ideas first suggested by N. S. Trubeckoj; cf. above, pp. 127-8) was placed in a broader theoretical framework in a discussion of the relationship of syntagmatic and paradigmatic phonology (Birnbaum 1967b: esp. 333-4). Trubeckoj's and my reevaluation of the CS (and Early OCS) nasal vowels were considered by Huntley (1968) in his discussion of "Two Cases of Analogical Feature Substitution in Slavic," the OCS nasal vowels, and especially the anomalous nasal vowel grapheme attested in certain OCS participles, being a case in point (501-3).

The volume *Obščeslavjanskoe značenie problemy akan'ja* (1968), published by the Bulgarian Academy of Sciences, contains contributions by four scholars, two

Bulgarian (V. I. Georgiev, who also served as the editor of the volume, and S. I. Stojkov, the well known Bulgarian dialectologist) and two Soviet (V. K. Žuravlev and F. P. Filin). These scholars attempt to summarize and vindicate the hypothesis, elaborated by Georgiev on the basis of certain suggestions made earlier by A. Vaillant and G. Y. Shevelov, according to which the so-called *akan'e* found in South Russian dialects (and in the standard Moscow pronunciation of contemporary literary Russian) as well as in Belorussian, must be considered an archaism preserving the original *a*-colored pronunciation of the CS short back vowel (< PIE *o* and *a*, and — where not dropped — *ə*), a pronunciation which is now believed by a majority of Slavists to have prevailed through most, but not all of the CS period. In other words, while nowadays most experts on Slavic diachronic phonology accept the view that Balto-Slavic and PS *ă* became distinctively rounded (flat, labialized) only toward the end of the CS period and that this late labialization (and concomitant partial closing or narrowing, rendering the vowel at least phonetically non-compact while remaining nondiffuse) at that time — presumably in the 8th/9th centuries — embraced all of the Slavic linguistic territory, Georgiev and his followers maintain that the open (compact), unrounded (nonflat or "natural") pronunciation of this vowel would have been retained in a portion or, to be exact, in several unconnected areas of the Slavic language territory. The other pillar on which Georgiev built his hypothesis is the fact that some of the so-called Rhodope dialects of Bulgarian exhibit certain features in their vocalism, comparable, though not identical with East Slavic *akan'e*; as has since been shown, they are genetically unrelated and of a different date, however. In all fairness it should be noted that the contributions (in the volume here under consideration) authored by the other three scholars take a considerably more circumspect position with respect to the main tenets of the hypothesis in question (antiquity of East Slavic *akan'e*, its genetic identity with the Bulgarian and some other Slavic phenomena, etc.), and that there is some indication that Georgiev himself now also recognizes the untenability of his hypothesis in its extreme, original form (cf. Georgiev 1970: 372-3). Of the three other contributions in the volume, Žuravlev's theoretical argumentation, applying his concept of group-phonemes, only in part supports Georgiev's hypothesis, while the separate studies by Filin, suggesting an early date for East Slavic *akan'e*, namely, the

8th/9th century (questionable but still not fully in agreement with Georgiev's nor, to be sure, even Shevelov's view that *akan'e* might simply preserve the Balto-Slavic and PS *a*-timbre of the short back vowel), and by Stojkov, examining the dialectal Bulgarian data without, however, arriving at any conclusive evidence of high antiquity, let alone CS origin of the relevant peculiarities of the vowel system concerned, can hardly be cited as an unequivocal underpinning of Georgiev's far-fetched and — in my view — essentially erroneous thinking in this matter. While not without some further adherents (cf., e.g., Aitzetmüller 1967: 90-1, or Weiher 1967: 88-9, both, to be sure, prior to the definitive formulation of Georgiev's hypothesis), the theory about "the CS significance of the problem of *akan'e*" has been severely criticized by P. Ivić (1969), J. Rigler (1969), and myself, among others (cf. Birnbaum 1970c: 47-61, with a summary also of Ivić's and Rigler's criticism, 58-61; cf. further Birnbaum 1971b). Of earlier critical voices, note in particular also Bernštejn (1961: 292), eminently competent to judge not only the East Slavic but also the relevant Bulgarian data. See now also Shevelov (1971: 303, esp. n. 4), "most emphatically" dissociating himself from Georgiev's relevant views.

If *akan'e* and comparable local phenomena in other parts of the Slavic language area cannot, therefore, be seriously considered as contributing to our insight into the vowel system of CS and its eventual spatial differentiation, the same is not necessarily true of some other developments of vocalism still observable in the writing system of the earliest texts with its imperfections and inconsistencies. This applies, for example, to the last major phonological process shared by all Early Slavic dialects (or, if you will, languages), the fall and vocalization of the *jers* (the two interrelated developments subsumable under the general term *jer* shift, proposed by Isačenko 1970a: 73), at least by one school of thought (adhered to, with some qualifications, by the present writer) considered to mark the final development in the evolution of CS in the broad sense. Prehistoric — preliterary, that is — in all branches of Slavic but OCS and Old Russian, the *jer* shift seems to have taken place relatively latest on East Slavic soil, reaching its ultimate completion in North East Slavic only by the late 12th and early 13th centuries; it can therefore, and in view of the rather ample evidence provided by a multitude of written records, best be studied on the basis of Old Russian

textual material. Continuing his earlier inquiry into
the fall of the *jers* (1964), V. V. Kolesov, studying
some phonetic characteristics of the Early Old Russian reduced vowels (1968), arrived at the conclusion that there
existed a causal connection between the fall of the *jers*
in weak position (and its corollary, the vocalization,
i.e., in effect, compensatory lengthening and merging with
e, *o* of the *jers* in strong position) and the breakdown of
the system of phonemically relevant syllabemes (closely
related to Žuravlev's group-phonemes, only representing an
even further development and systematization of one particular level of the sound pattern of CS). In the light of
some acute observations on the synchronic morphophonemics
of the vowel/zero alternations of contemporary standard
Russian (with some diachronic inferences), made some time
ago by D. S. Worth, V. Kiparsky in a recent article (1969d)
reexamined the role of stress in the treatment (i.e., fall
vs. vocalization) of CS ь, ъ in historically attested
Slavic, notably Russian and, to a somewhat lesser extent,
Serbo-Croatian. Concurring with Worth as to the importance of studying the morphophonemic mechanisms governing,
to some extent at least, seeming exceptions to the regular
treatment of the *jers* (following, by and large, "Havlík's
law," though supplemented by some specially conditioned
developments) and recognizing, it seems, the necessity of
going beyond the "obvious surface structure" (suggesting a
"deeper level" of representation also in phonology*),
Kiparsky, in concluding, feels compelled to concede "dass
wir immer noch nicht mit Sicherheit sagen können, ob die
slavischen Wörter wie *sъnъ*, *dъnъ* u. dgl. ursprünglich Oxy-
tona oder Barytona gewesen waren." Also the more all-
inclusive attempt at a reinterpretation of the Common East
Slavic *jer* shift on a morphophonemic basis, undertaken
some years ago by A. V. Isačenko (1970a), "was inspired by
D. S. Worth's important observations," this time "on the
behavior of certain Russian derivations" (73). What Isačenko set out to accomplish in his essay "East Slavic Morphophonemics and the Treatment of the Jers in Russian: a
Revision of Havlík's Law" is no less than to suggest a
sweeping reassessment of the driving forces behind the

---

*In my view, reserving the notion of "deep structure"
for semantically based units and their prelinear combination, "more abstract" would be a more appropriate term
than "deeper."

development (to zero and full vowel) in the eastern branch of what, with Durnovo, Trubeckoj, Toporov, and others, may be termed disintegrating Late CS. Isačenko has indeed covered, without any substantial gaps, the whole field of regular and irregular treatments of *jers* in Russian proper (rather than in all of East Slavic, i.e., including Ukrainian and Belorussian), accounting for and offering new, intriguing — mostly morphophonemically motivated — explanations for what at first glance appears to be a highly inconsistent development of the original, Late CS *jers*. After an initial definitional statement on "the jer shift," he discusses and analyzes in great detail "the strong jers" (suggesting, among other things, a "strong jer rule" where /ь/ is directly shifted to /o/ in all instances other than before a soft consonant), "the vowel/zero alternation" (involving a set of complex rules with different treatments for genuine Russian and "Slavonian"), "some general morpheme structure rules," "the type *mestь/mesti*," "multiple vowel/zero alternations," "elimination of multiple zero/vowel alternations," "some isolated cases," "the type *Smolensk*," "derived neuter nouns in {-#c-o}," "derived feminine nouns in {#c-a}," "derived masculine nouns in {#c}," "the groups *trьt, *tlьt, etc." and "the type *podošva*." To be sure, Isačenko's interpretation covers the whole time range of relevant phenomena, from the prehistoric period up to the Petrine epoch (and, occasionally, even later) in the history of Russian. Undoubtedly this is a most significant contribution to a new and probably better understanding also of the factors and conditions determining the "final process of Late CS" in its dialectal, East Slavic portion.

"Initiated by A. V. Isačenko's stimulating study," to quote the author (257), J. Marvan has recently examined "some structural aspects of the development of jers" (1971), focusing in particular on the crucial question of the relative chronology as regards *jer* shift (or "jer breakdown") and vowel contraction, another of the largely dialectal, Late CS (or possibly post-CS, Early Slavic) processes, and drawing on his own previous and simultaneous research on vowel contraction (cf. Marvan 1966, 1968a, 1968b, 1968c, 1968d, 1972). Marvan notes (253-4) that

> the 10th century is the time when the jers were disappearing in the West and South Slavic dialects. This process, however, is not homogeneous either

territorially or typologically. The Bulgarian data
prove that this area was one center of this process
while the contraction indicates Czech as its other
source. Bulgarian and other SouthSl[avic] dialects
exhibit certain exceptions to 'Havlík's rule' (e.g.,
in the first syllable), while WestSl[avic] followed
it consistently at that time. Thus, 'Havlík's rule'
applies to the system for which it has been formulated. Its automatic and unconditional generalization is not only inexact, as proved particularly by
Isačenko, but is also a source of criticism of facts
never stated by the man with whose name the rule is
connected.

And Marvan goes on to state his position on the chronological relationship between *jer* shift and vowel contraction
(255):

The jer-shift, preceded by the contraction which
principally disintegrated the Slavic area . . . cannot be a Protoslavic process, not even the very
last. Nevertheless, the process is so similar in
all Slavic languages that it is not distinguished
. . . But a critical approach to the similarities is
not only possible but also necessary for the interpretation of the process and its causes. The similarity is evidently motivated by the 'same conditions', common structural prerequisites, and common
changes as well.

Despite the basic similarity of the *jer* shift in all of
the Slavic linguistic territory, acknowledged by Marvan,
he does not consider this a truly CS (= PS) process; not
even vowel contraction, centered in West Slavic (especially Proto-Czech) and northwestern South Slavic (especially
Proto-Slovenian), is attributed CS status by him. Thus,
already in one of the opening sections of his article he
claims (250) that

The attempts to ascribe common Slavic character to
the contraction must be consistently refused as they
contain certain basic mistakes concerning the space
(contracting in North Russian without a proper transition in South Russian and Ukrainian), chronology
(the process is still in progress in North Russian
while in the West it was completed by 1100), and
typology (the Bulgarian and Macedonian groups with x
are not only new but also completely different from

those which were contracted in the West.

While a panchronic and typological interpretation of Slavic vowel contraction is of course possible (cf. also Bernštejn 1968a), it would seem unreasonable to deny the Late
CS nature of "the prehistoric contraction which changed
not some particular phonetic and morphologic details, but
the whole phonemic and morphologic structure of the dialects in half of the Slavic area" (*ibid.*). At least if
conceived broadly, vowel contraction in its earliest manifestations (to be subsequently repeated in a similar vein
on various occasions and in various subareas of Slavic in
the historical period), should therefore be included in
the last phase of Late CS dialectal disintegration. In my
present thinking, a similar reasoning would also apply,
for example, to a geographically limited, but obviously
prehistoric sound shift such as $g > \gamma$ ($> h$); cf. Birnbaum
1965b: 3-4; 1966a: 156-7; and, more recently and with a
different emphasis, Birnbaum 1970c: 28-9. See further also
below, pp. 266-7. The controversial relative chronology
of vowel contraction (after the dropping of intervocalic
j) and *jer* shift is, as was already hinted, also the topic
of an interesting paper by S. B. Bernštejn (1968a), presented at the Sixth International Congress of Slavists in
Prague, where this problem is viewed in connection with
some aspects of syllable structure. Noting that Trubeckoj
(1928/29) had already considered vowel contraction, in
part at least, as preceding the fall of the *jers* (a view,
as we have seen, shared also by Marvan), Bernštejn attempts to make a case — not fully convincing, I would
claim — for the opposite opinion, namely that while, to be
sure, taking place in Slavic at various times and under
various conditions, vowel contractions occurred in Slavic
"always after the loss of the ultra-short vowels [= *jers*,
H. B.], i.e., after the breakdown of the PS syllable
structure (syllabemes)" (29). W. Mańczak (1966), in his
study of data illustrating prehistoric as well as historic
vowel contraction in Slavic, is less concerned with chronology and more eager to use the case of Slavic vowel contraction as another instance of his frequency-determined
theory of relative word length and irregular sound change.
In a recent article dealing with some aspects of Slavic
vowel contraction, F. V. Mareš (1971b) has primarily been
interested in the quality (timbre) of the new vowel resulting from contraction and the factors determining it,
while confining himself to a few passing remarks about the

258

period of the earliest instances of these types of phonological processes. It seems that Mareš considers them
Proto-Czech, Proto-Slovak, etc., i.e., Early Slavic rather
than strictly CS.

Of work on another problem of the vowel system in
the Late CS or, rather, Early Slavic period, Z. Stieber's
succinct statement (1966) on the substitution for Latin $\bar{o}$
(*Rōma*), $\ubreve{u}$ (*crŭcem*), and $\bar{u}$ (*iūdaeus*) uniformly by Slavic *i*
(rather than by a conceivable *y*) in *Rimъ*, *križъ*, *židъ*, deserves mention. Referring to his earlier discussion of
the phonetic value of CS *y* (Stieber 1963) and to Bidwell's
paper on the chronology of certain sound shifts in CS as
evidenced by loans from Vulgar Latin (1961), Stieber elu-
cidates some moot points in these substitutions while
identifying one, for the time being, inexplicable prosodic
detail, namely, why the Slavs adapted *židъ* with a long
root vowel despite the fact that in Romance it was unstressed and must thus have been shortened (*iūdaeus* >
*žudêu, or, rather, *žudêu; cf. It *Giudeo*).

9.3. The Common Slavic Consonant System. Work on CS consonantism has proceeded along several lines during recent
years. Among studies discussing problems of the Early CS
(PS) consonant system and its relationship to earlier —
PIE or dialectal IE — phases in the evolution of the sound
pattern, the monograph by V. V. Martynov, *Slavjanskaja i
indoevropejskaja akkomodacija* (1968), is of considerable
interest. In it, the author argues for an uninterrupted
continuity between the consonant systems of the IE protolanguage and the ancestral language of the Slavs. In particular, Martynov's study examines the process of palatalization and depalatalization from PIE to PS, endeavors
to reconstruct the qualitative (timbre) correlations of
various groups of phonemes (vocalic as well as consonantal) during the two main periods concerned, and attempts
to demonstrate that syllabic synharmonism was not, in
fact, a Slavic innovation but was inherited from a preceding period. The two major portions of the book analyze
in some detail "the accomodation of dentals and the establishment of the PS state of affairs" (24-75) and "the accomodation of velars and the establishment of the pre-
Slavic (IE) state of affairs" (76-164). The introduction
(3-23) discusses recent relevant accomplishments achieved
by Comparative IE Linguistics and, to some extent, Slavic
Linguistics, pointing especially to the significant advances brought about by the introduction of typological

considerations and aspects of the theory of linguistic universals into the work on reconstructing protolanguages. Operating with the whole range of contemporary linguistic techniques and concepts and analyzing a great number of diagnostic lexical items, this monograph in its general methodological outlook appears to be quite close to the general position taken by V. K. Žuravlev and to his over- all interpretation. It is greatly surprising, therefore, that, as far as I have been able to determine, there is not a single reference to the relevant work of Žuravlev — for many years active in Minsk like Martynov! — while oth- er relevant studies (by Jakobson, Benveniste, Martinet, Trubeckoj, Milewski, Machek, Mareš, Illič-Svityč, Trubačev, and many others) are frequently cited. Well aware of the largely hypothetic nature of his conclusions, Martynov, in a final section of his book (165-70), formulates a set of tentative statements characterizing, in general terms, the sound system of PS (including, incidentally, also vocal- ism, viewed in the framework of the assumed syllabic syn- harmonism) and the relationship between Early CS (PS) and the preceding IE (Late PIE, pre-Slavic) stage of develop- ment partially expressible in a set of IE-PS correspond- ences reflecting the Slavic development of a variety of posited PIE velars (and velar clusters). Among the lat- ter, Martynov assumes also a set of pre-Slavic velar fric- atives (x, h, H) claimed to be identical with the so- called laryngeals of IE; cf. 168-9. The highly hypothetic nature of some of Martynov's conclusions is mitigated, to some extent, by his own acknowledgment of the merely ex- ploratory character of his explanations suggested in an area of considerable controversy indeed.

Among the lexical items adduced in Martynov's dis- cussion is CS *gǫsь* 'goose' (cf. Lith *žąsìs*) whose irregu- lar initial consonantism (*g*- for expected *z*- < PIE *g'h*-) has given rise to various explanations (dissimilation due to following, word-medial -*s*-; reflex of PIE so-called velar alternation, G *Gutturalwechsel*; influence of German- ic *gans*). Martynov now adds still another, hardly more likely explanation of CS *g*- in this word as reflecting PIE *H* < *H'* (164). Fairly recently, a new interpretation was proposed by J. B. Rudnyćkyj (1970) who — not very convinc- ingly, in my opinion – identified the Ukrainian interjec- tion *dzus*, *dzus'* < **zus'* (cf. Ukr *dzerkalo* < *zerkalo*, *dzvin* < *zvonь*, etc.) with the Slavic word for 'goose', thus supposedly allowing him to formulate the following conclusions (416):

(1)   The Indo-European word **$ghansis$ [= *$g'hansis$?
H. B.] 'goose', despite its 'kentumization' in all
Slavic languages, is preserved in its *satem*-form in
Ukrainian $dzu\overset{\frown}{s}$.   (2)   This word confirms the general
acceptance of the original Slavic, Baltic, etc.
change of $\acute{k}$-, $\acute{g}$- to *satem*-type consonants leaving no
doubts as to their changes into sibilants.

Even if the Ukrainian interjection could be identified
with the Slavic word for 'goose' (although its purely onomatopoetic character seems at least equally likely), the
factors responsible for the g-form in all or most of Slavic remain unaccounted for.

The sound shift /r/ > /tr/ after /s/ or, put differently, the change (insertion) $sr > str$ (further, similarly
and secondarily, $zr > zdr$) found in Slavic, but known also
from Germanic and, partly, Baltic as well as some extinct
Balkan IE languages, and therefore occasionally considered
a pre-Slavic (dialectal Late PIE) process, was briefly
discussed by H. Andersen (1972: 38) in terms of distinctive feature theory. He utilizes the notion of markedness
and treats this and some typologically comparable developments in the framework of a new overall theory of diphthongization as instances of intra-segmental variation
with a distribution of the opposite values of the feature
[±vocalic] within the segment in the order unmarked-
marked.

It is also Andersen who can be credited with a new,
ingenious if somewhat far-fetched explanation for the CS
reflex x < PIE s in the position after $\breve{\bar{\imath}}$, $\breve{\bar{u}}$, r, k (and its
allophones), paralleled, in part, in Baltic by the shift
$s > \check{s}$ (with a further counterpart, under somewhat different conditions, in Indo-Iranian). Assuming an early, Late
PIE split of s into two positional variants, one unmarked
(denoted s_1), the other one marked (in the position indicated above, s_2), Andersen (1968) suggests that the marked
variant of PIE s (s_2) yielded $\check{s}$ in Baltic (represented by
Lithuanian), but x in Slavic. PIE k' (partly < g') is
said to have coincided in Slavic with the unmarked s (s_1)
while merging with the marked variety of that sound (s_2)
in Baltic. In this different treatment of PIE k' Andersen
sees the first isogloss separating Baltic from Slavic (cf.
for some further thoughts on this also Andersen 1970a).
As an explanation for the puzzling fact that the shift
discussed occurred in the position after a set of largely
heterogeneous sounds, he suggests that all four of these

sounds (and their allophones) represent the marked members of the specific subcategories to which they belong: i and u, being diffuse, are the marked members of the vowel class (whose optimal member, a, is compact); k (and g) is marked for compactness in the consonant class (the optimal consonant, t, being diffuse); and r is the marked member in the opposition abrupt/nonabrupt (continuous), characteristic for liquids (or perhaps even the whole class of sonorants and glides). It is thus, according to Andersen, by virtue of this — to be sure, highly abstract — markedness assimilation that the marked variant of s (s_2) in the position after $\breve{i}$, $\breve{u}$, r, k developed. Brilliant as this explanation no doubt is, it suffers, however, also from certain shortcomings. For a more detailed assessment of Andersen's theory as well as for a discussion of some additional problems of this sound shift (e.g., the question of whether an intermediate stage $\breve{s}$ must be posited also for the Slavic change $s > x$ as well as the proper evaluation of the parallel Baltic and Indo-Iranian developments), see Birnbaum 1971a. For some additional considerations, continuing Andersen's line of thinking and suggesting some further "explorations into markedness" cf. Shapiro 1972: 361-3.

As is well known, PIE s is not the only source of Slavic x. For earlier work pertaining to CS x in word-initial position, see above, pp. 147-8. Yet another origin of Slavic x may have been its occurrence as an affective (emotive) means of expression. Such a possibility was explored at some length already, for example, by V. Machek (1939) and G. Y. Shevelov (1964: esp. 132-4; see also further references, 138) and has newly been reexamined by J. Otrębski (1970a) who concludes (60):

> Die slavischen Konsonanten s, k (g) und sk wurden durch das ch [= x, H. B.] ersetzt, wenn es galt eine besondere, meist augmentative bzw. deteriorierende Bedeutungsnuance der betreffenden Wörter zu bezeichnen.

He hastens to add, however (*ibid.*):

> Es ist leider zur Zeit noch nicht möglich, die Geschichte des expressiven ch in allen Einzelheiten darzustellen.

Cf. also above, p. 99.

The CS and Early Slavic Palatalization of Velars have continued to capture the attention of linguists up to

the present. In particular, several scholars have tried
to come to grips with the highly controversial problem of
relative chronology by adopting various, partly new approaches. Since the order between the First and Second
(regressive) Palatalizations is noncontroversial, it is
only natural that this well-established time succession
has been made a test case by linguists interested in (and
partly committed to) the claim of early generative theory
as to a far-reaching parallelism said to obtain between
the synchronic order of phonological rules (including the
important technique of rule reordering), on the one hand,
and relative chronology derived from diachronic change, on
the other. This claim was challenged by V. Zeps (1967),
among others, in a paper on the Palatalizations of Velars
as evidenced by OCS. Pointing out at the beginning of his
discussion (145) that "it is a commonplace that morphophonemics to some degree mirrors history, i.e., that historical changes survive as morphophonemic alternations," he
proceeds to demonstrate, on the basis of the two regressive palatalizations reflected in OCS, that the undisputed
relative chronology of these two historical processes and
the set of ordered generative rules devised to account for
both alternations in a unified fashion cannot be conceived
as matching each other in a one-to-one relationship. As a
result, after exploring several alternatives by either reshaping the order of rules so as to indeed parallel the
presumed historical order or unifying the two crucial —
palatalization — rules into one (with its components, however, in a reversed, "non-historical" order), Zeps suggests
not only "the strong possibility that the synchronic and
diachronic order of rules can disagree," but also questions "the credibility of internal reconstruction, especially if it involves the type of details and time depth
in reconstructions of Proto-IE from IE, and the like"
(150). It is thus not in this, now rather generally abandoned, claim that Zeps, a collaborator of M. Halle, sees
the major contribution of formal (generative) grammar to
diachronic linguistics. The obvious limitations and inherent inconsistencies resulting from the belief in this
sort of nonaccidental parallelism between the synchronic
and diachronic order of rules were further discussed and
demonstrated on a related set of data, until quite recently believed noncontroversial in terms of relative chronology (First and Progressive Palatalizations of Velars as
attested in OCS), in my paper "Rekonstrukcja wewnętrzna,
kolejność synchronicznych reguł gramatyki syntetycznej i

zagadnienie najdawniejszych stosunków między językami bałtyckimi i słowiańskimi" (Birnbaum 1968b), available also
in a slightly revised and extended English version (1970b:
92-122, adding a discussion of Zeps 1967 and Chomsky &
Halle 1968: 420-30). In their detailed and more comprehensive treatment of Slavic palatalizations — including
also the palatalizations of dentals (t, d, s, z) when combined with a following j, but excluding, like Zeps, the
results of the progressive (Baudouin) palatalization from
their considerations — N.Chomsky and M. Halle arrive at an
order of rules, different from those proposed by Zeps,
which indeed seems to parallel the well-established relative chronology of the two regressive palatalizations (for
some new thoughts on the reflexes of CS tj, dj, see, e.g.,
Pavlović 1966/67). This excursus in a monograph otherwise
devoted primarily to *The Sound Pattern of English* (1968),
which at the same time, however, represents a major statement on the then attained positions of generative phonology, obviously reflects primarily Halle's earlier thinking
on these matters. As I have commented on Chomsky's and
Halle's relevant conclusions elsewhere (Birnbaum 1970b:
111-13), I can here confine myself to stating that their,
to be sure, quite sophisticated and detailed, if often
arguable, analysis of the relevant data seems, to me at
least, quite unpersuasive as to the claim that any nonaccidental, indeed motivated, parallelism between relative
chronology of diachronic sound change and the order in the
application of synchronic generative rules to account more
adequately for the observable phonetic surface data, as
tested on the CS (and Early Slavic) Palatalizations of
Velars and related phenomena, can in fact be ascertained.
Thoughts of a somewhat different kind were voiced by J.
Hamm (1969) who deals primarily with some as yet controversial issues of causality and chronology regarding the
modifications of velars in CS. Discussing above all the
Third (Baudouin) Palatalization, which he does not consider simply progressive, Hamm interprets this process as,
in part at least, morphologically conditioned (and thus
largely a phenomenon describable in morphophonemic terms).
In this, his position comes close to that advocated earlier especially by J. Otrębski (1948), even though Hamm's
approach is, of course, a more modern one. Hamm's re-
liance on "deep (derivational) morphology," in recent
years theoretically elaborated with Slavic data by D. S.
Worth in particular, also for resolving or rather rendering largely insubstantial the controversial chronology of

this palatalization (in relation to the Second — regressive — Palatalization of Velars), seems on the whole less convincing.

While the relative chronology of the Second (regressive) Palatalization and the Third (by some linguists numbered Second, progressive, or Baudouin) Palatalization of Velars continues to be a much debated issue (cf., e.g., of recent specialized research on this problem, Thümmel 1967, Jeżowa 1968, Otrębski 1970b — all, in addition, discussing other aspects of the progressive palatalization), the CS and, indeed, PS nature of the Second Palatalization of Velars (type $k\breve{e}_2 > c\breve{e}$) had not been seriously questioned until recently. However, on the basis of some revealing observations of NW Russian dialectal material made by Gluskina (1966), supplemented by evidence pointing in the same direction gathered from a Russian dialect atlas (reporting on relevant data from the area east of Moscow, 1957), Z. Stieber in a recent article (1968a) concluded that the Second Palatalization of Velars cannot have been a strictly CS (let alone PS) process in view of the reported instances of unshifted or only partly shifted consonants (i.e., retention of k', etc., or incomplete change to t', etc.). Therefore, at most this sound change could have been CS in the broad sense of including dialectally differentiated Early Slavic; the Second Palatalization is thus dated by Stieber to approximately the 6th/7th centuries; cf. also above, pp. 50, 136. In addition, Stieber suggests that the shift $kv' > cv'$, etc., was neither Proto-Russian (Common East Slavic) nor, in all probability, even generally Russian (Great Russian). For a more detailed discussion of Stieber's findings, see also Birnbaum 1970c: 42-6. Prompted by Gluskina's and Stieber's observations and suggestions, Ferrell (1970) added some interesting but, in my view, perhaps not sufficiently warranted surmises and reinterpretations, attempting to establish a connection between the resistance to various degrees to dorsal palatalization (yielding hissing palatals at first) in all regions of East Slavic and the dialectal phenomenon referred to as $cokan'e$ (i.e., coalescence of the hissing and hushing series of, at least originally, palatal affricates and fricatives into one series, usually of the hissing type).

Phenomena of CS palatalization, yielding palatal (subsequently in part again depalatalized) consonants in alternation with nonpalatal ("hard") consonants, were further studied from a morphophonemic and morphological (derivational) point of view, analyzing the processes and alternations involved in the formation of diminutives, in R. I. Avanesov's contribution (1968) to the Sixth International Congress of Slavists, Prague, "K istorii čeredovanija soglasnyx pri obrazovanii umen'šitel'nyx suščestvitel'nyx v praslavjanskom." For some possible factors (influence of Baltic Finnic substratum) restraining the spread of forms exhibiting the results of the progressive Baudouin Palatalization (-*ica*, competing with -*ika*) in Russian, see Kiparsky 1970 (cf. also below, p. 286).

A dialectal innovation of Late CS, the shift $g > \gamma$ ($> h$) and some related processes, were reexamined from a new theoretical angle by H. Andersen in his thought-provoking paper "Lenition in Common Slavic" (1969a). To quote the brief abstract prefacing his article,

Three different reflexes of Proto-Slavic *g and the reflex of *$d\underset{\sim}{i}$ changed to fricatives in early Slavic. A hitherto unnoticed sequential constraint in Common Slavic, along with the geographical limitations of these changes, permits us to date them relative to the loss of syllable-final obstruents in CSl., to the fall of the jers, and to one another. Typological analysis shows that the source of the phonetic changes was a pronunciation rule implying phonemically tense vs. lax obstruents in CSl. The relative chronology established is significant for several problems of chronology within Slavic and for its relation to Baltic; and the set of concentric isoglosses defined throws light on the pattern of expansion of early Slavic.

Combining in this way an imaginatively interpreted distinctive feature theory with sound dialectological method and applying them to prehistoric Slavic linguistic data is, in my opinion, the kind of work from which our knowledge of the sound pattern of reconstructed CS and Early Slavic can still be significantly advanced. For some highly critical remarks on lenition in CS, see, however, Shevelov 1971: 323. The same keen insight and apt methodology is characteristic also for Andersen's recent study (1969b) on another Central Slavic innovation of dialectal CS, the change of *ot*(ь) to *od*, for which a purely phonological interpretation ("voicing sandhi") is offered in lieu of earlier, less satisfactory explanations (by Baudouin de Courtenay, Rudnicki, and Machek). For a recent discussion of the shift $g > \gamma > h$ in part of the Slavic

language area, focusing especially on the somewhat controversial question of chronology but commenting as well
on the purely phonetic aspect of this change (or, rather,
these two successive changes), see F. V. Mareš 1971a.

*9.4. Patterning Factors of Common Slavic Sound Change:
Syllable Structure, Auslaut, Morphophonemics.* In the late
sixties, V. K. Žuravlev, the originator of the theory of
group-phonemes in CS, continued to develop the theoretical
framework of this concept, having its roots in R. Jakobson's assumption of syllabic synharmonism as one of the
governing principles of CS phonology; cf. above, pp. 86
-7 and 142-4. Thus, in an article published in 1966,
Žuravlev endeavored to define the group-phoneme (closely
akin to the syllabeme but not fully identical with it) as
the basic phonological unit of CS. And in a paper, presented in 1966 at the International Phonologist Meeting,
Žuravlev outlined a phonological (phonemic) interpretation
of the CS group-phonemes in the framework of a theory of
languages of the 'syllabemic' type (Žuravlev 1967a). While
not without certain indisputable merits and characterized
by forceful reasoning, as most of the Soviet linguist's
work, the line supposedly separating his group-phonemes
from full-fledged syllabemes (i.e., phonemically relevant
units coinciding in range with the syllable) becomes thin
indeed. Moreover, it is not clear, at least to the present writer, how units of qualitatively and quantitatively
different kinds (phonemes and group-phonemes) can, on
theoretical grounds, be assumed at any time to have coexisted at the same level of representation, granted even
that group-phonemes at a given period represented the
"basic" units of phonology. As I pointed out in the discussion after the presentation of Žuravlev's paper (cf.
op. cit.: 155),

> it is difficult to see the basic difference between
> the theory of . . . Žuravlev and the notion of syn-
> harmonism as originally formulated by Jakobson.
> This theory was strongly criticized by van Wijk . . .
> Žuravlev would have to prove that the group-
> phonemes are indeed inseparable units. We do not
> really need to operate with two units, both on the
> same level of abstraction, phonemes and group-
> phonemes, unless we can actually show that there is
> something in the combination $C + V$ which makes it
> inseparable (and not a mere succession of two

267

segments characterized by certain suprasegmental features).

These critical remarks notwithstanding, I do, as was mentioned, recognize some merit inherent in Žuravlev's theory. Also, I was gratified to note that, in replying to my comments, Žuravlev took a clearer stand on the distinction between group-phoneme and syllabeme by pointing out (157) that "synharmonism in CS was not syllabic, there existed only a tendency in this direction." And he added that

> a certain negligence on the part of R. O. Jakobson did harm to his theory and brought to a standstill the advancement of the theory of CS for several decades. But the further development of this theory can, whether we like it or not, only be achieved by a revision and more precise definition of the hypothesis regarding synharmonism.

Taking as their point of departure not Jakobson's concept of syllabic synharmonism in CS but A. Martinet's illustration of his typologically based theory of open-syllable languages (cf. above, p. 142), G. Y. Shevelov and J. J. Chew, Jr., in a recent joint paper, "Open Syllable Languages and their Evolution: Common Slavic and Japanese" (1969), closely examined on a contrastive basis these two totally unrelated languages, viewing Japanese largely in a diachronic perspective. While heavily relying for CS on Shevelov's earlier comprehensive treatment of its phonology (Shevelov 1964), suggesting, however, a few chronological revisions, the sound changes of Japanese are traced in their presumed chronological order and "for each sound change a motivation is sought in conjunction with the problem of 'open syllable languages,' a comparison with CS is tentatively drawn, and the reasons for similarity, or the lack of it, are suggested" (254-5). As it turns out, a great number of striking resemblances, all explicable in typological terms, can be ascertained between the diachronic development of Japanese and CS or Early Slavic (cf. 272). Just as the similarities — pointed out by Martinet — between Old French and CS, for all intents and purposes unrelated, can be explained largely in terms of the trend toward open syllables and, before completion, its breakdown and ultimate reversion, a considerable parallelism in the phonological evolution of Japanese and prehistoric and early attested Slavic can be shown to exist. In all three cases, vowel syn- and

268

apocope (*i*, *u* in Japanese, ь, ъ in Slavic, *e muet* in
French) seem to have been the decisive factor for revers-
ing the general trend in the development of the respective
phonological systems (*ibid.*). This is a perfect instance
of demonstrating the fruitfulness of applying typological
considerations (yielding universal criteria and typologically definable generalizations) to linguistic diachrony
for the purpose of gaining deeper and more meaningful insights into the moving forces behind the changes in a dynamic, ever developing sound system. The fact that this
is a truly integrated study, finding its expression in
Shevelov's — the Slavist's — commenting from a compara-
tive-typological position also on the Japanese data, only
enhances its value.

It is somewhat less fortunate when a specialist in
one field (or even several fields) tries his hand at a
body of data and a set of corresponding problems without
the close advice of an expert in the field. This is the
case with two, to be sure, interesting papers dealing with
the controversial question of the treatment of word-final
position in CS, written by two Romanists, of which one is
also a trained phonetician (and expert in computational
linguistics) while the other can claim expertise in matters of general linguistic theory even though his outlook
is characterized by a heavy anti-structuralist bias and an
almost monomaniac preoccupation with the statistically interpreted relationship between frequency and word-length
(accounting for what he subsumes under the notion of "irregular sound change"). Of the two papers in question, H.
Lüdtke's "Gibt es urslavische Auslautgesetze?" (1966) no
doubt covers more ground and is, generally speaking, more
ambitious. The short paper by W. Mańczak, "W sprawie końcówek prasłowiańskich" (1970b), continuing his endeavors
in this direction (Mańczak 1967, 1969 and 1970a), discussed above and below (pp. 244-5 and 282), and polemicizing, in particular, with some views expressed by F. V.
Mareš, has a more limited goal but is essentially only
another variation of his recurrent theme (echoing Zipf)
about the causal impact of frequency on — irregular —
phonetic change. Although marked by certain basic similarities in the tenor of their conclusions, Lüdtke's well-
argued (if not always quite accurate) assessment of the
Slavic linguistic data (of which his knowledge seems to be
primarily derivative) deserves by and large more attention
than Mańczak's rather one-sided mechanistic (reductionist)
view of the high-frequency treatment of CS auslaut.

Rejecting, first (with Kuryłowicz), the positing of PIE
intonation contrasts as relevant for Balto-Slavic, second,
the assumption that PIE /ā̆/ and /ō̆/ developed differently
while coalescing in Balto-Slavic, and third, the postulate
of qualitative auslaut rules, Lüdtke, in closing, suggests
two hypotheses instead: (1) the existence of a rigorous
principle determining the modification of word-final vocalism after /j/ and palatal consonants (hitherto neither
denied nor consistently asserted); and (2) qualitative
variation (allophony) of the CS vocalic phoneme reflecting
PIE /ā̆ = ŏ/. Contrary to the refuted qualitative rules
for auslaut, quantitative (i.e., reductive) rules governing word-final position are being assumed as before: loss
of word-final consonants and denasalization. Lüdtke continues also to consider the avoidance of homonymy an important factor accounting for phonetic differentiation of
inflectional endings. Further morphological considerations (such as productivity or regression of various declensional stem classes) are taken into account while former (PIE) quantity differences in diphthongs are attributed no significance. Even if the validity of Lüdtke's
general conclusions, arrived at mostly on the basis of
secondary interpretations of the Slavic data (including
Slavic borrowings from and loans into other languages)
need to be tested further, his unprejudiced and fundamentally sound approach certainly must be considered in future discussions of the treatment of word-final position
in CS. In his concluding remarks, Lüdtke also touched
upon the already much debated problem of the dialectal CS
doublets in $-e/-\breve{e}_3$ (< $-jens$) and $-y/-a$ (< $-ons$ < $-ans$ or
possibly < $*-\bar{o}n/-\bar{o}$); cf. above, pp. 145, 157. A new, rather
complex explanation for these doublets, drawing analogies
with Baltic and positing "two sets of competing morphemes
for the same minimal unit of content," was some time ago
proposed by W. R. Schmalstieg (1968: 52). Cf. now further
Ferrell 1971, briefly discussed below (pp. 280-1). For some
additional considerations on the development of Early CS
(PS) auslaut, see also Duridanov 1968a, who considers the
shifts $-\bar{e} > -\bar{\imath}$ and $-\bar{o} > -\bar{u}$ (> $-y$), accounting for such
forms as OCS *dъšti* (cf. Lith *duktě̃*) and *kamy* (cf. Lith
akmuõ), the earliest exclusively Slavic, i.e., post-Balto-
Slavic, phonological development (cf. 19).

    Problems of CS and Early Slavic morphophonemics were
discussed or implicitly dealt with in the last few years
in articles by Avanesov (1968), Dybo (1968), Georgiev
(1968 and 1969), Hamm (1966 and 1969), and Isačenko

(1970a), referred to above and below, in addition to previously recorded current research on ablaut. A new attempt at a systematic presentation of Slavic morphophonemics, viewed on a comparative basis (within the limits of
the Slavic languages) and integrating some new observations and insights with generally accepted, standard knowledge, was made by S. Bernštejn in his essay "Vvedenie v
slavjanskuju morfonologiju" (1968b), conceived as a sort
of continuation of (or, rather perhaps, chapter in a
forthcoming sequel to) his 1961 introduction to Comparative Slavic Linguistics (cf. above, pp. 90 - 4) and appropriately dedicated to the memory of P. S. Kuznecov (cf.
especially Kuznecov 1954, briefly discussed above, p. 149).
It goes without saying that a great many of the morphophonemic alternations ascertainable in the modern literary
Slavic languages and surveyed by Bernštejn go back to prehistoric, CS times. The report on "Slavic Morphophonemics
in its Typological and Diachronic Aspects" by E. Stankiewicz (1966b; cf. also Stankiewicz 1960 and 1964, mostly
discussing modern data, however), although relevant to
some extent also to CS morphophonemic, especially vowel ~
zero, consonantal, and accentual alternations, reports on
research in the field but also bears on the linguistic
data, including Late CS, and its interpretation.

10. CURRENT RESEARCH ON THE WORD FORM SYSTEM OF COMMON SLAVIC

10.0. New Approaches to Common Slavic Morphology. The remarks opening the section on Morphology in Part One of this report on the particular methodological predicament of research on prehistoric Slavic morphology are applicable also to the following discussion and therefore again called to the reader's attention. Note, too, the reference to some reasoning of a similar kind in Andersen 1971 and Birnbaum 1973. As Andersen aptly put it (950),

> The student of the prehistorical morphology of Slavic faces formidable problems . . . as a consequence of regular phonological developments in prehistoric Slavic . . . the Slavic data alone are not sufficient for the reconstruction of a Proto-Slavic . . . system. Such a system can be posited on the basis of other Indo-European languages; but this reduces the study of Slavic prehistoric morphology to the task of reconciling the attested desinences with what can reasonably be posited for Proto-Slavic and postulating ad hoc changes for those difficult desinences whose attested forms are not directly related to their supposed Proto-Slavic etyma by general, regular phonological changes.

In other words, there is a vast gap separating the readily recoverable word form system of Late CS (as it can be reconstructed on the strength of the attested Slavic, especially Early Slavic, evidence, in most cases identical with that of OCS, the few exceptions and deviations being easily derivable from other ancient Slavic data, notably Old Russian) and the initial phase of Early PS, just emerged from dialectal Late PIE (or possibly a common

Balto-Slavic linguistic structure). Thus, while the polarization between the Early PS and Late CS state of affairs is considerable, the method of internal reconstruction providing techniques for establishing relative chronologies and recovering lost evolutionary phases is poorly
developed and quite inadequate when it comes to morphological change. Nonetheless, in recent years research on
charting and tracing the diachronic dynamics of paradigmatic — inflectional and derivational — variation of the
word form system in the CS (and Early Slavic) period has
made some progress by reassessing earlier positions concerning the morphological structure of prehistoric Slavic
and exploring new approaches and devices of linguistic inquiry. Some of these advances are, incidentally, already
reflected in the overall treatments of CS morphology as
presented in the framework of some of the more modern
textbooks and reference works designed for university use
(cf., e.g., the parts dealing with morphology in such
texts and outlines as Bräuer 1961/69; *Vstup* . . . 1966;
Vaillant 1950/66; and, in particular, Stieber 1969/71 and
1970; see further also Watkins 1969, and Szemerényi 1970).
Yet most of the relevant exploratory work on theory and
method can be found so far in article and occasionally
monograph form.

An attempt to explore some new avenues of approach
to certain problems of Slavic diachronic — largely prehistoric — morphology was ventured by J. Hamm in his 1966 essay "Entropy in Slavic Morphology." Hamm uses the term
entropy neither in the meaning which it has in thermodyna-
mics nor even in communication theory, as one might expect, but rather in accordance with its etymological
(Greek) meaning "to denote the turning of sound features
into distinctive morphological units" (40). Pointing out
that the introduction of new technical terms is justified
in linguistics if, and only if, the new terminology serves
the purpose of expressing a truly new and powerful set of
concepts and techniques (as was the case, for example,
with the Latin-Greek terminology coined by J. Baudouin de
Courtenay, cited by way of illustration), and referring
briefly to the 'means-ends model of language' sketched by
R. Jakobson, Hamm, after some preliminary remarks concerning the proper interpretation of certain phonological and
morphological developments from PIE through Late CS (as
represented by OCS), discusses "the question of morphophonemic clues concerning inflexional patterns, and to what
extent they can be used for closer diachronic identifica-

273

tion" (43). "Theoretically," the Croat-Austrian Slavist goes on, "every sound — vowel or consonant — possesses the capability of becoming entropic, of causing — or expressing — particular changes in morphological structure. But in reality we know that only a few vowels and consonants are capable of displaying morphologically distinctive functions . . ." (*ibid.*). He then comments on his notion of '(morphological) entropy' which, although "a concomitant feature, . . . always represents a full, phonologically as well as morphonologically distinct unit, equalizing the one heading the string of features in question" (*ibid.*). Applying these (and some related) somewhat nebulous concepts to the diachronic sequence PS - CS - OCS (the third link in this chain, to be sure, "already individually marked"), Hamm proceeds to examine the development of a crucial segment of Slavic declension, namely the feminine -$\bar{a}$ and masculine -o and -u stems, commenting also on some other stem classes, feminine -i and -r stems, and adducing comparative IE evidence especially from Baltic. By pursuing this line of reasoning and pointing up certain superficial (phonological) as well as deep-seated (semantic) links and interrelations determining the restructuring of this segment of inflectional morphology in Slavic (and Baltic), Hamm, with this sketchy and somewhat unsystematic study, has contributed a number of interesting new ideas which deserve to be further pursued and more rigorously organized, tested, and formalized.

The interplay between phonological and morphological units and factors, as applied to prehistoric Slavic and Early Slavic data, is also at the heart of some exploratory studies in this field by V. Georgiev. His article, "Fonematičeskij i morfematičeskij podxod k ob"jasneniju fleksii slavjanskix jazykov" (1968), is rather of a programmatic and illustrative nature, discussing the conceptual framework of "phonemes and morphophonemes" and formulating some presumably universal "morphemic laws," applicable to the case system (here illustrated with Slavic, mostly OCS — in Georgiev's terminology, Old Bulgarian — data, with some additional comments on its pre-Slavic antecedents), and elaborating at some length on "cases and syntactic categories," using medieval and modern Slavic (primarily OCS and CSR) examples. The Bulgarian linguist's 1969 monograph, *Osnovni problemi na slavjanskata diaxronna morfologija*, pursues a more ambitious goal, granted its title is patently misleading since Georgiev's book, in its major, second part (chapters three through

twelve), is concerned exclusively with the development of
the Slavic nominal declensions, stem class by stem class
(chapters 3-11) in addition to "the origin of the present
active participle inflection" (chapter 12). The much
shorter, first part of Georgiev's monograph (chapters 1-2)
presents his theoretical premises, "the phonemic and morphological approaches to the explanation of Slavic inflection" (chapter 1, largely, but not in its entirety, merely
a variant of his 1968 Russian paper) and "phonemic changes
in final syllables (chapter 2). Three sections of the
Russian resumé (167-78), despite slightly rephrased subheadings, repeat the text of his 1968 Russian article ver-
batim, and only the concluding fourth section contains
some new and interesting ideas, extracting a number of
thought-provoking generalizations from the data observed
and interpreted in the bulk of his monograph (179-81).
And even though Georgiev's attempt at analyzing the underlying factors and forces shaping the evolution of Slavic
morphology — or, rather, declensional inflection and, to a
lesser extent, nominal derivation — is perhaps not really
revolutionizing and not even always very convincing, this
writer, for one, finds the judgment of one of the review-
ers of Georgiev's book overly harsh. Thus, Andersen,
after first having accurately noted that "the two parts of
the book are independent in the sense that it is possible
to reject the theoretical premises presented in Ch. 1-2
and still accept some of the explanations proposed in the
remainder of the book; on the other hand, complete acceptance of G's theoretical position in no way binds the reader to accept all or any of the explanations," concludes by
stating (1971:953): "Some Slavists may find Georgiev's
book entertaining, but it must be recognized that it does
not advance our knowledge. Inasmuch as it fails to distinguish between facts and suppositions, it may have the
effect of obfuscating the extent of our ignorance. This
is to be regretted." True, Georgiev's inability — or unwillingness? — to draw a clear line between incontestable
explanation and tentative hypothesis (no matter how ingenious) must be considered a shortcoming of this monograph
(as well as of much of his writing in general); yet it
would not be fair to deny the occurrence in his *Osnovni
problemi* of both some subtle observations and at least
potentially insightful interpretations, offered for more
than merely "entertaining some Slavists."

10.1. Problems of Common Slavic Inflection. Some of the
unresolved or only tentatively solved problems of prehistoric and early recorded Slavic inflectional morphology,
declension as well as conjugation, have continued to challenge diachronically inclined Slavists and comparative
linguists (including Baltologists) in the past few years.
Various novel approaches have therefore been explored and
new hypotheses advanced. In this connection increasing
attention has often been paid to the intricate interaction
discernible between the formal manifestation of the inflectional categories (case forms, tenses, etc.), on the
one hand, and, on the other hand, the phonological segments expressing them (morphophonemes, 'systematic phonemes') and the semantic meanings (including the more abstract syntactic functions) inherent in them. In the following, a few recent studies on CS (as well as pre-Slavic,
i.e., Balto-Slavic, and Early Slavic) declension and conjugation will be briefly surveyed.

10.1.1. Nominal (and/or Pronominal) Inflection. Continuing his previous research on the CS and Early Slavic declension system and its development from the PIE stage up
to the period attested by OCS (Mareš 1962a, 1963a, 1963c,
1963d, 1964; see above, especially pp.155-6), F. V. Mareš
published a study in two parts (1967b and 1968) on "The
Historic Development of the Slavic Noun Declension," part
one of which discusses "The System of Categories" while
part two addresses itself to "The Development of Forms."
To be sure, this study focuses primarily on the development of the Slavic substantival inflection as recorded in
the various literary languages, seeking to establish underlying factors and forces determining its diachronic reshaping, different in different languages (or language
groups) but at the same time also exhibiting a number of
common traits, presumably at least in part inceptive already in the prehistoric CS period. Specifically, part
one discusses the basic nominal categories (gender/anima-
tion, number, case) before sketching the various types of
declension and their remodeling from a CS and Early Slavic
stem class organization to a largely gender-dominated set
of paradigms, making frequent reference to the prehistoric
Slavic and even PIE situation. Part two, surveying the
development of individual case forms, viewed as parts in
an integrated whole, and tracing such phenomena as case
syncretism and homophony on various linguistic levels,
summarizes the discussion by comparing the main evolu-

276

tionary trends with those prevailing in the preliterary,
CS epoch as follows (42):

> (1) The morphological development of [the] Slavic
> languages is to a high degree homogeneous; in all
> languages the same motives are at work, in all are
> to be found the same means and ways of solving the
> problems. Most differences derive only from differ-
> ent phonological premises, from different 'wave'
> chronology, from a different rate of development
> and, of course, from the various variants of the
> system of semantic and grammatical categories. (2)
> It is possible to state the motives (stimuli) and
> ways of morphological development in a similar way
> as has been done for the Proto-Slavic and Early
> Slavic period. (3) The motives are much more
> numerous (for Proto-Slavic there are properly only
> two: the inconvenient homophony of forms and the
> stem alternation). The ways of solution are more
> varied. (4) Summing up, we can state that the his-
> torical development of the Slavic declension of
> nouns is more complicated than the Proto-Slavic and
> Early Slavic evolution, but it is no less free of
> fortuitous analogies, no less regular; it has per-
> fectly coped with the new situation created by [the]
> essential remodeling of the system of semantic and
> grammatical categories.

While the preceding CS development of the declension is
used here primarily as a point of comparison (allowing for
some genetic-diachronic as well as typological-panchronic
inferences), this comparison also indirectly implies a
general characterization of the CS situation and the overall tendencies governing its evolution.

H. Schelesniker's 1967 article, "Beiträge zur historischen Kasusentwicklung des Slavischen," written in
response to two reviews of his monograph with the same
title (1964), one by E. Dickenmann, the other one by L.
Sadnik, was already briefly referred to above (p. 157) and
need not concern us here as its relevance does not essentially extend beyond taking issue with his two critics.

The development of the $-\bar{a}$ declension as a whole,
i.e., in the substantives, adjectives, and, where applicable, pronouns, and in both its varieties ($-\bar{a}$ and $-j\bar{a}$),
was not long ago (1971) discussed at some length by W. R.
Schmalstieg who, as usual, also adduces comparative Baltic
evidence, adding two notes basically unrelated to the main

topic of the paper but providing further illustration of a phonological point argued. Proceeding from the assumption that the shortening of original long diphthongs in word-final position was a Balto-Slavic (i.e., pre-CS) process, and distinguishing between nine various chronological stages (or periods), Schmalstieg not only offers a fairly complex set of explanations for the complete -ā/-jā nominal-pronominal paradigm of CS — not all of which seem fully convincing, however — but also digresses further to other controversial points of CS auslaut treatment, e.g., the -a vs. -y contrast in the nominative singular masculine of the present active participles (dealt with also in Schmalstieg 1968; cf. above, p. 270) where the American comparatist argues for a double development, first *-an[t]s > *-ās (> -a) and later, as a result of a shift induced by analogy, *-an[t]s > *-uns > *-ūs > -y (134-5). Schmalstieg sees the origin of the double reflex -(j)ě vs. -(j)ę in the long-form ('definite') adjective where the regular form *-jęjē in the transition from stage VIII A to stage IX could either be denasalized altogether (> -jějē) or fully nasalized (> -jęję) and from which the double reflex presumably subsequently spread to the other — substantival — forms (genitive singular, nominative and accusative plural of the -jā stems, likewise the accusative plural of the -jo stems; cf. 142-4). While not without a certain degree of ingenuity and worthy of consideration also because it adduces revealing Baltic parallel material, this contribution resorts by and large to traditional methods. Even if some of Schmalstieg's results will ultimately prove tenable, they could have been arrived at — in principle, at least — decades ago.

The emphasis is clearly on the interpretation of the Baltic facts even though corresponding — and usually secondary — Slavic developments are also discussed in a number of recent contributions on certain individual Balto-Slavic case forms; cf., e.g., Mažiulis 1966, and Kazlauskas 1968 (on the dative plural and dual); Schmalstieg 1967 (on the accusative singular and plural of certain stem classes). Proceeding from J. J. Mikkola's view (supported also, e.g., by E. Koschmieder 1956) that -o was the only regular (nonanalogical) reflex of an earlier *-os, J. B. Rudnyćkyj in 1966 once more tackled "The Problem of Nom. Sg. Endings of o-Stems in Slavic," suggesting that not only such OCS phonetic variants as rodo sъ, glagolo sъ, pozoro sъ, prazdьniko sъ, miro sъ (usually explained as due to ъ > o in strong position) but also such "onomastic archaisms" as *Samo* (7th century), OP *Boglo*, *Falo*, *Sędo*, *Żyro* (*Žiro*), MUkr *Suslo*, *Kozlo et al.* testify to the original reflex -*o* (< -*os*) in Slavic. Even if theoretically such a reflex is indeed plausible and perhaps even likely (cf. *slovo* < PIE *k'leyos*, etc.), the evidence adduced to corroborate such a development is by no means incontestable, least of all, of course, the relatively late (17th century) Ukrainian name forms (cf. also, e.g., OCS, OR, etc., *Petrъ* : Ukr *Petro* and the like). The article "On the Prehistory of the Locative Singular of the Common Slavic Consonant Stems" by J. Ferrell, contributed to the Jakobson *festschrift* (1967), is of great interest. After a thorough analysis and careful consideration of several possibilities, the American Slavist, impressively conversant also with Comparative IE Linguistics, reaches the following conclusion (661):

> There appears to be good evidence that a locative case differentiated from the dative existed in Indo-European. The locative singular desinence in Indo-European was either -*i* or zero. Baltoslavic inherited a locative desinence -*i* in all or most of the consonant stems. This ending was lost both in Baltic and Slavic though traces exist in some Baltic adessive forms. In Slavic replacement of the locative desinence -*i* in the consonant nouns was motivated by the syncretism of locative and accusative singular desinences in the non-neuter. The -*i* locative was replaced by the -*e* (-*es*?) of the genitive singular under several concurrent motivating factors. The Common Slavic adverbial ending -ъ may have had its source in the older form of the locative of the consonant stems, as may the accusative of 'point of time'.

This well-argued, cautiously phrased hypothesis appears highly plausible, to say the least. Two papers on Early Slavic locative plural forms (or what has been interpreted as such) also deserve mention here, especially in view of the previously discussed — in my view very questionable — hypothesis advanced by J. Trypućko (1949, 1952, 1957; cf. pp. 188 - 9) according to which the plural endings and especially the locative plural desinences were integrated only at a relatively late point into the CS (or pre-CS?) case system while they originally were particles (or reflexes thereof) with an adverbial function. H. Orzechowska (1966), discussing the locative plural in -*oxъ* in

Slavic, considers two possible explanations for this ending: (1) a phonetic one (< -ъхъ < *-usu), and (2) a morphological one (assuming that the vowel -o- may have been introduced by analogy from other case forms containing an -o-, namely, -o stems and also -u stems: dative singular -ovi, nominative plural -ove, genitive plural -ovъ). The author indicates her preference for the second explanation, dating the morphological leveling back to Late CS, possibly limited to a certain dialect area. The attested history of the ending in question is said to represent the phase of its already losing, not gaining ground. S. Rospond (1969) rejects the hitherto rather generally held view that Old Czech, Old Slovene, rarely Polabian toponyms in -as (type OCz Dolas) reflect an archaic (= PS) locative plural in *-asъ and explains these forms, attested from the 12th through 16th centuries (with an intensity height in the 13th century) as artificial, "bookish" forms due to German influence. This, then, is another instance where sound skepticism (here on the basis of solid, thorough toponomastic research) seems called for as regards claimed dialectal archaisms occasionally equated with a CS (or even Early PS) stage of development; cf. also Birnbaum 1970c: 35-62, 1971b, and below, pp. 327-8.

The similarities, often pointed out before (cf. also above, p. 20) and, in particular, the substantial differences obtaining between the long-form (compound) adjective inflection in Baltic and Slavic was discussed a few years ago by J. Kuryłowicz (1969), in terms of both formal (phonological and morphological) traits and functional (syntactic and semantic) aspects, utilizing the appropriate terminological apparatus of the Polish comparatist's established linguistic (including typological-linguistic) conceptual framework. As a result the complexity and conditional nature partly attributable to considerable chronological discrepancies of this Balto-Slavic isogloss have become even more emphatically apparent.

Recently, J. Ferrell (1971) has once again tackled the much debated, seemingly coinciding Late CS isogloss features, setting off North Slavic against South Slavic, namely -y vs. -a (in the present active participles) and -ę vs. -ě₃ in certain "soft" declensional endings. After having weighed this intricate twin problem from all possible angles, including some previously overlooked or not yet sufficiently considered aspects, Ferrell is able to offer some interesting new observations and insights —

partly of a purely phonological nature — pointing toward a future solution without, however, being able to come up with a fully satisfactory and conclusive answer to all of the many special questions which this complex problem poses.

10.1.2. *Verbal Inflection*.

Recent work by Lightner (1966), Gustavsson (1969), Mathiassen (1969), and Watkins (1969), in one way or another pertinent to CS and Early Slavic conjugation, has previously been discussed in this report. Other studies relevant to verbal derivation (Damborský 1967, Aitzetmüller 1968) will be surveyed below (pp. 287 - 8). In this particular section we can therefore limit ourselves to briefly mentioning a few works published in the last few years that primarily concern verbal inflection in CS and Early Slavic.

Certain problems of the Slavic imperfect and aorist (*o*-aorist) were recently discussed by G. Bech (1971: 5-48). Of particular interest is the Danish linguist's view of a gradual development in three phases of the Slavic imperfect (cf. 16-25, 26-9).

Some years ago, J. Kuryłowicz, in an article entitled "Sur une particularité de la conjugaison slave" (1968b), returned to the problem of the secondary ending OCS -*tъ* (OR -*tь*) of the 2nd and 3rd person singular of certain aorist forms, concomitant with or dependent upon circumflex intonation of the root vocalism. This correlation had been observed earlier by N. van Wijk (1926, cf. above, p. 163) and had also been discussed in the treatments of the Slavic verb by Stang and Vaillant. Further studying the accentual peculiarities of these forms, Kuryłowicz suggests that it was from the athematic root verbs that these secondary aorist forms spread to some other types; thus, first *$\tilde{e}d$-tъ*, *$d\tilde{a}d$-tъ* > $\tilde{e}stъ$, $d\tilde{a}stъ$ (where the secondary ending -*tъ* was originally introduced as a redundant element, taken from the present tense inflection, which was distinguished from the aorist by accentual differentiation: present *$\acute{e}stъ$*, *$dast\acute{u}$* vs. aorist *$\tilde{e}$*, *$d\tilde{a}$*) and only subsequently *klętъ*, *pitъ*, etc. The spread of the redundant element -*tъ* is thus said to be limited by the following conditions: (1) -*tъ* is added only to roots, never to (complex) stems (i.e., root + suffix); (2) this ending occurs only with aorist forms marked by circumflex intonation. The striking connection between the occurrence of this secondary (and, as it turns out, redundant) desinence and the -*to* suffix of the past

passive participles, noted by van Wijk, is also ultimately
due to prosodic conditions and is thus only indirect. Re-
viving a half-forgotten theory advanced by J. M. Kořínek,
Kuryłowicz in another contribution, published in the Jakobson *festschrift*, "Slavic *damь*: A Problem of Methodology" (1967), suggests that this athematic verb was not
originally a reduplicated formation in Slavic (as had been
frequently claimed), but that the "unorganic" -*d* and its
reflex -*s* (before *t*-) was introduced by "assimilation of
the forms of the subordinate type **dō* to those of **ēd*, not
vice versa" (1130). Moreover, "according to what has been
said about **dō*, we may consider the *d* of *idǫ* as an element
which originated, in the old athematic inflection of the
verb" and "the genealogy of the *d* of the semantically related *jadǫ* seems to be the same" (1131). The explanation
favored by Kuryłowicz (and modifying earlier theories,
e.g., by Kořínek) along with other interpretations were
considered by V. V. Ivanov in his most instructive and
thorough essay "Otraženie dvux serij indoevropejskix glagol'nyx form v praslavjanskom" (1968, cf. 242-7 and esp.
255-7). Discussing a number of complex problems connected
with the remodeling and redistribution in CS and pre-CS of
the original two PIE series of verb forms, represented by
the Hittite -*mi* and -*ḫi* verbs, Ivanov, in this compara-
tively designed study, continues his important inquiry
into the prehistory of Slavic morphology reported in previous work, in particular in part three of Ivanov 1965
(cf. above, pp. 67-8).

　　　The two contributions relevant to verbal inflection
by W. Mańczak (1967, on the development of the 3rd person
singular and plural of the present indicative in Slavic)
and J. Marvan (1968a, on vowel contraction and conjugation) fall within the broader framework of the particular
sets of problems — irregular phonetic change in word-final
position, studied by Mańczak, and Early Slavic vowel contraction, investigated by Marvan — chosen by these scholars as their field of specialized research (cf. above, pp.
244-5, 269, and 256-8).

10.2. Problems of Common Slavic Word Formation. A good
deal of recent research falling under this heading has already been mentioned in the preceding sections on current
studies concerning CS (as well as pre-CS and Early Slavic)
inflectional morphology as it is not always easy to draw a
sharp line separating this portion of morphology from derivation (or 'thematology', G *Stammbildungslehre*), the two

being intimately interrelated and relevant research frequently dealing with both. In addition, some of the studies published in the last few years treating aspects of
prehistoric Slavic lexicology occasionally touch upon
problems of derivation proper as well; the more important
among them will be briefly discussed below (pp. 301-5).
Although some of the work to be briefly surveyed here has
yielded valuable new insights or provided useful overviews
of interrelated phenomena, it has by and large resorted to
more traditional methods and approaches rather than exploring altogether new techniques and theoretical models.
Among general recent works of this kind treating infixation as a means of IE word formation, with much consideration given to Balto-Slavic data, see, for example, the
posthumous monograph on this subject by H. Karstien (1971).

10.2.1. Noun Formation. Of specialized studies in this
field that have appeared recently, my paper "Indo-European
Nominal Formations Submerged in Slavic" (Birnbaum 1972a)
is perhaps the one broadest in scope. Attempting to give
a systematic survey (to be sure, illustrated with selected
examples only) of all types of nominal formations inherited from PIE that have not survived as such in Slavic but
have undergone various modifications which have integrated
them into the recast system of nominal stem classes of CS,
I arrived at the following conclusions (161-3):

> Early Slavic, inheriting a great number of nominal
> formations from Late IE, where necessary, restruc-
> tured many of them to fit a simplified, gender-
> determined three-declensional system . . . Some
> nominal formations of IE were undoubtedly lost in
> Slavic altogether and replaced by others; or, they
> may partly be reflected only in secondary deriva-
> tions of more or less opaque origin. The precise
> reasons for adopting the primary distinction by gen-
> der in the substantive of Early Slavic are not fully
> understood. It has been convincingly argued, how-
> ever, that this criterion was taken over by the
> substantives from the adjectives and (gendered) pro-
> nouns. In addition to a certain amount of IE nouns
> not continued in Slavic and to a considerable num-
> ber of inherited substantives not subject to any
> substantial *morphological* (but only to phonological)
> remodeling (masc. and neut. *-o/-jo* stems, fem. and
> some masc. *-ā/-jā* stems, fem. *-ī* stems), others

underwent some structural reshaping before being integrated into the main, prevailing declensional patterns. As a rule, however, this process of adaptation and integration has left some apparent traces in the form of deviations from the regular set of inflectional endings, particularly salient in the attested phase of Early Slavic. This applies to the *-u/-ju* stems merging with the *-o/-jo* stems, to the bulk of the masc. *-i* stems adopted by the former *-jo* stem declension, to the fem *-y/-v* stems inflected as original fem. *-i* or, partly, *-ā* stems, to irregularities in some former consonantal stems, especially fem. *-r* and the neut. *-men* stems, and to some more instances. In still other cases, original IE stem classes or subclasses were not as such carried over to Early Slavic, and to the extent items originally belonging to these categories nonetheless appear also in Slavic they were so thoroughly remodeled or reinterpreted that the identification of their original membership can only be ascertained by resorting to the comparative method of IE linguistics. This applies, in particular, to original root nouns and other athematic (consonantal) formations: to heteroclitic (*-r/-l/-n*) stems; to masculine *-r* stems; to formerly feminine *-o* stems; to neuter *-u* (and *-i*) stems; and, possibly, to onetime (masculine and, mostly, feminine) *-ē* (*-ijē*) stems. As regards the basic processes by means of which these modified formations were achieved in Early Slavic, the following, in particular, should be mentioned: (1) *Gender switching* (with, at least initial, retention of original stem class) — Examples: *xodъ* (f —→ m *-o* stem), *medъ* (n —→ m *-u* stem), possibly, *domъ* (f? —→ m *-u* stem).   (2) *Suffixation* (with or without gender change; frequently by means of *-i* suffix added to athematic or old consonantal-suffixal formations; further, with 'thematic' *-o/-ā* suffix) — Examples: *noštь, solь, zvěrь; lakъtь, nogъtь; sněgъ, nosъ; srěda.*   (3) *Suffix substitution* (usually with retention of original gender) — Examples: *snъxa, *berza, mъzda* (f *-o* —→ *-ā* stem); *moŕe* (n *-i* —→ *-jo* stem . . .).   (4) *Phonologically conditioned suffix modification* (with or without change of gender) — Examples: *voda* (n *-r/-n* —→ f *-ā* stem); *doba* (n *-r* —→ n/f *-ā* stem).   (5) *Suffix expansion* (yielding complex suffixes . . . The first element of the complex

284

suffix often indicates the original stem formation
type. Among second suffixal components, preceding
the final, 'thematic' -o (-jo) / -ā (-jā) suffix,
-k- elements are particularly frequent.) — Examples: srьdьce, slъnьce; měsęcь (unless an original
compound . . .), zajęcь; vesna; vydra, vědro; orьlъ;
drěvo, drъva; bratrъ, sestra, stryjь (?), *jętry,
děverь; jablъko, pěsъkъ; vladyka, językъ, kamykъ.

As can be seen even from this highly selective listing, a
comprehensive derivational analysis oriented toward a
particular goal (here, the tracing of nominal formations
inherited from PIE but remodeled and adapted to systema-
tized declensional classes in Slavic) can yield interesting new insights not only for prehistoric word formation
but, indirectly, also for CS and Early Slavic inflectional
morphology (here, substantival declension).

   A much more narrowly limited segment of prehistoric
and Early Slavic nominal derivation was not so long ago
examined in great detail by S. B. Bernštejn in his article
"Sledy konsonantnyx imennyx osnov v slavjanskix jazykax.
(Sledy osnov na -s)" (1970), adducing not only many reconstructed CS items, as well as some comparative data
from other IE languages, but also abundant attested Slavic
evidence from contemporary standard, dialectal, and Old
Slavic (OCS, OR, etc.) texts. Pointing out at the beginning of his presentation that CS had inherited from PIE
three different -s stem types, namely, (1) nominal stems
in -os/-es, (2) adjectival stems (of the comparative
form) in -ējьs/-jьs, and (3) past active participle stems
in -u̯ъs/-ъs (or, more precisely, -u̯ŭs/-ŭs > -vъs/-ъs), the
Soviet Slavist proceeds to investigate more closely only
the type of nominal (substantival) stem formations in -os/
-es which in Slavic all have neuter gender only, while in
other IE languages (notably Italic and Greek) the two
other genders, especially the masculine, were also represented. Analyzing a considerable number of Slavic nouns,
most of them, to be sure, previously well established as
old -s stems (such as nebo, slovo, čudo, divo, tělo, isto,
oko, uxo, kolo, lože, etc.) and their various — mostly
adjectival — derivations, particularly indicative of the
-s stem origin of these nouns, Bernštejn is able to add
some further items whose original -s stem membership, exclusively or alternatively, has not been incontestably
substantiated earlier; cf., e.g., *ojes- (< *ojos-),
*runo (< *rou̯nos-), *udo-/*udos- (< *au̯do-/au̯dos-),

285

*pero-/*peros-, *jьgo-/*jьgos- (/*jьžes-), *liko- (/*lice-)
/ *likos- (/*ličes-), *tęgā / *tęžь (< *tęgjo-) / *tęgos-
(/*tęžes-), and others. Bernštejn's article concludes
with a few remarks on the semantic range of the CS -s
nouns, largely inherited from PIE (cf. however also such
a secondary Slavic formation as *zvenos-/*zvones-, attested in Polabian and probably a local innovation) and
passed on to recorded Slavic, though largely remodeled,
and on the archaic accentuation of this type: barytone
(stem stress) in the singular, oxytone (desinential
stress) in the plural.

Certain nominal -i stems occurring in part of the CS
area, or in some CS dialects only (*xǫtь, *xъtь?; *večerь;
*zetь?, *zьtь?) were discussed a few years ago by Eckert
(1971).

For the noticeable restriction in Russian of the
use of the nominal suffix -(n)ica, competing in Late CS
and Early Slavic with its phonetic variant -(n)ika — the
former derivable from the latter as a result of the progressive Palatalization of Velars — Kiparsky (1970) has
offered the explanation that the marked preference for the
unshifted form of the suffix in Russian, especially in
North Russian designations of berries, is due to the influence of the Baltic Finnic substratum with its well attested suffixes -ikka, -ukka. There is therefore no need
to here assume two originally different suffixes or secondary Russian innovation. On the other hand, the term
'allomorphs', used by Kiparsky in the title of his paper,
is hardly accurate here since the two phonetic variants of
the same suffix are not in morphophonemic alternation. On
some characteristics of suffixation in deverbative nouns
in CS as evidenced by Old Russian data, see Varbot 1967.

Nominal compounds with the (optional, irregularly
occurring) prefix a-/ja-, ultimately traceable to PIE ō-/
ē- (Slavic ja- in part derivable also from a- < PIE ō-
with secondary prothetic j-) and nonproductive, it seems,
probably already in the Slavic protolanguages, were treated in a fairly systematic way in a recent contribution by
O. N. Trubačev (1971a). The Slavic suffix -(d)lo as a
characteristic of the semantically defined group of nomina
loci was the subject of a short comparative study by Zett
(1971), concluding (412),

> dass die in allen slavischen Sprachen begegnenden,
> obschon in vergleichsweise geringem Masse produk-
> tiven Nomina loci auf -(d)lo einen Bestandteil des

urslavischen Wortbildungssystems bildeten, in
welchem sie — auch in ihrer lokalen Funktion, die
sich aus der instrumentalen herleitet — als ein
Erbe aus indogermanischer Zeit angesehen werden
können.

10.2.2. Verb Formation. As was mentioned before, the as-
signment of the formation of participles to verbal derivation rather than to nominal word formation (as an inflectional class here lumped together with other declinable
word classes) is somewhat arbitrary and dictated by practical rather than any theoretical considerations. This
slight ambiguity becomes particularly apparent in the case
of the Slavic participles in *-l* (frequently referred to as
past active participles II) which were finally made the
subject of monographic treatment a few years ago in J.
Damborský's thorough dissertation, defended at Warsaw University, *Participium l-ové ve slovanštině* (1967), where
this category is viewed both synchronically and diachronically and both morphological and syntactic aspects are
applied. Damborský distinguishes between two homonymic
categories on functional-semantic grounds. In his view,
the first of these consists of original deverbative adjectives in *-lo* which were integrated early — in prehistoric
times — into the paradigmatics of the verb system and became an integral component of the perfect tense (type
jesmь pisalъ) and of the conditional. They were thus reinterpreted as participles, a CS development, incidentally, with parallels in Tocharian and Armenian. The
second category is composed of deverbative adjectives
(represented by P *przybyły, powstały, dbały, wściekły*, and
their Czech counterparts), which, while not integrated
into the tense and mood system of the Slavic verb, retain
their semantic ties with the verb (cf. P *przybyć, wstać,
dbać, wściec się*) and therefore are labeled by the Czech
Slavist 'participles proper' (in contrast to the past
tense component, termed by him the 'preterite base', Cz
l-ový základ). Other *-l* adjectives do not (or, at any
rate, not fully) qualify as being *-l* participles proper in
the sense suggested by Damborský (cf., e.g., OCS *zrělъ,
ostalъ, gnilъ*, despite corresponding verbs *zrěti, ostati,
gniti*). Pointing to IE deverbative adjectives with an *-l*
suffix and a similar semantic shade expressing inclination
(type Lat *credulus*), Damborský suggests that, contrary to
a widespread view, the Slavic adjectives in *-l*, referred
to by him as participles proper, represent the continua-

287

tion of an earlier situation, prior to the paradigmatiza-
tion of many – adjectives, rather than originating from
the – formations constituting an integral part of the
Slavic tense and mood system. To be sure, he allows for a
number of transitional types and takes into account the
complexity of the processes involved. While going considerably beyond the time limitations of prehistoric Slavic and Early Slavic and discussing, in addition to derivational aspects, problems of inflectional morphology, particularly functional syntax and semantics, this recent
study is a significant contribution also to the field of
CS verbal derivation.

In addition to some phonological and lexical-semantic considerations, both inflectional and derivational
factors are taken into account in R. Aitzetmüller's discussion (1968) of the alleged Slavic vestiges of a former,
IE future characterized by the suffix -s as positable for
OCS *byšęšt-/*byšǫšt-, and attested in Russian Church
Slavic byšašč-/byšušč-. Reexamining the relationship,
function, and meaning of the two quoted forms as well as
that of some potentially cognate forms (OCz probyšúcný;
OCS byšьnъ, byšьstvo, byšьstvovati), Aitzetmüller takes a
skeptical view of the often claimed future meaning of
these forms or their predecessors (cf. Lith búsiąs, Av
búšyant-) and is rather inclined to consider its 'aorist'
meaning primary ('geworden seiend', possibly also 'wer-
dend', cf. also OCS bǫdǫšt-). This conclusion, argued on
the basis of solid philological evidence, seems at least
conceivable. For a brief discussion of the earlier, traditional view, see Birnbaum 1958a: 15-16 and 282-3 (notes
17-20).

Morphological (derivational), syntactic (functional),
and semantic considerations were brought up also in some
further discussions of recent date concerning various general aspects of major verbal categories such as tense,
aspect, voice, and the semantic-formal category of causatives, best definable perhaps as one of the several 'modes
of action' ascertainable in the Slavic verb. The formal-
semantic interrelation of aspect and tense was reexamined
from new premises by J. Dombrovszky in his paper "Über den
Ursprung und die Herausbildung des Aspekt-Tempussystems
des slavischen Verbums" (1967, summarizing a 1964 Budapest
dissertation) without, however, contributing any new major
insights, but rather developing only some controversial
ideas previously formulated by E. Koschmieder and T. Milewski.

288

Continuing his previous inquiry into the prehistory
of the Slavic aspect system, H. Kølln, in "Aspekt und Diathese im Slavischen" (1966), investigates some further
problems connected with the origin of the categories of
aspect and voice in Slavic. Summing up his findings,
based as usual on a firm grasp of the comparative IE data
and marked by subtle discernment, Kølln notes (79) that,

> die slavischen Aoristbildungen ursprünglich nach
> Terminativität und Diathese differenziert waren.
> Der starke Aorist (der *e/o*-Aorist und der Wurzel-
> aorist) sowie der *ě*-Aorist hatten ineffektive Bedeu-
> tung, und diese Aoriste waren wahrscheinlich beson-
> ders geeignet, die Vorstellung vom Anfang eines Zu-
> standes wiederzugeben. Es kann daher auch nicht
> befremden, dass die Verba mit dem starken Aorist,
> die zugleich eine Affinität zur terminativen Auf-
> fassung zeigten, besonders häufig perfektiv sind:
> ihre Semantik ermöglichte ihren Derivaten auf *-ati*
> *-ajǫ* und *-ati* *-jǫ*, nicht nur in Zustandsbedeutung,
> sondern auch in eigentlicher imperfektiver Funktion
> aufzutreten. Dem starken Aorist entspricht normal
> ein Nasalpräsens, und man kann deswegen mit Kury-
> łowicz den Typus *dvignǫti* : *dvidzati* als den Ausgangs-
> punkt für die Bildung weiterer Aspektpaare betrach-
> ten.

Whereas the category of voice played only a relatively subordinate role in the article just quoted, it is
this category and its formal expression that is the center
of attention in one of Kølln's other recent studies, this
time going beyond Slavic and viewing the Slavic evidence
in a broader comparative IE framework. Also in this brief
monograph, *Oppositions of Voice in Greek, Slavic, and Baltic* (1969), it is the various forms of the aorist in Greek
and Slavic and the *-ā* and *-ē* preterites of Baltic that
provide the diagnostic data. Taking issue with or sub-
scribing to views expressed by Indo-Europeanists from
Meillet to Watkins and Ivanov and being well versed also
in the specialized literature of the three IE language
subfields concerned, Kølln arrives at some interesting
conclusions (61-2):

> In Slavic the perfect disappeared as well as the
> distinction between active and middle endings; thus
> there was little support in the Slavic conjugation
> for a preservation of the opposition as an opposi-

tion of voice . . . This might be the explanation
why the opposition . . . in Slavic is rather an opposition of transitivity (*bljusti* tr. 'watch' : *vьz-*
bъnǫti intr. 'awake', *za-byti* tr. 'forget' : *byti* 'to
be') . . . It seems to me that the agreement between
Greek and Slavic in the application of the aorists
is too special to be the result of a parallel development . . . The opposition of voice found in
Greek and Slavic then to all appearance is very old.

And, commenting at some length on the similarities and
differences between Slavic and Baltic in this respect,
Kølln finally concludes (64-5):

> that the Baltic opposition of voice rests on a dis-
> tinction between the sigmatic and the strong aorist
> and that the opposition as such is as old as the
> opposition found in Slavic or Greek. I suppose that
> this triad of language groups has inherited an old
> opposition of voice in the aorist.

Even if some details of Kølln's relevant findings may occasionally seem controversial, his overall control of the
linguistic facts and their acute interpretation add to the
weight of his conclusions in this branch of comparative
diachronic linguistic research. It goes without saying
that his work falls into the field of verbal derivation as
much as into that of functional syntax (theory of grammatical categories).

Whereas Kølln's research on aspect, voice, and tense
(especially the aorist) in the Slavic verb is in the best
tradition of Comparative IE Linguistics as now practiced
with great insight and imagination by J. Kuryłowicz and a
host of younger comparatists (V. V. Ivanov and C. Watkins,
among them), a clearly transformational-generative approach to the problems of reconstructed (as well as attested) Slavic morphology was some time ago attempted by
Z. Gołąb in his paper "The Grammar of Slavic Causatives,"
one of the American contributions to the Sixth International Congress of Slavists, Prague (1968). Drawing on
theoretical foundations laid by others (e.g., Kuryłowicz
and L. Tesnière, to name just a few), Gołąb's aim, as he
put it (93), was merely "to call attention to these problems and to propose some directions of future research,"
but not to present an exhaustive treatment of all the
problems at hand. In closing his contribution he formulates "some conclusions concerning Slavic causatives in

their typological development" as follows (93):

(1) There is a general trend towards a linguistic economy. This trend expresses itself in the passage from the primary IE type of causatives (*vortiti*) through two subsequent stages, a) *běliti*, b) *ženiti* towards the last type . . . called syntactic-contextual. The primary IE type is maximally characterized (vocalic apophony + suffixation), the two intermediary types represent medium characterization: *běliti* if opposed to *bělěti* shows a different suffixation only, *ženiti* if opposed to *ženiti sę* shows dereflexivization. The morphological characterization of the last type is Ø, the causative function of a given verb being 'catalyzed' by a corresponding syntactic context. (2) There is an intimate connection between causative and *nomen* (especially *nomen deverbale*) expressed already in Common IE where the *u̯ortéi̯e-* type is primarily a denominal derivative based upon a deverbal adjective *u̯ortó-*. This connection reappears in Slavic where prehistorically and historically the denominal type of causatives (*bělъ* ⟶ *běliti*) is productive, eventually bringing about the replacement of old causatives by new ones which are clearly denominal in Slavic terms, e.g., *moriti* replaced already in OCS by *u-mrьtviti* or *u-sъmrьtiti*, etc.

These and other observations, not summarized in Gołąb's conclusions and arrived at by the application of a new method, certainly deserve further examination.

Of other recent work pertinent to verb formation, the articles by Sadnik (1966) on OCS *rekǫ* : *rьci*, Otrębski (1966/67), discussing as "some Slavic words with nonidentified infixed nasal," the verbs *kǫpati*, **tǫpiti*, P *wędzić* and *gnębić*, and Ivanov (1970), citing a few Slavic parallels when briefly discussing "Suffix **-sk̂-* > Baltic *-šk-* and the Problem of Verbs Denoting Sounds," have all been referred to previously in various contexts.

For some derivational considerations regarding the formation of the Slavic imperfect and *o*-aorist, see now also Bech 1971; cf. further p. 281, above.

11. FURTHER EXPLORATIONS INTO COMMON SLAVIC PHRASE AND SENTENCE STRUCTURE

11.0. Problems and Methods. In recent years, the search for an underlying structure determining the overt patterns of phrase and sentence structure as they can be ascertained in attested Early Slavic has been intensified. Methods serving this end have been further refined and inferences have been made from the thus constructed generalized (though not altogether universal) 'deep structure' as to its presumed relative stability and continuity. This points, it would seem, to an essentially identical set of deep-seated categories and their abstract, i.e., not yet 'linearized' or otherwise manifest, combinations and relationships prevailing also in the prehistoric period of Slavic linguistic evolution. Such an avenue of research, seeking to establish at least some fragments of CS syntax — ultimately hopefully to be put together into a coherent system — by means of recovering some facets of its presumed, semantically-based 'deep structure', has in the last few years yielded some new, to be sure only tentative, results. Some of them will be briefly accounted for in the following together with more traditional work aiming at the — particularly difficult — task of reconstructing CS phrase and sentence structure.

It goes without saying that several of the studies commented upon in the preceding sections, notably in those on derivational morphology, examine formal characteristics, and, in part, analyze the functional-semantic aspects of certain grammatical categories (e.g., tense) and their specific exponents (e.g., the aorist) relating individual word forms to each other within the boundaries of syntactic phrases (syntagms); these studies will not be cited again here, but the relevant titles are marked by

the appropriate numerical symbol for content identification in the appended Bibliography to which the reader is
therefore referred.

The two approaches discussed previously (pp. 182-3)
that have been explored to gain some insight into CS syntactic structure — namely, (1) comparison of phrase and
sentence characteristics in Slavic and Baltic, and (2)
identification and subsequent elimination of foreign syntactic patterns ascertainable in recorded Early Slavic,
notably syntactic Grecisms in OCS — are represented in recent publications by, on the one hand, R. Eckert's 1968
paper "Minimale Textfragmente im Slavischen und ihre Entsprechungen im Baltischen" and, on the other hand, R. Růžička's two articles "O ponjatii 'zaimstvovannyj sintak-
sis' v svete teorii transformacionnoj grammatiki" (1966)
and "Betrachtung zur Lehnsyntax im Altslavischen" (1971).
While the factual yield of Eckert's findings is not overly
rich, his comparisons being limited to the juxtaposition
of individual, syntactically interpreted items and phrases
(word-groups), Růžička, in his two papers, demonstrates
the potentials of a transformational-generative approach
to the intricate problem of isolating the Greek component
firmly integrated into the syntactic surface data of OCS.
The East German linguist presents the new powerful technique for identifying syntactic foreignisms in the rule
component of a language with a few examples of syntactic
Grecisms in OCS (embedded participles, replacement of
Greek preposition-plus-infinitive phrases by OCS dative
absolute constructions), an approach which he brilliantly
applied in his earlier (1966) article and which in less
explicit terms is also discussed in my work on the subject
(Birnbaum 1968a). However, in his more recent short contribution to the volume *Studia palaeoslovenica*, honoring
J. Kurz, Růžička voices a growing skepticism as to the
prospects of swiftly and successfully solving the problems
of loan syntax in OCS and hence of establishing CS syntactic patterns, both in view of the as yet largely lacking
methodological premises in terms of syntactic and semantic
theory and the complicated heuristic and textual situation
at hand (for a quite similar assessment, cf. also Birnbaum
1968a).

11.1. Word Forms and Word Classes: Their Syntactic Use.
Of recent publications falling under this heading and not
previously discussed, articles by Vaillant, Bednarczuk,
Kiparsky, Jacobsson, and H. Andersen deserve particular

attention. A. Vaillant, in his analysis "Le supin et ses
limitations d'emploi" (1967), first surveys in some detail
various instances of supine usage in OCS (after a few
opening remarks warning against blind trust in the complete and standardized paradigms of our manuals), pointing
out, in particular, some subtle semantic differences between the use of the supine and that of the infinitive
(which in most Slavic languages was to replace the supine)
and indicating that for some verbs the supine either is
not attested at all or only poorly attested, some instances being questionable on philological grounds. The
French Slavist goes on to outline briefly the occurrence
of this verb form in other Slavic languages (Low Sorbian
and Slovenian) and concludes by contrasting the Slavic
supine with its IE cognates, in Lithuanian and Latin, noting a derivational as well as functional difference between the supine in Latin and in Balto-Slavic. This,
then, is a precise if brief description of the Slavic supine and its specific use, allowing also for some conclusions as to its status in CS.

Continuing his previous research on Slavic conjunctions (cf. pp. 194-5), L. Bednarczuk, in his article "Pleonastyczne użycie spójników parataktycznych w językach
słowiańskich na tle indoeuropejskim" (1967), analyzes various instances of observed pleonastic use of paratactic
conjunctions, especially in compound sentences, formally
expressing coordination even in instances where the relationship denoted by the two clauses is actually one of
subordination. Bednarczuk's discussion is of considerable
merit because of its extensive comparisons with other IE
languages, but does not go essentially beyond previous
findings and explanations in its interpretation of the
Slavic material. Yet, as an indicator of our present
state of knowledge in this area, his paper is of some relevance also for CS syntax, especially as regards the
phase of incipient transition from paratactic to hypotactic sentence structure.

In his two articles, published in the late 1960s, V.
Kiparsky (1967, 1969a) has continued his discussion of the
so-called nominative object with the infinite, analyzed
earlier by him and a host of other linguists with various
results. According to Kiparsky, the construction of the
type *ryba loviti*, *zemlja paxati*, found in Old Russian,
modern Russian (especially North Russian) dialects, but
occasionally also elsewhere in Slavic (Czech, for example),
is not due to any substratum influence from some unrelated

language or language group (previous linguists often
claimed its Finnic origin), but can be considered a reflection of an earlier Balto-Slavic (and ultimately PIE)
state of affairs. While one can perhaps agree with Kiparsky's general conclusion as to the IE origin of this archaic construction, some details, e.g., whether these
clauses, originally must always have had an explicit copula verb or its equivalent (*ryba jestъ loviti, etc.) or
why this type has been preserved only with feminine -a
nouns, await further clarification. For a generative interpretation of this construction, shedding light also on
its historical and prehistoric evolution, see the interesting article "Zur Frage vom Nominativ als Kasus des di-
rekten Objekts im Slavischen" by G. Jacobsson (1965).

Recently the much-debated and highly controversial
problem of the dative absolute and its origin in Slavic
was again tackled by H. Andersen in a thought-provoking
paper "The Dative of Subordination in Baltic and Slavic"
(1970b). As I had an opportunity to point out elsewhere
(Birnbaum 1970b: 45),

> while I cannot quite agree with Andersen when he en-
> tirely rules out any influence whatsoever of Greek
> on the rise — or, as I would prefer to put it, acti-
> vation — of the dative absolute construction in
> (Old) Church Slavic, his monogenetic theory, favored
> over a polygenetic view, to explain the origin of
> the absolute case constructions in various Indo-
> European languages as well as his arguments, largely
> along Jakobsonian lines of semantic reasoning, jus-
> tifying the choice of the dative in Baltic and Slav-
> ic (as well as Gothic, representing Germanic at
> large) are, in my view, indeed fully convincing.

In other words, the attempt to identify an underlying,
typologically defined IE 'deep structure' of absolute case
construction to connote syntactic subordination, while
considering the choice of a particular case form a matter
of language-specific semantics, seems to me a plausible
approach to this difficult problem. Still, contrary to
Andersen, I would not disregard the possibility or even
probability of some influence of the Greek model (genitive
absolute) on the development of this category in OCS and,
secondarily, Russian Church Slavic; cf. further also Birnbaum 1968a: 57-60, 1970b: 43-6.

11.2. Clauses and Sentences. The line separating the study of syntactic phrases (word-groups, syntagms), on the one hand, and clauses and sentences, on the other, is fine indeed. For example, the article by Bednarczuk (1967), referred to above, touches as much on questions of sentence structure as it discusses the pleonastic use of the paratactic subtype of the specific word class of conjunctions. Similarly, an article like the one by A. V. Isačenko, discussing "Hortativsätze mit *a*, *i*, *ti*, *to* im Ostslavischen" (1970b), while limiting itself to only one branch of dialectally differentiated Late CS and its immediate continuation, but having implications for all of Slavic and hence also for CS, is relevant both to problems of functional syntax (here, the use of certain conjunctions) and to the theory of sentence structure (here, a certain type of clause); or, rather, this double relevance only shows the artificiality, at least from a theoretical point of view, of drawing such a dividing line.

In my Prague congress paper, "Obščeslavjanskoe nasledie i inojazyčnye obrazcy v strukturnyx raznovidnostjax staroslavjanskogo predloženija" (Birnbaum 1968a), I continued my previous research in this field (cf. Birnbaum 1958b). After answering some of my critics (especially J. Kurz) and determining the range of texts from which to gather data for the purpose of investigating OCS syntax, I then proceeded to classify all sentences of OCS into three main types: (a) simple sentences, (b) compound and complex sentences, and (c) so-called complicated sentences (R *osložnennye predloženija*). The latter type is represented by sentences in which the main clause is amplified by means of an 'isolated phrase' (R *obosoblennyj oborot*), i.e., a subordinate infinitive or participial construction. Commenting briefly on recent research concerning the OCS simple sentence, notably by C. Bartula, and pertinent scholarship in the field of the complex sentence of OCS, where S. Słoński's 1908 dissertation still provides the basis for all further discussion, I subsequently turned to the four 'isolated phrases', namely, (1) the dative absolute, (2) the accusative with a participle, (3) the accusative with the infinitive, and (4) the dative with the infinitive, all four constructions being condensed substitutes for full-fledged subordinate clauses. By applying a transformational-generative approach, pioneered in the field of OCS syntax by R. Růžička, I was able to arrive at some new conclusions concerning the exact nature of the syntactic foreignisms of the oldest literary language of

the Slavs, establishing, among other things, the need for
revising the formerly rather generally held view of the
high degree of 'penetrability' of syntax in comparison
with other components of linguistic structure. Yet, precisely because of the better understanding achieved for
the linguistically "mixed" structure of OCS syntax, I expressed (as was already indicated) some serious doubts in
the conclusion of my paper as to the possibility of fully
and accurately utilizing the syntactic data provided by
OCS for the purpose of reconstructing CS sentence structure and pointed to the abundantly attested evidence of
Early Old Russian, in part much less affected by Greek
models, as a potentially more significant source for such
reconstruction.

Of recent studies discussing some specific aspects
of CS and Early Slavic clause and sentence structure,
three may be singled out as being of particular conse-
quence. In his brief outline, "K razvitiju otnositel'nyx
pridatočnyx predloženij v slavjanskix jazykax" (1967), J.
Bauer suggested the following characterization of the CS
situation with regard to the emergence of subordinate relative clauses (54):

> In Proto-Slavic the relative clauses were in the
> initial stage of their evolution. Best established
> were the relative clauses with jьže and those with
> an adverb formed from the stem $*i̯o-$; however, even
> the structures with these clauses were not always
> fully unequivocally hypotactic, as suggested by the
> residues of an anaphoric function of jьže in Slavic.
> Relative clauses with new relative words, derived
> from interrogative words, emerge later; at most the
> very beginning of their emergence can be dated to
> Proto-Slavic.

A fairly precise and detailed picture of the prehistoric
Slavic state of affairs as regards a variety of impersonal
expressions (i.e., sentences without a personal subject),
some of them highly archaic, others fully developing only
during the historic period of Slavic linguistic evolution,
can be found in V. L. Georgieva's well documented and in
general cogently argued essay, "Bezličnye predloženija po
materialam drevnejšix slavjanskix pamjatnikov (osobenno
staroslavjanskix)" (1969). By and large it seems to follow from Georgieva's reasoning that, while the syntactic-
semantic premises for the development of impersonal sentences existed or were shaped already in CS times, the

full-fledged development of this sentence type belongs only to the historical epoch. Finally, in his comparative study, "On Some Conditional Clause Indicators in Slavic and Germanic Languages" (1968), J. Ferrell makes a few interesting observations and formulates some as yet merely tentative suggestions as to the origin of formally conditional clauses in prehistoric Slavic. Considering at least the possibility, but no more, of syntactic borrowing from Germanic to Slavic and juxtaposing in a number of instances parallel Old Germanic (mostly Gothic) and Old Slavic (primarily OCS or Old Russian) syntactic structure, Ferrell ends his contribution to the Martinet *festschrift* on a cautious note (111):

> At the beginning of the paper I stated that no certain evidence of borrowing could be produced and the statement is manifestly true. However, it would be, in the absence of proof that conditional clause indicators of the types shown here are of high frequency in languages generally, difficult to believe that borrowing direct or indirect from one side or the other does not play a role in at least part of the instances.

While, to be sure, Ferrell's concluding remarks do not necessarily apply only to the preliterary period but, it would seem, are meant to also refer to the recorded history of Germanic (here, German) and Slavic (Czech, Polish, Serbo-Croatian, etc.), his surmise, if borne out by future research, would again suggest penetrability or susceptibility at the surface-syntactic level only between two languages or language groups rather than any deep-seated syntactic instability, the presumably analogical 'deep structure' in Slavic and Germanic (representing the IE linguistic type or a subtype thereof) perhaps promoting precisely such borrowing in the overt syntactic structure (cf. the Greek-OCS "mixed" syntactic structure, discussed above).

12. CURRENT ATTEMPTS AT RECONSTRUCTING THE VOCABULARY OF COMMON SLAVIC

12.0. Preliminary Remarks. Work exploring the lexical structure of prehistoric Slavic has been carried on with considerable intensity over more recent years. While the publication of major etymological dictionaries, which was initiated and in progress during the fifties and early sixties, continued in the late sixties and early seventies (in some instances, reviewed partly also from a broadly IE point of view; cf., e.g., E. P. Hamp's notes on Sławski's Polish etymological dictionary, 1968 and 1971, and Szemerényi 1967, discussed below), the effort that went into other dictionary projects began to appear in print only in the late sixties and early seventies. Occasionally this was due simply to a delay of a technical nature (as, e.g., in the case of Skok 1971/73, already referred to above, p. 202), but in other instances the collective work of a whole team of researchers has only recently borne fruit. This is true, for example, of the research conducted at the Brno Etymological Section of the now defunct Institute of Languages and Literatures of the Czechoslovak Academy of Sciences. After a sample issue published in 1966, the first issue (authored by F. Kopečný) of this group's large-scale Slavic etymological dictionary, *Etymologický slovník slovanských jazyků*, has now finally appeared (cf. Kopečný 1973). The Moscow group of etymologists, headed by O. N. Trubačev, has produced four additional volumes in the *Ètimologija* series (1967, 1968, 1969, and 1971); some of the essays appearing in these collective volumes, written mostly by Soviet linguists, will be briefly referred to in the following.

Also, in the last few years, some further general, partly programmatically tinged state-of-the-art and

specific progress reports on Slavic etymological research
have appeared. Thus, for example, O. Szemerényi discussed
at some length "Slavic Etymology in Relation to the IE
Background" (1967), formulating a set of rigid but generally well-argued rules applicable to Slavic etymology
that, in his opinion, should govern all relevant research.
To illustrate his rules, he reexamined a number of Slavic
lexical items such as *radi* (and its relationship to OPers
radiy), *želěti* and *žьlděti*, *pętь*, *roniti*, **ārdla-* (Cz *rádlo*,
OCS *ralo*, etc., and its relationship to Lith *árklas* <
*ārtla-, on the one hand, and Gk ἄροτρον, Lat *arātrum*,
etc., on the other, all pointing to a PIE **arətro-*), *dъva-*
šьdi, *trišьdi* (once at considerable length but unsuccess-
fully analyzed by Trypućko 1947 — though Szemerényi's explanation, too, remains problematic), *ryba*, *gnětiti*,
*skovorda (or **skovordy*), *žeravlь* (R *žuravl'*), *godъ*, *mod-*
liti, *jezero*, and some others. In a separate section of
his paper he then discusses some additional items considered — or at one time or another suspected — to be loanwords. Among them we find *golǫbь*, believed by Szemerényi
to be a loan from Latin despite Vasmer's and Hofmann's objections (cf. *columba, palumbes*); OR *pьrě*, traced to Greek
rather than — as generally assumed — Finnic (which, according to Szemerényi, only borrowed it from Old Russian);
pora, possibly also a Greek loan (cf. φοφά); R *ráduga*, for
which the Hungarian-German comparatist considers the possibility of Iranian origin; and *rъžь* which he, on the
other hand, thinks to be an inherited item (G *Erbwort*)
from PIE rather than a Thracian loan to Germanic-Balto-
Slavic. While perhaps not all of Szemerényi's ideas and
suggestions will ultimately prove tenable, some of his observations and comparative data are certainly most valuable.

Two interesting progress reports in this field by
O. N. Trubačev have appeared. In his article "Rabota nad
ětimologičeskim slovarem slavjanskix jazykov" (1967b), the
Soviet etymologist exemplifies the principles and guide-
lines followed by his research group with a discussion of
some controversial lexical items, and briefly accounts also for other Slavic etymological dictionary projects currently in progress. Trubačev's sequel paper "O sostave
praslavjanskogo slovarja (problemy i rezul'taty)" (1968c;
cf. also Trubačev 1963d) surveys briefly some recent relevant research in the field of CS and Early Slavic with a
particular emphasis on lexical studies. Discussing also
my recent survey of the dialects of CS (Birnbaum 1966a),

the Soviet Slavist, not without reason, notes that I — on
the basis of research then available to me — had attached
too little significance to the evidence of lexical data,
which points, as we now know (thanks in particular to his
own research in this field), to a somewhat different
grouping of dialectal CS and probably already PS; cf. especially Trubačev 1963a and 1966; see, too, above, pp.
203, 211, and below, p. 329.   Referring to some of his
own relevant work, Trubačev further sketches some of his
basic themes regarding certain phenomena of dialectal CS
(secondary "occidentalization" of Sorbian, Iranian-Slavic
lexical contacts, etc.; cf. Trubačev 1967a and 1966) and
concludes his contribution by suggesting a new etymology
for Slavic *jьnьjь (R *inej*).

    Certain "universal formulae" allegedly applicable,
if not binding, in etymological research, and in particular the one designed some time ago by J. B. Rudnyćkyj,
were discussed — somewhat too appreciatively, in the
opinion of the present writer — by V. Kiparsky in his
state-of-the-art paper "Zum gegenwärtigen Stand der ety-
mologischen Untersuchungen" (1971). As in some of Kiparsky's other writings, his directly data-oriented comments
and interpretations are, by and large, much sounder and of
greater interest and value than his attempts to evaluate
new or rediscovered — and occasionally abstruse — purely
theoretical positions and claims.

12.1. *Current Research on the Common Slavic Inherited
Word Stock*. Obviously, in what follows, not all relevant
research of the last few years can be accounted for; some
references will be found in other sections of Part Two of
this volume; other titles will only be listed (and appropriately marked) in the appended Bibliography without any
mention in the text of this report; still other work in
this field was omitted because it was not deemed sufficiently significant; and some research the present writer
may be unaware of. The following is therefore merely a
selection of some pertinent items of the post-1965 (and
pre-mid-1972) period. É. Benveniste's monumental and, as
unfortunately it seems, last monograph on the vocabulary
of IE institutions (1969), ranging over the terminology of
economy, kinship, society, government, law, and religion,
discusses also a great number of Slavic lexical items as
even a glance at the index (326-7), listing 105 separate
Slavic words, mostly OCS (a few of them, to be sure, repeated in Russian), will reveal. Among them are many

controversial and previously analyzed items such as, e.g., many kinship terms, treated earlier by A. V. Isačenko and O. N. Trubačev in particular (cf. pp. 207 - 8), as well as established or presumed Slavic loanwords from Iranian most recently discussed by Benveniste himself (1967, see below, p. 309). Of other interesting lexical items touched upon by Benveniste (1: 95), one is Slavic *gospodь* (and its IE cognates), some years ago given a somewhat new interpretation by V. Machek (1968), for which an original meaning 'hôte-seigneur' rather than the previously assumed 'maître des hôtes' is suggested. The great and unique achievement of Benveniste's two-volume monograph does not, however, lie primarily in the number of new or modified etymologies that he proposes — at least this cannot be said with regard to his interpretation of the Slavic data — but rather in the superior ability to integrate the well-established as well as the tentatively interpreted nomenclature of a crucial segment of the IE vocabulary, as attested by the lexical data of a number of IE languages, into one coherent, complex system where each semantic subfield forms a well-defined whole and, on the other hand, the evidence of each separate language group again can be viewed as a self-contained entity. Put somewhat differently, Benveniste, not specializing in Slavic Linguistics, may with his last great work not so much have advanced Slavic etymological research per se as he has rather, by aptly utilizing the findings of current relevant scholarship, related its results with, and integrated them into, the overall semantic macrostructure of the major segments of economic, human-relational, sociological, and religious terminology of the ancient Indo-Europeans.

Some pertinent observations and comments on the particular relationship between etymological research and Slavic (and generally IE) mythology, discussed at some length by Benveniste and previously dealt with also, for example, by V. V. Ivanov and V. N. Toporov (cf. above, esp. pp. 209 - 10), were contributed a few years ago by J. Schütz (1968) and, again, V. N. Toporov (1969); on the etymology of the name of the Slavic god *Velesь*, discussed by Schütz, (along with the etymology of *Svarogь*), see further, in particular, Jakobson 1968 and 1969. Toporov's remarks are devoted to elucidating the Slavic mythological names *Kupala*, *Jarila*, *Sovij*, *Usyni* (*Usynja*) and to some Slavic echoes (*mir-*, *jat-*) of the Mithraic cult. The etymological equation Slavic *mirь* = Skt *mitra-*, Av *miϑra* is further considered by Abaev (1971: 11) who also discusses a number of other controversial Slavic etymologies (among them, *azъ*, *inъ*, *Dažьbogъ*, **vermę*). A number of controversial etymologies, mostly East Slavic but partly presumably of dialectal CS origin, are analyzed by Merkulova (1971), suggesting, among other things, a late CS form **stъpь* (**stъpъ*, **stъpa*, R *step'*) meaning 'back, crest, mountain'. Cf. further also the CS dialectal items with a morphological limitation (*-i* stems) discussed in Eckert 1971.

Various aspects of the close connection between etymology and grammar (including 'grammatical words') were studied in the last few years especially by O. N. Trubačev (1971b), L. Sadnik (1971), and F. Kopečný (1969a, 1969b, 1971, 1973), the latter interested particularly in the origin of Slavic prepositions (especially *kъ* and prepositions originating from pronominal adverbs as well as postposed particles).

The additional resources for reconstructing the CS vocabulary provided by one Slavic language (in this case, Serbo-Croatian) were discussed and a portion of a list juxtaposing reconstructed CS lexical items with their Serbo-Croatian counterparts (*a-* through *l'u-*) was drawn up by I. P. Petleva (1969, 1971), supplementing earlier work along similar lines by Lehr-Spławiński (1938), Orłoś (1958), and Radewa (1963).

Some potential Balto-Slavic word equations were recently reexamined by Karaliūnas (1968b; Lith *stragùs* = Slavic *strogъ*) and Otrębski (1970c; Lith *šakà* = Slavic *soxa*), the latter also contributing to the further elucidation of some OCS adjectives and adverbs (1969a *nyněšьnь*; 1969b *pěšь*).

E. Havlová (1966) has, once again, taken up for discussion the controversial etymology of the Early Slavic compound *čelověkъ*, suggesting that only the just quoted form, but not its presumed variant **čьlověkъ* (cf. OCS *člověkъ*, SCr *čòvjek*, *čõvjek*, P *człowiek*, etc.) should be considered truly CS; the **čьlo-*, *člo-* variants must, according to Havlová, be considered dialectal Late CS, i.e., in effect South and West Slavic allegro forms (cf. also SCr dial. *ček*, OP and P dial. and substandard *człek*, etc.). As the original meaning of this etymon, the Czech etymologist posits 'der als (Mitglied) in einer Soldaten- oder Dienertruppe wirkende' yielding 'Mann' on the one hand, and 'Untertan' on the other. The etymology of OCS *smrьdъ*, discussed some time ago with other semantically close items by Schuster-Šewc (1964b; cf. above, p. 212), was recently reexamined by R. Aitzetmüller (1971), who, by

pointing to the Greek counterpart of a related verb in
OCS, suggests the meaning 'entstellt, abgerackert', rather
than 'von unansehnlichem, unangesehenem Stand, plebeius',
and, assuming the initial *s*- to be '*s* mobile', points to a
number of IE cognates. The same Slavist contributed some
interesting "etymological marginalia" (1970), commenting
on a few controversial items (CS *dastā*, *dastī*; OCS
kъńiga, P *księga*; R *ovrag*, *očen'*, Slavic *otrokъ*; on the
last item see also Kopečný 1968).

Some special methodological problems of etymological
research were discussed by F. V. Mareš (1967a) in a detailed analysis of the etymologies of Slavic bird names,
some of them CS in origin, which can be onomatopoetic
formations.

Considering Gmc (Goth) *skatts* a borrowing from *skotъ*
and not vice versa (cf. also Kiparsky 1934: 186-8; Martynov 1963b: 183-7), R. Jakobson (1965b: 86) and — more
elaborately and independently from Jakobson — E. Stankiewicz (1968) derived the Slavic word from earlier **skop-
tъ*, the root morpheme of which, in their view, can be
identified with that of *skopiti* 'to castrate'.

A good example of a virtually exhaustive study of a
specific lexical morpheme in its overall semantic setting
is G. Eriksson's thorough dissertation *Le nid* prav- *dans
son champ sémantique. Recherches sur le vocabulaire slave*
(1967). Summing up her grammatical and semantic investigation of the Slavic word family (or 'semantic nest', R
semantičeskoe gnezdo) *prav-*, the Swedish Slavist concludes
(228):

> L'analyse sémantique du nid p r a v - a démontré que
> le sens concret 'ligne droite' de l'adjectif p r a v ъ
> est sécondaire et que le point de départ du nid doit
> être cherché dans le verbe p r a v i t i . Les re-
> cherches étymologiques ont indiqué que le nid
> p r a v - n'a pas de parents dans les autres langues
> indo-européennes, et, en outre, que, probablement,
> le nid p r a v - n'a pas débuté avant le premier
> groupement dialectal — slave de l'Ouest — slave de
> l'Est.

Dating the Slavic coinage *praviti* to the period of the
first Slavic-Germanic contacts and conflicts, Eriksson
then proceeds to summarize her views of how the other
Slavic words derived from the root *prav-* (*pravъ*, **pravь*,
pravьda, etc.) were created and how the antonyms *pravъ* ~
krivъ and *pravъ* ~ *lěvъ* came to be conceived.

Another, to be sure, less detailed study of a whole
semantic field and its many ramifications is G. Jacobsson's well-documented and well-argued study (1968) on the
Slavic verb *koxati (= *kochati, P kochać 'to love'), suggesting some interesting and generally quite plausible explanations. The diagram at the end of his article summarizes graphically the spread of the evidence (centered
in Polish), the types of formation, and, most important,
the complexities and interrelations of semantic shades and
transitions.

12.2. *Further Explorations into Lexical Meaning*. Clearly,
several of the recent studies just referred to, and in
particular the last two by Eriksson and Jacobsson, focus
on problems of semantics. Still, all or most of them also
discuss some other aspects of lexicology — phonological,
derivational, syntactic, or phraseological. In the following, a few additional works will be briefly surveyed
where considerations of meaning, either from a theoretical
point of view or as applied to some specific semantic
field, are even more in the foreground or, in some instances, are the exclusive concern of the particular researcher. Previously mentioned studies, discussing also —
but not only — problems of lexical meaning and therefore
not cited again here, will be found in the Bibliography at
the end of this volume appropriately marked for semantics,
among other things.

N. I. Tolstoj's essay (in two parts) "Iz opytov tipologičeskogo issledovanija slavjanskogo slovarnogo so-
stava" (1963/66) does not, to be sure, deal primarily with
CS material but rather uses comparative and contrastive
Slavic lexical data for the purpose of typological modeling of semantic fields (especially 'microfields') and
'networks' ('models'). Discussing and redefining such
concepts as 'lexeme' and 'sememe' and operating with sets
of semantic distinctive features (arranged in matrixes),
Tolstoj explores the potentials and new techniques of typological and areal linguistics not only for synchronic,
descriptive Slavic lexicology but, to some extent, also
for a diachronic analysis of the historically attested as
well as reconstructed, prehistoric vocabulary of the
Slavs. Thus, commenting on some of the implications of
applying the methods of typological and areal linguistics
to reconstructing fragments of the CS word stock, Tolstoj
states, for example (II: 20):

The turning to a certain spatially limited dialectal
continuum — to a compact dialectal landscape and not
to separate dialects from various language zones —
finds its explanation in the endeavor to use such a
landscape as some sort of a typological analogue of
the CS existence. This existence, as was noted by
N. S. Trubeckoj and many other students of CS, we
also conceive of in the form of a particular dialectal continuum, within which both divergent and
convergent processes took place. In reconstructing
the internal mechanism of CS (its system), typological criteria and indicators derived from contemporary languages and dialects are frequently resorted
to. Taking into consideration typologically similar
extralinguistic factors, structures, and situations
may prove to be no less important, however, for re-
storing the CS state of affairs ('existence').

Returning at the end of his study to CS, after some concrete exemplification, Tolstoj then asserts (II: 36):

In principle, it is difficult to assume for CS the
development of as rich a synonymy as in actuality
cannot be found in any single one of the contemporary Slavic literary languages and dialects, but
which implicitly can be derived when reducing the
meanings of the individual CS lexemes to the invariant ones.

And he concludes by suggesting some constraints inherent
in the relationship of typological possibilities and indicators, maximal lexeme load on — and permissible distribution over — a given semantic 'network', as well as various other factors (including derivational ones, lexical
borrowing, chronologically conditioned modifications,
etc.) which all have to be taken into account when attempting to reconstruct, on the basis of recorded data,
the lexical and semantic structure (namely, micro- as well
as macrostructure) of a protolanguage such as CS. While
Tolstoj's reasoning is, by and large, highly theoretical —
and the above brief account represents only a small sample — with cited factual data serving merely as illustrative examples, his study seems of considerable importance
also for the further elaboration of a more powerful and
adequate method for the reconstruction of the CS vocabulary. (Cf. for some further theoretical considerations
along similar lines Tolstoj 1968).

More directly concerned with methodological problems
of reconstructing the CS vocabulary and utilizing the notion of 'semantic microstructures' is V. V. Martynov's
paper "Analiz po semantičeskim mikrosistemam i rekonstruk-
cija praslavjanskoj leksiki" (1971, citing previous relevant work by the same author) which, in addition to Slavic
material, adduces some revealing comparative IE, notably
Germanic, linguistic data. Displaying considerable erudition and generally convincingly argued, this is a less innovative contribution to the problems of method than Tolstoj's longer and more broadly conceived study. Even more
limited in scope and thus less ambitious but nonetheless
instructive and not without interest from the methodological point of view is G. Jacobsson's 1969 note "Celi i metody ėtimologizacii slov, vyražajuščix nekotorye abstrakt-
nye ponjatija," drawing on the Swedish Slavist's experience from his etymological and semantic work on Slavic
(and other IE) words expressing the concept of time. For
a further study in this broad semantic field, see also
Havlová 1969 (on Slavic words for 'age' in the double
meaning of this concept, viewed against their IE background).

A major contribution of relatively recent date to
Slavic etymology, exploring one particular semantic sphere,
is the impressive 1966 monograph *Remeslennaja terminologija v slavjanskix jazykax (ėtimologija i opyt gruppovoj rekonstrukcii)* by the ranking Soviet etymologist O. N. Trubačev; this is the book-length sequel to his earlier, more
theoretical and limited study (1963b, focusing especially
on Early Slavic textile terminology) which was briefly
discussed above (p. 211). Treating in three major sections (1) "the terms of the textile craft" (5-143), (2)
"the terminology of woodworking" (144-72), and (3) "the
terminology of crafts connected with the use of fire" (a.
pottery, 173-308; b. smithery, 309-89), followed by a
short summing up of the "results" (390-3) and appended
illustrative "fragments from folklore and literature," an
updating note, and indexes, this is a most erudite, well-
argued, and pioneering study, combining a modern, complex
methodology with a traditional "Wörter-und-Sachen" type
approach. Utilizing, with much ingenuity, his linguistic
findings for the purpose of elucidating the history of
material culture (having established the intimate ties between the two planes), Trubačev is able to demonstrate,
among other things, the origin of pottery in plaiting and
the linguistic reflexes of this relationship. On the

purely linguistic side, the Soviet scholar notes the archaizing nature of all traditional, folk terminology and, in particular, comments on some lexical isoglosses and their geographic distribution. Trubačev's data seems to corroborate his assumption of a secondary "occidentalization" of Sorbian, to point to partly early lexical ties between Serbo-Croatian and Ukrainian (and to some extent also Belorussian) or, rather, the dialectal groups underlying these languages, and to allow for a more precise charting of the isogloss border separating the southwestern (subsequently Ukrainian and Belorussian) portion of the Eastern Slavs and the predecessors of the Russians (Great Russians) proper. Most interesting, perhaps, is the juxtaposition of relevant lexical items illustrating early Slavic-Germanic, Slavic-Latin (or generally Slavic-Italic), and Slavic-Baltic lexical ties, with many items reflecting an Early PS or even pre-Slavic period. The fact that the number of Slavic-Germanic lexical parallels is largest while that of Slavic-Baltic is relatively smallest (at least in the particular semantic sphere investigated by Trubačev) suggests a fundamental reassessment of the problem of the linguistic relationship between Baltic and Slavic; according to Trubačev, an earlier orientation of the Slavs toward Central Europe, entering into contact with Germanic and Italic tribes, prior to establishing closer ties with the Balts, seems more likely than a reverse chronology which would posit the establishment of more direct communications between Slavic, Germanic, and Italic peoples only after a loosening of any presumed original, intimate connections between Slavs and Balts. Even if this latter hypothesis may not easily be accepted by a majority of specialists in the field of Balto-Slavic Linguistics, Trubačev's observations and theories most certainly deserve serious and unprejudiced consideration.

Of other, minor specialized studies recently examining some particular semantic subfield of potentially high antiquity, L. V. Kurkina's two shorter essays (1969, 1971) on Slavic designations for swamps, roads, and paths may serve as representative examples.

12.3. A New Look at Some Loanwords in Common Slavic and Early Slavic. While, as we have just seen, some lexical Slavic - non-Slavic (Germanic, Latin, Baltic) parallels pointing to a common heritage rather than to borrowing, have received considerable attention also in recent years, not too much significant and novel has been published after 1965 concerning CS and Early Slavic loanwords and their proper assessment. Still, a few relevant studies are worth mentioning.

Z. Stieber's note (1966) on Late CS *Rimъ*, *križь*, and *židъ*, all borrowed from Late Latin or, probably, Early Italian or Rhaeto-Romance of the northeastern region (roughly Friul, or possibly from West Balkan Romance, i.e., Dalmatian) and interesting him primarily as regards the root vocalism of these items, was already referred to above (p. 259).

The ancient Slavic-Iranian linguistic relationship was reexamined in the light of lexical data by É. Benveniste, "Les relations lexicales slavo-iraniennes" (1967). According to the leading French comparatist, one has to distinguish between at least three kinds of lexical agreements found to exist between Slavic and Iranian, namely such coincidences which are explicable in terms of (1) a common IE heritage; (2) direct borrowing (loanwords); and (3) semantic calques. Common heritage Benveniste sees in Av *spənta-*, OCS *svętъ* (and, secondarily Lith *šveñtas*) 'holy'; also for Av *fšarəma-* and OCS *sramъ* 'shame' common IE origin is assumed. The French linguist surmises direct borrowing in instances such as Sogd *ku*, Slavic *kъ* (but cf. also Kopečný 1969b) or OPers *rādiy*, OCS *radi* (cf., however, Szemerényi 1967). Finally, Benveniste sees semantic calques in such instances as Av *sravah-*, Slavic *slovo*, in the special meaning 'word', and Iranian *baga-*, Slavic *bogъ* 'god', again with this specialized meaning.

Of great interest in this context is further the study "Iz slavjano-iranskix leksičeskix otnošenij" by O. N. Trubačev (1967a) which attempts to get away from the previous concept of contacts between a homogeneous ancient Iranian and an equally homogeneous CS ethnolinguistic group. Suggesting that the traditionally recognized East Slavic-Iranian lexical ties not be equated with the earliest Slavic-Iranian relationships, Trubačev then goes on to identify a series of tentative West Slavic (essentially Polish) — Iranian lexical agreements shedding new — and quite unexpected — light on the question of the dialectal place and membership of the ancestors of the Poles (and some other Western Slavs; cf. also his theory of the secondary "occidentalization" of the Sorbs) within the overall CS community. Yet another title deserving mention here is V. N. Toporov's paper (1971) "on an Iranianism in Slavic: **bazuriti*" (this lexical item of the NE Slavic area is related to its original doublet **baduriti* of NW

Slavic, the areal distribution reflecting an early isogloss division).

Two much debated lexical items, entering Slavic
toward the end of the CS period (or in Early Slavic) and
both, most likely, from Germanic, were reexamined in the
volume *Orbis Scriptus* (*festschrift* Čyževs'kyj [Tschižev-
skij]). H. G. Lunt (1966b) surveys some, but not all,
earlier and recent explanations of Slavic **korl'ъ* (**kărl'ъ*,
OCS **kraljъ?*), attested in the form *korol-* in the 12th/13th
century Russian Church Slavic copy (forming part of the
Uspenskij Sbornik) of the *Vita Methodii* but first actually
recorded from ca. 1100 (in the form *kralъ* in the Old Croatian Glagolitic Baška inscription), and concludes (488)
that

> there is no evidence that an OCS **kraljъ* 'king' ex-
> isted. The citations from VM are modifications of
> the personal name *Karl* which arose through the mis-
> understanding of the East Slavic scribes long after
> the fall of the Greater Moravian state.

Little can be said against Lunt's philological rather than
linguistic conclusions except that he, too, leaves certain
controversial questions concerning this item unanswered;
so, for example, why was this word integrated into Slavic
as a 'soft' stem? Perhaps because the Slavic word was
originally conceived as a possessive adjective modifying a
soon-to-be-suppressed noun, such as *mǫžь* or even *kъnęzь*?
(Cf. also Birnbaum 1972a: 167-8). Of the two seriously
considered possible foreign sources for Slavic *cьrky* (OCS
crъky, etc.), Greek κυρι(α)κόν or OBav *kirkō* (OHG *chirihha*,
OSax *kirika*, etc.) — Gunnarsson's derivation (1937) from
Lat (*ba*)*silica* via Balkan Romance (Romanian) has long been
refuted — K. H. Menges (1966) opts for the Greek source,
notwithstanding certain phonetic and morphological problems. Phonetic as well as some cultural-historical considerations, drawn from IE Armenian and non-IE (Kartvel-
ian) Georgian, which also adapted the Greek word, seem to
lend further support to Menges (and his predecessors')
theory.

Finally, mention should be made here of R. Auty's
recent reexamination (1969) of "The Western Lexical Elements in the Kiev Missal," probably the oldest extant
Slavic text (if we disregard here some still earlier Slavic inscriptions and glosses) dating from the 10th century
and most consistently preserving intact the reduced vowels
of CS. Commenting on the "western" words of the *Kiev*

Leaflets, a manuscript fragment based, it is believed, on a Latin original and representing a Late CS dialect mixture rather than any homogeneous dialect (say, of the Pannonia region; cf. also above, p. 11), Auty, contrary to the heretofore prevailing opinion which maintained that most if not all of them can be traced back to Latin models, concludes (p. 6):

> All of them, with the single exception of *prěfacija*, can be satisfactorily explained as loan-words from OHG. In view of what we now know of the pre-Cyrillo-Methodian missionary activities in Moravia this cannot surprise us. The soil had been prepared by others; but it was the seed sown by the Thessalonian brothers that bore fruit in the Slavonic language and the Slavonic liturgy.

Cautiously phrased (as regards the linguistic analysis), Auty's conclusion is reasonably plausible, though not really cogent in all instances, and the cultural-historical context seems at least not to controvert its possibility.

13. CURRENT CONCEPTS OF THE EMERGENCE, EVOLUTION, AND DISINTEGRATION OF COMMON SLAVIC

13.0. Reassessment of Definitions, Methods, and Goals in Reconstructing Common Slavic. There can be little doubt that recent and current advances in recreating (in concrete terms as well as in the form of abstract, underlying linguistic models) substantial segments of the structure of the Slavic preliterary protolanguage has led to a fundamental reevaluation of the very goals and potentials of such linguistic reconstruction, of the definition of CS (including its earlier phase, here termed PS) and, in particular, its time limits, and of the approaches and techniques most suitable for attaining as precise and realistic a reconstruction as possible of the various stages — especially the initial and final phases — in the evolution of the protolanguage common to all ancestors of the historically attested and present-day Slavic peoples. Symptomatic of such a reassessment of the theoretical premises for reconstructing CS is V. K. Žuravlev's contribution in the memorial volume for P. S. Kuznecov — one of the modern pioneers in the field — entitled "Ešče raz o predmete, metode, celjax i zadačax nauki o praslavjanskom jazyke" (1970). He reasons in a rather informal fashion about the methodological problems and possibilities of recovering the lost Slavic protolanguage, conceiving of it as an abstract, dynamic model capable of "generating those processes and phenomena that have been established in the Slavic languages and dialects, and their history" (91) rather than viewing CS as a concrete, homogeneous, largely invariable language and — quite correctly, in my view — assumes dialectal differences to have existed also in earlier phases of its development, their subsequent total obliteration alone accounting for our inability to recon-

struct them. In concluding his article, Žuravlev formulates some main principles on which, in his opinion, all
reconstruction of CS ought to be based (91-2):

> Thus, the *goal* of the theory of CS is to explicate
> the origin of the specifics of the Slavic languages
> as contrasted with other IE languages and, to some
> extent, also as contrasted among themselves, to elu-
> cidate the genesis and initial evolution of the
> specifically Slavic phenomena. The *task* of the the-
> ory of CS is to reconstruct the history of CS as the
> history of an evolving linguistic system. The *ob-
> ject* of the theory of CS is the history of the CS
> linguistic system. The theory of CS does not, and
> cannot, have at its disposal any data proper. The
> theory of CS abstracts from and generalizes the data
> of comparative Slavic and IE grammar and restores
> theoretically the processes which, for obvious rea-
> sons, we cannot observe directly. For immediate in-
> spection we dispose merely of the facts gathered by
> historical grammar and dialectology, facts that can
> be treated as the consequence of reconstructable CS
> processes. Naturally, these facts occupy their
> proper place in the historical processes of the in-
> dividual Slavic languages and dialects; these facts
> can attain their full development and explanation
> [only] in the system of subsequent facts and in the
> historical grammar [of individual languages, H. B.].
> But this by no means implies that any given fact
> cannot also carry with it the traces of some earlier
> processes. The *method* consists of systematizing, by
> applying techniques of structural analysis and
> structural typology, and of rectifying the data ob-
> tained by the comparative-historical method. In
> phonology, for example, these are the methods of
> diachronic phonemics.

While phrased rather casually, these and the preceding remarks by Žuravlev touch, in my estimation, on some essential points and previous weaknesses in the objectives and
methods of reconstructing the CS protolanguage. An even
more far-reaching but generally well-argued assessment of
the tasks of linguistic reconstruction can be found in another relatively recent paper by Žuravlev, discussing primarily the nature of the Balto-Slavic linguistic relationships (1968) where the Soviet linguist, commenting on the
determining role of what he terms the "leading" (R *peredo-*

voj) dialect within a given protolanguage, conceived as a loosely grouped isogloss area, states (174-5):

> There is some reason to assume that Old Prussian as well as the languages of the Jatvingians and Golindians originally formed part of the PS isogloss area but later, after having split off from it, attached themselves to that of Baltic (Letto-Lithuanian) possibly becoming the epicenter of the irradiation of Common Balto-Slavic processes. In turn, Letto-Lithuanian probably for some period joined the Proto-Germanic isogloss area, but having separated from it and joined that of Balto-Slavic, was up to the time of new contacts with the Germanic languages the irradiation epicenter of certain Germanic-Balto-Slavic tendencies. The details and chronology of the redistribution of isogloss areas must remain controversial so far — the relative chronology of the earliest processes has not yet been established, their hierarchy has not been ascertained, and the data obtained by means of internal reconstruction on the basis of material from one language has not yet been confronted with data from another language or language family. Therefore, for the time being we can only speak in general about the possibility of redistributing isogloss areas.

Again, while some of the assumptions made by Žuravlev (for example, concerning the original place of the predecessors of the West Baltic languages, previously to be sure, also considered by Bernštejn and Gornung) must be held to be highly controversial, his general interpretation of the prehistoric situation and relationships as regards ancestral languages certainly has considerable merit and deserves further exploration.

Commenting at some length on Žuravlev's position and attempting to point to some possibilities of reconciling seemingly conflicting views regarding the time of the crystallization of CS (or PS), as recently expressed in particular by, on the one hand, Z. Stieber (1970) who dates the emergence of CS to the beginning of the first millennium A. D., and, on the other hand, V. Georgiev (1970) who suggests that Balto-Slavic as a unified linguistic entity took form already in the third millennium B. C., I discussed, in my paper presented at the Seventh International Congress of Slavists in Warsaw (Birnbaum 1973), various approaches to reconstructing the earliest phase of CS (PS). Following some suggestions advanced more than fifty years ago by N. S. Trubeckoj (1922) and adopting the view first formulated by Ivanov and Toporov (1961) according to which the abstract language model underlying attested Slavic can be deduced from its Baltic counterpart but not vice versa, I defined this phase of CS (PS) as essentially identical with the abstract and dynamic isogloss area (in the sense of Žuravlev 1968) of Balto-Slavic. In addition, I ventured, very tentatively, some ideas for a reassessment of the age-old and much-debated problem of the original homeland of the Slavs, proposing the possibility of combining the linguistically based concept of Early PS, briefly sketched in the major portion of my paper, with some recent archeological indications of an initial southward migration of the Slavs away from an earlier area of settlement, coterritorial with — or, at any rate, immediately adjacent to — the original sites of the primitive Balts. In a subsequent paper to be summarized in the sequel to this progress report, I have further elaborated on this concept, reverting essentially to the earlier hypothesis of an "eastern", or rather "southeastern" original homeland of the Slavs, in the "Pontic" area north of the Black Sea and, in the east, reaching at least up to, if not beyond, the mid-Dnieper region.

13.1. *Some New Views on Common Slavic and Its Indo-European Cognates, Especially Baltic; the Problem of a Possible Non-Indo-European Substratum and Its Traces in Late Common Slavic.*

A further indication (not yet particularly emphasized in my Warsaw congress contribution) of the establishment of a first Slavic habitat in a relatively southern or southeastern area — presumably somewhere between the upper and central Vistula and the central and lower Dnieper — could possibly be seen in the early Slavic-Iranian and Slavic-Italic contacts (in addition to the already well-established early Slavic-Germanic ties), recently rather convincingly demonstrated by O. N. Trubačev to have been more intensive than previously assumed; cf. especially Trubačev 1963b, 1966, 1967a; see further relevant research by A. A. Zaliznjak 1962 and É. Benveniste 1967 and Toporov 1971 concerning Slavic-Iranian, by J. Safarewicz 1963, 1964 regarding Slavic-Italic, and by V. V. Martynov, especially 1963b, as regards Slavic-Germanic lexical agreements. For some Slavic-Armenian isoglosses, see the recently published posthumous article by R. A. Ačarjan (1968), updated in footnotes by É. A. Makaev. For some additional comments on Baltic, Slavic, and Iranian, consult now also V. Pisani 1969. A brief statement pertaining to the present research situation as regards Baltic, Germanic, and Slavic with a few notes of a programmatic nature was made by A. Klimas (1970) in the *Donum Balticum* for C. S. Stang who himself since has contributed a major study on Germanic-Balto-Slavic lexical agreements to be reported in the planned sequel to this state-of-the-art account.

In his paper "Common Slavic and Indo-European" (1970) V. Georgiev primarily strove to demonstrate with a few selected examples the new insights gained in recent years by Comparative Indo-European Linguistics, making possible, according to the Bulgarian comparatist, a more adequate understanding and correct assessment of some phenomena of the Slavic protolanguage, especially in its earlier phase. In particular, he stressed the considerable time-depth that, in his view, can be posited also for CS or, at any rate, Balto-Slavic. As was indicated in the preceding, such a chronological concept is plausible, to my mind, only if Early CS (PS) can be equated, given some qualifications, with Balto-Slavic; whereas, when it comes to the CS processes proper, I am rather inclined (with Stieber 1970 and elsewhere in his recent writings) to consider most of them as relatively late, in most instances not much earlier than the beginning of the Christian era (cf. also Birnbaum 1973). From a somewhat different point of view, and cautiously taking into account also the recent findings of other disciplines, notably archeology, the problem of the emergence of a Slavic ethnic and linguistic community was discussed by F. P. Filin in his instructive article "Nekotorye problemy slavjanskogo ètno- i glottogeneza" (1967). While I, for one, can only subscribe to Filin's skepticism when it comes to the utilization of archeological findings for the purpose of linguistic reconstruction (a methodological limitation pointed out, incidentally, also in my 1973 Warsaw congress paper), I would personally disagree with the Russian Slavist when he, already at the outset of his article, characterizes (28) "the ancient CS language as a linguistic reality which existed during many centuries and ceased to exist approximately in the 6th-7th cc. of our era." As the reader of this report will have noticed and as will be further elaborated (pp. 327, 339-40), I prefer to assume the CS period (in the broad sense) to have lasted until — and in fact, into — the first centuries of literary

attestation, considering, with Durnovo, Trubeckoj, and
Toporov (but contrary, for example, to Belić and, more recently, Weiher), the *jer* shift (fall and vocalization) of
the 10th/12th centuries the *terminus ad quem* for CS. For
a slightly modified and generally more acceptable view,
see now Filin 1972: 6-30.

The whole range of problems connected with the special relationship obtaining between Slavic and Baltic as
evidenced by a number of exclusive agreements (phonological, grammatical, and lexical) found to exist between
these two language groups was again discussed in recent
years by the Lithuanian linguist S. Karaliūnas in his essay "Kai kurie baltų ir slavų kalbų seniausiųjų santykių
klausimai" (1968a; cf. also the shorter Russian variant,
Drevnejšie otnošenija baltijskix i slavjanskix jazykov,
1967). Traditional in its basic approach, Karaliūnas's
study nonetheless introduces a number of new elements and
points of view, arguing that, while originating from the
same Late PIE dialectal base, Baltic and Slavic share a
great number of specific features not because of their going back to a common Balto-Slavic protolanguage of post-
PIE date but as a result of instances of prehistoric convergence between the two linguistic branches of IE. Although full of keen observations and original interpretations of linguistic detail, C. S. Stang's approach to the
complex problem of Balto-Slavic is also traditional in essence. Summing up his thinking in these matters in his
monumental *Vergleichende Grammatik der Baltischen Sprachen*
(1966), Stang concludes his opening discussion of the relationship between Baltic and Slavic (10-21) with the following statement:

> Welcher Schluss soll nun aus allen diesen Fakten ge-
> zogen werden? Wohl dieser, dass in nachindoeuropäi-
> scher Zeit ein balto-slavisches Dialektgebiet exi-
> stierte, das gewisse Variationen umfasste, und das
> vielleicht niemals ganz homogen war, das aber doch
> in dem Sinne eine Einheit bildete, dass es eine
> Reihe gemeinschaftlicher Neuerungen durchführte,
> während andere Neuerungen nur einen Teil des Gebiets
> umfassten und das spätere baltische Gebiet durch-
> schnitten. Methodisch bedeutet dies, dass man kein
> Recht hat, in allen Fällen mit baltoslavischen
> Grundformen zu rechnen. Aus dieser rein linguisti-
> schen Analyse ergibt sich somit folgende Reihe von
> Strata: (1) Urindoeuropäisch, (2) Das baltoslavische

Dialektgebiet, (3) Das baltische Dialektgebiet und
die annähernd einheitliche urslavische Grundsprache.

As can be seen even from this short quotation, Stang thus,
on the basis of a thorough analysis of the relevant linguistic data, arrived at a general picture of the common
point of departure for the Baltic and Slavic linguistic
evolution not too different from that sketched in recent
years by Soviet comparatists and Slavists (especially
Ivanov & Toporov 1961; Žuravlev 1968). Their view is
largely the result of some theoretical considerations,
supported, to be sure, by concrete linguistic data, and
the application of the relatively new method of linguistic
modeling. Yet, when it comes to Stang's assumption of a
"virtually uniform CS original language," Žuravlev (and
some other scholars with him, e.g., Filin) would now disagree, claiming that earlier dialectal differences, originating as spatially limited phenomena occurring here and
there, must also be assumed to have existed in Early PS
though they may be much more difficult and partly even impossible to retrace in view of their subsequent efface-
ment.

A. Senn's repeatedly expressed view of the nature of
the Balto-Slavic linguistic ties is less novel and more
dogmatic than Stang's. The gist of his 1966 paper on "The
Relationships of Baltic and Slavic" was already briefly
accounted for above (cf. p. 65) and therefore need not be
repeated here. In his more recent study, "Slavic and Baltic Linguistic Relations," contributed to the *Donum Balticum* for C. S. Stang (1970), he, while essentially reiter-
ating his basic position of rejecting the notion of any
particular Balto-Slavic unity and claiming that "the theory of a Balto-Slavic unity owes its origin largely to the
prominence attributed . . . to the *literary* Lithuanian
language of the 16th-18th centuries which was replete with
Polish loanwords" (485-6), labors on some peculiar definitions and criteria, supposedly applicable and admissible
for the purpose of establishing such notions and phenomena
as 'linguistic unity' and 'genetic kinship of languages'.
Thus, we read in his article (486):

> The term *linguistic unity* in its traditional usage
> means: 'original sameness of language based on
> blood relationship (consanguinity) with innovations
> limited to its own area'.

And further:

What criteria can be reliably used in an attempt to
establish genetic kinship of languages? Apparently,
syntax and vocabulary must be omitted . . . Syntax
and style are *supraracial elements* of language.

One cannot but be surprised to find this kind of argumentation in a scholarly publication of 1970! Still, even if
Senn was presumably unaware of the concept of semantic-
syntactic 'deep structure' which makes syntactic structure
a sphere for some meaningful inter-linguistic comparison
not to be entirely discarded even in attempts to substantiate or, on the contrary, render unlikely a closer genetic relationship between two language groups, his cautioning (487) against using certain syntactic features of Baltic and Slavic as proof of particularly close ties between
these language groups supposedly pointing to a Balto-Slavic linguistic unity (or common protolanguage) in a remote,
prehistoric past, must undoubtedly be considered justified. Making some very arguable comments on phonological
and morphological (or, rather, morpho-syntactic) phenomena
— namely, interpreting East Baltic *ie* as "the Slavic sound
ě transferred to the Lithuanian and Lettish cognates of
Slavic words" (487) and restating his highly controversial
theory of the development of verbal aspect in ancient Germanic, Slavic, and Baltic — and qualifying his rejection
of lexical data as a yardstick for measuring the degree of
genetic relationship ("the vocabulary can only be of limited usefulness," 489), Senn then sketches his view of the
"chronological order of events and conditions in the development of the Proto-Slavic and Proto-Baltic languages
and people" (489-93):

> (1) Pre-Slavs and Pre-Balts as an undistinguishable
> part of the Proto-Indo-European mass of population.
> (2) Existence (in the second millennium B. C.) of a
> separate community, still speaking Proto-Indo-Euro-
> pean but consisting only of the ancestors of the
> later Proto-Slavs, Proto-Balts, and Proto-Germanic
> people. (3) This pre-Slavic-Baltic-Germanic commu-
> nity was destroyed by a Persian invasion sometime
> between 1000 B. C. and 500 B. C. The Pre-Balts were
> driven off to the north of the Pripet Marshes into
> absolute isolation, out of touch with any other In-
> do-Europeans, even the Slavs. The Pre-Slavs were
> conquered, occupied, and ruled for a while by the
> Persians, and became Proto-Slavs. (4) The *Slavic-
> Baltic* contacts started (1) in the southwest toward

(i.e. before) the beginning of the Christian era, as
a result of the westward drive of the Balts, and (2)
in the east as late as the sixth Christian century,
as a result of the Slavic expansion . . . There are
quite a number of agreements limited to Slavic and
Baltic. Inasmuch as they refer only to Russian and
Lithuanian, Russian and Lettish, or Polish and Lithuanian, they may be considered later innovations
(Lithuanian or Lettish borrowings).

While, on the whole, Senn's concept and interpretation of
the origin and nature of the Balto-Slavic linguistic relationships remain unacceptable to the present writer (cf.
also Birnbaum 1973), it should of course not be denied
that certain elements of his theory deserve further consideration.

An essentially different view of the Balto-Slavic
problem was expounded in some of my own writing of relatively recent date. Thus, in commenting "On the Reconstruction and Predictability of Linguistic Models" (Birnbaum 1967a), I elaborated on some of the implications of
the then presumed but subsequently largely abolished view
of the close parallelism between the order of 'systematic
phonemic' (i.e., roughly morphophonemic) rules of — synchronic — generative theory and the time sequence of diachronic processes recoverable by internal reconstruction,
using some Balto-Slavic data and exploring the concept of
the primacy of Baltic (Common Baltic) over Slavic (CS)
launched by Ivanov and Toporov (1961). Considerations of
a similar kind were further discussed also in a final section of my paper "Rekonstrukcja wewnętrzna, kolejność synchronicznych reguł gramatyki syntetycznej i zagadnienie
najdawniejszych stosunków między językami bałtyckimi i
słowiańskimi" (1968b; expanded English version 1970b: 92-
122, especially 113-20; but cf. also 87-8). For some
further thoughts along these lines and some development of
the original underlying concept, see also Birnbaum 1970c:
especially 14-20 ("Baltoslavisch und/oder Frühurslavisch?")
and Birnbaum 1973. The "modeling approach" to Balto-Slavic, based largely on internal reconstruction, was briefly
discussed, along with other, more traditional ones (to
wit, the ultimately neogrammarian *Stammbaum* approach, the
concept, originated by Meillet, viewing Baltic and Slavic
as two closely related but separate offshoots of IE, and
the *Sprachbund* or convergence approach) in my contribution
to the Stang *festschrift*, "Four Approaches to Balto-

Slavic" (1970a), where, after a brief characterization and comparison, I suggested (74)

> that . . . the concept and method here labeled the modeling approach (which relates to, but also substantially modifies, the traditional view of an assumed Balto-Slavic protolanguage) combined with the interpretation referred to as the *Sprachbund* or convergence approach appears most apt to adequately account for the resemblant, yet in many respects different data of Baltic and Slavic.

The possibility of ascertaining and interpreting specific lexical conformities between only a particular part of the Slavic linguistic territory, especially Bulgarian, and Baltic or a certain portion thereof (notably Old Prussian or West Baltic in general), earlier contemplated by S. B. Bernštejn (1961), was in recent years again discussed in several studies by I. Duridanov (1968b, 1969, 1970). The relevant data seems to suggest that the Slavic ancestors of the Bulgarians (including the branch subsequently emerging as Macedonians, and possibly even a larger group of predecessors of the South Slavs), on the one hand, and the Proto-Prussians (or, generally, the ancestors of the Western Balts, if indeed we may assume that they were already speakers of an identifiable Baltic language or dialect), on the other, may in a remote past have settled in contiguous territories.

Taking as his point of departure the view advanced by V. M. Illič-Svityč (1961, cf. above, p. 148) of the different treatment of word-initial PIE $sg(h)$- in Slavic ($> x$-) and Baltic ($> sk$-, CS sk- being the reflex only of PIE sk- but not of PIE sg-, sgh-, as in Baltic and Germanic), H. Andersen ("On Some Old Balto-Slavic Isoglosses," 1970a) sees in this as well as in a few other early differences in the development of the IE consonant system peculiar to the two language branches (and treated by him elsewhere) some of the earliest isogloss features separating Baltic from Slavic and thus causing their subsequent independent evolution.

Considerations of linguistic geography are very much in the foreground of the otherwise fairly traditional discussion of the Balto-Slavic problem by V. Falkenhahn, "Die sprachgeographische Lage der balto-slawischen Sprachen als Ursache für ihre Besonderheiten" (1968). The significant though contestable contribution of this article is the East German Slavist's assumption of the decisive role

allegedly played by a Finno-Ugric substratum in the formation of the Baltic and Slavic language groups and their
underlying protolanguages. To be sure, it seems that the
role of this assumed substratum of a non-related language
group (or of an only very distantly related language family, if we are to take seriously the recent theories regarding a larger group of "nostratic" languages, expounded
in particular by the late V. M. Illič-Svityč) is grossly
exaggerated in Falkenhahn's article which closes, sympto-
matically, with the announcement (made in footnote 12):

> Der Verf. hofft, eine historische Grammatik der bal-
> tischen und slawischen Sprachen abschliessen zu kön-
> nen, in der sämtliche sich vom Indo-Europäischen
> unterscheidenden Besonderheiten dieser Idiome in der
> oben angegebenen Weise durch Mitberücksichtigung
> auch der finno-ugrischen und anderer Sprachen be-
> leuchtet und vielleicht erklärt werden sollen.

Clearly, the theory adopted by T. Lehr-Spławiński and G.
Gerullis and referred to at the outset of Falkenhahn's article as his point of departure, according to which the
emergence of the Balts and Slavs was triggered by an inva-
sion of IE tribes into previously Finno-Ugric territories
between the Oder and the Pripet (Pripyat') in the second
millennium B. C., must today be considered obsolete or at
any rate in need of substantial revision.

A sobering and much more realistic assessment of the
possible impact of a Finnic linguistic substratum on East
Slavic was recently presented by V. Kiparsky in his instructive and well-argued essay "Gibt es ein finnougrisches Substrat im Slavischen?" (1969c). After briefly
discussing the merits and hazards of the substratum theory, originally launched by Ascoli but espoused and given
added prestige in the twenties and thirties by such repu-
table linguists as E. Lewy and J. Pokorny (both assuming
the existence of a Finno-Ugric substratum for CS) and further embraced also by leading Polish Slavists (J. Baudouin
de Courtenay, J. Rozwadowski, and T. Lehr-Spławiński, to
mention just the most renowned ones), Kiparsky then goes
on to state (p. 4):

> Im Lichte der heutigen Ortsnamenforschung, lingui-
> stischen Paläontologie, Geschichte und Archäologie
> kann man jedoch für ziemlich sicher halten, dass die
> Urheimat der Slaven einerseits und diejenige der
> Finnougrier andererseits sich so weit voneinander

befanden, dass jedenfalls vor unserer Zeitrechnung keine unmittelbaren Berührungen zwischen diesen ethnischen Gruppen möglich waren.

A Finno-Ugric substratum thus cannot reasonably have played any major role in the formation of Baltic and Slavic as independent branches within the IE language family, contrary to what Falkenhahn seems to have been inclined to believe. On the other hand, such a substratum may have played, and indeed probably did play, a certain — though generally subordinate — role during the end phase of CS (in the broad sense) and in the early period of preliterary and historically recorded East Slavic (Proto-Russian). In concluding his detailed analysis, Kiparsky summarizes his findings as follows (27):

> Finnougrisches Substrat ist im Russischen zweifellos im Lautsystem und in der Syntax vorhanden. Sicher beruhen auf finnougrischen Modellen das Fehlen des Verbums *haben* und das nordrussische Cokanje. Wahrscheinlich mordwinischer Herkunft ist das mittel- und südrussische und das weissrussische Akanje. Sicher beruht die Bewahrung des Nominativobjekts des Infinitivs in nordrussischen Mundarten auf ostseefinnischer 'Kühlschrankfunktion'. Im Wortschatz ist das finnougrische Substrat kaum, im Formemsystem überhaupt nicht zu spüren. Die Erscheinungen, die zum letzteren gezählt wurden, sind entweder einheimischer Herkunft (-*ka* als 'Intimitätsimperativformans') oder sie gehören in die Syntax (postponierter Artikel, Komparation der Substantive).

In this context it should be noted that Kiparsky now unequivocally rejects the possibility of explaining East Slavic *akan'e* as a residual archaism from the CS period as claimed by V. Georgiev (cf. above, pp. 252-4, and below, 328).

13.2. From the Ongoing Discussion of the Time Limits, Periodization, and Chronology of Common Slavic. The treatment of topical questions concerning details of chronology as they pertain to various CS developments (notably sound shifts and, to some extent, morphological modifications) has been discussed in previous sections of this report and therefore need not concern us here. Likewise, the problem of establishing an upper and lower time limit for the CS (PS) period, setting it off against dialectal

Late PIE or possibly Common Balto-Slavic, on the one hand, and, on the other, against the attested history of the individual Slavic languages, discussed also in recent years, has in part — as regards the initial phase of CS — already been touched upon in the preceding section (13.1., discussing, incidentally, also some aspects of periodization, namely, recent views regarding the nature of the early phase of CS or PS) and will be reviewed further in the next section of this account of the pertinent ongoing debate (13.3.) where, in particular, recent and current views regarding the ultimate breakup of the relative linguistic unity of CS and the Late CS dialectal differentiation will be briefly discussed. The reader interested in the bulk of the relevant recent literature on the time limits, periodization, and chronology of CS not mentioned in the present short section on this subject is therefore referred to the respective sections just indicated and, especially, to the appended Bibliography where relevant titles are marked with the appropriate numerical symbol (VI:2). In what follows only a few studies and, in particular, a recent relevant essay in which I discussed at some length the time limits of CS, will be commented upon.

The unique relevance of onomastic data, which frequently can be dated incontestably, to problems of chronology, in particular for prehistoric periods for which no written records and thus no evidence datable on paleographic or other grounds are available, has long been recognized, of course. As regards prehistoric Slavic language material, the relevant studies by M. Vasmer, E. Moór, A. C. Sós, C. E. Bidwell, and, in recent years, Z. Stieber, to mention just a few, bear eloquent testimony to the merits and potentials of utilizing this source of information. It will therefore come as no surprise that the report "Prasłowianie w świetle onomastyki" (1968a), prepared for the First International Congress of Slavic Archeology by one of the ranking Polish experts in the field of Slavic onomastics, S. Rospond, not only sheds new light on many controversial questions of Slavic prehistory but also is a veritable mine of important, partly fresh data. In particular, it should be noted that Rospond does not limit himself to analyzing and interpreting relevant toponymic data, on the whole no doubt the most significant single source of onomastic information germane to linguistic prehistory; rather he extends his study to include also Early Slavic ethnonyms (cf. also Rospond 1966 and 1968b) and anthroponyms (cf., e.g., also Rospond 1965).

Thus, the picture that we can now conceive of the primitive Slavs on the basis of place names (as well as, it should be noted, hydronyms), ethnic denotations, and personal names not only supplements the relevant, but in terms of linguistic identification much less reliable data and findings of archeology and prehistory, but also substantially contributes to the concept of CS as formed on the basis of linguistics proper, i.e., as suggested by considerations of phonology, morphology, syntax, and lexicology. By taking into account also research such as that reported by Rospond, Z. Stieber in a series of recent studies (especially 1965c, 1968b, 1968c, 1969/71, 1970) was able to modify and establish more precisely the chronology of a number of CS and post-CS Early Slavic changes, notably sound shifts.

Some problems of relative chronology in CS or, to be more specific, of the time sequence establishable for the CS (and partly post-CS, Early Slavic) Palatalizations of Velars and some related phenomena of vowel mutation were briefly discussed by me, in addition to work reported earlier (cf. Birnbaum 1967a and 1968b), in my article "On Reconstruction and Prediction: Two Correlates of Diachrony in Genetic and Typological Linguistics" (1969), an expanded version of a paper read at the Tenth International Congress of Linguists, Bucharest (1967); see also Birnbaum 1970b: 71-91, especially 74-6.

A general stock-taking of the problems relevant to defining the time limits of CS was attempted by me in a recent essay entitled "Zur Problematik der zeitlichen Abgrenzung des Urslavischen" (1970c; an abridged Russian variant of its last portion, 35-62, subtitled "Über den Aussagewert als Archaismen angesprochener mundartlicher Erscheinungen," 1972b, appearing in the *festschrift* for R. I. Avanesov). After first briefly discussing some pertinent terminological problems, especially the mutual relationship between the terms 'language' and 'dialect' and the realities they cover (using Slavic as well as non-Slavic examples), and the partly analogical difficulties in defining the limits of time and space of CS, the latter being tantamount to the problems inherent in identifying the original homeland of the Slavs, I then proceeded to discuss in three subsequent sections the terminological and methodological problems that can be paraphrased by the three questions: "Urslavisch und/oder Gemeinslavisch?" (6-14), "Baltoslavisch und/oder Frühurslavisch?" (14-20), and "Spätgemeinslavischer Dialekt und/oder Ureinzel-

slavine?" (20-35). After having suggested some tentative
answers to these questions, I endeavored, in the remainder
of my paper (35-62), to illustrate with a number of concrete examples the hazards of incautiously interpreting
certain locally restricted phonological features ("dialec-
talisms") which have the appearance of representing an archaic state of affairs (and occasionally in fact have residual character, the precise time-depth remaining arguable, however) as reflecting or indeed preserving a CS
stage of development in the sound system or a portion
thereof.

Echoing my earlier suggestion (Birnbaum 1966a: 153-
4) to utilize the existing possibility in German (as well
as in English, French, and Russian, for example) of making
a terminological distinction between at least two phases
in the evolution of the Slavic protolanguage, I ventured
to propose, in answering the first of the three posed
questions (13-14),

> . . . dass u. E. keine ernsten Bedenken dagegen be-
> stehen, die sich . . . anbietende Möglichkeit einer
> Unterscheidung zwischen Urslavisch und Gemeinsla-
> visch in dem Sinne zu nutzen, dass ersterer Terminus
> für das frühere, durch innere (vom Gemeinslavischen
> ausgehende) und komparative (das Zeugnis anderer in-
> dogermanischer Sprachzweige berücksichtigende) Re-
> konstruktion wenigstens in seinen Grundzügen er-
> schliessbare Stadium der slavischen Grundsprache,
> letzterer für das spätere, durch Vergleichung der
> Einzelslavinen (in ihrer heutigen und besonders in
> ihrer altüberlieferten Form, in normierter Schrift-
> sprache und frei gewachsenem Dialekt) ermittelte
> Stadium des vorliterarischen Slavisch verwendet
> wird.

And adopting the previously discussed modeling approach to Balto-Slavic, I answered the second question as
follows (20):

> Zusammenfassend sei die . . . gestellte . . . Frage
> dahin beantwortet, dass es u. E. zwar durchaus sinn-
> voll erscheint, eine dem Frühurslavischen zeitlich
> vorausgehende baltoslavische Zwischenstufe in der
> vorliterarischen Entwicklung des Slavischen und sei-
> ner Vorgänger anzusetzen (was entsprechend dagegen
> für das Urbaltische wenig Sinn hätte, da Baltosla-
> visch und Frühbaltisch kaum zu trennen wären), wobei

es aber immerhin methodologisch und terminologisch problematisch bleibt, ob eine solche baltoslavische Zwischenstufe als wirklich je vorhandene, undifferenzierte, konkrete Spracheinheit verstanden werden darf. Eher sollte man sich darunter so etwas wie einen besonderen, altertümlich-konservativen spätgemeinindogermanischen Dialekt vorstellen. Wegen der sehr beschränkten Möglichkeiten, eine — jedenfalls nur recht unvollständig erschliessbare — Sprachstruktur zu entwerfen, empfiehlt es sich dabei überdies, besser von einem abstrakt konzipierten baltoslavischen (oder frühurbaltischen) Sprachmodell als etwa von einer im einzelnen rekonstruierbaren, konkreten Grund- oder Ursprache auszugehen.

For some further thoughts along these lines, see now also Birnbaum 1973 (as well as a recent rebuttal to Weiher, to be summarized in the planned sequel to this report).

And, finally, commenting on the problem paraphrased in my third question, I stated (31-2):

Es ist u. E. durchaus möglich, eine Periode der slavischen Sprachentwicklung anzunehmen, die *gleichzeitig* als die bereits mundartlich stark differenzierte Endphase des Gemeinslavischen (bzw. des Späturslavischen) und dabei als die Anfangsphase einzelsprachlicher slavischer Sprachentwicklung gelten kann; welcher Aspekt hervorzuheben ist, bestimmt der jeweilige Zusammenhang, worin diese Periode von dem einen oder anderen Forscher für den einen oder anderen wissenschaftlichen Zweck gesehen wird . . . Wir bemühen uns nach Möglichkeit die slavische Sprachentwicklung in natürliche, von sprachinhärenten Kriterien bestimmte Perioden aufzugliedern. Der Schwund der schwachen Jer-Vokale markiert u. E. (und nach Meinung vieler anderer Gelehrter, darunter besonders der von Trubeckoj, Durnovo und Toporov) den Abschluss einer solchen natürlichen Entwicklungsstufe.

For some harsh criticism of my, to be sure, deliberately relativistic position by Weiher (1971) with whom I had felt compelled to polemicize, and for some additional comments in this context, see below (pp. 330-1).

Among illustrative examples of alleged archaisms, believed by some scholars to have perpetuated a CS state of affairs, I discussed in the concluding section of my

essay, after first having pointed out some incontestable
instances of recorded Late CS phonetic forms, (1) the
dialectal Polish so-called Podhale archaism (P *archaizm
podhalański*), (2) the spelling *atče* (for regular *ače*) in
one of the Old Novgorod birchbark letters, discussed by me
and others elsewhere, (3) the rare spellings *v*(ь)*x-* instead of regular *vьs-* (represented, e.g., by *vxu* = *vьs'u*)
in some other Old Novgorod texts, (4) the unshifted or
only partially shifted consonants (for expected results of
the Second Palatalization of Velars) in some Great Russian
dialects (observed and interpreted by Gluskina, Stieber,
and others), and — last but not least — (5) the interpretation of East Slavic *akan'e* and some seemingly similar
but, as it turns out, genetically quite unrelated phenomena elsewhere in the Slavic language area, notably in the
Bulgarian so-called Rhodope dialects, considered by V.
Georgiev and earlier, in a less outspoken and not quite as
definite form, also by A. Vaillant and G. Y. Shevelov, a
survival of the CS pronunciation *ă* of the short, back,
nondiffuse — or, in other words, non-high — vowel. While
admitting the possibility, if not the probability, of interpreting the phenomena listed sub 3 and 4 as true archaisms stemming from the CS period, I denied this possibility for the instances discussed, sub 1 and 2. Likewise,
though in more vigorous terms, I argued in some detail
against the extreme interpretation (sub 5) of the "CS significance of *akan'e*" proposed by Georgiev (cf. also above,
pp. 253 - 4). As was mentioned before, my inability to accept Georgiev's reasoning has since been shared by a great
number of other Slavists (Bernštejn, Kiparsky, Rigler, and
Ivić, among others).

Based on his study of the first contacts between, on
the one hand, Balkan Slavic and, on the other hand, Greek
and Danubian Romance (Early Romanian), I. Pătruţ, in a recent article (1972), arrived at the conclusion that up to
the 8th century all Slavic dialects remained fundamentally
CS in nature, while beginning with the 9th century the
Slavic influences on Greek and Romanian assume a new, primarily markedly Bulgarian, character.

*13.3. Current Notions and Controversies Concerning the
Disintegration and Differentiation of Common Slavic.* In
my study "The Dialects of Common Slavic" (1966a, already
briefly referred to (cf. pp. 65-6), I had taken as my primary point of departure the generally very thorough account of the disintegration of CS and of the then current

state of its investigation given by A. Furdal in his 1961 book on "the disintegration of PS in the light of the phonetic evolution," reporting on, discussing, and, in part, reinterpreting the conclusions arrived at by him. In addition to considering, above all, phonological criteria, I further ventured to assess some morphological features suitable for purposes of classification, briefly discussed also by Furdal and generally corroborating (or in any event not contradicting) the dialectal divisions based on phonological characteristics. On the other hand, as I also pointed out in one of the introductory sections of my essay (160),

> the latest contribution to our topic, F. P. Filin's book *Obrazovanie jazyka vostočnyx slavjan* (. . . 1962), containing also a chapter on "The Beginning of the Disintegration of Common Slavic" . . . where particularly lexical data are taken into account . . . became available to me only while I was writing this report. In fact, it seems to constitute a first attempt to systematize lexical data for the purpose of classifying CSl dialects."

And I went on to say (160-1):

> Although, in Filin's words, 'a detailed study of the ancient lexical dialectal features is a task for the future' . . . some of his conclusions point in the same direction as those based on phonological as well as on certain morphological features to be reported in this paper.

It seems that my preliminary and, to be sure, very tentatively phrased impression derived from reading Filin was premature, at least to judge by O. N. Trubačev's criticism referred to above (p. 301), reproaching me precisely for not having paid sufficient attention to lexical data which, in his view, considerably upsets the by and large traditional picture of CS dialectology at which I had arrived. For some more recent studies by Filin on this subject (1968, 1970, 1972), see below (pp. 335-8). Contrary to Trubačev's criticism of my concept of the dialects of CS for being supported by too narrow a base of data (my evidence being almost exclusively phonological and morphological), some other objections — primarily of a terminological and, as regards CS phonology, theoretical nature — were raised in a couple of reviews (or, in the second instance, rather a review article) of my essay by R.

Aitzetmüller (1967) and, in much greater detail, his disciple E. Weiher (1967). I attempted to answer my critics in my above cited essay on the time limits of CS (Birnbaum 1970c), unfortunately, as it appears, without being able to convince at least one of them who has felt called upon to polemicize once more primarily with some of the underlying theoretical premises assumed by me (cf. Weiher 1971). Unable to accept my suggested specialized usage of the term CS (G *Gemeinslavisch*) to designate the, broadly speaking, later phase in the evolution of the Slavic ancestral language (while readily admitting, of course, the theoretical — though hardly practiced — possibility of attributing another connotation to that term, namely, that of pan- or achronic Slavic, 'Pan-Slavic' or 'Generalized Slavic'), Aitzetmüller and, in particular, Weiher objected to my late dating of the *terminus ad quem* for CS (or PS in the broad sense, to wit, in effect to the 10th/12th centuries, i.e., the time of the *jer* shift, in this respect, as has been shown, following the — in my view — well-argued reasoning of scholars such as Durnovo, Trubeckoj, and Toporov). Thus, Weiher posits a rather artificially and arbitrarily conceived intermediary period of "nachurslavisch-vorliterarisch [Slavisch]" (c.f. especially Weiher 1967: 85; 1971: 118). For some further considerations of the terminological problem concerned, see also above, paragraph 1.0. in the Introduction to this report. Among more substantial, and not merely terminological, disagreements between myself and the Würzburg Slavists, our different phonological interpretations of CS e, by them conceived as in fact /'ǎ/, i.e. distinct from CS /ǎ/ (= traditional o) only by — phonemic? — iotation or "softness" (sharping) of the preceding consonant (or consonantal cluster), can be noted. It is naturally also a disagreement in substance when Weiher assumes the PS (CS) period to have ended already somewhere around the 4th or 5th century A. D. while I, following, on the one hand, Stieber's more recently proposed late chronologies for some of the major CS sound shifts, and on the other hand, adopting, with some qualifications, the dynamic modeling concept of Balto-Slavic and Early PS developed by Ivanov and Toporov (1961) and especially Žuravlev (1968 and 1970), would consider the specifically and exclusively Slavic linguistic evolution to have set in only in the centuries immediately preceding (rather than those closely following) the beginning of the Christian era (cf. especially Birnbaum 1970c and 1973). Also Weiher's gross misinterpretation (1971:

119) of my view on the merits and shortcomings of the traditional *Stammbaum* concept of linguistic evolution and —
nota bene — branching (while, in fact, I reject only its
exclusive, dogmatic, and overly schematic application but
do not consider it altogether worthless) is surprising, to
say the least. As was already indicated, a rebuttal to
his distorted presentation of my certainly in no way revolutionizing views on CS dialectology has since appeared in
the same journal that published his polemics against me
and will be reported in the updating supplement to the
present publication.

In addition to the controversy stirred in recent
years by my fairly traditional (and, to be sure, imperfect) analysis of the dialects of CS, the same subject as
a whole was dealt with in the late sixties also by Z.
Stieber, one of the most prominent experts in the field.
Applying his precise, theoretically well-founded method
(resorted to previously both in Slavic Historical and Comparative Linguistics and in Slavic, especially West Slavic
dialectology) and utilizing his succinct exposition and
lucid style, the Polish Slavist has discussed problems of
CS dialectology particularly in three fairly recent contributions (Stieber 1965c, 1968b, 1968c). As in his other
research on CS and Early Slavic, and especially in their
phonological aspect, Stieber, when discussing the earliest
ascertainable CS dialectal features, relies heavily on
onomastic (primarily toponymic) data and on loanword material. As one of the main results of Stieber's relevant
reasoning, one may note his definite rejection of the earlier view (in somewhat modified form still adhered to,
e.g., by Bernštejn 1961) that the ancestors of the Southern Slavs came to the Balkans and the Eastern Alps only
from originally East Slavic territory. The relatively
late chronologies of some sound changes previously held to
fall entirely within the CS period but now believed to
have begun only toward the end of that period (notably the
Second and Third Palatalizations of Velars) as well as
some conspicuous agreements between, on the one hand, Slovenian and partly also Serbo-Croatian and, on the other,
West Slavic, naturally especially its Southern portion
(i.e., Czech and Slovak or, rather, the Late CS dialect
underlying these languages), suggest early ties also between the predecessors of the Western Slavs and the western branch of the Southern Slavs. These ties reflect in
part as yet uncharted movements of peoples and tribes during the period of the Slavic migrations in the 6th and 7th

centuries and were severed only by the advent of the Magyars and their ultimate landtaking in once Slavic-populated Pannonia; cf. also above pp. 12-13. Summing up his
most recent and detailed discussion devoted specifically
to the problems of the oldest differences between the
Slavic dialects (1968b), Stieber concludes (108):

> On voit que des quatre traits proposés par Bernštejn
> et des deux qu'établit Lehr-Spławiński en tant que
> critères d'une division, antérieure à l'an 500, du
> domaine linguistique slave en parties orientale et
> occidentale, on ne saurait retenir (avec certaines
> restrictions) qu'un seul, c'est-à-dire la disparité
> du sort des groupes slaves commun *tl dl* à l'Est et
> à l'Ouest. Beaucoup de choses indiquent que la
> chute de *d* et de *t* dans ces groupes est un phénomène
> ancien dans l'Est, mais on ne peut reconnaître cela
> comme démontré. A la lumière de tout ce qui a été
> dit, il semble que le domaine slave était, avant
> l'an 500 étonnamment homogène sous le rapport lin-
> guistique. On ne saurait expliquer cela qu'en sup-
> posant qu'encore peu avant cette date (donc, ap-
> proximativement, jusqu'aux environs du IVe s. de n.
> è.), les Slaves n'avaient habité qu'un territoire
> relativement très restreint, à l'intérieur duquel
> les communications et les échanges de population
> entre les diverses tribus avaient été aisés et fré-
> quents. Le premier changement dont on soit certain
> qu'il a été effectué de façons différentes (bien
> que, en principe, sur le territoire slave tout en-
> tier, à la seule exception possible de la périphérie
> Nord-Est), ce sont les résultats de la deuxième
> palatalisation des vélaires. Ceci n'a de quoi éton-
> ner, puisque la deuxième palatalisation s'est pro-
> duite à une époque (VIIe s.) où les Slaves habi-
> taient des espaces énormes, depuis l'Adriatique et
> la mer Egée au Sud jusqu'à la Baltique et près du
> golfe de Finlande au Nord. Sur de si vastes terri-
> toires, il devait déjà apparaître des différences
> nettes d'un dialecte slave à l'autre.

I tend to agree with this conclusion even though I believe
with Žuravlev (1968, 1970) and others that earlier innovations which originally may have had a limited range within
Slavic territory subsequently could have been generalized,
thus obliterating any possible earlier dialectal differentiation. Viewed in the historical context of Polish

Slavic linguistic studies, Stieber's new concept of the
spatial and temporal diffusion and differentiation of the
CS protolanguage, preliminary to its gradual disintegration (and the subsequent regrouping of Slavic linguistic
units) may be considered a departure from the earlier notion of CS in Polish Slavistics bearing the imprint of T.
Lehr-Spławiński and his school (A. Furdal and, in a way,
J. Nalepa — cf. below — being two of its last members).

A relatively independent though usually fairly traditional position has been taken in Polish linguistics by
T. Milewski, in some respects agreeing with Lehr-Spławiński's views on prehistoric Slavic but occasionally also
strongly differing with them. Of relevant contributions
by Milewski, his article discussing the range of the Slavic liquid metathesis (as well as some other Late CS and/or
Early Slavic processes, all falling into the period be
tween the 8th and 12th centuries), "Zasięg terytorialny
słowiańskiej przestawki płynnych," published in the year
of his death (1966), deserves mention. Considering the
only partial metathesis in Slavic (and some other sound
shifts carried out inconsistently or incompletely), Milewski arrives at the conclusion that all these processes and
their seemingly irregular occurrence ought to be viewed
(and in part explained) in terms of center versus peripheral areas (of various degrees and varying distance)
within the extended Slavic language territory, the heart-
land of that territory in this Late CS - Early Slavic period, and with it the epicenter of phonological innovations, having shifted from north of the Carpathian Mountains to the south, i.e., to somewhere in Pannonia and the
adjacent regions, only subsequently inundated and de-
stroyed as such by the expansion of the Magyars, the Ger-
mans, and the Romanians.

Considerations of a similar kind come to mind when
reading J. Marvan's latest contributions to his theory of
Slavic vowel contraction viewed in the light of the disintegration of Late CS and stressing, particularly in his
most recent paper, the repercussions of the primarily phonetic process of vowel contraction on the breakup of the
relative unity of Slavic in terms of morphological structure (Marvan 1968b and 1972). As was mentioned before,
Marvan considers Slavic vowel contraction in its earliest
phase a process preceding in time the fall of the weak
jers, while realizing, of course, and taking into consideration the unsystematic, "spotty", and chronologically
irregular nature of this phenomenon, definable in typo-

logical rather than genetic-diachronic terms (cf. especially Marvan 1971).

A significant contribution to one particular aspect
and phase in the disintegration of Late CS is the monograph *Słowiańszczyzna północno-zachodnia. Podstawy jedności i jej rozpad* (1967/68) by J. Nalepa. Although its
author was particularly well prepared to undertake this
study on objective premises, having received training both
as a historian (and prehistorian) and as a linguist, well
versed, in particular, also in the field of onomastics,
this is a strongly opinionated book, many remarkable merits notwithstanding. It is arranged in four major sections: (1) "the original homeland and the migrations of
the Slavs as the basis for the formation of the linguistic
unity of the Northwestern Slavs," (2) "the early medieval
unity of Northwestern Slavdom and its disintegration in
the light of linguistic data," (3) "the causes for the
disintegration of the linguistic unity of the Northwestern
Slavs," and (4) "conclusions and final remarks." Nalepa
is an ardent adherent of the school of Polish "neoautoch-
thonists" (represented by such names as Kostrzewski, Lehr-
Spławiński, Czekanowski, and Rudnicki, but opposed among
Polish scholars particularly by K. Moszyński whose counterarguments Nalepa deals with exceedingly lightly). To
underpin his contention of the original western homeland
of the Slavs, Nalepa quotes, following J. Pokorny, a number of alleged Slavic-Celtic lexical parallels and cites
onomastic (toponymic) data supposedly supporting the view
of an original Baltic-Northwest Slavic area of settlement
of the as yet undifferentiated or merely slightly differentiated primitive Balts and Slavs. One of Nalepa's main
theses, namely, that the Northwestern Slavs long formed a
relatively homogeneous linguistic unity, is generally well
argued; the same can be said about the — for quite some
time no longer seriously challenged — theory of the original sites of the ancestors of the Southern Slavs north of
the Carpathians. Here, incidentally, may lie the key to
the earlier close contacts between portions of the Western
and Southern Slavs, clearly demonstrated also by Stieber.
Nalepa's extreme views regarding the original homeland of
the Slavs as a whole are in need of some substantial revision, however. Testifying to its author's great erudition
and citing a wealth of linguistic (and historical) data as
well as secondary literature, this is a study that future
researchers in the field cannot afford to ignore. For
some additional assessment of the merits and shortcomings

of Nalepa's monograph, see, e.g., Popowska-Taborska 1970, and Urbańczyk 1971.

Finally, and turning to the East Slavic area, three new works by F. P. Filin, relevant to the problem of the disintegration and dialectal differentiation of Late CS and, in particular, its eastern portion, ought to be mentioned here: his 1968 contribution to the Sixth International Congress of Slavists, "Nekotorye problemy rekonstrukcii drevnerusskix dialektov"; his 1970 article "Drevnerusskie dialektnye zony i proisxoždenie vostočnoslavjanskix jazykov"; and — last but not least — the long Introduction (5-96) to his recent book *Proisxoždenie russkogo, ukrainskogo i belorusskogo jazykov* (1972). Since the latter includes a revised version of the two preceding papers, and the book as a whole, while it does not actually replace, in some respects nonetheless supersedes Filin's thinking and findings of his 1962 monograph on the formation of East Slavic, we can here confine ourselves to commenting briefly on his most recent publication.

The introductory chapter of Filin's new book consists of three sections, subtitled "On the Original Homeland of the Slavs, the Breakup of Common Slavic, and the Formation of East Slavic" (6-30), "From the History of the Problem of the Old Russian Dialects and the Origin of Russian, Ukrainian, and Belorussian" (30-83), and "Some Problems of Reconstructing the Old Russian Dialects" (84-96). Even though the discussion in section two (surveying (1) "the 'tripartite' concept of A. A. Šaxmatov," (2) "the 'bipartite' hypothesis of T. Lehr-Spławiński and N. S. Trubeckoj," (3) "the works of Soviet linguists of the thirties and forties," and (4) "the research of the fifties and the sixties") and in section three (the latter, in particular, restating in slightly modified form much of the argumentation of the 1968 and 1970 essays) is of some relevance to the problem of the disintegration and dialectal differentiation of Late CS (Early Old Russian dialects of the pre-*jer*-shift period qualifying, in our broad conception, for being considered Late CS dialects as well), it is of course especially the views and notions expounded in part one of the Introduction that are of primary interest for our purpose.

Here, the Soviet Slavist sketches a picture of some of the basic problems of the emergence, evolution, and dissolution of CS which is fully up-to-date with current, advanced thinking in these matters; Filin not only exhibits intimate familiarity with the immediately relevant secondary literature (though some of his judgments seem occasionally very unfair), but also demonstrates his acquaintance with some of the most weighty achievements in related disciplines such as Comparative IE Linguistics, Archeology and Prehistory, Anthropology and Folklore. In discussing the formation and development of CS, Filin refers, with guarded approval, to the relevant views of B. V. Gornung (as especially expounded in his booklet of 1963, *Iz predystorii obrazovanija obščeslavjanskogo jazykovogo edinstva*, Gornung's contribution to the Sofia Congress of Slavists; cf. further Gornung 1958 and 1959). According to this Soviet Slavist, the notion of an original Balto-Slavic linguistic unity must be considered a mere fiction, the many ascertainable Balto-Slavic conformities largely being the result of secondary convergence and mutual influences (beginning in the 5th/6th centuries and lasting until the times of the Grand Duchy of Lithuania). Further, the original status of a homogeneous Baltic linguistic group is, in his view, highly questionable as he considers the ancestors of the Prussians, Jatvingians, and Golindians originally to have formed part of the PS ethno-linguistic sphere and only subsequently to have joined the predecessors of the Lithuanians and Latvians, thereby converging into a "secondary Baltic community"; cf. for a similar view also Žuravlev 1968. Gornung conceives of the primitive Slavs (or rather their forefathers) as having originally belonged to the "southeastern zone" of the IE territory, i.e., as being in close contact with the ancestors of the Greeks, the Armenians, the Indo-Iranians, the Tocharians, and the "Anatolians", and only at a later stage as having migrated northwestward and making contact with the predecessors of the Baltic and Germanic tribes (cf. some analogical views expressed by O. N. Trubačev and others). Subsequently, outlining the two basic hypotheses concerning the so-called original homeland (G *Urheimat*, R *prarodina*) of the primitive Slavs, the western ("autochthonic" or "Vistula-Oder") theory, adhered to particularly by a number of Polish scholars but also, for example, by the Soviet linguist V. V. Martynov, and the eastern (or "mid-Dnieper") theory, embraced by L. Niederle, M. Vasmer, and K. Moszyński, to mention a few, but in recent years having gained new adherents (the present writer, among them), Filin discusses the merits and hazards of these theories, but is at first, understandably, unable to arrive at any definite standpoint of his own. However, after a fairly thorough discussion of the present

state of studies concerning lexical borrowings (stressing,
in particular, the increasing significance attributed to
early Slavic-Iranian contacts) and botanic and zoological
terminology, he indicates his preference to locate the
earliest ascertainable sites of the Protoslavs somewhere
on the central Dnieper and the adjacent western territories. Discussing in the following the difficulties of
identifying linguistically the oldest layers of topo- and
hydronyms (including, incidentally, the hydronymics of the
upper Dnieper, investigated by Toporov and Trubačev, and
usually held to be either Proto-Baltic or possibly Balto-
Slavic), not to speak of the various prehistoric "cul-
tures" defined in archeological terms (the classical controversial example being provided by the so-called Lusatian culture, identified by some with the earliest Slavs —
without sufficient evidence, in my opinion), Filin briefly
comments on the relative value of ancient ethno- and anthroponyms and notes that the Slavic-inhabited area was
vastly expanded during the first centuries of our era and
even more so in the 6th and 7th centuries. He then proceeds to survey the more significant among the phonological criteria usually adduced to illustrate the beginning
differentiation of the Slavic linguistic area into locally
delimited subgroups and subregions. Finally, pointing out
that some linguists because of the late date of the *jer*
shift would assume a coexistence of Late CS and the early
historical phases of individual Slavic languages in the
10th/13th centuries, Filin takes exception to such a view
and suggests that CS came to an end shortly before the appearance of the first extant written documents (in the
10th/11th centuries). I have argued in this volume on
several occasions for the possibility of assuming precisely such a coexistence (or time overlap) between the last
phase of a disintegrating common ancestral language and
the first beginnings of individual daughter languages —
the point of view largely to be determined by the particular orientation of a given researcher in a given situation, but also because of the undeniable closeness between,
not to say, near-identity of, in particular, OCS and Early
Old Russian, suggesting merely dialectal differences rather than a clear-cut difference in distinct languages
(granted the well-known difficulties of defining 'language' as opposed to 'dialect'). Nonetheless, I will
readily concede that Filin's well-informed and cautious
appraisal of the problems of CS and its speakers, as currently conceived, is more than merely adequate. In more

337

than one way, it could serve as an exemplary capsule
statement of our present knowledge of CS.

Of recent work introducing some new criteria into
the study of Late CS dialectisms, R. Eckert's brief contribution (1971) on the geographically distributed -*i*
stems in CS has previously been mentioned (see pp. 286 and
303, above).

14. Conclusion: OVERVIEW AND OUTLOOK

If, in concluding our progress and state-of-the-art report on past, recent, and ongoing research relevant to CS, its prehistory, immediate continuation, as well as its external setting and conditions, we were to assess in retrospect the overall accomplishments attained in the field to date and, as a final note, venture to make a few remarks on the prospects for future advances or even breakthroughs, we would have to say that, on the whole, the achievements thus far are most impressive indeed, and that, with the increasingly sophisticated tools of linguistic research — applicable in particular also to linguistic reconstruction — at our disposal, there is every reason to expect in the foreseeable future further important insights into the structure and functioning of the Slavic protolanguage.

Obviously, a combination of favorable factors can be cited to provide at least a partial explanation for the, generally speaking, extraordinarily high level of achievement as regards the reconstruction of CS. Above all, the available linguistic data itself accounts for a good deal of the success of scholarship in this field. Depending on the interpretation of the upper time limit of CS, there is either merely a relatively very small time gap of some two to three hundred years separating the end phase of the common ancestral language of all Slavs and the first appearance of written texts in Slavic (the earliest OCS translations having been made in the second half of the ninth century with the oldest extant texts dating to — probably, the second half of — the tenth century); or, if we take a less conservative view and consider the earliest OCS and Old Russian textual and epigraphic evidence of the

10th through 12th centuries barely more than local varieties of dialectally markedly differentiated Late CS, in
the process of final disintegration — a view advocated in
the preceding pages while, to be sure, not considered the
only conceivable one — we can even speak of a certain
overlap between the very last phase of CS and historically
attested Early Slavic. Undoubtedly, the fairly complete
and coherent linguistic structure that can be derived (for
phonology and morphology in any event) from the earliest
recorded data of Slavic, in a few, precisely defined instances supplemented, it would seem, by archaic features
of subsequent periods, provides a solid basis for all further reconstruction of the preceding phases of CS. Such
earlier stages in the linguistic evolution can either be
recovered internally by identifying primary sounds and
sound sequences as well as protoforms and original patterns, and by establishing relative chronologies; or they
can be ascertained and corroborated by comparison of the
Slavic linguistic evidence with cognate data of other,
more or less closely related IE languages. While not
quite as ideal as in the case of, for example, the Romance
languages with their abundantly attested common ancestral
language, Latin, or of the northern branch of Germanic
(i.e., Scandinavian, Nordic) with a small but significant
body of Runic inscriptions in Proto-Nordic preserved, the
situation in Slavic, as regards the earliest attested linguistic data (in relationship to the reconstructed sounds
and forms, functions and meanings, and their patterning)
and its sequential arrangement in the underlying protolanguage, compares most favorably to the state of affairs
prevailing with regard to several other IE language fami-
lies and groupings such as, for instance, Indo-Iranian,
the Anatolian languages, Celtic, or Baltic. The contrast,
in particular, to the latter language group (the one no
doubt most closely related to Slavic) when it comes to the
discrepancy between protolanguage and historical attestation — a discrepancy which in the case of Baltic may
amount to many centuries or even a millennium or two — is
most conspicuous. It is in part at least this wide time
gap separating the earliest Baltic texts (the first Old
Prussian source, the Elbing Vocabulary, dating to ca.
1400, the first Old Lithuanian texts to the early 16th
century) from a common Baltic ancestral language (if the
existence of such a protolanguage can actually even be assumed, which is somewhat doubtful in view of the profound
differences cutting through Baltic) that has also blurred

the picture of the precise nature of the close and unique
ties ascertainable between Baltic as a whole (or a substantial portion thereof) and Slavic. If, therefore, it
may seem legitimate to claim that the continued controversy concerning the chronology of the end phase of CS (in
which recently this writer, too, has been embroiled) is
largely one of terminology and, to some extent perhaps, of
linguistic theory and conception, the as yet largely un-
reconciled differences of opinion when it comes to the
Balto-Slavic problem are undoubtedly of a more substantial
nature.

Another reason for the many accomplishments and successful solutions of difficult problems of reconstruction
in the field of Slavic linguistic prehistory can undoubtedly be found in the fact that some of the most ingenious
and erudite linguists of modern times have devoted their
particular efforts to central and crucial aspects of Slavic linguistic reconstruction. Illustrious names such as
Meillet, Trubeckoj, Lehr-Spławiński, van Wijk, Vasmer,
Jakobson, Kuryłowicz are prominently written in the history of Slavic Comparative and Historical Linguistics.
Their work has been or is being continued by scholars of
such stature as Vaillant and Shevelov, Stang and Arumaa,
Stieber and Machek, Kuznecov and Bernštejn. And in recent
years remarkable results have been accomplished by a host
of younger imaginative and dedicated linguists — Ivanov
and Toporov, Trubačev, Illič-Svityč and Žuravlev, Mareš
and Andersen, to mention just a few of the most outstanding and innovative among them.

In some areas of linguistic reconstruction where
modern systematic treatments covering the whole range of
interrelated phenomena and processes are currently available (as, e.g., in phonology; cf. Shevelov 1964, or Stieber 1969/71, 1), new syntheses, taking into consideration
the latest theoretical insights and improvements, will
have to be developed; in other fields as yet less thoroughly investigated (such as, e.g., derivational morphology or syntax, individual work of great merit such as that
by Machek, Bauer, or Ivanov notwithstanding), first comprehensive treatments, adequate by contemporary linguistic
standards and affording an insightful grasp of the factors
and forces at work while at the same time accurately and
systematically accounting for the relevant data, will have
to be elaborated in the near future.

Not satisfied with merely reinterpreting second-hand
data along traditional lines, but continuing to explore

new approaches and to test new methods as well as gathering and sifting fresh material, this generation of linguists now active in the field has every qualification and prerequisite for breaking new ground and opening up previously unknown avenues for a better and deeper understanding of the common protolanguage — not accessible to direct inspection or at most revealing itself only in its very last phase of local variation and incipient modification — from which the historically recorded Slavic languages, so vigorous and widespread today, have evolved.

As already indicated, a sequel to this state-of-the-art report, covering relevant literature which (will have) appeared between mid-1972 (or shortly thereafter) and 1977, is planned for publication in early 1978, prior to the VIIIth International Congress of Slavists to be held in Ljubljana and Zagreb in the late summer of that year.

Selective Bibliography

Note: Of the titles listed below, those either discussed
or referred to in the text of this book are marked by double asterisk (**) or simple asterisk (*), respectively.
All entries are listed in alphabetical order. For purposes of content identification, a system of numerical
symbols, given after each entry, was devised. Where
deemed necessary, content identification is made by means
of two, three, or exceptionally even more numerical symbols for cross reference. To the extent possible, the
specific order of these symbols quoted with each title reflects an order of decreasing general significance or particular relevance to the subject matter dealt with; however, frequently the first two symbols are interchange-
able. Except for titles identified for Morphology (where
two- or three-digit symbols are used; see Special Note,
below), each symbol consists of two digits, a Roman numeral indicating the broad area within which a given title
falls, and an Arabic number specifying the particular subfield (e.g., II:4 or VI:1).

Key to numerical symbols used for content identification:

I	G e n e r a l T r e a m e n t s o f C S (Including CS Viewed in a Broader Framework)
I:1	General Treatments of CS
I:2	Comparative Slavic Linguistics
I:3	Comparative IE Linguistics
I:4	CS as Prehistory of Individual Slavic Languages (Diachrony of Individual Slavic Languages)
I:5	Problems Related to CS (Ethnogenesis, Prehistory, and Early History of the Slavs; Original Home- land and Early Migrations of the Slavs; Earliest Slavic Texts; Onomastic Evidence of CS and Early Slavic)
II	P h o n o l o g y
II:1	Monographic Treatments & General Problems of CS Phonology

II:2	Accentology
II:3	Vocalism (Including Ablaut and CS Modification of Diphthongs in Liquids and Nasals; Syllabic Liquids and Nasals)
II:4	Consonantism
II:5	Special Factors Conditioning CS Sound Change: Syllable Structure, Word-Final and Word-Initial Position
II:6	Morphophonology (Morphophonemics, Other Than Ablaut Alone)
III	M o r p h o l o g y
III:1	Monographic Treatments & General Problems of CS Morphology
III:2	Inflection
III:3	Derivation (Including Other Processes of Word-Formation, Primarily Composition)
III:4	Noun (and/or Pronoun), Nominal (and/or Pronominal)
III:5	Verb, Verbal

Special Note: Content identification re Morphology may be by way of two- or three-digit symbols; e.g., III:2 = Morphology, Inflection, without specification of whether a given title treats Nominal (and/or Pronominal) Inflection (Declension) or Verbal Inflection (Conjugation), but usually implying that both problems of Declension and Conjugation are discussed; III:5 = Morphology, Verb, without specification of whether only Verbal Inflection (Conjugation), Verbal Derivation, or both aspects of the Morphology of the Verb are examined, though usually suggesting the latter; III:2:4 = Morphology, Inflection, Nominal and/or Pronominal (Declension); III:3:5 = Morphology, Derivation, Verbal.

IV	S y n t a x
IV:1	General Problems of CS Syntax
IV:2	Grammatical Functions (Meanings) & Grammatical (Morphosyntactic) Categories
IV:3	Sentence (& Clause) Structure
IV:4	Deep Structure (Semantic Structure Underlying

AfslPh	Archiv für slavische Philologie
AnzfslPh	Anzeiger für slavische Philologie
BPTJ	Biuletyn Polskiego Towarzystwa Językoznawczego
BSL	Bulletin de la Société de linguistique de Paris
IF	Indogermanische Forschungen
IJSLP	International Journal of Slavic Linguistics and Poetics
IORJaS	Izvestija otdelenija russkogo jazyka i slovesnosti AN SSSR
JF	Južnoslovenski filolog
KZ	Zeitschrfit für vergleichende Sprachforschung auf dem Gebiete der indogermanischen Sprachen. Begründet von A. Kuhn ("Kuhn's Zeitschrift")
LF	Listy filologické
MSL	Mémoires de la Société de linguistique de Paris
NTS	Norsk tidsskrift for sprogvidenskap
PF	Prace filologiczne
RES	Revue des études slaves
RFV	Russkij filologičeskij vestnik
RS	Rocznik slawistyczny
ScSl	Scando-Slavica
SEEJ	Slavic and East European Journal
SEER	Slavonic and East European Review
Skr. utg. av K. Hum. Vetensk.- Samf. i Uppsala	Skrifter utgifna af K. Humanistiska Vetenskaps-Samfundet i Uppsala
SlOcc	Slavia Occidentalis
Sprache	Die Sprache. Zeitschrift für Sprachwissenschaft
SR	Slavistična Revija
TCLP	Travaux du Cercle linguistique de Prague
TLP	Travaux linguistiques de Prague
VJa	Voprosy jazykoznanija
VslJa	Voprosy slavjanskogo jazykoznanija
WdSl	Die Welt der Slaven
WslJb	Wiener slavistisches Jahrbuch
ZfSl	Zeitschrift für Slawistik
ZfslPh	Zeitschrift für slavische Philologie

Abaev, V. I.
1957   * "Opyt ètimologii slavjanskogo *mědъ*,"   V:2
            Ezikovedski izsledvanija . . ., 321-
            328.
1971   ** "Neskol'ko zamečanij k slavjanskim   V:2
            ètimologijam," *Problemy istorii i
            dialektologii slavjanskix jazykov.
            Sbornik statej k 70-letiju člena-kor-
            respondenta AN SSSR V. I. Borkovsko-
            go*, F. P. Filin, ed. (Moscow: "Nau-
            ka"), 11-15.
Abernathy, R.
1963   * "Some theories of Slavic Linguistic   II:3
            Evolution," *American Contributions*   VI:3
            *to the Fifth International Congress
            of Slavists*, 7-26.
1968   ** "The Slavic Liquid-Metathesis,"   II:3
            American Contributions to the Sixth   VI:3
            International Congress of Slavists,
            9-27.
Ačarjan, R. A.
1968   * "Armjano-slavjanskie izoglossy," *VJa*   VI:1
            5, 102-105.
Agrell, S.
1925/26   * *Zur Geschichte des indogermanischen*   III:4
            Neutrums (Lund: Gleerup).   I:3
Aitzetmüller, R.
1954   * "Zur slavischen *-nt-* Deklination,"   III:2:4
            KZ 71, 65-73.
1962a   * "Slav. *iměti* und das idg. Perfekt,"   III:5
            Sprache 8, 250-262.   VI:1
1962b   "Über Präfixe bei nicht-durativen
            Verben vom Typus *mrěti*," *ZfslPh* 30,   III:3:5
            310-336.
1962c   * "Zu *imamъ*," *ZfslPh* 30, 375-377.   III:2:5
1965   * "Die Relation *'e* : *'o* bzw. *o* in den
            ostslavischen Sprachen," *WdSl* 10,   II:3
            1-8.   VI:3
1967   ** Review of "The Dialects of Common   VI:3
            Slavic" by H. Birnbaum, *Sprache* 13,
            89-91.
1968   ** "Das angebliche *s*-Futurum des Slavi-   III:5
            schen," *Studien zur Sprachwissen-*   IV:2
            *schaft und Kulturkunde. Gedenk-
            schrift für Wilhelm Brandenstein
            (1898-1967)* (= *Innsbrucker Beiträge*

348

              zur Kulturwissenschaft 14), M. Mayr-
              hofer, ed. (Innsbruck: AM OE), 11-16

1970   * "Etymologische Randbemerkungen,"   V:2
              AnzfslPh 4, 83-89.

1971   * "Abg. *smrъdъ*, Verdeutlichung einer   V:2
              Etymologie," *Studia palaeoslovenica*, V:3
              B. Havránek, ed. (Prague: Academia),
              17-19.

American Contributions . . .

1963   *American Contributions to the Fifth*
              International Congress of Slavists,
              Sofia, September 1963. I: *Linguistic*
              Contributions (= *Slavistic Printings*
              and Reprintings 46) (The Hague: Mou-
              ton).

1968   *American Contributions to the Sixth*
              International Congress of Slavists,
              Prague, 1968, August 7-13. I: *Lin-*
              guistic Contributions (= *Slavistic*
              Printings and Reprintings 80), H.
              Kučera, ed. (The Hague: Mouton).

Ancient Indo-European Dialects . . .

1966   ** *Ancient Indo-European Dialects: Pro-* I:3
              ceedings of the Conference on Indo- VI:1
              European Linguistics, Held at the   VI:3
              University of California, Los Ange-
              les, April 25-27, 1963, H. Birnbaum
              & J. Puhvel, eds. (Berkeley-Los An-
              geles: University of California
              Press).

Andersen, H.

1968   ** "IE *s after *i, u, r, k* in Baltic   II:4
              and Slavic," *Acta Linguistica Haf-* VI:1
              niensia 11 (Copenhagen: Nordisk
              Sprog- og Kulturforlag), 171-190.

1969a   ** "Lenition in Common Slavic," *Lan-*   II:4
              guage 45, 553-574.   VI:3
                                         VI:2

1969b   ** "The Change of *ot* to *od,*" *WdSl*   II:4
              14, 315-330.   II:5
                                        VI:3

1970a   ** "On Some Old Balto-Slavic Iso-   VI:1
              glosses," *Donum Balticum*, 14-21. II:4

1970b   ** "The Dative of Subordination in Bal-
              tic and Slavic," *Baltic Linguistics*, IV:2
              T. F. Magner & W. R. Schmalstieg, III:2:4

349

eds. (University Park-London: Penn-   IV:4
sylvania State University Press),   VI:1
1-9.

1971   ** Review of *Osnovni problemi na sla-*   III:1
vjanskata diaxronna morfologija by   III:2:4
V. Georgiev, *Language* 47, 949-954.   II:5
    IV:2
    II:6

1972   ** "Diphthongization," *Language* 48,   II:3
11-50.   II:4

Anttila, R.
1969   ** *Proto-Indo-European Schwebeablaut*   II:3
(= *University of California Publica-*
tions, Linguistics 58) (Berkeley-Los
Angeles: University of California
Press).

Arntz, H.
1933   ** *Sprachliche Beziehungen zwischen*   VI:1
Arisch und Baltoslavisch (= *Indoger-*   V:4
manische Bibliothek III, 13) (Heidelberg: Winter).

Arumaa, P.
1948/49   * "Sur l'histoire des adjectifs en -*u*   III:3:4
en balto-slave," *Årsbok, Slaviska*   VI:1
Institutet vid Lunds Universitet,
24-105.

1955   * "Die Verwandtschaftsverhältnisse   VI:1
zwischen Baltisch und Slavisch,"
ZfslPh 24, 9-28

1963   * "De l'unité balto-slave," *ScSl* 9,   VI:1
70-86.

1964   ** *Urslavische Grammatik: Einführung in*   I:1
das vergleichende Studium der slavi-
schen Sprachen. I: *Einleitung; Laut-*
lehre, 1. Teil: *Vokalismus,* 2. Teil:
Betonung (Heidelberg: Winter).

Auty, R.
1964   * "Community and Divergence in the   I:1
History of the Slavonic Languages,"
SEER 42, 257-273.

1969   ** "The Western Lexical Elements in the   I:5
Kiev Missal," *Slawisch-Deutsche*   V:4
Wechselbeziehungen in Sprache, Lite-   VI:3
ratur und Kultur (= *Deutsche Akade-*
mie der Wissenschaften zu Berlin.
Veröffentlichungen des Instituts für

Slawistik 44), W. Krauss, Z. Stieber,
J. Bělič & V. I. Borkovskij, eds.
(Berlin: Akademie), 3-6.

Avanesov, R. I.
1947   * "Voprosy obrazovanija russkogo ja-   II:3
       zyka v ego govorax," *Vestnik Moskov-*   VI:3
       skogo Gosudarstvennogo Universiteta
       9, 109-158.

1955   "Problemy obrazovanija jazyka rus-   VI:3
       skoj (velikorusskoj) narodnosti,"
       VJa 5, 20-42.

1968   ** "K istorii čeredovanija soglasnyx   II:4
       pri obrazovanii umen'šitel'nyx   III:3:4
       suščestvitel'nyx v praslavjanskom,"   II:6
       Slavjanskoe jazykoznanie VI . . . ,
       3-18.

Bălgarski etimologičen rečnik
1962-   * *Bălgarski etimologičen rečnik*, V.   V:1
       Georgiev, I. Gălăbov, J. Zaimov, &
       S. Ilčev (1-) (Sofia: BAN).

Bauer, J.
1958   ** "Problema rekonstrukcii praslavjan-   IV:3
       skogo složnogo predloženija," *Sbor-*
       ník prací filosofické fakulty brněn-
       ské university 7, 43-55.

1963a   * "Osnovnye problemy sravnitel'no-   IV:1
       istoričeskogo izučenija sintaksisa
       slavjanskix jazykov," *VJa* 4, 4-13.

1963b   ** "Úkoly a metody rekonstrukce pra-   IV:1
       slovanské syntaxe," *Československé*
       přednášky pro V. Mezinárodní sjezd
       slavistů v Sofii, B. Havránek *et al.*,
       eds. (Prague: Nakl. ČSAV), 75-81.

1967   ** "K razvitiju otnositel'nyx pridatoč-   IV:3
       nyx predloženij v slavjanskix ja-   VI:3
       zykax," *VJa* 5, 47-59.

Bech, G.
1971   ** *Beiträge zur genetischen idg. Ver-*   III:5
       balmorphologie (= *Det Kongelige*   VI:1
       Danske Videnskabernes Selskab. His-
       torisk-filosofiske Meddelelser 44,5)
       (Copenhagen: Munksgaard).

Bednarczuk, L.
1962/63   ** "Uwagi o słowiańskich spójnikach   IV:2
       alternatywnych," *RS* 22, 13-20   IV:3
                                              V:2

1963   ** "Zasób prasłowiańskich spójników pa-   IV:2
rataktycznych," *Studia linguistica*   IV:3
. . .,61-65.   V:2

1967   ** "Pleonastyczne użycie spójników pa-   IV:2
rataktycznych w językach słowiań-   IV:3
skich na tle indoeuropejskim," *RS*   V:2
28, 21-30   VI:1

Belić, A.

1913   * "Promene akcenata u praslovenskom   II:2
jeziku," *JF* 1, 38-66.

1914   * *Akcenatske studije* I (= *Posebna iz-*   II:2
danja 42. *Nauke filosofske i filo-*
loške 11) (Belgrade: SAN)

1920   * "Un système accentologique du slave   II:2
commun," *MSL* 21, 149-165.

1921   * "Najmlađa (treća) promena zadnje-   II:4
nepčanih suglasnika *k*, *g* i *h* u pra-   VI:2
slovenskom jeziku," *JF* 2, 18-39.

1922   ** "O praslovenskom jeziku," *Slavia* 1,   VI:2
8-11.   I:1

1925   * "Zur slavischen Akzentlehre (Aus   II:2
Anlass von D. Bubrich's Aufsatz über
'Die Akzentlehre' von A. Belić),"
ZfslPh 2, 1-28.

1928   * "La troisième ou la plus récente   II:4
palatalisation des gutterales," *RES*   VI:2
8, 50-67.

1950/   ** *Istorija srpskohrvatskog jezika* II.   I:4
51/60   1: *Reči sa deklinacijom*, 1950; 2:   VI:3
Reči sa konjugacijom, 1951 (Bel-   III:2
grade: "Naučna knjiga').
Osnovi istorije srpskohrvatskog je-   I:4
zika I. *Fonetika*, 1960 (Belgrade: VI:3
Nolit), [4]1969 (Belgrade: "Naučna   II:1
knjiga").

1955/56 ** "O glagolima sa dva vida," *JF* 21, 1-   IV:2
13. Russian résumé "O glagolax,   III:5
imejuščix dva vida," *Beogradski Me-*
đunarodni slavistički sastanak, 483-
484.

Benveniste, É.

1935   ** *Origines de la formation des noms en*   III:3:4
indo-européen, deuxième tirage   VI:1
(Paris: Librairie Adrien-Maisonneuve).

1956   ** "Une corrélation slavo-iranienne,"   VI:1
Festschrift für Max Vasmer, 70-73.   V:2

1967 ** "Les relations lexicales slavo-ira- V:4
niennes," *To Honor Roman Jakobson* I, VI:1
197-202.

1969 ** *Le vocabulaire des institutions in-* V:2
do-européennes. 1: *Économie, parenté,* V:3
société; 2: *Pouvoir, droit, religion* VI:1
(Paris: Les Éditions de Minuit).

Beogradski Međunarodni slavistički sastanak . . .
1957 *Beogradski Međunarodni slavistički*
sastanak (*15-21. IX. 1955*), K. Tara-
novski, ed. (Belgrade: Izdanje Orga-
nizacionog Odbora).

Berneker, E.
1899 * "Von der Vertretung des idg. ĕu̯ im II:3
baltisch-slavischen Sprachzweig," *IF* VI:1
10, 145-167.

1900 ** *Die Wortfolge in den slavischen* IV:3
Sprachen (Berlin: Behr). VI:3

1913/14 * *Slavisches etymologisches Wörter-*
buch. 1: *A-L*, 1913; *M-morъ*, 1914; V:1
²1924 (Heidelberg: Winter).

Bernštejn, S. B.
1954 * "Osnovnye zadači, metody i principy I:2
'sravnitel'noj grammatiki slavjanskix jazykov'," *VJa* 2, 49-67 (=
VslJa 1, 1954, 5-23).

1958 ** "Balto-slvjanskaja jazykovaja so- VI:1
obščnost'," *Slavjanskaja filologija,*
45-67.

1961 ** *Očerk sravnitel'noj grammatiki sla-* I:2
vjanskix jazykov (Moscow: Izd-vo AN II:1
SSSR).

1963 ** "K istorii sloga v praslavjanskom II:5
jazyke," *Slavjanskoe jazykoznanie*
V . . ., 53-69.

1968a ** "Kontrakcija i struktura sloga v II:3
slavjanskix jazykax," *Slavjanskoe* VI:3
jazykoznanie VI . . ., 19-31. II:5
                 VI:2

1968b ** "Vvedenie v slavjanskuju morfonolo- II:6
giju," *VJa* 4, 43-59.

1970 ** "Sledy konsonantnyx imennyx osnov v III:3:4
slavjanskix jazykax. (Sledy osnov na VI:1
-s)," *VJa* 3, 71-86.

Bidwell, C. E.
1961 ** "The Chronology of Certain Sound VI:2

　　　　　　　　Changes in Common Slavic as Evi-　　II:1
　　　　　　　　denced by Loans from Vulgar Latin,"　V:4
　　　　　　　　Word 17, 105-127.
1963　　　** *Slavic Historical Phonology in Tabu-*　II:1
　　　　　　　　lar Form (The Hague: Mouton).
Birnbaum, H.
1956　　　 * "Zu urslav. *kv-*," *ScSl* 2, 29-40.　　II:4
　　　　　　　　　　　　　　　　　　　　　　　　　　　II:5
　　　　　　　　　　　　　　　　　　　　　　　　　　　VI:3
1958a　　** *Untersuchungen zu den Zukunftsum-*
　　　　　　　　schreibungen mit dem Infinitiv im　　IV:2
　　　　　　　　Altkirchenslavischen. Ein Beitrag　III:2:5
　　　　　　　　zur historischen Verbalsyntax des　　VI:3
　　　　　　　　Slavischen (= *Acta Universitatis*
　　　　　　　　Stockholmiensis, Études de philolo-
　　　　　　　　gie slave 6) (Stockholm: Almqvist &
　　　　　　　　Wiksell).
1958b　　** "Zur Aussonderung der syntaktischen　IV:1
　　　　　　　　Gräzismen im Altkirchenslavischen　　VI:1
　　　　　　　　Einige methodische Bemerkungen,"　　VI:3
　　　　　　　　ScSl 4, 239-257.
1963　　　** "Reinterpretacje fonologiczne no-　　II:3
　　　　　　　　sówek słowiańskich (Na podstawie
　　　　　　　　materiału prasłowiańskiego, staro-
　　　　　　　　słowiańskiego, i polskiego)," *Ameri-*
　　　　　　　　can Contributions to the Fifth In-
　　　　　　　　ternational Congress of Slavists,
　　　　　　　　27-48.
1965a　　** "Lautwandel und Phonolgisierung. Ein　II:1
　　　　　　　　chronologisches Problem, erläutert　　VI:3
　　　　　　　　an zwei dialektischen Erscheinungen
　　　　　　　　des Spätgemeinslavischen," *ZfslPh* 32,
　　　　　　　　281-289.
1965b　　 * "On Some Problems of Common Slavic　VI:3
　　　　　　　　Dialectology," *IJSLP* 9, 1-19.
1965c　　 * Review of *Russische historische*　　I:4
　　　　　　　　Grammatik. I: Die Entwicklung des　　VI:3
　　　　　　　　Lautsystems by V. Kiparsky, *ZfslPh*　II:1
　　　　　　　　32, 375-418.
1966a　　** "The Dialects of Common Slavic,"　　VI:3
　　　　　　　　Ancient Indo-European Dialects,
　　　　　　　　153-197.
1966b　　 * Review of *Urslavische Grammatik.*　　I:1
　　　　　　　　Einführung in das vergleichende Stu-
　　　　　　　　dium der slavischen Sprachen. I:
　　　　　　　　Einleitung. 1. Teil: *Vokalismus*, 2.

Teil: *Betonung* by Peeter Arumaa,
IJSLP 10, 165-178.

1967a ** "On the Reconstruction and Predict-　VI:1
ability of Linguistic Models: Balto-Slavic Revisited," *ScSl* 13, 105-
114.

1967b ** "Syntagmatische und paradigmatische　II:3
Phonologie," *Phonologie der Gegen-*　II:1
wart, J. Hamm & G. Wytrzens, eds.
(= *WslJb* 6) (Graz-Vienna-Cologne:
Hermann Böhlaus Nachf.), 307-352.

1968a ** "Obščeslavjanskoe nasledie i inoja-　IV:3
zyčnye obrazcy v strukturnyx razno-　IV:1
vidnostjax staroslavjanskogo pred-　IV:2
loženija," *American Contributions to*　VI:1
the Sixth International Congress of　VI:3
Slavists, 29-63.

1968b ** "Rekonstrukcja wewnętrzna, kolejność　VI:1
synchronicznych reguł gramatyki syn-　VI:2
tetycznej i zagadnienie najdawniej-　II:4
szych stosunków między językami bał-　II:3
tyckimi a słowiańskimi," *IJSLP* 11,
1-24. Revised English version "Internal Reconstruction, Order of Synchronic Rules in Generative Grammar,
and the Problem of Early Balto-Slavic Relations," *Problems of Typologi-*
cal and Genetic Linguistics Viewed
in a Generative Framework (= *Janua*
Linguarum, Series minor 106, 1970)
(The Hague: Mouton), 92-122.

1969 * "On Reconstruction and Prediction:　VI:2
Two Correlates of Diachrony in Gene-　VI:1
tic and Typological Linguistics,"　II:4
Folia Linguistica 2, 1-17 (= *Prob-*
lems of Typological and Genetic Lin-
guistics Viewed in a Generative
Framework = *Janua Linguarum*, Series
minor 106, 1970, The Hague: Mouton,
71-91).

1970a ** "Four Approaches to Balto-Slavic,"　VI:1
Donum Balticum, 69-76.

1970b ** *Problems of Typological and Genetic*　VI:1
Linguistics Viewed in a Generative　II:4
　　　　　　　　　　　　　　　　　　　　　II:3
Framework (= *Janua Linguarum*, Series　VI:2
minor 106) (The Hague: Mouton).　IV:4

355

1970c   ** "Zur Problematik der zeitlichen Ab-   VI:2
      grenzung des Urslavischen (Über die   VI:1
      Relativität der Begriffe Baltosla-   VI:3
      visch/Frühurslavisch bzw. Spätge-   II:3
      meinslavischer Dialekt/Ureinzelsla-   II:4
      vine)," *ZfslPh* 34, 1-62.

1971a   ** "Noch einmal zur Problematik des   I:4
      Lautwandels idg. *s* > usl. *x*," *ScSl*   VI:1
      17, 235-247.

1971b   * Review of *Zarys gramatyki porównaw-*   I:2
      czej języków słowiańskich: Fonologia
      by Z. Stieber, *SEEJ*, 347-351.

1972a   ** "Indo-European Nominal Formations   III:3:4
      Submerged in Slavic," *The Slavic*   VI:1
      Word, 142-168.

1972b   * "O stepeni dokazatel'nosti dialek-   II:1
      tizmov-'arxaizmov'," *Russkoe i sla-*   VI:3
      vjanskoe jazykoznanie. K 70-letiju   VI:2
      člena-korrespondenta AN SSSR R. I.
      Avanesova (Moscow: "Nauka"), 43-48.

1973   ** "O możliwości odtworzenia pierwot-   I:1
      nego stanu języka prasłowiańskiego   VI:1
      za pomocą rekonstrukcji wewnętrznej   VI:2
      i metody porównawczej (Kilka uwag o
      stosunku różnych podejść)," *American*
      Contributions to the Seventh Inter-
      national Congress of Slavists.

Bogoljubova, N. D. & T. A. Jakubajtis
   1959   * "Istorija razrabotki voprosa o bal-   VI:1
      to-slavjanskix jazykovyx otnošeni-
      jax," *Rakstu krājums*, 331-375.

Borkovskij, V. I. & P. S. Kuznecov
   1965   ** *Istoričeskaja grammatika russkogo*   I:4
      jazyka, 2nd aug. ed. (Moscow: "Nau-   VI:3
      ka").

Borodič, V. V.
   1953   * "K voprosu o formirovanii soveršen-   III:3:5
      nogo i nesoveršennogo vida v sla-   IV:2
      vjanskix jazykax," *VJa* 6, 68-86.

Braun, M.
   1947   ** *Grundzüge der slawischen Sprachen*   I:2
      (Göttingen: Vandenhoeck & Ruprecht).

Bräuer, H.
   1961/69   ** *Slavische Sprachwissenschaft. I:*   I:2
      Einleitung, Lautlehre (= *Göschen*
      1191/1191 a; 1961) II: *Formenlehre,*

1. Teil (= *Göschen* 1192/1192 a/
1192 b; 1969) III: *Formenlehre*, 2.
Teil (= *Göschen* 1236/1236 a; 1969)
(Berlin: Walter de Gruyter).

Brodowska-Honowska, M.
1960   ** *Słowotwórstwo przymiotnika w języku*   III:3:4
staro-cerkiewno-słowiańskim (= *Mono-
grafie slawistyczne* 2) (Cracow-
Wrocław-Warsaw: Ossolineum).

Brugmann, K.
1902/04 ** *Kurze vergleichende Grammatik der*   I:3
indogermanischen Sprachen, 1.-3.
Lieferung (Strassburg: Trübner). Un-
veränderter Neudruck, 1933 (Berlin-
Leipzig: Walter de Gruyter).

Brugmann, K. & B. Delbrück
1893-   ** *Grundriss der vergleichenden Gram-*   I:3
1916   *matik der indogermanischen Sprachen.*
I-V = 9 vols., I-III, 2. Bearbeitung
(Strassburg: Trübner). Unveränder-
ter photomechanischer Nachdruck,
1967 (Berlin: Walter de Gruyter).

Brückner, A.
1923   ** "Slavische *ch*-," *KZ* 51, 221-242.   II:5
                                                       II:4

1927   * *Słownik etymologiczny języka pol-*   V:1
skiego, [2]1957 (Warsaw: Wiedza Pow-
szechna).

1931   * "*ą*- und *u*-Dubletten im Slavischen,"   II:3
ZfslPh 8, 436-441.

Bubrix, D. V. (Bubrich)
1919   "Iz praslavjanskoj fonetiki," *IORJaS*   II:3
24, 246-284.   VI:2
                                                     II:5

1922   * "O trudax A. A. Šaxmatova v oblasti   II:2
slavjanskoj akcentologii," *IORJaS*
(1920) 25, 198-207.

1925   "Beiträge zur urslavischen Laut-   II:3
lehre. 1. Über die relative Chrono-   VI:2
logie der Monophtongierung von
Nasaldiphtongen im Urslavischen. 2.
Der Umlaut im Urslavischen," *ZfslPh*
2, 121-124.

1926   * "Du système d'accentuation en slave   II:2
commun," *RES* 6, 175-215.

Budziszewska, W.

1965　** *Słowiańskie słownictwo dotyczące*　V:3
　　　　　　przyrody żywej (= *Monografie sla-*　V:2
　　　　　　wistyczne 6) (Wrocław: Ossolineum,　III:3:4
　　　　　　PAN).

Bulaxovs'kyj, L. A. (Bulaxovskij)

1927　　 *Vstup do porivnjal'noji hramatyky*　II:1
　　　　　　slov'jans'kyx mov. Fonetyka pra-　I:2
　　　　　　slov'jans'koji movy (Kharkov:
　　　　　　[bibliographical data not avail-
　　　　　　able]).

1946　　 * "Vostočnoslavjanskie jazyki kak　II:2
　　　　　　istočnik rekonstrukcii obščeslavjan-　VI:3
　　　　　　skoj akcentologičeskoj sistemy,"
　　　　　　IORJaS 5, 467-477.

1947　　 * "Akcentologičeskij zakon A. A. Šax-　II:2
　　　　　　matova," *A. A. Šaxmatov, 1864-1920.*
　　　　　　Sbornik statej i materialov, S. P.
　　　　　　Obnorskij, ed. (= *Trudy Komissii po*
　　　　　　Istorii AN SSSR 3) (Moscow-Lenin-
　　　　　　grad: AN SSSR), 399-434.

1950　　 * *Akcentologičeskij kommentarij k*　II:2
　　　　　　pol'skomu jazyku (Kiev: Izd-vo Kiev-　VI:3
　　　　　　skogo gos. univ. im. T. G. Ševčenko).

1953/56　 * *Akcentologičeskij kommentarij k*　II:2
　　　　　　češskomu jazyku, vyp. 1, 1953; vyp.　VI:3
　　　　　　2-3, 1956 (Kiev: Izd-vo Kievskogo
　　　　　　gos. univ. im. T. G. Ševčenko).

1955　　 * "Udarenie starokrymskogo bolgarskogo　II:2
　　　　　　govora," *Sbornik v čest na akademik*　VI:3
　　　　　　Aleksandăr Teodorov-Balan po slučaj
　　　　　　devetdeset i petata mu godišnina, M.
　　　　　　Dimitrov, ed. (Sofia: BAN), 131-143.

1956　　 * "Grammatičeskaja indukcija v sla-　III:2:4
　　　　　　vjanskom sklonenii," *VJa* 4, 14-30.

1957　　 * "Grammatičeskaja indukcija v sla-　III:2:4
　　　　　　vjanskom sklonenii. Indukcija akku-
　　　　　　zativa (vinitel'nogo padeža)," *VJa*
　　　　　　3, 3-19.

1958a　　 * *Bolgarskij jazyk kak istočnik dlja*　II:2
　　　　　　rekonstrukcii drevnejšej slavjanskoj　VI:3
　　　　　　akcentologičeskoj sistemy (Moscow:
　　　　　　Izd-vo AN SSSR). Résumé in *IV Mež-*
　　　　　　dunarodnyj s"ezd slavistov. Mate-
　　　　　　rialy diskussii II: *Problemy sla-*
　　　　　　vjanskogo jazykoznanija, N. I. Tol-

stoj (Moscow: Izd-vo AN SSSR), 343-344.

1958b   * "Otraženija tak nazyvaemoj novoaku-   II:2
tovoj intonacii drevnejšego slavjan-   VI:3
skogo jazyka v vostočno-slavjan-
skix," *VJa* 2, 87-92.

1959   * "Akcentologičeskaja problematika vo-   II:2
prosa o slavjano-baltijskom jazy-   VI:1
kovom edinstve," *Rakstu krājums*, 55-77.

Burlakova, M.
1962   "Predystorija slavjanskix zadnenëb-   II:4
nyx," *VslJa* 6, 46-65.

Calleman, B.
1950   ** *Zu den Haupttendenzen der ursla-*   II:1
vischen und altrussischen Lautent-   VI:2
wicklung (Uppsala: Almqvist & Wik-   VI:3
sell).

Chomsky, N. & M. Halle
1968   ** *The Sound Pattern of English* (New   II:4
York-Evanston-London: Harper & Row).   VI:2

Cronia, A.
1952   "Revision der slavischen Eigennamen   I:5
im alten Evangeliar von Cividale,"
WslJb 2, 6-21.

Czekanowski, J.
1932   ** "Różnicowanie się dialektów prasło-   VI:3
wiańskich w świetle kryterium ilo-
ściowego," *Sborník prací* . . ., 485-504.

1957   * *Wstęp do historii Słowian. Perspek-*   I:5
tywy antropologiczne, etnograficzne,
archeologiczne i językowe, wydanie
II na nowo opracowane (Poznań: In-
stytut Zachodni).

Čejka, M. & A. Lamprecht
1963   ** "K otázce vzniku a diferenciace   II:1
slovanských jazyků," *Sborník prací*   VI:2
filosofické fakulty brněnské univer-   VI:3
sity 12, 5-20.

Černyx, P. J.
1962   ** *Istoričeskaja grammatika russkogo*   I:4
jazyka. Kratkij očerk, 3rd ed. (Mos-   VI:3
cow: Učpedgiz). German transl.
(Tschernych) *Historische Grammatik*
der russischen Sprache (Halle-Saale:

Niemeyer), 1957.

Damborský, J.

1967   ** *Participium* l-*ové ve slovanštině* (=   III:3
Dissertationes Universitatis Varso-   III:2:5
viensis 15) (Warsaw: PWN).   V:3
   IV:2

Darden, B. J.

1972   ** "Rule Ordering in Baltic and Slavic   II:2
Nominal Accentuation," *SEEJ* 16, 74-   VI:1
83.   III:2:4

Decaux, É.

1957   * "Le passage de *g* à *h* et le groupe   II:4
zg," *RES* 34, 46-50.   VI:3

Décsy, G.

1958   ** "Die Entsprechungen der gemeinsla-   II:3
vischen Halbvokale im Finnischen und   VI:1
Ungarischen," *WdSl* 3, 369-387.   VI:3

Dejna, K.

1968   ** "Prasłowiańskie systemy fonologicz-   II:1
ne," *Łódzkie towarzystwo naukowe.*
Sprawozdania z czynności i posiedzeń
naukowych 22, [p. reference not
available].

Diels, P.

1914   * "-*ě* und -*ę* der Endungen der slavi-   III:2:4
schen Deklination," *AfslPh* 35, 321-   II:5
324.   VI:3

1932/34   * *Altkirchenslavische Grammatik mit*
einer Auswahl von Texten und einem   I:4
Wörterbuch. I: *Grammatik*; II: *Ausge-*   VI:3
wählte Texte und Wörterbuch (= *Samm-*
lung slavischer Lehr- und Handbücher
1:6), [2]1963 (Heidelberg: Winter).

Diver, W.

1955   * "The Problem of Old Bulgarian *št*,"   II:4
Word 11, 228-236.   VI:3

Dolobko, M.

1925   * "Die enklitischen Formen des Prono-   III:2:4
mens der 1. und 2. Person im dat.
dual. des Urslavischen," *ZfslPh* 1,
336-342.

1926   "Der sekundäre *v*-Vorschlag im Russi-   II:2
schen," *ZfslPh* 3, 87-144.   VI:3

1926/27   * "Noč' - nočés', ósen' - osenés',   II:2
zimá - zimús', léto - létos',"   VI:3
Slavia 5, 678-717.

360

Dombrovszky, J.
1962   * "La question d'origine des aspects   III;3:5
             verbaux slaves," *Slavica* 2, 25-36.   IV;2
1967   ** "Über den Ursprung und die Heraus-
             bildung des Aspekt-Tempussystems des   III:3:5
             slavischen Verbums," *Slavica* 7, 41-   IV:2
             50.

Donum Balticum . . .
1970   *Donum Balticum. To Professor Chris-*
             tian S. Stang on the occasion of his
             seventieth birthday, 15 March 1970,
             V. Rūḳe-Draviņa, ed. (Stockholm:
             Almqvist & Wiksell).

Dostál, A.
1953/54   "Některé otázky vývoje slovanské   III:2:5
             konjugace a jejích rešení s hlediska
             vývoje gramatické stavby slovanských
             jazyků," *Slavia* 22, 267-275.
1954   ** *Studie o vidovém systému v staroslo-*   III:3:5
             věnštině: Z prací Slovanského ústavu   IV:2
             Československé Akademie Věd (Prague: VI:3
             Státní Pedag. Nakl.).
1958   "Původ a vývoj slovanské jazykové   I:2
             skupiny," *Československé přednášky*
             pro IV. Mezinárodní sjezd slavistů
             v Moskvě, K. Horálek, ed. (Prague:
             Nakl. ČSAV), 215-219.
1963   ** "Několik úvah o praslovanštině,"   VI:2
             Studia linguistica . . ., 71-79.   I:1
1967   ** *Historická mluvnice česká.* II: *Tva-*   I:4
             rosloví 2. *Časovaní* (Prague: Státní   VI:3
             Pedag. Nakl.).   III:5

Duridanov, I.
1963   "Praslav. *sъsьnъ, *sъsьnъ," *Studia*   V:2
             linguistica . . ., 81-86.
1968a   ** "Za praslavjanskija vokalizăm,"   II:3
             Slavistični izsledvanija (Sofia: II:5
             Fakultet po slavjanski filologii pri   VI:2
             Sofijskija universitet "Kliment Ox-
             ridski"), 17-25.
1968b   * "Zum baltoslav. *verp-," *Baltistica*   V:2
             4, 55-58.   VI:1
1969   * "Südslawisch-baltische Übereinstim-   V:2
             mungen im Bereiche der Wortbildung,"   V:3
             Baltistica 5, 21-27.   VI:1
                                                         III:3

1970   * "Baltico-Bulgarica," *Donum Balticum*,   V:2
          107-109.   VI:1
Durnovo, N. N.
1924   ** *Očerk istorii russkogo jazyka* (Mos-   I:4
          cow-Leningrad: Gosizdat). Reprint   VI:3
          (The Hague: Mouton), 1959.
1924/25   * "Spornye voprosy obščeslavjanskoj   II:5
          fonetiki. 1. Načal'noe *e* v ob. sl.   II:3
          jaz.," *Slavia* 3, 225-271.
1926   * "Le traitement de *sk* dans les   II:4
          langues slaves," *RES* 6, 216-223.
1927/28   * "Spornye voprosy obščeslavjanskoj   II:3
          fonetiki. 2. Glasnye iz *en*, *em* pered   VI:3
          nosovymi v ob. sl. jaz.," *Slavia* 6,
          209-232.
1932a   ** "K voprosu o vremeni raspadenija   VI:3
          obščeslavjanskogo jazyka," *Sbornik*   VI:2
          prací . . ., 514-526.
1932b   "Manuscrits russes distinguant l'an-   II:2
          cien '*o* acuté' et l'*o* d'une autre   VI:3
          origine," *Annales Academiae Scien-*
          tiarum Fennicae B, 27 (Helsinki:
          Suomalainen Tiedeakatemia), 7-13.
Dvornik, F.
1956   * *The Slavs: Their Early History and*   I:5
          Civilization, 2nd printing 1959
          (Boston: American Academy of Arts
          and Sciences).
Dybo, V. A.
1958   * "O drevnejšej metatonii v slavjan-   II:2
          skom glagole," *VJa* 6, 55-62.
1961   * "Sokraščenie dolgot v kel'to-italij-   II:2
          skix jazykax i ego značenie dlja   VI:1
          balto-slavjanskoj i indoevropejskoj
          akcentologii," *VslJa* 5, 9-34.
1962   * "O rekonstrukcii udarenija v pra-   II:2
          slavjanskom glagole," *VslJa* 6, 3-27.   III:5
1963   * "Ob otraženii drevnix količestvennyx   II:2
          i intonacionnyx otnošenij v verxne-   VI:3
          lužickom jazyke," *Serbo-lužickij*
          lingvističeskij sbornik, L. È. Kal-
          nyn', ed. (Moscow: AN SSSR), 54-83.
1968   ** "Akcentologija i slovoobrazovanie v   II:2
          slavjanskom," *Slavjanskoe jazyko-*   III:3:4
          znanie VI . . ., 148-224.   II:6
1969a   * "Drevnerusskie teksty kak istočnik

dlja rekonstrukcii praslavjanskogo   II:2
udarenija (Praesens)," *VJa* 2, 114-   VI:3
122.

1969b   * "Srednebolgarskie teksty kak istoč-   II:2
nik dlja rekonstrukcii praslavjan-   VI:3
skogo udarenija (Praesens)," *VJa* 3,   III:2:5
82-101.

1971   * "Zakon Vasil'eva - Dolobko i akcen-   II:2
tuacija form glagola v drevnerusskom   VI:3
i srednebolgarskom," *VJa* 2, 93-114.   III:2:5

Dybo, V. A. & V. M. Illič-Svityč

1963   ** "K istorii slavjanskoj sistemy ak-   II:2
centuacionnyx paradigm," *Slavjanskoe*   III:2
jazykoznanie V . . ., 70-87.

Džurovyč, D. P.

1913   *Govory obščeslavjanskogo jazyka. S*   VI:3
lingvistieskoj kartoj (Warsaw:
[bibliographical data not avail-
able]).

Ebeling, C. L.

1963   ** "Questions of Relative Chronology in   II:1
Common Slavic and Russian Phonology,"   VI:2
Dutch Contributions to the Fifth In-   VI:3
ternational Congress of Slavicists,
Sofia 1963 (= *Slavistic Printings*
and Reprintings 45) (The Hague: Mouton), 27-42.

1967   ** "Historical Laws of Slavic Accentua-   II:2
tion," *To Honor Roman Jakobson* I,   VI:2
577-593.

Eckert, R. (Ékkert)

1959   * "K voprosu o sostave gruppy imen   III:3:4
suščestvitel'nyx s osnovoj na -ŭ v
praslavjanskom jazyke," *VslJa* 4,
100-129.

1963   * "Reste indoeuropäischer heterokli-   III:3:4
tischer Nominalstämme im Slawischen   VI:1
und Baltischen," *ZfSl* 8, 878-892.

1965   "Zur slawischen Hochzeitsterminolo-   V:3
gie," *ZfSl* 10, 185-211.   V:2

1968   * "Minimale Textfragmente im Slavi-   IV:1
schen und ihre Entsprechungen im   VI:1
Baltischen," *Baltistica* 4, 79-91.

1971   ** "Praslavjanskie dialektizmy sredi   III:3:4
imennyx osnov na -ĭ," *Issledovani-*   VI:3
ja . . ., 486-496.

Eckert, R., G. Kirchner, R. Růžička & W. Sperber
1966   ** *Russische Wortkunde*, ²1969 (Halle-   I:4
        Saale: Niemeyer).   VI:3
                                            II:1
                                            V:1

Eisner, J.
1948   "Les origines des slaves d'après les   I:5
        préhistoriens tchèques," *RES* 24,
        129-142.

Ekblom, R.
1915/16 * "Eine gemeinslavische Umwandlung des III:2:4
        Participiums Präsentis Aktivi," *Le*   III:3:5
        monde oriental 10, 1-44.
1925   * "Der Wechsel (*j*)*e*- ~ *o*- im Slavi- II:5
        schen," *Skr. utg. av K. Hum. Ve-* II:3
        tensk.-Samf. i Uppsala 22:4.
1927/28 * "Zur Entwicklung der Liquidaverbin- II:3
        dungen im Slavischen," *Skr. utg. av*
        K. Hum. Vetensk.-Samf. i Uppsala
        24:9, 1927; 25:4, 1928.
1928   * "Le développement de *dl*, *tl* en II:4
        slave," *Symbolae grammaticae in* VI:3
        honorem Ioannis Rozwadowski II (Cra-
        cow: Gebethner & Wolff), 57-70.
1930   ** "Zur Entstehung und Entwicklung der II:2
        slavo-baltischen und der nordischen VI:1
        Akzentarten," *Skr. utg. av K. Hum.*
        Vetensk.-Samf. i Uppsala 26:2.
1935   ** "Die Palatalisierung von *k*, *g*, *ch* II:4
        im Slavischen," *Skr. utg. av K. Hum.*
        Vetensk.-Samf. i Uppsala 29:5.
1951   * *Die frühe dorsale Palatalisierung im* II:4
        Slavischen (Uppsala: Almqvist & Wik- VI:2
        sell).
1956   "L'origine des intonations nouvelles II:2
        en slave," *ScSl* 2, 3-12.

Endzelīns, J. (Ėndzelin, I.)
1911   ** *Slavjano-baltijskie ėtjudy* (Kharkov: VI:1
        Zil'berberg).
1931   * "Zur slavisch-baltischen Konjuga- III:2:5
        tion," *Commentationes Ordinis Philo-* VI:1
        logorum Universitatis Lithuaniae.
        Archivum philologicum 2, 38-46.
1938   "Bemerkungen zu J. Kuryłowiczs An- II:2
        sichten über die baltisch-slavischen VI:1
        Intonationen," *ZfslPh* 15, 348-354.

1939   * "Über den slavisch-baltischen Reflex   II:4
         von idg. $\widehat{sk}$," *ZfslPh* 16, 107-115.   VI:1

1952   * "Drevnejšie slavjansko-baltijskie   VI:1
         jazykovye svjazi," *Izvestija Akade-*
         mii Nauk Latvijskoj SSR 3, 33-46 (=
         Trudy Instituta jazyka i literatury,
         AN LSSR 2, 1953, 67-72).

Entwistle, W. J. & W. A. Morison
1949   ** *Russian and the Slavonic Languages*   I:2
         (London: Faber & Faber).

Erhart, A.
1958   * "Zum Problem der baltisch-slavischen   VI:1
         Spracheinheit," *Sborník filosofické*
         fakulty University Komenského v Bra-
         tislavě 7, 123-130.

Eriksson, G.
1967   ** *Le nid* prav- *dans son champ séman-*   V:2
         tique. Recherches sur le vocabulaire   V:3
         slave (= *Acta Universitatis Stock-*
         holmiensis. Études de philologie
         slave 12) (Stockholm-Gothenburg-
         Uppsala: Almqvist & Wiksell).

Ètimologija . . .
1963   * *Ètimologija. Issledovanija po rus-*   V:1
         skomu i drugim jazykam (Moscow:
         AN SSSR).

1965   * *Ètimologija 1964. Principy rekon-*   V:1
         strukcii i metodika issledovanija
         (Moscow: "Nauka").

1967   * *Ètimologija 1965. Materialy i is-*   V:1
         sledovanija po indoevropejskim i
         drugim jazykam (Moscow: "Nauka").

1968   * *Ètimologija 1966. Problemy lingvo-*   V:1
         geografii i mež"jazykovyx kontaktov
         (Moscow: "Nauka").

1969   * *Ètimologija 1967. Materialy Mežduna-*   V:1
         rodnogo Simpoziuma "Problemy sla-
         vjanskix ètimologičeskix issledova-
         nij v svjazi s obščej problematikoj
         sovremennoj ètimologii" (Moscow:
         "Nauka").

1971   * *Ètimologija 1968* (Moscow: "Nauka").   V:1

Etymologický slovník . . .
1966   * *Etymologický slovník slovanských ja-*   V:1
         zyků: Ukázkové čislo, E. Havlová,
         ed. (Brno: ČSAV, Ústav jazyků a

literatur).

Ezikovedski izsledvanija . . .
1957   *Ezikovedski izsledvanija v čest na akademik Stefan Mladenov*, V. Georgiev, ed. (Sofia: BAN).

Falk, K.-O.
1958   * "Slavjanskoe nazvanie duba," *ScSl* 4, 265-285.   V:2 / V:3 / VI:1

Falkenhahn, V.
1956   "Entstehung, Entwicklung und Ende der urslavischen Sprachgemeinschaft in polnischen Veröffentlichungen von T. Lehr-Spławiński," *ZfSl* 1:2, 49-88.   VI:2

1968   ** "Die sprachgeographische Lage der balto-slawischen Sprachen als Ursache für ihre Besonderheiten," *ZfSl* 13, 226-235.   VI:1

Feist, S.
1939   * *Vergleichendes Wörterbuch der gotischen Sprache mit Einschluss des Krimgotischen und sonstiger zerstreuter Überreste des Gotischen*, dritte neubearbeitete und vermehrte Auflage (Leiden: Brill).   V:1 / V:4

Ferrell, J. O.
1963   ** "Some Notes on Slavic Gendered Pronominal Inflection," *American Contributions to the Fifth International Congress of Slavists*, 59-112.   III:2:4

1965   * "Some Observations on the Form of the Nominative and Vocative Singular of the *O*- and *Ĭo*-stems in Common Slavic," *ScSl* 11, 93-109.   III:2:4 / II:3 / II:5

1967   ** "On the Prehistory of the Locative Singular of the Common Slavic Consonant Stems," *To Honor Roman Jakobson* I, 654-661.   III:2:4

1968   ** "On Some Conditional Clause Indicators in Slavic and Germanic Languages," *Word* 24, 99-111.   IV:3 / VI:1 / IV:4

1970   ** "Cokan'e and the Palatalization of Velars in East Slavic," *SEEJ* 14, 411-422.   II:4 / VI:3

1971   ** "On the Slavic Nom. Sg. Masculine   III:2:4

and Neuter of the Present Active
Participle and the Problem of ě Ter-
tium," *Studia palaeoslovenica*, B.
Havránek, ed. (Prague: Academia),
85-93.

Festschrift . . .
1956   *Festschrift für Max Vasmer zum 70.*
Geburtstag am 28. Februar 1956 (=
Veröff. d. Abt. f. slav. Spr. u.
Lit. d. Osteuropa-Instituts [*Sla-*
visches Seminar] *an der Freien Uni-*
versität Berlin 9) (Wiesbaden: Harrassowitz).

Filin, F. P.
1962   ** *Obrazovanie jazyka vostočnyx sla-*
vjan (Moscow-Leningrad: Izd-vo AN
SSSR).

1967   ** "Nekotorye problemy slavjanskogo
ètno- i glottogeneza," *VJa* 3, 28-41.

1968   * "Nekotorye problemy rekonstrukcii
drevnerusskix dialektov," *Slavjan-*
skoe jazykoznanie VI . . ., 379-392.

1970   * "Drevnerusskie dialektnye zony i
proisxoždenie vostočnoslavjanskix
jazykov," *VJa* 5, 3-14.

1972   ** *Proisxoždenie russkogo, ukrainskogo*
i belorusskogo jazykov (Leningrad:
"Nauka").

Filip, J.
1946   *Počátky slovanského osídlení v Čes-*
koslovensku (= *Knihovna Společnosti*
přátel starožitnosti 5) (Prague:
Společnost přátel starožitností).

For Roman Jakobson . . .
1956   *For Roman Jakobson. Essays on the*
Occasion of his Sixtieth Birthday,
11 October 1956 (The Hague: Mouton).

Fraenkel, E.
1926   * "Der prädicative Instrumental im
Slavischen und Baltischen und seine
syntaktischen Grundlagen," *AfslPh*
40, 77-117.

1950a   * *Die baltischen Sprachen: Ihre Bezie-*
hungen zu einander und zu den indo-

	II:5
	VI:3
	I:4
	VI:3
	V:1
	VI:1
	I:5
	VI:3
	I:4
	VI:3
	I:4
	VI:3
	VI:1
	VI:2
	I:4
	1:5
	I:5
	IV:2
	III:2:4
	VI:1
	VI:1
	I:3

germanischen Schwesteridiomen als Einführung in die baltische Sprachwissenschaft (Heidelberg: Winter).

1950b   * "Zum baltischen und slavischen Verbum," *ZfslPh* 20, 236-320.   III:5 / VI:1

1962/65   * *Litauisches etymologisches Wörterbuch*. I, 1962; II:, 1965 (Heidelberg: Winter; Göttingen: Vandenhoeck & Ruprecht).   V:1 / VI:1

Freisinger Denkmäler . . .

1968   * *Freisinger Denkmäler. Brižinski Spomeniki. Monumenta Frisingensia. Literatur-Geschichte-Sprache-Stilart-Texte-Bibliographie*, J. Pogačnik, ed. (= *Geschichte, Kultur und Geisteswelt der Slowenen* II) (Munich: Trofenik).   I:5

Furdal, A.

1961   ** *Rozpad języka prasłowiańskiego w świetle rozwoju głosowego* (= *Prace Wrocławskiego Towarzystwa Naukowego* A:70) (Wrocław: Ossolineum).   VI:3 / II:1 / III:1

Galton, H.

1962   ** *Aorist und Aspekt im Slavischen. Eine Studie zur funktionellen und historischen Syntax* (Wiesbaden: Harrassowitz).   IV:2 / III:2:5 / VI:3

Gasparini, E.

1952   "La cultura lusaziana e i protoslavi," *Richerche slavistiche* 1, 67-92.   I:5

Georgiev, V. I.

1957   "Koncepcija ob indoevropejskix guttural'nyx soglasnyx i ee otraženie na ètimologii slavjanskix slov," *Beogradski Međunarodni slavistički sastanak*, 511-517.   II:4 / VI:1 / V:2

1958a   * "Balto-slavjanskij, germanskij i indo-iranskij," *Slavjanskaja filologija*, 7-26.   VI:1

1958b   * "Balto-slavjanskij i toxarskij jazyki," *VJa* 6, 3-20.   VI:1

1959   * "Baltoslavjanskij i germanskij," *Slavia* 28, 1-11.   VI:1

1960   * *Bălgarska etimologija i onomastika* (Sofia: BAN).   V:1 / V:2

1963   ** "Russkoe akan'e i ego otnošenie k   II:3

	sisteme fonem praslavjanskogo ja- zyka," *VJa* 2, 20-29.	VI:3 VI:2
1965a	"Problèmes phonématiques du slave commun," *RES* 44, 7-17.	II:1
1965b	"Značenie nekotoryx zaimstvovanij v finskom jazyke dlja praslavjanskoj fonemnoj sistemy," *Lingua viget* 56- 60.	II:1 VI:1 V:4
1968	** "Fonematičeskij i morfematičeskij podxod k ob"jasneniju fleksii sla- vjanskix jazykov," *VJa* 4, 32-42.	III:1 III:2:4 II:5 IV:2 II:6
1969	** *Osnovni problemi na slavjanskata diaxronna morfologija* (Sofia: BAN).	III:1 III:2:4 II:5 IV:2 II:6
1970	** "Common Slavic and Indo-European," *Mélanges Marcel Cohen. Études de linguistique, ethnographie et sci- ences connexes offertes par ses amis et ses élèves à l'occasion de son 80e anniversaire* (= *Janua Linguarum*, Series maior 27) (The Hague: Mouton), 368-374.	VI:1 VI:2

Georgiev, V. I., V. K. Žuravlev, F. P. Filin & S.
I. Stojkov

1968	** *Obščeslavjanskoe značenie problemy akan'ja* (Sofia: Izd-vo BAN).	II:3 VI:2 VI:3

Georgieva, V. L.

1969	* "Bezličnye predloženija po materi- alam drevnejšix slavjanskix pamjat- nikov (osobenno staroslavjanskix)," *Slavia* 38, 63-90.	IV:3 VI:3

Gimbutas, M.

1971	* *The Slavs* (= *Ancient Peoples and Places* 74) (London: Thames & Hudson).	I:5

Gluskina, Z. (Głuskina)

1966	* "O drugiej palatalizacji spółgłosek tylnojęzykowych w rosyjskich dialek- tach północno-zachodnich," *Slavia Orientalis* 15, 475-482.	II:4 VI:3 VI:2

Gołąb, Z.

1967	** "The Traces of *Vr̥ddhi* in Slavic,"	II:3

369

To Honor Roman Jakobson I, 770-783.   III:3:4

1968   ** "The Grammar of Slavic Causatives,"   III:3:5
American Contributions to the Sixth   IV:2
International Congress of Slavists,
71-94.

Gołąb, Z. & K. Polański

1960   * "Z badań nad słownictvem [sic!] pra-   V:1
słowiańskim," *Slavia* 29, 525-540.

Gornung, B. V.

1958   * "K diskussii o balto-slavjanskom ja-   VI:1
zykovom i ètničeskom edinstve," *VJa*
4, 55-62.

1959   * "Iz istorii izučenija baltijsko-   VI:1
slavjanskix jazykovyx otnošenij,"
Rakstu krājums, 109-132.

1963   ** *Iz predystorii obrazovanija obšče-*   VI:1
slavjanskogo jazykovogo edinstva.
V Meždunarodnyj s"ezd slavistov.
Sofija, sentjabr' 1963. Doklady
sovetskoj delegacii (Moscow: Izd-vo
AN SSSR).

Grickat-Virk, I.

1951/52   * "Još o trećoj palatalizaciji," *JF*   II:4
19, 87-110.   VI:2

Grünental, O.

1947   "Zur Liquidametathese," *ZfslPh* 19,   II:1
323-324.

Gudkov, V. P.

1963   "Iz istorii slavjanskogo glagol'nogo   III:3:5
vida," *VJa* 1, 86-89.   IV:2

Gunnarsson, G.

1937   ** *Das slavische Wort für Kirche* (=   V:4
Uppsala Universitets Årsskrift 7)
(Uppsala: Almqvist & Wiksell).

Gustavsson, S.

1969   ** *Accent Paradigms of the Present*   II:2
Tense in South Slavonic. East and   III:2:5
Central South Slavonic (= *Acta Uni-*   VI:3
versitatis Stockholmiensis. Stock-
holm Slavic Studies 3) (Stockholm:
Almqvist & Wiksell).

Güntert, H.

1916   * *Indogermanische Ablautprobleme. Un-*   II:3
tersuchungen über Schwa secundum,
einen zweiten indogermanischen Mur-
melvokal (= *Untersuchungen zur indo-*

germanischen Sprach- und Kulturwissenschaft 6) (Strassburg: Trübner).

Halle, M.
1951   ** "The Old Church Slavonic Conjuga-   III:2:5
tion," *Word* 7, 155-167.   VI:3

Hamm, J.
1957   * "Praslav. *ê* i njegov izgovor," *Beo-*   II:3
gradski Međunarodni slavistički
sastanak, 549-550.

1962   "Iz prošlosti slavenske fleksije,"   III:2:4
Slavica Pragensia IV, 157-169.

1963   ** "Slavenski komparativ," *IJSLP* 7,   III:3:4
1-13.

1966   ** "Entropy in Slavic Morphology,"   III:1
IJSLP 10, 39-51.

1969   ** "Die Verschiebung der Velarkonso-   II:4
nanten," *WslJb* 15, 38-58.   VI:2

1970   ** "Phonologische Erwägungen: Das Ur-   II:1
slavische," *WslJb* 16, 54-76.

Hamp, E. P.
1969   * "Notes on Słownik etymologiczny   V:1
języka polskiego III, 2," *RS* 30,
43-45.

1971   * "Notes on Słownik etymologiczny   V:1
języka polskiego III, 3," *RS* 32,
67-72.

Havlová, E. (Gavlova)
1966   ** "Slav. *čelověkъ*," *ScSl* 12, 80-86.   V:2
    V:3
    III:3:4

1968   "Slav. *gъlъkъ* 'kuvšin'," *Ètimologija*   V:2
1966, 97-99.

1969   * "Slavjanskie terminy 'vozrast' i   V:3
'vek' na fone semantičeskogo razvi-   V:2
tija ètix nazvanij v indoevropejskix   VI:1
jazykax," *Ètimologija 1967*, 36-39.

Havránek, B.
1939a   ** "Aspect et temps du verbe en vieux   IV:2
slave," *Mélanges de linguistique of-*   III:5
ferts à Charles Bally (Geneva: Georg   VI:3
& Cie), 223-230.

1939b   "Da li se dijalekti praslovenskog   VI:3
jezika mogu odrediti ne samo na os-
novu dvojnih ili trojnih glasovnih
pojava, nego i na osnovu paralelnih
oblika u svima delovima gramatičke

strukture?," *III Međunarodni Kongres
Slavista. Odgovori na pitanja. Dopune* (Belgrade: Izdanja Izvršnog Odbora 3), 20.

1939c   * "Ein phonologischer Beitrag zur Ent-   II:4
wicklung der slavischen Palatalrei-   VI:3
hen," *TCLP* 8, 327-334.   VI:2

1939d   "Pitanje glagolskog vida prasloven-   III:3:5
skog jezika: njegova morfologija.   IV:2
Odnos među perfektivnim i perfekti-
ziranim glagolima, imperfektivnim i
imperfektiziranim, i njihov značaj
za razumevanje slovenskog glagolskog
vida," *III Međunarodni Kongres Slavista. Odgovori na pitanja. Dopune*
(Belgrade: Izdanja Izvršnog Odbora
3), 13.

Hermann, E.
1935   * "Entstehung der slavischen Substan-   III:3:4
tiva auf *-yńi*," *ZfslPh* 12, 119-120.

Herne, G.
1954   * *Die slavischen Farbenbenennungen.*   V:2
Eine semasiologisch-etymologische   V:3
Untersuchung (= *Publications de
l'Institut slave d'Upsala* 9) (Uppsala: Almqvist & Wiksell).

Hirt, H.
1921/37 ** *Indogermanische Grammatik.* I-VII   I:3
(Heidelberg: Winter).

Hjelmslev, L.
1937   * "La syllabation en slave," *Zbornik*   II:5
lingvističkih i filoloških raspra-   VI:1
va . . ., 315-324.

Holub, J. & F. Kopečný
1952   * *Etymologický slovník jazyka českého,*   V:1
3. přepracovane vyd. (Prague: Státní
Nakl. Učebnic).

Horálek, K.
1959   * "N. S. Trubetzkoy und die Phonologie   II:1
des Urslavischen," *WslJb* 7, 5-13.

1960/61   * "Zum gegenwärtigen Stand der sla-   II:2
vischen Akzentologie," *ZfslPh* 29,
357-379.

1962   ** *Úvod do studia slovanských jazyků,*   I:2
2nd ed., [1]1955 (Prague: Nakl. ČSAV).

372

Hujer, O.

1910   * *Slovanská deklinace jmenná* (Prague: III:2:4
Nakl. České Akademie Cisaře Fran-
tiška Josefa pro vědy, slovesnost a
uměni).

1911   * "K slovanské deklinaci zájmenné,"   III:2:4
Sborník filologický 2 (Prague: Nakl.
České Akademie Cisaře Františka Josefa pro vědy, slovesnost a uměni),
188-207.

1920/21   * *Praslovanské tvarosloví*. I: *Praslo-*   III:2:4
vanské skloňování (Prague: [biblio-
graphical data not available]).

Huntley, D. G.

1968   ** "Two Cases of Analogical Feature   II:3
Substitution in Slavic," *Language*
44, 501-506.

Il'inskij, G. A.

1902   *O nekotoryx arxaizmax i novoobrazo-*   I:1
vanijax praslavjanskogo jazyka   II:1
(Prague: [bibliographical data not   III:1
available]).

1907   * "Der Reflex des indogermanischen   II:3
Diphthongs *ēu* im Urslavischen,"
AfslPh 29, 481-497.

1916   * *Praslavjanskaja grammatika* (Něžin: I:1
Tipo-lit. "Pečatnik," byvš. nasl.
V. K. Melenevskago).

1917   "Mnimaja assimiljacija reducirovan-   II:3
nyx glasnyx v praslavjanskom ja-
zyke," *IORJaS* 22, 188-204.

1922   "Problema praslavjanskoj prarodiny   I:5
v naučnom osvěščenii A. A. Šaxma-
tova," *IORJaS* 25, 419-436.

1923/24   * "K voprosu o čeredovanii glasnyx   II:5
rjada *o*, *e* v načale slov v slavjan-   II:3
skix jazykax," *Slavia* 2, 232-276.

1925/26   * "Ešče raz o praslavjanskix dubletax   II:5
tipa *jelenь* : *olenь*," *Slavia* 4, 387-   II:3
394.

1930   * "K istorii infinitiva v praslavjan-   III:5
skom jazyke," *Doklady Akademii Nauk
SSSR* V:6, 100-104.

1962   "Vzgljad na obščij xod izučenija   I:1
praslavjanskogo jazyka," *VJa* 5, 124-
129.

Illič-Svityč, V. M.

1959   * "O nekotoryx refleksax indoevropej-   II:1
          skix 'laringal'nyx' v praslavjan-   II:2
          skom," *VJa* 2, 3-18.   VI:1

1961   ** "Odin iz istočnikov načal'nogo *x*- v   II:5
          praslavjanskom. (Popravka k 'zakonu   II:4
          Zibsa')," *VJa* 4, 93-98.

1963   ** *Imennaja akcentuacija v baltijskom*   II:2
          i slavjanskom. Sud'ba akcentuacion-   VI:1
          nyx paradigm (Moscow: AN SSSR).   III:2:4

1964   * Review of *Das prosodische System des*   II:2
          Urslavischen und seine Weiterent-   VI:3
          wicklung im Serbokroatischen by Hel-
          mut Lüdtke, *Slavjanskaja i baltij-*
          skaja akcentologija (= *Kratkie soob-*
          ščenija Instituta slavjanovedenija
          41) (Moscow: "Nauka"), 87-88

Isačenko, A. V. (Issatchenko, Issatschenko)

1939   * "Zur phonologischen Deutung der Ak-   II:2
          zentverschiebungen in den slavischen   VI:3
          Sprachen," *TCLP* 8, 173-183.

1940   "Tense and Auxiliary Verbs, with   III:2:5
          Special Reference to Slavic Lan-
          guages," *Language* 16, 189-198.

1943   * *Jazyk a pôvod Frizinských Pamiatok.*   I:5
          Sprache und Herkunft der Freisinger   VI:3
          Denkmäler (Bratislava: SAVU).

1953   ** "Indoevropejskaja i slavjanskaja   V:2
          terminologija rodstva v svete mark-   V:3
          sistskogo jazykoznanija," *Slavia* 22,   VI:1
          43-80.

1954   * "Príspevok k štúdiu najstarších   V:2
          vrstiev základného fondu slovanských   III:3:4
          jazykov: Slovanské neutrá na -*men*,"
          K šedesátým narozeninám akademika
          Bohuslava Havránka (= *Studie a práce*
          linguistické 1), J. Bělič, M. Doku-
          lil, K. Horálek & A. Jedlička, eds.
          (Prague: Nakl. ČSAV), 114-130.

1955   ** "O vozniknovenii i razvitii 'katego-   IV:2
          rii sostojanija' v slavjanskix ja-
          zykax," *VJa* 6, 48-65.

1970a   ** "East Slavic Morphophonemics and the   II:3
          Treatment of the Jers in Russian: A   II:6
          Revision of Havlík's Law," *IJSLP* 13,   VI:3
          73-124.

374

1970b   * "Hortativsätze mit *a, i, ti, to* im   IV:3
Ostslavischen," *ScSl* 16, 189-203.   V:2
     VI:3

Issledovanija . . .
1971   *Issledovanija po slavjanskomu jazykoznaniju. Sbornik v čest' šesti-
desjatiletija professora S. B. Bern-
štejna* (Moscow: "Nauka").

Ivanov, V. V.
1957   ** "O značenii xettskogo jazyka dlja   VI:1
sravnitel'no-istoričeskogo issledo-   II:2
vanija slavjanskix jazykov," *VslJa*   III:2
2, 3-28.   III:3
1958   * "K étimologii baltijskogo i slavjan-   V:2
skogo nazvanij boga groma," *VslJa* 3,   VI:1
101-111.
1965   ** *Obščeindoevropejskaja, praslavjan-*   I:1
skaja i anatolijskaja jazykovye sis-   I:3
temy (Moscow: "Nauka").   VI:1
1968   ** "Otraženie dvux serij indoevropejskix glagol'nyx form v praslavjan-   III:5
skom," *Slavjanskoe jazykoznanie*
VI . . ., 225-276.
1970   * "Suffix *-śk-* > Baltic *-šk-* and the   III:3:5
Problem of Verbs Denoting Sounds,"   VI:1
Donum Balticum, 206-210.   V:3

Ivanov, V. V. & V. N. Toporov
1961   ** "K postanovke voprosa o drevnejšix   VI:1
otnošenijax baltijskix i slavjanskix
jazykov," *Issledovanija po slavjan-*
skomu jazykoznaniju, N. I. Tolstoj,
ed. (Moscow: Izd-vo: AN SSSR), 273-
305.
1963   ** "K rekonstrukcii praslavjanskogo   IV:1
teksta," *Slavjanskoe jazykoznanie*   V:3
V . . ., 88-158.   IV:4
1965   ** *Slavjanskie jazykovye modelirujuščie*   V:3
semiotičeskie sistemy: Drevnij pe-   IV:1
riod (Moscow: "Nauka").

Ivić, P.
1965   ** "Roman Jakobson and the Growth of   II:1
Phonology," *Linguistics* 18, 35-78.
1967   ** "Nouveaux phonèmes et possibilités   II:1
distinctives," *Word* 23, 344-349.
1969   * "O drevnosti akan'ja v slavjanskix   II:3
jazykax," *VJa* 3, 59-69.   VI:3
     VI:2

1970   ** "Rasširenie inventarja fonem i čislo   II:1
        distinktivnyx vozmožnostej," *VJa* 3,
        3-9.

Ivšić, S
1970   ** *Slavenska poredbena gramatika*, J.   I:2
        Vrana & R. Katičić, eds. (Zagreb:
        "Školska Knjiga").

Jacobsson, G. (Jakobsson)
1947   ** *Le nom de temps* lěto *dans les*   V:2
        langues slaves (=*Études de philolo-*   V:3
        gie slave publ. par l'Institut russe
        de l'Université de Stockholm 1)
        (Uppsala: Almqvist & Wiksell).

1958a   * *L'histoire d'un groupe de mots bal-*   V:2
       to-slaves (=*Slavica Gothoburgensia*   V:3
       1) (Gothenburg: Almqvist & Wiksell).   VI:1

1958b   * "Razvitie ponjatija vremeni v svete   V:3
       slavjanskogo *časъ*," *ScSl* 4, 286-307.   V:2

1960   * "Polysemie und semantische Struktur.
       Betrachtungen anlässlich des slavi-   V:3
       schen Wortes *lěto*," *ScSl* 6, 189-   V:2
       195.

1961   * "La racine **tep-* 'couper' en slave,"   V:2
       ScSl 7, 252-259.   V:3

1963   * "The Slavic Active Participles:
       Original Structure and Interfer-   III:5
       ence," *ScSl* 9, 123-138.   III:2:4

1965   ** "Zur Frage vom Nominativ als Kasus   IV:2
        des direkten Objekts im Slawischen,"   VI:1
        Lingua viget, 71-82.   IV:4
                                     VI:3

1968   ** "Das slavische **kochati*," *ScSl* 14,   V:2
        99-115.   V:3

1969   ** "Celi i metody ètimologizacii slov,
        vyražajuščix nekotorye abstraktnye   V:3
        ponjatija (Primerom služit ponjatie   V:2
        'vremja')," *Ètimologija 1967*, 32-35.

Jakobson, R.
1929   ** *Remarques sur l'evolution phonolo-*   II:1
        gique du russe comparée a celle des   VI:2
        autres langues slaves (=*TCLP* 2)   VI:3
        (=*Selected Writings*. I: *Phonologi-*
        cal Studies, 1962, The Hague: Mouton,
        7-116).

1935   ** "Les enclitiques slaves," *Atti del*   IV:3
        III Congresso Internazionale dei

Linguisti (*Roma, 19-26 Settembre 1933-XI*), B. Migliorini & V. Pisani, eds. (Florence: Felice Le Monnier), 384-390 (= *Selected Writings*. II: *Word and Language*, 1971, The Hague: Mouton, 16-22).

1948   * "Russian Conjugation," *Word* 4, 155-167.   III:2:5

1949   ** *Slavic Languages: A Condensed Survey*, ²1955 = Columbia Slavic Studies (New York-London: King's Crown Press).   I:2

1952   * "On Slavic Diphthongs Ending in a Liquid," *Word* 8 (= *Slavic Word* 1), 306-310 (= *Selected Writings*. I: *Phonological Studies*, The Hague: Mouton, 1962, 443-448).   II:3   VI:3

1962a   * "Comparative Slavic Phonology," *Selected Writings*. I: *Phonological Studies* (The Hague: Mouton), 413-417.   II:1

1962b   ** "Die urslavischen Silben $\bar{u}r$-, $\bar{u}l$-," *Selected Writings*. I: *Phonological Studies* (The Hague: Mouton), 546-549.   II:5   V:2

1962/71   * *Selected Writings*. I: *Phonological Studies*, 1962; II: *Word and Language*, 1971 (The Hague: Mouton).

1963   ** "Opyt fonologičeskogo podxoda k istoričeskim voprosam slavjanskoj akcentologii. Pozdnij period slavjanskoj jazykovoj praistorii," *American Contributions to the Fifth International Congress of Slavists*, 153-178.   II:2   VI:3

1965a   ** "Information and Redundancy in the Common Slavic Prosodic Pattern," *Symbolae linguisticae* . . ., 145-151.   II:2   VI:3

1965b   * "Uščekotalъ skača," *Lingua viget*, 83-89. (= *Selected Writings*. IV: *Slavic Epic Studies*, The Hague: Mouton, 1966, 603-610).   V:2   V:3   V:4

1966   * "Nikolaj Sergejevič Trubetzkoy," *Portraits of Linguists. A Biographical Source Book for the History of*   I:1

Western Linguists, 1746-1963. II:
*From Eduard Sievers to Benjamin Lee
Whorf*, T. A. Sebeok, ed. (Blooming-
ton-London: Indiana University
Press), 526-542.

1968   * "Voprosy sravnitel'noj indoevropej-   V:2
skoj mifologii v svete slavjanskix   VI:1
pokazanij," *American Contributions
to the Sixth International Congress
of Slavists*, 125-128.

1969   * "The Slavic god *Veles* and his Indo-   V:2
European cognates," *Studi Linguisti-   VI:1
ci in Onore di Vittore Pisani* (Bre-
scia: Editrice Paideia), 579-599.

Jakubinskij, L. P.
1953   ** *Istorija drevnerusskogo jazyka* (Mos-   I:4
cow: Učpedgiz).   VI:3
                                             I:5

Jażdżewski, K.
1948/49 * *Atlas to the Prehistory of the Slavs.* I:5
I-II (Łódź: Łódzkie Towarzystwo
Naukowe, Wydział II).

1968   * *Z problematyki początków Słowiań-*   I:5
szczyzny i Polski. Część I (Wrocław:
[Łódź: Łódzkie Towarzystwo Naukowe.
Wydział II, Nauk historycznych i
społecznych] Ossolineum).

1970   * "Praojczyzna Słowian," *Słownik*   I:5
starożytności słowiańskich, IV:
301-305.

Jeżowa, M.
1968   * *Z problemów tak zwanej trzeciej pa-*   II:4
latalizaciji tylnojęzykowych w   VI:2
językach słowiańskich (Wrocław:
Ossolineum).

Jokl, N.
1906   "Ein urslavisches Entnasalierungs-   II:3
gesetz," *AfslPh* 28, 1-17.

Jurkowski, M.
1963   * "Losy prasłowiańskich grup *kъ-*,   II:4
gъ-, *xъ-*," *Z polskich studiów*   II:5
slawistycznych. Seria 2 *Języko-*   VI:3
znawstwo (Warsaw: PWN).

Kalima, J.
1929   * "Zur Herkunft der slavischen Lehn-   V:4
wörter im Ostseefinnischen," *ZfslPh*

378

6, 154–172.

1956   * *Die slavischen Lehnwörter im Ostsee-*   V:4
        finnischen (= *Veröff. d Abt. f.*
        slav. Spr. u. Lit. d. Osteuropa-
        Instituts [*Slavisches Seminar*] *an*
        der Freien Universität Berlin 8)
        (Wiesbaden: Harrassowitz).

Kalnyn', L. Ė.
1961   ** *Razvitie korreljacii tverdyx i*   II:4
        mjagkix soglasnyx fonem v slavjan-   VI:3
        skix jazykax (Moscow: Izd-vo AN
        SSSR).

Karaliūnas, S. (Karaljunas)
1967   * *Drevnejšie otnošenija blatijskix i*   VI:1
        slavjanskix jazykov (Vilnius: Vil'-
        njusskij gosudarstvennyj universi-
        tet).

1968a   ** "Kai kurie baltų ir slavų kalbų   VI:1
        seniausiųjų santykių klausimai,"
        Lietuvių kalbotyros klausimai 10
        (Vilnius: "Mintis"), 7–100.

1968b   * "Lie. *stragùs* = Sl. *strogъ*," *Bal-* V:2
        tistica 4, 259–267.   VI:1

Karaś, M.
1965   * "Z historii prasłowiańskiej dekli-   III:2:4
        nacji spółgłoskowej," *Symbolae lin-*   III:3:4
        guisticae . . ., 159–169.

Karstien, H.
1936   * "Slavische Instrumentalformen auf   III:2:4
        -*a*," *ZfslPh* 13, 109–128.

1956a   * "Das slav. Imperf. und der arm.   III:2:5
        -*aǫe*- Aor. Ein Beitrag zum slav.-   VI:1
        arm. Verwandtschaftsverhältnis,"
        Festschrift für Max Vasmer, 211–229.

1956b   * "Das slav. Imperfekt und seine idg.   III:2:5
        Verwandten," *ZfslPh* 25, 67–112.   VI:1

1971   ** *Infixe im Indogermanischen* (*Gekürzte* III:3
        Fassung) (Heidelberg: Winter).   VI:1

Klazlauskas, J. (I.)
1968   * "O balto-slavjanskoj forme datel'-   III:2:4
        nogo pad. mn. i dv. č.," *Baltistica*   VI:1
        4, 179–183.

Kiparsky, V. (Kiparskij)
1934   ** *Die gemeinslavischen Lehnwörter aus*   V:4
        dem Germanischen (= *Annales Acade-*
        miae Scientiarum Fennicae B, 32₂)

379

(Helsinki: Suomalainen Tiedeakatemia).

1948   * "Chronologie des relations slavo-   VI:2
baltiques et slavofinnoises," *RES*   VI:1
24, 29-47.   V:4

1954   ** "Sur la chronologie de quelques   VI:2
altérnations phonétiques en slave,"   II:3
ScSl 1, 19-21.   II:4

1958   ** "O xronologii slavjano-finnskix
leksičeskix otnošenij," *ScSl* 4,   V:4
127-136.   VI:2

1962   * "Wie haben die Ostseefinnen die   VI:1
Slaven kennengelernt?," *Commenta-*   V:4
tiones Fenno-Ugricae in honorem
Paavo Ravila (Helsinki: Suomalais-
Ugrilainen Seura), 223-230.

1963/67 ** *Russische historische Grammatik.* I: I:4
Die Entwicklung des Lautsystems,   VI:3
1963; II: *Die Entwicklung des For-*   II:1
mensystems, 1967 (Heidelberg: Win-   III:2
ter).

1967   ** "Nochmals über das Nominativobjekt   IV:2
des Infinitivs," *ZfslPh* 33, 263-   VI:1
266.   IV:4
VI:3

1969a   ** "Das Nominativobjekt des Infinitivs   IV:2
im Slavischen, Baltischen und Ost-   VI:1
seefinnischen," *Baltistica* 5, 141-   IV:4
148.   VI:3

1969b   * Review of *A Prehistory of Slavic* by
G. Y. Shevelov, *ZfslPh* 34, 427-434.   II:1

1969c   ** *Gibt es ein finnougrisches Substrat* VI:1
im Slavischen? (= *Annales Academiae* II:3
Scientiarum Fennicae B, 153₄) (Hel-   II:4
sinki: Suomalainen Tiedeakatemia),   IV:3
3-27.

1969d   ** "Über die Betonung der urslav. ь,   II:2
ь," *ScSl* 15, 187-192.   II:3
VI:3

1970   ** "Über slav. -*ika* und -*ica* als Allo- II:4
morphe," *ScSl* 16, 137-142.   VI:1
III:3:4

1971   ** "Zum gegenwärtigen Stand der etymo-   V:1
logischen Untersuchungen," *PF* 21,
265-275.

Klemensiewicz, Z.
1961   ** *Historia języka polskiego*. I: *Doba*   I:4
        staropolska. Od czasów najdawniej-   VI:3
        szych do początków XVI wieku (War-
        saw: PWN).
Klemensiewicz, Z., T. Lehr-Spławiński & S. Urbańszyk
1964   ** *Gramatyka historyczna języka pol-*   I:4
        skiego, 2nd ed. (Warsaw: PWN).   VI:3
Klimas, A.
1970   * "Baltic, Germanic and Slavic," *Donum*   VI:1
        Balticum, 263-269.
Kniezsa, I.
1933   "Ungarn zur Zeit der Landnahme," *RS*   I:5
        11, 1-25.
1948   "Zur Geschichte der Jugoslavismen im   VI:3
        Mittelslovakischen," *Études slaves*
        et roumaines 1, 139-147.
1955   ** *A magyar nyelv szláv jövevényszavai*   V:4
        I: 1-2 (Budapest: Akadémiai Kiadó).
Knutsson, K. P.
1926   * *Über die sog. zweite Palatalisierung*   II:4
        in den slavischen Sprachen (= *Lunds*   VI:2
        Universitets Årsskrift, N. F. Avd.
        1, 24:9) (Lund: Gleerup; Leipzig:
        Harrassowitz).
1929   * *Die germanischen Lehnwörter im Sla-*   V:4
        vischen vom Typus buky (= *Lunds Uni-*
        versitets Årsskrift, N. F. Avd. 1,
        21:9) (Lund: Gleerup; Leipzig: Har-
        rassowitz).
Kolesov, V. V.
1964   * "Padenie reducirovannyx v statisti-   II:3
        českoj interpretacii," *VJa* 2, 30-44.   VI:3
1968   ** "K fonetičeskoj xarakteristike redu-   II:3
        cirovannyx glasnyx v russkom jazyke   VI:3
        XI v.," *VJa* 4, 80-86.
Komárek, M.
1958   ** *Historická mluvnice česká*. I: *Hlás-*   I:4
        kosloví (Prague: Státní Pedag Nakl.).   VI:3
        II:1
Kondrašov, N. A.
1962   ** *Slavjanskie jazyki*, 2nd ed. (Moscow: I:2
        Učpedgiz).
Koneczna, H. (Świderska)
1932   "Próba objaśnienie przegłosu w języ-   II:3
        kach słowiańskich," *Sprawozdania z*

posiedzeń Towarzystwa naukowego war-
szawskiego. Wydział 1, 25 (Warsaw:
Nakł. Towarzystwa Naukowego Warszaw-
skiego), 48-69.

1934   "Wzdłużenie zastępcze," *2. Między-*   II:3
narodowy zjazd slawistów. Księga   VI:3
referatów. Sekcja 1: *Językoznawstwo*
(Warsaw: Druk. Bankowa), 56-60.

Koneski, B.
1965   ** *Istorija na makedonskiot jazik*   I:4
(Skopje: "Koco Racin"). SCr transl.   VI:3
Istorija makedonskog jezika, 1966
(Belgrade: Prosveta).

Kopečný, F. F. (Kopečnyj)
1958   ** "Zu den deverbativen *l*-Formationen   III:3
im Slavischen," *Mélanges linguis-*
tiques offerts à Emil Petrovici,
269-282.

1962a   Review of *Proisxoždenie nazvanij*   V:2
domašnix životnyx v slavjanskix ja-
zykax by O. N. Trubačev, *Slavia* 31,
460-465.

1962b   * "Zur Entstehung der Futurbedeutung   IV:2
beim perfektiven Präsens im Slavi-   III:3:5
schen," *ScSl* 8, 171-181.

1968   * "K étimologii slav. *otrokъ*," *Étimo-*   V:2
logija 1966, 54-61.

1969a   * "Problemy étimologii grammatičeskix   V:2
slov," *Étimologija 1967*, 22-31.   IV:2

1969b   * "Slavisch *kъ*," *AnzfslPh* 3, 5-12.   V:2
   IV:2

1971   * "Prépositions slaves issues d'ad-   V:2
verbes pronominaux," *Studia palaeo-*   IV:2
slovenica, B. Havránek, ed. (Prague:
Academia), 179-183.

1973   * *Etymologický slovník slovanských*   V:1
jazyků. Slova gramatická a zájmena.
1: *Předložky. Koncové partikule.*
(Prague: Academia).

Kořínek, J. M.
1948   ** *Od indoeuropského prajazyka k pra-*   I:1
slovančine (Bratislava: Slovenská   VI:1
Akadémia Vied a Umení).

Koschmieder, E.
1956   * "N. van Wijks Einwand gegen die 2.   II:2
Metatonie," *Festschrift für Max*

        Vasmer, 235-244.

1958a ** "Die Aussprache der Nasalvokale im   II:3
             Altkirchenslavischen," *WdSl* 3, 236-   VI:3
             247.

1958b ** "Schwund und Vokalisation der Halb-   II:3
             vokale im Ostslavischen," *WdSl* 3,   VI:2
             124-137.   VI:3

1959   ** "Die Palatalitätskorrelation im   II:4
             Slavischen," *ZfslPh* 27, 245-255.   VI:3

1966   ** "Die sogenannten leicht palatali-
             sierten Konsonanten des Urslavi-   II:4
             schen," *Orbis Scriptus*, 433-438.   VI:3

Kostrzewski, J.
1946   * *Prastowiańszczyzna. Zarys dziejów*   I:5
             i kultury prastowiańskiej (Poznań:
             Księgarnia akademicka).

Kølln, H.
1957   * "Vidové problémy v staroslověn-   III:3:5
             štině," *Universitas Carolina, Philo-* IV:2
             logica 3, R. Foustka, ed. (Prague: VI:3
             "Práce"), 67-100.

1958   * "Die Entstehung des slavischen Ver- III:3:5
             balaspektes. Die imperfektiven Ab- IV:2
             leitungen zu präfigierten Verben in
             ihrem Verhältnis zur Determinations-
             kategorie und zum System der Verbal-
             formen," *ScSl* 4, 308-313.

1961   ** "Die *e/o*-Verba im Slavischen," *ScSl* III:3:5
             7, 260-285.

1966   ** "Aspekt und Diathese im Slavischen," III:3:5
             ScSl 12, 57-79.   IV:2

1969   ** *Oppositions of Voice in Greek, Slav-* III:3:5
             ic, and Baltic (Copenhagen: Munks- IV:2
             gaard).   VI:1

Krajčovič, R.
1962   * "O príčinách vzniku zapadoslovanskej II:3
             kontrakcie," *Slavica Pragensia IV*,   VI:3
             111-115.   II:5

Krogmann, W.
1956   * "Slav. *gospodъ*," *Festschrift für*   V:2
             Max Vasmer, 253-258.   III:3:4

Kuraszkiewicz, W.
1954   * *Zarys dialektologii wschodnio-*   I:2
             stowiańskiej (z wyborem tekstów   VI:3
             gwarowych), [2]1963 (Warsaw: PWN).
1955   * "Ugrupowanie języków wschodnio-   I:2

                           słowiańskich," *BPTJ* 14, 94-102.   VI:3

Kurkina, L. V.

1969   * "Nazvanija bolot v slavjanskix ja-   V:3
            zykax," *Ètimologija 1967*, 129-144.   V:2

1971   * "Iz nabljudenij nad nekotorymi
            nazvanijami dorog i tropinok v   V:3
            slavjanskix jazykax," *Ètimologija*   V:2
            1968, 92-105.

Kuryłowicz, J. (Kurilovič, E.)

1929   * "La genèse d'aspects verbaux   III:3:5
            slaves," *PF* 14, 644-657.   IV:2

1931   * "Le problème des intonations bal-   II:2
            to-slaves," *RS* 10, 1-80.   VI:1

1932   * "Pochodzenie słowiańskich aspektów
            czasownikowych," *Sborník prací . . .*,   III:3:5
            572-576 (= *Sprawozdania Towarzystwa*   IV:2
            Naukowego we Lwowie 9, 70-74).

1937   * "La structure de l'imparfait slave,"   III:2:5
            Mélanges linguistiques offerts à M.
            Holger Pedersen, 385-392.

1938   * "Intonation et morphologie en slave   II:2
            commun," *RS* 14, 1-66.   III:2

1950   * "Le degré long en balto-slave," *RS*   II:3
            16, 1-14.   VI:1
                                                      III:3:5

1951   ** "Związki językowe słowiańsko-germań-   VI:1
            skie," *Przegląd Zachodni* 7 (Poznań: V:4
            Instytut Zachodni).

1952   ** *L'accentuation des langues indo-*   II:2
            européennes (= *PAU*, *PKJ* 37) (Cracow: VI:1
            Nakl. PAU) (^{2}1958 = *PAN KJ Prace*
            Językoznawcze 17, Wrocław: Ossoli-
            neum, PAN).

1956   ** *L'apophonie en indo-européen* (= *PAN*, II:3
            KJ, *Prace Językoznawcze* 9) (Wrocław: VI:1
            Ossolineum, PAN).

1957   * "O jedności językowej bałto-słowiań-   VI:1
            skiej," *BPTJ* 16, 70-114. R transl.
            "O balto-slavjanskom jazykovom
            edinstve," *VslJa* 3, 1958, 15-49.

1958   * "Na marginesie ostatniej syntezy ak-   II:2
            centuacji słowiańskiej," *RS* 20, 40-   VI:1
            53.

1959   * "Réflexions sur l'imparfait et les   III:5
            aspects en v. slave," *IJSLP* 1/2, 1-   IV:2
            8.

1962a * "O nekotoryx fikcijax sravnitel'nogo   II:2
         jazykoznanija," *VJa* 1, 31-36.
1962b ** "Personal and Animate Genders in   IV:2
         Slavic," *Lingua* 11, 249-255.
1964 ** *The Inflectional Categories of Indo-* III:1
         European (Heidelberg: Winter).   III:2
                                                 I:3
                                                 VI:1
                                                 III:3

1965 ** "Indoeuropejskie perfectum w sło-   III:2:5
         wiańskim," *Studia z filologii pol-*   VI:1
         skiej i słowiańskiej 5 (Warsaw:
         PWN), 53-58.
1967 ** "Slavic *damъ*: A Problem of Methodol- III:5
         ogy," *To Honor Roman Jakobson* II,
         1127-1131.
1968a ** *Indogermanische Grammatik*. II: *Ak-* I:3
         zent, Ablaut (Heidelberg: Winter).   II:2
                                                 II:3

1968b ** "Sur une particularité de la conju-   III:2:5
         gaison slave," *Annuaire de l'Insti-*   II:2
         tut de Philologie et d'Histoire
         Orientales et Slaves 18 (Brussels:
         Université libre de Bruxelles), 249-
         253.
1969 ** "Fleksii prilagatel'nogo v baltij-   III:2:4
         skom i slavjanskom," *VJa* 3, 3-11.   VI:1
Kurz, J.
1958 ** "K otázce doby vzniku slovanských   III:4
         adjektiv složených a jejich původ-   IV:2
         ního významu," *Studie ze slovanské*   VI:2
         jazykovědy. Sborník k 70. narozeni-
         nám akademika Františka Trávníčka,
         V. Machek, ed. (Prague: Státní
         Pedag. Nakl.), 211-219.
Kuznecov, P. S.
1952   "Voprosy sravnitel'no-istoričeskogo   I:2
         izučenija slavjanskix jazykov," *VJa*
         5, 38-55.
1954 ** "Čeredovanija v obščeslavjanskom   II:6
         'jazyke-osnove'," *VslJa* 1, 24-67.   II:3
                                                 II:4
1958   * "O povedenii sonantov na granice   II:3
         osnov glagolov III i IV klassov v   II:4
         slavjanskix jazykax," *Slavjanskaja*   II:5
         filologija. Sbornik statej 3,   III:3:5

              posvjaščennyj IV Meždunarodnomu
              s"ezdu slavistov, V. V. Vinogradov
              et al., eds. (Moscow: Izd-vo AN
              SSSR), 5-37.

1961a   ** *Očerki po morfologii praslavjanskogo*   III:1
             jazyka (Moscow: Izd-vo AN SSSR).

1961b   ** "Razvitie indoevropejskogo sklone-   III:2:4
             nija v obščeslavjanskom jazyke,"   VI:1
             Issledovanija po slavjanskomu ja-   II:5
             zykoznaniju, N. I. Tolstoj, ed.
             (Moscow: Izd-vo AN SSSR), 114-164.

1964   * "K voprosu o proisxoždenii akan'ja,"   II:3
             VJa 1, 30-41.   VI:3
                                          VI:2

Lamprecht, A.
1956   "Neskol'ko zamečanij k razvitiju   III:1
             fonetičeskoj sistemy praslavjanskogo
             jazyka," *Sborník filosofické fakulty*
             University Komenského v Bratislavě
             5, 19-23.

Lang, P.
1922   * "Slovanská dvojice jelenь - olenь,   II:5
             lanьji," *Časopis pro Moderní Filolo-* II:3
             gii a Literaturu 8 (Prague: Nákl.
             Klubu Moderních Filologů), 97-101,
             202-205.

Laziczius, G. (J.)
1933   * "Zur Wandlung idg. *s* > slav. *ch*," *IF* II:4
             51, 196-199.   II:5

Lehr-Spławiński, T. (Ler-Splavinskij)
1911   * "Nowsze poglądy na niektóre zjawiska II:4
             t. zw. drugiej palatalizacji," *RS*   VI:2
             4, 141-148 (=*Studia i szkice*, 153-
             158).

1917   ** *Ze studjów nad akcentem słowiańskim*   II:2
             (=*PAU*, *PKJ* 1) (Cracow: Nakl. PAU).

1918a   ** *O prasłowiańskiej metatonii* (=*PAU*,   II:2
             PKJ 1) (Cracow: Nakl. PAU) (=*Studia*
             i szkice, 52-93).

1918b   * "Prasłowiańskie *jь*- w językach za-   II:5
             chodnio-słowiańskich," *RS* 8, 152-156 VI:3
             (=*Studia i szkice*, 215-218).   II:3

1918c   * "Ślady dawnych różnic intonacyjnych
             w językach ruskich. Z powodu prac   II:2
             Szachmatowa, Rozwadowskiego i Endze- VI:3
             lina," *RS* 8, 250-263 (=*Studia i*

          szkice, 303-313).

1921/22   * "O jakości intonacji prasłowiańskich.   II:2
        Z powodu prac K. H. Meyera, N. Tru-
        bieckiego i R. Ekbloma," *RS* 9, 254-
        294 (= *Studia i szkice*, 93-124).

1926   * "Les voyelles nasales dans les   II:3
        langues léchites," *RES* 6, 54-65.   VI:3

1928a   "Kilka uwag o wspólności językowej   VI:3
        praruskiej," *Sbornik statej v čest'*
        akademika Alekseja Ivanoviča Sobo-
        levskogo (Leningrad: Izd-vo AN
        SSSR), 371-377 (= *Studia i szkice*,
        295-302).

1928b   * "Najstarsze prasłowiańskie prawo   II:2
        cofania akcentu," *Symbolae grammati-*
        cae in honorem Ioannis Rozwadowski
        II (Cracow: Gebethner & Wolff), 85-
        100 (= *Studia i szkice*, 125-140).

1929a   * "Kilka uwag o nosówkach prasłowiań- II:3
        skich," *PF* 14, 635-643 (= *Studia i*
        szkice, 168-173).

1929b   ** "Les emprunts latins en slave com- V:4
        mun," *Eos* 32, 705-710 (= "Zapoży-
        czenia łacińskie w języku prasło-
        wiańskim," *Studia i szkice*, 196-
        200).

1931a   * "Jedna z izofon północno-zachodnio- VI:3
        słowiańskich. Formy typu *w Polszcze* II:4
        itp.," *SłOcc* 10, 153-159 (= *Studia i*
        szkice, 251-256).

1931b   * "O mieszaniu prasłowiańskich połą- II:3
        czeń *telt* z *tolt* w językach północ- VI:3
        no-słowiańskich," *PF* 15:2, 345-361
        (= *Studia i szkice*, 219-230).

1931c   * "O tzw. przestawce płynnych w ję- II:3
        zykach słowiańskich. Z powodu prac VI:3
        R. Ekbloma i T. Milewskiego," *RS* 10,
        116-137 (= *Studia i szkice*, 231-
        250).

1932   * "O dialektach prasłowiańskich,"   VI:3
        Sbornik prací . . ., 577-585 (=
        Studia i szkice, 207-214).

1935   * "Sur les origines des intonations en II:2
        slave commun," *Atti del III Con-*
        gresso Internazionale dei Linguisti
        (Roma, 19-26 Settembre 1933-XI),

B. Migliorini & V. Pisani, eds.
(Florence: Felice Le Monnier), 379-
383.

1937a   Review of "Le problème des intona-   II:2
         tions balto-slaves" by André Vail-
         lant, *RS* 13, 1-8 (=*Studia i szkice*,
         145-150).

1937b * "Dwie etymologie prasłowiańskie   V:2
         (*dąbrava ognь*)," *Zbornik lingvistič-
         kih i filoloških rasprava* . . ., 411-
         416 (=*Studia i szkice*, 201-206).

1937c * "Zu den slavischen *q*- und *u*-Dublet-   II:3
         ten," *Mélanges linguistiques offerts
         à M. Holger Pedersen*, 379-384 (= "O
         dubletach słowiańskich z *q* i *u*,"
         Studia i szkice, 191-195).

1938 ** "Element prasłowiański w dzisiejszym   V:2
         słownictwie polskim," *Studia histo-
         ryczne ku czci Stanisława Kutrzeby*
         II (Cracow: Nakładem Komitetu), 469-
         484.

1946a * *O pochodzeniu i praojczyźnie Słowian*   I:5
         Poznań: Wydawnictwo Instytutu Za-
         chodniego).

1946b * *Początki Słowian* (Cracow: Wydawnict-   I:5
         wo Studium Słowiańskiego U. J.).

1950   "Zagadnienie tzw. prajęzyków," *BPTJ*   VI:1
         10, 106-121.

1951a ** *Język polski. Pochodzenie, powsta-*   I:4
         nie, rozwój, 2nd ed. (Warsaw: Arct).   VI:3
         R transl. *Pol'skij jazyk* (Moscow:
         Izd-vo inostr. lit.), 1954.

1951b   "Powstanie, rozrost i rozpad wspól-   I:1
         noty prasłowiańskiej," *Przegląd Za-
         chodni* 7 (Poznań: Instytut Zachodni),
         350-378.

1952a ** "Przyczynek do zagadnienie genezy   II:5
         prasłowiańskiego *x*- nagłosowego,"   II:4
         *Sprawozdania Polskiej Akademii
         Umiejętności* 53, 343-344 (= *Studia
         i szkice*, 151-152).

1952b   "Zagadnienie rodzin językowych i ję-   VI:1
         zyka prasłowiańskiego w świetle dys-   I:1
         kusji językoznawczej w Związku
         Radzieckim (1950-1951)," *Slavia* 21,
         494-510 (=*Studia i szkice*, 25-41).

1953   * "Wspólnota językowa bałto-słowiańska VI:1
a problem etnogenezy Słowian," I:5
Slavia Antiqua 4, 1-21. Résumé in
Slovenski jezik (Ljubljana: Sla-
vistično društvo), 1952/53, 35-38
(=*Studia i szkice*, 174-190).

1954   * "Próba datowania tzw. II palatali- II:4
zacji spółgłosek tylnojęzykowych w VI:2
języku prasłowiańskim," *Studia z filologii polskiej i słowiańskiej* 1
(Warsaw: PWN), 375-383 (=*Studia i
szkice*, 159-167).

1955   "Problem ugrupowania języków sło- I:2
wiańskich," *BPTJ* 14, 112-121 (= VI:3
Studia i szkice, 42-51).

1956a   ** "Bemerkungen zu N. van Wijks Perio- VI:2
disierung des Urslavischen," *WslJb*
5, 5-9.

1956b   * "Kilka uwag o stosunkach językowych VI:1
celtycko-prasłowiańskich," *RS* 18,
1-10.

1956c   "Nacrt na istorijata na prasloven- I:1
skiot jazik," *Makedonski jazik* 7:2,
145-173.

1957a   * "O pochodzeniu prasłowiańskich róż- II:2
nic intonacyjnych," *Studia i szkice*,
141-144.

1957b   *Studia i szkice wybrane* (Warsaw:
PAN).

1957c   * "Z dziejów języka prasłowiańskiego VI:2
(Urywek z większej całości)," *Ezikovedski izsledvanija* . . ., 255-261.

1957/58 * "Zur Frage nach der Stellung des VI:1
Slavischen und des Tocharischen in-
nerhalb der indoeuropäischen Spra-
chenwelt," *WslJb* 6, 138-146.

1958a   * "Balto-slavjanskaja jazykovaja obšč- VI:1
nost' i problema étnogeneza Slavjan," I:5
VslJa 3, 5-14.

1958b   * "Podstawy indoeuropejskiej wspólnoty VI:1
językowej bałto-słowiańskiej," *Z
polskich studiów slawistycznych.
Prace językoznawcze i etnogenetyczne
na IV Międzynarodowy Kongres Slawistów w Moskwie 1958*, P. Zwoliński, ed.
(Warsaw: PWN), 125-136.

1958c   ** "Szkic dziejów języka prasłowiań-   I:1
              skiego," *Studia z filologii polskiej*   VI:1
              i słowiańskiej 3 (Warsaw: PWN), 243-   VI:2
              265.

1960a   * "K sovremennomu sostojaniju problemy   I:5
              proisxoždenija slavjan," *VJa* 4, 20-
              30.

1960b   "Rozmieszczenie geograficzne prasło-   I:5
              wiańskich nazw wodnych," *RS* 21, 5-
              22.

1964a   * "O severo-vostočynyx okrainax pra-   VI:1
              slavjanskogo jazyka. (Po povodu   I:5
              knigi V. N. Toporova i O. N. Truba-
              čeva o gidronimike verxnego Podnep-
              rov'ja)," *VJa* 1, 134-136.

1964b   "Z zagadnień językowych północno-   VI:1
              indoeuropejskich," *RS* 23, 3-17.

1965   ** "Szczątki odmiany medialnej w koniu-   III:2:5
              gacji prasłowiańskiej," *Studia z*   VI:1
              filologii polskiej i słowiańskiej
              5 (Warsaw: PWN), 59-62.

Lehr-Spławiński, T. & F. Sławski
1958   * "Z pracowni Słownika prasłowiań-   V:1
              skiego," *RS* 20, 1-15.

Lehr-Spławiński, T. & K. Polański
1962-   * *Słownik etymologiczny języka Drze-*   V:1
              wian połabskich. 1- (Wrocław-Warsaw-
              Cracow: Ossolineum).

Lehr-Spławiński, T., P. Zwoliński & S. Hrabec
1956   ** *Dzieje języka ukraińskiego w za-*   I:4
              rysie, T. Lehr-Spławiński, ed. (War- VI:3
              saw: PWN).

Lehr-Spławiński, T., W. Kuraszkiewicz & F. Sławski
1954   ** *Przegląd i charakterystyka języków*   I:2
              słowiańskich (Warsaw: PWN).

Lekov, I.
1934   * *Praslavjanskite glagolni formi i*   III:5
              otraženijata im v dnešnite slavjan-   VI:3
              skite ezici (Sofia: BAN).

1960   ** *Nasoki v razvoja na fonologičnite*   II:1
              sistemi na slavjanskite ezici   I:2
              (Sofia: BAN).

Leskien, A.
1919a   ** *Grammatik der altbulgarischen (alt-* I:4
              kirchenslavischen) Sprache, 2. u. 3. VI:3
              Auflage (Heidelberg: Winter).

1919b   * *Litauisches Lesebuch. Mit Grammatik*   I:3
             und Wörterbuch (Heidelberg: Winter).   VI:1

1962   ** *Handbuch der altbulgarishen (alt-*   I:4
             kirchenslavischen) Sprache. Gram-   VI:3
             matik-Texte-Glossar, 8. verbesserte
             und erweiterte Auflage, ^{5}1910, post-
             humous eds. ^{6}1922 & ^{7}1955 (Heidel-
             berg: Winter).

Leumann, M.
1955   * "Baltisch und Slawisch," *Corolla*   VI:1
             Linguistica. Festschrift Ferdinand
             Sommer zum 80. Geburtstag am 4. Mai
             1955 (Wiesbaden: Harrassowitz), 154-
             162 (= *Kleine Schriften*, Zürich-
             Stuttgart: Artemis, 1959, 389-398).

Liewehr, F.
1956   "Einiges über slawische Flexionsen-   III:2:4
             dungen," *ZfSl* 1:3, 10-21.   III:2:5

1963   * "Besonderheiten der -*en*- und -*ū*-   III:3:4
             Stämme im Slawischen," *ZfSl* 8, 874-   III:2:4
             878.

Lightner, T. M.
1966   ** "On the Phonology of the Old Church   II:1
             Slavonic Conjugation," *IJSLP* 10,   III:2:5
             1-28.   VI:3

Lingua viget . . .
1965   *Lingua viget. Commentationes slavi-*
             cae in honorem V. Kiparsky, I. Vah-
             ros & M. Kahla, eds. (Helsinki: Suo-
             malaisen Kirjallisuuden Kirjapaino
             Oy Helsinki).

Ljapuškin, I. I.
1968   * *Slavjane Vostočnoj Evropy nakanune*   I:5
             obrazovanija Drevnerusskogo gosu-
             darstva (VIII - pervaja polovina IX
             v.). Istoriko-arxeologičeskie očerki
             (= *AN SSSR. Institut Arxeologii.*
             Materialy i issledovanija po arxeo-
             logii SSSR 152) (Leningrad: "Nauka").

Lohmann, J. F.
1930   * "Zum slavischen Gen. Sing. der *ā*-   III:2:4
             Deklination," *ZfslPh* 7, 372-377.   II:5

Lotko, E.
1965   * "O powstaniu i dyferencjacji języków   VI:3
             słowiańskich (metodą glottochronolo-
             gii)," *RS* 24, 21-24.

Lunt, H. G.
1956   ** "On the Origins of Phonemic Pala-   II:4
           talization in Slavic," *For Roman*   VI:3
           Jakobson (The Hague: Mouton), 306-
           315.
1963   * "On the Study of Slavic Accentua-   II:2
           tion," *Word* 19, 82-99.
1966a   * Review of *A Prehistory of Slavic:*   II:1
           The Historical Phonology of Common
           Slavic by G. Y. Shevelov, *SEEJ* 10,
           85-92.
1966b   ** "Old Church Slavonic '*kraljь'?,"   V:4
           Orbis Scriptus, 483-489.   VI:3
1968   * *Old Church Slavonic Grammar*, 5th ed.   I:4
           [6th ed., completely revised & extend-
           ed, 1974] (=*Slavistic Printings and*   VI:3
           Reprintings 3) (The Hague: Mouton).

Lüdtke, H.
1959   ** "Das prosodische System des Ursla-   II:2
           vischen und seine Weiterentwicklung   VI:3
           im Serbokroatischen," *Phonetica*,
           Supplementum ad Vol. 4, *Symposion*
           Trubetzkoy, 125-156.
1966   ** "Gibt es urslavische Auslautge-   II:5
           setze?," *Annali dell'Istituto Uni-*   III:2
           versitario Orientale, *Sezione Slava.*
           Napoli 9, 117-141.

Lytkin, V. I.
1965   * "Ešče k voprosu o proisxoždenii   II:3
           russkogo akan'ja," *VJa* 4, 44-52.   VI:3
                                                      VI:2

Łoś, J. (Los', I.)
1890   "Ob udvoenii v oblasti cerkovno-   III:3
           slavjanskago jazyka," *RFV* 23, 55-76.   VI:3

Machek, V.
1937   ** "Zur Herkunft der slavischen Verbal-   III:5
           klasse auf -*ujǫ*//-*ovati*," *ZfslPh* 14,
           272-278.
1938   * "Die Herkunft des *nǫ*-Stammes in der   III:5
           slavischen II. Verbalklasse," *ZfslPh*
           15, 85-92.
1939   ** "Untersuchungen zum Problem des an-   II:5
           lautenden *ch* im Slavischen," *Slavia*   II:4
           16, 161-219.
1942   ** "Die Stämme der slavischen Verba auf   III:5
           -*ěti* und -*iti*," *ZfslPh* 18, 61-72.

1949	*	"Origine des thèmes nominaux en -ęt- du slave," *Lingua Posnaniensis* 1, 87-98.	III:3:4
1951/52	**	"Slav. *bǫdǫ* 'ich werde sein'," *ZfslPh* 21, 154-158.	III:5 IV:2 V:3
1956		"Slav. *ot-*, balt. *at-*," *ZfSl* 1, 3-10	V:3 VI:1 II:3
1957a	**	"Etyma latino-slavica," *Ezikovedski izsledvanija* . . ., 355-362.	V:2 V:3 VI:1
1957b	*	*Etymologický slovník jazyka českého a slovenského* (Prague: ČSAV).	V:1
1957c	*	"Slavische Verba mit suffixalem *sk*," *SR* 10, 67-80.	III:5 IV:2
1958a	*	"Sur l'origine des aspects verbaux en slave," *Slavjanskaja filologija. Sbornik statej* 3, *posvjaščennyj IV Meždunarodnomu s"ezdu slavistov*, V. V. Vinogradov *et al.*, eds. (Moscow: Izd-vo AN SSSR), 38-60.	III:3:5 IV:2
1958b	*	"Zur Erklärung der sog. Baudouin-schen Palatalisierung im Slavischen und im Baltischen," *Mélanges linguistiques offerts à Emil Petrovici*, 327-335.	II:4 VI:1 VI:2
1961	**	"Nochmals über die Adjektivdubletten auf -*ont* im Slavischen," *ZfSl* 6, 579-587.	III:3:4 V:3 VI:1
1963	*	"Zur Frage der slawisch-keltischen sprachlichen Beziehungen," *Studia linguistica* . . ., 109-120.	VI:1
1964	*	"Alternance *ǫ//u* en slave -- affaire du traitement des consonnes gemi-nées?," *PF* 18:2, 57-66.	II:3
1965a	**	"Mots slaves a *k^s* indo-européen," *Symbolae linguisticae* . . ., 192-198.	II:4 VI:1
1965b	**	"Slaw. *bǫdǫ*, Hilfsverbum zur Bildung des analytischen Futurums," *Studia z filologii polskiej i słowiańskiej* 5 (Warsaw: PWN), 67-75.	III:5 IV:2 V:3
1965c	*	"Zu den slavischen Benennungen fur unfreie Personen," *Lingua viget*, 90-96.	V:3 V:2

1968   ** "Sl. *gospodь*, lat. *hospes* et lit.   V:2
               viešpats," *Slavica* 8, 155-158.   V:3
                                                III:3:4
                                              VI:1

Mańczak, W.

1966   ** "Contraction des voyelles dans les   II:3
               langues slaves," *AnzfslPh* 1, 52-58.   VI:3
                                                II:5
                                                VI:2

1967   * "Rozwój końcówki 3 os. ind. praes.
              w językach słowiańskich," *BPTJ* 25,   III:2:5
              193-202.   II:5

1969   ** "Nieregularny rozwój fonetyczny
               spowodowany częstością użycia w pra-   II:1
               słowiańskim," *Slavia* 38, 52-62.   II:5

1970a   * "Prawo nieregularnego rozwoju fone-   II:5
              tycznego spowodowanego frekwencją,"   II:1
              Z zagadnień językoznawstwa ogólnego   III:2
              (Wrocław-Warsaw-Cracow: Ossolineum),   III:1
              62-94.

1970b   ** "W sprawie końcówek prasłowiań-   II:5
               skich," *Slavia* 39, 218-222.   III:2

Mann, S. E.

1957   ** *Czech Historical Grammar* (London: I:4
               Athlone Press).   VI:3
                                                I:3

1958/59   * "Initial *X/Š* in the Slavonic Lan-   II:5
               guages," *SEER* 37, 131-140.   II:4

Mareš, F. V.

1956   * "Vznik slovanského fonologického   II:1
              systému a jeho vývoj do konce období
              slovanské jazykové jednoty," *Slavia*
              25, 443-495.

1958a   * "Palatalizacija slavjanskix veljar-   II:4
              nyx i al'veoljarnyx soglasnyx v   VI:3
              sočetanii s *u - v* (*cvětь, zvězda,*
              umr'štvenь)," *Mélanges linguistiques*
              offerts à Emil Petrovici, 345-351.

1958b   * "Vývoj skupiny *gn* (*kn*) v období slo-   II:4
              vanské jazykové jednoty," *Českoslo-*
              venské přednášky pro IV. Mezinárodní
              sjezd slavistů v Moskvě, K. Horálek,
              ed. (Prague: Nakl. ČSAV), 109-123.

1959   * "Střídnice *i*-ových a *u*-ových dif-   II:3
              thongů v období slovanské jazykové
              jednoty," *Slavia* 28, 347-349.

1962a   ** "Rannij period morfologičeskogo raz-   III:2:4
vitija slavjanskogo sklonenija," *VJa*
6, 13-21.

1962b   ** "The Slavic Verbal Forms of the 3rd   III:5
Person Plural '*bǫdǫ*' and '*bǫ*',"
IJSLP 4, 28-30.

1963a   * "Powstanie i wczesny rozwój deklina-   III:2:4
cji słowiańskiej," *Zeszyty naukowe
Uniwersytetu Jagiellońskiego* 60 (=
Prace językoznawcze 5), 423-428.

1963b   * "Proisxoždenie slavjanskogo nosovogo   II:3
ǫ (*jǫ*)," *VslJa* 7, 7-11.

1963c   * "Słowiański celownik liczby pojedyn-   III:2:4
czej," *Studia linguistica* . . .,
121-125.

1963d   ** "Vznik a raný vývoj slovanské dekli-   III:2:4
nace," *Československé přednášky pro
V. Mezinárodní sjezd slavistů v
Sofii*, B. Havránek, ed. (Prague:
Nakl. ČSAV), 51-69.

1964   ** "The Proto-Slavic and Early Slavic   III:2:4
Declension System," *TLP* 1, 163-172.

1965a   * *Die Entstehung des slavischen pho-*   II:1
*nologischen Systems und seine Ent-
wicklung bis zum Ende der Periode
der slavischen Spracheinheit* (Munich: Sagner).

1965b   * *The Origin of the Slavic Phonologi-*   II:1
*cal System and Its Development Up To
the End of Slavic Language Unity*,
transl. by J. F. Snopek & A. Vitek
(= *Michigan Slavic Materials* 6) (Ann
Arbor: Dept. of Slavic Langs. &
Lits.).

1967a   * "K metodice etymologického bádáni: V:2
Etymologie některých slovanských
pojmenování ptáků onomatopoického
původu," *Slavia* 36, 345-373.

1967b   ** "The Historic Development of the   III:2:4
Slavic Noun Declension. 1. The Sys-   IV:2
tem of Categories," *Slavia* 36, 485-   VI:3
506.

1968   ** "The Historic Development of the   III:2:4
Slavic Noun Declension. 2. The De-   VI:3
velopment of Forms," *Československé
přednášky pro VI. Mezinárodní sjezd*

        slavistů v Praze, B. Havránek, ed.
        (Prague: Academia, Nakl. ČSAV), 37–
        46.

1969   ** *Diachronische Phonologie des Ur- und*   II:1
          Frühslavischen (Munich: Sagner).

1971a   ** "Chronologie změny $g > \gamma > h$ [v]   II:4
          slovanských jazycích," *Miscellanea*   VI:2
          Linguistica, Acta Universitatis Pa-   VI:3
          lackianae Olomucensis - facultas
          philosophica (Ostrave: Profil), 27–
          31.

1971b   ** "Kontrakce vokálů v slovanských ja-   II:3
          zycích," *Slavia* 40, 525–536.   VI:3
                                             II:5
                                           VI:2

Martinet, A.
1951   "Concerning Some Slavic and Aryan   II:4
          Reflexes of IE *s*," *Word* 7, 91–95.   VI:1

1952   ** "Langues à syllabes ouvertes: le
          cas du slave commun," *Zeitschrift*   II:5
          für Phonetik und allgemeine Sprach-
          wissenschaft 6, 145–163.

1955   ** *Économie des changements phonétiques*   II:5
          (Berne: Francke).

Martynov, V. V.
1961   * "K lingvističeskomu obosnovaniju   I:5
          gipotezy o vislo-oderskoj prarodine   V:4
          slavjan," *VJa* 3, 51–59.

1963a   * *Lingvističeskie metody obosnovanija*   I:5
          gipotezy o vislo-odrskoj prarodine   V:4
          slavjan (Minsk: Izd-vo AN BSSR).

1963b   ** *Slavjano-germanskoe leksičeskoe*   V:4
          vzaimodejstvie drevnejšej pory. K   I:5
          probleme prarodiny slavjan (Minsk:
          Izd-vo BSSR).

1968   ** *Slavjanskaja i indo-evropejskaja*   II:4
          akkomodacija (Minsk: "Nauka i Tex-"   VI:1
          nika").

1971   ** "Analiz po semantičeskim mikrosis-   V:3
          temam i rekonstrukcija praslavjan-
          skoj leksiki," *Ètimologija 1968*
          (Moscow: "Nauka"), 11–23.

Marvan, J.
1966   * "Z historie kontrakce. Osud intervo-   II:4
          kalického *j*," *Slavia* 35, 345–356.   II:3
                                               II:5

1968a   * "Kontrakce a Konjugace," *LF* 91, 163-   III:2:5
169.   II:3
   VI:3

1968b   ** "Kontrakce období rozpadu slovanské   VI:3
jednoty," *Československé přednášky*   II:3
pro VI. Mezinárodní sjezd slavistů
v Praze, B. Havránek, ed. (Prague:
Academia, Nakl. ČSAV), 11-15.

1968c   * "Kontrakce v systému slovanských   II:3
izoglos," *Slavia* 37, 1-20.   VI:3
   II:5
   VI:2

1968d   * "Místo slovanské kontrakce ve vý-   II:3
voji systému," *Slavia* 37, 210-225.   VI:3
   II:5
   VI:2

1971   ** "Some Structural Aspects of the De-   II:3
velopment of Jers," *ScSl* 17, 249-   II:5
258.   VI:2
   VI:3

1972   ** "On the Morphologic Disintegration   VI:3
of Slavic Unity. Morphologic De-   III:1
velopment of the Contraction,"   III:2
Slavic Word, 312-334.

Maslov, J. S.
1959   * "Zur Entstehungsgeschichte des sla-   III:3:5
wischen Verbalaspektes," *ZfSl* 4,   IV:2
560-568.

1961   * "Rol' tak nazyvaemoj perfektivacii   III:3:5
i imperfektivacii v processe voz-   IV:2
niknovenija slavjanskogo glagol'nogo
vida," *Issledovanija po slavjanskomu*
jazykoznaniju, N. I. Tolstoj, ed.
(Moscow: Izd-vo AN SSSR), 165-195.

Mathiassen, T.
1969   ** "On the Problem of Lengthened Ablaut   II:3
Degree and the Slavic Sigmatic Ao-   III:5
rist," *ScSl* 15, 201-214.

1970a   ** "Baltisch und Slawisch. Zur Chrono-   II:3
logie und Bedeutung der Kürzung lan-   VI:1
ger Diphthonge," *Donum Balticum*,   VI:2
322-333.

1970b   * *Studien zum slavischen und indo-*   II:3
europäischen Langvokalismus (Oslo: VI:1
Universitetsforlaget).

Mátl, A.
1954   ** "Abstraktní význam u nejstarších   V:3
            vrstev slovanských substantiv (kmenů   III:3:4
            souhláskových)," *K šedesátým naroze-*
            ninám akademika Bohuslava Havránka
            (= *Studie a práce linguistické* 1)
            (Prague: Nakl. ČSAV), 131-151.

Matthews, W. K. (Mět'jus, V. K.)
1957   * "The Phonetic Basis of Pleophony in   II:3
            East Slavonic," *SEER* 36, 94-99.   VI:3
1958   * "O vzaimootnošenii slavjanskix i
            baltijskix jazykov," *Slavjanskaja*   VI:1
            filologija, 27-44.
1960   ** *Russian Historical Grammar* (London: I:4
            Athlone Press).   VI:3

Mayer, A.
1939   ** "Die zeitliche Bestimmung der ur-   VI:2
            slavischen Periode," *Govori i Preda-*
            vanja. III Međunarodni Kongres Sla-
            vista (*Slovenskih Filologa*) (Bel-
            grade: Izdanja Izvršnog Odbora 4),
            45-55.

Mažiulis, V. (Mažjulis)
1958   * *Zametki k voprosu o drevnejšix otno-*   VI:1
            šenijax baltijskix i slavjanskix
            jazykov (Vilnius: Gos. izd-vo polit.
            i naučn. lit. Litovskoj SSR).
1965   * "Nekotorye fonetičeskie aspekty bal-   III:2
            to-slavjanskoj fleksii," *Baltistica*   II:5
            1, 17-30.   VI:1
1966   * "K balto-slavjanskoj forme dativa
            (mn. i dv. č.)," *Baltistica* 2, 43-   III:2:4
            53.   VI:1

Meillet, A. (Meje)
1897   * *Recherches sur l'emploi du génetif-*   IV:2
            accusatif en vieux-slave (= *Biblio-* III:2:4
            thèque de l'École des hautes études   VI:3
            publiée sous les auspices du Minis-
            tère de l'instruction publique.
            Sciences philologiques et histo-
            riques 115) (Paris: É. Bouillon).
1902   * "O nekotoryx anomalijax udarenija v   II:2
            slavjanskix imenax," *Sbornik statej*   III:4
            posvjaščennyx učenikami i počita-
            teljami akad. F. F. Fortunatovu (=
            RFV 48) (Warsaw: Tipografija Varšav-

skago Učebnago Okruga), 193-200.

1902/05 ** *Études sur l'étymologie et le voca-*   III:3
bulaire du vieux slave (Première   V:2
partie, 1902; Seconde partie, 1905   IV:2
(= *Bibliothèque de l'École des
hautes études publiée sous les auspices du Ministère de l'instruction
publique. Sciences historiques et
philologiques* 139) (Paris: É. Bouil-
lon); [2]1961 (Paris: Librairie Champion).

1903   ** *Introduction a l'étude comparative*   I:3
des langues indo-européennes, [8]1937,
reprint 1949 (Paris: Librairie Ha-
chette).

1906/08   * "Les alternances vocaliques en vieux   II:6
slave," *MSL* 14, 193-209.   II:3

1908a   ** *Les dialectes indo-européens* (Paris: I:3
Librairie Champion). E transl. by S.   VI:1
N. Rosenberg, *The Indo-European Dialects* (University, Alabama: University of Alabama Press), 1967.

1908b   "Notes sur quelques formes verbales   III:2:5
slaves," *MSL* 15, 32-59.

1908c   "Sur l'aoriste sigmatique," *Mélanges*   III:2:5
*de linguistique offerts à M. Ferdi-
nand de Saussure* (= *Collection Linguistique publiée par la Société de
Linguistique de Paris* 2) (Paris:
Librairie Champion), 81-106

1913   * "Sur la flexion des démonstratifs   III:2:4
slaves au féminin pluriel et duel,"
MSL 18, 432-436.

1914/15   * "De quelques finales slaves," *RS* 7,   II:5
1-8.   II:3

1916   * "Sur le traitement de *o* en syllabe   II:5
finale slave," *MSL* 19, 282-289.   II:3

1920a   ** "À propos du genre grammatical en   IV:2
slave," *RS* 9, 18-23.   III:2:4

1920b   "L'unité linguistique slave," *Scien-*   I:1
tia 27 (Bologna: Nicola Zanichelli),
41-51.

1921   "De l'unité slave," *RES* 1, 7-14.   I:1

1922a   "Des innovations charactéristiques   II:1
du phonétisme slave," *RES* 2, 206-
213.

1922b	** "Des innovations du verbe slave," *RES* 2, 38-46.	III:5
1922c	* "Du nominatif-accusatif masculin en slave commun," *BSL* 23, 87-93.	III:2:4 IV:2
1922d	* "Sur *ju-* initial en slave," *Slavia* 1, 197-199.	II:5 II:4 II:3
1923	** "Les formes nominales en slave," *RES* 3, 103-204.	III:4 IV:2
1924	** *Le slave commun*, ²1934, reviewed and augmented in collaboration with A. Vaillant (Paris: Librairie Champion). Russian transl. (Meje) *Obščeslavjanskij jazyk*, perevod i primečanija P. S. Kuznecova (Moscow: Izd-vo inostr. lit.), 1951	I:1
1925a	* "Les origines du vocabulaire slave. I. Le problème de l'unité balto-slave," *RES* 5, 5-13.	V:2 VI:1
1925b	* "Les origines du vocabulaire slave. II. De quelques noms de nombre," *RES* 5, 177-182.	V:2 III:3:4
1926	* "Le vocabulaire slave et le vocabulaire indo-iranien," *RES* 6, 165-174.	V:4 V:2 VI:1
1927	* "De quelques anciennes alternances vocaliques," *BSL* 27:1, 124-128.	II:6 II:3

Mélanges . . .

1958   *Mélanges linguistiques offerts à Emil Petrovici par ses amis étrangers à l'occasion de son soixantième anniversaire* (= *Cercetări de lingvistică* 3, *Supliment*) (Cluj: Editura Academiei Republicii Populare Romîne).

1937   *Mélanges linguistiques offerts à M. Holger Pedersen à l'occasion de son 70-ième anniversaire 7 avril 1937* (= *Acta Jutlandica* 9) (Aarhus: Universitetsforlaget; Copenhagen: Levin & Munksgaard).

Mel'nyčuk, O. S. (Mel'ničuk, A. S.)

1968   "Koren' *kes-* i ego raznovidnosti v   V:2
        leksike slavjanskix i drugix indoev-
        ropejskix jazykov," *Ètimologija 1966*
        194-240.

Menges, K. H.
1966 ** "Wieder einmal zum slavischen Wort   V:4
           für 'Kirche'," *Orbis Scriptus*, 543-
           550.
Merkulova, V. A.
1963 * "Slav. *-žab-; praslav. *žarovъji   V:2
           'vysokij, prjamoj'," *Ètimologija*,
           72-80.
1965a * "O nekotoryx principax ètimologii   V:2
           nazvanij rastenij," *Ètimologija 1964*, V:3
           72-87.
1965b * "Ob otnositel'noj xronologii sla-   V:2
           vjanskix nazvanij gribov (Voprosy   V:3
           lingvističeskoj rekonstrukcii i re-   VI:2
           konstrukcii material'noj kul'tury),"
           Ètimologija 1964, 88-99.
1971 * "Zametki po istorii i ètimologii   V:2
           slov," *Ètimologija 1968*, 79-   V:3
           91.
Meyer, K. H.
1920 * *Slavische und indogermanische Into-*   II:2
           nation (= *Slavica* 2) (Heidelberg: VI:1
           Winter).
Mikkola, J. J.
1904 * "Woher lit. *iau* und slav. *ju*?," *IF*   II:3
           16, 95-101.   VI:1
1913/ ** *Urslavische Grammatik: Einführung in*   I:1
42/50   *das vergleichende Studium der slavi-*
           schen Sprachen. I: *Lautlehre, Voka-*
           lismus, Betonung, 1913; II: *Konso-*
           nantismus, 1942; III: *Formenlehre*,
           1950 (Heidelberg: Winter).
1921 * "La question des syllabes ouvertes   II:5
           en slave commun," *RES* 1, 15-19.
1937 * "Zum slavischen Suffix *-dlo*," *Mé-*   III:3:4
           langes linguistiques offerts à M.
           Holger Pedersen, 409-413.
Miklosich, F. (Miklošič)
1852/ * *Vergleichende Grammatik der slavi-*   I:2
1926   *schen Sprachen.* I: *Lautlehre*, 1852,
           ²1879; II: *Stammbildungslehre*, 1875;
           III: *Formenlehre/Wortbildungslehre*,
           1856, ²1876; IV: *Syntax*, 1868/74
           (Vienna: Wilhelm Braumüller). Manul-
           neudruck der Erstausgabe, 1926, vols.
           II and IV only (Heidelberg: Carl

401

Winter).

Milewski, T.
1927   * "Przyczynki do fonetyki lechickiej.   II:3
            1. W sprawie rozwoju prasł. grupy   VI:3
            tort w lechickie *tart*. 2. Nagłosowa
            grupa *ja*," *PF* 14, 582-590.

1929   * "Przyczynek do charakterystyki wy-   II:3
            mowy prasł. *y*," *Sprawozdania z
            czynności i posiedzeń PAU w Krakowie*
            34, 14-20.

1931a   ** "Drobiazgi z fleksji prasłowiań-   III:2:4
            skiej," *PF* 15, 265-274.   III:2:5
                                                     II:5

1931b   * "O powstaniu prasłowiańskich samo-
            głosek nosowych," *RS* 10, 80-115.   II:3

1932   ** "Rozwój fonetyczny wygłosu prasło-   II:5
            wiańskiego," *Slavia* 11, 1-32; 225-   II:3
            264.

1933   * "O zastępstwie ps. grup *tårt*, *tålt*, II:3
            tert, *telt* w językach lechickich,"   VI:3
            SlOcc 12, 96-120.

1937a   * "Kilka uwag o genezie aspektów sło-   III:3:5
            wiańskich," *Zbornik lingvističkih i   IV:2
            filoloških rasprava . . . .*, 431-438.

1937b   Review of "Die Palatalisierung von   II:4
            k, *g*, *ch* im Slavischen" by R. Ek-
            blom, *RS* 13, 8-20.

1938   * "O genezie aspektów słowiańskich,"   II:3:5
            RS 15, 1-13 + "Uwaga" by J. Safare-   IV:2
            wicz, 13-14.

1950   * "Paralele hetycko-słowiańskie w   VI:1
            ewolucji kategorii rodzaju," *RS* 16,   IV:2
            14-24.

1960/61   "Dwa ujęcia problemu granic prasło-   I:5
            wiańskiego obszaru językowego," *RS*   VI:1
            21, 41-76.   VI:3

1962/63   * "Pochodzenie słowiańskich imion   III:3:4
            osobowych z pierwiastkiem werbalnym   IV:3
            w pierwszym członie," *RS* 22, 3-11.

1965   ** "Ewolucja prasłowiańskiego systemu   II:3
            wokalicznego," *RS* 24, 5-18 (= *Z za-
            gadnień językoznawstwa ogólnego i
            historycznego*, Warsaw: PWN, 1969,
            309-326).

1966   ** "Zasięg terytorialny słowiańskiej   VI:3
            przestawki płynnych," *RS* 26, 9-20   II:3

(= *Z zagadnień językoznawstwa ogól-* II:4
nego i historycznego, Warsaw: PWN,
1969, 327-341).

1967   * "The Evolution of the Common Slavic II:3
[Vowel] System," *To Honor Roman Ja-
kobson* II, 1362-1372.

Mirčev, K.
1963   ** *Istoričeska gramatika na bălgarskija* I:4
ezik, 2nd ed. (Sofia: "Nauka i iz- VI:3
kustvo").

Mladenov, S.
1929   ** *Geschichte der bulgarischen Sprache* I:4
(Berlin-Leipzig: Walter de Gruyter). VI:3
1941   * *Etimologičeski i pravopisen rečnik* V:1
na bălgarskija knižoven ezik (Sofia:
Danov).

Moór, E.
1930   "Die slavischen Ortsnamen der I:5
Theissebene," *Zeitschrift für Orts-
namenforschung* 6, 3-37; 105-140.
1936   *Westungarn im Mittelalter im Spiegel* I:5
der Ortsnamen (Szeged: Städtische
Druckerei & Buchverlags A. G.).

Moszyński, K.
1957   * *Pierwotny zasiąg języka prastowiań-* I:5
skiego (Wrocław-Cracow: Ossolineum,
PAN).
1962   *O sposobach badania kultury mate-* I:5
rialnej Prastowian (Warsaw: Ossoli-
neum).

Moszyński, L (Mošinskij)
1960   * *Wyrównania deklinacyjne w związku z* II:4
mazurzeniem polskim, ruskim, potab- VI:3
skim (= *PAN*, *KJ*, *Prace Językoznawcze*
21) (Wrocław: Ossolineum).
1965a   "K fonologii prosodičeskix élementov II:2
v slavjanskix jazykax (O fonologi-
českoj nerelevantnosti izolirovan-
nogo prosodičeskogo priznaka)," *VJa*
2, 3-14.
1965b   ** "Przyczyny rozkładu prasłowiańskiego VI:3
systemu językowego," *Studia z filo-
logii polskiej i słowiańskiej* 5
(Warsaw: PWN), 77-85.
1969   ** "K razvitiju praslavjanskix sonan- II:3
tov," *VJa* 5, 3-10.   VI:1
                                 VI:3

Nahtigal, R.

1952   ** *Slovanski jeziki*, 2nd reviewed &   I:2
augmented ed. (Ljubljana: "Jože
Moškrič"). G transl. *Die slavischen
Sprachen: Abriss der vergleichenden
Grammatik* (Wiesbaden: Harrassowitz),
1961. Russian transl. *Slavjanskie
jazyki* (Moscow: Izd-vo inostr. lit.),
1963.

Nalepa, J.

1967/68 ** *Słowiańszczyzna północno-zachodnia.*   VI:3
Podstawy jedności i jej rozpad (=   I:5
Prace Komisji Historycznej 25) (Lund: VI:1
Duplica-Offset AB, Malmö, 1967;
Poznań: Poznańskie Tow. Przyjaciół
Nauk, Wydz. Hist. i Nauk Społeczn.,
1968).

Nandriş, G.

1959   ** *Old Church Slavonic Grammar* (London: I:4
Athlone Press).   VI:3

Němec, I. (J.)

1956   * "Kategorie determinovanosti a inde-   III:3:5
terminovanosti jako základ slovanské   IV:2
kategorie vidu," *Slavia* 25, 496-534.

1958   * *Geneze slovanského systému vidového*   III:3:5
(Prague: Nakl. ČSAV) (= *Rozpravy*   IV:2
ČSAV 68/7).

1964   * "K původu slovanských transitiv *n*-   III:3:5
ových," *PF* 18:2, 87-92.   IV:2

Nieminen, E. K.

1956   * "Slavisch (*j*)*ustro*, (*j*)*utro* und Ver-   V:2
wandte," *ScSl* 2, 13-28.   II:5
                                     II:4
                                     VI:1

1957a   * "Die urslavische Benennung der Be-
kleidung der Beine **gatję* bzw.   V:2
*gatjě," *ScSl* 3, 224-235.   V:3

1957b   ** "K voprosu o vlijanii praslavjan-   VI:1
skogo jazyka na pribaltijskofinskie   V:4
jazyki," *Beogradski Medunarodni*   VI:3
slavistički sastanak, 497-502.

1958   "Über ein vermeintliches urslavi-   V:4
sches Lehnwort im Ostseefinnischen,"
WdSl 3, 101-123.

Nitsch, K. (C.)

1926   * "Nature et chronologie de la seconde   II:4

                    palatalisation en slave commun," *RES*   VI:2
                    6, 42-53.
Noha, M.
    1924   * "Praslovanská dvojice -ę//-ě," *LF*   III:2:4
                    51, 244-263.   II:3
                                                             II:5
                                                             VI:3
    1927   "Zum Alter der urslavischen Nasal-   II:3
                    vokale," *ZfslPh* 4, 64-68.   VI:2
Nonnenmacher-Pribić, E.
    1961   * *Die baltoslavischen Akzent- und In-*   II:2
                    tonationsverhältnisse und ihr quan-   VI:1
                    titativer Reflex im Slovakischen   VI:3
                    (Wiesbaden: Harrassowitz).
Orbis Scriptus . . .
    1966   *Orbis Scriptus. Dmitrij Tschiževskij*
                    zum 70. Geburtstag, D. Gerhardt, W.
                    Weintraub & H.-J. zum Winkel, eds.
                    (Munich: Fink).
Orłoś, T. Z.
    1958   * "Element prasłowiański w dzisiejszym V:2
                    słownictwie czeskim," *Studia z filo-*
                    logii polskiej i słowiańskiej 3
                    (Warsaw: PWN), 267-283.
Orzechowska, H.
    1966   ** "Locativus pluralis na *-oxъ w języ-   III:2:4
                    kach słowiańskich," *RS* 26, 35-50.
Ossowski, L. (Ossovskij)
    1965   * "Tzw. prawo A. A. Szachmatowa w sło-   II:2
                    wiańskim," *Symbolae linguisticae* . . .,
                    220-222.
    1971   * "Zapadnoe Poles'e — prarodina sla-   I:5
                    vjan," *VJa* 1, 112-113.   VI:1
Otrębski, J. S. (Otrembskij)
    1921   * "Słowiańskie formacje na -ę//-ě i na   II:5
                    -y//-a," *Prace lingwistyczne ofiaro-*   III:2:4
                    wane Janowi Baudouinowi de Courtenay   VI:3
                    (Cracow: Drukarnia Uniwersytetu Ja-
                    giellońskiego), 10-16.
    1938   * "Über die Herkunft des slavischen   III:2:5
                    Imperfekts," *ZfslPh* 15, 302-311.   VI:1
    1948   * "Pochodzenie tzw. Baudouinowskiej
                    palatalizacji w językach słowiań-   II:4
                    skich," *SlOcc* 19, 23-62.   VI:2
    1954   * "Slavjano-baltijskoe jazykovoe   VI:1
                    edinstvo," *VJa* 5, 27-42; 6 28-46.

                                405

1957	* "O jedności językowej bałto-słowiań-	VI:1
	skiej," *BPTJ* 16, 70-113.	
1958	* "Rozwój wzajemnych stosunków między	VI:1
	grupą językowa bałtycką a słowiań-	
	ską," *Z polskich studiów slawistycz-*	
	nych 1 (Warsaw: PWN), 146-148.	
1966/67	* "Einige slavische Wörter mit nicht	III:3
	erkanntem infigiertem Nasal," *ZfslPh*	V:2
	33, 313-321.	
1969a	* "Aksl. *nyněšьнь* usw.," *ZfslPh* 34,	V:2
	350-353.	III:3:4
1969b	* "Aksl. *pěšь* und Verwandtes," *WdSl*	V:2
	14, 312-314.	III:3:4
1970a	* "Das expressive *ch* im Slavischen,"	
	WdSl 15, 51-60.	II:4
1970b	* "Die Sonderfälle der 2. slavischen	II:4
	Palatalisation," *ZfslPh* 35, 63-76.	VI:2
1970c	* "Lit *šakà* und Verwandtes," *Donum Bal-*	V:2
	ticum, 361-364.	II:4
		VI:1

Pătruţ, I.

1972	* "Pierwsze kontakty językowe słowiań-	VI:2
	sko-romańsko-greckie a okres trwania	VI:1
	języka prasłowiańskiego," *RS* 33, 7-	VI:3
	19.	II:3
		II:4

Pavlović, M.

1966/67	* "Simbioza procesa i diferenciranje	II:4
	praslovenskog *tj*, *dj*," *JF* 27, 143-	VI:3
	164.	

Peciar, Š.

1939	* "Otázka metathese likvid a klasifi-	II:3
	kace slov. jazyků," *Časopis pro Mo-*	VI:3
	derní Filologii a Literaturu 25	
	(Prague: Nakl. Klubu Moderních Filo-	
	logu), 272-285.	
1941	* "Vznik praslovan. slabičných likvidů	II:3
	ḷ, *ṛ*," *Linguistica Slovaca* 3, 49-	
	53.	
1952	* "Kritický prehl'ad prác o tzv. meta-	II:3
	téze likvid," *Jazykovedný sborník*	VI:3
	Slovenskej akadémie vied a umeni 6,	
	59-93.	

Pešikan, M

| 1966/67 | ** "O poreklu slovenskih akcenatskih | II:2 |
| | tipova. Osvrt na studiju sovetskog | |

akcentologa V. M. Iliča-Svitiča,"
JF 27, 237-266.

Petleva, I. P.
1969 * "Dopolnitel'nye resursy dlja rekon- V:2
strukcii praslavjanskoj leksiki (Na VI:3
materiale serboxorvatskogo jazyka),"
Ètimologija 1967, 173-179.

1971 * "Praslavjanskij sloj leksiki serbo- V:2
xorvatskogo jazyka, I," *Ètimologija* VI:3
1968, 114-156.

Pisani, V.
1961 ** *Glottologia indeuropea. Manuale di* I:3
grammatica comparata delle lingue
indeuropee con speciale riguardo del
greco e del latino, terza edizione
completamente riveduta accresciuta e
aggiornata (Torino: Rosenberg & Sel-
lier).

1969 * "Baltisch, Slavisch, Iranisch," *Bal-* VI:1
tistica 5, 133-140.

Piuk, K.
1950 "Zur Frage der Slaven in Pannonien I:5
im 9. Jahrhundert," *WslJb* 1, 112-
130.

Plevačevá, H. (G.)
1968 * "K slav. *žabrьjь," *Ètimologija 1966*, V:2
90-96.

Pokorny, J.
1959/69 * *Indogermanisches etymologisches Wör-* V:1
terbuch. I, 1959; II: *Vorrede, Re-*
gister, Abkürzungen, 1969 (Berne-
Munich: Francke).

Polák, V.
1969 * "Die Entstehung des Urslavischen im I:5
Lichte der neueren Forschung," *Das* VI:1
heidnische und christliche Slaventum
(= *Annales Instituti Slavici*, F. Za-
giba, ed., II/1) (Wiesbaden: Harrassowitz), 26-33.

Popović, I.
1950 "Die Einwanderung der Slaven in das I:5
Oströmische Reich im Lichte der
Sprachforschung," *ZfSl* 4, 705-721.
1960 ** *Geschichte der serbokroatischen* I:4
Sprache (Wiesbaden: Harrassowitz). VI:3

Popowska-Taborska, H.

1970   * Review of *Słowiańszczyzna płtnocno-*   VI:3
           zachodnia by J. Nalepa, *RS* 31, 78-   I:5
           88.   VI:1

Porzeziński, W. (Poržezinskij, V.)

1911   * "Die baltisch-slavische Sprachge-   VI:1
           meinschaft," *RS* 4, 1-26.

1914   * *Sravnitel'naja grammatika slavjan-*   I:2
           skix jazykov. Vyp. I: *Vvedenie.*   I:1
           Obščeslavjanskij jazyk v světě dan-   VI:1
           nyx sravitel'noistoričeskoj gramma-
           tiki indoevropejskix jazykov (*Fone-*
           tika. Formy sklonenija), ^{2}1916 (Mos-
           cow: Tipografija T-va I. N. Kušnerev
           i Ko.).

Porzig, W.

1954   ** *Die Gliederung des indogermanischen*   I:3
           Sprachgebiets (Heidelberg: Winter).   VI:1

Pravdin, A. B.

1957   ** "K voprosu o praslavjanskix značeni-   IV:2
           jax datel'nogo padeža," *VJa* 6, 81-   III:2:4
           83.

Preobraženskij, A. G.

1910/   * *Etimologičeskij slovar' russkogo*   V:1
49/58   *jazyka.* I: A-O; II: P-S (Moscow:
           Tipografija G. Lissnera & D. Sovko)
           + *Trudy Instituta russkogo jazyka*
           I: telo-jaščur, 1949 (Moscow-Lenin-
           grad: AN SSSR) = *Etimologičeskij*
           slovar' russkogo jazyka (Moscow:
           Gos. izd-vo inostrannyx i nacional'-
           nyx slovarej), 1958.

Preveden, F. R.

1932   * "Some Balto-Slavic Terms of Acoustic   V:2
           Perceptions," *Language* 8, 145-151.   V:3
                                         VI:1

Radewa, S.

1963   * "Element prasłowiański w dzisiejszym   V:2
           słownictwie bułgarskim," *Studia z*
           filologii polskiej i słowiańskiej 4
           (Warsaw: PWN), 141-199.

Rakstu krājums . . .

1959   *Rakstu krājums veltījums akadēmiķim*
           profesoram Dr. Jānim Endzelīnam viņa
           85 drīves un 65 darba gadu atcerei
           (Riga: Latvijas PSR Zinātņu Akadēmi-

jas Izdevniecība).

Ramovš, F.

1924/35	**	*Historična gramatika slovenskega je-* *zika.* II: *Konzonantizem*, 1924; VII: *Dialekti*, 1935 (Ljubljana:"Učitelj-ska Tiskarna").	I:4 VI:3 II:4
1927	*	"O naravi psl. *tort* in *tert* v pra-slovenščini," *Časopis za slovenski jezik, književnost in zgodovino* 6 (Ljubljana: "Učiteljska Tiskarna"), 22-26.	II:3
1936	**	*Kratka zgodovina slovenskega jezika* I (Ljubljana: Akademska založba).	I:4 VI:3 II:3
1944	*	"Fonetična vrednost psl. *ě*," *Razpra-ve Akademije Znanosti in Umetnosti v Ljubljani, Filozofsko-filološko-historični razred* 2, 211-224.	II:3
1950	*	"Relativna kronologija slovenskih akcentskih pojavov," *SR* 3, 16-23.	II:2 VI:2
1951	*	"O praslovanski metatoniji," *SR* 4, 157-161.	II:2
1952	**	*Morfologija slovenskega jezika* (Ljubljana: Državna založba Slove-nije).	I:4 VI:3 III:1

Red'kin, V. A.

1962		"K voprosu o proisxoždenii novogo akuta," *VJa* 2, 56-62.	II:2

Regnéll, C. G.

1944	**	*Über den Ursprung des slavischen Verbalaspektes* (Lund: Håkan Ohlssons boktryckeri).	III:3:5 IV:2

Reichenkron, G.

1961		"Urslavisch *ŏ* im Rumänischen," *WdSl* 6, 40-54.	II:3 VI:1

Rigler, J.

1964	*	"K probleme akan'ja," *VJa* 5, 36-45.	II:3 VI:3 VI:2
1969	*	"Obščeslavjanskoe značenie problemy akan'ja," *VJa* 3, 47-58.	II:3 VI:3 VI:2

Romportl, M.

1953	*	"Zůstaly v češtině stopy praslovan-ských intonací?," *Slavia* 22, 361-368.	II:2 VI:3

Rosenkranz, B.
1955   ** *Historische Laut- und Formenlehre*   I:4
           des Altbulgarischen (Altkirchen-   VI:3
           slavischen) (Heidelberg: Winter).

1958   * "Zur Entstehungsgeschichte des be-   III:3:4
           stimmten Adjektivs des Baltischen   IV:2
           und Slavischen," *WdSl* 3, 97-100.   VI:1

Rospond, S.
1954   * "Palatalizacja, dyspalatalizacja a   II:4
           tzw. mazurzenie," *BPTJ* 13, 21-50.   VI:3

1962   "Perspektivy razvitija slavjanskoj
           onomastiki," *VJa* 4, 9-19.   I:5

1965   * "Struktura i klassifikacija drevne-   VI:3
           vostočnoslavjanskix antroponimov   III:3:4
           (imena)," *VJa* 3, 3-21.

1966   * "Struktura pierwotnych etnonimów   I:5
           słowiańskich," *RS* 26, 21-32.   III:3:4
                                                             V:1

1968a   ** "Prasłowianie w świetle onomastyki,"   VI:2
           I Międzynarodowy Kongres Archeolo-   I:5
           gii Słowiańskiej, Warszawa, 14.-18.
           IX. 1965 I (Wrocław-Cracow: Ossoli-
           neum), 109-170.

1968b   * "Struktura pierwotnych etnonimów   I:5
           słowiańskich. 2. Formacje po roz-   III:3:4
           padzie dialektalnym (IX w. i nn.),"   V:1
           RS 29, 9-28.   VI:3

1969   ** "Rzekomy staroczeski loc. plur. na   III:2:4
           -as," *RS* 30, 5-26.   VI:1

Rozwadowski, J.
1912   * "O pierwotnym stosunku wzajemnym   VI:1
           języków bałtyckich i słowiańskich,"
           RS 5, 1-36.

1914/15 * "Rozwój pierwotnego wygłosowego *-os*   II:5
           w słowiańskim i tzw. pierwsza woka-   II:3
           lizacja jerów," *RS* 7, 14-18.

Rudnicki, M.
1959/61 * *Prasłowiańszczyzna-Lechia-Polska.* I: I:5
           Wyłonienie się Słowian spośród ludów   VI:1
           indoeuropejskich i ich pierwotne   VI:3
           siedziby, 1959; II: *Wspólnota sło-*
           wiańska-Wspólnota lechicka-Polska,
           1961 (Poznań: PWN).

Rudnyc'kyj, J. B.
1962-   * *An Etymological Dictionary of the*   V:1
           Ukrainian Language, parts 1-5, 1966;

410

parts 1-5, 2nd rev. ed., 1971; parts
6-10, 1971; introductory Part (0/11),
1972 (Winnipeg: Ukrainian Free Academy of Sciences-UVAN).

1966   ** "The Problem of Nom. Sg. Endings of   III:2:4
O-Stems in Slavic," *Orbis Scriptus*,   II:5
655-658.

1970   ** "Lithuanian *žąsìs* — Ukrainian *dzuś*,"   II:4
Donum Balticum, 414-417.   V:2

Růžička, R.

1961   ** "Struktur und Echtheit des altslavi-   IV:2
schen dativus absolutus," *ZfSl* 6,   III:2:4
588-596.   VI:3

1962   * "Zur Genesis des slavischen Verbal-   III:3:5
aspekts," *IJSLP* 5, 16-27.   IV:2

1966   ** "O ponjatii 'zaimstvovannyj sintak-   IV:4
sis' v svete teorii transformacion-   IV:1
noj grammatiki," *VJa* 4, 80-96.   VI:1
   VI:3

1971   ** "Betrachtung zur Lehnsyntax im Alt-   IV:1
slavischen," *Studia paleoslovenica*,   IV:4
B. Havránek, ed. (Prague: Academia),   VI:1
303-308.   VI:3

Sadnik, L.

1957   * "Akzentstudien," *SR* 10, 230-236.   II:2

1959   ** *Slavische Akzentuation*. I: *Vorhis-*   II:2
torische Zeit (Wiesbaden: Harrasso-
witz).

1960   * "Das slavische Imperfekt (Ein Bei-   III:2:5
trag zur Erforschung des urslavi-
schen Verbalsystems)," *WdSl* 5, 19-
30.

1962   * "Die Nasalpräsentia und das frühur-   III:5
slavische Verbalsystem," *Sprache* 8,
238-249.

1966   ** "Aksl. 'rekǫ : rьci'," *Orbis Scriptus*,   II:3
659-662.   III:3:5
   IV:2

1969   ** "Idg. **ei* - slav. **iḫ* in heterosyl-   II:3
labischer Stellung," *AnzfslPh* 3,
1-4

1971   * "K probleme ètimologičesko-grammati-   V:2
českix svjazej," *Ètimologija 1968*   III:3:5
(Moscow: "Nauka"), 3-10.

Sadnik, L. & R. Aitzetmüller

1955   * *Handwörterbuch zu den altkirchen-*   V:1

slavischen Texten (= *Slavistic Print-*
ings & Reprintings 6) (The Hague:
Mouton).

1963-   * *Vergleichendes Wörterbuch der Sla-*   V:1
vischen Sprachen, Lieferung 1-
(Wiesbaden: Harrassowitz).

Safarewicz, J.

1945   * "Przyczynki do zagadnienia wspólnoty VI:1
bałtosłowiańskiej," *Sprawozdania z*
czynności i posiedzeń PAU w Krakowie
46, 199-202.

1963   * "Ze związków słownikowych słowiań- VI:1
sko-italskich. Czasowniki," *Studia*   V:2
linguistica . . ., 133-142.

1964   * "Przedhistoryczne związki językowe VI:1
italsko-słowiańskie," *RS* 23, 19-25. V:2

1966   "Rozwój fonemów szczelinowych i
zwartoszczelinowych w językach   II:4
bałtyckich i słowiańskich," *RS* 26, VI:1
3-7.

Samilov, M.

1964   ** *The Phoneme Jat' in Slavic* (The   II:3
Hague: Mouton).   VI:3

Sborník . . .

1932   *Sborník prací I. Sjezdu slovanských*
filologů v Praze 1929. Sv. II: *Před-*
nášky, J. Horák, M. Murko, M. Weingart a S. Petíra, eds. (Prague:
"Orbis").

Scatton, E.

1968   ** "On the Loss of Proto-Slavic Liquid II:3
Diphthongs," *Studies Presented to* VI:3
Professor Roman Jakobson by His Stu-
dents, C. E. Gribble, ed. (Cambridge: Slavica Publishers), 281-
288.

Schelesniker, H.

1959   * "Entstehung und Entwicklung des sla- III:3:5
vischen Aspektsystems," *WdSl* 4, 390- IV:2
409.

1963   * "Slavisch *kogo, togo, jego, česo*," III:2:4
WslJb 10, 69-72.

1964   ** *Beiträge zur historischen Kasusent-* III:2:4
wicklung des Slavischen (Graz-Vien- IV:2
na: Böhlaus Nachf.).

1967   * "Beiträge zur historischen Kasusent- III:2:4

wicklung des Slavischen," *AnzfslPh*   IV:2
2, 122-130.

1967/68 ** "Die 'Vokallängung' in den urslavi-   II:3
schen Lautverbindungen *(t)art,*   VI:3
(t)alt," *WslJb* 14, 68-72.

1969   * "Slavisch *rabъ* und *robъ,*" *AnzfslPh*   II:3
3, 13-17.   V:3
    VI:3

Schmalstieg, W. R.

1956   "The Phoneme /v/ in Slavic Verbal   III:3:5
Suffixes," *Word* 12, 255-259.   II:4

1959a   "The Indo-European Semivowels in   II:4
Balto-Slavic," *Language* 35, 16-17.   VI:1

1959b   ** "The Slavic Stative Verb in -$\bar{\imath}$-,"   III:3:5
IJSLP 1/2, 177-183.   IV:2

1960a   * "A Note on Slavic Verbs of the Type   III:3:5
zějǫ : *zĭjati*," *Word* 16, 204-206.   II:3

1960b   * "-$\bar{\imath}$- as a Marker of the Determina-   III:3:5
tive Aspect in Pre-Historic Slavic,"   IV:2
Annali, Sezione linguistica 2, *Isti-*
tuto Universitario Orientale, W.
Belardi, ed. (Naples: Ist. Univ.
Orientale di Napoli), 191-199.

1964   "A Balto-Slavic Structural Paral-   II:3
lelism," *Word* 20, 35-39.   VI:1
    III:3:5

1965   * "Slavic o- and $\bar{a}$-Stem Accusatives,"   III:2:4
Word 21, 238-243.   II:5

1967   * "A Note on Certain Balto-Slavic Ac-   III:2:4
cusatives," *Baltistica* 3, 47-55.   II:5
    VI:1

1968   ** "Slavic Morpheme Alternants in $\check{e}$/$ę$ II:5
and a/y," *SEEJ* 12, 44-52.   III:2:4
    VI:1

1971   ** "Die Entwicklung der $\bar{a}$-Deklination   III:2:4
im Slavischen," *ZfslPh* 36, 130-146.   VI:2

Schriften . . . (see also *sub* Vasmer)

1971   *Schriften zur slavischen Altertums-*
kunde und Namenkunde I = Veröffent-
lichungen der Abteilung für slavi-
sche Sprachen und Literaturen des
Osteuropa-Instituts [Slavisches Se-
minar] an der Freien Universität
Berlin 38 (Wiesbaden: Harrassowitz).

Schröpfer, J.

1966   "Slavisches in Ortsnamen des Pelo-   I:5

ponnes, besonders der Argolis. Eine
Nachlese," *Orbis Scriptus*, 679-706.

Schuster-Šewc, H.

1964a   * "Noch einmal zur Behandlung der Li-   II:4
quidaverbindungen *tl, dl* in den   VI:3
slawischen Sprachen," *Slavia* 33,   VI:2
359-368.

1964b   * "Zur Bezeichnung des Bauern im Sla-   V:3
wischen **cholpъ, *kъmetь, *smȓdъ*."   V:2
ZfSl 9, 241-255.

Schütz, J.

1963   * "Zur Abstufung und Erweiterung in   II:3
diphthongischen Wurzeln im Slavi-   III:3
schen und Baltischen," *WdSl* 8, 337-   VI:1
347.

1968   ** "Die slavische Mythologie und die   V:2
Etymologie," *Annuaire de l'Institut*   V:3
de Philologie et d'Histoire Orien-   VI:1
tales et Slaves 18 (Brussels: Uni-
versité libre de Bruxelles), 335-
346.

Schwartz, E.

1927a   * "Zur Chronologie der slavischen Li-   II:3
quidenumstellung in den deutsch-   VI:2
slavischen Berührungsgebieten,"   VI:3
ZfslPh 4, 361-369.

1927b   * "Zur Chronologie von asl. $a > o$,"   II:3
AfslPh 41, 124-136.   VI:2

1929   * "Zur Chronologie von asl. $\bar{u} > y$,"   II:3
AfslPh 42, 275-285.   VI:2

Sedov, V. V.

1970   * *Slavjane verxnego Podneprov'ja i*   I:5
Podvin'ja (= *Materialy i issledova-*
nija po arxeologii SSSR 163) (Moscow: "Nauka").

Seliščev, A. M.

1931   * "Sokan'e i šokan'e v slavjanskix   II:4
jazykax," *Slavia* 10, 718-741.   VI:3

1941   * *Slavjanskoe jazykoznanie.* I: *Zapad-*   VI:3
no-slavjanskie jazyki (Moscow: Uč-   I:2
pedgiz).

1951/52   ** *Staroslavjanskij jazyk.* I: *Vvedenie.*   I:4
Fonetika, 1951; II: *Teksty. Slovar'*   VI:3
Očerki morfologii, 1952 (Moscow: Uč-
pedgiz).

Senn, A.

1941   ** "On the Degree of Kinship between   VI:1
Slavic and Baltic," *SEER* 20, 251-
265.

1949   ** "Verbal Aspects in Germanic, Slavic   III:3:5
and Baltic," *Language* 25, 402-409.   IV:2
   VI:1

1954   ** "Die Beziehungen des Baltischen zum   VI:1
Slavischen und Germanischen," *KZ*
71, 162-188.

1966   ** "The Relationships of Baltic and   VI:1
Slavic," *Ancient Indo-European Dia-
lects*, 139-151.

1970   ** "Slavic and Baltic Linguistic Rela-   VI:1
tions," *Donum Balticum*, 485-494.

Shapiro, M.

1972   * "Explorations into markedness,"   II:4
Language 48, 343-364.   VI:1

Shevelov, G. Y.

1963   ** "Prothetic Consonants in Common   II:5
Slavic. An Historical Approach,"   II:4
*American Contributions to the Fifth
International Congress of Slavists*,
243-262 (= *Teasers and Appeasers*,
35-49).

1964   ** *A Prehistory of Slavic. The Histori-*   III:1
cal Phonology of Common Slavic (Hei-
delberg: Winter; New York: Columbia
University Press, 1965).

1965a   ** "Dwie uwagi o słowiańskim ě," *Studia*   II:3
z filologii polskiej i słowiańskiej   VI:3
5 (Warsaw: PWN), 93-100 (= *Teasers
and Appeasers*, 71-77).

1965b   * "On Endings with Nasal Consonants   II:5
after Palatal and Palatalized Conso-   III:2:4
nants. An Inquiry into the Allopho-   II:3
nic Structure of Common Slavic,"
WdSl 10, 233-244 (= *Teasers and Appeasers*, 50-59).

1971   *Teasers and Appeasers. Essays and
Studies on Themes of Slavic Philology* [Reprints of earlier published
essays plus a newly written study,
"Issues and Non-Issues. Five Years
after *A Prehistory of Slavic*," 297-
326] (= *Forum Slavicum* 32) (Munich:

Fink).

Shevelov, G. Y. & J. Chew, Jr.
1969   ** "Open Syllable Languages and their   II:5
        Evolution: Common Slavic and Japa-   VI:1
        nese," *Word* 25, 252-274 (= *Teasers*
        and Appeasers, 15-34).

Skok, P.
1971/73   * *Etimologijski rječnik hrvatskogo ili*   V:1
        srpskogo jezika, I-III (Zagreb: JAZU).

Slavjanskaja filologija . . .
1958   *Slavjanskaja filologija. Sbornik*
        statej 1, IV Meždunarodnyj s"ezd
        slavistov, S. B. Bernštejn, ed.
        (Moscow: Izd-vo AN SSSR).

Slavjanskoe jazykoznanie . . .
1963   *Slavjanskoe jazykoznanie. V Meždu-*
        narodnyj s"ezd slavistov (*Sofija,*
        sentjabr' 1963). *Doklady sovetskoj*
        delegacii, B. V. Gornung, ed. (Mos-
        cow: Izd-vo AN SSSR).
1968   *Slavjanskoe jazykoznanie. VI Meždu-*
        narodnyj s"ezd slavistov (*Praga, av-*
        gust 1968 g.). *Doklady sovetskoj de-*
        legacii, V. V. Vinogradov, S. B.
        Bernštejn & N. I. Tolstoj, eds.
        (Moscow: "Nauka").

Sławski, F.
1947   * "Oboczność *ǫ* : *u* w językach słowiań-   II:3
        skich," *SlOcc* 18, 246-290; French
        résumé 539.
1952-   * *Słownik etymologiczny języka pol-*   V:1
        skiego, 1- (Cracow: Nakł. Tow.
        Miłośników Języka Polskiego).
1955   * "Ugrupowanie języków południowo-   I:2
        słowiańskich," *BPTJ* 14, 103-111.   VI:3
1957   * "Principi za săstavjane na etimolo-
        gičen rečnik na slavjanski ezik,"   V:1
        Ezikovedski izsledvanija . . ., 263-
        271.
1962   * *Zarys dialektologii języków połud-*   I:2
        niowo-słowiańskich (*z wyborem*   VI:3
        tekstów gwarowych) (Warsaw: PWN).

Słownik prasłowiański . . .
1961   * *Słownik prasłowiański. Zeszyt prób-*   V:2
        ny (Cracow: Ossolineum, PAN).

Słownik starożytnosci słowiańskich . . .
  1961/72- *Słownik starożytności słowiańskich.*
            Encyklopedyczny zarys kultury Sło-
            wian od czasów najdawniejszych do
            schytku wieku XII, I-IV-, W. Kowa-
            lenko, G. Labuda & T. Lehr-Spławiń-
            ski, eds. (IV, 1970/72, G. Labuda &
            Z. Stieber, eds.) (Warsaw-Cracow:
            Ossolineum, PAN).

Sós, A. C.
  1969   * "Zur Frage der Kontinuität der pan-   I:5
            nonischen Slaven im 9. Jahrhundert,"   VI:3
            Das heidnische und christliche Sla-
            ventum (= *Annales Instituti Slavici,*
            F. Zagiba, ed., II/1) (Wiesbaden:
            Harrassowitz), 153-157.

Sørensen, H. C.
  1952   * "Die sogenannte Liquidametathese im   II:3
            Slavischen," *Acta Linguistica* 7   VI:3
            (Copenhagen: Munksgaard), 40-61.

Specht, F.
  1944   ** *Der Ursprung der Indogermanischen*   III:2:4
            Deklination (Göttingen: Vandenhoeck   VI:1
            & Ruprecht, Neudruck 1947).

Stang, C. S.
  1939a   * "Einige Bemerkungen über das Ver-   VI:1
            hältnis zwischen den slavischen und
            baltischen Sprachen," *NTS* 11, 85-98
            (= *Opuscula linguistica,* 53-64).

  1939b   * "Slavische indeklinable Adjektiva   III:3:4
            auf -ь," *NTS* 11, 99-103.

  1942   ** *Das slavische und baltische Verbum*   III:5
            (Oslo: Jacob Dybwad).   VI:1

  1949   * "L'adjectif slave istъ," *NTS* 15,   V:2
            343-351 (= *Opuscula linguistica,*   III:3:4
            83-89).

  1956   * "Slavonic sъ with the Accusative in   IV:2
            Expressions of Measure," *For Roman*   V:2
            Jakobson, 514-517 (= *Opuscula lin-*
            guistica, 104-108).

  1957a   ** "Eine preussisch-slavische (oder   V:2
            baltisch-slavische?) Sonderbildung,"   V:3
            ScSl 3, 236-239 (= *Opuscula linguis-* VI:1
            tica, 69-72).

  1957b   ** *Slavonic Accentuation* (= *Skr. utg.* II:2
            av Det Norske Vidensk.-Akad. i Oslo

                I: *Hist.-fil. Kl.* 3) (Oslo: Asche-
houg W. Nygaard).

1961   ** "Zum baltisch-slavischen Verbum,"   III:3:5
           IJSLP 4, 67-74 (= *Opuscula linguis-* V:2
           tica, 73-80).   VI:1

1963   * "Über das Verhältnis zwischen den
           slavischen und baltischen Sprachen," VI:1
           Prace Językoznawcze 5 (= *Zeszyty*
           naukoweUniwersytetu Jagiellońskiego
           60), 393-395 (= *Opuscula linguisti-*
           ca, 65-72).

1964   ** "De l'instrumental singulier des   III:2:4
           themes en *-o-* en slave commun," *RES*
           40, 191-194 (= *Opuscula linguistica*,
           109-112).

1965   * "Russisch *devjanosto*," *Lingua viget*, V:2
           124-129 (= *Opuscula linguistica*,   III:3:4
           113-118).

1966   ** *Vergleichende Grammatik der Balti-* VI:1
           schen Sprachen (Oslo: Universitets- I:3
           forlaget).

1970   *Opuscula linguistica: Ausgewählte,*
           Aufsätze und Abhandlungen (Oslo:
           Universitetsforlaget).

Stanislav, J.
1947/48   "Zo štúdia slovanských osobných mien I:5
           v Evanjeliu cividalskom (Ev. Civ.),"
           Slavia 18, 87-100.

1948   *Slovenský juh v stredoveku* I-II (= I:5
           Spisy Jazykovedného odboru Matice
           slovenskej B, 1-2) (Turč. sv. Mar-
           tin: Matica slovenská).

1957/58 ** *Dejiny slovenského jazyka.* I: *Úvod* I:4
           a hláskoslovie, 2nd aug. ed.; II: VI:3
           Tvaroslovie, I & II, 1958; III:
           Teksty, 1957 (Bratislava: Vyda-
           tel'stvo SAV).

Staniševa, D. S.
1966   "Konstrukcija tipa *zemlja paxat'* v IV:2
           sisteme sintaksičeskix vostočno-   VI:1
           slavjanskix jazykov," *Slavia* 35, IV:4
           1-16.   VI:2

Stankiewicz, E.
1960   * "The Consonantal Alternations in the II:6
           Slavic Declension," *Word* 16, 183- II:4
           203.

1962   * "The Etymology of Common Slavic   V:2
     *vъnǫkъ/*vъnukъ." *SEEJ* 6, 28-33.

1963   * Review of *Slavic Historical Phonol-*   II:1
     ogy in Tabular Form by C. E. Bid-
     well, *SEEJ* 7, 419-425.

1964   * "Trubetzkoy and Slavic Morphophone-   II:6
     mics," *WslJb* 11, 79-90.

1966a   * "The Common Slavic Prosodic Pattern   II:2
     and Its Evolution in Slovenian,"   VI:3
     IJSLP 10, 29-38.

1966b   ** "Slavic Morphophonemics in Its Typo-   II:6
     logical and Diachronic Aspects,"
     Current Trends in Linguistics. III:
     Theoretical Foundations, T. A.
     Sebeok (The Hague: Mouton), 495-520.

1968   ** "The Etymology of Common Slavic   V:2
     skot'ъ [sic!] 'cattle' and Related   V:3
     Terms," *Studies in Slavic Linguis-*   V:4
     tics and Poetics in Honor of Boris
     Unbegaun, R. Magidoff *et al.*, eds.
     (New York: NY University Press),
     219-226.

Stankiewicz, E. & D. S. Worth
   1966   *A Selected Bibliography of Slavic*
     Linguistics I (= *Slavistic Printings*
     & Reprintings 49) (The Hague: Mou-
     ton).

Stender-Petersen, A.
   1927   * *Slavisch-Germanische Lehnwortkunde,*   V:4
     eine Studie über die ältesten ger-
     manischen Lehnwörter im Slavischen
     in sprach- und kulturgeschichtlicher
     Beleuchtung (= *Göteborgs Kungl. Ve-*
     tensk.- o. Vitterhetssamh. Handl. IV,
     31:4) (Gothenburg: Elanders boktr.).

Stepanova, Z. P.
   1965   "Areal rasprostranenija glagolov na   I:3
     -ē- v indoevropejskix jazykax," *VJa*   III:3:5
     4, 110-118.

Stieber, Z. (Štiber)
   1955   * "Wzajemne stosunki języków zachod-   I:2
     nio-słowiańskich," *BPTJ* 14, 73-93.   VI:3

   1956   * *Zarys dialektologii języków zachod-*   I:2
     nio-słowiańskich z wyborem tekstów   VI:3
     gwarowych) (Warsaw: PWN).

   1963   * "Jak brzmiało prasłowiańskie 'y'?,"   II:3

Z polskich studiów slawistycznych.
Seria 2. *Językoznawstwo* (Warsaw:
PWN), 19-21.

1964   ** "Jak brzmiało prasłowianskie jat?,"   II:3
PF 18:2, 131-137.

1965a   ** "Prsłow. *věža* (*veža*) i znaczenie   V:3
tego wyrazu," *Zbornik za filologiju*   V:2
i lingvistiku 7 (Novi Sad: Matica
Srpska), 45-47.

1965b   * "Przyczynek do zagadnienia przestaw-   II:3
ki płynnych," *RS* 24, 19-20.   VI:3

1965c   ** "W sprawie pierwotnego podziału
dialektalnego języka prasłowiań-   VI:3
skiego," *Symbolae linguisticae* . . .,
304-308.

1966   ** "Rzym, krzyż i Żyd," *RS* 26, 33-34.   II:3
    V:4
    VI:2

1967   ** "Nowe osiągnięcia gramatyki porównawczej języków słowiańskich," *RS*   I:2
28, 3-20.

1968a   ** "Druga palatalizacja tylnojęzykowych   II:4
w świetle atlasu dialektów rosyj-   VI:2
skich na wschód od Moskwy," *RS* 29,   VI:3
3-7.

1968b   ** "Problem najdawniejszych różnic   VI:3
między dialektami słowiańskimi,"
*I Międzynarodowy Kongres Archeologii
Słowiańskiej. Warszawa 14.-18. IX.
1965* I (Wrocław-Warsaw-Cracow: Ossolineum, PAN), 88-108, French transl.
98-108.

1968c   ** *Problèmes fondamentaux de la lin-*   I:2
guistique slave (Wrocław-Warsaw-   VI:3
Cracow: Ossolineum, PAN).

1969/71 ** *Zarys gramatyki porównawczej języków*   I:2
słowiańskich. Fonologia, 1969; Cz.
2. zesz. 1: *Fleksja imienna,* 1971
(Warsaw: PWN).

1970   ** "Prasłowiański język," *Słownik*   I:1
starożytności słowiańskich, IV,
309-312.

1971   * "O jazyke Kievskogo missala," *Is-*   I:5
sledovanija . . ., 106-109.   VI:3
    II:4

Studia linguistica . . .
1963   *Studia linguistica in honorem Thad-*
        dai Lehr-Spławiński, T. Milewski, J.
        Safarewicz & F. Sławski, eds. (Cra-
        cow: PWN).
Symbolae linguisticae . . .
1965   *Symbolae linguisticae in honorem*
        Georgii Kuryłowicz, A. Heine *et al.*,
        eds. (= *PAN, KJ, Prace Językoznaw-*
        stwa 5) (Wrocław-Warsaw-Cracow: Osso-
        lineum, PAN).
Szemerényi, O.
1948   * "Zwei Fragen des urslavischen Ver-   III:5
        bums," *Études slaves et roumaines* 1,
        7-14.
1957   * "The Problem of Balto-Slav Unity —   VI:1
        A Critical Survey," *Kratylos* 2,
        97-123.
1967   ** "Slavic Etymology in Relation to the   V:1
        IE Background," *WdSl* 12, 267-295.   V:2
                                                 VI:1
1970   ** *Einführung in die vergleichende*   I:3
        Sprachwissenschaft (Darmstadt: Wis-
        senschaftliche Buchgesellschaft).
Szober, S.
1927   * "Słowiański Nom.-Acc. sg. neutr.   III:2:4
        tematów na -o-, -es-," *PF* 12, 563-
        571.
1930   * "Prasłowiańskie formy dopełniacza i   III:2:4
        biernika liczby pojed. (gen. sg.,
        acc. sg.) zaimków osobowych," *PF* 15:
        1, 229-235.
Šanskij, N. M.
1963-   * *Étimologičeskij slovar' russkogo ja-* V:1
        zyka, 1- (Moscow: Moskovskij Univer-
        sitet).
Šaxmatov, A. A. (Schachmatov)
1910   * "Die gespannten (engen) Vokale ь und   II:3
        ъ im Urslavischen," *AfslPh* 31, 481-   VI:3
        506.
1915   ** *Očerk drevnejšago perioda istorii*   I:4
        russkago jazyka (= *Ènciklopedija*   VI:3
        slavjanskoj filologii I, vyp. 11)
        (Petrograd: Tipografija Imperator-
        skoj AN) (= *Russian Reprint Series*
        61, 1967, The Hague: Mouton).

Šur, S. M.
1963   * "K istorii slavjanskogo imennogo   III:3:4
tipa s suffiksom -*ti," VslJa 7,
82-102.

Tedesco, P.
1948   ** "Slavic ne-Presents from Older je-   III:3:5
Presents," Language 24, 346-387.

1951   ** "Slavic *pilьnь and naglъ: Two Ety-   V:3
mologies Based on Meaning," Language   V:2
27, 18-33.

Tesnière, L.
1933   * "Les diphones tl, dl en slave: essai   II:4
de géolinguistique," RES 13, 51-100.   VI:3

The Slavic Word . . .
1972   The Slavic Word. Proceedings of the
International Slavistic Colloquium
at UCLA, September 11-16, 1970, D.
S. Worth, ed. (The Hague & Paris:
Mouton).

Thümmel, W.
1967   * "Die dritte oder Baudouinsche Pala-   II:4
talisierung im Slavischen," ScSl 13,   VI:2
115-145.

To Honor Roman Jakobson . . .
1966   To Honor Roman Jakobson. Essays on
the Occasion of his Seventieth
Birthday 11 October 1966 I-III (=
Janua Linguarum, series maior, 31-
33) (The Hague: Mouton).

Tolkačev, A. I.
1959   * "K voprosu o drevnejšix (dopis'men-   III:2:4
noj pory) izmenenijax v sisteme
sklonenija složnyx prilagatel'nyx
v slavjanskix jazykax," Doklady i
soobščenija Instituta jazykoznanija
12 (Moscow: Izd-vo AN SSSR), 87-107.

Tolstoj, N. I.
1963/66 ** "Iz opytov tipologičeskogo issledo-   V:3
vanija slavjanskogo slovarnogo so-
stava. I," VJa 1, 1963, 29-45; II,
VJa 5, 1966, 16-36.

1968   * "Nekotorye problemy sravnitel'noj   V:3
slavjanskoj semasiologii," Slavjan-
skoe jazykoznanie VI . . ., 339-365.

Toporov, V. N.
1958   * "Novejšie raboty v oblasti izučenija   VI:1

balto-slavjanskix jazykovyx otnošenij," *VslJa* 3, 134-161.

1959a   ** "Nekotorye soobraženija otnositel'-   I:1
no izučenija istorii praslavjanskogo   VI:2
jazyka," *Slavjanskoe jazykoznanie.*   VI:3
Sbornik statej, V. V. Vinogradov,
ed. (Moscow: Izd-vo AN SSSR), 3-27.

1959b   * "Očerk istorii izučenija drevnejšix   VI:1
balto-slavjanskix otnošenij," *Učenye*
zapiski Instituta Slavjanovedenija
AN SSSR 17, 248-274.

1961a   * "K voprosu ob èvoljucii slavjanskogo   III:5
i baltijskogo glagola," *VslJa* 5, 35-   VI:1
70.

1961b   ** *Lokativ v slavjanskix jazykax* (Mos-   IV:2
cow: Izd-vo AN SSSR).   III:2:4
  VI:3

1962   * "O praslavjanskom **kot-*," *VslJa* 6,   V:2
172-176.   V:3

1963   * "K ètimologii slav. *myslъ*," *Ètimo-*   V:2
logija, 5-13.

1969   ** "Iz nabljudenij nad ètimologiej   V:2
slov mifologičeskogo xaraktera,"   V:3
Ètimologija 1967, 11-21.   VI:1

1971   ** "Ob odnom iranizme v slavjanskom: VI:1
*bazuriti," *Issledovanija* . . .,   VI:3
450-458.   I:5

Toporov, V. N. & O. N. Trubačev
1962   * *Lingvističeskij analiz gidronimov*   I:5
verxnego Podneprov'ja (Moscow: Izd-   VI:1
vo AN SSSR).

Torbiörnsson, T.
1901/03   * *Die gemeinslavische Liquidametathese*   II:3
I-II (Uppsala: Akademische Buch-
druckerei Edv. Berling/Adakemiska
Bokhandeln [C. J. Lundström]).

1922   * "Métathèse des liquides et voyelles   II:3
nasales en slave commun," *RES* 2,   VI:3
214-216.

1922/23   * "Die altbulgarische Umbildung der   III:2:4
Partizipialformen," *Slavia* 1, 208-   III:3:5
214.

Trautmann, R.
1923   * *Baltisch-Slavisches Wörterbuch* (Göt-   V:1
tingen: Vandenhoeck & Ruprecht).   VI:1
1947   ** *Die slavischen Völker und Sprachen.*   I:2

Eine Einführung in die Slavistik
(Göttingen: Vandenhoeck & Ruprecht).

Trávníček, F.

1935　　** *Historická mluvnice československá.*　　I:4
Úvod, hláskosloví a tvarosloví　　VI:3
(Prague: Melantrich).

1963　　** *Historická mluvnice česká.* III:　　I:4
Skladba, 2nd ed., prepared by A.　　VI:3
Vašek, 1st ed. 1956 (Prague: Státní　　IV:1
Pedag. Nakl.).

Treimer, K.

1954　　*Ethnogenese der Slawen* (Vienna:　　I:5
Gerold & Co.).

1957/58 ** "Skythisch, Iranisch, Urslavisch.　　VI:1
Ethnogenetische Erwägungen," *WslJb*　　I:5
6, 105-112.

Tret'jakov, P. N.

1948　　* *Vostočnoslavjanskie plemena* (Moscow-　　I:5
Leningrad: Izd-vo AN SSSR).

1966　　* *Finno-ugry, balty i slavjane na*　　I:5
Dnepre i Volge (Moscow-Leningrad:
"Nauka").

Trost, P.

1958a　　* "K otázce baltoslovanských jazyko-　　VI:1
vých vztahů," *Československé před-*
nášky pro IV. Mezinárodní sjezd
slavistů v Moskvě, K. Horálek, ed.
(Prague: Nakl. ČSAV), 221-227.

1958b　　* "O baltoslovanských vztazích v ob-　　VI:1
lasti syntaxe," *K historickosrovná-*　　IV:1
vacímu studiu slovanských jazyků,
J. Bělič, J. Daňhelka & A. Isačenko,
eds. (Prague: Státní Pedag Nakl.),
124-127.

Trubačev, O. N.

1957a　　* "K ètimologii nekotoryx drevnejšix　　V:2
slavjanskix terminov rodstva (i.-e.　　V:3
*ǧenǝ-, slav. *rodъ, plemę,* obъtjo-*),"
VJa 2, 86-95.

1957b　　* "Principy postroenija ètimologi-　　V:1
českix slovarej slavjanskix jazy-
kov," *VJa* 5, 58-72.

1957c　　* "Slavjanskie ètimologii 1-7," *VslJa*　　V:1
2, 29-42.

1957d　　* "Slavjanskie ètimologii 8-9," *Eziko-*　　V:1
vedski izsledvanija . . ., 337-339.

1958   * "Slawische Etymologien 10-19," *ZfSl*   V:1
3, 668-681.

1959a   ** *Istorija slavjanskix terminov*   V:2
rodstva i nekotoryx drevnejšix   V:3
terminov obščestvennogo stroja
(Moscow: Izd-vo AN SSSR).

1959b   * "Slawische Etymologien 20-23," *ZfSl*   V:1
4, 83-87.

1960a   ** *Proisxoždenie nazvanij domašnix*   V:3
životnyx v slavjanskix jazykax   V:2
(Moscow: Institut slavjanovedenija
AN SSSR).

1960b   * "Slavjanskie ètimologii 24-27,"   V:1
Ezikovedsko-etnografski izsledvanija
v pamet na akad. Stojan Romanski
(Sofia: BAN), 137-143.

1960c   * "Slavjanskie ètimologii. 28. Bolgar-   V:1
skoe dialektnoe *măkắ* 'skot'," *Ètimo-*
logičeskie issledovanija po russkomu
jazyku I (Moscow: Izd-vo Moskovskogo
Universiteta), 87-89.

1962   * "Slavjanskie ètimologii 29-39," *Èti-*   V:1
mologičeskie issledovanija po rus-
skomu jazyku II (Moscow: Izd-vo Moskovskogo Universiteta), 26-43.

1963a   * *Etimologičeskij slovar' slavjanskix*   V:1
jazykov (praslavjanskij leksičeskij
fond): Prospekt. Probnye stat'i
(Moscow: Izd-vo AN SSSR).

1963b   ** "Formirovanie drevnejšej remeslennoj   V:3
terminologii v slavjanskom i nekoto-   V:2
ryx drugix indoevropejskix dialek-   VI:1
tax," *Ètimologija*, 14-51.

1963c   ** "O praslavjanskix leksičeskix dia-   V:2
lektizmax serbo-lužickix jazykov,"   VI:3
Serbo-lužickij lingvističeskij sbor-
nik (Moscow: AN SSSR), 154-172.

1963d   * "O sostave praslavjanskogo slovarja   V:1
(Problemy i zadači)," *Slavjanskoe*
jazykoznanie V . . . ., 159-196.

1964   * "Slavjanskie ètimologii 40. Slav.   V:1
gotovъ," *PF* 18:2, 153-156.

1965   * "Slavjanskie ètimologii 41-47,"   V:1
Ètimologija 1964, 3-12.

1966   ** *Remeslennaja terminologija v sla-*   V:3
vjanskix jazykax. Ètimologija i opyt   V:2

        gruppovoj rekonstrukcii (Moscow:
        "Nauka").

1967a ** "Iz slavjano-iranskix leksičeskix   V:4
        otnošenij," *Ėtimologija 1965*, 3-81.

1967b ** "Rabota nad ėtimologičeskim slovarem V:1
        slavjanskix jazykov," *VJa* 4, 34-45.

1968a   "Iz opyta issledovanija gidronimov   I:5
        Ukrainy," *Baltistica* 4, 31-53.

1968b   *Nazvanija rek Pravoberežnoj Ukrainy.* I:5
        Slovoobrazovanie. Ėtimologija. Ėtni- III:3
        českaja interpretacija (Moscow: V:2
        "Nauka").

1968c ** "O sostave praslavjanskogo slovarja V:1
        (Problemy i rezul'taty)," *Slavjan-*
        skoe jazykoznanie VI . . ., 366-378.

1971a ** "Iz praslavjanskogo slovoobrazovani- III:3:4
        ja: imennye složenija s pristavkoj   V:2
        a-," *Problemy istorii i dialektolo-*
        gii slavjanskix jazykov. Sbornik
        statej k 70-letiju člena-korrespon-
        denta AN SSSR V. I. Borkovskogo, F.
        P. Filin, ed. (Moscow: "Nauka"),
        267-272.

1971b   * "Zametki po ėtimologii i sravnitel'- V:2
        noj grammatike," *Ėtimologija 1968* VI:1
        (Moscow: "Nauka"), 24-67.

Trubeckoj, N. S. (Trubetzkoy, Troubetzkoy)
  1921   * "De la valeur primitive des intona- II:2
        tions du slave commun," *RES* 1, 171-
        187.

  1922   ** "Essai sur la chronologie de cer- II:1
        tains faits phonétiques du slave   VI:2
        commun," *RES* 2, 217-234.

  1922/23 ** "O nekotoryx ostatkax isčeznuvšix III:3:4
        grammatičeskix kategorij v obšče- III:2:5
        slavjanskom prajazyke," *Slavia* 1, II:2
        12-21.   V:2

  1923   * "Les adjectifs slaves en -ькъ," *BSL* III:3:4
        24, 130-137.

  1924   * "Zum urslavischen Intonationssystem," II:2
        Streitberg-Festgabe (Leipzig: Mar-
        kert & Petters), 359-366.

  1925a   * "Die Behandlung der Lautverbin- II:4
        dungen *tl, dl* in den slavischen   VI:3
        Sprachen," *ZfslPh* 2, 117-121.

  1925b ** "Einiges über die russische Laut- II:1

	entwicklung und die Auflösung der	VI:3
	gemeinrussischen Spracheinheit,"	VI:2
	ZfslPh 1, 287-319.	
1925c	* "Les voyelles nasales des langues	II:3
	léchites," *RES* 5, 24-37.	VI:3
1927	* Urslav. *dъždžь* 'Regen'," *ZfslPh* 4,	II:4
	62-64.	II:5
		V:2
		III:3:4
		VI:3
1927/28	* "Ob otraženijax obščeslavjanskogo	II:3
	ę v češskom jazyke," *Slavia* 6, 661-	VI:3
	684.	
1928/29	* "K voprosu o xronologii stjaženija	II:3
	glasnyx v zapadnoslavjanskix ja-	II:5
	zykax," *Slavia* 7, 805-807.	VI:2
		VI:3
1930	** "Über die Entstehung der gemeinwest-	II:4
	slavischen Eigentümlichkeiten auf	VI:3
	dem Gebiete des Konsonantismus,"	VI:2
	ZfslPh 7, 383-406.	
1933	"Zur Entwicklung der Gutturale in	II:4
	den slavischen Sprachen," *Sbornik v*	VI:3
	čest na prof. L. Miletič za sedemde-	
	setgodišninata ot roždenieto mu	
	(1863-1933) (Sofia: Makedonskija	
	Naučen Institut), 267-279.	
1936	* "Die altkirchenslavische Vertretung	II:4
	der urslav. **tj, *dj*," *ZfslPh* 13,	VI:3
	88-97.	
1954	* *Altkirchenslavische Grammatik.*	I:4
	Schrift-, Laut- und Formensystem, R.	VI:3
	Jagoditsch, ed. (= *Österreichische*	
	Akademie der Wissenschaften, Philo-	
	sophisch-historische Klasse 228/4)	
	(Vienna: Rohrer).	
Trypućko, J.		
1947	* *Słowiańskie przysłówki liczebnikowe*	V:2
	typu stcsł. dvašdi, trišti (Uppsala:	III:3:4
	Almqvist & Wiksell).	
1949	* *Russe* vtoropjáx *'dans la précipita-*	IV:2
	tion', contribution a l'étude des	III:3:4
	adverbes slaves (= *Språkvetenskapli-*	V:2
	ga sällskapets i Uppsala Förhandlin-	
	gar 1949-1951).	
1952	** *Le pluriel dans les locutions adver-*	IV:2

       biales de temps et de lieu en slave   III:3:4
       (= *Uppsala Universitets Årsskrift* 7)   V:2
       (Uppsala: Almqvist & Wiksell).

1957   * "Stcsł. *radoštami* i pokrewne," *SR*   IV:2
       10, 81-93.   III:3:4
           V:2

Tvoritel'nyj padež . . .
1958   ** *Tvoritel'nyj padež v slavjanskix ja-*   IV:2
       zykax, S. B. Bernštejn, ed. (Moscow: III:2:4
       Izd-vo AN SSSR).   VI:3

Ułaszyn, H.
1959   * *Praojczyzna Słowian* (= *Łódzkie To-*   I:5
       warzystwo Naukowe. Wydział 1. Prace
       37) (Łódź: Ossolineum).

Urbańczyk, S.
1971   * Review of *Słowiańszczyzna północno-*   VI:3
       zachodnia by J. Nalepa, *AnzfslPh* 5,   I:5
       124-127.   VI:1

Vaillant, A.
1929   * "Le vocalisme des comparatifs   II:3
       slaves," *RES* 9, 5-12.   III:3:4

1930/31a * "Les noms slaves masculins en **-ēn,*"   III:3:4
       Slavia 9, 490-496.   IV:2

1930/31b * "L'impératif-optatif du slave,"
       Slavia 9, 241-256.   III:2:5

1931   * "Le comparatif slave en *-ějĭ,*" *RES*   III:3:4
       11, 5-11.

1934   * "L'élimination des présents athéma-   III:2:5
       tiques et le slave **možĭ,*" *RES* 14,
       26-35.

1935   * "Le génitif pluriel en **-ŏn,*" *RES*   III:2:4
       15, 5-11.   II:5

1936   * "Le problème des intonations balto-   II:2
       slaves," *BSL* 37, 109-115.   VI:1

1937   ** "L'origine des présents thématiques
       en *-e-* // *-o-,*" *BSL* 38, 89-101.   III:5

1939a   * "L'aspect verbal du slave commun; sa   III:3:5
       morphologisation," *RES* 19, 289-314.   IV:2

1939b   * "L'imparfait slave et les prétérits   III:2:5
       en *-ē-* et en *-ā-,*" *BSL* 40, 5-30.   VI:1

1940/48   "Les traits communs des langues   I:2
       slaves," *Conférences de l'Institut*
       de linguistique de l'Université de
       Paris 8, 17-31.

1948   * *Manuel de vieux slave*. I: *Grammaire*;   I:4
       II: *Textes et Glossaire* (= *IES*,   VI:3

Collection de manuels 6) (Paris:
Institut d'études slaves). Russian
transl. (Vajan) *Rukovodstvo po sta-
roslavjanskomu jazyku* by V. V. Borodič (Moscow: Izd-vo inostr. lit.),
1952.

1950/66 ** *Grammaire comparée des langues*   I:2
slaves. I: *Phonétique*, 1950; II:
Morphologie, 1. *Flexion nominale*, 2.
Flexion pronominale, 1958, I & II
(Lyon-Paris: Éditions IAC); III: *Le
Verbe*, Première partie & Deuxième
partie, 1966 (Paris: Éditions
Klincksieck).

1953/54 * "La désinence -tǔ de 2ᵉ--3ᵉ personne III:2:5
du singulier de l'aoriste," *JF* 20,
29-37.

1957 * "L'unité linguistique balto-slave," VI:1
Filologija 1, 23-35.

1963 ** "Slave *rota* '(prestation de) ser- V:2
ment'," *RES* 42, 122.   II:5
                                    II:4

1965 "L'accentuation du participe en II:2
-*l*-," *Lingua viget*, 157-160.   III:3:5

1967 ** "Le supin et ses limitations d'em- IV:2
ploi," *RES* 46, 9-13.   III:5

Van Campen, J. A.

1963 ** "Vowel Alternations in Old Church II:3
Slavonic Conjugation," *IJSLP* 6, 58- III:3:5
64.

1966 * "On the Appearance of a New Work on II:1
Common Slavic Phonology," *IJSLP* 10,
52-81.

Varbot, Ž. Ž.

1963a * "O slovoobrazovatel'nom analize v V:2
ètimologičeskix issledovanijax," III:3:4
Ètimologija, 194-212.

1963b ** "Slav. *vad* 'priučat'; privyčka, V:2
priučenie," *Ètimologija*, 213-216.

1965 * "Zametki po slavjanskoj ètimologii V:2
(slav. *naglъjь*, *naprasьnъjь*,
pakostь, *lězo*, *lězivo*)," *Ètimologija 1964*, 27-43.

1967 * "O nekotoryx xarakteristikax suf- III:3:4
fiksal'nogo imennogo otglagol'nogo V:2
slovoobrazovanija v praslavjanskom

jazyke (na materiale drevnerusskogo
jazyka)," *Ètimologija 1965*, 82-122.

Vasmer, M.

1923   * *Untersuchungen über die ältesten*   I:5
Wohnsitze der Slaven. I: Die Iranier V:4
in Südrussland (= *Veröff. d. balt.*
u. slav. Inst. a. d. Univ. Leipzig
3) (= *Schriften zur slavischen Al-*
tertumskunde und Namenkunde I, 106-
170).

1924   * "Iranisches aus Südrussland,"   I:5
Streitberg-Festgabe (Leipzig: Mar- V:4
kert & Petters), 367-375 (= *Schriften*
zur slavischen Altertumskunde und
Namenkunde I, 171-178).

1925   "Beiträge zur slavischen Grammatik. II:4
1. Meillet's urslavisches Sibilan-
tendissimilationsgesetz," *ZfslPh* 2,
54-58.

1926   * "Die Urheimat der Slaven," *Der ost-* I:5
deutsche Volksboden, W. Volz, ed.
(Breslau: Ferdinand Hirt), 118-143
(= *Schriften zur slavischen Alter-*
tumskunde und Namenkunde I, 37-56.

1927   Review of *Wstęp do historji Słowian.* I:5
Perspektywy antropologiczne, etno-
graficzne, archeologiczne i językowe
by J. Czekanowski, *ZfslPh* 4, 273-
285 (= *Schriften zur slavischen Al-*
tertumskunde und Namenkunde I, 57-
68).

1938   "Die ältesten Bevölkerungsverhält- I:5
nisse Russlands im Lichte der
Sprachforschung," *Geistige Arbeit*
5:21, 1-3 (= *Schriften zur slavi-*
schen Altertumskunde und Namenkunde
I, 73-79).

1941a   *Die alten Bevölkerungsverhältnisse* I:5
Russlands im Lichte der Sprachfor-
schung (= *Preuss. Akad. d. Wiss.,*
Vorträge und Schriften 5) (Berlin:
Walter de Gruyter) (= *Schriften zur*
slavischen Altertumskunde und Namen-
kunde I, 80-99).

1941b   *Die Slaven in Griechenland* (= *Abh.* I:5
d. Preuss. Akad. d. Wiss., Philos.-

                  hist. Kl. 12) (= *Subsidia Byzantina*
                  Lucis Ope Iterata IV, 1970, Leipzig:
                  Zentralantiquariat der DDR).

1953/58   * *Russisches etymologisches Wörterbuch.*   V:1
(1964/73)   I–III (Heidelberg: Winter). Russian
                  transl. (M. Fasmer) *Ètimologičeskij*
                  slovar' russkogo jazyka, I–IV, O. N.
                  Trubačev, transl. & ed. (Moscow:
                  "Progress").

1957   * "Baltisch-slavische Wortgleichungen,"   V:2
                  Ezikovedski izsledvanija . . ., 351–   V:3
                  353.   VI:1

1971   *Schriften zur slavischen Altertums-*   I:5
                  kunde und Namenkunde, H. Bräuer, ed.,   VI:1
                  I–II ([Berlin] Wiesbaden: Harrasso-
                  witz).

Važný, V.
1964   ** *Historická mluvnice česká.* II: *Tva-*   I:4
                  rosloví. 1. *Skloňování* (Prague: VI:3
                  Státní Pedag. Nakl.).   III:2:4

Večerka, R.
1959   * "Ke genezi slovanských konstrukcí   IV:2
                  participia praes. act. a praet. act.
                  I," *Sborník prací filosofické fakul-*
                  ty brněnské university 8, 37–49.

Vey, M.
1931   ** "Slave *st-* provenant d'i.-e. *$^*pt$-,*"   II:5
                  BSL 32, 65–67.   II:4

Vondrák, V. (W.)
1903   * "Zur Liquidametathese im Slavi-   II:3
                  schen," *AfslPh* 25, 182–211.   VI:3
1923/24   * "O pozdějších palatalisacích v pra-   II:4
                  slovanštině," *Slavia* 2, 17–25.   VI:2
1924/28 ** *Vergleichende slavische Grammatik.*   I:2
                  I: *Lautlehre und Stammbildungslehre,*
                  zweite stark vermehrte und ver-
                  besserte Auflage, 1924; II: *Formen-*
                  lehre und Syntax, zweite Auflage
                  neubearbeitet von O. Grünenthal,
                  1928 (Göttingen: Vandenhoeck &
                  Ruprecht; 1st ed., 1906/08).

Vstup . . .
1966   ** *Vstup do porivjal'no-istoryčnoho*   I:2
                  vyvčennja slov'jans'kyx mov, O. S.
                  Mel'nyčuk, ed. (Kiev: Naukova dum-
                  ka).

Walde, A.

1927/30   * *Vergleichendes Wörterbuch der indo-*   V:1
germanischen Sprachen. I, 1930; II,
1927, J. Pokorny, ed. (Berlin-Leipzig: Walter de Gruyter).

Wanstrat, L.

1933   ** *Beiträge zur Charakteristik des*   V:2
russischen Wortschatzes (= *Veröf-*   VI:3
fentlichungen des Slavischen Insti-
tuts an der Friedrich-Wilhelms-Uni-
versität Berlin 7) (Leipzig: Markert
& Petters); Nendeln-Liechtenstein:
Kraus Reprint 1968).

Watkins, C.

1965   ** "Evidence in Balto-Slavic," *Evidence*   II:1
for Laryngeals, W. Winter, ed., pre-   II:2
liminary version 1960 (The Hague: VI:1
Mouton), 116-122.

1969   ** *Indogermanische Grammatik.* III: *For-*   I:3
menlehre. 1. *Geschichte der Indoger-*   III:5
manischen Verbalflexion, J. Kuryłowicz, ed. (Heidelberg: Winter).

Weiher, E.

1967   ** "Urslavisch-Gemeinslavisch-Dialekte   VI:3
des Gemeinslavischen(?)," *AnzfslPh*
2, 82-100.

1971   ** "Nochmals zu H. Birnbaums 'Dialekten   VI:3
des Gemeinslavischen'," *AnzfslPh* 5,
117-119.

Weingart, M.

1919   * *Praslovanský vokalismus*, [2]1923   II:3
(Prague: [bibliographical data not
available]).

Węglarz, W.

1937/38a   "Metafonie spółgłosek na tle palata-   II:4
lizacyjnym w prasłowiańskim," *Slavia*
15, 511-516.

1937/38b   * "Problem t. zw. mazurzenia w świetle   II:4
fonologii," *Slavia* 15, 517-524.   VI:3

Widnäs, M.

1953   ** *La position de l'adjectif épithète*   IV:3
en vieux russe (= *Societas Scientia-*   III:4
rum Fennica. Commentationes Humana-   VI:3
rum Litterarum 18:2) (Helsinki: Cen-
traltryckeriet).

432

Wieczorkiewicz, B. & R. Sinielnikoff
1959   ** *Elementy grammatyki historycznej*   I:4
          języka polskiego, z ćwiczeniami   VI:3
          (Warsaw: Państwowe Zakłady Wydaw-
          nictw Szkolnych).

Wijk, N. van (Vejk)
1916a   * "ę und ě im Akk. Plur. der *jo*-Stämme   III:2:4
          und im Gen. Sing., Nom. Akk. Plur.   II:5
          der *jā*-Stämme," *AfslPh* 36, 460-464.   VI:3

1916b   * "Zur sekundären steigenden Intona-   II:2
          tion im Slavischen, vornehmlich in
          ursprünglich kurzen Silben," *AfslPh*
          36, 321-377.

1923   ** *Die baltischen und slavischen Ak-*   II:2
          zent- und Intonationssysteme. Ein   VI:1
          Beitrag zur Erforschung der bal-
          tisch-slavischen Verwandtschaftsver-
          hältnisse (= *Verhandelingen der*
          Koninklijke Akademie van Wetenschap-
          pen te Amsterdam. Afdeeling Letter-
          kunde. Nieuwe reeks, deel 23:2)
          (Amsterdam: Uitgave der Koninklijke
          Akademie van Wetenschappen). ^{2}1958 =
          Janua Linguarum, Studia memoriae
          Nicolai van Wijk dedicata 5 (The
          Hague: Mouton).

1923/24 * "Zur Aussprache des urslavischen ě,"   II:3
          Slavia 2, 593-595.

1925   ** "Zur Entwicklung der partizipialen   III:2:4
          Nominativendung *-onts* in den slavi-   II:3
          schen Sprachen," *ZfslPh* 1, 279-286.   II:5

1926   ** "Die slavischen Partizipia auf *-to-*   III:5
          und die Aoristformen auf *-tъ-*," *IF*   VI:1
          43, 281-289.

1927   ** "O dwóch okresach w rozwoju języka   VI:2
          prasłowiańskiego i o ich znaczeniu
          dla językoznawstwa ogólnego," *PF* 12,
          395-404.

1929a   * "Sur l'origine des aspects du verbe   III:3:5
          slave," *RES* 9, 237-252.   IV:2

1929b   ** "Zu den Verbaldubletten auf *-ai̯ǫ,*   III:3:5
          -ati; -ěi̯ǫ, -ěti," *ZfslPh* 6, 70-74.

1931   ** *Geschichte der altkirchenslavischen*   I:4
          Sprache. I: Laut- und Formenlehre   VI:3
          (Berlin-Leipzig: Walter de Gruyter).
          Russian transl. by V. V. Borodič,

433

Istorija staroslavjanskogo jazyka
(Moscow: Izd-vo inostrannoj litera-
tury), 1957.

1934   ** "Een phonologiese parallel tussen   II:3
            Germaans, Slavies, en Balties," *Me-*   VI:1
            dedeelingen der Koninklijke Akademie
            van Wetenschapen. Afd. Letterkunde
            77A, 29-35.

1937a   * "Eine bisher unbekannte altkirchen-   III:2:5
            slavische 3. Pers. Sg. Aor. auf
            -tъ," *ZfslPh* 14, 270-272.

1937b   * "La décadence et la restauration du   II:3
            système slave des quantités voca-   II:2
            liques," *Mélanges linguistiques of-*
            ferts à M. Holger Pedersen, 373-378.

1937c   ** "Le slave commun dans l'ensemble in-   I:1
            doeuropéen," *Le Monde slave* 14, 472-   VI:1
            499. Reprint *Les langues slaves. De*   I:2
            l'unité à la pluralité (= *Janua Lin-*
            guarum, Studia memoriae Nicolai van
            Wijk dedicata 2) (The Hague: Mouton),
            1956, 1-24.

1937d   ** "Parallélisme et divergence dans   VI:2
            l'évolution des langues slaves," *Le*   I:2
            Monde slave 14, 419-446. Reprint *Les*
            langues slaves. De l'unité à la plu-
            ralité (= *Janua Linguarum, Studia*
            memoriae Nicolai van Wijk dedicata
            2) (The Hague: Mouton)., 1956, 25-
            48.

1937/38   * "La génèse de la mouillure des con-   II:4
            sonnes dans les langues slaves,"   VI:3
            Slavia 15, 24-42.

1939/40   "Zu den Phonemen $i̯/j$ und $u̯/w/v$,   II:1
            speciell im Slavischen," *Linguistica*   II:6
            Slovaca 1/2, 77-84.

1941a   ** "Zum urslavischen sogenannten Syn-   II:5
            harmonismus der Silben," *Linguistica*   II:1
            Slovaca 3, 41-48.

1941b   * "Zur nordkašubischen Polytonie,"   II:2
            ZfslPh 17, 34-42.   VI:3

1941/42   * "Die slavischen Metatonien im
            Lichte der Phonologie," *IF* 58, 51-   II:2
            66.

1949/   ** "K istorii fonologičeskoj sistemy v   II:1
50a   obščeslavjanskom jazyke pozdnego   VI:2
            perioda," *Slavia* 19, 293-313.   VI:3